CNE Short Course

Dorothy Cady

Drew Heywood

Blaine Homer

Emmett Dulaney

Matt Arnett

Debra Niedermiller-Chaffins

NEW RIDERS
PUBLISHING

New Riders Publishing, Indianapolis, IN

CNE Short Course

By Dorothy Cady, Drew Heywood, Blaine Homer, Emmett Dulaney, Matt Arnett, Debra Niedermiller-Chaffins

Published by:
New Riders Publishing
201 West 103rd Street
Indianapolis, IN 46290 USA

Copyright © 1995 by New Riders Publishing

Printed in the United States of America 1 2 3 4 5 6 7 8 9 0

```
Cady, Dorothy L., 1953-
        CNE Short Course / Dorothy L. Cady, Drew
        Heywood, Blaine Homer,
              p.        cm.
        Includes index
        ISBN 1-56205-446-5 : $60.00
        1. NetWare (Computer file)  2. Operating systems
     (Computers)  3. Local area network (Computer
     networks)  I. Heywood, Drew.  II. Homer, Blaine,
     1964-     .  III. Title
     QA76.76.063C334    1995
     005.7'1369—dc20                        94-47042
                                               CIP
```

Warning and Disclaimer

Publisher	Don Fowley
Associate Publisher	Tim Huddleston
Product Development Manager	Rob Tidrow
Marketing Manager	Ray Robinson
Director of Special Projects	Cheri Robinson
Managing Editor	Tad Ringo

Product Director
Emmett Dulaney

Acquisitions Editor
Stacey Beheler

Software Specialist
Steve Weiss

Production Editor
Cliff Shubs

Copy Editors
Amy Bezek, Fran Blauw, John Kane, Sarah Kearns, Rob Lawson, Stacia Mellinger, John Sleeva, Suzanne Snyder, Phil Worthington, Lillian Yates

Technical Editor
Kurt Schernekau

Marketing Copywriter
Tamara Apple

Acquisitions Coordinator
Tracey Turgeson

Publisher's Assistant
Karen Opal

Cover Designer
Dan Armstrong

Book Designer
Kim Scott

Production Team Supervisor
Katy Bodenmiller

Graphics Image Specialists
Dennis Sheehan
Clint Lahnen

Production Analysts
Dennis Clay Hager
Angela Bannan
Bobbi Satterfield

Production Team
Georgiana Briggs, Don Brown, Michael Brumitt, Jama Carter, Charlotte Clapp, Terrie Deemer, Michael Dietsch, Terri Edwards, Judy Everly, Donna Haigerty, Louisa Klucznik, Ayanna Lacey, Kevin Laseau, Shawn MacDonald, Brian-Kent Proffitt, Linda Quiqley, Beth Rago, Erich Richter, SA Springer, Jill Tompkins, Tina Trettin, Scott Tullis, Mark Walchle, Jeff Weissenberger, Holly Wittenberg, Michelle Worthington

Indexer
Jeanne Clark

About the Authors

Dorothy L. Cady is a senior technical writer at Novell, Inc. in Provo, Utah. Ms. Cady started with Novell in 1990 as the team leader for the Software Testing Department's Documentation Testing Team, helping to ensure the quality of the documentation that ships with NetWare 2, 3, and 4, NetWare Lite, and Personal NetWare products. She is a Certified NetWare Instructor (CNI), a Certified NetWare Engineer (CNE), and a Certified NetWare Administrator (CNA). Aside from her duties as a technical writer, Ms. Cady also is a member of the adjunct faculty at Utah Valley State College and a freelance writer. Dorothy has over twenty years experience in the computer industry inculding both in private and public service. She also is the author of *CNA Study Guide* and *New Rider's Guide to NetWare Certification*, as well as co-authoring many other New Riders books.

Drew Heywood is a Product Development Specialist for New Riders, where he is responsible for developing books about computer networking and enterprise computing. For over fifteen years, Mr. Heywood has been involved with personal computers as an educator, and application programmer, and a system manager of local area networks and minicomputers. Mr. Heywood is a Certified NetWare Engineer (CNE) and has been working with Novell NetWare for eight years. In addition to his activities as a PDS for New Riders, Mr. Heywood has been a contributing author to several NRP books about networking.

Blaine Homer is a technical editor for *LAN Times*. He writes previews, reviews, and product comparisons. His technical beats includes network hardware, Novell products, network management applications and tools, and network security. Before joining the *LAN Times* Testing Center, Mr. Homer worked for Novell's internal network management team. He also worked for Novell's IS department repairing hardware and supporting the end user. Mr. Homer does private network installation and consulting. He has a B.S. degree from Brigham Young University's Marriott School of Management, with an emphasis in Information Systems.

Emmett Dulaney is a Product Development Specialist for New Riders Publishing. The author and co-author on several computer books, including *Inside UNIX* (NRP) and *Voodoo NetWare* (Ventura Press), he also is a frequent contributor to several magazines. An Associate Professor at Indiana-Purdue University of Fort Wayne, IN, Emmett has taught continuing education classes in Unix and writing, among other things, for several years.

Matthew Flint Arnett is a Product Reviews Editor for *LAN Times* magazine. He works in the *LAN Times* Testing Center in Provo, Utah where his beats include Internet/online services, optical storage, printing, RAID, security, storage management/tape backup, UPSes, Unix, and virus protection. Matt's background includes analog and digital hardware development and industry listing testing. He has also has extensive experience designing Secure Compartmented Information Facilities (SCIF) intruder detection systems for multiple government locations. Immediately prior to working with *LAN Times*, Matt owned and operated a network consulting company in Southern California where he stressed disaster prevention and data recovery.

Debra Neidermiller-Chaffins is Education Director for Computer Data, Inc. in Madison Heights, Michigan. Ms. Neidermiller-Chaffins started the education department at Computer Data in 1988 to help organizations develop autonomy and self sufficiency in training future Certified NetWare Engineers operations. She is a Certified NetWare Instructor and a CNE, specializing in training future CNEs. In addition to teaching, Ms. Neidermiller-Chaffins also supports a small client base, which provides her with a background of real-world networking scenarios. She is the author of *Inside Novell NetWare*, Special Edition, and *Inside NetWare Lite*, also published by New Riders Publishing.

Trademark Acknowledgments

Contents at a Glance

Introduction

Part I: NetWare 3.1x Administration

1 Understanding NetWare 3.1x Functions and Services 7
2 Understanding and Implementing NetWare 3.1x Network Security 23
3 Accessing NetWare 3.1x Network Services 39
4 Managing NetWare Services from the File Server Console 53
5 Preparing NetWare 3.1x Printing Services for Users 67
6 Preparing Other NetWare 3.1x Services for Users 83
7 Protecting the NetWare 3.1x Network 99

Part II: NetWare 3.1x Advanced Administration

8 Understanding NetWare 3.1x Server Basics 109
9 Understanding Memory and Performance in NetWare 3.1x Servers 129
10 Working with NetWare 3.1x Clients 147
11 Setting Up and Maintaining NetWare Print Services 163
12 Maintaining and Monitoring Netware 3.1x Servers 177
13 Supporting and Protecting Netware 3.1x Servers 195

Part III: NetWare 2.2 Administration

14 Comparing NetWare 2.2 and NetWare 3.12 207
15 Additional NetWare 2.2 System Management Information 221

Part IV: Networking Technologies

16 Computer Network Concepts 233
17 Network Services 239
18 The OSI Layered Protocol Model 255
19 Tranmission Media 261
20 Transmission Media Connections 291
21 OSI Physical Layer Concepts 311
22 OSI Data Link Layer Concepts 329
23 OSI Network Layer Concepts 345

24 OSI Transport Layer Concepts 355

25 OSI Session Layer Concepts 359

26 OSI Presentation Layer Concepts 363

27 OSI Application Layer Concepts... 369

28 Protocol Suites 377

29 Other Protocols and Standards 413

30 Tasks of Network Administrators 429

Part V: Service and Support

31 Troubleshooting the Network.. 435

32 Using Research Tools in Troubleshooting 443

33 Working with Network Adapter Cards and Cabling 457

34 Troubleshooting Network Storage Devices 491

35 Troubleshooting the DOS Workstation................................. 523

36 Troubleshooting Network Printing....................................... 535

37 Network Optimization and Disaster Recovery 541

Part VI: NetWare 3.1x Installation

38 Preparing for a NetWare Installation 561

39 Installation and Configuration 567

40 Migrating a 3.11 Server to a 3.12 Server 583

41 Installing Client Software 593

42 Tuning for Performance 607

Part VII: DOS/Microcomputer Basics

43 DOS Concepts for NetWare Administrators 621

44 Microcomputer Concepts for NetWare Administrators 641

Index 671

Table of Contents

Introduction   **1**

Who Should Read This Book? 2
How *CNE Short Course* Helps You 2
New Riders Publishing 2

Part I: Netware 3.1*x* Administration

1   Understanding NetWare 3.1*x* Functions and Services   **7**

Network Functions and Services 8
The Network Communication Process 9
    Link Support Layer 10
    Communications Protocol 11
    NetWare DOS Requester 11
    LAN Driver 11
The Network File System 11
    LOGIN 14
    MAIL 15
    PUBLIC 15
    SYSTEM 15
    ETC 15
    DELETED.SAV 16
    DOC 16
NetWare Utilities 16
    DOS Text Utilities 16
    Command-Line Utilities 17
    Graphical Utilities 17
The ElectroText Electronic Documentation 17
Questions 19
    Answers 21

2   Understanding and Implementing NetWare 3.1*x* Network Security   **23**

Manipulating NetWare Network and File System Security 24
    Login Security 24
    Rights Security 26
    Attributes Security 29
    File Server Security 29
Setting Up and Securing User and Group Accounts 31
Implementing Network and File System Security 32
Implementing File Server Console Security 34
Questions 36
    Answers 37

3   Accessing NetWare 3.1*x* Network Services   **39**

    Installing and Configuring a Network Client 40
    Connecting a Workstation to the Network 42
    Accessing the Network File System 43
    Viewing and Managing File System Information 44
        VOLINFO 45
        CHKVOL 45
        SLIST 45
        LISTDIR 46
        NDIR 46
        NCOPY 46
        FILER 47
        SALVAGE 48
        PURGE 50
    Questions 51
        Answers 52

4   Managing NetWare Services from the File Server Console   **53**

    Using Console Commands 54
        Configuration Console Commands 54
        Installation Console Commands 55
        Maintenance Console Commands 55
        Screen Display Console Commands 56
    Using NetWare Loadable Modules 56
        Disk Driver NLMs 57
        Management and Enhancement Utility NLMs 58
        LAN Driver NLM 61
    Accessing a Server Console from a Workstation 61
        REMOTE.NLM 61
        RSPX.NLM 62
        RS232.NLM 62
    Questions 64
        Answers 65

5   Preparing NetWare 3.1*x* Printing Services for Users   **67**

    Network Printing Services 68
        Basic Network Printing Components 68
        Network Print Services Setup 69
    Setting Up Network Printing Services 70
        Creating a Print Queue 70
        Creating a Print Server 71
        Configuring a Print Server 71
        Bringing Up a Print Server 72

Redirecting Print Jobs to Network Printers 74
Managing Network Print Jobs.. 75
Questions 79
    Answers 80

6   Preparing Other NetWare 3.1x Services for Users   83

Adding Network Application Software 84
The Function of Login Scripts 85
Build System and User Login Scripts 85
The NetWare Menu System 89
Create and Run a NetWare 3.12 Menu........................... 91
Convert Older NetWare Menus 93
Understand NetWare Basic MHS 93
Set Up and Administer Basic MHS 93
    Install Basic MHS 93
    Add a User 93
    Create a Distribution List 93
Use First Mail 93
    Send Mail Using First Mail 94
    Read Mail Using First Mail 94
Questions 95
    Answers 97

7   Protecting the NetWare 3.1x Network   99

Understanding System Fault Tolerance 100
Understanding Storage Management Services 102
Backup and Restore NetWare File Servers 103
Questions 105
    Answers 106

Part II: NetWare 3.1x Advanced Administration

8   Understanding NetWare 3.1x Server Basics   109

Understanding Server Components 110
    NetWare 3.1x Server Hardware Components 110
    NetWare 3.1x Server Software Components 112
Working with Server Configuration Files 115
    STARTUP.NCF 116
    AUTOEXEC.NCF 117

Describing Network Communication 118
Supported Name Spaces 118
Supported Frame Types 119
Supported Protocols 120
Understanding Name-Space Support 123
Starting a NetWare 3.12 Server 123
Questions 124
Answers 127

9 Understanding Memory and Performance in NetWare 3.1x Servers   129

How Server Memory Works 130
Memory Pools 130
NetWare File Server Memory Components 132
NetWare Server Memory 134
Determining Server Memory Requirements 135
Using Memory-Related Console Commands 138
The MEMORY Console Command 138
The REGISTER MEMORY Console Command 138
Optimizing Performance Using SET Parameters 140
How Protocols Affect Performance 142
LIP 142
Packet Burst 143
Questions 144
Answers 145

10 Working with NetWare 3.1x Clients   147

The ODI Environment 148
Installing and Updating Client Workstations 150
Installing Client Workstations 151
Updating Client Workstations 153
Working with the NetWare DOS Requester 154
Supporting Read-Only and Diskless Network Devices 159
Questions 161
Answers 162

11 Setting Up and Maintaining NetWare Print Services   163

Advanced Printing Services 164
Creating Default Print Job Settings 166
Printing Documents Using Default Settings 169
Maintaining Network Printing Services 170
Checking Printer Status 170
Stopping and Restarting Print Jobs 170

Mounting Forms 170

Adding Users to the Printer Notify List 171

Assigning a Print Queue to a Printer 171

Questions 173

Answers 175

12   **Maintaining and Monitoring NetWare 3.1x Servers**   **177**

Understanding Network Performance 178

Monitoring Server Information 180

Resource and Processor Utilization Information 181

Memory Statistics 184

Hard Disk Drive Status 185

Performing Server Maintenance 186

BINDFIX and BINDREST 187

VREPAIR 187

SBACKUP 189

Setting Server Time 189

Understanding Routing Information 190

Creating File Server Batch Files 191

Questions 192

Answers 193

13   **Supporting and Protecting NetWare 3.1x Servers**   **195**

Implementing Virus Protection 196

Backups and Restores 198

Backing Up a File Server Bindery 199

Backing Up a Network Client 200

Questions 202

Answers 203

Part III: NetWare 2.2 Administration

14   **Comparing NetWare 2.2 and NetWare 3.12**   **207**

NetWare 2.2 File System and Directory Structure 208

Accessing the NetWare 2.2 Network 209

NetWare 2.2 Security 210

NetWare Commands and Utilities 211

NetWare 2.2 Printing Services 214

Ensuring Compatibility of Network Applications 216

Login Scripts 216

Questions 218

Answers 219

15 **Additional NetWare 2.2 System Management Information** **221**

NetWare 2.2-Only Objectives 222
    System Manager Responsibilities 222
    Filling in a NetWare Log 222
    General System Management Resources 223
    Defining a Network 224
    Hardware Components 224
    Software Components 224
    Choosing and Loading IPX and the Shell 224
    The Best Option for Expanding Your Network 225
    The Distributed Processing Environment 225
The NetWare 2.2 Menu System 225
The NetWare 2.2 Backup and Restore Software 227
Questions 229
    Answers 230

Part IV: Networking Technologies

16 **Computer Network Concepts** **233**

Models of Network Computing 234
    Centralized Computing 234
    Distributed Computing 234
    Collaborative Computing 235
Local, Metropolitan, and Wide Area Networks 235
Components of Computer Networks 235
    Network Services 236
    Transmission Media 237
    Protocols 237
Questions 238
    Answers 238

17 **Network Services** **239**

File Services 240
    File Transfer 240
    File Storage 241
    File Archiving 242
    File-Update Synchronization 242
Print Services 243
    Providing Multiple Access 243
    Servicing Simultaneous Print Requests 243
    Operating without Distance Limitations 244

Managing Specialized Equipment Types 244
Providing Facsimile (Fax) Service 245
Message Services 245
Electronic Mail 245
Integrated Electronic Mail and Voice Mail 245
Object-Oriented Applications 246
Workgroup Applications 246
Directory Services 247
Application Services 247
Database Services 248
Implementing Services in Centralized and Distributed Environments 249
Control of Resources 250
Server Specialization 251
Selecting Network Operating Systems (NOS) 251
Questions 252
Answers 253

18 The OSI Layered Protocol Model   255

Rules and the Communication Process 256
The OSI Reference Model 256
How Peer Layers Communicate 258
Questions 260
Answers 260

19 Transmission Media   261

Network Transmission Media 262
Characteristics of Transmission Media 263
Bandwidth 263
Attenuation 264
Electromagnetic Interference 264
Cable Media 264
Coaxial Cable 264
Twisted-Pair Cables 266
Fiber-Optic Cable 270
Summary of Cable Characteristics 272
Wireless Media 273
Radio 273
Microwave 278
Infrared Systems 281
Summary of Wireless Media 283
Public and Private Network Services 284
The Public Telephone Network 284

The Internet 288
Questions 289
    Answers 290

20   Transmission Media Connections   291

Connecting Hardware 292
    Connectors for Multi-Wire Cable 292
    Connectors for Twisted-Pair Cables 293
    Connectors for Coaxial Cable 294
    Connectors for Fiber-Optic Cable 295
Network Connectivity Devices 296
    Network Interface Boards 296
    Hubs 297
    Repeaters 299
    Bridges 300
    Multiplexors 301
    Modems 301
Internetwork Connectivity Devices 302
    Routers 303
    Brouters 305
    CSU/DSUs 305
Important Terms from this Chapter 305
Questions 307
    Answers 309

21   OSI Physical Layer Concepts   311

Connection Types 312
Physical Topologies 312
    Physical Topologies Based on Multipoint Connections 312
    Physical Topologies Based on Point-to-Point Connections 314
Digital and Analog Signaling 317
    Digital Signaling Techniques 318
    Analog Signaling 319
Bit Synchronization 321
    Asynchronous Communication 322
    Synchronous Communication 322
Baseband and Broadband Transmissions 323
Multiplexing 324
    Frequency-Division Multiplexing 324
    Time-Division Multiplexing 325
Questions 326
    Answers 327

22 OSI Data Link Layer Concepts   **329**

Logical Topologies 330

Media Access Control 332

   Contention 332

   Token Passing 333

   Comparing Contention and Token Passing......................... 335

   Polling... 335

   Summary of Access Control Methods.................................. 336

Addressing.. 337

Transmission Synchronization 337

   Asynchronous Transmission 338

   Synchronous Transmission 339

   Isochronous Transmission 340

Connection Services 340

   Flow Control at the LLC Sublayer 341

   Error Control 341

Questions 343

   Answers 344

23 OSI Network Layer Concepts   **345**

Addressing.. 346

   Logical Network Addresses 346

   Service Addresses 346

   Addressing Summary 346

Switching 347

   Circuit Switching 347

   Message Switching 348

   Packet Switching 349

Routing Algorithms 350

   Distance Vector Routing 351

   Link-State Routing 352

Connection Services 352

   Network Layer Flow Control 352

   Network Layer Error Control 352

   Packet Sequence Control 353

Gateway Services 353

Questions 353

24 OSI Transport Layer Concepts   **355**

Addressing.. 356

   Connection Identifiers... 356

   Transaction Identifiers.. 356

Address/Name Resolution 356
    Service-Requester-Initiated Address/Name Resolution 356
    Service-Provider-Initiated Address/Name Resolution 357
Segment Development 357
Connection Services 357
    Segment Sequencing 357
    Error Control 357
    End-to-End Flow control 358
Questions 358

25 OSI Session Layer Concepts   **359**

Dialog Control 360
Session Administration 361
    Connection Establishment 361
    Data Transfer 362
    Connection Release 362
Questions 362

26 OSI Presentation Layer Concepts   **363**

Data Translation 364
    Bit Order 364
    Byte Order Translation 364
    Character Code Translation 364
    File Syntax Translation 365
Encryption 365
    Private Keys 367
    Public Keys 367
Questions 367

27 OSI Application Layer Concepts   **369**

Advertising Services 370
    Active Service Advertisement 370
    Passive Service Advertisement 370
Service Use Methods 370
    OS Call Interruption 370
    Remote Operation 371
    Collaborative Computing 371
Questions 372
    Answers 375

28   Protocol Suites   **377**

     Models and Protocols 378
     NetWare IPX/SPX 379
     Internet Protocols.. 382
     AppleTalk 389
     Digital Network Architecture 394
     Systems Network Architecture (SNA) 401
         SNA and the OSI Reference Model 401
         Network Addressable Units 403
         Key SNA Protocols 406
     Questions 410
         Answers 411

29   Other Protocols and Standards   **413**

     The IEEE 802 Family 414
         IEEE 802.2 414
         IEEE 802.3 414
         IEEE 802.4 416
         IEEE 802.5 417
         IEEE 802.6 417
         IEEE 802.9 417
         IEEE 802.11 417
         IEEE 802.12 418
     Fiber Distributed Data Interface 418
     Serial Line Internet Protocol and Point-to-Point Protocol 420
     CCITT/ITU X.25 421
     Frame Relay 422
     ISDN and B-ISDN 423
     Synchronous Optical Network and the Synchronous Digital Hierarchy 424
     Asynchronous Transfer Mode (ATM) 425
     Switched Multimegabit Digital Service (SMDS) 427
     Questions 428
         Answers 428

30   Tasks of Network Administrators   **429**

     Configuration Management 430
     Fault Management 430
     Performance Management... 431
     Security Management.. 432
     Accounting Management 432

Part V: Service and Support

31 Troubleshooting the Network   435

    Problem Prevention 436
        Physical Problems 436
        Electrical Problems 436
        Security 437
        Viruses 438
    Troubleshooting 438
        Documents and Records 439
        Diagnostic Software 440
    Questions 442
        Answers 442

32 Using Research Tools in Troubleshooting   443

    NSEPro 444
        Installing NSEPro 444
        Using NSEPro 445
        Running Queries 445
    What's New 447
        NetWare Support Encyclopedia Modules 447
    NetWire 449
    Micro House Technical Library (MHTL) 449
    Questions 456
        Answers 456

33 Working with Network Adapter Cards and Cabling   457

    Exploring ARCnet Specifications 459
        ARCnet Board Settings 460
        ARCnet Cabling 460
        ARCnet Troubleshooting 462
    Understanding Ethernet Specifications 463
        Ethernet Board Settings 464
        Ethernet Cabling 465
        Ethernet Frame Types 471
        Ethernet Troubleshooting 473
    Understanding Token Ring Specifications 474
        Token Ring Board Settings 474
        Token Ring Cabling 475
        Token Ring Troubleshooting 478

Understanding FDDI 481
   Advantages of Using FDDI 482
   Disadvantages of Using FDDI 483
   FDDI Cabling.. 484
   FDDI Troubleshooting 484
Which Topology Should I Use? 485
Questions 487
   Answers 489

34   Troubleshooting Network Storage Devices   491

Hard Drives 492
   Types of Hard Drive Interfaces 492
   Setting Up Hard Drives... 499
   Understanding Disk Mirroring and Disk Duplexing 511
Working with CD-ROM Drives 517
   Tips for Working with CD-ROM Players 517
Working with Magneto-Optical Drives... 518
Questions 519
   Answers 521

35   Troubleshooting the DOS Workstation   523

Working with IPX/NETX.. 524
   What To Do If You Cannot Connect to the Server 524
   The Watchdog 525
Working with ODI 525
   Troubleshooting ODI 525
Working with DOS Requester 526
   Installing the DOS Requester 527
Working with Remote Boot 527
Troubleshooting with TRACK 528
Diagnosing Conflicts... 528
Conflict Resolution 529
Working with PC Memory 530
   Memory Types 531
DR DOS.. 532
Questions 533
   Answers 534

36   Troubleshooting Network Printing   535

Preventing Problems 536
Troubleshooting... 536
   Physical Problems 536
   Print Queues 537

Print Servers 537
Remote Printers 537
Printer Configuration 538
Printer Utilities 538
PostScript Printers 538
Questions 539
Answers 539

37   Network Optimization and Disaster Recovery   541

The SET Parameter 542
Communications Parameters 542
Memory Parameters 543
File Caching Parameters 543
Directory Caching Parameters 544
File System Parameters 544
Lock Parameters 546
Transaction Tracking Parameters 546
Miscellaneous Parameters 547
Performance Modifications and Considerations 548
Monitoring with MONITOR 549
Connection Information 549
Disk Information 550
LAN Information 551
System Module Information 552
Lock File Server Console 552
File Open/Lock Activity 552
Resource Utilization 553
PATCHMAN 553
Bridges, Routers, and Hubs 554
Protocol Analyzers 555
Third-Party Disaster Recovery Products 556
Burst Mode Advantages and Drawbacks 556
Questions 558
Answers 558

Part VI: NetWare 3.1x Installation

38   Preparing for a NetWare Installation   561

Terms and Files 562
Finding Third-Party Drivers and NLMs 563
Required Software 564

Required Hardware 564
Questions 566
    Answers 566

39   Installation and Configuration   567

Performing a NetWare 3.12 Installation 568
    Partitioning the Hard Disk for DOS 568
    Formatting the Hard Disk with DOS 568
    Entering a Server Name 569
    Assigning a Unique Internal IPX Number 570
    Entering Local Support Codes 570
    Selecting the File Name Format 570
    Loading the Disk Driver 571
    Loading INSTALL.NLM 571
    Creating a NetWare Partition 571
    Creating a NetWare Volume 572
    Mount Volume SYS 573
    Copying Public and System Files 573
    Loading the LAN Driver 574
    Creating AUTOEXEC.NCF and STARTUP.NCF Files 577
Differences between a NetWare 3.11 and NetWare 3.12 Installation 579
    CD-ROM Installation Issues 579
    NetWare 3.12's INSTALL.BAT File 580
    The Automatically Installed File System 580
Questions 581
    Answers 582

40   Migrating a 3.11 Server to a 3.12 Server   583

Overview 584
Across-the-Wire Migration 586
The Same-Server Method 587
Performing the 3.11 to 3.12 Upgrade Steps 589
Post-Migration Procedures 590
Questions 591
    Answers 591

41   Installing Client Software   593

Client Support in NetWare 3.12 594
    Macintosh 594
    OS/2 594
    Unix 594
    DOS 594

Differences between the Shell and Requester 595
NET.CFG File 598
    Performance 599
Performing Workstation Installation Steps 600
    Installation Methods 601
Installation Steps 602
Questions 605
    Answers 605

42 Tuning for Performance   **607**
NetWare 3.11 Server Components 608
    Memory Pools 608
    File System Adjustments 611
    Communications Subsystems 612
    System Processor 616
Questions 617
    Answers 617

Part VII: DOS/Microcomputer Basics

43 DOS Concepts for NetWare Administrators   **621**
The DOS File System 622
    File Names 622
    Types of Files 623
    File Attributes 623
Booting DOS 623
Using DOS Commands 624
    Internal Commands 624
    External Commands 625
    Command Parameters 625
    Command Switches 625
    Case Insensitivity 625
    Error Messages 625
Procedures Used with Disks 626
    Formatting Floppy Disks 626
    Formatting Hard Disks 626
    DOS File Storage Methods 626
    Changing Disk Volume Labels 627
    Creating Boot Disks 627
    Selecting a Default Disk 627
    Accessing Files on Non-Default Disks 627
    Copying Disks 628

Directories and Subdirectories 628
  Creating Directories 628
  Deleting Directories 628
  The Default Directory 629
  Relative Directory Paths 629
  Using a DOS Path 629
  How DOS Searches for Commands 629
File Management Procedures 630
  The DIR Command 630
  TYPE 630
  Copying Files 630
  Copying Input to a File 631
  DEL and ERASE 631
  Wild Cards 631
  ATTRIB 631
  XCOPY 632
Utility Commands 633
  DATE and TIME 633
  VER 633
  PROMPT 633
  CLS 633
  PRINT 633
  Redirection 634
Batch Files 634
  REM 634
  ECHO 634
  PAUSE 635
AUTOEXEC.BAT 635
Installing and Configuring DOS 635
  Partitioning Hard Drives 635
  Formatting the DOS Partition 636
  Configuring CONFIG.SYS 637
  Questions 638
  Answers 639

44 Microcomputer Concepts for NetWare Administrators   641

Basic Functions of a Computer 642
Microcomputer Hardware 642
  Microprocessor Characteristics 642
  The Expansion Bus 648
  Microcomputer Memory 654

Disk Storage 658
Hard Disk Drives 661
Ports 663
Display Devices 665
Configuration Issues for PCs 666
Configuring CMOS 667
Booting the Computer 667
Questions 668
Answers 670

Index　　　**671**

INTRODUCTION

CNE Short Course *is designed for NetWare system administrators who are seeking certification as Certified NetWare Engineers. It breaks the seven tests necessary to obtain such certification into parts and gives the information required to comprehend and master test objectives.*

Who Should Read This Book?

CNE Short Course is designed for advanced NetWare system administrators who have only one purpose in mind—to pass the certification tests. It does not purport to teach you networking or NetWare. Rather, it assumes that you have a working knowledge of both and want to know the minute details that you rarely deal with as an administrator, but which quickly become test fodder.

How *CNE Short Course* Helps You

The tests are broken into parts to make studying easier and immediately alert you as to which test you are reading information for. The first part covers NetWare 3.1*x* administration—the only test you need to take if you want to be a Certified NetWare Administrator. If you want to go further, the CNA certification is a good first step toward that of CNE.

The second continues the theme and addresses advanced administration, presenting the material and knowledge necessary to prepare for that test.

Part 3 focuses on NetWare 2.2 administration, comparing and contrasting it with what was learned in the preceding two parts. This serves as the elective requirement in the CNE curriculum.

The fourth part looks at networking technologies. Almost since the beginning, all other vendors offering certification programs have accepted that of Novell's as a substitute for theirs—a tribute to how encompassing it is.

Part 5 concentrates on service and support—the most difficult of all aspects of CNE certification. It fully covers NSEPro, and the MicroHouse Technical Library, a copy of which is included on the accompanying CD.

The sixth part reviews NetWare 3.1*x* installation and configuration. Do not be fooled by the name; there are many items which can be grouped under the heading of Configuration, and the existing test does so with all of them.

The seventh, and last, part looks at DOS and microcomputer concepts and prepares you for that test.

It must be noted that command lines that you enter are sometimes interrupted on contiguous lines by the ➥ symbol, which indicates the text should be entered on a single line on your computer. We simply were unable to fit it on one line.

On this book's disk:

The accompanying disk contains a copy of the MicroHouse Technical Library so you can familiarize yourself with it before attempting to take the Service and Support test. Additionally, there is a complete copy of Test Prep, the New Riders' test engine that enables you to evaluate your skills before taking any of the actual tests.

New Riders Publishing

The staff of New Riders Publishing is committed to bringing you the very best in computer reference material. Each New Riders book is the result of months of work by authors and staff who research and refine the information contained within its covers.

As part of this commitment to you, the NRP reader, New Riders invites your input. Please let us know if you enjoy this book, if you have trouble with the information and examples presented, or if you have a suggestion for the next edition.

Please note, however, that the New Riders staff cannot serve as a technical resource for NetWare or NetWare certification-related questions, including hardware- and software-related problems. Refer to the documentation that accompanies your NetWare operating system or NetWare application package for help with specific problems.

If you have a question or comment about any New Riders book, there are several ways to contact New Riders Publishing. We will respond to as many readers as we can. Your name, address, or phone number will never become part of a mailing list or be used for any purpose other than to help us continue to bring you the best books possible. You can write us at the following address:

New Riders Publishing
Attn: Associate Publisher
201 W. 103rd Street
Indianapolis, IN 46290

If you prefer, you can fax New Riders Publishing at (317) 581-4670.

As well, you can leave a voice mail message to New Riders at (317) 581-3871.

You can send electronic mail to New Riders from a variety of sources. NRP maintains several mailboxes organized by topic area. Mail in these mailboxes is forwarded to the staff member who is best able to address your concerns. Substitute the appropriate mailbox name from the list below when addressing your e-mail. The mailboxes are as follows:

ADMIN	Comments and complaints for NRP's Publisher
APPS	Word, Excel, WordPerfect, other office applications
ACQ	Book proposals inquiries by potential authors
CAD	AutoCAD, 3D Studio, AutoSketch and CAD products
DATABASE	Access, dBASE, Paradox and other database products
GRAPHICS	CorelDRAW!, Photoshop, and other graphics products
INTERNET	Internet
NETWORK	NetWare, LANtastic, and other network-related topics
OS	MS-DOS, OS/2, all OS except Unix and Windows
UNIX	Unix
WINDOWS	Microsoft Windows (all versions)
OTHER	Anything that doesn't fit the above categories

If you use an MHS e-mail system that routes through CompuServe, send your messages to:

mailbox @ NEWRIDER

To send NRP mail from CompuServe, use the following to address:

MHS: *mailbox* @ NEWRIDER

To send mail from the Internet, use the following address format:

mailbox@newrider.mhs.compuserve.com

NRP is an imprint of Macmillan Computer Publishing. To obtain a catalog or information or to purchase any Macmillan Computer Publishing book, call (800) 428-5331.

Thank you for selecting *CNE Short Course*!

PART I

Netware 3.1x Administration

1   *Understanding NetWare 3.1x Functions and Services* 7

2   *Understanding and Implementing NetWare 3.1x Network Security* 23

3   *Accessing NetWare 3.1x Network Services* 39

4   *Managing NetWare Services from the File Server Console* 53

5   *Preparing NetWare 3.1x Printing Services for Users* 67

6   *Preparing Other NetWare 3.1x Services for Users* 83

7   *Protecting the NetWare 3.1x Network* 99

1

Understanding NetWare 3.1x Functions and Services

Access to resources is provided by NetWare through three types of utilities—DOS text, command-line, and graphical—which interact with the file server through functions and services. The purpose of this chapter is to cover those functions and services, so you can do the following effectively:

- *Describe network functions and services*
- *Use the network communication system*
- *Use the NetWare file system*
- *Use NetWare utilities*
- *Use the ElectroText Electronic Documentation*

Network Functions and Services

The basic function of a network is to enable you to access shared network resources and provide services to clients. Those services can and often do include:

- File storage and retrieval
- Distributed and centralized processing
- Security
- Printing
- Back up and protection of network data
- Inter-office/department communication
- Network connectivity

File storage and retrieval is provided through physical means—hard disk drives on network file servers—and through logical means—networking software that provides access to the physical hard disks.

Distributed processing is provided through microprocessors found on the system boards of each network workstation. NetWare offers centralized processing by providing network clients with access to mainframes and minicomputer systems that also can be part of the network.

Security features can be implemented at the level of your choice.

Printing services are provided through printers attached to the network at different locations.

NetWare enables you to make backup copies of your network data and NetWare's bindery (user-

related information) as well as to choose the type of backup device and software to be used. The SBACKUP utility is provided by default, but you also have the option of using more sophisticated or user-friendly backup programs provided by third-party vendors.

NetWare provides communication across network lines from office to office, workgroup to workgroup, company to company, even country to country. Communication is the key to networking, and communication is provided by NetWare's operating system software. The physical connection enabling communication is accomplished with *network interface cards* (NICs), also known as network boards.

The function of a NetWare file server is to provide network users with the services and functions they need. Those services, described previously, include but are not limited to the following:

- File storage and retrieval services
- Security services
- Printing services

For NetWare file servers to provide these services, special software must be loaded into file server memory (RAM). This software consists of two main pieces: the core *operating system* (OS) and *NetWare Loadable Modules* (NLM).

The core operating system provides three basic services, as follows:

- File storage
- Security (including Packet Signature)
- Routing

NetWare Loadable Modules provide other networking services including:

- Printing services

- File storage management

- Server management and monitoring

- Remote console access

- Network protection services through *uninterruptible power supply* (UPS) management

- Network communication services

To access services and functions, network users connect various types of computers and other devices to the network. Any device connected to the network and capable consequently of requesting services from the network is called a *network client.* Computers connected to the network are included in this group, but most often are referred to as *workstations* rather than network clients.

NetWare supports not only *Disk Operating System* (DOS)-based computers (clients), but the following types of clients as well:

- Microsoft Windows

- Macintosh

- Unix

- OS/2

The Network Communication Process

Hardware requirements for communication include the addition of a network board into an available slot in your computer. Furthermore, the board is then physically connected to the network cabling system, using a specific type of cable and connectors (see fig. 1.1).

Figure 1.1
Basic network communication.

Network Cable

Network Board

Client

Network Board

Client

File Server

Network Board

Your workstation can connect to another network using a different type of cabling and network board scheme. This other connection is accomplished through a network router—a device capable of routing network communications between unlike networks.

After a physical (hardware) connection is made, a software connection must be established. To make a software connection to the network, several files must be loaded into the workstation's memory (see fig. 1.2).

The software your workstation needs to accomplish network communication includes the following:

■ LSL.COM (referred to as the Link Support Layer)

■ LAN driver (such as NE2000.COM or NE2.COM)

■ IPXODI.COM (the communications protocol)

■ VLM.EXE (the NetWare DOS Requester)

For the software to function properly, it must be loaded into the workstation's memory in the same order listed. These software elements perform a variety of tasks.

Link Support Layer

The *Link Support Layer* (LSL) implements the ODI specification (see communications protocol). Its primary function is to route network information between the LAN driver and the appropriate communication software. In this capacity, it functions much like a switchboard—it ensures that all communication is sent to its proper destination. The LSL is implemented at each workstation when you load the LSL.COM file.

Figure 1.2

Files used for network communication.

Communications Protocol

The Communications Protocol is a set of rules loaded into workstation memory that determine how communication takes place. NetWare 3.12 follows the *Open Data-Link Interface* (ODI) communications protocol when you load the IPXODI.COM file.

NetWare DOS Requester

The purpose of the NetWare DOS Requester is to allow connection of DOS-based workstations to the network. It functions as a connection point between the workstation's local operating system and the network. A series of files called *Virtual Loadable Modules* (VLM), along with the VLM Manager (VLM.EXE), make up the NetWare DOS Requester. When you load the VLM.EXE file at your workstation, it loads the other required VLMs.

LAN Driver

The LAN driver activates and controls the network board in your workstation. You must load a LAN driver that matches the network board installed in your workstation. NetWare provides LAN drivers for many common network boards. If you are using a network board for which NetWare does not supply a matching LAN driver, simply load the appropriate LAN driver supplied with the network board when you purchased it.

 Not all LAN drivers support the ODI specification. You must use a LAN driver that does support ODI when running on a NetWare 3.12 network. These drivers are referred to as *Multiple Link Interface Drivers* (MLID).

All the network communication files are loaded at the workstation by typing these file names at the DOS prompt or by putting them into your workstation's startup file. After this software is loaded into your workstation's memory, the workstation can send requests for services and data, as well as receive responses and information across the network.

 To help you remember all the software associated with network communications, remember the following sentence, which is also noted in figure 1.2:

To ensure successful communication, remember to **AD**d the **VIL**lai**N** to your workstation:

1. **A.** Applications software

2. **D.** DOS (or other supported workstation operating system)

3. **V.** VLM.EXE

4. **I.** IPXODI.COM

5. **L.** LSL.COM

6. **N.** NE2000 (LAN card for your network board)

Now that your workstation is connected to the file server, you can access network information. To optimize that access, you must understand how the information is arranged on the file server.

The Network File System

NetWare 3.12 file servers provide storage and retrieval of files by giving network clients access to its hard disk(s). Each hard disk is organized into logical structures containing volumes and directories.

Volumes are logical divisions of the hard disk. They are the highest logical level on a NetWare file server (see fig. 1.3). Volumes contain directories, which are the second logical level. Subdirectories and files comprise the third logical level. They cannot be stored directly at the volume level; they are stored in directories, which are stored on volumes.

The NetWare operating system has requirements of its own in order for it to function and provide network services. The logical division into volumes is one of those requirements. Another is that of specific NetWare directories into which NetWare can store and retrieve various files it needs to perform requested functions and to provide required services.

In the DOS environment, NetWare volumes are the logical equivalent to the DOS root. As with the DOS directory structure, the highest level you can

access on a NetWare file server hard disk is the root (volume). Also, as with the DOS root, there are specific technical requirements associated with volumes. These specifications include the following:

■ A volume name must be two to fifteen characters long and follow the same basic naming conventions as DOS (0-9 and A-Z). However, NetWare volume names can include symbols such as the underscore (_). Volume names are identified by the colon (:) that immediately follows them, so a colon cannot be used in the volume name.

■ Each volume name on a file server must be unique to that file server, although the same volume name can be used on other file servers.

Figure 1.3

NetWare file system structure.

For example, every NetWare file server has a SYS: volume, but no NetWare file server can have two volumes called SYS.

■ A volume can be as large as 32 TB and can span as many as 32 hard disks.

■ A file server can have a maximum of 64 volumes on it, but the total size for all volumes is limited to 32 TB.

Directories are the next-highest level in the NetWare file system structure. Directories can have files and other directories (subdirectories) beneath them. NetWare, like DOS, uses a hierarchical file storage system (see fig. 1.4).

The main function of a NetWare directory structure is to provide organization for files and subdirectories. Each directory, subdirectory, and file has its own name, a name unique within a particular area of the directory structure. You can have more than one subdirectory with the same name if each of these subdirectories are stored beneath a different directory. Because directories, subdirectories, and files are accessed by name, no directory, subdirectory, or file can have the same name as another directory, subdirectory, or file at the same level within the file system structure.

NetWare's directory structure uses drive letters and specific paths. A path begins with the name of the file server and is followed by a volume name, a directory name, and, if appropriate, the names of any subdirectories below that point in the directory structure. A typical NetWare directory path might look similar to the following:

F:Acct_Server/SYS:Public/Users/Sam

The letter F is the drive letter assigned to this specific path, as noted by the colon which follows it. In DOS, only drive letters representing actual

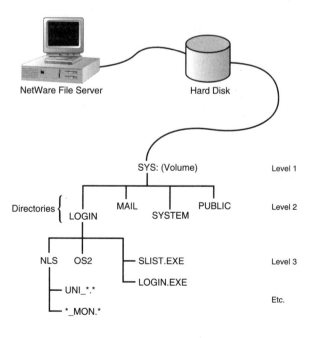

Figure 1.4
NetWare's hierarchical file storage system.

physical drives or logical drives formed by creating DOS partitions are used. In NetWare, every letter of the alphabet can be used as a NetWare drive, assuming your workstation does not need the drive letter to represent a physical or logical DOS drive.

Acct_Server is the name of the file server on which the remainder of this path can be found. When specifying a NetWare path, the name of the file server must be followed by either a forward (/) or a backward (\) slash.

SYS represents the name of the NetWare volume and must be followed by a colon, which indicates that the name that precedes it is a NetWare volume.

USERS is the name of a directory which can be found on the SYS: volume. It is followed by a slash, which is used from here on out in the NetWare path to indicate subdirectories.

SAM is the name of a subdirectory found below the USERS directory. In many network environments, this path would represent the home directory for a network user called SAM, who would use this home directory to file all his personal files. In it he can create other subdirectories and extend the NetWare directory structure to as many levels as the operating system allows.

NetWare requires specific directories to set up and access the files it needs to operate. When you install NetWare, it creates seven directories and installs the files it requires into these directories. The directories NetWare installation creates include the following:

- LOGIN
- MAIL
- PUBLIC
- SYSTEM
- ETC

These directories are all created below the SYS: volume in the file system structure.

LOGIN

The first directory you access on a NetWare file server is the LOGIN directory. It contains several files important to your initial file server access, including SLIST.EXE and LOGIN.EXE.

SLIST

SLIST.EXE is a NetWare utility used to see the names of all file servers that the file server to which you are logging in can see. To make it easier for you to find a particular file server's name, SLIST.EXE provides the list of known file servers in alphabetical order. In addition, SLIST.EXE provides some basic information about each file server. This information includes the following:

- Network
- Node address
- Status

The network address is the assignment of the ipx internal net for the server. The node address in 3.*x* is always 1.

The status information for a workstation is a little more complex. There are three types of status that can be displayed: blank, Default, and Attached. The status displayed indicates the relationship of this workstation to the file server, not the actual or physical status of the file server.

A blank or no status indicates that there is no current relationship between this workstation and this file server. The fact that the file server is included in the list indicates that the workstation can see this server, but otherwise the workstation and file server have no established relationship.

A Default status indicates the workstation is currently connected to this file server and this is the file server from which you are running any NetWare-related commands.

An Attached status indicates that the workstation has loaded the appropriate files and has established communication with this file server. It often indicates that this was the first server to which the workstation was able to establish a network connection (attachment), so that it could see the LOGIN directory and gain access to the appropriate file server by running the LOGIN.EXE file.

LOGIN

The LOGIN.EXE file enables you to identify yourself to the network using your assigned network USERID (assigned login name), and if applicable, related password. After you successfully identify yourself to the network, you are able to access network files and resources to which you have been given rights.

MAIL

The MAIL directory contains a mail subdirectory that is named with a unique one to eight digit hexidecimal number for each NetWare user. These directories are created for each user when given a USERID and account on the network. These subdirectories contain a user's personal login script, as well as any printer definition files created for the user's personal use. These files are identified as

PRINTCON.DAT files. The Supervisor's mail subdirectory is always identified with just the numeral 1.

PUBLIC

The PUBLIC directory contains all the utilities and commands that most network users are allowed to and might need to access. It also contains files used for defining printers (printer definition files—PDF files), and files the NetWare OS uses when it has to perform various system subroutines (overlay—OVL files). In addition, the PUBLIC directory contains all the help files (*.HLP) for the utilities and commands located in this directory. These help files give you online information related to these utilities and commands to help you properly execute and use them.

SYSTEM

The SYSTEM directory contains those NetWare utilities and command-line commands that only network supervisors and users of equivalent status can use. It also contains the NetWare Loadable Modules (NLM) and files intended for use by the NetWare operating system. Three other directories are sometimes created, as well:

- ETC
- DELETED.SAV
- DOC

ETC

Because correct connectivity is important in the NetWare environment, this directory contains files to be used with TCP/IP connectivity. These files are text files that provide connectivity information about other network devices.

DELETED.SAV

The DELETED.SAV directory contains files that have been deleted and files that at one time were stored in a directory that no longer exists. NetWare enables you to undelete files you have deleted. Furthermore, when configured to do so, it saves the files you have deleted in the directories in which they were originally stored. If you also delete those directories, the deleted files, of course, cannot be stored there and are instead stored in the DELETED.SAV directory.

Deleted files do not appear on the file list when you request a directory listing. To see which files have been deleted and might be recoverable, you must use NetWare's salvage feature.

DOC

NetWare 3.12 ships with a full set of documentation on CD-ROM. It also includes various files required to access this online documentation set. This directory stores the electronic versions of the NetWare manuals, if you choose to install them.

NetWare Utilities

As discussed previously, several of the system-created directories contain utilities that both regular users and network administrators can use. There are three types of *interfaces* (methods of access and control) used by these utilities. The type of interface that a utility uses also is used to identify the type of utility. The three types of network utilities available on a NetWare network include the following:

- DOS text utilities
- Command-line utilities
- Graphical utilities

Though the interface used by a given NetWare utility might differ from that of another utility, together, all these NetWare utilities provide the basic functionality needed to administer and use network resources.

DOS Text Utilities

All DOS text utilities use a menu-based interface. Information shown includes the name of the utility, the version number, the current date and time, the name of the user accessing this utility, and the name of the file server the user is currently accessing. All this information is displayed on the command line.

Figure 1.5 shows the SYSCON main screen.

Within all DOS text utilities you can use function keys to perform basic tasks or functions. The available function keys include the following:

- **F1** Opens the help (HLP) file for this utility
- **F3** Enables you to choose an option to modify it
- **F5** Lets you mark multiple items upon which to simultaneously perform the same action
- **ALT+F10** Enables you to exit the utility at any given point

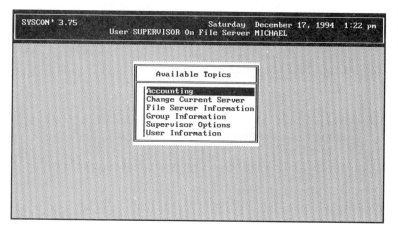

Figure 1.5
SYSCON DOS text utility main screen.

Command-Line Utilities

Command-line utilities have no menu interface and are often provided as an alternative to using either the DOS text utilities or the graphical utilities.

Graphical Utilities

Graphical utilities have a *graphical-user interface* (GUI). Figure 1.6 shows a graphical utility.

As with the command-line utilities, it might not always be easy or instinctive for you to understand how to use a particular utility or how to perform a given task using that utility. To help you, NetWare utilities provide online (on-screen) help that you can access from within the utility. How you access this online help depends on the type of utility you are using—text, command-line, or graphical.

To access help from within a DOS text utility, press F1. DOS text utility help is contact sensitive; meaning, wherever you are within the utility, pressing F1 displays a help screen related to the area of the utility. In the SYSCON utility, for example (refer to fig. 1.5), if you chose the first menu item from the Available Topics menu, you could press F1 to see a help screen related to that specific menu item.

To access help from a command-line utility, type the utility name followed by a blank space, a slash, and a question mark.

To access help from within a graphical utility, choose the Help button from the button bar. The Help button shown previously in figure 1.6 is the question mark displayed as the last button in the button bar.

The ElectroText Electronic Documentation

NetWare provides another online help resource called *Novell ElectroText*, an electronic copy of the entire NetWare 3.12 manual set. If you install it, the ElectroText software can be stored on the file server, a workstation, or accessed from the CD-ROM disk.

Novell's ElectroText software is provided through three major components, as follows:

■ **Search engine.** Locates information in NetWare's electronic manual set

Figure 1.6

*A NetWare graphical
utility.*

Figure 1.6

*A NetWare graphical
utility.*

■ **Bookshelf.** Contains the NetWare 3.12 set of electronic manuals

■ **Viewer.** Enables you to move through, read, and print Novell's electronic documentation

You can only run ElectroText through Windows. From within Windows, select the ElectroText icon. After ElectroText opens, choose the NetWare 3.12 manuals; then open one of the books, such as Concepts or System Administration. Furthermore, before users can access Novell's ElectroText software, you must set up each user's MS Windows workstation to display the icon for starting the feature.

After you have opened a book, you can activate the search engine by using the Search field found at the bottom of either a library or *bookshelf window* (a window containing the collection of available documents) to search for a specific topic. You also can use the outline to choose specific information that you want to read.

Novell's ElectroText software also provides a viewer that is used to open books, navigate through books, and print portions of books; that is, the viewer is used to activate and navigate Novell ElectroText.

Before anyone can use Novell's ElectroText, certain related software must be installed on the network. To install ElectroText, your system must meet the minimum requirements, which include the following:

■ At least 30 MB of available disk storage space

■ A copy of the program software, ET.EXE

■ A copy of the NetWare 3.12 electronic book set

Once you meet these minimum requirements, you can set up the ElectroText software so users can access it from any of the following:

■ A Microsoft Windows client

■ A NetWare 3.12 file server

■ A CD-ROM drive

Questions

1. Which of the following is NOT a service provided by NetWare 3.12?

   ○ A. File storage and retrieval

   ○ B. Distributed and centralized processing

   ○ C. Security

   ○ D. Interoffice telephone communication

2. Of the following, which THREE are provided by the NetWare core operating system?

   ☐ A. File storage

   ☐ B. Packet Signature

   ☐ C. Network management

   ☐ D. Routing

3. The file whose primary function is to route network information between the LAN driver and the appropriate communication software is called _____.

   ○ A. LSL.COM

   ○ B. LAN driver

   ○ C. IPXODI.COM

   ○ D. NetWare DOS Requester

4. The set of rules that determine how the network and workstation communicate is implemented at each workstation when you load the _____ file.

   ○ A. LSL.COM

   ○ B. LAN driver

   ○ C. IPXODI.COM

   ○ D. NetWare DOS Requester

5. The main function of a NetWare directory structure is to do which of the following?

   ○ A. Provide file and directory organization

   ○ B. Emulate the DOS environment

   ○ C. Allow storage of Macintosh files on disk

   ○ D. Provide advanced file system security

6. The directory containing all the utilities and commands that most network users are able to and might need to access is the _____ directory.

   ○ A. SYSTEM

   ○ B. PUBLIC

   ○ C. MAIL

   ○ D. ETC

7. In which directory are the NLMs stored?

   ○ A. SYSTEM

   ○ B. PUBLIC

   ○ C. MAIL

   ○ D. ETC

8. Of the three types of NetWare 3.12 utilities, which type does NOT provide online help?

   ○ A. DOS GUI

   ○ B. Command-line

   ○ C. DOS text

   ○ D. Graphical

9. To activate and navigate DOS text utility help, press the _____ key while the utility is running.

   ○ A. F1

   ○ B. F3

   ○ C. F5

   ○ D. Alt+F10

10. If you choose the help button (?), for which type of utility will you be activating online help?

   ○ A. DOS text

   ○ B. Command-line

   ○ C. NetWare User Tools

   ○ D. GUI

11. The _____ utility requires you to type /? to activate help.

   ○ A. DOS text

   ○ B. command-line

   ○ C. GUI

   ○ D. ElectroText

12. The help system that must be started from inside MS Windows is called _____.

   ○ A. DOS text

   ○ B. command-line

   ○ C. GUI

   ○ D. ElectroText

13. The primary file used to install ElectroText is called _____.

   ○ A. INSTALL.NLM

   ○ B. DYNATEXT.INI

   ○ C. SYSDOCS.CFG

   ○ D. ET.EXE

14. Basic information NOT shown on the main screen of DOS text utilities is _____.

   ○ A. the name of the utility

   ○ B. the utility's version number

   ○ C. the current date and time

   ○ D. None of the Above

15. Login security is provided by _____.

   ○ A. requiring each user to have a
        unique network identification

   ○ B. making passwords mandatory

   ○ C. providing Packet Signature at the
        file server, client, and file server and
        client levels

   ○ D. creating SYS volume at installation

Answers

1. D	9. A
2. A B D	10. D
3. A	11. B
4. C	12. D
5. A	13. D
6. B	14. D
7. A	15. A
8. A	

Understanding and Implementing NetWare 3.1x Network Security

There are several aspects of NetWare security that you need to understand, such as the overall design and availability of security, as well as how to implement it. The chapter is broken into the following four sections:

- *Manipulating NetWare network and file system security*

- *Setting up and securing user and group accounts*

- *Implementing network and file system security*

- *Implementing file server console security*

Manipulating NetWare Network and File System Security

The levels of network security and how they work are illustrated in figure 2.1. They consist of the following:

- Login
- Rights
- Attributes
- File server

NetWare's four security levels control access to information on the network. Login security controls user access to the network. Rights security controls user access to network resources. Attributes security controls what users can do with or to network resources. File server security controls user access to the file server through the file server console.

Login Security

This is the first and most rudimentary level of network security. Components consist of a valid network *user ID* (also called the username) and an associated password.

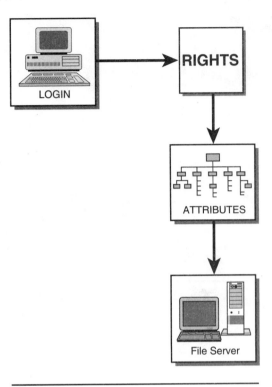

Figure 2.1
The NetWare security levels.

The first step in the login security process is *validating* the user, which involves the following:

- Checking for password requirements
- Matching the user's ID and password
- Checking user account restrictions

NetWare's security system validates network users by checking the login information that the user provides (user ID and password) against the information stored in the NetWare bindery about that user.

Note The NetWare bindery is a database containing three types of information, including the following:

■ **Objects.** Physical or logical entities, such as users and groups

■ **Properties.** Characteristics of each object in the NetWare bindery, such as password requirements and group members

■ **Data sets.** Values assigned to each bindery property, such as the actual password used by a given user

After a network user's ID and password have been checked, the user's request for access is then checked against any restrictions placed on their user account.

User account restrictions control several aspects of network access and use. Restrictions can be set, for example, that specify the days of the week and times of day that a user can log into the network. Other restrictions can limit the number of clients (workstations) from which a user can log in. Intruder detection is a user account restriction feature that locks a user's account after a predetermined number of incorrect user login attempts have been made.

Most of the account restrictions are related to a user's rights to log into the network. There are different types of restrictions that can be set. Figure 2.2 shows the SYSCON utility's User Information menu.

Some of the different types of user account restrictions you can set—which are included on the SYSCON User Information menu shown in figure 2.2—include the following:

■ **Account restrictions.** You can specify account-related restrictions, such as whether a user must have a password, what the minimum length of that password must be, whether the user can change the password, whether the user must periodically change the password, whether the account has an expiration date, and whether the user's connections should be limited.

■ **Station restrictions.** You can restrict which network clients a user can log in from.

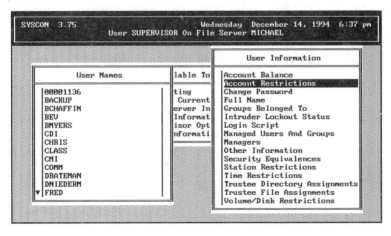

Figure 2.2
SYSCON's User Information menu.

■ **Time restrictions.** You can restrict the times of day during which a user can access the network (see fig. 2.3).

■ **Volume disk restrictions.** You can limit the amount of space the user can have for file storage on any particular network volume.

You can also set another particularly useful security feature of NetWare known as intruder account detection. *Intruder account detection* enables you to choose whether the network detects and tracks unsuccessful attempts to log in using an invalid network user ID or password, or an incorrect combination of user ID and password.

The SYSCON utility enables you to see the status of a user's intruder account detection. Figure 2.4 shows the status of FRED's intruder account detection—this user's detection feature has not been triggered.

Rights Security

For a validated user to access network resources, the user must have the necessary *rights*, which are the access privileges you give network users. They are an integral part of network security, even though they are oriented toward file system security.

These rights, granted by the network administrator, can be assigned to individual network users (regular users) as well as to other pre-defined types of network users.

 NetWare defines several different types of users. They include the following:

■ **Supervisor.** Has all rights to everything on the network

■ **Supervisor equivalent.** Has the same rights as the Supervisor

■ **Workgroup manager.** Has limited control over a select group of other users, including the right to create or delete users (within that group)

■ **Account manager.** Has limited control over a select group of users specifically assigned to him or her (the account manager)

■ **PCONSOLE operator.** Can manage existing print queues or print servers but cannot add new ones

■ **FCONSOLE operator.** Can manage the network file server using FCONSOLE, if that user has supervisor equivalent rights

■ **User.** (Includes regular users and a special user known as Guest.) Can log in to the network and access the network resources granted to them

You protect NetWare's file system using various security features, described as the following:

■ Trustees

■ Directory and file rights

■ Inheritance

■ Inherited Rights Mask (IRM)

■ Effective rights

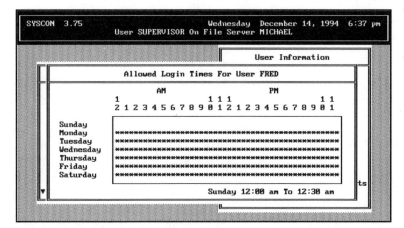

Figure 2.3
SYSCON utility display of Allowed Login Times For User FRED.

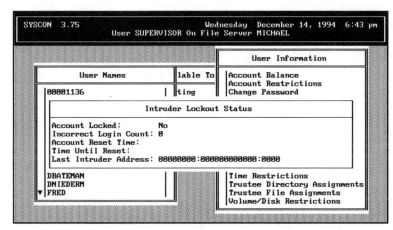

Figure 2.4
The Intruder Lockout Status for user FRED.

You grant rights to users for access to network files and directories by making them trustees of various network files and directories. Use the SYSCON utility to make users trustees, then to grant specific rights to those users. You also can use the SYSCON utility to see which directories a user is a trustee of.

Figure 2.5, for example, shows both the list of Trustee Rights Granted to user FRED and the Trustee Rights Not Granted user FRED to his mail directory.

Rights you can give to network users include the following:

■ **Access Control.** Enables you to modify trustee assignments and the IRM for a directory or file

■ **Create.** Enables you to create files and subdirectories

■ **Erase.** Enables you to delete files and directories

■ **File Scan.** Enables you to see files and direc-tories when you request a directory listing

■ **Modify.** Enables you to change file and directory attributes

■ **Read.** Enables you to open files and read or run them

■ **Supervisory.** Gives you all rights to files and directories

■ **Write.** Enables you to open a file and write to it

One other method in which rights security is implemented is through the use of *Inherited Rights Masks* (IRMs). An IRM is provided for each file and directory at the time it is created. By default, the IRM grants all rights to the file or directory. You can modify the IRM to filter out any rights you do not want users to have for a particular file or directory.

By changing the IRM for a given directory to remove a right, any user who would have inherited that right will no longer have it. The IRM takes effect from the point in the directory at which the

IRM is modified, on down through the balance of that portion of the directory structure.

 An *inherited right* is a right you receive to all subdirectories or files below the level at which the right was granted. Once granted, rights flow through the directory structure until either another set of rights are granted to you or the IRM prevents you from inheriting those rights.

IRMs cannot filter out the Supervisory right. If you give the Supervisory right to an individual, you cannot prevent them from having full access to all files and directories from there on, until you go back and remove the Supervisory right.

Because rights can be granted, can be blocked out, and can flow down through the directory structure, a user's rights at one point in the directory structure can be different than his or her rights at another point in the directory structure. The rights the user ends up with at any point in the directory structure are the user's effective rights.

Figure 2.5
User FRED's Granted and Not Granted Trustee Rights.

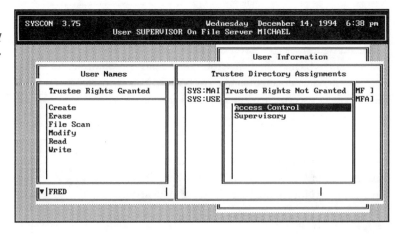

A user's effective rights are determined by looking at the user's inherited rights, the IRM, and any group affiliations or equivalencies the user might have.

In most cases, the explicit rights granted to a user are the same as the user's effective rights. If a user has rights granted because that user is a member of a group, those explicit rights are added to the explicit rights granted to the user at that level in the directory structure, to equal the user's effective rights.

When no rights are explicitly granted to the user, and no rights are granted based on the user's association with a group, the user's effective rights are those that have been granted elsewhere at a higher level in the directory structure, with one exception, the IRM. If an IRM is applied, the rights the IRM filters out are taken away from that user. The only exception is the Supervisory right, which cannot be removed with an IRM.

In addition to enhancing or restricting a user's access to network directories and files using rights, you also can restrict what users can do with directories and files by assigning directory and file attributes.

Attributes Security

Rights are given to users. *Attributes* are attached to files and directories and are given to files by using FLAG and to directories by using the FLAGDIR command. Figure 2.6 shows the FLAG command help screen, which lists the available attributes.

The available attributes include the following:

- **Read Only.** File can be opened and read but cannot be modified

- **Read Write.** File can be opened, read, and modified

- **Sharable.** File can be accessed by multiple users at the same time

- **Hidden.** File is not displayed when a directory listing is requested

- **System.** File is a system file

- **Transactional.** File is one to which the *Transactional Tracking System* (TTS) security feature can be applied

- **Purge.** File is to be completely eliminated so as not to be recoverable when deleted

- **Archive needed.** File is to be archived

- **Read Audit.** Not implemented in NetWare 3.1*x*

- **Write Audit.** Not implemented in NetWare 3.1*x*

- **Copy Inhibit.** File cannot be copied (for use with MAC files only)

- **Execute only.** File can only be run (executed)

- **Delete Inhibit.** File cannot be deleted

- **Rename Inhibit.** File cannot be renamed

File Server Security

File server security refers to the physical security of the network file servers. To make a network file server secure from physical access by others, place the server in an area where physical access can be restricted, such as a locked file server room.

Figure 2.6

*FLAG Help screen
displaying attributes.*

```
Z:\PUBLIC>flag /?
USAGE:  FLAG [path [ option ! [+!-] attribute(s) ] [SUB]]

386 Attributes:
---------------
RO Read Only
RW Read Write
S  Sharable
H  Hidden
Sy System
T  Transactional
P  Purge
A  Archive Needed
RA Read Audit
WA Write Audit
CI Copy Inhibit
X  Execute only
DI Delete Inhibit
RI Rename Inhibit

All All
N   Normal
SUB

Z:\PUBLIC>
```

Two other methods of restricting physical file server console access include setting a console password and setting a password on the remote console utility.

You set a file server console password using the Lock File Server Console option from the MONITOR NLM's Available Topics main menu. When prompted to enter a password, enter a password for the file server console. Then, no user can access the console to load modules or make changes without first knowing the console password.

Whenever you run RCONSOLE, you are prompted for a password. When you load the RCONSOLE-related *NetWare Loadable Modules* (NLM) on the file server, you set that password. RCONSOLE-related NLMs include:

- REMOTE.NLM

- RSPX.NLM

Another important security feature of NetWare 3.1*x* is known as Packet Signature.

Packet Signature is defined at both the NetWare file servers and clients. Once defined, the level of Packet Signature you set is added to network packets to provide a user/client identification for packets being sent between a particular client and the file server. Packet Signature prevents users from forging network packets to gain greater access to the network than that user was originally granted.

Higher levels of Packet Signature cause greater burden on network traffic. NetWare's Packet Signature security feature, therefore, is designed to let you set the level for the NCP Packet Signature. At the maximum level, when a client logs into a NetWare 3.12 server, the server and client agree upon a single, shared identification key called the *session key*, which is included in every packet sent between the file server and this client until the connection is broken. Each client receives a unique session key each time it connects to the network.

After a client is logged in and a session key is established, the file server checks each packet to make sure it has the client's unique signature, ensuring that each packet it receives is a valid packet. Packets with correct signatures are processed, and all others are discarded. Figure 2.7 shows the NCP Packet Signature process.

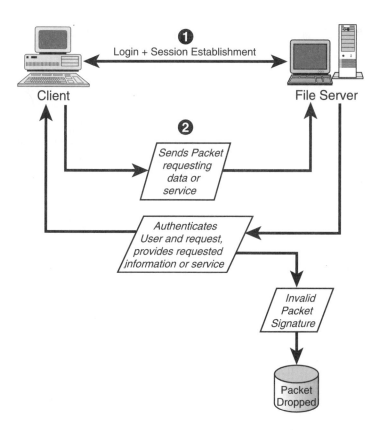

Figure 2.7
The Packet Signature process.

There are various Packet Signature levels you can set. The level is set as a number ranging from 1 to 4 inclusive. Level 1 provides the least amount of security. Level 4 provides the greatest amount of security.

You set signature levels for each server and client by adding **SET NCP PACKET SIGNATURE OP-TION** = *number* at the server console *or* in the server's AUTOEXEC.NCF file. To set the Packet Signature level at the client, put **SIGNATURE LEVEL** = *number* in the client's NET.CFG file, indented under the NetWare DOS Requester heading.

Performance issues associated with Packet Signature are discussed in Chapter 12, "Maintaining and Monitoring NetWare 3.1*x* Servers."

Setting Up and Securing User and Group Accounts

Network security entails much more than just understanding what it is. You must also understand how to implement it. There are different tasks associated with the different types of security features.

Before users can access the network, for example, they need to have a user account on the network. To ensure that users access only those network services to which they are entitled, user network accounts need to have appropriate account restrictions applied to them. In addition, you need to work with and manage both group and user accounts.

Setting up user accounts requires three steps. First, you must establish the account for the user. Second, you must determine whether each user account should have a password associated with it. Third, you must decide whether user accounts will have restrictions applied to them, then implement any restrictions you have chosen to apply.

To simplify the setup of user accounts, you can also establish group accounts. Using group accounts enables you to simultaneously apply rights and restrictions to a group of network users.

Use the SYSCON utility to create user and group accounts. Create user accounts by choosing the User Information option from SYSCON's main menu. Pressing Insert and following the prompts then enables you to create users.

SYSCON also enables you to create group accounts. The process for creating group accounts is very similar to that of creating user accounts. The main difference is that you choose the Group Information option from SYSCON's main menu, instead of the User Information option.

 Note You can automate the creation of user accounts using the USERDEF and MAKEUSER utilities. These two utilities enable you to define various aspects of user accounts, which will be applied to all user accounts when created.

Implementing Network and File System Security

You implement Network and file system security using the SYSCON and FILER utilities. SYSCON enables you to create users and groups and also enables you to establish user- and group-related security. You can create Workgroup Managers and User or Group Account Managers, as well as Console Operators using SYSCON.

You can also make trustee assignments and apply rights using the SYSCON and FILER utilities.

You make trustee assignments by adding users or groups as trustees of the current directory. To accomplish this task, start the FILER utility and choose Current Directory Information from the Available Topics menu (see fig. 2.8).

When the Directory Information For screen opens, choose Trustees. To add trustees, press Insert, then choose users and groups to be added. If you want to add more than one user or group, first mark each user or group using the F5 key, then press Enter to accept your choices.

You then can give those users and trustees specific rights to that directory or file by returning to the Available Topics FILER menu, choosing Current Directory Information, choosing the trustees to receive rights, pressing Insert to see a list of available rights, marking (F5) those rights that you want to grant, and then pressing Enter.

In addition to granting or revoking rights and trustee assignments using the SYSCON and FILER utilities, you can also use various command-line utilities, including the following:

Figure 2.8
FILER's Available Topics menu.

- RIGHTS

- TLIST

- GRANT

- ALLOW

- REVOKE

- REMOVE

Use these utilities to implement security on your network. You can accomplish the same basic tasks with these command-line utilities as you accomplish using the SYSCON and FILER utilities.

 Note You can use the SYSCON utility, for example, to set account restrictions. Account restrictions are used to determine whether or not a user can log in to the network, at what times they can log in, and from which workstations they can log in.

You set account restrictions for individual users. You choose the user for whom you want to set account restrictions, therefore, from the User Information screen in SYSCON, then choose

Account Restrictions. From there you choose which account restrictions you want to implement.

You perform the following in SYSCON to set account restrictions:

- Disable the user's account so that the user cannot log into the network at all

- Enable the user's account if it has been disabled

- Set user's account to expire and provide an expiration date on that user's account

- Remove an expiration date restriction

Command-line utilities are used to accomplish various security-related tasks.

RIGHTS is used to view your effective rights in a given directory, subdirectory, or file. To use RIGHTS, type **RIGHTS [*path*]** and press Enter. Replace *path* with the directory path in which you want to view your rights.

TLIST is used to see the list of trustees assigned to a given directory, subdirectory, or file. To use TLIST, type **TLIST [***path* **[USERS | GROUPS]]** and press Enter. Replace *path* with the directory path, and type either **USERS** or **GROUPS** to view either the users or the groups with rights to this directory, subdirectory, or file.

GRANT is used to give trustee rights to a given directory, subdirectory, or file for a specific user or group. To use GRANT, type **GRANT** *rights* **[FOR** *path***] TO [USER | GROUP]** *name* and press Enter. Replace *rights* with the list of rights you want to grant, inserting a space between each right. To grant Read and File Scan, for example, type **R F** in place of *rights*. Replace *path* with the path to the directory or file, and replace *name* with the name of the user or group to whom you are granting the rights.

ALLOW is used to change the IRM for a directory, subdirectory, or file. To use ALLOW, type **ALLOW [***path* **[TO INHERIT]** *rights* and press Enter. Replace *path* with the path to the directory, subdirectory, or file, and replace *rights* with the list of rights you want to prevent from flowing down. As with the GRANT command, rights must be separated with a space.

REVOKE is used to take trustee rights to a directory, subdirectory, or file away from a specific user or group. To use REVOKE, type **REVOKE** *rights* **[FOR** *path***] FROM [USER | GROUP]** *name* **[/***option***]** and press Enter. Replace *rights* with the list of rights to be revoked, separating each with a space. Replace *path* with the path to the directory, subdirectory, or file from which the rights are to be revoked. Replace *name* with the user or group name which the REVOKE command is intended to affect. If you want, you can replace *option* with **-SUB** to revoke the rights to all subdirectories within the specified path, or **-F** to revoke the rights

to all files within the path, and within any subdirectories if you also used the -SUB option.

REMOVE is used to remove a user or a group from the list of trustees associated with a directory, subdirectory, or file. To use REMOVE, type **REMOVE [USER | GROUP]** *name* **[[FROM]** *path* **[***option***]** and press Enter. Replace *name* with the name of the user or group. Replace *path* with the path that points to the directory, subdirectory, or file. Replace *option* with one or both of the available options. You can type **-SUB** to remove the users or groups from the trustee list associated with all subdirectories within the specified path, or **-F** to apply the REMOVE command to all files within the path, and within any subdirectories (if you also used the -SUB option).

Implementing File Server Console Security

Securing user access to the network and its resources is an important security system implementation. It is not, however, the only security measure you should take. You should also physically protect your file servers from unauthorized access.

There are two ways to physically protect your file servers from unauthorized access. The first is to lock the file server in a secure area; the second is to provide the console with a password.

You implement console password security from either the file server console or by running one of the remote console utilities—RCONSOLE or ACONSOLE. RCONSOLE is run from a network workstation, ACONSOLE from a workstation that gains access to the network through a modem. The use of a modem and an additional file, which you load at the file server, make up the main difference between using RCONSOLE and ACONSOLE.

Whether you use RCONSOLE, ACONSOLE, or directly access the file server's console, you set the file server password by first loading the MONITOR NLM, then choosing Lock File Server Console from the Available Topics menu. Next, you type a password used to lock the keyboard. You can use any password, including the Supervisor's.

Questions

1. Of the following, which is NOT a level of network security?

   ○ A. Login

   ○ B. Rights

   ○ C. Group accounts

   ○ D. File and directory attributes

2. Which network security level is affected by the user's password?

   ○ A. Login

   ○ B. Rights

   ○ C. User accounts

   ○ D. Attributes

3. To access a NetWare network, a user must first pass through the _____ security level.

   ○ A. login

   ○ B. rights

   ○ C. user accounts

   ○ D. attributes

4. Which utility can be used to set user account password requirements?

   ○ A. GRANT

   ○ B. SYSCON

   ○ C. FILER

   ○ D. TLIST

5. Which of the following restrictions CANNOT be turned on or off for individual network user accounts?

   ○ A. Intruder detection

   ○ B. Account restrictions

   ○ C. Time restrictions

   ○ D. Station restrictions

6. Which key is used to choose more than one user or group for simultaneously applying account restrictions?

   ○ A. F1

   ○ B. F3

   ○ C. F5

   ○ D. Alt+F10

7. Effective rights are equal to which of the following?

   ○ A. User's granted rights at the level granted

   ○ B. Supervisor's rights

   ○ C. User's inherited rights less applied IRM

   ○ D. User's granted rights plus granted group rights

8. The file server console can be secured with a password using _____.

   ○ A. AUTOEXEC.NCF

   ○ B. MONITOR.NLM

   ○ C. SYSCON.EXE

   ○ D. FILER.EXE

9. You delete a user or group from the trustee list of a file using the _____ utility.

   ○ A. REMOVE

   ○ B. REVOKE

   ○ C. TLIST

   ○ D. GRANT

10. You CANNOT use the SYSCON utility to complete which of the following tasks?

    ○ A. Change a user's group

    ○ B. Modify a user's security equivalence

    ○ C. Change a user's directory assignment

    ○ D. Calculate a user's effective rights

11. Of the following, which THREE are NetWare rights?

    ☐ A. F

    ☐ B. W

    ☐ C. S

    ☐ D. B

12. To see a list of files in a directory, you must have the _____ right.

    ○ A. F

    ○ B. A

    ○ C. M

    ○ D. E

13. Another way of describing rights that flow down throughout the NetWare directory structure is _____.

○ A. Trustee

○ B. Inheritance

○ C. Effective

○ D. Granted

14. To prevent an executable file from being deleted accidentally, set the _____ attribute on the file.

    ○ A. R

    ○ B. C

    ○ C. X

    ○ D. A

15. Which TWO tasks should be used to implement console security features on the server?

    ☐ A. Lock the file server in a secure place

    ☐ B. Load FDISK at the file server console

    ☐ C. Add a console password

    ☐ D. None of the above

Answers

1. C	9. A
2. A	10. D
3. A	11. A B C
4. B	12. A
5. A	13. B
6. C	14. C
7. D	15. A C
8. B	

Accessing NetWare 3.1x Network Services

*W*hen a user's client is prepared to access the network, the user needs to understand how to access and use the network file system. This chapter provides instructions related to preparing a client for network access and to finding and using the network resources the client's user needs, including the following:

■ *Installing and configuring a network client*

■ *Connecting a workstation to the network*

■ *Accessing the network file system*

■ *Viewing and managing file system information*

Installing and Configuring a Network Client

Providing networking services requires special hardware and software; so, too, does accessing those services. On a NetWare 3.12 file server, the operating system software provides the services. On a NetWare network client, the client software provides the access to those services. Just as the 3.12 operating system and related files must be installed on the file server, the network client software must be installed on the client.

After backing up your PC's configuration files, change to the drive containing the WSDOS_1 disk. Type **INSTALL** and press Enter to start the client installation. The NetWare Client Install screen opens (see fig. 3.1).

Five steps must be completed to install the NetWare client software. Each is represented on the NetWare Client Install screen.

■ Step 1 requires you to provide a path and directory into which the client files will be installed. The C:\NWCLIENT directory is the default. The client installation creates this directory, if it does not already exist. Change the default path if you want the client files installed into a directory other than C:\NWCLIENT.

■ Step 2 enables you to choose whether the installation program automatically updates your configuration files as needed. If you answer Yes, the LASTDRIVE=Z statement is added to the client's CONFIG.SYS file, and the CALL STARTNET.BAT statement is added to the client's AUTOEXEC.BAT file.

■ Step 3 automatically installs support for Microsoft Windows clients. If your workstation runs Microsoft Windows, type **Yes** at the prompt.

Step 3 also requires you to provide the path and directory name into which you installed Microsoft Windows. If you installed Microsoft

Figure 3.1

The NetWare Client Install screen.

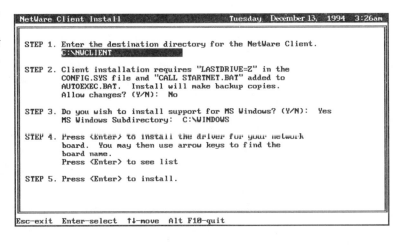

Windows into a directory other than the MS Windows default of C:\WINDOWS, change this field to reflect the actual location of these files.

■ Step 4 requires you to specify your device driver. By highlighting this field and pressing Enter, you are presented with a list of device drivers from which to choose. Your choice depends on the network board installed in your workstation. When possible, the installation software determines which board is installed and fills in the appropriate device driver. You then need to choose the device driver and indicate the settings on your network board.

■ Step 5 starts the installation. Highlight its field and press Enter. The balance of the installation is completed automatically. You only have to make changes to your configuration files if you typed No instead of Yes in step 2. If you typed Yes, your original configuration files are saved in their original location with a BNW extension. You can now reboot your PC, and it will load the appropriate files to boot your workstation as a network client.

Now that you have installed the DOS and Microsoft Windows client software, you can log in to the network. In the event that you cannot access the network, or you have to modify your configuration files at some later date, however, you should know what these files must contain for your workstation to access the network.

CONFIG.SYS provides configuration information for the computer to use when it boots.

The AUTOEXEC.BAT file contains DOS commands to help set up your working environment.

When you install the NetWare client, a command to run the STARTNET.BAT file is added to the AUTOEXEC.BAT file.

The NET.CFG file is not a standard computer configuration file. It is used on NetWare clients to provide commands to help your computer establish and maintain a network connection.

The CONFIG.SYS file must include the LASTDRIVE=Z command, which is added to it by the INSTALL program for the DOS Requester. The NetWare 3.12 client files work with DOS. Unless you include the LASTDRIVE=Z command in the CONFIG.SYS file, DOS assumes that the last available drive is the last drive it can recognize, which is usually represented as drive E. By including this command in the CONFIG.SYS file, you have all other drive letters available for network access.

The AUTOEXEC.BAT file uses a series of commands to load the appropriate network client files. These commands can also be placed in a file called STARTNET.BAT, in which case STARTNET.BAT is called from the AUTOEXEC.BAT file to run the following commands:

```
C:
CD \NWCLIENT
LSL.COM
NE2000 (replace with your LAN driver)
IPXODI
VLM
F:
LOGIN fileserver_name/username
```

These AUTOEXEC.BAT or STARTNET.BAT commands work with the NET.CFG file. The BAT file runs the commands, and the NET.CFG file provides the parameters needed to properly configure the commands when they are run.

The NET.CFG file must include the following lines of information with parameters set to match your LAN board and first network drive.

```
Link Driver NE2000
    INT 5
    PORT 340
    MEM D0000
    FRAME ETHERNET_802.2
NetWare DOS Requester
    FIRST NETWORK DRIVE=F
```

Information needed in the NET.CFG file includes the following:

■ **INT number.** The interrupt setting on the network board.

■ **PORT number.** The port setting for the network board.

■ **MEM address.** The memory address used by the network board.

■ **FRAME type.** The frame number used by the network to which you are connecting; NetWare 3.12 uses a default frame type of ETHERNET_802.2.

The NET.CFG file also contains a FIRST NET-WORK DRIVE= command. The client installation automatically updates the NET.CFG file with the FIRST NETWORK DRIVE=F line, if you chose Yes in Step 2.

Connecting a Workstation to the Network

Four specific files must be run to access the network. These four files, which must be run in the order listed, include the following:

1. LSL.COM
2. LAN Driver
3. IPXODI.COM
4. VLM.EXE

LSL.COM enables the routing of Network information of different protocols between the LAN driver and the software. LSL.COM is also called the *Link Support Layer.*

Once LSL.COM is run, load the LAN driver for your workstation to your workstation's network board, thus allowing it to establish a connection between the client software and the physical components of the network.

The third file that must be loaded into the workstation's memory is the IPXODI.COM file. When run, this file loads the NetWare IPX protocol, which processes network requests, passing the required information between the NetWare DOS Requester and the Link Support Layer.

Running the VLM.EXE file and its associated files (also referred to as the NetWare DOS Requester) provides a connection point between DOS and applications being run on the client, and the services provided by the network.

Once all these files have been run, your workstation is a network client. You can use it to log in to the network and access available resources.

Accessing the Network File System

Understanding the MAP command is critical to undertanding how to efficently access the NetWare server.

To run the NetWare MAP command, type the following and press Enter:

```
MAP [option] drive_letter:=directory_path
```

With the MAP command, you specify a drive letter (from those specified in the FIRST NETWORK DRIVE and LAST NETWORK DRIVE parameters set in your configuration files), followed by a colon (:), to indicate that it is a drive letter, then you provide the exact path.

Options available with the command include the following:

■ **ROOT.** Specifies that the drive is to appear as though it is a root directory, even though the drive can point to a subdirectory several levels deep within the NetWare directory structure.

■ **N.** Tells the MAP command to use the next available drive letter instead of waiting for you to specify a letter.

■ **DEL.** Lets the MAP command know that you want to remove an existing drive mapping. When you use this option, you must tell the MAP command which drive letter you want it to delete.

You can also use the MAP command without any options, which displays a list of your current drive mappings.

In NetWare, the exact path includes the file server name (if it is not your current default server),

followed by a slash, then the volume name, followed by a colon, and finally, the directories and subdirectories that point to the final destination. Each directory and subdirectory is separated by a slash.

To map drive letter P to the PAYROLL directory on the HR volume of the ACCOUNTING file server, for example, type the following line and press Enter:

```
MAP P:=ACCOUNTING/HR:PAYROLL
```

You can map two types of network drives: regular and search. A *search drive* functions like a DOS path drive. NetWare uses mapped search drives to find executable files. Network drives are used to find data files.

To access network applications, you must specify the network drive letter when searching for a data file. When searching for an executable program with a NetWare search drive mapped, however, you can just type the name of the program. NetWare then searches all its mapped search drives until it finds and runs the program.

To map a search drive, you must tell NetWare that you want the mapping to be a search drive. To do so, replace the drive letter in the previous example with **S16**. Using S16 tells NetWare to assign the next available search drive. You can also specify a particular search drive by specifying the numeric order associated with the search pattern.

You can, for example, make the search drive you are mapping the first drive to be used when looking for a program file by replacing the drive letter with **INS S1**. INS indicates that the search drive should be placed in the order indicated, and that existing search drives should be renumbered. The S1 indicates that it is a search drive and that it should be placed in the first position. To map a search drive to the DOS directory so it will search it first whenever it is looking for an executable program, the MAP command would look similar to the following:

```
MAP INS S1:=SYS:PUBLIC/DOS
```

If you fail to include INS, a new directory mapping will be assigned for the specified drive. Omit INS, therefore, when you are reassigning a drive. Include INS when you are adding a new search drive to a particular position in the search drive order.

You can use the MAP command to map to NetWare volumes or to specific directories on NetWare volumes. Once a drive is mapped to at least the volume level on a NetWare file server, you can then use the DOS CD command to move through the NetWare directory structure, if necessary.

After you have mapped search and network drives, you can navigate through the NetWare file server's volume and directory structure to find the network resources you need, using these mappings.

After a drive map has been created, you can access the mapped volume and directories by simply changing your default drive letter to the letter that represents the drive you mapped. You can then access data files stored at that path.

If you mapped search drives to the location of an executable file, you do not have to change first to that search drive to run the program. You can run it from anywhere on the network by typing the program name and letting NetWare's search drive capabilities find and start the program. You should, however, add to your DOS path statement the drive letters that represent your network search drives.

In the following DOS PATH statement of a network client, for example, you can see that two search drives—Z and Y—have been added:

```
PATH C:\;C:\WP51;C:\DOS;C:\
WINDOWS;C:\MOUSE;Z:.;Y:.
```

Because directories are searched for executable files in the same order they're displayed in the DOS path, these two NetWare search drives are the last drives searched when an executable file needs to be found. Keeping your DOS path statement relatively short is an important factor for timely access of files. Include, therefore, only those drive letters that contain executable files and which you use most frequently. Because Z is most often used to represent the search path to the NetWare utilities found in the SYS:PUBLIC directory, you should always include it in the DOS PATH statement.

Viewing and Managing File System Information

Using network and search drives, you can display, modify, and otherwise access available network resources.

NetWare provides several commands and utilities to help you access, view, and manage the NetWare file system. These utilities and commands include the following:

- ◼ FILER
- ◼ VOLINFO
- ◼ CHKVOL
- ◼ SLIST

VOLINFO

The VOLINFO utility provides information about each volume on the current NetWare file server, including the volume's name, the amount of storage space available on it, how much of that storage space is still available (unused), the total number of directory entries allowed on this volume, and the number of currently available directory entries (see fig. 3.2).

This screen also shows a menu from which you can choose to view volume information about other file servers.

In addition, the VOLINFO utility enables you to determine how frequently the volume information display is updated (use the Update Interval option from the Available Options menu).

CHKVOL

Use the CHKVOL utility to see information about the current volume. Type **CHKVOL [*path*] [/Continuous]** and press Enter. Replace *path* with the path pointing to the specific volume. Add the /Continuous option to see all the information displayed without stopping.

SLIST

The SLIST utility provides information about NetWare network file servers. To use SLIST, type **SLIST [*Server*] [\Continue]**, and press Enter. Replace *Server* with the file server name, and add \Continue if you want to see a continuous display.

Using SLIST, you can view several items of information, including the following:

- Network file server names
- Network numbers
- Each file server's node address
- The client's current relationship to each server

The network file server name represents the unique name given to that file server when it was installed. No two file servers on the same network can have the same name.

When more than one network exists, the network number identifies one NetWare network from another. It is the number (in hexadecimal format) assigned to the network cable segment for that network.

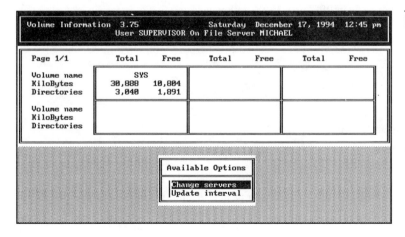

Figure 3.2
The VOLINFO screen.

Each client, file server, directly attached printer or other peripheral device must have something to identify it as unique to the network. This identifier is called the *node address* and is displayed using the SLIST utility.

The status fields show the current relationship of this network client to the listed file server. It does not show the operational status of the file server itself. A status of Default indicates that this is your client's current default directory. The Attached status indicates that this client is currently attached to or logged into this file server. You cannot have any drives mapped to the file server, but if you have a connection, the status is indicated as Attached.

A status of No indicates that you are neither attached nor logged in to this file server.

You can manipulate and otherwise manage directories on NetWare file servers using three basic DOS commands, including the following:

- MD
- RD
- RENDIR

The following two NetWare utilities can be used to obtain information about network directories:

- LISTDIR
- NDIR

LISTDIR

The LISTDIR command enables you to see a listing of network directories.

Type **LISTDIR** [*drive | path*] and press Enter. Replace *drive* with a mapped NetWare drive letter

or replace *path* with a full NetWare directory path, including the name of the file server.

LISTDIR shows all subdirectories found in the specified path, as well as the total number of directories found.

NDIR

The NDIR utility enables you to view information about directories that meet a specific search criteria that you specify.

You can also use NetWare and DOS utilities to manage files on the network. File management includes copying, moving, deleting, salvaging, and purging files.

DOS commands used to copy, move, or delete files include the following:

- **COPY.** Makes a duplicate of a file in another directory

- **REN.** Changes a file name, or moves that file from one directory to another

- **DEL.** Eliminates a file

NetWare utilities used for file management include the following:

- NCOPY
- FILER
- SALVAGE
- PURGE

NCOPY

The NetWare NCOPY command is used to accomplish the same types of tasks that the DOS

COPY or XCOPY commands accomplish. NCOPY, however, is designed to let you manage network files. It can handle extended file information, such as file attributes, which DOS COPY and XCOPY commands cannot.

NCOPY can also verify a successful and accurate copy. The most impressive feature of NCOPY, however, is its capability to use full NetWare paths, including the file server and volume names.

To use NCOPY, type **NCOPY** [*path*] [[**TO**] *path*] *option* at the prompt and press Enter. Replace the first *path* with the NetWare path pointing to the file to be copied and the name of the file. Replace the second *path* with the ending location for the copied file. Replace *option* with any of NCOPY's available option parameters.

NCOPY's available option parameters include the following:

- **/S.** Copies all subdirectories

- **/S/E.** Copies all subdirectories, even if they contain no files

- **/F.** Copies sparse files

- **/I.** Informs the user when non-DOS file information will be lost

- **/C.** Copies only DOS information

- **/A.** Copies all files that have the archive bit set

- **/M.** Copies all files that have the archive bit set, then clears that archive bit

- **/V.** Verifies that each write can subsequently be read

- **/H** or **/?.** Views the help screen associated with the NCOPY utility

You can manage directories and files using either DOS or NetWare command-line commands. You can also manage directories and files using three NetWare utilities: FILER, SALVAGE, and PURGE.

FILER

The FILER utility enables you to perform such directory and file management tasks as accessing, viewing, and managing information about network file servers, volumes, directories, and files. From the FILER Available Topics menu you can choose any of the following options:

- **View information about the current directory.** Self explanatory

- **Current Directory Information.** Displays directory information, such as the directory's owner, creation date and time, directory attributes, inherited rights that have been masked out, directory trustees, and your current effective rights in this directory

- **Directory Contents.** Displays a list of all files and subdirectories in the current directory

- **Select Current Directory.** Modifies your current default directory

- **Set Filer Options.** Modifies the defaults used for directory and file information display when using FILER

- **Volume Information.** Displays details about the current volume, including file server and volume names, the disk type and size, and the number of directory entries

If you choose the Current Directory Information option, a screen similar to that shown in figure 3.3 appears.

Figure 3.3
*The current Directory
Information for SYSTEM
screen.*

If you choose the Directory Contents option, a screen similar to that shown in figure 3.4 appears.

If you choose the Select Current Directory option, a screen showing the current directory path appears, and you can modify the path if you want.

If you choose Set Filer Options, a screen similar to that shown in figure 3.5 appears.

If you choose Volume Information, a screen similar to that shown in figure 3.6 appears.

SALVAGE

NetWare's SALVAGE utility enables you to retrieve files that were previously deleted. Although the deleted files are no longer included on the list when you issue a directory command, they are still available on the hard disk until purged or written over. Even if you delete the directory in which the file was stored, NetWare saves the directory's deleted files in a directory, DELETED.SAV, found at the root level of the volume containing the deleted files.

To recover deleted files, type **SALVAGE** and press Enter. The main menu for the SALVAGE utility opens, and you can choose from among four available options (see fig. 3.7).

The available four options perform the following:

■ **Salvage From Deleted Directories.** Specifies a file pattern to be used by the SALVAGE utility to search for and display deleted directories from which you can choose to recover files

■ **Select Current Directory.** Changes from the current directory to another directory, if necessary

■ **Set Salvage Options.** Determines sort order when SALVAGE presents the list of deleted files or directories from which you can recover files (see fig. 3.8)

■ **View/Recover Deleted Files.** Specifies the Erased File Name Pattern To Match that Salvage is to use when searching for recoverable files and directories

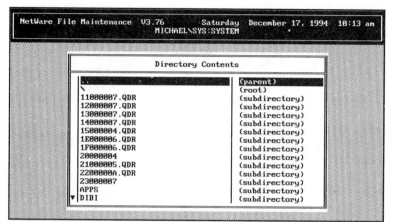

Figure 3.4
The Directory Contents screen.

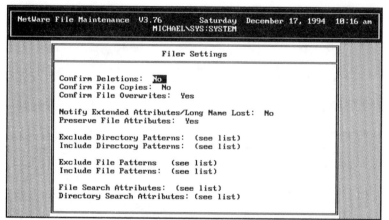

Figure 3.5
The Filer Settings screen.

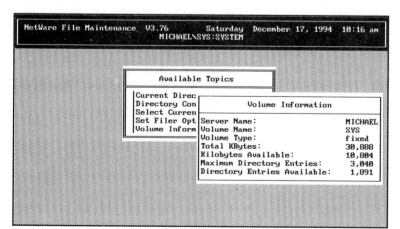

Figure 3.6
The Volume Information screen.

Figure 3.7

*The SALVAGE Main
Menu Options screen.*

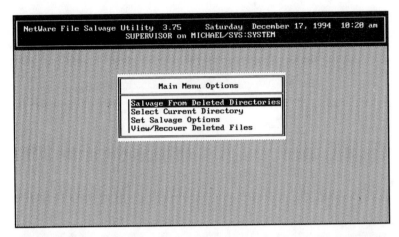

Figure 3.7

*The SALVAGE Main
Menu Options screen.*

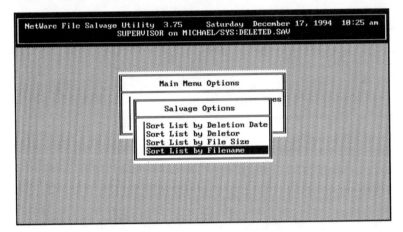

Figure 3.8

*The Salvage Options
screen.*

PURGE

Deleted files can be salvaged unless one of two things have happened. At some point, new files overwrite deleted files, starting with the files that have been deleted the longest time. In that case, files remain salvageable for a period of time determined by the free space available on the volume.

It might be desirable to remove files from the volume completely. The process of purging deleted files to make room for new files retards the server. Additionally, you might not want sensitive files to

be salvageable. You remove deleted files using the NetWare PURGE command-line utility. Once purged, files and directories cannot be recovered.

To use the PURGE command, type the following at the system prompt and press Enter:

`PURGE [file_name ¦ wildcard] [/ALL ¦ /A]`

Replace *file_name* ¦ *wildcard* with either a specific file name or a wild card (that is, ? or *) to request all files with a given filename character(s). You can also use PURGE with the /ALL or the /A option to remove all files from the current directory path.

Questions

1. Of the following, which THREE are steps in the DOS and Microsoft Windows client installation process?

   ☐ A. Install DOS

   ☐ B. Copy files to C:\WINDOWS directory

   ☐ C. Copy client files to the C:\NWCLIENT directory

   ☐ D. Select your network board driver

2. The disk used to install the client is called _____.

   ○ A. INST_1

   ○ B. DOS_INS1

   ○ C. SYSTEM_1

   ○ D. WSDOS_1

3. The directory in which the client files are installed (unless you specify otherwise) is the _____ directory:

   ○ A. C:\WINDOWS

   ○ B. C:\NWCLIENT

   ○ C. C:\WINDOWS\SYSTEM

   ○ D. C:\

4. If you need to recover your modified configuration files after the client installation is complete, you can find them by looking for files with the _____ extension.

   ○ A. BNW

   ○ B. BFR

   ○ C. BKU

   ○ D. OLD

5. Which NetWare client installation step requires that you choose and configure the driver for the network board installed in your computer?

   ○ A. 1

   ○ B. 2

   ○ C. 3

   ○ D. 4

   ○ E. 5

6. Which TWO configuration files do computers generally have before they are set up as network clients?

   ☐ A. CONFIG.SYS

   ☐ B. STARTNET.BAT

   ☐ C. NET.EXE

   ☐ D. AUTOEXEC.BAT

7. Which file contains the NetWare DOS Requester configuration parameters?

   ○ A. CONFIG.SYS

   ○ B. STARTNET.BAT

   ○ C. NET.CFG

   ○ D. AUTOEXEC.BAT

8. Which file contains the LASTDRIVE=Z statement?

   ○ A. CONFIG.SYS

   ○ B. STARTNET.EXE

   ○ C. NET.CFG

   ○ D. AUTOEXEC.BAT

9. The drive letter used most commonly as the drive letter for accessing the LOGIN.EXE file is drive _____.

   ○ A. D

   ○ B. F

   ○ C. G

   ○ D. Z

10. In which order must you load client files to connect to the network?

    ○ A. VLM.EXE, IPXODI.COM, LAN driver, and LSL.COM

    ○ B. LSL.COM, IPXODI.COM, VLM.EXE, and LAN Driver

    ○ C. LSL.COM, LAN driver, IPXODI.COM, and VLM.EXE

    ○ D. IPXODI.COM, LAN driver, LSL.COM, and VLM.EXE

11. Use the _____ utility to see a list of directories in the current path.

    ○ A. RENDIR

    ○ B. MKDIR

    ○ C. NDIR

    ○ D. NEWDIR

12. Use the _____ NetWare command-line utility to make a duplicate of a file with extended file information such as attributes.

    ○ A. NCOPY

    ○ B. COPY

    ○ C. SALVAGE

    ○ D. DUPE

13. You can see the owner of a directory by choosing the _____ option from the FILER Available Options screen.

    ○ A. Current Directory Information

    ○ B. Volume Information

    ○ C. Select Current Directory

    ○ D. Set Filer Options

14. The SALVAGE utility uses the _____ directory to store deleted files when the files' original directory has also been deleted.

    ○ A. DIRECT.DEL

    ○ B. DELETED.SAV

    ○ C. SAVED.FIL

    ○ D. SALVAGE.DIR

15. To permanently remove files that have been deleted, use the _____ utility.

    ○ A. NCOPY

    ○ B. SALVAGE

    ○ C. PURGE

    ○ D. DELETE

Answers

1. B C D	9. B
2. D	10. C
3. B	11. C
4. A	12. A
5. D	13. A
6. A D	14. B
7. C	15. C
8. A	

Managing NetWare Services from the File Server Console

This chapter explains the available NetWare console commands and the steps needed to access the file server console from a workstation. These steps enable you to manage your network file servers from any workstation, rather than having to be in the same physical proximity as the file server console.

The three sections of this chapter address the following:

- Using Console Commands

- Using NetWare Loadable Modules (NLMs)

- Accessing a Server Console From a Workstation

Using Console Commands

NetWare's operating system loads into memory on each file server when you boot that file server. The *core* operating system files provide basic network services, including file storage and retrieval, network security, and routing.

For users to have access to additional network services, such as printing, storage management, and communications, additional server software must be loaded. You provide these additional services by running console utilities, and loading NetWare Loadable Modules (NLMs) on each file server.

When you load the NetWare operating system, you also load software that enables you to manage the network. This software is accessed from the file server console and is therefore referred to as *console commands*.

NetWare provides four types of console commands, which follow:

- Configuration commands

- Installation commands

- Maintenance commands

- Screen display commands

NetWare commands are similar to DOS commands. Just as DOS commands provide DOS operating system access and instructions, NetWare commands provide NetWare operating system access and instructions. DOS commands can be run from any workstation with DOS loaded into its memory. NetWare console commands can be run from any PC with the NetWare operating system loaded into its memory (a NetWare file server).

NetWare console commands—unlike regular NetWare commands, which can be issued from any NetWare client—can only be issued from the NetWare file server console. NetWare console commands can be issued from a NetWare client, however, if they are issued while running a remote session using NetWare's remote console utility, which is discussed later in this chapter.

Understanding the function, purpose, and use of NetWare console commands makes it easier for you to monitor and maintain your network file servers. Each of the four types of NetWare 3.12 console commands are discussed in this chapter.

Configuration Console Commands

Configuration console commands relate to tasks performed to configure various aspects of the NetWare file server. Some of the more important NetWare configuration console commands include the following:

- CONFIG

- NAME

- TIME

- UPS STATUS

- VOLUMES

Installation Console Commands

Installation console commands relate to tasks associated with installing NetWare on the file server. Some of the important NetWare installation console commands include the following.

BIND

Links the local area network (LAN) driver to a communication protocol and to a specific file server LAN board. Type **BIND** *protocol* [**TO**] *LANdriver\boardname* [*driver_parameter*] [*protocol_parameter*] and press Enter. *Protocol* is IP, IPX, and so on. *LANdriver\boardname* is the driver name for the file server's network board. *Driver_parameter* is comprised of the following: DMA number, FRAME name, INT number, MEM number, PORT number, and SLOT number. *Protocol_parameter* is comprised of any parameters unique to the protocol you are binding to the LAN driver.

LOAD

Places an NLM in file server memory. Type **LOAD** [*path*] *NLM_name* [*parameter*] and press Enter. Replace *path* with the full directory path pointing to where the NLMs are stored, if they are not stored in SYS:SYSTEM. Replace *parameter* with any of the valid parameters, as needed. For example, if loading a LAN drive, use the following parameters as needed: DMA number, FRAME name, INT number, MEM number, PORT number, and SLOT number.

MOUNT

Readies a volume for access by NetWare users. Type **MOUNT** *volume_name* and press Enter. Replace *volume_name* with the name of the volume to be mounted or type **ALL** to mount all file server

volumes. Mount a CD-ROM disk to use as a read-only volume by typing **CD MOUNT** [*device number*] [*volume_name*] and pressing Enter. Replace *device number* with the CD-ROM device number. Replace *volume_name* with the volume name assigned to the CD-ROM disk.

Maintenance Console Commands

Maintenance console commands relate to tasks associated with maintaining your NetWare file server. Some of the more important NetWare installation console commands include the following.

CLEAR STATION

Disconnects a client from the file server, thus closing any files or tables the client had open. Use this command to clear a client whose workstation has become *hung* (locked up and nonresponsive). Type **CLEAR STATION** *n* (replace *n* with the client's station number) and press Enter.

DISABLE LOGIN

Prevents network users from logging in to the file server. Type **DISABLE LOGIN** and press Enter. Currently logged-in users are not disconnected, but no other users will be able to log in.

DOWN

Closes all open files, writes all dirty cache buffers to disk, and updates the DET and FAT tables before rebooting the file server. Type **DOWN** and press Enter.

ENABLE LOGIN

Enables users to log in to the network if the DISABLE LOGIN command was previously issued. If you downed the file server after using the DISABLE LOGIN command, then rebooted the file server, login is automatically reenabled. Type **ENABLE LOGIN** and press Enter.

REMOVE DOS

Unloads the DOS operating system from the file server's memory. Reboots the server when EXIT is typed after downing the server. Type **REMOVE DOS** and press Enter.

UNBIND

Unlinks a LAN driver from a communication protocol or from the file server's LAN board. Type **UNBIND** *protocol* **[FROM]** *LANdriver* [*driver_parameter*] and press Enter. Replace *protocol* with the communication protocol bound to the LAN driver, and *LANdriver* with the name of the driver previously bound to the LAN board, installed in the file server. *Driver_parameters* may include DMA number, INT number, MEM number, PORT number, or SLOT number.

UNLOAD

Removes NLMs from file server memory. Type **UNLOAD** *loadable_module* and press Enter, replacing *loadable_module* with the name of the NLM to be removed from memory. Use this command to unload LAN drivers, Name Space Modules, Disk drivers, and NLM utilities.

Screen Display Console Commands

Screen display console commands relate to the display of information on the NetWare file server's monitor. The more important NetWare screen display console commands include the following.

BROADCAST

Sends messages to users who are currently logged in or attached to the file server. Type **BROADCAST** *"message"* **[TO]** and press enter, replacing *message* with the 55-character maximum message you want to send.

CLS

Clears the file server's display. Type **CLS** at the console and press Enter. (You can use the OFF command to accomplish the same task.)

EXIT

Restores control of the computer to DOS. Type **EXIT** and press Enter, after first issuing the DOWN command. You can then issue DOS commands at the DOS prompt, update NetWare file server configuration files using DOS commands, or boot the file server.

SEND

Causes a message to be displayed on the client monitors of all users (or specified users) currently logged in or attached to the file server. Type **SEND** *"message"* **[TO]** *username|connection number*] [**[AND,]** *username|connection number*] and press Enter, replacing *message* with the text to be sent, and *username|connection number* with either the name or NetWare file server connection number of the user(s) to receive the message.

Using NetWare Loadable Modules

NetWare Loadable Modules (NLMs) are files loaded into file server memory to provide additional functionality. The NetWare operating system provides basic functionality, such as file management. NLMs provide additional functionality, such as file server monitoring capabilities. NetWare provides a variety of NLMs. Figure 4.1 shows a listing of those NLMs stored in the SYS:SYSTEM directory of a NetWare 3.12 file server.

There are four types of NLMs. The functions they provide are name-space support, disk drivers, NLM utilities, and LAN drivers.

 To help you remember these four types of NLMs, remember that working with NLMs is *Never DUL.*

N = Name space

D = Disk driver

U = Utilities (Management and Enhancement)

L = LAN Drivers

Disk Driver NLMs

Disk driver NLMs are loaded on the file server to enable communication between the NetWare operating system and the file server's hard disk controller. There are different types of hard disk controllers and, consequently, different types of disk driver NLMs. You need to load the disk driver NLM that is compatible with the disk controller installed in the file server.

To load a disk driver, type **LOAD** *driver_name parameters* and press Enter. Replace *driver_name* with the disk driver to be loaded and *parameters* with any parameters that you need and that relate to this disk driver.

You can load the disk driver from the file server console and must do so when you first install NetWare 3.12. If, however, in the process of installing 3.12 and creating the file server configuration files (AUTOEXEC.NCF and STARTUP.NCF), you load the disk driver before creating the configuration files, the command to load the disk driver is included in the configuration file. Then, each time you boot the file server, the disk driver NLM is run and automatically loaded into file server memory.

```
F:\SYSTEM>dir *.nlm /w

    Volume in drive F is SYS
    Directory of  F:\SYSTEM

F: CDROM    NLM : INSTALL  NLM : KEYB     NLM : NUT      NLM : RS232    NLM
F: VREPAIR  NLM : V_MAC    NLM : V_OS2    NLM : 3CBOOT   NLM : ADAPTEC  NLM
F: AFTER311 NLM : AIO      NLM : AIOACI   NLM : AIOCOMX  NLM : AIOCXCFG NLM
F: AIODGCX  NLM : AIODGMEM NLM : AIODGXI  NLM : AIOESP   NLM : AIOWNIM  NLM
F: BREBUILD NLM : BROUTER  NLM : BSETUP   NLM : BSPXCOM  NLM : BSPXSTUB NLM
F: BTRIEVE  NLM : BTRMON   NLM : BUTIL    NLM : CONLOG   NLM : DIBIDAI  NLM
F: DIRECTFS NLM : DPTSIM   NLM : EDIT     NLM : ETHERTSM NLM : FDDITSM  NLM
F: IPCONFIG NLM : IPXS     NLM : LLC8022  NLM : MATHLIB  NLM : MATHLIBC NLM
F: MONITOR  NLM : MSM31X   NLM : NFSFIX   NLM : NFSSHIM  NLM : NLICLEAR NLM
F: NMAGENT  NLM : NOVADIBI NLM : NWSNUT   NLM : PCN2LTSM NLM : PFIXUP   NLM
F: PING     NLM : PROTO    NLM : PSERVER  NLM : REMFILFX NLM : ROUTE    NLM
F: RPL      NLM : RXNETTSM NLM : SBACKUP  NLM : SMDR31X  NLM : SNMP     NLM
F: SNMPLOG  NLM : SPXCONFG NLM : SPXS     NLM : STREAMS  NLM : TAPEDC00 NLM
F: TCPCON   NLM : TCPIP    NLM : TLI      NLM : TOKENTSM NLM : TPING    NLM
F: TSA311   NLM : TSA312   NLM : TSA_DOS  NLM : UINSTALL NLM : UPS      NLM
F: WANGTEK  NLM : WS_MAN   NLM : RSPXSTUB NLM : RSPX     NLM : CLIB     NLM
F: REMOTE   NLM
        81 File(s)  11059200 bytes free

F:\SYSTEM>
```

Figure 4.1
Directory Listing of NetWare 3.12 NLMs.

Management and Enhancement Utility NLMs

Various utility NLMs are used to provide network management and operating system enhancement capabilities. The three major management and enhancement utility NLMs include the following:

- INSTALL

- MONITOR

- UPS

The purpose of the *INSTALL* NLM is to enable you to install and then maintain your NetWare 3.12 file server. The purpose of the *MONITOR* NLM is to provide you with a way to monitor your file server's efficiency and to provide file server console security using the Lock File Server Console option. The purpose of the *UPS* NLM is to provide a software connection between the *Uninterruptible Power Supply* (UPS) and the UPS NLM.

To load any of these three NLMs, **LOAD** *NLM_name parameter* at the file server prompt and press Enter. You can also load these NLMs from the file server's configuration file. If the NLM you want to load is not stored in the SYS:SYSTEM directory, include the path to the directory containing the NLM before you type the name of the NLM.

When you load a 3.12 NLM, replace *NLM_name* with the actual name of the NLM, such as MONITOR. If the NLM you are loading requires any specific parameters—such as NS used with MONITOR to turn off the "Snake" screen saver, or -P to display the MONITOR main menu with the Processor Utilization option included (see fig. 4.2)—then replace *parameter* with any needed parameters.

INSTALL.NLM

NetWare 3.12 provides the INSTALL NLM so you can install and maintain your 3.12 file server. From the Installation Options menu, you can perform tasks related to the hard disk installed in the file server, volumes on the file server, configuration files, files in the SYSTEM and PUBLIC directories, or additional Novell products.

Figure 4.2
The MONITOR NLM screen.

```
NetWare v3.12 (250 user) - 12/18/94          NetWare 386 Loadable Module

                        Information For Server Michael

      File Server Up Time:    14 Days  4 Hours 36 Minutes 22 Seconds
      Utilization:                   14    Packet Receive Buffers:    400
      Original Cache Buffers:     3,590    Directory Cache Buffers:    21
      Total Cache Buffers:        1,865    Service Processes:           3
      Dirty Cache Buffers:            1    Connections In Use:          2
      Current Disk Requests:          0    Open Files:                 38

                          Available Options
                       ┌──────────────────────────┐
                       │Connection Information     │
                       │Disk Information           │
                       │LAN Information            │
                       │System Module Information  │
                       │Lock File Server Console   │
                       │File Open / Lock Activity  │
                       │Resource Utilization       │
                       │Processor Utilization      │
                       │Exit                       │
                       └──────────────────────────┘
```

Figure 4.3 shows the Available Disk Options menu that opens when you choose Disk Options from the Installation Options menu. From the Available Disk Options menu, you can perform tasks such as formatting the hard disk, viewing and managing partitions, mirroring the file server's hard disks, or performing a surface test on the hard disks.

MONITOR.NLM

The MONITOR NLM provides a variety of information related to the status and configuration of your NetWare file server. It provides the following information:

■ **Connection Information.** Users currently connected to the file server

■ **Disk Information.** Number and type of disk drives

■ **LAN Information.** LAN drivers installed and related configuration information

■ **System Module Information.** List of modules currently loaded on the file server

■ **Lock File Server Console.** Capability to provide a password for the console to prevent unauthorized access

■ **File Open / Lock Activity.** Option to see which files have been locked

■ **Resource Utilization.** Information about file server memory, including statistics such as the current size of each memory pool

■ **Processor Utilization.** Option to see active processes from which you can choose to view related statistics

Figure 4.4 shows the information screen for the AES No Sleep Process. This screen opens when you choose AES No Sleep Process from the Available Processes & Interrupts menu. (The Available Processes & Interrupts menu opens when you choose Processor Utilization from the Available Options menu.)

```
NetWare Server Installation V3.12          NetWare 386 Loadable Module

  Installation Options
  Disk Options
  Vo
  Sy  Available Disk Options
  Pr
  Ex  Format (optional)
      Partition Tables
      Mirroring
      Surface Test (optional)
      Return To Main Menu




        Use the arrow keys to highlight an option, then press <ENTER>.
```

Figure 4.3
The NetWare Server Installation screen.

UPS.NLM

The UPS NLM is not a menu-based NLM. Loading it activates UPS monitoring (once you have connected the UPS hardware to the file server on which you are loading the UPS NLM). After the UPS is attached and you have loaded the UPS NLM, you can verify the current status of UPS by typing **UPS Status** and pressing Enter.

You can also use the UPS NLM to customize the UPS software to fulfill your network's UPS-related needs. When you load UPS, supply the NLM with information about UPS configuration. You can accept the default configuration information supplied by the NLM (see fig. 4.5), but you must use the UPS type and port value specific to the UPS you have attached to the file server.

If your UPS is not correctly configured, is powered off, or is not connected to the file server, a message similar to the one shown in figure 4.6 appears.

Figure 4.4
The AES No Sleep Process screen.

Name	Time	Count	Load
AES No Sleep Process	3,277	18	0.28%
Total Sample Time:	1,179,557		
Histogram Overhead Time:	14,601	(1.23 %)	
Adjusted Sample Time:	1,165,100		

Figure 4.5
UPS NLM configuration defaults.

```
MICHAEL:load ups
Loading module UPS.NLM
  NetWare 386 UPS Monitor
  Version 1.11    December 18, 1990
Available UPS Types: 1-DCB 2-EDCB 3-STANDALONE 4-KEYCARD 5-MOUSE 6-OTHER
UPS TYPE: 1
Support I/O port values are 346, 34E, 326, 32E, 386, 38E
I/O port: 346
Discharge time range:  1   3976031 minutes
Discharge time: 20
Recharge time range:  1 - 3976821 minutes
Recharge time: 60
```

Figure 4.6
UPS NLM warning message.

```
WARNING:  Commercial power detected off during UPS installation.
          Check commercial power lines or the UPS.
WARNING:  UPS battery is low.  Repair or replace battery.
WARNING:  UPS hardware configuration error was detected.
          Check for errors in your UPS hardware configuration settings.
Module initialization failed.
Module UPS.NLM NOT loaded
```

LAN Driver NLM

LAN driver NLMs establish a communication link between the network board and the driver. Once installed into file server memory, the LAN driver NLM facilitates communication between the file server and the network. To load, type **LOAD** [*path*] *driver* [*parameters*] and press Enter.

Replace *path* with the full path to the directory containing the LAN driver NLM, if it is other than SYS:SYSTEM. Otherwise, the path entry is optional. Replace *driver* with the name of the driver NLM for the file server's network board. Replace *parameters* with any of the appropriate LAN driver parameters and place them inside a pair of square brackets. Parameters that might be needed include: DMA number, FRAME name, INT number, MEM number, NAME board name (if assigned during installation), NODE number, PORT number, and SLOT number.

Accessing a Server Console from a Workstation

You can access the file server's console from the actual file server, or remotely from a workstation (called an *SPX connection* or a *snychronous connection*), using a utility called RCONSOLE, which enables you to emulate the file server's console on the monitor of a workstation connected to the file server. You can also use a utility called ACONSOLE to emulate the file server's console, if you access it from an asynchronous device such as a modem rather than from a workstation connected to the network.

To access a NetWare file server using either a synchronous or an asynchronous connection, you must run the appropriate files at both the file server and the client.

Two NLMs must be loaded at the file server, regardless of whether you are going to access it through an SPX or asynchronous connection. The two NLMs are as follows:

- REMOTE.NLM
- RSPX.NLM

 Note For an asynchronous connection to this file server, the RS232 NLM must be loaded as well.

REMOTE.NLM

The REMOTE NLM is responsible for the exchange of information between the file server and the client. To load the REMOTE NLM, include the LOAD REMOTE command in the file server's AUTOEXEC.NCF configuration file or type it at the file server console. The correct format for using the REMOTE NLM is as follows:

```
LOAD [path]REMOTE [password]
```

When loading the REMOTE NLM, replace *path* with the drive letter mapped to the directory containing the REMOTE NLM, if it is not stored in the SYS:SYSTEM directory.

Replace *password* with a password you assign to the REMOTE NLM. This password, or the Supervisor's password, can then be used when you later run the RCONSOLE or ACONSOLE utility.

RSPX.NLM

The RSPX NLM loads the SPX driver used by the REMOTE NLM. In addition, it tells the active network clients that it is available. The RSPX NLM *advertises* its presence by sending a specific packet across the network, telling network clients and file servers that it is available for remote access.

Load the RSPX NLM after loading the REMOTE NLM. It, too, can be loaded using the file server's AUTOEXEC.NCF configuration file, or by typing it directly at the console.

To load the RSPX NLM, use the following format, replacing *path* with the drive letter mapped to the directory containing the RSPX NLM, if it is not located in the SYS:SYSTEM directory:

LOAD [*path*]RSPX

 Because NetWare requires you to load REMOTE.NLM before loading RSPX.NLM, NetWare will autoload the REMOTE NLM if you issue the LOAD RSPX command before issuing the LOAD REMOTE command.

RS232.NLM

The RS232 NLM is loaded on the file server when the connection to that server is going to be asynchronous. One of the main functions of this NLM is to initialize the modem software. Load the RS232 NLM after loading REMOTE.NLM. To load this NLM, type the following line or place this command into the file server's AUTOEXEC.NCF configuration file:

LOAD [*path*]RS232

As with the other NLMs, replace *path* with the path pointing to the location of the RS232 NLM, if it is not stored in the SYS:SYSTEM directory.

After you have loaded the REMOTE NLM and RSPX NLM at a file server (as well as the RS232 NLM if making an asynchronous connection), you can access that server using either the RCONSOLE or ACONSOLE utility. Use the RCONSOLE utility for SPX network connections (through a workstation cabled to the network). Use the ACONSOLE utility for asynchronous network connections (through a modem).

To use RCONSOLE, log in to the network, type **RCONSOLE** at a network client, and press Enter. The Connection Type menu opens. Choose the SPX option and choose the file server to which you want to establish a SPX remote connection. If prompted, provide the password.

After you have connected to the file server, the RCONSOLE utility opens an Available Options menu. Depending on the option you choose, you can perform a variety of tasks. The options available are as follows:

- Select a Screen to View
- Directory Scan
- Transfer Files to Server
- Copy System and Public Files
- End Remote Session with Server (Shift+Esc)
- Resume Remote Session with Server (Esc)

In addition to choosing from the Available Options menu, you can use different keys and key combinations to perform various tasks. Those keys include the following:

*	Displays the RCONSOLE menu
+	Moves forward through server console screens
-	Moves backward through server console screens
Shift+Esc	Exits the RCONSOLE utility
Esc	Resumes your remote console session

 For the first three keys, you must use the numeric keypad. The number and special character keys on the regular keypad will not function.

For all asynchronous connections to a network file server, use the ACONSOLE utility rather than the RCONSOLE utility.

To use the ACONSOLE utility, type **ACONSOLE** at a network client and press Enter. Then choose the Connect to Remote Location option from the ACONSOLE main menu. Provide the phone number to be dialed to access the modem connected to the file server. After the phone connection is made and the Available Servers list opens, choose the file server you want. If prompted, provide the remote console password. From the file server console screen, you can now perform a variety of management tasks. You can perform the same tasks using the ACONSOLE utility as you can using the RCONSOLE utility.

Questions

1. Of the following, which THREE are NetWare console commands?

   □ A. Screen

   □ B. Setup

   □ C. Installation

   □ D. Maintenance

2. Which TWO console commands CANNOT be used to send messages?

   □ A. SEND

   □ B. BROADCAST

   □ C. RCONSOLE

   □ D. ACONSOLE

3. You can use the CLS command at workstations and file server consoles. Which other command can you use at the file server console to accomplish the same task as using CLS?

   ○ A. BROADCAST

   ○ B. EXIT

   ○ C. CLEAR

   ○ D. OFF

4. Which TWO of the following are installation console commands?

   □ A. BIND

   □ B. EXIT

   □ C. MOUNT

   □ D. REMOVE DOS

5. You know you are looking at a console command if the file has any one of the following THREE extensions:

   □ A. NLM

   □ B. DRV

   □ C. NAM

   □ D. NDS

6. Which of the following console commands is used to link the LAN driver to a communication protocol?

   ○ A. MOUNT

   ○ B. BIND

   ○ C. LINK

   ○ D. EXIT

7. To access a NetWare volume, you must first _____ the volume.

   ○ A. bind

   ○ B. load

   ○ C. mount

   ○ D. format

8. Type _____ to mount a read-only CD-ROM device as a volume.

   ○ A. CD MOUNT 1

   ○ B. MOUNT READONLY CD

   ○ C. CD MOUNT ALL

   ○ D. MOUNT ALL/CD

9. If a user's workstation has hung, use the _____ maintenance console command to remove the connection.

   ○ A. CLEAR ALL

   ○ B. DISABLE LOGIN

   ○ C. EXIT

   ○ D. CLEAR CONNECTION

10. Which THREE commands are configuration commands?

    ☐ A. NAME

    ☐ B. VOLUMES

    ☐ C. MODULES

    ☐ D. CONFIG

11. The THREE most common NetWare NLMs used by a network administrator include _____, _____, and _____.

    ☐ A. MONITOR

    ☐ B. UPS

    ☐ C. RCONSOLE

    ☐ D. INSTALL

12. To see drive status information for one of the file server's hard disks, use the _____ NLM.

    ○ A. MONITOR

    ○ B. CONSOLE

    ○ C. CONFIG

    ○ D. INSTALLATION

13. You cannot choose the _____ option from MONITOR's Available Options menu.

    ○ A. LAN Information

    ○ B. Lock File Server Console

    ○ C. Disk Options

    ○ D. Resource Utilization

14. Which NLM is NOT used for remote console access?

    ○ A. RSPX.NLM

    ○ B. REMOTE.NLM

    ○ C. ASYNC.NLM

    ○ D. RS232.NLM

15. The remote network connection made through a modem is referred to as a/an _____ connection.

    ○ A. REMOTE

    ○ B. INDIRECT

    ○ C. ASYNCHRONOUS

    ○ D. SPX

Answers

1.	A C D	9.	D
2.	C D	10.	A B D
3.	D	11.	A B D
4.	A C	12.	A
5.	A B C	13.	C
6.	B	14.	C
7.	C	15.	C
8.	A		

Preparing NetWare 3.1x Printing Services for Users

This chapter discusses how NetWare provides shared printing services and how to set up the network so users can access those services. It shows how to redirect print jobs to network printers and how to manage those print jobs after they have been sent to NetWare's printing system. The topics are broken as following:

- *Understanding network printing services*

- *Setting up network printing services*

- *Redirecting print jobs to network printers*

- *Managing network print jobs*

Network Printing Services

The five basic components associated with network printing are as follows:

- Clients
- Printers
- Print queues
- Print servers
- File servers

The four basic steps required to set up network printing include the following:

- Configuring network printing
- Initializing network print servers
- Connecting printers to the network
- Customizing printing services

Basic Network Printing Components

Of the five network printing components, three—printers, file servers, and clients—are very common and should, therefore, be easy to remember. The other two are print queues and print servers.

By now, you should know what file servers and clients are and how they fit into the overall network design. You no doubt know what a printer is, but you need to familiarize yourself with some aspects

of using printers on a NetWare network. Consider the following information concerning network printers:

- Printers can be connected to the network in any of three ways. They can be connected to a print server, a workstation, or directly to the network cabling system.

- A printer that is connected to a print server is called a *local* printer, and one connected to a workstation or to the network cable is called a *remote* printer.

- A maximum of 16 printers can be connected to one print server. Because *print servers* (computers running the related print server software) do not have 16 physical ports available—they have only five—printers can be either physically attached to the print server, or logically attached to it. A *physical* connection means the printer is attached by cable to a printer port on the computer. A *logical* connection means the printer is physically attached to either a network workstation or the network cabling and makes a software connection to the print server using the related NetWare printing software. You can physically connect a maximum of five of the 16 printers to ports on the print server.

As just noted, a print server is a computer running special NetWare software. Print servers control network printers. They are responsible for taking print jobs stored in print queues and sending them to the appropriate network printer (see fig. 5.1).

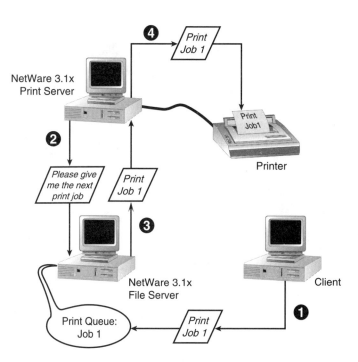

Figure 5.1
*The function of a
print server.*

A *print queue* is simply a directory on a NetWare 3.12 file server that temporarily holds *print jobs* (files waiting to be printed) until the assigned print server can collect the job and send it to a printer.

Network Print Services Setup

To set up network print services, you must complete the following four basic processes:

1. Configure network printing

2. Initialize network print servers

3. Connect printers to the network

4. Customize printing as needed

You configure network printing by defining each network print server, print queue, and printer used on the network. You define these network printing components using the PCONSOLE utility.

 Note This installation step easily qualifies as the most tedious of all installation steps. It involves several tasks that must be performed once the PCONSOLE utility is issued. These steps include the following:

■ Creating and configuring print servers

■ Defining the types of printers being used on your network

■ Establishing a logical connection between these different components

The following section discusses the last step in detail.

After defining each print server, print queue, and printer used on the network, you then initialize each of your network print servers.

To initialize a network print server, you load the print server software. Because print servers can be attached to either a NetWare server or to a *dedicated workstation* (one being used for a single function, such as providing access to a network printer), you type **LOAD PSERVER** *print_server_name* at the NetWare server console or **PSERVER** *print_server_name* at the workstation and press Enter. Replace *print_server_name* with the name you assigned to the print server when you first created it.

After the network print servers have been initialized, you must make certain that all network printers are correctly connected to the network. If you intended for printers to be connected directly to the network cable, then connect those printers to the cable. If you intended for some of the printers to be connected to various NetWare file servers or workstations, connect those printers to the appropriate file servers and workstations.

When you define print servers using the PCONSOLE utility, you specify the type of print server you are defining (local or remote). When you make the physical connection, therefore, be sure to connect them in the same way they were defined.

After you have connected the printer to the network, you can make any modifications needed to customize printing services.

You can, for example, establish default print job configurations for users or define printer forms to be used if not all of your network printing will be done on standard letter-size plain bond paper.

The last section of this chapter explains how to use the PRINTDEF and PRINTCON utilities to customize network print jobs.

Setting Up Network Printing Services

Network printing is configured by defining each network print server, print queue, and printer used on the network. The PCONSOLE utility is used for this task. You run PCONSOLE from a workstation attached to the network. Log in to the network as a user with Supervisor or equivalent rights, then start the PCONSOLE utility.

Creating a Print Queue

To create a print queue, choose Print Queue Information from the PCONSOLE Available Options menu. The Print Queues screen opens. Press Insert to open the New Print Queue Name box. Type the name of the print queue you want to create and press Enter. The print queue is created, and its name is added to the Print Queues list.

Figure 5.2 shows the Print Queues screen. In this figure, the print queue called PANASONIC_Q is being created. A print queue called LASER_Q already exists.

Figure 5.2

Screen associated with creating a print queue.

Creating a Print Server

To create a print server, choose Print Server Information from the PCONSOLE Available Options menu. The Print Server screen opens. If you have not previously created any print servers, it will be empty. Press Insert to open the New Print Server Name box. Type the name of the print server you want to create and press Enter. The print server is created, and its name is added to the list of Print Servers.

Figure 5.3 shows the Print Server screen. In this figure, the print server called LEE_PS is being created. A print server called MICHAEL_PS already exists.

Configuring a Print Server

After creating your print servers, you need to configure each one. To configure a print server, choose it from the Print Servers list. Choose Print Server Configuration from the Print Server Information screen, then choose Printer Configuration to open the Configured Printers list (see fig. 5.4).

If you have not yet configured any printers, the list displays every printer number as Not Installed. Choose a printer number, fill out the form that opens, press Esc, and answer Yes when prompted to save the changes.

The Printer Configuration form requires information about the printer, such as its name, type, and the interrupts and IRQ it uses.

With the printer configured, choose Queues Serviced by Printer from the Print Server Configuration Menu, then choose the printer you defined. When the screen opens displaying the File Server, Queue, and Priority for this print server (blank if no print queues have been added yet), press Insert to display a list of print queues from which to choose (see fig. 5.5). Choose a print queue by highlighting it and pressing Enter. Assign a priority to this print queue (priority 1 has the highest priority). It is now added to the list of print queues to be serviced by this printer.

Figure 5.3
Screen associated with creating a print server.

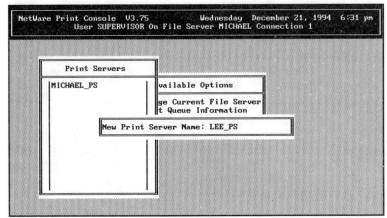

Figure 5.4
The Configured Printers screen.

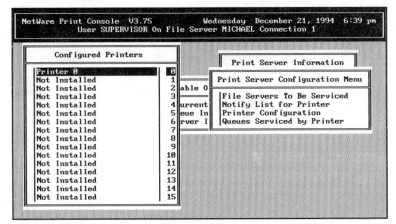

Bringing Up a Print Server

After completing these basic tasks, you must bring up the print server by loading the PSERVER software. Choose Print Queue Information from the PCONSOLE Available Options menu. Then choose the print queue from the Print Queues list. Finally, choose Currently Attached Servers from the Print Queue Information menu and view the name of the print server displayed in the Currently Attached Servers window, as shown in figure 5.6.

To see the name of the print server displayed in the Currently Attached Servers window, you must connect the printer to the file server, workstation, or cable and provide configuration information.

The steps in the previous section explained how to set up the printing-related configuration (print servers, print queues, and printers) using PCONSOLE. The most common mistake people make when setting up printing services is choosing the wrong printer type when filling in the Printer Configuration information (see fig. 5.7).

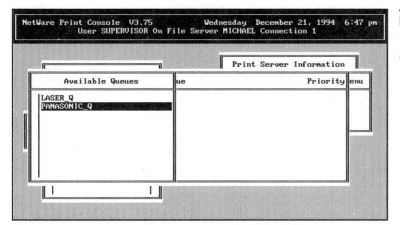

Figure 5.5
Choosing print queues to be serviced by a printer.

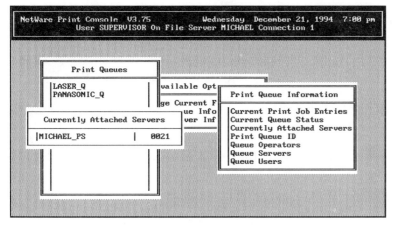

Figure 5.6
The Currently Attached Servers window confirms successful printing installation and configuration.

Local printers are printers that are directly attached to the print server, which may be running as an NLM on a file server or as an EXE on a dedicated print server. For local printers choose either Parallel, LPT1 (or LPT2 or LPT3), or Serial, COM1 (or COM2, COM3, or COM4).

If you did not attach the printer to either a file server with PSERVER.NLM loaded on it or to a PC with PSERVER.EXE running, then choose one of the Remote Parallel, Remote Serial, or Remote Other/ Unknown printer types.

Using printers attached to workstations can pose a problem. If the workstation to which the printer is attached is not being used as a dedicated print server, but is being used as a regular workstation with a printer attached, you must run the RPRINTER.EXE utility on the workstation. That way, network users can access the printer attached to a non-dedicated workstation.

Figure 5.7
The Printer Types list.

```
NetWare Print Console  V3.75          Wednesday  December 21, 1994  7:11 pm
                     User SUPERVISOR On File Server MICHAEL Connection 1

      Co                            Printer types                        ion
   Michae Name: Michael          Parallel, LPT1                       on Menu
   Not In Type: Parallel,        Parallel, LPT2
   Not In                        Parallel, LPT3                       iced
   Not In Use interrupts:        Serial, COM1
   Not In IRQ:                   Serial, COM2
   Not In                        Serial, COM3                         ter
   Not In Buffer size in         Serial, COM4
   Not In                        Remote Parallel, LPT1
   Not In Starting form:         Remote Parallel, LPT2
   Not In Queue service m        Remote Parallel, LPT3 ed
   Not In                        Remote Serial, COM1
   Not In Baud rate:             Remote Serial, COM2
   Not In Data bits:             Remote Serial, COM3
   Not In Stop bits:             Remote Serial, COM4
   Not In Parity:                Remote Other/Unknown
   Not In Use X-On/X-Off:        Defined elsewhere
```

Redirecting Print Jobs to Network Printers

After the printing environment is properly set up, users can send print jobs to network printers. Users can send print jobs from inside application programs, or from the DOS prompt. If the application program understands and uses network printing (if it is *network-aware*), and if the application's print services have been set up to redirect print jobs away from the computer's LPT1 or serial port and toward a network printer, send print jobs using the application directly. There is no need for NetWare's CAPTURE or NPRINT utilities.

If you print directly from applications which are *not* network-aware, or you want to print jobs from a DOS prompt (such as capturing the contents of your monitor's screen to a printer), then NetWare provides two utilities you can use, CAPTURE and NPRINT.

Use the CAPTURE utility (at the DOS prompt) to redirect print jobs from your workstation's LPT or serial ports to network printers. Type **CAPTURE /[*option*]** and press Enter. In place of *option*, you can use any of the available CAPTURE command options.

You can, for example, use /SH to display the current status of the CAPTURE command. Use /Server=*servername* to specify which file server to use. Use /Queue=*queuename* to specify which print queue to use. Figure 5.8 shows the help screen for the CAPTURE command. It displays all the available CAPTURE options.

 Note   NetWare also provides a graphical approach to using the CAPTURE command. You can set CAPTURE options using the User Tools for Windows application.

Use the NPRINT utility (also used from the DOS prompt) to print files outside an application. NPRINT uses most of the same options that CAPTURE uses. You can also use PRINTCON to set NPRINT options.

```
F:\SYSTEM>capture /?
USAGE: CAPTURE /SHow /Job=jobname /Server=fileserver /Queue=queuename /Local=n
/Form=form or n /CReate=path /Copies=n (1-255) /TImeout=n /Keep /Tabs=n (1-18)
/No Tabs /Banner=bannername /NAMe=name /No Banner /FormFeed /No FormFeed
/AUtoendcap /No Autoend /NOTIfy /No NOTIfy /DOmain=domain
 /EndCapture /CAncel /ALL

F:\SYSTEM>
```

Figure 5.8

The CAPTURE command help screen displaying available options.

Managing Network Print Jobs

Once you send print jobs to a network print queue, occasions arise when you need to make modifications to, or otherwise manage, those print jobs.

Using the PCONSOLE utility, you can choose Current Print Job Entries from the Print Queue Information menu to then choose a print job to manage.

The Print Queue Entry Information screen opens (see fig. 5.9).

It displays information about the current print job. From this screen, you can choose any of the options shown in table 5.1 and perform the associated actions.

If you submitted the print job, you can modify most of these fields. Some of these fields can only be modified by a user with Supervisor rights or who has been assigned as a print queue operator.

When you submit a print job, many of the fields displayed on the Print Queue Entry Information screen for this job are already filled because they have default entries. You can set some of these defaults by customizing your print job defaults using the PRINTDEF and PRINTCON utilities.

The PRINTCON utility lets you customize print job configurations. Using PRINTCON, you can create special printer setup configurations, edit existing print job configurations, or copy print job configurations from one network user to another.

Note Users can have their own print job configurations. To make a copy of one user's print job configuration so it can be used by another user, choose the Copy Print Job Configurations option from the Configure Print Jobs Available Options menu. You are prompted for the *Source* User (whose print job configuration file you want to make a copy of), as well as the *Target* user (the user to whom you want to give the copy of the print job configuration file).

To create a print job configuration, use the Edit Print Job configurations option in the Configure Print Jobs Available Options menu. A list of available print jobs is displayed. To create a print job, press Insert, provide a name for the print job, and set configuration information in the Edit Print Job Configuration screen. As figure 5.10 shows, many of the same fields that are included in the Print Queue Entry Information screen are included in the Edit Print Job Configuration screen (refer to fig. 5.9).

Figure 5.9
*The Print Queue Entry
Information screen.*

```
┌─────────────────────────────────────────────────────────────────────┐
│ NetWare Print Console  V3.75           Wednesday  December 21, 1994  7:54 pm │
│                  User SUPERVISOR On File Server MICHAEL Connection 1 │
├─────────────────────────────────────────────────────────────────────┤
│                     Print Queue Entry Information                     │
│  Print job:         928            File size:       250               │
│  Client:            SUPERVISOR[1]                                     │
│  Description:       NEW.TXT                                           │
│  Status:            Ready To Be Serviced, Waiting For Print Server    │
│                                                                       │
│  User Hold:         No             Job Entry Date:  December 9, 1993  │
│  Operator Hold:     No             Job Entry Time:  8:33:20 am        │
│  Service Sequence:  3                                                 │
│                                                                       │
│  Number of copies:  1              Form:                             │
│  File contents:     Byte stream    Print banner:    Yes              │
│  Tab size:                         Name:            SUPERVISOR       │
│  Suppress form feed: No            Banner name:     NEW.TXT          │
│  Notify when done:  No                                               │
│                                    Defer printing:  No               │
│  Target server:     (Any Server)   Target date:                     │
│                                    Target time:                     │
└─────────────────────────────────────────────────────────────────────┘
```

Table 5.1
Print Queue Entry Information Options

Option	Action
Description	Delete or modify the contents to describe this file more accurately.
User Hold	Prevent this file from printing now by placing a user hold. You can later use this field to remove the hold.
Operator Hold	Prevent another user's file from printing immediately— if you have the rights (must be Supervisor or Print Queue Operator)—or remove the hold.
Service Sequence	Change the position of the job in the queue, if you are the Print Queue Operator.
Number of Copies	Specify how many copies will be printed.
File Contents	Specify whether the formatting of this file is to be designated by the application that submitted it (Byte stream), or by the printer (Text), which converts tabs in the document into spaces.
Suppress Form Feed	Advance the printer's paper to the top of the next page after your job is printed (No), or do not advance it (Yes).
Notify When Done	Specify that you want a broadcast message to tell you when your print job is printed (Yes), or not (No).

Option	Action
Target Server	Choose the file server you want to have service your print job if you want to indicate a specific server or let any server take care of it for you (Any Server).
Form	Choose a predefined form from the list of defined forms.
Banner	To identify print jobs being submitted by other users, choose Yes if you want a header page to print before your print job.
Name	If you chose Yes to Banner, enter the text you want to have displayed on the banner. The default is your network UserID, but you can type something else if you want.
Banner Name	Type in the file name being printed—or any other information you want printed on another area of the banner page.
Defer Printing	Choose Yes to print it at a specified date and time, then fill the Target date and Target time fields. Choose No and the print job will print as soon as it becomes priority one at the print queue.
Target Date	Insert the date you want the print job to be printed if you chose to defer the print job.
Target Time	Insert the time of the day you want the job to be printed if you chose to defer its printing to a later time.

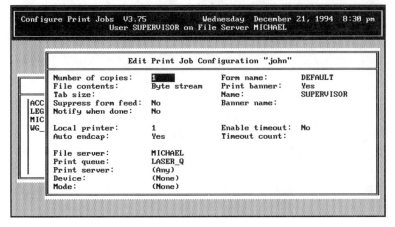

Figure 5.10

The Edit Print Job Configuration screen.

Use the PRINTDEF utility to add printer definitions and names, or form definitions for printing. To start this utility, type **PRINTDEF** and press Enter.

From the Printer Definition Utility PrintDef Options menu, you can choose either Printer Devices or Forms. If you choose Printer Devices, you can do the following:

- Create printer names and definitions

- Edit printer names and definitions

- Delete printer names and definitions

- Import a printer name and definition

- Export a printer name and definition

You can customize how your printer prints. For example, if you want your printer to condense the type when it prints a specific document, you can set up a series of printer escape sequences (series of *ASCII codes*) that tells the printer precisely how to print in condensed mode. You then save these

escape sequences as a function. To each function, you assign a function name, so you can use the function whenever you want to print a file using the printer sequences defined by it.

You can also use the Printer Definition utility to define forms to be used on your network printers. If, for example, you want to print on paper that is 5×7 inches instead of 8 1/2×11, you can define such a form using this utility.

To create a form, choose Forms from the Printer Definition Utility PrintDef Options menu. When the Forms screen opens, press Insert to open the Form Definition screen (see fig. 5.11). Name the form, assign a form number, and provide the length (number of lines on the form) and width (number of characters per line) of the form.

In the preceding example of a 5×7-inch form, and if your printer prints 6 lines per inch of length and 10 characters per inch of width, you would type **42** (seven times six) in the Length field and **50** (five times ten) in the Width field.

Figure 5.11
The Form Definition screen.

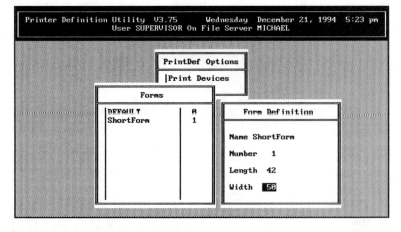

Questions

1. The network printing component to which you can logically connect a printer is the _____.

   ○ A. file server

   ○ B. client

   ○ C. print queue

   ○ D. print server

2. When you send a job to be printed, it goes first to the _____.

   ○ A. file server

   ○ B. client

   ○ C. print queue

   ○ D. print server

3. The second step in the basic printing setup is to _____.

   ○ A. configure network printing

   ○ B. connect the printers to the network

   ○ C. initialize network print servers

   ○ D. customize printing

4. To initialize a network print server, load _____ at the _____.

   ○ A. PSERVER.EXE, file server

   ○ B. PSERVER.NLM, file server

   ○ C. PRINTCON, file server

   ○ D. PRINTCON, workstation

5. Which utility do you use to create print queues?

   ○ A. PSERVER

   ○ B. PRINTCON

   ○ C. PRINTDEF

   ○ D. PRINTER

6. Of the following, which is NOT an item of information provided on the Printer Configuration form?

   ○ A. Printer Name

   ○ B. Interrupt

   ○ C. Print Queue

   ○ D. IRQ

7. How can you tell that you were successful at completing all the printing services setup tasks?

   ○ A. You can send jobs to print queues.

   ○ B. The Current Attached Servers window displays the name of the print server.

   ○ C. You can load the print server on a file server.

   ○ D. You can change printer types without effecting the quality of print services.

8. The THREE utilities used to send print jobs to network printers by redirecting them include:

   ☐ A. User Tools

   ☐ B. PRINTCON

   ☐ C. CAPTURE

   ☐ D. NPRINT

9. Change the _____ field to prevent your print job from being printed until a later date.

   ○ A. Operator Hold

   ○ B. Service Sequence

   ○ C. Suppress Form Feed

   ○ D. User Hold

10. If you have rights, you can modify the _____ job field to specify when a job is to print.

    ○ A. Operator Hold

    ○ B. Service Sequence

    ○ C. Suppress Form Feed

    ○ D. User Hold

11. To customize print jobs, use the _____ utility.

    ○ A. PRINTDEF

    ○ B. PCONSOLE

    ○ C. PRINTCON

    ○ D. PSERVER

12. You CANNOT _____ with the PRINTDEF utility.

    ○ A. edit printer names and definitions

    ○ B. create special printer setup configu-rations

    ○ C. create printer names and definitions

    ○ D. import a printer name and defini-tion

13. Which utility lets you copy one user's print job information to another user?

    ○ A. PRINTCON

    ○ B. PCONSOLE

    ○ C. PRINTDEF

    ○ D. PSERVER

14. Which THREE are valid ways to connect a printer to the network physically?

    □ A. Attach it directly to the cable

    □ B. To a NetWare file server running PSERVER

    □ C. To a workstation

    □ D. To a workstation running PCONSOLE

15. You can connect a maximum of _____ printers to a NetWare 3.12 print server.

    ○ A. 5

    ○ B. 8

    ○ C. 11

    ○ D. 16

Answers

1. D

2. D

3. C

4. B

5. B

6. C

7. B

8. A C D

9. D

10. A

11. C

12. B

13. A

14. A B C

15. D

Preparing Other NetWare 3.1x Services for Users

*A*s a network administrator, it is your job to help make it easier for your users to access the network, including the services, programs, and data files that they need. This chapter discusses the guidance and suggestions that Novell provides, as well as those features of NetWare that help you to make the user's access to the network and its services as easy as possible. Topics include:

- Adding network application software
- Understanding login scripts and their function
- Building system and user login scripts
- Understanding the NetWare menu system

■ Creating and running a NetWare 3.12 menu

■ Converting older NetWare menus

■ Understanding NetWare basic MHS

■ Setting up and administering basic MHS

■ Using first mail

Adding Network Application Software

When choosing application software to put on your network, consider these seven suggested guidelines to make your choices easier and more successful:

■ Choose application software that is compatible with your network operating system.

■ Choose and verify that the software is designed for multiple users.

■ Establish a directory structure into which you can place the application software before you install it and place different application software files in subdirectories within that directory. Load it all in one area of the network directory structure.

■ After the directory structure is in place, install the application software, following the installation instructions provided by the application software's manufacturer.

■ After the application software files are installed, flag them as Shareable/Read Only (S, RO) to secure against viruses and to

enable multiple users to access the files without changing, copying, or deleting the files.

■ Ensure that users have a search drive mapped to the directory containing the application software's executable files. In addition, grant the Read (R) and File (F) scan rights to each group or individual network user so they have the right to run these programs.

■ If necessary, increase the number of memory buffers and the number of files that can be opened simultaneously in the CONFIG.SYS file on the file server, as well as on user's workstations. Do not make this modification to CONFIG.SYS unless you have determined that the current settings for these two parameters are insufficient.

To load applications software, complete the following steps:

1. Create a directory structure for the application software (if it does not already exist).

2. Copy the application software to its specific directory.

3. Create or update the CONFIG.SYS file (as previously discussed).

4. INSTALL the application software by following the instructions that came with the application program.

5. Flag the application program files so no one can delete, copy, or modify them, as well as to provide some virus protection.

6. Verify that the application runs correctly.

7. Grant users and groups the necessary rights (R and F) to the application software.

8. Create a search drive to the directory. If you put the search drive into the system login script (see the following section for information on login scripts), all the users can access it without having to create search drives for themselves.

The Function of Login Scripts

There are three types of NetWare login scripts:

- System
- User
- Default

System login scripts set up the network environment with general-use information. The system login script, for example, is the most common place to put a search drive mapping to network applications. By placing this search drive mapping in the system login script, which is run first whenever a user logs in to the network, necessary search drive mappings are created for each user.

The user login script enables you or the user to establish a user-specific environment. User login scripts, for example, can contain network drive mappings to the user's home directory and related subdirectories.

The default login script is part of the LOGIN.EXE file. If no user login script exists, the default login script runs, setting up essential environment variables, such as a drive mapping to the SYS:PUBLIC directory. After a user login script is created, the default login script is not run for that user. (This is true even if the user's login script contains only blank lines.) If you want to prevent the default login script from running even when no user login script exists, enter the **NO_DEFAULT** command in the system login script.

Build System and User Login Scripts

Although the default login script is part of the LOGIN.EXE file, and, as such, does not need to be created by the network administrator or by a user, the same is not true of the system and user login scripts.

Table 6.1 shows the available login script commands. These commands can be used in both system and user login scripts, with one exception: You *must* place the NO_DEFAULT command into the system login script if you do not want the default login script to be run when a user does not have a user login script.

 Note Login script commands that have a percent sign (%) in front of them are called identifier variables. An *identifier variable* is a special command that, when run, is replaced by the actual item of information that the identifier variable represents. The LOGIN_NAME identifier variable, when included as %LOGIN_NAME in a login script command, for example, is replaced by the actual UserID of the user running this login script.

Table 6.1
Login Script Commands

Command	Purpose	Example
#	Is followed by a program name, runs an external DOS program, then returns to the login script.	#PS.EXE
*	Indicates the following is a remark—for information purposes only—and is not run as a command.	* This section is only run on Mondays
BREAK	Used with ON or OFF to let the user stop or not stop the login script from running.	BREAK OFF
COMSPEC	Tells where to find the DOS COMMAND.COM file.	COMSPEC=C: \COMMAND.COM
DISPLAY	Types a text file to the screen.	DISPLAY Z:USER.TXT
DRIVE	Specify first (default) drive for user after login script is run.	DRIVE F:
END	Used with IF...THEN...ELSE to specify the end of this conditional statement.	IF MEMBER OF "HR" THEN ATTACH HR1\PR: END
FDISPLAY	Types a text file to the screen, but removes printer and other codes.	FDISPLAY Z:USER.TXT
FIRE PHASERS	Sets the user's computer to repeat a sound for a given number of times.	FIRE PHASERS 3
GREETING_TIME	Specifies time of day such as morning or evening.	WRITE "GOOD % GREETING_TIME"

Command	Purpose	Example
HOUR24	Determines the hour based on a 24-hour day.	IF HOUR24 "18" THEN WRITE "Go home!" END
IF...THEN...ELSE	Lets you run nested (up to 10 levels) condition statements.	IF TUESDAY THEN WRITE "Meet at 3" ELSE...WRITE "Hello" END
INCLUDE	Runs a DOS text file as part of the login script.	INCLUDE Z:TUES.TXT
LOGIN_NAME	Use's the user's login name.	WRITE "Hello %LOGIN_NAME"
MACHINE	Determines computer type if not an OS/2 computer.	S3:=S2\SYS:PUBLIC\ %MACHINE\%OS\ %OS_VERSION
MAP	Creates or modifies a drive mapping or displays current drive mappings.	MAP F:=SYS:USERS\ %LOGIN_NAME
NDAY_OF_WEEK	Determines day of week, using 1 through 7 (Sunday through Saturday).	IF NDAY_OF_WEEK = "02" THEN WRITE "Oh No!" ELSE WRITE "We made it! END
OS	Determines the type of DOS running on the user's PC.	S3:=S2\SYS:PUBLIC\ %MACHINE\%OS\ %OS_VERSION
OS_VERSION	Determines the DOS version running on the user's PC.	S3:=S2\SYS:PUBLIC\ %MACHINE\%OS\ %OS_VERSION
PAUSE	Stops program execution until user presses a key.	PAUSE

continues

Table 6.1, Continued
Login Script Commands

Command	Purpose	Example
REMARK	Indicates that what follows is a remark—for information purposes only—and is not run as a command.	* This section is only run on Tuesdays.
SET	Sets DOS variables.	SET PROMPT = "PG"
STATION	Displays the client's connection number.	WRITE "Your connection number is %STATION
WRITE	Prints information inside quotations to the monitor.	WRITE "Hello"

You can create login scripts by completing the following steps:

1. Log in to the network with Supervisor rights if you want to create a system login script or a user login script for someone other than yourself.

2. Start the SYSCON utility.

3A. If you want to create a system login script, choose Supervisor Options from the SYSCON Available Topics menu, then choose System Login Script system login.

3B. Choose User Information from the SYSCON Available Topics menu, then choose a user's name to create your own user login script, or, if you have Supervisor rights, another user's login script.

4. If you are creating a user login script, you can choose to copy another user's login script. Type the name of the user whose user login script you want to copy when you are prompted with Read Login Script From User, as shown in figure 6.1.

5. Modify a user script copied from another user or create a login script by using the commands shown in table 6.1.

6. Press Esc to exit the login script file and click on Yes to save the file.

Figure 6.2 shows the system login script for the file server called MICHAEL.

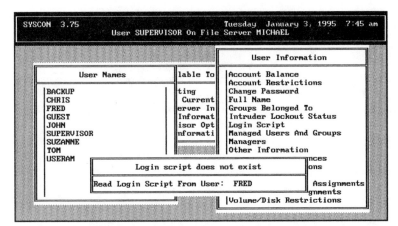

Figure 6.1
*The Read Login Script
From User prompt.*

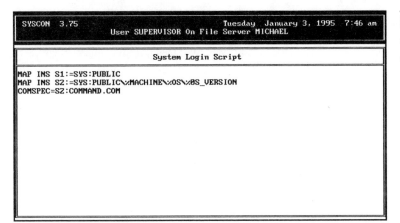

Figure 6.2
*Sample System
Login Script.*

The NetWare Menu System

A *menu* is a screen from which you can choose various options to accomplish various tasks. Some NetWare utilities, such as SYSCON and FILER, provide a menu from which you can make your selections.

NetWare lets you create custom menus using any DOS text editor, and its menuing software program—MENUMAKE.

NetWare menus consist of the following four basic components:

- The main menu
- Submenus

■ Commands

■ Prompts for user input

The main menu must have a title and contain a list of options from which the user can choose. Each option must include commands to be executed when the option is chosen. Submenus must also have a title, as well as options and commands.

There are two types of commands used in a NetWare menu: Organizational and Control. *Organizational commands* determine the layout or arrangement of the menu. *Item commands* define the options available in each menu.

The following are Organizational commands:

■ MENU

■ ITEM

The MENU command identifies the start of each menu. Use the MENU command by including it in the text file, followed by a two- to three-character menu number (01 through 255), a comma, and a menu name. This MENU command must be left-justified whenever it is used.

Use the MENU command as shown in the following example:

```
MENU 01, User Utilities
```

The ITEM command specifies the options to be included on the menu. ITEM lines are indented beneath MENU lines. Include one ITEM line for each option on the menu.

For example, use the ITEM command as shown in the following line:

```
MENU 01, User Utilities
    ITEM Word Processing
```

The ITEM command also has options that can be used with it:

■ **BATCH.** Removes the menu program from RAM and runs the CHDIR option

■ **CHDIR.** Returns the user to the default directory after the chosen menu option has completed its last associated command

■ **PAUSE.** Suspends action until the user presses a key

■ **SHOW.** Displays in the upper left corner of the screen the name of a DOS command being run, if it is being run because of a user's choice of a specific menu option

These ITEM options are used below the ITEM command. They must be indented farther than the ITEM command.

For example, use the EXEC ITEM option as shown below:

```
MENU 01, User Utilities
    ITEM Word Processing
        EXEC WP
```

In addition to the two Organizational commands, there are six Control commands:

■ **EXEC.** Runs the command whose executable file name follows the EXEC command

■ **GETO.** Accepts but does not require the user to provide input to a prompt that is displayed as the result of the user choosing a menu option

■ **GETP.** Stores the user's input for later use, as specified based on numbered identifier variables preceded by a percent sign

■ **GETR.** Requires that the user input valid information (such as a numeric when a numeric is required) before the menu will continue

GET commands prompt the user to provide input. You can use up to 100 GET commands per ITEM.

You must place any GET commands between the ITEM and EXEC lines associated with them.

When you use GET commands, the command must be entered as follows, using {curly braces} when indicated, and replacing unused parameters with commas:

```
GETxinstruction{prepend}length,prefill,
   ➥SECURE{append}
```

Replace *instruction* with what you want to appear on the screen.

Replace *prepend* with any information that you want placed in front of the user's response. Place the prepended information in curly braces.

Replace *length* with the number of characters allowed for the user's response.

Replace *prefill* with any information you want to put into the user's answer field as a default answer.

Use SECURE to cause only asterisks to be shown when the user types a response.

Replace *append* with information to be placed at the end of the user's typed input.

■ **LOAD.** Suspends the current menu to load and run another menu that is stored in a separate file.

■ **SHOW.** Retrieves the submenu as specified by the submenu number. The difference between the SHOW and the LOAD commands is that the SHOW command is used when the submenu is contained within the same file as the original menu. The LOAD command calls a menu contained within a separate file.

Create and Run a NetWare 3.12 Menu

After you have created a menu, such as the one shown in figure 6.3, you must prepare the menu to be used.

Figure 6.3
Sample NetWare menu.

To prepare a menu for use, complete the following steps:

1. Create or edit the menu as needed, using any DOS text editor.

2. Compile the menu by running the MENUMAKE utility, as shown in figure 6.4. To run this utility, type **MENUMAKE** *[path]textfile*, replacing *path* and *textfile* with the path and the name of the DOS text file containing the menu commands. Press Enter.

3. Run the menu by using the NMENU command, followed by the path to and the name of the DAT file created by the MEMUMAKE utility.

Create, for example, a text file with menu commands called USERMENU. Next, run the MENUMAKE utility to compile this file, creating a file called USERMENU.DAT. Then run the file by typing **NMENU USERMENU** and pressing Enter. The menu is displayed (see fig. 6.5).

Figure 6.4

Using MENUMAKE to create a menu file.

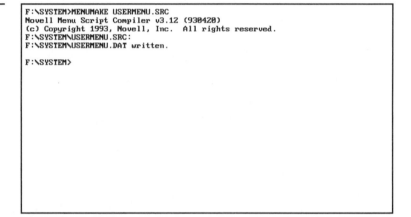

```
F:\SYSTEM>MENUMAKE USERMENU.SRC
Novell Menu Script Compiler v3.12 (930420)
(c) Copyright 1993, Novell, Inc.  All rights reserved.
F:\SYSTEM\USERMENU.SRC:
F:\SYSTEM\USERMENU.DAT written.

F:\SYSTEM>
```

Figure 6.5

User Utilities menu.

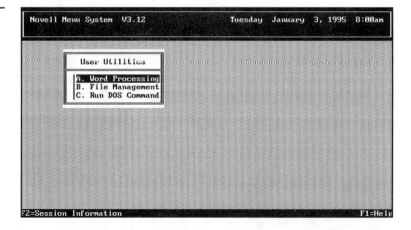

Convert Older NetWare Menus

Pre-NetWare 3.12 menu files had an MNU extension. To convert an older menu, run the MENUCNVT program. To run this program, type **MENUCNVT** *filename.mnu* and press Enter.

After you have converted the menu file, compile it using the MENUMAKE utility, as previously described.

Understand NetWare Basic MHS

Novell's NetWare Basic *Message Handling Service* (MHS) is the software that delivers electronic mail messages. NetWare Basic MHS lets users on a single-server network send electronic mail messages to each other. After Basic MHS receives a mail message from a mail application, it delivers it to the appropriate electronic mailbox.

Set Up and Administer Basic MHS

Basic MHS is installed at the file server console. Basic MHS can only be used on NetWare networks with a single file server. You install Basic MHS on the file server by accessing the server directly from the file server console.

Install Basic MHS

Basic MHS ships with NetWare 3.12 and is installed as if it were an optional Novell product, using the Prodcut Options selection from the INSTALL.NLM.

To start the installation of Basic MHS, type **LOAD INSTALL** at the file server console.

Add a User

Basic MHS installs an administration utility during installation. Before you can run and use this utility, you must run BREQUEST.EXE at the client. Then activate the administrative utility by typing **ADMIN** and pressing Enter.

To add a mail user, choose Users from the Admin Functions menu, press Insert, then type a name for the new user's account and fill in other information as needed. Add users by repeating this process.

Create a Distribution List

You also use the ADMIN utility to create a list of users to whom you can send mail messages. To create a distribution list, choose Distribution Lists from the Admin Functions menu and press Insert. Next, fill in the requested information and press Esc. Choose Yes to save the distribution list.

Use First Mail

As a network administrator, you use the ADMIN utility to prepare Basic MHS for users. Basic MHS provides the background processing and managing features for e-mail. Network users can run First Mail—the NetWare utility that provides the user interface for electronic messaging—or any other e-mail program that uses the *Standard Message Format* (SMF) to send, read, and manage their e-mail messages.

Send Mail Using First Mail

To create and send a mail message, type **MAIL** and press Enter. Choose Send a mail message from the Mail Options menu and type the recipient's user name in the To field. Then type a brief topic description in the Subj field and the message in the blank area, and press Ctrl+Enter to send the mail message.

Read Mail Using First Mail

To read a mail message, type **MAIL** and press Enter. Choose Browse mail messages from the Mail Options Menu, then choose the message you want to read. Press Esc to return to the list of messages and you can choose another message.

 To help you decide which messages are most important—which should be read promptly and which can wait—First Mail provides three useful items of information for each message displayed in the list of available messages. If the sender filled out all fields, you will see information that tells you the date and time the message was created, who sent the message, and to what the subject of the message relates.

Questions

1. Which TWO of the following are guidelines to consider when choosing application software?

   ☐ A. Usable by only one person at a time

   ☐ B. Flag files SRO ·

   ☐ C. Load before DOS

   ☐ D. Network OS compatibility

2. The correct order for loading application software is which of the following?

   ○ A. Create directory structure, copy software, update CONFIG.SYS file, INSTALL software, and flag files

   ○ B. Update CONFIG.SYS file, create directory structure, flag files, and INSTALL software

   ○ C. INSTALL software, update CONFIG.SYS file, create directory structure, and copy software

   ○ D. Create directory structure, copy software, flag files, and update CONFIG.SYS file

3. Which of the following is NOT a type of login script?

   ○ A. System

   ○ B. User

   ○ C. Network

   ○ D. Default

4. The login script that runs when no individual login script exists for a user is called the _____ login script.

   ○ A. System

   ○ B. User

   ○ C. Network

   ○ D. Default

5. The _____ login script sets up the network environment with general-use information.

   ○ A. System

   ○ B. User

   ○ C. Network

   ○ D. Default

6. To establish a specific environment for an individual, create a _____ login script.

   ○ A. System

   ○ B. User

   ○ C. Network

   ○ D. Default

7. Which of the following statements about the default login script is true?

   ○ A. It is part of the LOGIN.EXE file.

   ○ B. It executes after the user's login script.

   ○ C. It does not run if a system login script exists.

   ○ D. It runs before the network login script.

8. To run an external DOS command from inside a login script, preceed the command with _____.

   ○ A. #

   ○ B. *

   ○ C. %

   ○ D. INCLUDE

9. To run a DOS text file as part of the login script, use the _____ command.

   ○ A. #

   ○ B. *

   ○ C. %

   ○ D. INCLUDE

10. Which TWO statements about login scripts are true?

    □ A. To create a user menu, choose User Information in SYSCON.

    □ B. You can copy one user's login script to create a script for another user.

    □ C. You can create login scripts for any user regardless of your network rights.

    □ D. You create user login scripts to customize their environment and make access to network resources easier for the user.

11. The NetWare software used to create a menu is called _____.

    ○ A. SYSCON

    ○ B. FILER

    ○ C. MENUMAKE

    ○ D. MENUCNVT

12. Which command identifies the start of a NetWare menu?

    ○ A. MENU

    ○ B. START

    ○ C. ITEM

    ○ D. BATCH

13. Of the following, which is NOT an option of the ITEM command?

    ○ A. BATCH

    ○ B. CHDIR

    ○ C. SHOW

    ○ D. MENU

14. Use the _____ command to run a NetWare menu.

    ○ A. MENUMAKE

    ○ B. NMENU

    ○ C. USERMENU

    ○ D. DAT

15. NetWare menus created before NetWare 3.12 can be changed to run in a 3.12 environment using which TWO menu commands?

    □ A. NEWMENU

    □ B. MENUDAT

    □ C. MENUCNVT

    □ D. MENUMAKE

Answers

1.	B D	9.	D
2.	A	10.	A D
3.	C	11.	C
4.	D	12.	A
5.	A	13.	D
6.	B	14.	B
7.	A	15.	C D
8.	A		

Protecting the NetWare 3.1x Network

Features such as passwords, login user IDs, NCP Packet Signature, and others help protect your network from unauthorized access. Unauthorized access is not the only problem that you can experience with your NetWare file server, however. Power outages and hard disk crashes are two other problems from which your file server might suffer. NetWare helps you deal with these types of problems by providing three data integrity features. This chapter discusses those three features with topics including the following:.

- *Understanding system fault tolerance*
- *Understanding storage management services*
- *Backing up and restoring NetWare file servers*

Understanding System Fault Tolerance

System Fault Tolerance (SFT) is one of NetWare's network data protection systems. It includes a variety of approaches to maintaining the integrity of data on your NetWare file server.

SFT helps to ensure your network's data integrity through several key features (see fig. 7.1). These features include the following:

■ Disk mirroring

■ Disk duplexing

■ Duplicate FATs and DETs

■ Hot fix

■ Read-after-write verification

■ TTS

■ UPS Monitoring

Table 7.1 shows these SFT features and briefly describes each of them.

Figure 7.1

Features of SFT.

Table 7.1
NetWare's SFT Features

Feature	Description	Purpose
Disk Duplexing	NetWare duplicates data from the NetWare partition of one hard disk to that of another hard disk, using a different adapter, cable, and controller.	To protect data from hard disk failure.
Disk Mirroring	NetWare duplicates data from the NetWare partition of one hard disk to that of another hard disk, using the same adapter, cable, and controller.	To provide a second copy in case of hard disk failure.
Duplicate FATS and DETS	NetWare duplicates the *File Allocation Table* (FAT) and *Directory Entry Table* (DET) to different parts of the hard disk.	To ensure the OS always has access to these tables.
Hot fix	When a bad block is identified, hot fix redirects the data to another area on the hard disk.	To store data in a valid area of the hard disk.
Read-after-Write Verification	When data is stored in a block on the computer's hard disk, read-after-write verification checks that block of data to make certain it can be read. After several unsuccessful tries, it marks the hard disk block as bad and saves the data to another location.	To verify the readability of the data that it just wrote to disk.
TTS	Tracks database transactions to ensure either that all related database changes are saved to the database or that no changes are saved.	To protect the integrity of database files.
UPS	This software lets you control an *Uninterruptible Power Supply* (UPS) connected to your network server.	To protect your server from power outages/fluctuations.

Understanding Storage Management Services

Centralized data storage and access brings with it the increased possibility of the loss of a major amount of your network data due to a hard drive crash. NetWare provides a feature called *Storage Management Services* (SMS) to allow data to be stored and retrieved on your network.

NetWare provides SMS as a group of *NetWare Loadable Modules* (NLMs). One of the most important aspects of SMS is its design. SMS enables you to back up and restore your network's file system using the SMS-compatible backup software and hardware of your choice. SMS also lets you back up and restore files regardless of the local operating system that you are using. SMS supports DOS, OS/2, Macintosh, Windows, and Unix file systems.

One of the main ways to use a file storage management system is to make regular backups of your network's file system. The next section of this chapter shows you how to use the backup software NetWare provides. This software is called SBACKUP. To ensure data integrity, you must establish a regular schedule of backing your network's data, whether you use SBACKUP or another backup-and-restore software.

The regularity of network backup is important. If you have to restore a network backup, the more current and complete that backup is, the less work you will have to do to reconstruct your network data. Because regular and consistent backups are important, Novell describes some backup techniques that you should consider implementing in your network environment. These techniques include the following:

- Full backup

- Incremental backup

- Differential backup

A *full backup* involves backing up all files on a NetWare file server. You can back up the files on the file server that is running the backup software, or on any other NetWare file server. When you do a full backup, you back up all files on a file server, including bindery and system files. A full backup also causes the *modify bit* (a flag set on a file that indicates whether its contents have changed since the last time this file was backed up) to be reset for each file that is backed up. You should do the first full backup on your NetWare network shortly after you have installed it.

In addition to doing a full backup, you can also choose to back up any of the following:

- Certain directories

- All files that changed after you ran the last backup

- Files ending with a specific file name extension

If you choose to do a backup following one or more of these options, then you are not doing a full backup. Instead, you are doing either an incremental backup or a differential backup.

When you do an *incremental backup*, you back up all files that have been created in or copied to a specific directory since you ran the last backup. You also back up any files in the specified directory that have been modified since the last time you ran a backup. When you do an incremental backup, all file modify bits are cleared.

When you do a *differential back up*, you are backing up all data that has changed since you ran the last full backup. With a differential backup, it does not matter whether the changed files were backed up by an incremental backup because the modify bit is not cleared. This enables you to do an incremental backup later, and back up these files as well.

Knowing when to do network backups is only part of the process. You also need to know how to do those backups. If you are using a backup software package provided by anyone other than Novell, you must follow the instructions provided by that software package. If you choose to use the backup software provided with NetWare 3.12, then follow the instructions for using SBACKUP.

Backup and Restore NetWare File Servers

Before using SBACKUP, it might help you to be familiar with two of Novell's related terms, as follows:

- **Host.** The file server that has the backup device attached to it.

- **Target.** The file server (or workstation) that contains the files being backed up.

To back up files on a NetWare 3.12 file server or client, complete the following steps:

1. LOAD the TSA312.NLM on the target file server.

2. Load the backup device drivers on the host server if they have not already been loaded.

 Note   If you automated the process of loading the backup device drivers using the file server's AUTOEXEC.NCF file, you do not need to complete step 2.

3. Load SBACKUP at the host server.

4. Provide your supervisor user name if prompted, along with the password.

5. If the Select the Device Driver menu is displayed, choose the device driver for the backup hardware you have attached to your file server.

6. Choose Select Target to Backup/Restore option from the SBACKUP Main Menu to choose the file server or workstation whose files you will back up.

7. If prompted, provide a user name and password for the target server.

8. Choose Backup Menu from the Main Menu

9. When the Backup Menu window appears, as shown in figure 7.2, choose Select Working Directory and provide a path to where the backup session files, such as the error log, should be saved.

Figure 7.2
The Backup Menu.

10. When prompted, fill in the Backup Options fields, then press Esc.

11. When prompted to Proceed with Backup, choose Yes.

12. Choose Start Backup Now to begin the backup session.

13. When the backup is complete, press Enter to redisplay the Backup Menu, then press Esc to return to the Main menu.

 If you are backing up a network DOS client instead of a file server, you first must load the TSA_DOS.NLM at the host. Loading TSA_DOS.NLM, automatically loads the following additional NLMs:

- STREAMS.NLM

- SMDR31X.NLM

- TLI.NLM

- SPXS.NLM or IPXS.NLM

In addition, you must load the TSA_SMS.COM file at the workstation whose files you want to back up. The best way to do this is to modify the client's AUTOEXEC.BAT file to load the TSA_SMS.COM file, then reboot the client to load the TSA_SMS.COM file automatically.

After you have done this, continue with the step that has you loading the SBACKUP NLM at the file server.

You can also back up an OS/2 client by loading the TSA_OS2.NLM at the file server, just as you would load the TSA_DOS.NLM if you were backing up a DOS client.

Questions

1. To back up only files changed since the last backup, perform a/an _____ backup.

   ○ A. full

   ○ B. incremental

   ○ C. differential

   ○ D. custom

2. To back up a DOS client, run the _____ file at the DOS client.

   ○ A. SMDR.NLM

   ○ B. TSA_OS2.COM

   ○ C. TSA_DOS.COM

   ○ D. TSA_SMS.COM

3. Which of the following is NOT a feature of SFT?

   ○ A. Disk mirroring

   ○ B. Disk duplexing

   ○ C. Duplicate FATs and DETs

   ○ D. Hot Repair

4. The SFT feature that verifies the readability of data after it has been written to the hard disk is _____.

   ○ A. hot fix

   ○ B. UPS

   ○ C. read-after-write

   ○ D. duplicate FAT

5. Which THREE files are automatically loaded when you load DOS_TSA.NLM.

   ☐ A. STREAMS.NLM

   ☐ B. SMDR31X.NLM

   ☐ C. DOS_SMS.NLM

   ☐ D. TLI.NLM

6. The feature of SFT that lets you back up and restore your network's file system using compatible backup software and hardware is called _____.

   ○ A. SMS

   ○ B. UPS

   ○ C. SOS

   ○ D. FATS

7. If you are backing up a network DOS client instead of a file server, you must first load the _____ at the _____.

   ○ A. TSA_DOS.NLM, target

   ○ B. TSA_DOS.NLM, host

   ○ C. TSA_SMS.COM, target

   ○ D. TSA_SMS.COM, host

8. Tracking database transactions is a feature of _____.

   ○ A. TTS

   ○ B. SMS

   ○ C. UPS

   ○ D. NLM

9. To protect your network from failure of the hard disk channel, which SFT feature should you implement?

   ○ A. UPS

   ○ B. Duplicate FAT

   ○ C. Disk mirroring

   ○ D. Duplicate DET

10. The SFT feature that you should implement to protect against a bad disk drive adapter card is _____.

   ○ A. duplicate FAT

   ○ B. disk duplexing

   ○ C. disk mirroring

   ○ D. duplicate DET

Answers

1.	C
2.	C
3.	D
4.	C
5.	A B D
6.	A
7.	B
8.	A
9.	C
10.	B

PART

NetWare 3.1x Advanced Administration

8 *Understanding NetWare 3.1x Server Basics* 109

9 *Understanding Memory and Performance in NetWare 3.1x Servers* 129

10 *Working with NetWare 3.1x Clients* 147

11 *Setting Up and Maintaining Network Print Services* 163

12 *Maintaining and Monitoring NetWare 3.1x Servers* 177

13 *Supporting and Protecting NetWare 3.1x Servers* 195

Understanding NetWare 3.1x Server Basics

As a network administrator, server startup, monitoring, and maintenance are among your primary duties. To successfully maintain and monitor your network's NetWare 3.1x file servers, you must understand various aspects of the 3.1x operating system and its primary component—the NetWare file server. This chapter is designed to provide you with advanced information about the NetWare 3.1x file server.

After reading this chapter, you will be able to:

- *Understand server components*

- *Work with server configuration files*

- *Describe network communication*

- Understand name-space support

- Start a NetWare 3.12 server

Understanding Server Components

Personal computers consist of two primary components: hardware and software. The hardware of a PC includes such physical components as a monitor, keyboard, *central processing unit* (CPU), and so on. Software includes the operating systems, communication programs, and so on.

A NetWare 3.1*x* file server, which runs on an Intel-based PC, also consists of two primary components: hardware and software. By understanding the components of a 3.1*x* file server, you can better understand how a file server provides network services to multiple users. Consequently, you also can better understand how to successfully maintain and monitor your network's 3.1*x* file servers.

NetWare 3.1*x* Server Hardware Components

Because a NetWare 3.1*x* file server runs on an Intel-based PC, the hardware components of the file server are the same as those of a PC. Three of these common components, however, are especially important to a NetWare file server:

- Microprocessor

- Memory

- Hard disk

There is one other hardware component that is not originally part of a PC. It is, however, an important part of a file server (see fig. 8.1). That component is the network board and its associated cabling.

Microprocessor

To install NetWare 3.1*x* file server software on your PC, you must have at least an Intel 80386 microprocessor. Intel 80486 microprocessors generally are capable of processing service requests at a greater speed than are 80386 microprocessors. A PC with an 80486 microprocessor, therefore, often is more suitable as a NetWare file server than a PC with an Intel 80386 microprocessor, although both can be used.

Table 8.1 provides a quick comparison of some of the features of Intel 80386 and 80486 microprocessors.

Table 8.1
Intel 80386 versus 80486 microprocessors.

Feature	*80386*	*80486*
Register	32-bit	32-bit
Data Bus	32-bit	32-bit
Clock Speeds	16, 20, 25, and 33	25, 33, 50, and 66

PCs using the Intel Pentium microprocessor also can be used as NetWare 3.1*x* file servers. The Pentium microprocessor still uses the 32-bit address bus, but has a data bus with a 64-bit width. In addition, Pentiums currently run at 60 MHz and 66 MHz, although faster versions are planned.

The Pentium microprocessor also can execute two commands at once, instead of just one command at a time, which is what the 80386 and 80486 micro-processors currently are capable of doing. The Pentium has two data pipelines, not one. NetWare 3.1*x* is not designed, however, to take advantage of this Pentium microprocessor feature.

Memory

The NetWare 3.1*x* file server requires a minimum of 4 MB of random access memory (RAM) with which to temporarily store and retrieve needed data. The file server can access and use as much as 4 GB of RAM.

Hard Disk

One of the main benefits of networking is the capability to store data and program files on the network's file servers. Data and program files are stored on one or more file server hard disks. Those hard disks can be internal or external to the file server, but there must be at least one hard disk.

The first hard disk usually contains both a DOS partition and a NetWare partition. The DOS partition is used to boot the PC and to start the file server. (SERVER.EXE is stored on the DOS partition.) A DOS partition is not mandatory, however, because the PC can be booted and the SERVER.EXE file can be loaded from a floppy disk (not recommended).

The NetWare partition stores the other file server files. It is divided into one or more NetWare volumes. Each 3.1*x* file server must have at least one volume. That volume is always named SYS.

Figure 8.1
PC and file server components.

Each file server can have only one volume called SYS, but it can have more than one volume. Other volumes can be located on the same hard disk, or on additional hard disks, as long as no two volumes on any single NetWare 3.1*x* file server have the same name.

All NetWare volumes must be placed on NetWare partitions. These volumes cannot be placed on DOS partitions. You can, however, put more than one volume on a NetWare partition.

You can have more than one hard disk on your NetWare file server as well, as long as the total disk space does not exceed 32 TB (*terabytes*). Each additional hard disk must have its own NetWare partition, however, which you create by using the INSTALL utility.

Network Board and Cabling

Each NetWare file server must have at least one network board installed, although file servers can have several boards installed to enable communication among different networks. The network board is responsible for the physical communication between network file servers and clients. When multiple boards (up to a maximum of 16) are installed in a file server, that file server performs another duty—that of a network router.

The cabling system connects the network boards to each other. When different types of network boards are installed in a NetWare file server, different types of cabling systems might also be required.

NetWare 3.1*x* Server Software Components

In addition to the physical or hardware components required to create a network, software components are needed. The file server must contain three types of software:

- SERVER.EXE
- Disk driver
- LAN driver

This software is described in the following sections.

SERVER.EXE

The main operating system file, which is responsible for performing various NetWare operating system functions, is the SERVER.EXE file. It is loaded into file server memory as a DOS executable file. Once loaded, DOS no longer controls the PC, although it remains resident in memory and provides services if requested.

SERVER.EXE provides limited services. Its primary function is to provide a platform (software bus) to which other network services can attach. These other network services, provided through files known as *NetWare Loadable Modules* (NLMs), ensure that NetWare provides basic networking and advanced services.

Two of the most common and most important services include communication between the file server and the PC's hard disk, and communication between the file server and the PC's network board (see fig. 8.2). These services are provided through software files called disk drivers and LAN drivers.

Disk Driver

Most NLMs are files with an NLM extension. Disk driver NLMs have a DSK extension, however, because they are specialized NLMs. They are responsible for enabling communication between the LAN board installed in the PC with

SERVER.EXE loaded, and the *disk controller*—the PC's hard disk system interface.

As with SERVER.EXE, disk driver NLMs are stored in the server boot directory—SERVER.312. The disk driver NLM appropriate to the architecture of the disk controller in the PC is loaded into the file server's memory after SERVER.EXE has been loaded.

 Note   Common disk controller architectures supported by and shipped with NetWare 3.12 include the following:

- SCSI
- IDE
- ISA
- EISA
- Microchannel

Unlike SERVER.EXE, which is loaded into RAM by running the DOS-based SERVER executable file, NLMs are loaded into memory by executing a NetWare command called LOAD. You can load any NLM into file server RAM by using the LOAD command. The proper format for the LOAD command follows:

LOAD *NLM_name*

The purpose of the disk driver NLM is to enable communication between the NetWare server and the disk driver. Therefore, the NetWare server (SERVER.EXE) is loaded first, followed by the disk driver. Loading the disk driver then enables the file server to *mount* (prepare for network users to access and use the stored information) NetWare volumes. By default, loading the file server disk driver automatically mounts the required NetWare SYS volume.

Figure 8.2

Important services provided by NLMs.

Note You must tell the file server to mount any other volumes created when you installed NetWare. To mount other NetWare volumes, use the MOUNT command.

You can MOUNT any single volume by typing **MOUNT** *volume_name* at the file server console and pressing Enter, or by including this command in the file server's AUTOEXEC.NCF file (discussed in the following section).

You can MOUNT all other NetWare volumes by issuing the MOUNT ALL command, replacing *volume_name* with the word ALL. This command also can be issued at the file server console, or placed into the file server's AUTOEXEC.NCF file to automate its execution.

LAN Driver

After the server file (SERVER.EXE) and the disk driver file are loaded into RAM, and the file server volumes (SYS volume as a minimum) have been mounted, you must load the LAN driver into RAM. The LAN driver is responsible for providing a communication interface between the LAN board and the NetWare file server. LAN drivers also are specialized NLMs. These drivers have a LAN file extension.

One of the more common network boards is the NE2000 board. Its associated LAN driver file is NE2000.LAN. To load the NE2000 LAN driver file, type **LOAD NE2000** at the file server console and press Enter. As with loading disk drivers, this process can be automated by placing this command in the AUTOEXEC.NCF file.

Unlike the disk driver NLMs stored in the DOS SERVER.312 directory with SERVER.EXE, LAN NLMs are stored on the NetWare SYS volume in the SYSTEM directory (see fig. 8.3). Because LAN drivers are stored on the SYS volume, they cannot be loaded until the disk driver has been loaded. Loading the disk driver automatically mounts the SYS volume.

Loading the LAN driver into file server RAM is not, by itself, sufficient to enable communication between the NetWare server and the LAN board. To enable communication, the LAN driver also must have a software link established between the LAN driver and its related *communication protocol* (a set of rules that enables information to be prepared, sent, and received between two or more points on the network). To establish this communication, the NetWare BIND command must be issued.

To BIND the *Internetwork Packet Exchange* (IPX) protocol to the NE2000 LAN board, for example, after issuing the LOAD NE2000 command, type the command **BIND IPX TO NE2000** at the file server console and press Enter. You also can automate this command by placing it into the AUTOEXEC.NCF file following the LOAD *LAN_driver* command.

The file server, the network board, and the communication protocol are treated as separate entities. As such, each of these server components must have a network number assigned to it. This network number, also referred to as a *network address*, uniquely identifies each of the network components. These identifiers follow:

■ Server = IPX internal network number

■ Communication protocol = network address

■ Network board = node address

You tell the server what the server's IPX internal network number is after you load SERVER.EXE. The file server's IPX internal network number must be unique for each file server on the network.

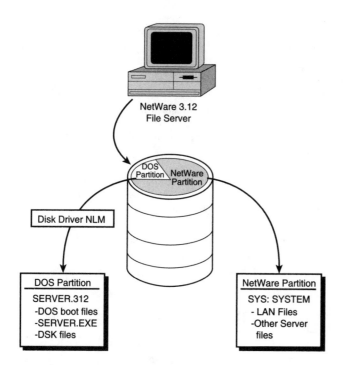

NetWare 3.12
File Server

Disk Driver NLM

DOS Partition
SERVER.312
-DOS boot files
-SERVER.EXE
-DSK files

NetWare Partition
SYS: SYSTEM
- LAN Files
-Other Server
 files

Figure 8.3
Location of file server software components.

You tell the server what the communication protocol network address is when you BIND the communication protocol to the LAN driver. The network address is common to all file servers on the network.

The server determines the node address for itself from information from the network board. Many boards, including Ethernet and Token-Ring, encode a unique number in the card's ROM. Some boards, such as ARCnet, require you to set address information on the board directly using dip switches. Some boards permit you to set the board number with the network board's configuration files prior to installing the board in the file server. The node address must be unique for each network board on the network.

Working with Server Configuration Files

You can load the NetWare server and associated startup files manually from the NetWare file server console. Loading the required files from commands contained in text files called server configuration files is a much easier process, however, and is less prone to error.

Like your PC, which has its own startup configuration files (CONFIG.SYS and AUTOEXEC.BAT), the NetWare file server also can have startup configuration files. These files are called STARTUP.NCF and AUTOEXEC.NCF.

Because the NetWare file server is loaded on a PC, the PC runs its own CONFIG.SYS and

AUTOEXEC.BAT files when you boot the PC. To then load the NetWare file server, you must run the DOS-based SERVER.EXE file. After SERVER.EXE is run, STARTUP.NCF and AUTOEXEC.NCF are executed, if available.

To automate the entire startup process so that SERVER.EXE is loaded each time you boot the PC containing the NetWare file server files, add the SERVER.EXE command to the PC's AUTOEXEC.BAT file. Then when you boot the PC, the required file server files are loaded and run, as shown in figure 8.4.

STARTUP.NCF

The STARTUP.NCF file is used to hold commands that configure the NetWare server. It is stored in the same directory as SERVER.EXE, which is the C:\NETWARE.312 directory created as the default during installation.

Two types of commands are found most frequently in the STARTUP.NCF file: the LOAD and SET commands.

The LOAD Command

The LOAD command, when used in the STARTUP.NCF file, is used primarily for loading

disk drivers. It also is used outside of the STARTUP.NCF file, however, to load LAN drivers, name-space modules, and NLMs.

Follow this format when using the LOAD command to load a disk driver:

```
LOAD [path]disk_driver [driver parameter...]
```

A typical LOAD statement in a STARTUP.NCF file might look similar to this example:

```
LOAD ISADISK port=1FO int=D
```

 Note Hexadecimal numbers, such as the D in int=D, are commonly used when specifying configuration parameters.

The SET Command

The SET command is used in the STARTUP.NCF file to configure operating system parameters. These parameters customize server features to better meet your networking needs.

Five categories of SET commands are commonly used in the STARTUP.NCF file:

- Communications
- Memory

Figure 8.4
Automating the loading of the NetWare server.

1. Power ON or Reset (CTRL+ALT+DEL)
2. POST (Power ON Self Test)
3. CONFIG.SYS
4. AUTOEXEC.BAT

   CD SERVER.312
   SERVER

5. SERVER
6. STARTUP.NCF
7. AUTOEXEC.NCF

- File caching
- Disk caching
- Miscellaneous

Use the following line when placing SET commands into the STARTUP.NCF file:

```
SET [parameter]
```

A typical SET command used in the STARTUP.NCF file might look similar to the following:

```
SET Minimum File Cache Buffers: 20
```

 Creating a STARTUP.NCF file to automate server startup procedures makes your life as a network administrator much simpler. If you occasionally need to load the server without running the STARTUP.NCF file, however, you can do so by typing the **SERVER** command followed by **-S*path\\filename*** and pressing Enter to load an alternate STARTUP.NCF file; or you can type **SERVER -NS** and press Enter to load SERVER.EXE.

AUTOEXEC.NCF

The AUTOEXEC.NCF file is used to hold information that the NetWare server needs when it is booting. This file is stored in the same directory as the LAN and other network files—SYS:SYSTEM. Four items of information that the server needs when booting are stored in this file:

- Name of the file server
- Internal network number
- Command to LOAD the LAN driver
- Command to BIND the protocol to the LAN driver

 As with the STARTUP.NCF file, you can load SERVER without running the AUTOEXEC.NCF file by typing **SERVER -NA** at the file server console and pressing Enter.

As mentioned previously, the LOAD command is used primarily for loading disk and LAN drivers. It also can be used in the AUTOEXEC.NCF file, however, to load name-space modules and other needed NLMs. For example, you can automatically load the MONITOR utility each time you boot your NetWare file server by placing the following command in the AUTOEXEC.NCF file:

```
LOAD MONITOR
```

The AUTOEXEC.NCF file also can contain *console commands* (commands that can be entered at the file server console), such as the following:

- **ABORT REMIRROR.** Stops the automatic remirroring of disks
- **BROADCAST.** Sends messages to network users
- **CD MOUNT.** Mounts a CD-ROM volume
- **DISPLAY SERVERS.** Displays a list of all NetWare servers that the router recognizes

These server configuration files can be created or edited from the file server console in either of two ways. You can create or edit the STARTUP.NCF and AUTOEXEC.NCF files by using the IN-STALL or EDIT NLM commands.

To create or edit these files using the INSTALL NLM, type **LOAD INSTALL** at the NetWare file server console. Choose System Options from the Installation Options menu, then choose one of the following from the Available System Options menu:

- Create AUTOEXEC.NCF file

- Create STARTUP.NCF file

- Edit AUTOEXEC.NCF file

- Edit STARTUP.NCF file

Fill in the blank file window or edit the existing information contained in the file window. Save your changes when you exit.

To create or edit these files using the EDIT NLM, type **LOAD EDIT** at the file server console and press Enter. Type the name of the file to be created or edited, preceded by the path for that file and press Enter. To edit the AUTOEXEC.NCF file, for example, type **SYS:SYSTEM\AUTOEXEC.NCF** and press Enter. Create or modify the file as needed, and save your changes before exiting.

You can also edit the AUTOEXEC.NCF file by using the SYSCON utility. To edit this file using SYSCON, log in to the file server from a network client. Log in as a user with Supervisor rights. Type **SYSCON** and press Enter. Next, choose Supervisor Options from the Available Topics menu. Then choose Edit System AUTOEXEC file from the Supervisor Options menu (see fig. 8.5). Be sure to save your changes when you have finished editing this file.

Figure 8.5

Using SYSCON to edit AUTOEXEC.NCF.

Describing Network Communication

Communication is key to any network. Without successful communication, you cannot access network application programs, store and retrieve data files, or print to any printer that is not directly attached to your computer. For network communication to be successful, however, the network operating system must be capable of dealing with differences between types of computers, the communication protocols they support, and the architecture of various files. NetWare 3.1*x* is capable of handling these differences.

One useful feature of 3.1*x* is that it enables you to store data files on network file servers that are not named using DOS naming conventions. NetWare also enables you to store non-DOS file names in their original file-name formats. In addition to retaining the file's non-DOS file name, 3.1*x* stores associated information about these files, such as the following:

- File attributes

- Special non-DOS legal characters

- Case-sensitivity

NetWare provides NLMs that support non-DOS file names. If you use OS/2, Macintosh, NFS, or FTAM file names, you can load the related NLMs onto your NetWare file servers to support these non-DOS file names.

Supported Name Spaces

NetWare 3.1*x* offers two name-space NLMs:

- OS2.NAM to support OS/2 file-naming conventions

■ MAC.NAM to support Macintosh file-naming conventions

If you also need to support NFS (Unix) and FTAM (GOSIP) file-naming conventions on your NetWare 3.1*x* network, you can purchase the NFS.NAM and FTAM.NAM NLMs for your network.

NetWare supports different operating environments, including those used by minicomputers, mainframe computers, network operating systems, and workstations. Supported name-space protocols are as follows:

■ OS2

■ MAC

■ NFS

■ FTAM

Supported Frame Types

In order for NetWare to support all these environments, it must support *multiple protocols* (conventions or rules used to define how different endpoints on the network will communicate), and a variety of *frame types* (specifications that indicate the format of the data being transmitted in a packet).

 Note Protocols are responsible for providing various operating systems with the following capabilities:

■ Accessing the network media

■ Transporting information across the network

■ Sharing resources on the network

Access to the network media enables clients to send *packets* (addressed and defined groups of

data) across the network. Each packet uses a specific frame type. Before another device on the network can accept a transmitted packet, that other device must be using the same frame type as the device that sent the packet.

NetWare 3.12 supports Ethernet 802.2 as its default frame type. It also, however, supports various Ethernet and Token-Ring frame types.

NetWare 3.12 supports the following Ethernet frame types:

■ Ethernet II

■ 802.2

■ 802.3 (Raw)

■ SNAP

The Ethernet II frame type supports both IPX and TCP/IP communication protocols. If you use one of these protocols in your NetWare server to bind that protocol to the network board, you include the following command in your startup file:

```
BIND protocol TO lan driver¦boardname [driver
parameters][protocol parameters]
```

For example, include entries similar to the following in your AUTOEXEC.NCF file if you use IPX, Ethernet II, and a NE2000 network board in your file server.

```
LOAD NE2000 PORT=300 PORT=300
FRAME=Ethernet_II
BIND IPX TO NE2000 NET=01DC01
```

The 802.2 frame type is also an Ethernet frame type. It also supports both IPX and TCP/IP communication protocols. If you use one of these protocols in your NetWare server, bind that protocol to the network board by including the BIND command in your AUTOEXEC.NCF file, as shown in the following example:

```
LOAD NE2000 INT=3 PORT=300 FRAME=802.3
BIND IPX TO NE2000 NET=01DC02
```

The 802.3 (Raw) frame type is another Ethernet frame type. It supports IPX, but does not support TCP/IP. If you use the IPX protocol with the 802.3 frame type in your NetWare server, bind this protocol to the network board using the BIND command in the AUTOEXEC.NCF startup file, as shown in the following example:

```
LOAD NE2000 INT=3 PORT=300 FRAME=802.3
Bind IPX TO NE2000 NET=01DD
```

The SNAP frame type is also an Ethernet frame type. It supports the AppleTalk communication protocol. If you use AppleTalk in your NetWare server, BIND this protocol to the network board using the BIND command in your AUTOEXEC.NCF startup file, as shown in the following example:

```
LOAD NE2000 INT=3 PORT=300
FRAME=Ethernet_SNAP
BIND AppleTalk TO NE2000
```

NetWare 3.12 supports the following Token-Ring frame types:

- Token-Ring
- Token-Ring_SNAP

The Token-Ring frame type supports the IPX communication protocol. If you use the IPX protocol with a Token-Ring frame type in your NetWare server, BIND this protocol to the network board by including the BIND command in your startup file, as shown in the following example:

```
LOAD Token INT=5 PORT=20a FRAME=Token_Ring
BIND IPX TO Token NET=2201AD
```

The Token-Ring_SNAP frame type is also a Token-Ring frame type. It supports the AppleTalk communication protocol, as well as the TCP/IP communication protocol. If you use either of these protocols with Token Ring in your NetWare server, BIND the chosen protocol to the network board by including the BIND command in your AUTOEXEC.NCF startup file, as shown in the following example:

```
LOAD Token INT=5 PORT=20a FRAME=Token-
Ring_SNAP
BIND IP TO Token ADDR=110.111.1.1
```

Supported Protocols

NetWare supports several communication protocols, which Novell refers to as the *NetWare Protocol Suite* (see fig. 8.6).

The communication protocols included in the NetWare protocol suite follow:

- Internetwork Packet Exchange (IPX)
- Sequenced Packet Exchange (SPX)
- Routing Information Protocol (RIP)
- Service Advertising Protocol (SAP)
- NetWare Core Protocol (NCP)
- Packet Burst

The IPX communication protocol is used by both NetWare file servers and *routers* (devices that transfer network packets between different networks).

The advantage of the IPX communication protocol is that it does not require the receiving client to acknowledge the packet's delivery, a process referred to as *connectionless delivery*. IPX addresses the data packet, sends it out to the proper network, and then delivers the packet based on the node address of the computer.

The SPX communication protocol layers on top of IPX to add reliable delivery service. SPX is a connection-oriented communication protocol that ensures that all data packets are received properly. If SPX does not receive a response to its request for verification of receipt, the data packet is retransmitted.

The RIP communication protocol is used by network routers to exchange information about network routes. It enables network clients to determine which path through the network is the best one to take in order to deliver a packet.

The SAP communication protocol is used by each device on the network to announce (advertise) its service, its name, and its network address. This protocol tells all other devices on the network what network service these devices can expect to find, and where they can expect to find it. A NetWare print server, for example, would advertise its provision of printing services, its print server name, and its network address.

 You can use the TRACK ON console command to see continuous information about RIP and SAP network packets that are being sent from and received by the file server. TRACK ON causes file-server, network-routing, and network-connection request information to be displayed continuously on the file server's monitor. To discontinue the display of RIP and SAP traffic, issue the TRACK OFF command at the file server console.

Each file server keeps a record of all RIP and SAP information that has been broadcast on the network. This information then can be used for routing packets across the network over the best route. Sometimes the routing information becomes corrupted. You can clear the router tables by issuing the RESET ROUTER console command. The previous router tables then are cleared, and a new router table is created.

Figure 8.6
The NetWare protocol suite.

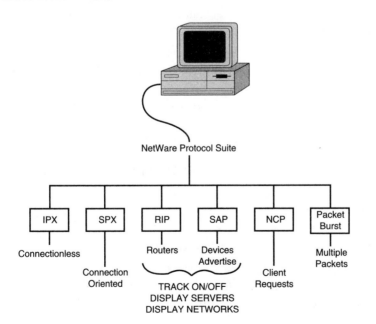

Because file servers keep information about other servers on the network, you can see a list of known services that have advertised with SAP by issuing the DISPLAY SERVERS console command, which also shows you how many network routers (known as the number of *hops*) a packet traveling from this file server to another file server must make to reach its destination.

The DISPLAY NETWORKS console command reveals the network numbers of all networks this file server can recognize and tells you how many hops are needed to reach each network.

The NCP communication protocol is used by the NetWare operating system to accept, interpret, and respond to requests from network clients for network services. When a user loads the connection files at his client and requests a network connection, for example, the related NCP responds to the client's connection request.

The Packet Burst communication protocol enables network clients to combine multiple packets and send them across the network in a series. Only after several packets have been sent is an acknowledgment of packet receipt required. The Packet Burst protocol reduces network traffic by reducing the number of acknowledgment packets that must be sent.

Packet Burst might be supported on some servers but not on others. Each network client, therefore, must negotiate with other network devices to determine whether they support Packet Burst. Network clients that support it also must negotiate with each other to determine the largest Packet Burst size that both clients can manage successfully.

Although not part of the NetWare protocol suite, support for the primarily Unix-based TCP/IP protocol is shipped with NetWare 3.1*x* in the form of

NLMs. These NLMs enable Unix clients or hosts to send packets through NetWare network file servers, and provide support for some Unix-based applications, such as NFS.

Before support for the Unix-based TCP/IP protocol is available on a NetWare 3.1*x* server, the TCP/IP-related NLMs must be installed on the NetWare server. As with all NLMs, the TCP/IP-related NLMs are installed on a NetWare file server using the LOAD console command.

To load the TCP/IP-related NLMs, type the following command at the NetWare file server console and press Enter:

LOAD TCPIP

NetWare then automatically loads six other related NLMs:

- **STREAMS.NLM.** Provides an interface between the NetWare operating system and various communication protocols, making the communication protocol transparent to the operating system.

- **SNMP.NLM.** (Simple Network Management Protocol.) Makes it possible for TCP/IP-based network management clients to share network node information.

- **CLIB.NLM**. Provides a library of C programs required by NLMs.

- **AFTER311.NLM.** Loads a post NetWare 3.11 NLM.

- **IPXS.NLM**. Provides a protocol stack for service NLMs that need STREAMS-based IPX protocol services.

- **TLI.NLM**. Provides a communication interface between STREAMS and user appli-cations.

Understanding Name-Space Support

NetWare supports different operating system's file naming conventions. It does so by providing NLMs that you can load. If you want to store files on the NetWare server that follow the Macintosh file naming conventions, for example, you can load the MAC.NAM NLM.

NetWare provides name-space support for DOS file names as part of the operating system files. You do not have to load an additional NLM to provide DOS name-space support.

In contrast, to use non-DOS file names, you do have to load separate NLMs to support OS/2 (OS2.NAM), Macintosh (MAC.NAM), Unix (NFS.NAM), and GOSIP (FTAM.NAM) name spaces.

Before you can use non-DOS file names, you must prepare the NetWare volume. Issue the following two commands:

```
LOAD name_space.NLM
ADD NAME SPACE TO volume_name
```

To use OS/2 file names on the SYS volume, type **LOAD OS2** and press Enter. Then type **ADD NAME SPACE TO SYS** and press Enter. To add Macintosh name-space support to the SYS volume, type **LOAD MAC** and press Enter.

You must issue the LOAD command for each name-space NLM you want to load. After all name-space NLMs are loaded, you issue the ADD NAME SPACE TO *volume_name* command. Even though you issue separate LOAD commands for each type of name space you want to use, you only issue the

ADD NAME SPACE TO *volume_name* command once for each volume to which you are adding name-space NLMs.

Starting a NetWare 3.12 Server

Before you can issue any console commands, including the LOAD command, you must start the NetWare file server. After the server's startup files are created, you can start the server automatically each time you boot the file server.

To start a NetWare file server, complete the following steps:

1. Boot DOS on the computer.

2. Change to the directory containing the SERVER.EXE file so it can be loaded into RAM.

3. Type **SERVER** and press Enter to load the NetWare operating system.

4. Load the disk driver from the DOS partition so the server can access the disk and see the NetWare partition and volumes.

5. Mount volume SYS and any other NetWare volumes so that file and bindery information can be cached into RAM for quicker access.

6. Load the LAN driver to activate the network board.

These steps start the NetWare file server. Each step, except for physically powering up the PC, can be automated using the computer's startup files and the file server's startup files.

Questions

1. THREE hardware components that are particularly important to a NetWare file server are the _____, the _____, and the _____.

    ☐ A.   Microprocessor

    ☐ B.   Printer

    ☐ C.   Memory

    ☐ D.   Hard disk

2. Which TWO of the following hardware components are exclusive to file servers and workstations and are not part of a standard PC?

    ☐ A.   Network board

    ☐ B.   Network cabling

    ☐ C.   Microprocessor

    ☐ D.   Hard disk

3. The minimum microprocessor required to run a NetWare 3.1*x* file server is_____.

    ○ A.   Intel 80286

    ○ B.   Intel 80386

    ○ C.   Pentium

    ○ D.   Motorola MC68000

4. Which of the following is NOT mandatory on a NetWare 3.1*x* file server?

    ○ A.   A minimum of 4 MB of RAM

    ○ B.   An Intel 80386 or higher microprocessor

    ○ C.   A DOS partition on the file server's hard disk

    ○ D.   A NetWare partition on each file server volume

5. You can use more than one hard disk on your NetWare file server as long as _____.

    ○ A.   you install a DOS partition on each hard disk

    ○ B.   all hard disks have a SYS volume

    ○ C.   you do not install more than three hard disks on any one file server

    ○ D.   the total hard disk space does not exceed 32 TB

6. The hardware responsible for the physical communication between the file server and network clients is the _____.

    ○ A.   network board

    ○ B.   LAN driver

    ○ C.   hard disk

    ○ D.   SYS volume

7. Installing more than one network board in a file server also makes it a network _____.

    ○ A.   client

    ○ B.   driver

    ○ C.   router

    ○ D.   workstation

8. The maximum number of Network boards that can be installed in a NetWare 3.1*x* file server is _____.

    ○ A.   8

    ○ B.   12

    ○ C.   16

    ○ D.   18

9. Which of the following is NOT considered a NetWare file server software component?

   ○ A. IPXODI.COM

   ○ B. SERVER.EXE

   ○ C. LAN driver

   ○ D. Disk driver

10. Which term best describes the primary function of the main NetWare operating system file?

    ○ A. Communication tool

    ○ B. Software bus

    ○ C. Connection driver

    ○ D. LAN driver

11. Of the following file-name extensions, which one is NOT a NetWare Loadable Module (NLM)?

    ○ A. NLM

    ○ B. NCF

    ○ C. NAM

    ○ D. LAN

12. Which TWO of the following are NOT NetWare file server startup files?

    ☐ A. AUTOEXEC.EXE

    ☐ B. AUTOEXEC.NCF

    ☐ C. CONFIG.NCF

    ☐ D. STARTUP.NCF

13. Which of the following statements is true?

    ○ A. SERVER.EXE is run after file server configuration files are run.

    ○ B. SERVER.EXE is run before STARTUP.NCF is run.

    ○ C. You can add SERVER.EXE as a line to the PC's CONFIG.SYS file to automate server startup.

    ○ D. STARTUP.NCF is stored in the SYS:SYSTEM directory.

14. Which TWO commands are used to customize server configuration files?

    ☐ A. LOAD

    ☐ B. SET

    ☐ C. INSTALL

    ☐ D. RUN

15. The SET command is NOT used to configure _____.

    ○ A. communications

    ○ B. memory

    ○ C. disk caching

    ○ D. installation

16. Which THREE NetWare utilities can you use to modify file server configuration files?

    ☐ A. SYSCON

    ☐ B. NAMESPACE

    ☐ C. INSTALL

    ☐ D. EDIT

17. Which TWO name-space NLMs must be purchased separately from NetWare 3.12 if you need to use them?

    ☐ A. NFS

    ☐ B. OS2

    ☐ C. MAC

    ☐ D. FTAM

18. Which of the following is NOT a name space the NetWare supports by loading a specific name-space module?

    ○ A. DOS

    ○ B. NFS

    ○ C. OS2

    ○ D. FTAM

19. The default frame type supported by NetWare 3.12 is _____.

    ○ A. Ethernet II

    ○ B. 802.2

    ○ C. 802.3

    ○ D. SNAP

20. The frame type that supports IPX but does not support TCP/IP is _____.

    ○ A. Ethernet II

    ○ B. 802.2

    ○ C. 802.3

    ○ D. SNAP

21. The Token-Ring frame type that supports AppleTalk is _____.

    ○ A. 802.2

    ○ B. 802.3

    ○ C. Token-Ring

    ○ D. SNAP

22. Which of the following protocols is NOT part of the NetWare protocol suite?

    ○ A. SAP

    ○ B. IPX

    ○ C. TCP/IP

    ○ D. Packet Burst

23. To install support for TCP/IP, you must load the _____ NLM at the NetWare file server console. Other related NLMs are loaded for you.

    ○ A. STREAMS

    ○ B. TCP/IP

    ○ C. CLIB

    ○ D. TLI

24. Which TWO console commands must be used to provide name-space support on a NetWare 3.1*x* file server?

    □ A. ADD NAME SPACE TO

    □ B. LOAD

    □ C. INSTALL

    □ D. TRACK ON

25. Which of the following shows the correct order for starting a NetWare file server?

    ○ A. Boot DOS, load disk driver, load SERVER, mount SYS

    ○ B. Boot DOS, load SERVER, load LAN driver, mount SYS

    ○ C. Boot DOS, load SERVER, load disk driver, mount SYS, load LAN driver

    ○ D. Boot DOS, load LAN driver, load disk driver, load SERVER, mount SYS

Answers

1. A C D		14. A B
2. A B		15. D
3. B		16. A C D
4. C		17. A D
5. D		18. A
6. A		19. B
7. C		20. C
8. C		21. D
9. A		22. C
10. B		23. B
11. B		24. A B
12. A C		25. C
13. B		

Understanding Memory and Performance in NetWare 3.1x Servers

The amount of system memory available to the NetWare 3.1x file server greatly affects its performance. To help ensure that the NetWare operating system has enough available memory, NetWare divides the available system memory into groups called memory pools. Each memory pool is set aside to be used in processing specific types of service requests, or for storing information about the status of a file server's resources.

NetWare file servers require a minimum of 4 MB of system memory, but can address as much as 4 GB of memory. This chapter discusses how NetWare 3.1x allocates and uses system memory, and the ways in which server performance is affected by NetWare's handling of system memory.

After reading this chapter, you will be able to do the following:

- Understand how server memory works
- Determine server memory requirements
- Use memory-related console commands
- Optimize performance using SET parameters
- Understand how protocols affect performance

How Server Memory Works

If your file server's hard disk drive is no larger than 80 MB, the NetWare 3.1x operating system can function with as little as 4 MB of system memory. Larger hard disks require greater amounts of memory. To address and use this wide range of available system memory, the NetWare operating system divides that memory into groups that it refers to as memory pools.

Memory Pools

NetWare uses six pools, as shown in figure 9.1.

The six NetWare 3.1x memory pools include the following:

- File cache buffer
- Permanent

- Semi-permanent
- Alloc short term
- Cache movable
- Cache non-movable

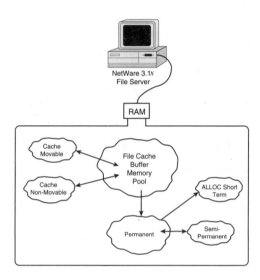

Figure 9.1
NetWare 3.1x memory pools.

Each memory pool has its own features, content, and method of using resources. Table 9.1 provides a comparison of some of the information related to these six memory pools.

Table 9.1
Comparison of NetWare 3.1*x* Memory Pools

Memory Pool	Features	Resource Use
File cache buffer	Takes all free memory when the server boots It is the memory pool from which other pools draw Cache files that users are accessing	Lends buffers to NLMs Allocates enough memory to cache volume's entire FAT Caches portions of volume's DET Uses buffers to build a directory name Hashing table Uses buffers to build Turbo FAT indexes for all open, randomly-accessed files
Permanent	Used as memory source for semi-permanent and alloc pools	Used by the NetWare operating system to store long-term information such as permanent tables, directory cache buffers, and packet receive buffers
Semi-permanent	Subdivision of the permanent memory pool Used for limited memory needs	Used by LAN drivers and disk drivers

Alloc short term	Supplies short term memory needs
	
	Also called *alloc memory*
	
	Released memory is returned to this memory pool
		Used by utilities with pop-up window
		
		Stores information related to:
		   Mappings & connections
		   Service requests
		   Open/locked files
		   Service advertising
		   Broadcast messages
		   NLM and Queue manager tables

continues

Table 9.1, Continued
Comparison of NetWare 3.1x Memory Pools

Memory Pool	Features	Resource Use
Cache movable	Gets its memory from file cache buffer pool	Used by FAT, Hash, and other system tables
	Also called *movable memory*	
	Its memory space is moved around to optimize memory	
	Returns unused memory to file cache buffer pool	
Cache non-movable	Used for loading modules into memory	Lists memory buffers temporarily assigned
	Handles large memory buffers	
	Does not move memory	
	Returns released memory to file cache buffer pool	

NetWare File Server Memory Components

Memory pools are NetWare's way of dividing and allocating available memory, which is used to manage NetWare's three major file server memory components, which follow:

- Cache buffers
- Tables
- Disk blocks

Cache Buffers

Cache buffers are areas of RAM where the most frequently accessed files are stored. NetWare's file cache buffer memory pool is used to accommodate the RAM requirements of cache buffers, of which there are three types:

- File cache buffers
- Directory cache buffers
- Packet receive buffers

File cache buffers are the primary type of cache buffer and the main portion of the file cache buffer pool. They are temporary storage areas for files—or portions of files—users need.

File cache buffers temporarily store files that have been read from the hard disk. When a user requests a file, the file is read from the hard disk and stored in a file cache buffer. Future requests by the user to read this file then can be fulfilled from the file cache buffer rather than the hard disk.

 Note File cache buffers make it possible for files to be read as much as 100 times faster than when read from disk.

File cache buffers also temporarily store files that have been modified by the user, but have not yet been written back to the hard disk. When the file cache buffers contain such modified files, the file cache buffers are called *dirty cache buffers.*

All user requests for files are serviced from the file cache buffers, which means that anytime a user requests a file, the server first checks the cache to determine whether the file is already there. If it is, the server provides the requested file. If the file is not already stored in a file cache buffer, the server checks the disk for the file. When the file is found, the server stores a copy in the file cache buffer, and then it provides a copy to the user's client (workstation).

Directory cache buffers are also a portion of server memory. Rather than hold files, however, directory cache buffers store directory table information.

Packet receive buffers temporarily hold packets as they are received from network clients. Once the file server is free to process and route the received packet, it retrieves the packet from the packet receive buffer and processes it as needed. Packet receive buffers are particularly useful when

network traffic and file server processing is heavy. Packets received when the server is too busy to immediately process them would be lost without a packet receive buffer temporary storage area.

Tables

Tables are used to find files stored on the hard disk and to track properties of those files. There are two types of tables:

- Directory tables
- File allocation tables

Directory tables are located on each volume, and they contain information related to the files, directories, and trustees (if appropriate) used by NetWare file server clients.

Directory tables contain various items of information (see fig. 9.2). The following are the two main categories of information:

- Name-space information
- Directory-related information

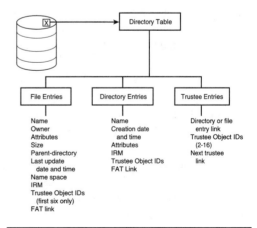

Figure 9.2
Directory table entry information.

Because of the increase in table entry size required for non-DOS name spaces, adding a name space to a NetWare volume requires that there be at least 10 MB of available disk space.

Disk Blocks

To store information on a disk, the disk first must be divided logically into storage areas called *disk blocks*. Disk blocks can be allocated in different sizes—4, 8, 16, 32, and 64 KB blocks are common sizes. Two types of blocks are created when a disk is divided:

- Disk allocation blocks
- Directory table blocks

Disk allocation blocks are used to store files. NetWare's default disk allocation block is 4 KB. If a file to be stored on a NetWare volume is larger than 4 KB, several disk allocation blocks can be used to store it.

 When multiple blocks are used to store a file, each block contains a link to the preceding and the following block. The FAT tracks the links, subsequently keeping track of which blocks contain all the pieces of any given file.

Directory table blocks are always set at the smallest block size—4 KB. Each 4 KB directory table block can contain up to 32 entries. Each entry can be as large as 128 bytes. Each NetWare volume can contain up to 65,536 directory entry blocks. Therefore, the maximum number of directory table entries per volume can be 2,097,152:

$$65,536 \times 32 = 2,097,152$$

To allow as much room on the disk as possible for use by files, NetWare initially allocates only six directory table blocks. If more directory table blocks are needed, NetWare allocates them one at a time.

NetWare Server Memory

Various aspects of the NetWare file server must have some server memory allocated to them. How well memory is allocated can affect how efficiently your NetWare file server performs.

 NetWare helps ensure that memory is allocated adequately because it can dynamically allocate needed memory. You must, however, make some decisions regarding memory as a NetWare administrator.

Your first decision relates to the loading of two specific NetWare resources, which follow:

- NLMs
- Name spaces

Your second decision, discussed in the following section, relates to calculating how much memory your file server must have to function.

NetWare Loadable Modules return memory to the pool once they are done using it. But you still need to know approximately how much memory you need to load and run the NLMs you want on your NetWare server.

When determining how much memory your NetWare server will need for NLMs, consider the following:

■ What other NLMs must be loaded when you load the specific NLM you have chosen? When you load the SBACKUP NLM, for example, you also must load the appropriate TSA NLM. You need to take into consideration how much memory all the related NLMs require.

■ Whether a particular NLM will require additional memory to run.

When adding name-space support to a NetWare volume, consider the following:

■ Extra cache memory will be needed to accommodate the increase in directory table information and size.

■ Partially due to its two forks (data and resource), Macintosh name-space support requires more memory than any other name space.

Determining Server Memory Requirements

Because of all the variables that go into the use of NetWare file server memory, it is important that you make sure your file server has sufficient memory to function. NetWare 3.1*x*'s minimum memory requirement of 4 MB is a good place to start. However, 4 MB is only enough to operate a NetWare file server using the minimum configuration. If you want your NetWare file server to function at its peak efficiency, you must determine how much memory is required for it to do so, and then ensure that an adequate amount of memory—or more—is provided.

Before you can determine the memory requirement for your NetWare 3.1*x* file server, you must have a good idea of the functions and services it must provide your network users. Once you understand what is needed from the network, you can calculate the memory requirements for each of your file servers.

Before attempting to calculate the memory requirements for each NetWare file server, consider the following variables:

■ NetWare 3.1*x*'s minimum memory requirement of 4 MB

■ Which NLMs will be loaded on the file server

■ Size of each file server hard disk

■ Size of each volume on the file server

■ Block size used (4, 8, 16, 32, or 64 KB)

■ Anticipated maximum number of entries in each volume's directory table

■ Number of file and directory cache buffers allocated for caching

To calculate each file server's total memory requirements, use the following information and formulas:

1. Calculate memory requirements for each *DOS volume* (a volume without name space loaded), using the following instructions:

   1a) Calculate the total MB of space on all of the file server's DOS volumes:

   Size (in MB) of 1st DOS volume

   + Size (in MB) of 2nd DOS volume

   + Size (in MB) of all other DOS volumes

   Total MB of DOS volume space

If the DOS volumes on your NetWare file server have not been set up so that the disk allocation block is the same for each volume (all configured to 4 MB or all configured to 8 MB, and so forth), do not add the space on each volume to get a total DOS volume space. Rather, multiply each DOS volume's space separately against the factor (.023) shown in the following step:

1b) Multiply the total MB DOS volume space by a factor of .023:

Total (MB) DOS volume space

.023 (2.3%)
_____

Total DOS volume space

1c) Divide the total DOS volume space by the disk allocation block size of the volume(s). The default is 4 KB on Net-Ware 3.1*x* file servers and is the size used in the following example:

Total DOS volume space

÷ 4 KB DOS volume block size
_____

Total memory required for DOS volumes

 Novell shows this step (for DOS volumes) as the following formula:

Memory (M) = .023 × volume size (in MB) ÷ block size

2. Calculate memory requirements for each *non-DOS volume* (a volume *with* name space loaded), using the following instructions:

2a) Calculate the total MB of space on all the file server's non-DOS volumes:

Size (in MB) of 1st non-DOS volume

+ Size (in MB) of 2nd non-DOS volume

+ Size (in MB) of all other non-DOS volumes
_____

Total MB of non-DOS volume space

 If the non-DOS volumes on your NetWare file server have not been set up so that the disk allocation block is the same for each volume (all configured to 4 MB or all configured to 8 MB, and so forth), do not add the space on each volume to get a total non-DOS volume space. Rather, multiply each non-DOS volume's space separately against the factor (.032) shown in the following step:

2b) Multiply the total MB non-DOS volume space by a factor of .032:

Total (MB) non-DOS volume space

× .032 (3.2%)
_____

Total non-DOS volume space

2c) Divide the total non-DOS volume space by the disk allocation block size of the volume(s). The default is 4 KB on Net-Ware 3.1*x* file servers, and is the size used in the following example:

Total non-DOS volume space

÷ 4 KB non-DOS volume block size
_____

Total memory required for non-DOS volumes

Novell shows this step (for non-DOS volumes) as the following formula:

Memory (M) = .032 × volume size (in MB) ÷ block size

3. Calculate the total file server memory requirements according to the following instructions:

3a) Add the total memory required for DOS volumes to that required for non-DOS volumes:

Total memory required for DOS volumes
+ Total memory required for non-DOS volumes
Total memory required for all volumes

 Novell shows this step (for adding DOS and non-DOS volume memory together) as the following formula:

Total Volume Memory (M) = $M_{DOSvol1}$ + $M_{DOSvol2}$ + $M_{notDOSvol}$

3b) Now add 2 MB of memory to the total memory required for all volumes (total volume memory):

Total volume memory
+ 2 MB
Total file server memory required (rounded to next highest MB)

 Novell shows this step (for calculating the total file server memory required) as the following formula:

2 MB + Total Volume Memory = Total MB (rounded to higher)

After NetWare 3.1*x* is installed, you can view memory usage information by using the MONITOR console utility (see fig. 9.3).

The MONITOR console utility provides information about the file server, including that which affects memory usage, such as the following:

■ **Original cache buffers.** Number of buffers you originally assigned for caching purposes.

■ **Total cache buffers.** Number of buffers available for caching files. Each time you LOAD an NLM, this number decreases.

■ **Dirty cache buffers.** Number of buffers currently in use. If this number is consistently close to the number of total cache buffers, you might need to increase the number of cache buffers for this file server. You might need to add more memory to this file server to add more cache buffers.

■ **Packet receive buffers.** Number of buffers set aside to provide temporary storage to network packets as they arrive at the file server.

```
NetWare v3.12 (250 user) - 11/11/94          NetWare 386 Loadable Module

                    Information For Server Michael

File Server Up Time:    14 Days  4 Hours 40 Minutes 45 Seconds
Utilization:              17        Packet Receive Buffers:    400
Original Cache Buffers:  3,590      Directory Cache Buffers:    21
Total Cache Buffers:     1,865      Service Processes:           3
Dirty Cache Buffers:         0      Connections In Use:          2
Current Disk Requests:       0      Open Files:                 38
```

Figure 9.3
The MONITOR console utility showing file server information.

■ **Directory cache buffers.** Number of buffers set aside to handle directory caching. Remember when assigning the maximum number of directory cache buffers that the more directory cache buffers you allow the operating system to assign, the fewer buffers there will be available for file caching. Careful balance between the two is important to the efficient operation of your file server.

Using Memory-Related Console Commands

The MONITOR console utility enables you to see a great deal of information about your NetWare file server. It is not, however, the only utility related to NetWare file server memory. In addition to the MONITOR console utility, there are two other console commands you can use to manage your NetWare 3.1*x* file server's memory.

The two NetWare file server console commands related to memory follow:

■ MEMORY

■ REGISTER MEMORY

These commands are discussed in the following sections.

The MEMORY Console Command

You use the MEMORY console command to see information about the total amount of addressable memory installed in your NetWare 3.1*x* file server.

After you type **MEMORY** at the file server console and press Enter, a display similar to the following appears:

```
Total server memory: 8,831 Kilobytes
```

By default, NetWare 3.1*x* automatically can address up to 16 MB of memory if the file server uses an *Enhanced Industry Standard Architecture* (EISA) bus. If the file server uses an *Industry Standard Architecture* (ISA) or microchannel bus, 3.1*x* can address memory above 16 MB, if it is configured to do so, by using the REGISTER MEMORY command.

 If your NetWare 3.1*x* file server has an AT bus disk adapter or network board installed, and it uses *Direct Memory Access* (DMA) or bus mastering, the file server cannot address memory above 16 MB. In this case, to prevent problems on your file server, you must enter the following SET parameter into the file server's STARTUP.NCF file:

```
Auto Register Memory Above 16 Megabytes=OFF
```

This SET parameter cannot be entered at the console prompt or in the AUTOEXEC.NCF file. To activate this set parameter from the STARTUP.NCF file, reboot the file server.

The REGISTER MEMORY Console Command

When you know you have more than 16 MB of memory in your file server, but the NetWare operating system is not recognizing that additional memory, you should suspect one of two conditions:

■ Your NetWare 3.1*x* file server has an AT bus disk adapter or network board installed that uses DMA or bus mastering.

■ You have not yet registered that additional memory with the NetWare operating system.

To register the additional memory with the NetWare 3.1*x* operating system, place the following console command in the file server's AUTOEXEC.NCF:

`REGISTER MEMORY start length`

Replace *start* with the hexadecimal number that represents the starting address of the additional memory. The usual address is 0×1,000,000, which equals 16 MB.

Replace *length* with the hexadecimal value that represents the end of the additional memory. If you have 24 MB of total memory installed in your NetWare file server, for example, you would use the following command:

`REGISTER MEMORY 0×1000000 800000`

Note

The *length* field must contain a hexadecimal number that is divisible by 10h×10. If you don't know the hexadecimal number for the amount of memory installed in your file server, you can find a chart listing start and length values for standard computers in Novell's NetWare 3.12 *System Administration* manual.

To place the REGISTER MEMORY command into the file server's AUTOEXEC.NCF file, you can use the SYSCON utility. As figure 9.4 shows, this command must be placed after the lines that provide the file server's name and its IPX internal network number.

Obviously, it is important that your NetWare file server be capable of accessing all the memory installed in it. It's also important that you are able to monitor and manage the file server's memory. Part of monitoring and managing your NetWare file server, including its memory, is setting parameters that optimize your NetWare 3.1*x* file server's performance. Various SET parameters can help you optimize your 3.1*x* file server's resources.

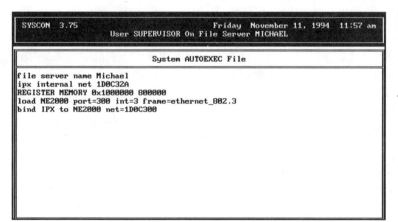

Figure 9.4

The REGISTER MEMORY command in the AUTOEXEC.NCF file.

Optimizing Performance Using SET Parameters

In addition to the MONITOR console utility and the two console commands used to manage the 3.1*x* file server's memory, there also are several SET parameters you can use. The SET AUTO REGISTER MEMORY ABOVE 16 MEGABYTES=OFF is just one of them.

The categories of other SET parameters include the following:

- Communications

- Memory

- File caching

- Directory caching

- Miscellaneous

The SET parameters engaged, coupled with how they interact with other SET parameters, can result in unexpected file server performance. Therefore, before learning which SET parameters can be used to optimize a NetWare 3.1*x* file server's performance, it is useful to understand just how SET parameters interact.

The 3.1*x* operating system is designed to configure dynamically many of its performance factors so that its performance is optimized by default. The key operating system functions NetWare dynamically optimizes include the following:

- The number of service processes it needs to handle disk reads and writes

- The number of packet receive buffers it allocates (up to the configured maximum) to handle all incoming packets

- The number of directory cache buffers (up to the configured maximum) it needs to cache as many of the directory information requests that it receives as possible

Although you can configure many SET parameters, some of the more important ones follow:

- Maximum physical receive packet size

- Maximum packet receive buffers

- Minimum packet receive buffers

- Maximum alloc short term memory

- Cache buffer size

- Minimum file cache buffers

- Maximum concurrent disk cache writes

- Immediate purge of deleted files

- Maximum directory cache buffers

- Minimum directory cache buffers

- Maximum service processes

Table 9.2 lists each of these SET parameters, reveals suggested or default settings for these parameters, and provides a brief summary of how changing each parameter might alter the performance of your NetWare 3.1*x* file server. Also note in the table that those parameters that must be set in the STARTUP.NCF file are shown in a **bold** typeface.

Table 9.2
SET Parameters that Affect File Server Performance

Parameter	Suggested or Default Setting	Performance Summary/Suggestions
MAXIMUM PHYSICAL RECEIVE PACKET SIZE	Token Ring=4204 Ethernet=1514 Range=618–24682	Set only to actual size of largest packet to prevent wasted buffer space
MAXIMUM PACKET RECEIVE BUFFERS	Default=400 Range=50–2000	Increase to prevent sudden peak usage, but impacts permanent memory pool
MINIMUM PACKET RECEIVE BUFFERS	Default=100 Range=10–1000	Increase to improve server response time
MAXIMUM ALLOC SHORT TERM MEMORY	Default=8 MB (8388608) Range=50000–33554432	Increase if server cannot do assigned tasks because pool is at its limit
CACHE BUFFER SIZE	Default=4096 bytes Options=4096, 8192, and 16384	Increase to improve server performance if block sizes are more than 4 KB, but optimum is buffer=block size
MINIMUM FILE CACHE BUFFERS	Default=20 Range=20–1000	Lower if too high a setting limits NLM loading due to insufficient memory
MAXIMUM CONCURRENT DISK CACHE WRITES	Default=50 Range=10–1000	Increase if a write-intensive network, decrease if a read-intensive network
IMMEDIATE PURGE OF DELETED FILES	Default=ON	Change to OFF to reduce server activity and enable salvage feature
MAXIMUM DIRECTORY CACHE BUFFERS	Default=500 Range=20–4000	Increase to speed up directory searches, or reduce to save memory
MINIMUM DIRECTORY CACHE BUFFERS	Default=20 Range=10–2000	Increase if MONITOR shows 100% or more, or if directory searches are slow
MAXIMUM SERVICE PROCESSES	Default=20 Range=5–40	Increase to fix low memory temporarily, until you can add more file server memory

SET parameters are not alone in affecting the NetWare 3.1*x* file server's performance. Some protocols are capable as well.

How Protocols Affect Performance

Two protocols NetWare 3.1*x* includes can have an important impact on your NetWare file server:

- Large Internet Packet (LIP)
- Packet Burst

LIP

The LIP protocol is active, by default, at both the NetWare 3.12 file server and the client. You can disable LIP if you choose to do so. To disable LIP, enter the following command at the file server console:

```
SET ALLOW LIP=OFF
```

Although you can disable LIP, leaving LIP enabled provides enhanced network performance whenever packets must be sent across *network routers* (a file server, dedicated computer, or a workstation that contains multiple network boards of different topologies).

Some routers have difficulty handling packet sizes larger than 576 bytes (512 bytes of data plus 64 bytes of header information). Because some routers can handle larger packet sizes, however, LIP enables larger packet sizes to be sent across routers, as long as both the server and the client agree to the negotiated larger packet size. The maximum size of a packet depends on what the file server can accommodate. This information may be hardcoded into the router, in which case, LIP has no effect.

Figure 9.5 shows the logic of LIP in a NetWare 3.12 network.

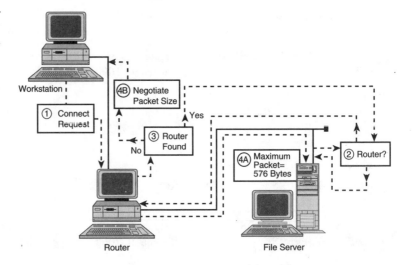

Figure 9.5
The logic of LIP.

Packet Burst

The Packet Burst protocol also affects the performance of the NetWare file server because it expedites the transfer of read-and-write *NetWare Core Protocol* (NCP) packet requests. By default, Packet Burst is enabled at NetWare 3.12 file servers. If the client requesting NetWare services is not capable of taking advantage of the Packet Burst protocol, the NetWare file server communicates with the client on a one-on-one request/response basis.

Packet Burst improves network performance because it does the following:

■ Reduces network traffic by not requiring that each individual packet be sequenced and acknowledged

■ Monitors the network for dropped packets and retransmits only those that were dropped

Questions

1. The type of memory pool used by a pop-up window such as the MONITOR utility is called _____.

    ○   A.   file cache buffer memory

    ○   B.   permanent memory

    ○   C.   semi-permanent memory

    ○   D.   alloc short term memory

2. LAN drivers and disk drivers are stored in the _____ memory pool.

    ○   A.   file cache buffer

    ○   B.   permanent

    ○   C.   semi-permanent

    ○   D.   alloc short term

3. A network packet that CANNOT be processed immediately would be stored temporarily in the file server's _____ memory pool.

    ○   A.   file cache buffer

    ○   B.   permanent

    ○   C.   semi-permanent

    ○   D.   alloc short term

4. Which memory pool CANNOT be used by NetWare Loadable Modules?

    ○   A.   File cache buffer memory

    ○   B.   Permanent memory

    ○   C.   Semi-permanent memory

    ○   D.   Alloc short term memory

5. All other memory pools obtain additional memory from the _____ pool.

    ○   A.   file cache buffer memory

    ○   B.   permanent memory

    ○   C.   semi-permanent

    ○   D.   alloc short term

6. Which of the following is NOT a major NetWare 3.1*x* file server memory component?

    ○   A.   Cache buffers

    ○   B.   ROM

    ○   C.   Tables

    ○   D.   Disk blocks

7. Areas of RAM where the most frequently accessed files are stored are known as _____.

    ○   A.   cache buffers

    ○   B.   ROM

    ○   C.   tables

    ○   D.   disk blocks

8. NetWare 3.1*x* used to finds files that have been stored on the hard disk by checking its _____.

    ○   A.   Cache buffers

    ○   B.   ROM

    ○   C.   Tables

    ○   D.   Disk blocks

9. The logical storage areas on the disk used to store files are called _____.

   ○ A.   cache buffers

   ○ B.   ROM

   ○ C.   tables

   ○ D.   disk blocks

11. The primary type of cache buffer is called the _____.

   ○ A.   file cache buffer

   ○ B.   directory cache buffer

   ○ C.   packet receive buffer

   ○ D.   dirty cache buffer

12. The cache buffer that temporarily stores files that have been read from, or are being written back to, the hard disk is called the _____.

   ○ A.   file cache buffer

   ○ B.   directory cache buffer

   ○ C.   packet receive buffer

   ○ D.   dirty cache buffer

13. Where in memory is directory table information stored?

   ○ A.   Directory entry table

   ○ B.   File allocation table

   ○ C.   Packet receive buffer

   ○ D.   Directory cache buffer

14. Buffers that hold service requests yet to be processed are _____.

   ○ A.   file cache buffers

   ○ B.   directory cache buffers

   ○ C.   packet receive buffers

   ○ D.   dirty cache buffers

15. Buffers that hold files not yet written back are called _____.

   ○ A.   file cache buffers

   ○ B.   directory cache buffers

   ○ C.   packet receive buffers

   ○ D.   dirty cache buffers

Answers

1. D	9. D
2. C	10. A
3. B	11. A
4. B	12. D
5. A	13. D
6. B	14. C
7. A	15. D
8. C	

Working with NetWare 3.1x Clients

File servers are a key component in any network. Another key component is the client (a workstation using appropriate NetWare software in order to access and use resources on the network). NetWare 3.12 networks can include several types of clients, such as DOS, Apple Macintosh, Unix, IBM OS/2, and Microsoft Windows. Regardless of the type of client you use, your ultimate goal is to gain access to the network so you can utilize the resources it provides.

As a network administrator, you are responsible for ensuring that each network client can connect to and access resources on the network. The better you understand the design and abilities of 3.1x client software, the easier it is for you to install, update, and maintain your network clients.

Although different client types can access a NetWare network, the most common types include DOS and Microsoft Windows clients. This chapter explains what you need to know about DOS and Windows clients in order to successfully install, update, and maintain them.

After reading this chapter, you will be able to:

■ Understand the ODI environment

■ Install and update client workstations

■ Work with the NetWare DOS Requester

■ Support read-only and diskless network devices

The ODI Environment

One area of network management that is often the source of major problems is client administration. Although a NetWare network might only have several NetWare file servers to maintain, it may have several hundred clients, many of which you might be responsible for managing. Even if you do not have total responsibility for client management, you may at least be responsible for setting up the client environment and making sure that it functions correctly.

On a NetWare 3.1*x* network, DOS and Windows clients follow the *Open Data-Link Interface*. ODI was chosen for 3.1*x* networks because it supports several protocols as well as multiple LAN drivers on 3.1*x* file servers.

ODI is one of two major client pieces that you enable at each network client to provide communication between the client and the network. The other major client piece is the NetWare DOS Requester.

 NetWare 3.1*x* clients use ODI communication and connection files. If the NetWare client also supports Windows, then additional Windows-related files must also be used on the client, and can be updated using WSUPDATE. The 3.1*x* DOS-based client, moreover, needs to have the NetWare DOS Requester loaded in order to access NetWare network resources.

Understanding both the NetWare DOS Requester and the architecture and related files of ODI makes it easier to set up and upgrade 3.1*x* network clients. Because ODI provides the model to which other client pieces belong, ODI is discussed here first.

ODI implements the *Open System Interconnection* (OSI) model. The OSI model was designed to provide companies with guidance and direction when developing methods of network communication, by establishing recommendations to be followed during development.

OSI defines seven layers (see fig. 10.1). At each layer, the procedure that should be followed in order for one computer to send information or requests across the network to another computer is defined. These definitions help developers see what particular processes should take place at any given point in the model. How those processes occur is up to the developer.

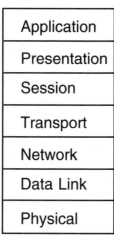

| Application |
| Presentation |
| Session |
| Transport |
| Network |
| Data Link |
| Physical |

Figure 10.1

The OSI reference model.

As you can see from figure 10.1, the name of each OSI layer is based on the primary function for which the layer provides development guidelines.

■ **Application.** Provides the communication interface between network applications and lower-layer protocols.

■ **Presentation.** Provides rules for encoding data so it can be successfully communicated between unlike computers.

■ **Session.** Provides a type of fault tolerance by ensuring that all activities related to a transaction are complete before the transaction is passed on to the next layer.

■ **Transport.** Provides a variety of transport services such as error recovery and reliability.

■ **Network.** Provides both connection-oriented and connectionless network services.

■ **Data Link.** Provides logical link control defined by various standards including IEEE 802.2, 802.4, and others.

■ **Physical.** Provides local area network standards that include the physical layer components of three IEEE standards—802.3, 802.4, and 802.5.

ODI implements the OSI reference model, choosing modules to implement that fill the particular communication need at various places in the communication process.

The ODI method of implementing OSI provides the following benefits:

■ Allows for maximum flexibility of the network

■ Makes client/server connections primarily transparent to the user

■ Requires no additional investment in network equipment

■ Supports multiple LAN drivers on each NetWare 3.1*x* file server and client

■ Supports multiple protocols on each NetWare 3.1x file server and client, including—but not limited to—IPX/SPX, TCP/IP, AppleTalk, OSI TP4, and DEC LAT

In some instances, the software that implements the OSI reference model is directly related, layer for layer, to the model itself. For example, the Network Board (also referred to as the *Network Interface Card* or NIC) is an implementation of the Physical layer of the OSI model. In addition, IPX (the communication protocol that Novell uses to send data packets between clients and servers) is an implementation of the network layer.

Other software that NetWare uses to implement the OSI reference model includes the *Link Support Layer* (LSL) and the *Multiple Link Interface Driver* (MLID). The LSL and MLID software are an implementation of the OSI model's data link layer (see fig. 10.2).

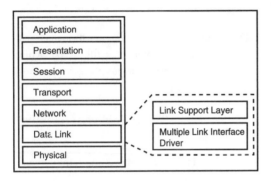

Figure 10.2
Software implementation of OSI layers.

The link support layer, implemented by means of LSL.COM, links the network board to the appropriate MLID. This link ensures that each packet is routed through the appropriate *protocol stack* (a group of communication protocols that establish the rules of communication across the network and which is used above the data link layer of the OSI Reference model). The LSL acts like a switchboard, routing network packets to their correct destination.

The MLID is somewhat less independent in its handling of network packets than the LSL, although its function is no less important. MLIDs are LAN driver files, such as NE3200.COM, that copy specific identification information about an incoming packet, and send that information along with the packet to the LSL. When a packet is being sent out of the file server, the MLID copies the needed packet identification information into the packet and sends it out to the network (see fig. 10.3).

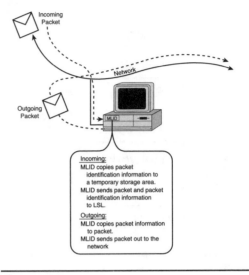

Figure 10.3
Functions of the MLID.

Other software required for connection to the network includes the protocol stack files. The makeup of the protocol stacks depends on the types of protocols used on the network.

A network using IPX, for example, would include the IPX protocol stack, which is implemented on a NetWare 3.1*x* client by loading the IPXODI.COM file.

Before a client can load the IPXODI.COM and other communication and control files, the client must have those files installed and any related files updated.

Installing and Updating Client Workstations

When you install or update a network client, several files are either copied to the client or modified. What occurs depends at least in part on whether or not the network client requires Windows support.

Installing Client Workstations

When you install client workstation files on a client that uses Windows, two processes occur.

First, two sets of files are copied to the client's hard disk, as shown in table 10.1. One set of files is copied to the \WINDOWS\SYSTEM directory. The second set is copied to the \WINDOWS directory.

Table 10.1
Microsoft Windows Files Affected During Client Installation

Directory Where File's Installed	Name of File	Function/Purpose of File
\WINDOWS	ET.INI	Initializes Novell's ElectroText (Electronic Documentation) file
\WINDOWS\SYSTEM	NETWARE.DRV	Allows access to the NetWare network from an MS Windows application
\WINDOWS\SYSTEM	NETWARE.HLP	Provides help for clients running MS Windows
\WINDOWS	NETWARE.INI	Provides configuration information to customize the MS Windows driver
\WINDOWS	NWADMIN.INI	Sets MS Windows user tools options
\WINDOWS\SYSTEM	NWPOPUP.EXE	Displays network-related messages inside MS Windows applications
\WINDOWS	NWUSER.EXE	Loads the MS Windows NetWare User Tools
\WINDOWS	NWUTILS.GRP	Provides access to the NWUSER group in the MS Windows Program Manager
\WINDOWS\SYSTEM	VIPX.386	Lets users run DOS-based applications from within Enhanced Mode MS Windows
\WINDOWS\SYSTEM	VNETWARE.386	Works with NETWARE.DRV and NWPOPUP.EXE to show broadcast messages

The second process that occurs when you install the NetWare 3.1*x* networking files on the client involves several changes made to the following three Microsoft Windows configuration files:

- PROGMAN.INI
- SYSTEM.INI
- WIN.INI

The PROGMAN.INI Windows configuration file is changed to include an additional entry under the [Groups] section. This entry specifies the group number and sets the path to the executable NWUSER file. Figure 10.4 shows a PROGMAN.INI file with the related group information in bold.

```
[Settings]
Window=66 29 578 365 3
display.drv=qvision8.drv
Order= 10 6 19 14 3 1 17 9 7 11 4 15 8 13 18 12 2 20 5
SaveSettings=1
AutoArrange=1
MinOnRun=0

[Groups]
Group1=C:\WINDOWS\MAIN.GRP
Group2=C:\WINDOWS\ACCESSOR.GRP
Group3=C:\WINDOWS\NAUTILUS.GRP
Group4=C:\WINDOWS\STARTUP.GRP
Group5=C:\WINDOWS\APPLICAT.GRP
Group6=C:\WINDOWS\NWUSER.EXE
н
```

Figure 10.4
Sample PROGMAN.INI file.

The SYSTEM.INI Windows configuration file is changed to include entries under three categories. The affected categories and their related changes are shown as bolded entries in figure 10.5.

```
[boot]
network.drv=netware.drv
taskman.exe=C:\WINDOWS\TASKMGR.EXE
mouse.drv=lmouse.drv
language.dll=English
keyboard.drv=keyboard.drv
system.drv=atmsys.drv

[keyboard]
type=4

[boot.description]
network.drv=NetWare.drv
keyboard.typ=Enhanced 101 or 102 key US and Non US keyboards
mouse.drv=Logitech
language.dll=English (American)
system.drv=MS-DOS System
codepage=437
display.drv=COMPAQ QVision, 640x480x256, sm. res.

[386Enh]
network=*vnetbios,vnetware.386,vipx.386
TimerCriticalSection=10000
OverlappedIO=off
device=fastback.386
32BitDiskAccess=OFF
```

Figure 10.5
Sample SYSTEM.INI file.

The WIN.INI MS Windows configuration file is changed to include an entry that loads the NWPOPUP.EXE file, as shown in bold characters in figure 10.6.

After the initial installation of client files, updates to these files may be periodically released by Novell. Updates should be implemented on your NetWare 3.1*x* file servers as soon as possible.

```
[windows]
spooler=yes
load=nwpopup.exe
Beep=yes
NullPort=None
BorderWidth=3
CursorBlinkRate=530
DoubleClickSpeed=452
Programs=com exe bat pif
Documents=
DeviceNotSelectedTimeout=15
TransmissionRetryTimeout=45
KeyboardDelay=2
KeyboardSpeed=31
ScreenSaveActive=1
ScreenSaveTimeOut=480
DosPrint=no
NetWarn=0
CoolSwitch=1
DefaultQueueSize=32
PrinterSetup=1
device=HP LaserJet IIIP PostScript,pscript,LPT1:

[Desktop]
Pattern=116 84 84 84 84 84 84 92
Wallpaper=butterly.bmp
```

Figure 10.6

Sample WIN.INI file.

Updating Client Workstations

You can update client files by running WSUPDATE from the DOS command line at the network client. WSUPDATE.EXE is, however, located on the NetWare file server, not the client. Therefore, you must be logged in to the NetWare 3.1*x* file server to run WSUPDATE.

You can automate client file updating by placing the WSUPDATE command and associated parameters into a file server's system login script. Using this method updates each client's files at the time the user logs in to the network. Because you only have to initiate the update once (at the login stage instead of with each client), the possibility for error is reduced considerably.

Automating client file updating is more efficient than physically moving from client to client, logging in, and running WSUPDATE from the client. You should, however, use great care when placing this command in the system login script, as different types of network clients often use different types of files.

 Note Although WSUPDATE is primarily used for updating client files, you can also use it to update files on other NetWare servers by using the /ALL option with it, as described later.

To use WSUPDATE for updating files, use the following syntax:

`WSUPDATE[`*source_path*`][`*destination_path*`][`*/options*`]`

Replace *source_path* with the full path and filename of the most current version of the file being used for updating other copies of this file. To make it possible for users to access this file, copy it into the SYS:PUBLIC directory, particularly if you are going to automate the update using the system login script.

Replace *destination_path* with only the predefined drive letter (do not specify a directory) followed by a colon and the name of the file being updated. If you want to specify a local drive, use ALL or ALL_LOCAL in place of the *destination_path* just described. Using ALL searches all network drives. Using ALL LOCAL searches all local drives.

Replace */options* with one or more option parameters, preceding each one you use with a slash (/). Available option parameters and additional details about the syntax for the WSUPDATE utility are shown in figure 10.7.

Figure 10.7
WSUPDATE
Help screen.

```
Usage: WSUPDATE [/F=<InFile>!<SourcePath>] <DestDrive:DestFile> [/option...]]
        /F=<InFile> - specify a configuration file or
          SourcePath - file to update
        DestDrive = <drive letter:> ! ALL: ! ALL_LOCAL:
        DestFile - the name of the file to update (optional)
        [/[C]opy over old ! /[R]ename old]
        /[S]ubdirectory - scan all subdirectories
        /read-[O]nly - update read-only files
        /[L]ogfile=filename - create a log file called filename
        /[N]ew file - create <DestFile>,<DestFile> must be full destination path
          with file name
        /[V] [=<drive letter>] - update config.sys with LASTDRIVE=Z
          use <drive letter> for boot drive if not C.
```

The options available for WSUPDATE include:

- Search options:

  /ALL or **/ALL_LOCAL.** Searches all network drives, or all local drives

  /S. Searches for the files to be updated in all subdirectories of the *destination_path*

- File update options:

  /O. Updates all files, even those flagged as Read-Only

  /C or **/R.** Use these options to **C**opy the new file over the old file without saving a backup of the old file, or to first **R**ename the old file

- Destination options:

  /F=[path/file]. Directs the WSUPDATE command to a file containing required WSUPDATE options so that no options used with this command are run

  /L=[path/file]. Directs the WSUPDATE command to the appropriate path for recording its operations in a log file

  /N. Creates a new file and path if one does not already exist

- Other options:

  /V=[<drive letter>]. Adds the LASTDRIVE= command to the CONFIG.SYS file (replaces <drive letter> with the actual last drive letter, usually the letter Z)

- Help:

  /?. Use this option to get help information online

The support of clients running Windows by installing or updating the client files is important for those clients. Regardless of whether or not the DOS client uses MS Windows, the DOS client requires the NetWare DOS Requester in order to access the 3.1*x* network.

Working with the NetWare DOS Requester

In addition to the communication and connection files previously discussed, DOS clients need other files in order to establish communication with network devices. These files are collectively referred to as the *NetWare DOS Requester*.

The NetWare DOS Requester consists of a series of files that provide services such as redirecting print jobs, maintaining network connections, and handling network packets. The NetWare DOS Requester also provides expanded and extended memory support, allows unneeded files to be swapped in and out of memory (thus making more efficient use of memory), and eliminates duplication of effort between the NetWare shell and DOS.

The modularity of the NetWare DOS Requester allows third-party and future NetWare services to be easily added to NetWare clients. Modularity is provided through a variety of program files called *Virtual Loadable Modules* (VLMs). Each VLM performs specific services.

 Some client VLMs are required, but a few VLMs are optional. You can save memory by not loading the optional VLMs. The load order of VLMs is important, however. If you choose not to load optional VLMs, the best way to prevent them from being loaded is to rename them. VLMs have a VLM extension. Rename unnecessary VLMs by changing their VLM extension to something else.

VLMs are of three types, as follows:

■ **DOS redirection VLMs.** REDIR.VLM provides DOS redirection services. It tricks the DOS client into believing it is looking at another DOS drive when it sees the NetWare file server.

■ **Service protocol VLMs.** NWP.VLM, FIO.VLM, and PRINT.VLM provide specific services to the network client. NWP.VLM is responsible for establishing and maintaining network connections. It also handles broadcast messages and the implementation of different Novell file server types, such as *NetWare Directory Services* (NDS), Bindery, and NetWare Lite. FIO.VLM handles the file transfer protocol, including cached, noncached, and burst mode read/write requests. PRINT.VLM provides printing services.

■ **Transport protocol VLMs.** TRAN.VLM provides services related to server connection maintenance, the transportation of network packets, and other transport-related services.

The NetWare DOS Requester modules available with NetWare 3.1*x* are shown in table 10.2.

Table 10.2
NetWare DOS Requester Virtual Loadable Modules

Module's File Name	Purpose of the Module	Parent VLM
AUTO.VLM	Automatically reconnects a client to a server when the server is available	
BIND.VLM	Lets clients on NDS networks access Bindery-based servers (NetWare 3.1x and earlier versions)	NWP.VLM
		continues

Table 10.2, Continued
NetWare DOS Requester Virtual Loadable Modules

Module's File Name	Purpose of the Module	Parent VLM
CONN.VLM	Tracks connection information and makes it available to other VLMs as needed	
FIO.VLM	Supports file access	
GENERAL.VLM	Provides general functions needed by other VLMs	
IPXNCP.VLM	Adds NCP header information to packets and passes them off to IPX	TRAN.VLM
NDS.VLM	Lets clients on Bindery-based NetWare servers access NDS-based (NetWare 4.*x*) servers	NWP.VLM
NETX.VLM	Provides backward compatibility for applications using the old NetWare shell	
NWP.VLM	Coordinates services with the VLMs for which it is responsible (its Child VLMs)	
PRINT.VLM	Redirects printing requests to the network	
RSA.VLM	Provides re-authentication for NDS	NWP.VLM
REDIR.VLM	Working with DOS, redirects non-DOS requests to the network	
SECURITY.VLM	Provides packet security when needed	

Only four of the VLMs listed in table 3.2 are considered optional. All others are required. The four optional VLMs include:

- NDS.VLM

- PRINT.VLM

- AUTO.VLM

- RSA.VLM

All VLMs are loaded and managed using the NetWare DOS Requester's VLM manager—VLM.EXE.

To load the NetWare DOS Requester, run the VLM.EXE file, followed by any parameters needed by your client's particular configuration. For example, you can load a portion of the NetWare DOS Requester into expanded memory (if available on the client) by typing **VLM /Me**, and pressing Enter at the client's system prompt. You can also load the NetWare DOS Requestor into extended memory (VLM IMX) or conventional memory. In addition, you can load the NetWare DOS Requester from either of two client startup files, including:

- AUTOEXEC.BAT

- STARTNET.BAT

Besides the /M parameter, which lets you specify the area of memory into which the NetWare DOS Requester is to be loaded, there are several other parameters available with VLM.EXE. Available parameters include:

- **/C=[path/]filename.ext.** If you use a configuration file other than NET.CFG, this parameter specifies that another configuration file is to be used, and where that file is located.

- **/D.** This parameter displays diagnostic information related to the NetWare DOS Requester.

- **/M*x*.** This parameter tells the NetWare DOS Requester which area of memory it is to load into. Replace *x* with C for conventional memory, X for extended memory, or E for expanded memory.

- **/PS=<*server name*>.** This parameter specifies which NetWare 3.1*x* file server the NetWare DOS Requester is to seek out and attach to (called the Preferred Server) when loading. Replace *server name* with the actual name of the file server.

- **/PT=<*tree_name*>.** This parameter specifies which NetWare 4.*x* network tree the NetWare DOS Requester is to seek out to establish the network connection when loading.

- **/U.** This parameter unloads the NetWare DOS Requester from the client's memory.

- **/V*x*.** This parameter provides details about the NetWare DOS Requester while it is loading. (V stands for verbose.) Four levels of detail are available. Replace *x* with the level you prefer. Available levels are numbered 0 through 4.

- **/?.** This parameter displays the help screen shown in figure 10.8.

You can use the NET.CFG file to configure the NetWare ODI environment and to specify configuration options for the NetWare DOS Requester.

Figure 10.8

*NetWare DOS Requester
(VLM) help screen.*

```
(C) Copyright 1993 Novell, Inc.  All Rights Reserved.
Patent pending.

Available command line options:
/?        Display this help screen.
/U        Unload the VLM.EXE file from memory
/C=[path\]filename.ext
          Specify a configuration file to use (Default is NET.CFG).
/Mx       The memory type the VLM.EXE file uses where x is one of the following:
          C = Conventional memory.
          X = Extended memory (XMS).
          E = Expanded memory (EMS).
/D        Display the VLM.EXE file diagnostics.
/PS=<server name>
          Preferred server name to attach to during load.
/PT=<tree name>
          Preferred tree name to attach to during load.
/Vx       The detail level of message display where x is one of the following:
          0 = Display copyright and critical errors only.
          1 = Also display warning messages.
          2 = Also display VLM module names.
          3 = Also display configuration file parameters.
          4 = Also display diagnostics messages.

C:\NWCLIENT>
```

To modify the NET.CFG file to include ODI-related configuration information, include the following:

■ A Link Driver section, which includes applicable information for naming your network driver and identifying various related hardware settings.

This section must have a left-justified section head titled **Link Driver *driver_name*.** (Replace *driver_name* with the name of the network board driver used in this client.)

The following lines of information, where applicable, must be included as options (indented at least one space) under this section head:

DMA [#1|#2] *channel number*

INT [#1|#2] *interrupt_request_number*

MEM [#1|#2] *hex_start_address[hex_length]*

PORT [#1|#2] *hex_start_address*

SLOT *number*

FRAME *frame_type*

■ A Link Support section is also needed. It, too, must be left-justified and is entered as **Link Support**.

The following lines of options, where applicable, are included, and must also be indented at least one space under this section head:

BUFFERS *number [size]*

MEMPOOL *number*

MAX BOARDS *number*

MAX STACKS *number*

To modify the NET.CFG file to include NetWare DOS Requester-related configuration information, include applicable options from the following list. Remember to indent each option at least one space under the left-justified heading called NetWare DOS Requester. The available options include:

AUTO RECONNECT=

AUTO RETRY=

BIND RECONNECT=

CACHE BUFFERS=

CACHE BUFFERS SIZE=

CACHE WRITES=

CHECKSUM=

CONNECTIONS=

FIRST NETWORK DRIVE=

LARGE INTERNET PACKETS=

LOAD CONN TABLE LOW=

LOAD LOW IPXNCP=

LOCAL PRINTERS=

MAX TASKS=

MESSAGE LEVEL=

PB BUFFERS=

PREFERRED SERVER=

PRINT BUFFER SIZE=

PRINT HEADER=

PRINT TAIL=

SEARCH MODE=

SIGNATURE LEVEL=

USE DEFAULTS=

VLM=

Figure 10.9 shows a sample NET.CFG file for a NetWare network client. It includes some of the most common parameters used by the NetWare DOS Requester.

```
Link support
    Buffers 8 1586
    MemPool 4096

Link driver NE2000
    INT 5
    PORT 340
    MEM D0000
    FRAME Ethernet_802.2

Netware DOS Requester
    FIRST NETWORK DRIVE = F
    NETWARE PROTOCOL = PNW,BIND,NDS
    PREFERRED SERVER = MICHAEL
    SHOW DOTS = ON
    VLM = NMR.VLM

Protocol IPX
        IPX SOCKETS 45
```

Figure 10.9
Sample NET.CFG File.

Supporting Read-Only and Diskless Network Devices

Currently, read-only devices are compact disc devices being used as CDROM volumes. NetWare 3.1*x* makes available an NLM called CDROM.NLM. As with all NLMs, you load this one by typing **LOAD CDROM** at the file server console, and pressing Enter. You also can include this NLM load command in the file server's startup file.

Once the CDROM.NLM is loaded, you must use the MOUNT command to make this volume available. Type **CD MOUNT** *[device_number]* *[volume_name]* and press Enter at the file server console to mount the CDROM volume. Replace *device_number* with the device or drive number that specifies the CD-ROM drive's system interface. Replace *volume_name* with the name assigned to this volume.

The CD utility, followed by an appropriate command word, allows you to obtain CD-ROM information.

You can see a list of available CD-ROM devices by typing **DEVICE LIST** at the file server console and pressing Enter.

You can obtain help information related to the CD-ROM device by typing **CD HELP** and pressing Enter.

You can also see information from the root directory of a CD-ROM volume by typing **CD DIR** [*device_number*] [*volume_name*] and pressing Enter.

Beside providing support for read-only devices, NetWare 3.1*x* also supports *diskless clients* (workstations with no attached hard disk or floppy disk drives).

As a network administrator, you must prepare the NetWare file server to support diskless clients. To prepare the file server, install the related NLM, called **RPL.NLM**, and bind it to the network board.

Any required bootstrap files must be located in the file server's SYS:LOGIN directory. Run the DOSGEN utility to create remote boot disk image files to be placed into the SYS:LOGIN directory.

Questions

1. ODI stands for _____.

   - A. Open Data-Link Interface
   - B. Open Data-Connect Interface
   - C. Open Data Interconnect
   - D. Open Data-Systems Interconnect

2. Which TWO of the following are supported by ODI?

   - A. Multiple file servers
   - B. Multiple protocols
   - C. Multiple LAN drivers
   - D. Multiple clients

3. Of the following, which is NOT an OSI layer?

   - A. Application
   - B. Transportation
   - C. Presentation
   - D. Physical

4. The purpose of the OSI model is to _____.

   - A. define exactly what procedure must be followed
   - B. separate software from hardware processes
   - C. show the processes that should take place at any given point
   - D. force companies to comply with communication rules

5. The layer of the OSI model that provides the interface between network applications and lower-layer protocols is _____.

   - A. application
   - B. presentation
   - C. session
   - D. network

6. The layer of the OSI model which provides rules for encoding data for successful communication is _____.

   - A. application
   - B. presentation
   - C. session
   - D. network

7. The _____ OSI model layer provides both connection-oriented and connectionless network services.

   - A. application
   - B. presentation
   - C. session
   - D. network

8. Which of the following is NOT a benefit of the modular implementation of the OSI reference module?

   - A. Flexibility
   - B. Transparent client/server connection
   - C. Concentration on a single network protocol
   - D. No additional equipment investment required

9. NetWare implements the Link Support Layer of the OSI reference model with the _____ file.

   ○ A. IPXODI.COM

   ○ B. NEx.COM

   ○ C. LSL.COM

   ○ D. NETX.COM

10. Which of the following is an MLID file?

   ○ A. IPXODI.COM

   ○ B. LSL.COM

   ○ C. NETX.COM

   ○ D. NE2000.COM

11. Which THREE are files copied to the \WINDOWS\SYSTEM directory during client installation?

   ☐ A. ET.INI

   ☐ B. NETWARE.DRV

   ☐ C. NETWARE.HLP

   ☐ D. NWPOPUP.EXE

12. During client installation, the _____ file is copied to the \WINDOWS\SYSTEM directory to let users run DOS-based applications from within Enhanced Mode MS Windows.

   ○ A. NETWARE.INI

   ○ B. NWUTILS.GRP

   ○ C. VIPX.386

   ○ D. VNETWARE.386

13. To see which group was added to Windows Program Manager during client installation, look at the _____ file.

   ○ A. NETWARE.INI

   ○ B. SYSTEM.INI

   ○ C. WIN.INI

   ○ D. PROGMAN.INI

14. Which of the following INI files is not modified during client installation?

   ○ A. NETWARE

   ○ B. SYSTEM

   ○ C. WIN

   ○ D. PROGMAN

15. The file used to update existing client files is _____.

   ○ A. CLIENT.UPD

   ○ B. INSTALL.EXE

   ○ C. WSUPDATE.EXE

   ○ D. NETWARE.EXE

Answers

1. A	9. C
2. B C	10. D
3. B	11. B C D
4. C	12. C
5. A	13. D
6. B	14. A
7. D	15. C
8. C	

Setting Up and Maintaining NetWare Print Services

To use NetWare 3.1x print services, you must first set up the printing environment. After that has been accomplished, you can concentrate on improving, customizing, and maintaining network print services using some of NetWare's advanced printing capabilities.

This chapter shows you how to use NetWare's advanced print services so that you can customize and maintain printing on your 3.1x network. After reading this chapter, you will be able to do the following:

- *Understand advanced printing services*
- *Create default print job settings*
- *Print documents using default settings*
- *Maintain network printing services*

Advanced Printing Services

When you set up basic printing services on your NetWare network, you completed the following four main steps:

1. Using PCONSOLE to configure basic printing environment components including print queues, print servers, and printers.

2. Running PSERVER at either a NetWare file server or a dedicated print server to initialize the print server.

3. Connecting all the network printers to the network.

4. Using NetWare 3.1x utilities such as PRINTCON and PRINTDEF to provide some basic customization of NetWare printing services.

Now that the basic printing services are running smoothly, consider ways in which you can customize and maintain those services. Before you jump right in and start making modifications to the network's printing environment, however, you might find it helpful to consider some advanced printing setup and management design.

Designing your network printing environment is relatively easy when your network is small and you have only one or two file servers and only one or two print servers. When your network begins to grow, however, printing setup and design issues become a little more complex. To implement and maintain advanced printing services successfully, you must consider the needs of your network and its users, as well as issues related to advanced printing setup and management design.

In assessing the print service needs of your network, you must consider the following higher-level performance issues:

■ **Capacity of your network printers.** By monitoring the print jobs in each print queue, you can determine when peak printing loads occur, then decide whether your current network printers are capable of handling those peak loads. If they are not, you can make modifications to accommodate the peak loads.

■ **Necessity for multiple print queues for each printer.** If after monitoring print jobs in print queues you determine that high-priority print jobs are not being serviced as soon as they should be, you can consider adding print queues to each printer.

■ **Priority assigned to each print queue.** By adding print queues and assigning them different priorities, you can ensure that high-priority jobs are printed before low-priority jobs.

■ **Necessity for multiple printers per print queue.** Again, monitoring print jobs in print queues helps you see whether you have enough network printers to handle all of your network's printing needs. If print job requests are always backlogged in the print queues, you might consider adding more printers to one or more of the print queues.

■ **Network printers of different types.** You can provide support on your NetWare 3.1x network for non-DOS-compatible printers, such as Unix or AppleTalk printers, by installing additional software, available from Novell authorized resellers, and using PCONSOLE to define these printers.

In addition to having to assess the printing requirements and needs of your network's users, you will be faced with the following two advanced printing setup and management design issues:

- Working with multiple file servers

- Designing multiple print queues

You can set up a network print server to accept print jobs from several network file servers. The number of file servers that you assign to a single print server depends on factors such as the following:

- How close the printer is to those file servers

- What logical groups of network users can reasonably access the associated printers

- The type of printing environment in your company (job shop or individual printing assignments)

Other factors can affect your decision as well. Regardless of the reasons, if you choose to service several NetWare file servers from a single print server, you must make the appropriate changes to your printing environment. The changes you need to make include the following:

1. Creating a print queue on each of the NetWare file servers that will be submitting print jobs to the print server.

2. Defining a print server on each file server. These print servers must have the same name as that of the print server. If the print server that will be providing the printing services is called PS_MICHAEL, for example, then you must define a print server on each file server and identify it as PS_MICHAEL.

3. Defining printers for each file server that also have the same printer number and printer name as the printers on the print server.

4. Assigning each printer to one of the print queues that you created.

5. Choosing the file servers for which the print server will service job orders.

 You make the choices in step 5 by selecting servers from the list of available servers. This list is displayed when you press the Insert key from within the Print Server Configuration menu of the File Servers to be Serviced screen in the PCONSOLE utility.

It is relatively easy to set up several print queues to service print jobs on the network. The important issue to consider is the design and use of those print queues.

This book assumes that you have some experience as a NetWare administrator, so an effective place to start is to look at the current print queues on your server. Checking the Current Queue Status option in PCONSOLE for each of your print queues shows you, among other things, print jobs currently in the queue. From this screen you might be able to determine such things as whether the print queue is servicing too many print jobs, if low-priority print jobs are beating out more important print jobs simply because they arrived at the queue first, and other related print job status information.

Gathering and reviewing information about the status of print jobs in print queues helps you decide if your current print queue design and setup is sufficient for your network's current and future needs. If you believe that some changes might benefit the network and its users, then you can consider making changes in some or all of the following areas:

■ **Assignments of print queue users.** Consider whether you can change the assignment of print queue users to make better use of workgroups or of the arrangement of print queue users.

■ **Print queue priorities.** If you have not assigned different priorities to different print queues, changing print queue priorities can help ensure that critical jobs are printed before those that can safely wait to be printed.

■ **Increasing or reducing the number of print queues.** If there simply are so many jobs in the print queue that there is always a wait for printing services, then perhaps you should add more print queues.

■ **Assignment of print queue and print server operators.** Consider delegating some of the responsibility for print queue and print server management to other company employees. Assigning other users to be print queue operators and print server operators can relieve you of some of the daily responsibilities associated with troubleshooting and problem solving related to print queues and print servers.

Careful consideration, effective design, and proper implementation of the use of multiple servers on the network, as well as effective design of print queues will enhance your network printing environment. In the case of print queue management, modifications such as those previously discussed also can relieve you of some of the daily burden associated with managing your network's printing environment.

Creating Default Print Job Settings

When using network print services, some aspects of printing can be a little more complex than if you simply had a printer attached to your workstation's LPT port. Tasks that often become a little more cumbersome include the following:

■ Redirecting screen displays to a network printer

■ Redirecting print jobs from within applications to a network instead of a local printer

■ Redirecting data to a network file

To simplify these types of printing tasks on a network, NetWare 3.1*x* provides utilities that enable you to specify and automate your printing configurations. NetWare also provides utilities that enable you to automate your printing configurations. The NetWare CAPTURE utility, for example, enables you to specify what to do with network print requests when the print jobs are not automatically network compatible. The NetWare PCONSOLE utility enables you to view print queues, print servers, and printers on the network, as well as view and manipulate your own network print jobs.

The NetWare PRINTCON utility enables you to automate your CAPTURE and PCONSOLE settings by specifying defaults to be used when printing jobs that are not automatically network compatible.

Before CAPTURE and PCONSOLE settings are automatic, you must create different print job settings that can be used when needed. These print job settings are called *default print job settings*. You create default print job settings using the PRINTCON utility.

To create a new default print job setting, run the PRINTCON utility and choose the Edit Print Job Configurations option from the Available Options menu to display the Print Job Configuration screen, as shown in figure 11.1.

From the Print Job Configuration screen, you add a new print job configuration by pressing Insert, typing a name for the new configuration, and pressing Enter. This action opens the Edit Print Job Configuration screen for the print job

configuration you are adding. Figure 11.2 shows the Edit Print Job Configuration screen that opened when creating a new print job called LEGAL.

If you do not create print job configurations, users need to specify CAPTURE options before printing jobs from their workstations' screens or from applications that are not network-compatible. Table 11.1 lists the fields included in the Edit Print Job Configuration screen and shows their equivalent CAPTURE option.

Figure 11.1
The Print Job Configurations screen.

Figure 11.2
The Edit Print Job Configuration screen.

Table 11.1
Print Job Configuration and CAPTURE Options

Edit Print Job Configuration Field Option	Description of Field	Related CAPTURE
Number of copies	Tells how many copies should be printed	/Copies=*n*
File contents	Indicates if file is a text file or a byte stream file	(none)
Tab size	Specifies number of spaces in a tab, if applications do not predefine the number of spaces	/Tabs=*n*
Suppress form feed	Specifies whether to feed a blank form after job is printed	/FormFeed
Notify when done	Indicates if a message should be sent to tell the user his job has finished printing	/NOTify
Local printer	Specifies that the LPT port is used to capture the job	/Local=*n*
Auto endcap	Sends data waiting to be printed to printer when the application is closed	/AUtoend
File server	Indicates which server should receive the print job	/Server=*name*
Print queue	Indicates which queue should receive the print job	/Queue=*name*
Print server	Indicates which print server is being used for the print job	(none)
Device	Specifies which device to use as defined in the file server's PRINTDEF database	(none)

Edit Print Job Configuration Field Option	Description of Field	Related CAPTURE
Mode	Specifies the mode to use as defined in the file server's PRINTDEF database	(none)
Form name	Indicates the form to use to print the job	/Form=*name* or *n*
Print banner	Tells whether to print a banner page before printing job	/No Banner
Name	Shows the name of the user submitting the print job	/NAMe=*name*
Banner name	Text to appear on lower part of banner page	/Banner=*name*
Enable timeout	Tells the program to print without exiting application after a specified time period has elapsed	(none)
Timeout count	Specifies the time period to use for Enable timeout	/TImeout=*n*

Printing Documents Using Default Settings

After a default print job configuration has been created using PRINTCON, users can issue print job requests using that default print job configuration.

When a print job configuration such as the one shown as LEGAL is created, users can tell print jobs to use this configuration. Specifying that jobs use a default configuration enables users to issue the CAPTURE command with only one option: that which specifies the configuration job to use.

Network users also can skip using the CAPTURE command. If they do not issue any capture command, the default print job configuration information is used.

To specify a job configuration defined in PRINTCON, use the following CAPTURE command:

`CAPTURE J=job name`

In the earlier Edit Print Job Configuration example, to use the previously created LEGAL job configuration, you would type **CAPTURE J=LEGAL** at your workstation and press Enter.

Maintaining Network Printing Services

After you have set up and configured network printing services, you then need to maintain those services. Maintenance issues can include items such as the following:

■ Managing printers

■ Converting remote printers to private status

■ Making permanent and temporary changes to printing features such as print queue settings and notification lists

Some of the printing management/maintenance tasks that you can perform with the PSC and PCONSOLE utilities include checking printer status, stopping and restarting print jobs, and mounting forms.

Checking Printer Status

You can check the status of a printer by using either the PSC utility or the PCONSOLE utility. To check the status of a printer using the PSC utility, type the following and press Enter:

`PSC PS=print_server_name P=printer_number Stat`

To check the status of a printer using the PCONSOLE utility, first run the PCONSOLE utility, then choose Print Server Information from the Available Options menu. Next, choose a print server from the Print Servers list; the Print Server Information menu opens. From that menu, select Printer. Now select the printer whose status you want to see. You now can see the printer status information for this printer.

Stopping and Restarting Print Jobs

You can stop and restart print jobs using either the PSC or PCONSOLE utilities. To stop a print job using PSC, type the following at the prompt and press Enter:

`PSC PS=print_server_name P=printer_number PAU`

To stop the printing of the current print job using PCONSOLE, and otherwise temporarily suspend printing on a printer, complete the following steps from inside the Status of *Printer_name* screen:

1. Choose Printer Control.

2. Choose Stop Printer from the Printer Control menu.

To restart a stopped print job using PSC, type the following command at the prompt, then press Enter:

`PSC PS=print_server_name P=printer_number STAR`

To restart a stopped print job using PCONSOLE, select Start Printer from inside the Printer Control menu.

Mounting Forms

You can mount forms using either the PSC utility or the PCONSOLE utility. To mount a form using the PSC utility, type the following at the prompt and press Enter:

`PSC PS=print_server_name P=printer_number MO F=n`

Replace *n* with the number of the form you want to mount. Forms must be predefined using the PRINTDEF utility.

To mount a specific form using the PCONSOLE utility, complete the following steps:

1. Start PCONSOLE.

2. Choose Print Server Information from the Available Options menu.

3. Choose a print server form the Print Servers list.

4. Choose Print Server Status/Control from the Print Server Information menu.

5. Choose a printer from the list of Active Printers.

6. Choose Mounted Form.

7. Type the number of the form you want to mount (as previously defined using the PRINTDEF utility), then press Enter.

You can use the PSC utility to accomplish another task: converting a remote network printer to a private workstation printer for local-only printing. To change a remote network printer from shared to private status, type the following command at the workstation's prompt and press Enter:

`PSC PS=print_server_name P=printer_number PRI`

To restore the now private printer to a network printer, type the following command at the workstation's prompt and press Enter:

`PSC PS=print_server_name P=printer_number SH`

Another management/maintenance task you can perform is that of changing print queue and notification lists settings. Some of these changes are permanent changes, such as creating print queues, whereas others are considered temporary, such as assigning a print queue operator.

You can use the PCONSOLE utility to make permanent changes, such as adding print queues, and temporary changes. Two temporary changes that you can make are adding users to the printer notify list and temporarily assigning a print queue to a printer.

Adding Users to the Printer Notify List

To temporarily add users to the printer notify list, first make sure that the print server is up and running, then run the PCONSOLE utility at your workstation and complete the following steps:

1. Choose Print Server Information.

2. Print Server Status and Control.

3. Choose Notify List for Printer.

4. Add users as needed.

 Some of the menu options for making changes are available only when the print server is running. The Print Server Status and Control option is one of them.

The users you add will continue to be part of the notify list until you down the print server.

Assigning a Print Queue to a Printer

Sometimes a print queue becomes overloaded with print job requests (too many requests or very large print jobs). To relieve the burden on a given printer, you can assign one or more of the print queues to different printers.

To temporarily assign a print queue to another printer, complete the following steps:

1. Start PCONSOLE at your workstation by typing **PCONSOLE** and pressing Enter.

2. Choose Print Server Information.

3. Choose Print Server Status and Control.

4. Choose Queues Serviced by Printer.

5. Reassign the print queue.

Questions

1. Which of the following is NOT a step involved in setting up basic print services?

   ○ A. Create default print job settings

   ○ B. Connect printers to the network

   ○ C. Run PSERVER

   ○ D. Configure print queues, servers, and printers

2. The advanced print setup consideration that takes into account peak printing loads is which of the following?

   ○ A. Priority assigned to the print queue

   ○ B. Multiple print queues for each printer

   ○ C. Multiple printers per queue

   ○ D. Capacity of network printers

3. Which of the following is NOT an advanced network printing environment design consideration?

   ○ A. Types of network printers

   ○ B. Number of printers per print queue

   ○ C. Location of printers on network

   ○ D. Capacity of network printers

4. The utility used to define non-DOS-compatible printers, such as Unix or AppleTalk, is the _____ utility.

   ○ A. PSC

   ○ B. PCONSOLE

   ○ C. PRINTCON

   ○ D. PRINTDEF

5. TWO advanced printing setup and management design issues to be considered include _____ and _____.

   ☐ A. print server location

   ☐ B. multiple file servers

   ☐ C. multiple print queues

   ☐ D. file server location

6. Which of the following is NOT a change that you must make to accommodate multiple print servers on your network?

   ○ A. Attaching a printer to each print server

   ○ B. Creating a print queue on each file server

   ○ C. Defining a print server on each file server

   ○ D. Choosing which file servers the print server will service

7. Which network printing task is NOT a reason to create default print job settings?

   ○ A. Print all documents to your local printer

   ○ B. Redirect screen displays to a network printer

   ○ C. Send print jobs to a file

   ○ D. Print from applications that are not designed for use on a network

8. The TWO utilities that enable you specify details such as number of copies and tab size for print jobs that must be redirected are _____ and _____.

   ☐ A. PRINTCON

   ☐ B. PRINTDEF

   ☐ C. PCONSOLE

   ☐ D. CAPTURE

9. The NetWare utility that enables you to automate print job details such as tab size is _____.

   ○ A. PRINTCON

   ○ B. PRINTDEF

   ○ C. PCONSOLE

   ○ D. CAPTURE

10. The equivalent CAPTURE command for the Suppress form feed field in the Print Job Configuration screen is _____.

   ○ A. /C=*n*

   ○ B. /F

   ○ C. /NAM=*n*

   ○ D. /FF

11. The _____ Print Job Configuration field specifies how many spaces should be used for tabs if the application does not have print formatting instructions.

   ○ A. File Server

   ○ B. Form Name

   ○ C. Enable Timeout

   ○ D. Tab Size

12. If you do NOT want a cover page to be printed before your print job, specify _____ in the CAPTURE command.

   ○ A. /NB

   ○ B. /B=name

   ○ C. /Q=name

   ○ D. /T=*n*

13. To print a document using a job configuration defined in PRINTCON, use the _____ CAPTURE command.

   ○ A. /N=name

   ○ B. /B=name

   ○ C. /J=name

   ○ D. /T=*n*

14. To stop a print job using the PSC command, which option should you add to the command?

   ○ A. STAT

   ○ B. PAUSE

   ○ C. START

   ○ D. MO F=*n*

15. To convert a remote network printer to private use, use the _____ command.

   ○ A. PCONSOLE

   ○ B. PSC

   ○ C. PRINTCON

   ○ D. PRINTDEF

Answers

1. A

2. D

3. C

4. B

5. B C

6. A

7. A

8. C D

9. A

10. D

11. D

12. A

13. C

14. B

15. B

12

Maintaining and Monitoring NetWare 3.1x Servers

NetWare file servers are the key components in the NetWare network. Without them, clients are only PCs cabled together using network boards and cabling. They can do little more than function as stand-alone computers.

Your network users may actually prefer the functionality of their stand-alone PCs to that of a network plagued with poor performance. It is your responsibility as a network administrator to keep the network functioning at peak performance.

The best way to ensure the performance of your network is to periodically monitor and adjust various performance factors. This maintenance requires a knowledge and understanding of those factors.

This chapter is designed to help you understand your network and some specific performance factors. After reading this chapter, you will be able to perform the following:

- Understand network performance
- Monitor server information
- Perform server maintenance
- Set server time
- Understand routing information
- Create file server batch files

Understanding Network Performance

The amount of storage space your file servers contain and the number and type of application programs they provide are important to your users. Slow or inadequate network performance, however, will bring more complaints from users than almost anything else. To keep the network running at peak performance, it must be maintained.

Maintaining network performance is mostly a balancing act. Four different factors must be kept in order, and they are as follows:

- Communication
- Hardware
- Environment
- Memory

Communication refers to the compatibility of the file server's bus architecture and the network boards used in the file server. If your file server's bus architecture is 32-bit, then using 32-bit network boards helps to ensure the efficient transmission of packets through the file server.

Hardware refers to computer equipment chosen for the network file server and clients. For quicker processing, choose PCs with CPUs that have higher speeds, as well as file servers and workstations with larger bus architectures. Slow workstations can bottleneck the network's processing and reduce network performance.

Environment refers to the needs and uses of your network. A network supporting large quantities of file server disk reads and writes functions less efficiently than one that requires fewer disk reads and writes, given the same hardware. Supporting large quantities of disk reads requires additional file server RAM for caching. Supporting large quantities of disk writes requires faster disk controllers and hard drive systems.

Memory refers primarily to file server memory. In NetWare 3.1x, memory is arranged into logical pools and allocated dynamically (as needed). The more RAM provided in the network file servers, the better response you can expect from your network servers. NetWare 3.1x also automatically balances memory pools after the server has been running for a period of time. You can change memory pool SET parameters to help expedite or customize memory pool balance.

Other aspects of NetWare can affect network performance, one of those being NCP Packet Signature.

NCP Packet Signature is a NetWare security enhancement that ensures that each packet received by a file server from a workstation is the same packet originally sent by that workstation. Its purpose is to prevent individuals from creating counterfeit packets, modified packets that grant the user greater rights to the network than were originally provided. NCP Packet Signature provides significant improvements in network security. Along with those improvements, however, comes additional network overhead. Additional NCP Packet Signature overhead can impact network performance, as can the types of services provided by your network.

For example, any load-intensive task on the network can have a negative impact on the client's performance when NCP Packet Signature is implemented. This is particularly noticeable to clients when they perform tasks such as transferring large databases or other files.

Network clients that commonly request less resource-intensive network services, such as word processing, are not likely to notice any performance degradation.

If you do experience a reduction in performance with the implementation of NCP Packet Signature, consider making the following changes or upgrades:

■ Changing file server hardware to PCs containing Intel 80486 CPUs running at a minimum of 50 MHz

■ Upgrading all clients to at least 80386 CPUs

■ Updating all NetWare utilities to those released with NetWare 3.12, especially the LOGIN and ATTACH utilities

■ Setting NCP Packet Signature levels at the client and file server to only the maximum level of security the network requires

NCP Packet Signature enables you to set the level of security to be provided.

 Note After you start the file server, you can increase the NCP Packet Signature level, but you cannot decrease it. Therefore, set the NCP Packet Signature to the lowest level with which you feel comfortable, and increase it later if it is not sufficient.

You have four NCP Packet Signature levels from which to choose: 0, 1, 2, and 3. Level 1 is the default for NetWare clients. Level 2 is the default for NetWare file servers. Levels 3 and 4 have the greatest impact on network performance. The higher you set the number, the higher the level of packet security. Higher security tends to increase network traffic, thus slowing network performance.

You set the NCP Packet Signature levels at file servers and client workstations. To set the NCP Packet Signature level for the file server, add the following to the file server's STARTUP.NCF file:

`SET NCP PACKET SIGNATURE OPTION=number`

To set the NCP Packet Signature level at the client workstation, add the following line to the client's NET.CFG file:

`SIGNATURE LEVEL=number`

The level set at any of the file servers can be different from the level set at each of the clients. Table 12.1 lists the available NCP Packet Signature levels.

Table 12.1
Levels of NCP Packet Signature

Level	Default	Description
0		The file server does not sign any packets.
1	Client	The file server will sign packets if the client requests that packets be signed.
2	Server	The file server will sign packets if the client is able to sign packets as well.
3		The file server will sign all packets and require the client to do so as well; if the client does not sign, the file server will not allow the client to log in.

Monitoring Server Information

Before you can improve the performance of your network, you must understand how well the network's individual file servers are currently performing. The MONITOR utility provides a great deal of information concerning your file server's performance. Run MONITOR on each file server and view several items of information, including the server's, which follow:

- Resource and processor utilization

- Memory statistics

- Hard disk drive status

MONITOR is a server console utility. You can access MONITOR from a workstation using NetWare's remote console feature. To start MONITOR, type the following command at the file server console:

`LOAD MONITOR`

 If you include the /P option with the LOAD MONITOR command, the Processor Utilization option also is displayed on the Available Options menu that opens.

When the MONITOR console utility is loaded, a screen appears displaying basic network information, including server memory statistics. The top of that screen is similar to the one shown in figure 12.1. It contains several items of information about your network, including information related to file server and network performance, and resource and processor utilization.

Six of the items on the MONITOR utility's main screen are particularly useful for verifying file server and network performance. These six items include the following:

- Utilization
- Total Cache Buffers
- Dirty Cache Buffers
- Packet Receive Buffers
- Directory Cache Buffers
- Service Processes

The Available Options menu contains the following two options from which to choose to view server memory statistics:

- System Module Information
- Resource Utilization

The six file server and network performance items, as well as each of the two Available Options menu memory statistics items, are discussed in this section to help you monitor and maintain your network's performance.

Resource and Processor Utilization Information

Table 12.2 provides important information related to the six file server and network performance items listed previously.

Figure 12.1
MONITOR Utility main screen.

Table 12.2
Relevant Resource and Processor Utilization Information

Item Name	Description	Information to Note
Utilization	The percent of file server processing currently being used.	Varies inversely to the Polling Process ability percentage shown in MONITOR's Process Utilization screen (LOAD MONITOR /P).
		High percentage might mean the following:
		Network board using CPU cycles
		NLM using processing time
		High percentage does not necessarily mean the CPU needs more processing power.
Total Cache Buffers	Quantity of RAM still available for cache buffers to use.	If server performs too slowly, add more RAM to increase cache buffers.
		If Cache Buffers statistic in Server Memory Statistics screen is below 20%, add more RAM.
		Cache Buffers should range from 40–60%.
Dirty Cache Buffers	Number (not %) of cache buffers that hold information not yet saved back to the hard disk.	Calculate percentage by dividing this number into Total Cache Buffers number.
		If over 70%, change MAXIMUM CONCURRENT

Item Name	Description	Information to Note
		DISK CACHE WRITES Set parameter to a higher number.
Packet Receive Buffers	Number of buffers the server uses to hold client service requests when the processor cannot immediately handle them.	Each buffer is equal to 1 KB of memory.
		The default value is 100.
		Can change using the MINIMUM and MAXIMUM PACKET RECEIVE BUFFERS Set commands.
		If there's an increase in the number of Service Processes, you can lower this number.
Directory Cache Buffers	Number of buffers for directory caching.	Increases in number of searches will increase this number to the maximum you allocated.
		Allocate with the MINIMUM and MAXIMUM DIRECTORY CACHE BUFFERS Set command.
Service Processes	Number of task handlers allocated for processing client requests.	The only way to remove memory given to service processes is to down and reload the server.
		Increase the default setting (by 5) if this number is close to 20, and there is enough available cache buffer memory.

Memory Statistics

To view file server memory statistics, use the following two MONITOR Available Options menu choices:

- System Module Information
- Resource Utilization

When you choose System Module Information from the Available Options menu, you will see a screen similar to the one shown in figure 12.2. It contains a list of system modules, such as the network card and the NetWare 386 Console Monitor.

Choosing a module from the System Module screen provides two basic items of information about that module, as follows:

- **Module Size.** The number of bytes of memory taken by this module while it is loaded

- **Load File Name.** The name of the NetWare Loadable Module that you placed into server memory using the LOAD command

A menu from which you can choose to view additional information about that network module is also shown. This menu is called Resource Tags (see fig. 12.3).

You can choose to view several items from the Resource Tags menu. What you choose depends on the type of information for which you are searching and on the system module you have selected.

For example, if you want to view information about the MONITOR utility's use of Alloc Short Term memory, first choose NetWare 386 Console Monitor from the System Modules screen, then choose Alloc Memory from the Resource Tags menu. Figure 12.4 shows the Resource Information window that appears after Alloc Memory has been selected.

Figure 12.2

The System Module screen.

```
NetWare v3.12 (250 user) - 12/03/94              NetWare 386 Loadable Module
┌──────────────────────────────────────────────────────────────────────────┐
│                        Information For Server Lee                          │
│   File Server Up                                          econds           │
│   Utilization:                                           Buffers:     400  │
│   Original Cache     Module Size:       51,718 Bytes      Buffers:     21  │
│   Total Cache Buf    Load File Name:    DSS.NLM          es:            3  │
│   Dirty Cache Buf                                        Use:           2  │
│   Current Disk Re                                                     38   │
│                                                                            │
│      ┌────────────────────────┐┌────────────────────────┐                 │
│      │     System Modules      ││      Resource Tags     │                 │
│      ├────────────────────────┤├────────────────────────┤                 │
│      │Document & Security Server││delay function          │                │
│      │IBM SCSI Adapter Device Driver│IPX/SPX sockets       │               │
│      │NetWare 386 Console Monitor  │Large memory allocations│              │
│      │NetWare 386 Remote Console   │Local semaphores       │               │
│      │NetWare 386 Remote Console SPX Dri│Medium memory allocations│        │
│     ▼│NetWare C NLM Runtime Library V3.1│▼│NetWare Streams │               │
│      └────────────────────────┘└────────────────────────┘                 │
└──────────────────────────────────────────────────────────────────────────┘
```

Figure 12.3

The Resource Tags menu.

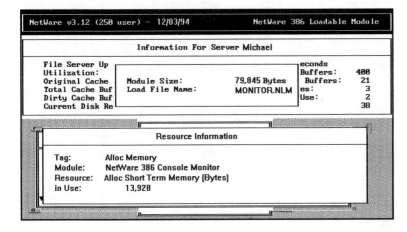

Figure 12.4

The Resource Information screen.

The Resource Information screen provides the following information:

■ **Tag.** The Resource Tag you chose to view

■ **Module.** The module for which you are viewing requested information

■ **Resource.** The type of resource you chose to view, and how it is provided—usually shown as bytes

■ **In Use.** The number of bytes currently being used by this module

Resource tags are NetWare's way of tracking the various memory-related resources your network is using. You can view this information to help deter-

mine whether or not you can unload some modules to temporarily free up memory. You can also use this information when adding new modules to help determine whether or not you want the modules loaded only as needed because of the quantity of resources that they may use.

Hard Disk Drive Status

You can also use the MONITOR utility to view information related to the health of the file server's hard disks.

To view disk-related information, choose Disk Information from MONITOR's Available Options menu. Several items of information about the hard disk will be displayed on the screen. These items include the following:

- Driver name (such as ISADISK.DSK)

- Disk size

- Number of partitions on the disk

- Status of disk mirroring (Mirrored or Not Mirrored)

- Status of Hot Fix

- Partition blocks

- Data blocks

- Redirection blocks

- Redirected blocks

- Reserved blocks

Of these items, three need to be watched in order to monitor the status of your file server's hard disk. They include the following:

- Redirection blocks

- Redirected blocks

- Reserved blocks

Approximately once a week, check these three numbers. Add together the number of Redirection Blocks and the number of Reserved Blocks. If the total number of Redirection plus Reserved Blocks is approximately half the number of Redirected Blocks, then your hard disk may be on the verge of failing. Consider backing up your hard disk, running the INSTALL utility to perform a hard disk surface test, and replacing the hard disk if the surface test fails.

Performing Server Maintenance

Understanding how your server is performing and making modifications to improve its performance is not always enough. Sometimes, problems with your network are the result of other unrelated problems.

For example, the NetWare file server's *bindery* (a database of network information such as users, account restrictions, and so forth) becomes corrupt. Problems with removing user accounts or changing a user's account restrictions cannot be fixed by adding more system memory. Instead, you must correct the bindery.

You can have other types of network problems as well, such as volume errors or corruption of network files. NetWare provides the following four utilities to help correct these types of problems:

- BINDFIX

- BINDREST

- VREPAIR

- SBACKUP

Run BINDFIX for any server you suspect might have corrupted bindery files. Running BINDFIX corrects problems such as user names that you cannot delete, and passwords that you cannot change.

Run BINDREST when you have run BINDFIX but need to restore the bindery to its previous version. That is, run BINDREST when you want to undo the bindery changes you made running BINDFIX.

Use VREPAIR to make volume repairs and to remove name space from a NetWare volume.

Use SBACKUP to make copies of files and programs on the NetWare file server. You also use SBACKUP to restore copies of files and programs that were made using SBACKUP.

BINDFIX and BINDREST

BINDFIX and BINDREST use the following three bindery files stored in the SYS:SYSTEM directory on the file server:

- NET$OBJ.SYS

- NET$PROP.SYS

- NET$VAL.SYS

When you run BINDFIX, it makes a copy of each of these three files, then renames the three bindery files with an OLD extension. BINDREST uses the files with the OLD extension to restore the previous bindery files.

Both BINDFIX and BINDREST are utilities run from the workstation. Log in to the file server as a user with Supervisor rights. After making sure that all users are logged out of the file server, change to the SYS:SYSTEM directory and run BINDFIX by typing **BINDFIX** and pressing Enter.

BINDFIX then runs several checks on the bindery, finding and repairing problems such as the following:

- Errors in the bindery causing bindery error messages to appear on the file server console

- The "unknown server" error message you might receive when printing to your default server

- User names, passwords, or rights you cannot change; or, in the case of user names, you cannot delete

When BINDFIX is complete, there will be corrected copies of the NET$OBJ.SYS, NET$PROP.SYS, and NET$VAL.SYS files. The previous versions exist as NET$OBJ.OLD, NET$PROP.OLD, and NET$VAL.OLD.

If running BINDFIX did not solve your bindery problems, you can restore the previous versions of these files by typing **BINDREST** and pressing Enter. BINDREST then restores the OLD files, effectively undoing all of the changes made when you ran BINDFIX.

VREPAIR

VREPAIR is a NetWare NLM. You use VREPAIR to accomplish two primary tasks.

One task for which you use VREPAIR is to make volume repairs. You also use VREPAIR to remove name space from a NetWare volume.

Other reasons to use VREPAIR include the following:

- A volume will not mount as the result of a hardware failure

- A hardware failure has caused disk read errors

- A volume is corrupted due to a hardware failure

■ Mirroring errors occur when the file server boots

■ Memory errors occur

■ A volume will not mount because name space has been added to it

Unlike most NLMs, VREPAIR is stored on the DOS partition of the NetWare file server. The name space NLMs are also stored on the DOS partition, instead of the NetWare partition.

 To run VREPAIR, you must first dismount the NetWare volumes that are to be repaired. When the volumes are dismounted, you cannot access them. If the SYS volume is dismounted, you cannot access VREPAIR.NLM to repair the SYS volume. Therefore, it is good practice to keep a copy of the VREPAIR.NLM file on the server's boot partition where the file can be accessed after SYS has been dismounted.

To run VREPAIR, notify all network users to log out of the file server. Once all users are logged out, you can dismount the volumes to be repaired and run VREPAIR.

To remove name space support from a volume, complete the following steps:

1. Notify all users to log out of the file server.

2. Make sure that the VREPAIR.NLM and the name space NLM (such as V_MAC.NLM or V_OS2.NLM) are stored on the DOS partition of the file server.

3. Issue the SEARCH ADD command and add the DOS path for these NLMs to the file server's NLM search path.

4. Type **LOAD INSTALL**, choose Volume options, select the volume to be dismounted, then choose status to dismount the volume containing the name space you want to remove. Or type **DISMOUNT volume_name** and press Enter.

5. From the console prompt, type **LOAD VREPAIR** and press Enter.

6. From the VREPAIR menu, choose option 2—Set Vrepair Options.

7. Change the Current Vrepair Configuration field to read Remove Name Space Support from the Volume, by choosing Option 1.

8. Choose the name space to be removed.

9. Choose Option 0 to return to the main menu.

10. Choose Repair a Volume from the main menu, and choose the volume to be repaired.

11. Start VREPAIR.

12. After VREPAIR has completed its process, it prompts you to tell it whether or not to write its repairs to the disk. Choose Yes to Write Repairs to the Disk. This removes name space from the volume.

If you need to remove other name spaces, repeat the process.

13. Choose Exit (Option 0) to exit from VREPAIR.

14. Remount the dismounted volume.

 You can also verify that name space has been removed by issuing the VOLUMES command at the file server console.

SBACKUP

The SBACKUP utility lets you back up several pieces of your network, including:

- DOS and OS/2 workstations
- Network file system
- BTRIEVE and NDS databases

SBACKUP also lets you restore any of these network pieces you previously backed up using SBACKUP.

SBACKUP consists of eight modules. Together, these modules provide the software you need to back up and restore your network's important files.

Of these eight modules, three are particularly important. They include:

- Storage Device Interface (SDI)
- NetWare Server TSAs
- Workstation TSAs

You load the SDI software on the file server to which your backup tape device is attached. Using device drivers, the SDI passes commands and information between the tape device and the backup utility. A file server with an attached backup device and the SDI software is called the host server.

You load NetWare Server TSAs on the file servers whose files you want to back up. These file servers are called target servers. The TSAs communicate with the file server backup software. A host server can also be a target server.

You load workstation TSAs on DOS or OS/2 workstations so you can back up the local hard disks on these workstations.

Software you back up is referred to either as parent or child software. A *parent* is any data set that is capable of having subordinate data sets. A *child* is any data set that cannot have subordinate data sets.

A directory, for example, can have subdirectories or files stored below them. Subdirectories can have other subdirectories or files stored below them. Therefore, directories and subdirectories are parents. A file cannot have directories or other files stored below it; therefore, a file is a child.

While NetWare provides SBACKUP, many companies choose alternative backup and restore utilities. SBACKUP is functional, but it is not the easiest to use of available backup software. Understanding the basics of SBACKUP, however, particularly the terms and features just described, is helpful to you as a network administrator.

There are other utilities NetWare provides to help you monitor and maintain your network. Two of those are the SET TIME and SET TIMEZONE commands.

Setting Server Time

Use the SET TIME command to set the clock time and date on the file server. Use the SET TIMEZONE command to set the time zone (such as Pacific Standard Time) for your file server.

To set the current date and time on your file server, type the following command at the file server console:

```
SET TIME mm/dd/yy h:m:s
```

Replace *mm/dd/yy* with the month, day, and year to which you want to set the server. For example, to set the server date to January 1, 1995, type **SET TIME 01/01/95** and press Enter.

You also use the SET TIME command to change the time on the file server. For example, to set the file server time to 1:32 a.m., type **SET TIME 1:32:00** and press Enter.

To set the time zone, use the SET TIMEZONE command. For example, to set the time zone on your file server to daylight savings time in the Pacific zone, type **SET TIMEZONE PST8PDT**.

Understanding Routing Information

Another important responsibility of a network administrator is understanding routing information.

The TRACK ON console utility enables you to view the traffic on your network. To use this utility, type **TRACK ON** at the file server console. Figure 12.5 shows the type of information displayed when the TRACK ON utility is used.

A *Routing Information Protocol* (RIP) packet exchanges information between network routers. This information is then used by each router to deter-

mine the best route to take between two points to send a packet to its final destination as quickly as possible.

A *Service Advertising Protocol* (SAP) packet advertises the service provided and the name and address of network devices that provide network services. For example, file servers and print servers are network devices that provide network services to network clients.

The TRACK ON utility provides information for each RIP and SAP packet sent in or out of the network file server. Packet information common to both RIPs and SAPs includes the following:

- ■ **Direction of the packet.** Indicates whether the packet was received (IN) by the file server or sent (OUT) by the file server. For example, a SAP packet can display on the screen as IN.

- ■ **Network address.** Shows the LAN address of the network card that sent or received the packet. For example, a network address looks something like 000004AD, followed by a colon, which separates it from the node address.

- ■ **Node address.** Shows the address of the device (server or router) on the network node. For example, in a RIP packet that is a broadcast message, the node address is displayed as a series of Fs (FFFFFFFFFFFF).

Figure 12.5

The TRACK ON utility displays information about RIP and SAP network packets.

```
IN   [ABCD0012:00001B01112B]        10:03:19AM      SERVER3    3
OUT  [ABCD003C:FFFFFFFFFFFF]        10:03:19AM      SERVER3    4
IN   [ABCD0012:00001B01112B]        10:10:03AM      SERVER1    5    SERVER3   3
     DOCSERVER       3              ISSERVER   2    ENGINEER   4    PROVO     6
     DOCMASTER       4
IN   [ABCD0012:00001B01112B]        10:10:04AM      SERVER1    5
     DOCSERV1        3              ISSERVER   4    ENGINEER   2
     DOCMASTER
<Use ALT ESC or CRTL ESC to switch screens, or any other key to pause>
```

■ **Packet time.** Indicates the time the packet was sent in or out. For example, time is displayed as hh:mm:ss, followed by either am or pm (11:05:33am).

■ **Net number.** Represents the number of the specific network (cabling system). For example, 000BAD1234 would be a valid net number.

■ **Hops and/or ticks.** The number of routers between the sending and receiving devices are *hops*. One hop equals one router. A *tick* is the number of $^1/_{18}$th-of-a-second increments it takes for the packet to reach its specified destination, when sent from this server. For example, in the case of SAPs, only the number of hops is shown (2). In the case of RIPs, both the number of hops and ticks are shown, separated by a slash ($^2/_3$).

Viewing route information using the TRACK ON utility can help you find problems with your network.

Creating File Server Batch Files

You can create batch files on the network file servers to help automate some of the processes that need to be performed. One of the most common uses for a server batch file is downing a file server from a remote console.

To create a server batch file, you can use the EDIT.NLM. You can also create a server batch file using any ASCII text editor. Your server batch file must be named with an NCF extension and must be stored in the SYS:SYSTEM directory of your NetWare file server.

To create a batch file that you can use to down a file server from a remote location, include the following three lines in the NCF file:

```
REMOVE DOS
DOWN
EXIT
```

To fully reboot a file server from a remote console using this server batch file, you must make sure that the AUTOEXEC.BAT file on the file server will automatically load the file server. To accomplish this, include the following two commands in the file server's AUTOEXEC.BAT file:

```
CD \SERVER.312
SERVER
```

After creating a batch file and updating the file server's AUTOEXEC.BAT file, when you log into this file server from a remote console and type the name of the NCF file you created, you will reboot the file server.

Questions

1. Which of the following is NOT a factor that affects network performance?

   ○ A. communications

   ○ B. hardware

   ○ C. software

   ○ D. memory

2. The compatibility of the file server's bus architecture and the network boards that you use in your file server is an example of the _____ factor that affects network performance.

   ○ A. communication

   ○ B. Hardware

   ○ C. Software

   ○ D. Memory

3. The network performance feature that is also a security feature is known as _____.

   ○ A. Communication

   ○ B. NCP Packet Signature

   ○ C. RAM

   ○ D. RIP

4. Implementing which TWO of the following changes will improve network performance if performance is reduced when implementing NCP Packet Signature?

   ☐ A. Upgrading file servers to 80486 processors

   ☐ B. Using only NetWare 3.12 utilities

   ☐ C. Setting NCP Packet Signature to level 4

   ☐ D. Upgrading clients to at least 80286 processors

5. Which of the following statements about NCP Packet Signature is true?

   ○ A. Level 2 is the default for clients.

   ○ B. Level 4 is the default for servers.

   ○ C. You must implement the same level at servers and clients.

   ○ D. It lets you set the level of security.

6. The level of NCP Packet Signature at which the file server will sign packets if the client is able is _____.

   ○ A. 1

   ○ B. 2

   ○ C. 3

   ○ D. 4

7. Which of the following is NOT an NCP Packet Signature level option?

   ○ A. 1

   ○ B. 2

   ○ C. 3

   ○ D. 4

8. What step must you take to see the Processor Utilization option in the MONITOR utility?

   ○ A. Choose Resource Utilization, then choose Processor from the MONITOR main menu

   ○ B. Add the /P option when running MONITOR

   ○ C. Load MONITOR before AUTOEXEC.NCF is loaded

   ○ D. Both A and B are options

9. Which item of information displayed on MONITOR's main menu is not used to verify file server and network performance?

   ○ A. Utilization

   ○ B. Total Cache Buffers

   ○ C. File Server Name

   ○ D. Service Processes

10. Which TWO Available Options menu choices let you view server memory statistics?

   ☐ A. System Module Information

   ☐ B. Resource Utilization

   ☐ C. Permanent Memory Pool

   ☐ D. Disk Options

11. To see the percent of file server processing capability currently being used, view the _____ information in MONITOR.

   ○ A. Utilization

   ○ B. Total Cache Buffers

   ○ C. System Module Information

   ○ D. Disk Options

12. If file server performance is too slow, add more _____ to the file server.

   ○ A. file server processes

   ○ B. total cache buffers

   ○ C. RAM

   ○ D. disk sspace

13. If Cache Buffers falls below _____ percent, add more RAM.

   ○ A. 10

   ○ B. 20

   ○ C. 40

   ○ D. 60

14. Total Cache Buffers should range from _____ to _____ percent.

   ☐ A. 10

   ☐ B. 20

   ☐ C. 40

   ☐ D. 60

15. Increases in the number of searches increases the number of _____ to the maximum that you allocated.

   ○ A. total cache buffers

   ○ B. directory cache buffers

   ○ C. packet receive buffers

   ○ D. service processes

Answers

1. C		9. C	
2. B		10. A B	
3. B		11. A	
4. A B		12. C	
5. D		13. B	
6. A		14. C D	
7. D		15. B	
8. B			

Supporting and Protecting NetWare 3.1x Servers

It doesn't matter how efficient your network file server is if it encounters a virus or if its hard disk crashes. Therefore, in addition to monitoring and improving your network's performance, you must also protect it.

You protect your servers from viruses by implementing several steps or approaches to network protection. You ensure that you can restore older versions of your network files by following a regular backup program. This chapter discusses these two topics.

After reading this chapter, you will be able to do the following:

- Implement virus protection

- Conduct backups and restores

Implementing Virus Protection

A computer *virus* is a software program that spreads throughout a computer (or network) in much the same way a virus spreads throughout your body. Protecting a computer or network from a virus is mostly a matter of prevention. It is much easier to prevent a virus from gaining access to any of your computers than it is to try to cure that virus later.

The best way to keep your body free of a virus is to prepare for it, to prevent it with good personal habits. Good security habits go a long way toward preventing your network from being infected as well.

Viruses come from many sources, including pre-packaged, shrink-wrapped, licensed software (though this occurrence is rare). Other sources might include:

- Bulletin board services (BBS)

- Data disks used on network clients

- Illegal copies of software programs

You can take several approaches to prevent your network from being invaded by a virus (see fig. 13.1).

Figure 13.1

Protecting your network from viruses.

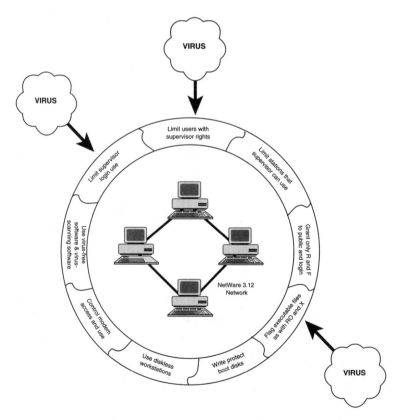

The greater your rights on the network, the more widespread the damage a virus can do. Because most viruses function by attacking the executable program files, a user with the right to change the read-only flag on executable files can make those files more susceptible to attack. To limit the amount of damage a virus can do when it enters the network because of something you did, only use your Supervisor login when necessary. In addition, limit the number of users with Supervisor or equivalent rights.

You should also limit the number of users on your network who have Supervisor rights. In addition, you can limit which network workstations from which the Supervisor user can log in.

For example, limit the Supervisor's login to your regular workstation and one other backup workstation. Then, no one can log in to the file server as user Supervisor, unless he or she is attempting to do so from your workstation, or from the alternate workstation.

Control access to the network and its files by implementing all or most of the following:

■ Grant all users only the Read and File Scan rights to common directories such as PUBLIC and LOGIN

■ Flag all executable NetWare system and software application files with the Read Only, and, if appropriate, Execute Only NetWare flags

■ Make sure all boot disks are designed as write-protected disks

■ Convert workstations to diskless workstations where possible

■ Control access to and use of modems on your network

Make every effort to ensure that disks used on your network are free of any viruses by implementing the following:

■ Purchase new software from reliable manufacturers and vendors

■ Only install software you have verified to be virus-free by running virus-scanning software on it before it is installed

■ Provide network users with access to virus-scanning software and insist they scan all disks prior to using them when attached to the network

■ Have users check-in any disks they are bringing into the office so they can be scanned

■ Only use working copies of disks that have been write-protected, using original disks only when you must

Two other important guidelines for protecting your network from viruses include:

■ Training and educating your network users as to the problems, symptoms, and procedures associated with network viruses

■ Maintaining adequate backups for restoring network files from tapes that have not been infected

Should your network become infected with a virus, you need to be prepared. Make certain you are familiar with the different types of viruses so you can recognize their symptoms. Also, train yourself in the procedures that must be followed to eradicate these viruses.

If you get a virus on your network that you cannot eliminate with virus-protection software, your next best option is to restore a backup that pre-dates the introduction of the virus into your network. It might not be possible for you to determine exactly when the virus was introduced. If you have maintained adequate protection measures, however, you might be able to determine approximately when the virus entered your network.

If you run antivirus software and make every effort to remove the virus from the network, but it does not eliminate the virus, you can choose and restore a backup. NetWare provides SBACKUP to ensure that you have at least a minimal backup and restore function for your network. Of course, you cannot restore network files using SBACKUP unless you originally made the backups using SBACKUP. In the event that you do not use an alternative backup

method, the next section of this chapter explains how to use SBACKUP to conduct network backups and restores.

Backups and Restores

As indicated in Chapter 12 of this course section, you can use the SBACKUP utility to back up and restore several pieces of your network (see fig. 13.2), including the following:

■ DOS and OS/2 workstations

■ Network file system

■ BTRIEVE and NDS databases

Figure 13.2

*Types of network
information you
can back up.*

SBACKUP provides eight modules with which to back up and restore your network's important files. Some of these modules you load on the *host server*, which is the file server to which your backup tape device is attached. For example, SBACKUP includes the *Software Device Interface* (SDI) module to pass commands and information between the tape device and the backup utility.

Some of these modules you load on *target servers*, which are the file servers whose files you want to back up, and some modules you load on the *target clients*, which are workstations whose local hard disks you want to back up.

Backing Up a File Server Bindery

Although you can back up and restore all data and files on your network, sometimes it is most important to back up and restore the file server's bindery files, particularly after NetWare is first installed, you have made many corrections to the bindery, or you have run BINDFIX to repair a corrupted bindery. You do not need to back up the file server's bindery each time you backup your network, as long as you have not made any bindery-related changes. If you add or delete users, change a user's rights, or perform other administrative tasks that affect the file server's bindery, then you should make a new backup of the file server's bindery.

To back up a file server's bindery and trustee assignments using NetWare's SBACKUP utility, complete the following steps:

1. Make a preliminary review of your file server and SBACKUP. This review includes the following:

    ■ Make sure there is sufficient memory on the host server. Load the MONITOR.NLM and verify that the file

server has at least 1 MB of available memory.

    ■ Know passwords for the user who will conduct the backup (Supervisor or other user with Supervisor rights) and, if you are conducting a client backup, for that workstation as well.

    ■ Remember any special path you are using for storing or retrieving session files.

2. Prepare the backup device (power it on, load the appropriate backup tape, and so forth).

3. Type **LOAD TSA312** at the target server console and press Enter. This command loads the NetWare 3.12 file server's *Target Service Agent* (TSA), so the file server's bindery can be backed up.

 Note   If backing up a NetWare 3.11 file server, use TSA311.NLM rather than TSA312.NLM.

4. Depending on the backup device you are using, load the related drivers at the console of the host server.

 Note   If you have not already done so, edit the DIBI2$DV.DAT file stored in SYS:SYSTEM of the host server before completing the next step.

Remove any lines for device drivers your backup device does not use. You may also have to add the driver name and controller board settings for your particular backup device.

Flag the DIBI2$DV.DAT file to Normal, then edit the DIBI2$DV.DAT file by typing the following command at the file server console and pressing Enter:

```
LOAD EDIT SYS:SYSTEM\DIBI\DIBI2$DV.DAT
```

If using a WANGTEK DIBI-II driver, you only have to load the SBACKUP NLM.

If using a DIBIDAI DIBI-II driver, type the following commands, where *nnnn* is the number of the host adapter, and press Enter after each:

LOAD AHA*nnnn*

LOAD TAPEDAI

If using a TAPEDC001 DIBI-II driver, type **LOAD ADAPTEC** and press Enter.

5. Type **LOAD SBACKUP.NLM** at the host server and press Enter.

6. When prompted, provide your user name and password.

7. If prompted, choose the appropriate device driver for the type of backup device you are using.

8. If prompted, choose a target to back-up.

9. From the Main menu, choose Backup Menu.

10. Choose Select Working Directory from the Backup menu and specify where the backup session files are to be stored.

11. In the Backup Options window, choose to back up the bindery in the What to back up: field. The default is NetWare Server.

12. Fill in other fields and make other choices as needed, then press Esc.

13. Choose Yes when prompted to Proceed with Backup.

14. Choose Start Backup Now and follow any additional prompts for inserting media (tapes), and so forth.

When the backup is complete, you can View the Error Log or just press Esc to return to the Main Menu. Then you can either exit SBACKUP, choose a different target to back up, restore previous backups, or choose to back up a network client.

Backing Up a Network Client

You can choose to back up a network client for any of several reasons. One good reason, particularly with DOS clients, arises when those clients are running Novell's Personal NetWare networking product. If they are, other users might also be accessing this client's hard disk. Backing up this client under this situation provides a measure of security for all network users who access the client.

Just as the SBACKUP utility is used to back up the file server's bindery, you employ SBACKUP to back up a client. However, some of the components needed to perform a client backup differ from those used to back up another file server on the network.

Prepare a NetWare DOS client for backup with the SBACKUP.NLM by completing the following steps:

1. Type **LOAD TSA_DOS** at the host server and press Enter. Several other NLMs are automatically loaded, including the following:

   ■ **STREAMS.NLM.** Provides a common interface between NetWare and the different transport protocols

   ■ **SMDR31X.NLM.** Provides an interface to the backup device driver for communication of device commands such as read, write, rewind, and eject

■ **TLI.NLM.** Provides an interface between STREAMS and end-user's application programs

■ **SPXS.NLM** or **IPXS.NLM.** Provides access between STREAMS and the related protocol: *Sequenced Packet Exchange* (SPX) or *Internetwork Packet Exchange* (IPX)

2. Modify the client's AUTOEXEC.BAT file to load TSA_SMS.COM. Then, reboot the client to automatically load the TSA_SMS.COM file.

 You only have to perform step 2 one time on each client whose hard disk you will be backing up. Thereafter, each time you boot any of these clients, the client's AUTOEXEC.BAT file automatically loads the TSA_SMS.COM file, preparing that client to be backed up.

3. Load SBACKUP at the host server.

4. Choose the client target you want to back up, and follow the prompts.

5. When the backup of the client is finished, exit SBACKUP.

 To back up an OS/2 client rather than a DOS client, follow the same procedure. However, load the TSA_OS2.NLM at the file server, rather than the TSA_DOS.NLM, and choose the OS/2 icon at the client instead of loading the TSA_SMS.COM file.

Questions

1. Which of the following statements about protecting your network from viruses is true?

   ○ A. The greater your rights on the network, the more damage the virus can do.

   ○ B. Limiting the Supervisor's number of login workstations has no effect on virus intrusion.

   ○ C. The only way to protect against viruses is to write-protect all disks.

   ○ D. Purchasing software from reputable vendors is a guarantee against virus intrusion.

2. To ensure that disks used on your network are free of any viruses, you can do all of the following EXCEPT:

   ○ A. Give network users access to virus scanning software.

   ○ B. Purchase new software from reliable vendors.

   ○ C. Install only software that has been virus tested.

   ○ D. None of these options help ensure network protection.

3. TWO additional guidelines you can implement to protect your network from viruses include:

   ☐ A. Training and educating network users

   ☐ B. Maintaining adequate backups

   ☐ C. Cleaning up all hard disks

   ☐ D. Installing virus software on each file server

4. Which of the following CANNOT be backed up using SBACKUP?

   ○ A. Network files

   ○ B. DOS workstations

   ○ C. OS/2 workstations

   ○ D. Macintosh workstations

5. In order to use SBACKUP on your network, your file server must have at least _____ of memory.

   ○ A. 1 MB

   ○ B. 2 MB

   ○ C. 4 MB

   ○ D. 8 MB

6. The file server to which the tape backup device is attached is called the _____.

   ○ A. parent

   ○ B. child

   ○ C. host

   ○ D. target

7. If you want to back up the files on the hard disk of a DOS client, which TWO files must be loaded?

   ☐ A. TSA_DOS on the file server

   ☐ B. TSA_DOS on the client

   ☐ C. TSA_SMS on the file server

   ☐ D. TSA_SMS on the client

8. To back up an OS/2 client, load the _____ file at the file server.

   ○ A. TSA_DOS

   ○ B. TSA_SMS

   ○ C. TSA_OS2

   ○ D. TSA_ICON

9. Which of the following files is NOT loaded when TSA_DOS is loaded?

   ○ A. STREAMS

   ○ B. SMDR31X

   ○ C. SPX

   ○ D. TSA

10. Of the following statements, which TWO are true?

   ☐ A. TSA_DOS.NLM is loaded at the host server.

   ☐ B. STREAMS.NLM is automatically loaded when TSA_DOS is loaded.

   ☐ C. You cannot load both TSA_SMS and TSA_DOS when backing up a DOS client.

   ☐ D. None of the above statements are true.

Answers

1. A	6. C
2. D	7. A D
3. A B	8. C
4. D	9. D
5. A	10. A B

NetWare 2.2
Administration

14   Comparing NetWare 2.2 and NetWare 3.12 207

15   Additional NetWare 2.2 System Management Information 221

Comparing NetWare 2.2 and NetWare 3.12

This chapter provides you with an overview of NetWare 2.2 based on its similarities to NetWare 3.12. Some of the 3.12 operating system is based on the 2.2 operating system. Consequently, much of the basic functionality of 2.2 is the same as that of 3.12. NetWare 2.2 basic functionality is discussed briefly in this chapter when it relates to test objectives.

To help you make the most of the information contained here, this chapter concentrates on citing the similarities between these two NetWare operating systems. This chapter is divided into major topic areas, such as security and accessing network files. Then, within these topic areas, the chapter discusses the

NetWare 2.2 System Manager test objectives that are similar to the test objectives for the NetWare 3.12 Administration test. This chapter also tells you where in this book you can find information related to the 3.12 Administration test objectives.

Finally, if the information you need to know about any of these test objectives differs between 3.12 and 2.2, this chapter tells you about those differences.

 Only the NetWare 2.2 System Manager test objectives are covered. The NetWare 2.2 Advanced System Manager test objectives are not covered in this section.

After reading this chapter, you will be able to do the following:

- Understand NetWare 2.2 file system and directory structure

- Access the 2.2 network

- Understand 2.2 security

- Use NetWare commands and utilities

- Understand 2.2 printing services

- Ensure compatibility of network applications

- Understand login scripts

NetWare 2.2 File System and Directory Structure

The levels of the NetWare directory structure (see fig. 14.1) include the following:

- File server name

- Volume name

- Directory

- Subdirectory

Figure 14.1

The NetWare Directory Structure.

Chapter 1, "Understanding NetWare 3.1*x* Functions and Services," covers this topic in more detail.

The required volume is SYS. The four required directories are SYSTEM, LOGIN, MAIL, and PUBLIC, all found at the root of the SYS volume. When accessing one of these directories, you first must specify the file server name followed by a slash (/), then the volume name followed by a colon (:), then the directory and any subdirectories separated by slashes.

To access the PUBLIC directory on a file server named MICHAEL, for example, your path should show as follows:

MICHAEL/SYS:PUBLIC

Three other NetWare 2.2 topics relate to these. The discussion of each is included in the same section. You should, however, be able to do the following:

■ Diagram possible directory structures given an organization and its needs

■ Create an organized and efficient directory structure

■ Construct a directory path using the required syntax

Chapter 1 also covers the topic of NetWare volume and directory structures in more detail. From the topics in that chapter, you should be able to do the following:

■ Describe a volume and its technical specifications

■ Describe a directory, including its main functions, hierarchical structure, directory name, and directory path

■ List the system-created directories on the SYS volume and describe their contents

Accessing the NetWare 2.2 Network

Accessing the NetWare 2.2 network involves setting up and then using NetWare paths. It also involves using specific NetWare and DOS commands.

The following are the seven commands you can use with NetWare 2.2:

■ COPY CON
■ CD or CHDIR
■ DIR
■ MD or MKDIR
■ PROMPT
■ RD or RMDIR
■ TYPE

Similar NetWare commands that improve DOS functionality also can be used. Four of the more useful commands include:

■ **LISTDIR.** To display the directory structure in an enhanced mode

■ **NDIR.** To make a global search of the NetWare file server directory structure

■ **RENDIR.** To rename a directory

■ **VOLINFO.** To view information about network volumes

Other NetWare 2.2 objectives also relate to the topic of NetWare directory structure access and use. They include:

■ Identifying the default drive pointers in both the DOS and NetWare environments

■ Using the MAP command to move through the directory structure

■ Differentiating between drive mappings and search drive mappings

■ Understanding the effects of the DOS CD command on MAP

Chapter 3, "Accessing NetWare 3.1x Network Services," provides additional information related to these topics.

NetWare 2.2 Security

Access to the network and its services is controlled by various NetWare security features. This section provides information about NetWare 2.2 security, as well as references to other chapters in this book that provide additional security-related information.

There are four levels of security in NetWare 2.2:

- Login/Password
- Directory
- Trustee
- File Attributes

Chapter 2, "Understanding and Implementing NetWare 3.1*x* Network Security," provides additional information related to these topics.

The following five command-line utilities are commonly used to apply NetWare security:

- **SETPASS.** Enables you to set or change a password.

- **ATTACH.** Enables you to access additional file servers.

- **WHOAMI.** Enables you to see your user name, the servers to which you are attached, your connections numbers, and the date and time you last logged in to the file server.

- **USERLIST.** Enables you to see who is currently logged in to the network or to view information about a specific user.

- **SLIST.** Displays a list of available file servers.

In NetWare 2.2, effective rights are calculated by combining directory rights and trustee assignments. As with 3.12, you receive 2.2 rights from trustee assignments granted to your user name, as well as from those granted to any groups to which you belong.

The primary difference between NetWare 2.2 rights and 3.12 rights relates to inherited rights and how they are blocked. More than anything, it is a matter of semantics. The implementation of rights blocking in 2.2 is called the *Maximum Rights Mask* (see fig. 14.2). In 3.12, it is called the *Inherited Rights Mask*. Its function is still basically the same.

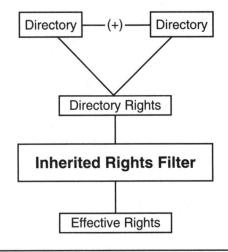

Figure 14.2
The Maximum Rights Mask.

Chapter 2 provides additional information related to these topics.

NetWare 2.2 defines several types of users, including:

■ **Supervisor.** A user who has all rights to everything on the network. This user is created when 2.2 is installed.

■ **Supervisor equivalent.** A user who has been assigned the same rights as the Supervisor.

■ **Workgroup manager.** A user who has limited control over a select group of other users. She functions like an assistant supervisor, with rights to create bindery objects, including users and groups.

■ **User account manager.** A user who has limited control over a select group of users that have been specifically assigned to her. She can manage user accounts but cannot create bindery objects such as users. Workgroup managers automatically are user account managers.

■ **Console operator.** A user who can manage file servers from her workstation using the FCONSOLE utility.

■ **Print Queue Operator.** A user who can manage a print queue using the PCONSOLE utility.

■ **Print Server Operator.** A user who can manage a print server using PCONSOLE. A print server operator cannot create new print servers and does not have the right to create other print server operators.

■ **Network User.** A user who can log in to the network and access network resources. The user's access depends on his rights.

NetWare Commands and Utilities

NetWare 2.2 provides a variety of commands and utilities for network users. Some utilities require Supervisor or equivalent rights for complete access. Some can be used by all types of network users.

Command-line utilities are programs that perform specific functions. To use them, you must type the command at the prompt, followed by any related and needed parameters.

Menu utilities group functions that would otherwise be provided by individual command-line utilities into a multiple-function menued program. The menu makes it easier to access the related functions and eliminates the need for you to memorize the specific syntax related to the individual command-line utilities.

Table 14.1 shows the 2.2 menu utilities and lists their associated command-line commands.

These three menu utilities are available in NetWare 3.12 and 2.2. There is a slight difference, however, between the 2.2 and 3.12 SYSCON utility. The 2.2 SYSCON User Information menu does not contain the following two options, which are contained on the 3.12 SYSCON User Information menu:

■ Account Balance

■ Intruder Lockout Status

Table 14.1
Menu and Command-Line Utilities

Menu Utility	Purpose	Associated Command-line Commands
FILER	To manage and control file server volume, and directory, subdirectory, and file information	FLAG LISTDIR NCOPY NDIR RENDIR XCOPY
SESSION	To control network file servers and access to the resources they contain	MAP SEND USERLIST WHOAMI
SYSCON	To configure and control network file servers	ATTACH GRANT REMOVE REVOKE RIGHTS SETPASS SLIST TLIST

Other NetWare 2.2 test objectives associated with these menu utilities and command-line commands include:

■ Identify the workstation commands incorporated in these menus

■ Recognize the specific tasks that can be accomplished within each menu utility

NetWare 2.2 provides the following menu utilities to accomplish tasks listed in this objective:

■ FILER

■ SESSION

■ SYSCON

In addition, these menu utilities have associated command-line commands, as shown in table 14.1.

You run Supervisor commands from a workstation and use them to manage your network.

Other Supervisor-command-related 2.2 objectives discussed include the following:

■ Identify the directory where Supervisor commands are located and the limitations of other users to this directory

■ Function within the special menu utilities reserved for Supervisor use

Supervisor commands are contained within the SYS:SYSTEM directory, which generally can only be accessed by a user with Supervisor or equivalent rights. Some of these Supervisor commands can be accessed by other network users. When the user does not have Supervisor rights, however, the feature list is limited.

The menu utilities and command-line commands that a Supervisor can use are the following:

- ATOTAL
- BINDFIX
- BINDREST
- DCONFIG
- DOSGEN
- DSPACE
- FCONSOLE
- FILER
- HOLDOFF
- HOLDON
- MAKEUSER
- NWSETUP
- PAUDIT
- PCONSOLE
- PRINTCON
- PRINTDEF
- SECURITY
- SYSCON
- USERDEF
- WSUPDATE

Of these utilities and commands, the following are not available as separate commands in NetWare 3.12:

- DCONFIG—Changes LAN driver configuration and related information
- HOLDOFF—Releases a lock placed on a file
- HOLDON—Opens and locks any file so other users cannot write to it while you are using it
- NWSETUP—Helps you quickly get started setting up users, including their login scripts and home directories

Parts I and II of this book discuss in greater detail the various Supervisor commands used in both 2.2 and 3.12.

You run console commands from the file server console or from a workstation using NetWare's remote console software. Chapter 4, "Managing NetWare Services from the File Server Console," provides the NetWare console commands (see table 4.1). The commands in table 4.1 that are also shipped with NetWare 2.2 are the following:

- BROADCAST
- CLEAR STATION
- CONFIG
- DISABLE LOGIN
- DISPLAY SERVERS
- DOWN
- ENABLE LOGIN
- NAME
- SET

■ TIME

■ UPS

The following are console commands included in 2.2, but not included in table 4.1 of Chapter 4:

■ **CLEAR MESSAGE.** Clears any message shown in the display area at the bottom of the file server's monitor

■ **DISABLE TRANSACTIONS.** This is called DISABLE TTS in 3.12

■ **ENABLE TRANSACTIONS.** This is called ENABLE TTS in 3.12

■ **VAP.** Displays a list of *Value Added Processes* (VAPs) loaded on the file server

■ **WATCHDOG.** Turns on file server connection monitoring

Commands included in NetWare 2.2 and 3.12 but not listed in table 4.1 include the following:

■ **DISPLAY NETWORKS.** Lists networks that this file server's router can see

■ **MONITOR.** Provides details about the efficiency of your NetWare file server

■ **OFF.** Clears the file server's console screen

■ **PURGE.** Makes deleted files unrecoverable

■ **RESET ROUTER.** Resets the file server's router table

■ **SPOOL.** Lists or modifies spooler assignments used to set up default print queues for use with NPRINT and CAPTURE commands

■ **TRACK OFF.** Turns off the display of network advertising packets received or sent by this file server

■ **TRACK ON.** Turns on the display of network advertising packets received or sent by this file server

NetWare 2.2 Printing Services

The difference between NetWare 3.12 and 2.2 is that 2.2 offers NetWare core printing. *Core printing* lets NetWare automatically set up basic defaults for print service access by network users. Versions of NetWare earlier than 2.2 also provided core printing services, but they did not give system managers the additional NetWare Print Server option provided in 3.12.

You should consider using NetWare's core printing services if:

■ Your network does not need more than five shared printers.

■ You can connect all network printers directly to a single NetWare file server.

You should consider using NetWare's print server if:

■ Your network needs more than five shared printers.

■ You have to connect your printers to locations other than the single file server.

■ The NetWare file server does not have sufficient memory (less than four file server processes are available).

■ You need to take advantage of local printing (printers attached directly to workstations).

Choose the type of printing services for your network based on your network's needs (see fig. 14.3).

To create print queues in NetWare 2.2, use the QUEUE command at the console. Enter the command using the following line:

`Q[ueue]`*`queue_name`*`CREATE`

Replace *queue_name* with the name to be assigned to this print queue.

You also can create queues using PCONSOLE.

The PCONSOLE utility in 3.12 is very similar to the PCONSOLE utility in 2.2. Therefore, if you are familiar with how to use the 3.12 PCONSOLE utility, you will be familiar with the 2.2 PCONSOLE utility.

To assign queues to printers in NetWare 2.2, use the PRINTER command at the console. Enter the command following this line:

`P[RINTER]`*`n`*`ADD[QUEUE]<`*`queue_name`*`>[AT][PRIORITY][`*`n`*`]`

Replace *n* with the printer number in the first instance and the priority in the second instance. Replace *queue_name* with the name of the print queue.

You also can assign queues to printers using PCONSOLE.

A *spooler assignment* directs print jobs to print queues and is used primarily to ensure that the printing setups in older versions of NetWare are compatible with 2.2. In addition, you can use spooler assignments whenever your printing setup requires printer numbers instead of queues. You also can use spool assignments to create a default queue for print jobs that use NPRINT and CAPTURE.

To use spooling, issue the SPOOL command at the console, following the line shown below:

`S[POOL]` *`printer_number`*`[TO][QUEUE]`*`queue_name`*

Replace *printer_number* with the number assigned to the printer. Replace *queue_name* with the name of the print queue.

Core Printing	(or)	NetWare Print Server
Maximum of 5 printers		Need more than 5 printers
All printers connect to one file server		Need printers connected to other than the file server
		Insufficient file server memory
		Need for local printing service

Figure 14.3
Choosing NetWare 2.2 printing services.

These three command-line commands also are available in NetWare 3.12, and they include CAPTURE and NPRINT. They are discussed in detail in Chapter 5, "Preparing NetWare 3.1*x* Printing Services for Users." Because 3.12 uses some automatic ENDCAP functionality, ENDCAP is not discussed in Chapter 5.

NetWare 2.2 uses an AUTOEXEC.SYS file as the login script for the file server. When the file server boots, it searches for and runs the AUTOEXEC.SYS file which is, therefore, useful for automating the setup of printing on your 2.2 network.

Any commands you can enter manually at the file server console, such as the printing services commands discussed previously, can be placed into this file. As with NetWare 3.12, you use SYSCON to create or change this file. Choose the Supervisor Options, then choose Edit System AUTOEXEC file to edit this file.

Ensuring Compatibility of Network Applications

Chapter 6, "Preparing Other NetWare 3.1*x* Services for Users," discusses the selection and placement of application software on your NetWare file server. The information contained in that chapter is applicable to 2.2 as well.

For an application to be *multiuser*, more than one user must be able to access the application at the same time, without overwriting or corrupting any files. The best way to determine whether an application program is multiuser is to review the application's documentation.

When determining where to place application programs, consider the user's needs. Also consider the rights that users need within the directory structure to access the application program.

After you establish that the application is network compatible and multiuser, install it into an area within the directory structure that allows for easy and secure access. Once installed, you flag application files as **S**hareable, **R**ead**O**nly. Next, grant rights to users so they can access and run the application's EXE files. To protect these files, users should be given only **R**ead and **F**ile scan rights to the directory containing the EXE files. If necessary, you then can ensure that users can access these applications by providing the correct drive mappings. Drive mappings can be established for users by placing them in login scripts.

Login Scripts

NetWare 2.2 login scripts and login script commands are mostly the same. Both use System and Default login scripts, as well as User login scripts.

Chapter 6 discusses login scripts. The NetWare 2.2 login script-related objectives covered there include the following:

■ Contrast the three login scripts used on the network

■ Identify and use login script commands to create a system and user login script

■ Identify vital mappings that must exist in the system login script

■ Debug problems in login script logic

· Note NetWare 3.12 test objectives do not include a specific objective that requires you to be able to debug login scripts. Part of understanding how to create a login script, however, requires that you be able to correct any mistakes that you make. Correcting mistakes in login scripts is the process of debugging a login script.

NetWare 3.12 objectives that cover the information you need to know for 2.2 login scripts (and that are found in Chapter 6) include the following:

■ Describe the types of login scripts and how they coordinate at login

■ Explain each login script command, propose standard procedures that are executed through login scripts, and plan a system of login scripts for users

■ Build and execute the plan using System and User login scripts

Questions

1. Which of the following is NOT one of the required NetWare 2.2 directories?

   ○ A. SYS

   ○ B. LOGIN

   ○ C. MAIL

   ○ D. PUBLIC

2. Of the following, which THREE NetWare commands are used to improve on DOS functionality?

   ☐ A. LISTDIR

   ☐ B. RMDIR

   ☐ C. RENDIR

   ☐ D. NDIR

3. Which one is NOT a level of security in NetWare 2.2?

   ○ A. Login/Password

   ○ B. Security Utility

   ○ C. Directory

   ○ D. File Attributes

4. TWO command-line utilities commonly used to apply NetWare security include _____ and _____.

   ☐ A. NDIR

   ☐ B. ATTACH

   ☐ C. WHOAMI

   ☐ D. RMDIR

5. A primary difference between NetWare 2.2 and 3.12 rights relates to which of the following?

   ○ A. The flow of rights

   ○ B. File attributes

   ○ C. Maximum Rights Mask

   ○ D. Group trustee assignments

6. The user who can use the FCONSOLE utility is the _____.

   ○ A. Workgroup manager

   ○ B. Print server operator

   ○ C. Print queue operator

   ○ D. Console operator

7. Which utility can be described as providing management and control of file server volume information?

   ○ A. FILER

   ○ B. FCONSOLE

   ○ C. SESSION

   ○ D. SYSCON

8. Which TWO SYSCON menu options included in NetWare 3.12 are NOT included in 2.2?

   ☐ A. Account Balance

   ☐ B. Change Current Server

   ☐ C. Supervisor Options

   ☐ D. Intruder Lockout Status

9. Which NetWare 2.2 utility lets you get a quick start on setting up users, including their login scripts and home directories?

   ○ A. DCONFIG

   ○ B. WSUPDATE

   ○ C. NWSETUP

   ○ D. SECURITY

10. You use the _____ command to list or modify spooler assignments used to set up default print queues for use with NPRINT and CAPTURE commands.

   ○ A. FCONSOLE

   ○ B. NDIR

   ○ C. SPOOL

   ○ D. SYSCON

Answers

1. A

2. A C D

3. B

4. B C

5. C

6. D

7. A

8. A D

9. C

10. C

Additional NetWare 2.2 System Management Information

he previous chapter discussed NetWare 2.2 System Manager objectives that were similar to the 3.12 Administration objectives. This chapter covers the 2.2 objectives that are not specifically covered in the 3.12 areas of this book. It also explores two areas of 2.2 that are substantially different from those same areas in 3.12. These two areas consist of the following:

- *Menus*
- *Backup*

NetWare 3.12 uses a menu system based on a different software than that used by 2.2. In addition, 3.12 uses a different backup and restore software than does 2.2. Therefore, the 2.2 menu system and backup and restore software are discussed in this chapter.

NetWare 2.2-Only Objectives

This first section discusses NetWare 2.2 objectives not included in 3.12.

System Manager Responsibilities

In NetWare 2.2, the individual who is responsible for the care and maintenance of the NetWare network is called the *system manager* or *network administrator*.

As a system manager/network administrator, you have various responsibilities, including the following:

■ Understanding NetWare, including software and hardware

■ Maintaining a secure network environment by managing trustees, the directory structure, and other related security issues

■ Monitoring network file servers using the supervisory utilities provided by NetWare

■ Maintaining the network using various NetWare console utilities

■ Managing applications software, including loading, upgrading, and flagging the software

■ Establishing a friendly environment for your network users by creating and maintaining login scripts and menus

■ Maintaining a usable and current backup of the network software, which might include user data

■ Ensuring that at least one other individual can perform supervisory tasks on the network in your absence

■ Creating and maintaining logs about the configuration of the network

■ Keeping your own networking technology knowledge and skills up-to-date

Filling in a NetWare Log

To help you maintain information about your NetWare 2.2 network, Novell provides a log form and suggests that you track the following information:

■ The name of your file server, the type of hardware it contains, the date it was installed, and who installed it

■ The version of the NetWare operating system that you are running, along with the date it was installed, and the name of the person who installed it

■ The file server purchase date, Internet address, and a description of its physical location

■ Information about each volume on each file server, including the name of the file server on which the volume resides, the volume's name, the hard disk number on which the volume resides, and the volume's size

■ Details about each workstation (client) on the network, including the names of all users who access the network from each workstation, the workstation's physical and node addresses, and the types of hardware and options of each workstation computer

■ The names of all applications loaded on network file servers, as well from whom the software was purchased, when it was purchased, and what version you have installed

General System Management Resources

Novell provides four types of resources for you to use as a system manager (see fig. 15.1). These resources include the following:

■ **Product documentation.** Includes a printed copy of the NetWare 2.2 manual set. NetWare 2.2 does not ship with an ElectroText version of the documentation set. Other product documentation is provided through Novell's online help facility.

■ **NetWire.** A 24-hour online electronic product information service that lets you submit questions to be answered by a Novell Technician or *System Operator* (SYSOP), and lets you access technical information, as well as software updates and modifications.

■ **NetWare Buyer's Guide.** Provides details about Novell products, its strategies, and its network solutions. Use it as a product reference, as well as a guide for planning and budgeting. It also includes a section to help you see what network management tools are available for your use, and a section that describes Novell's current education courses.

■ **NetWare's Online Help System.** Helps you find information about utilities, concepts, and system messages, without having to look at the paper copy of the manual set. It is available at your fingertips. Access it by typing **Help**, followed by the name of the command for which you want information.

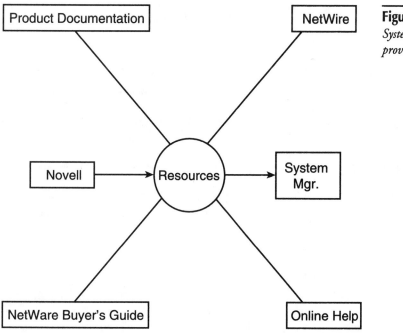

Figure 15.1
System manager resources provided by Novell.

Defining a Network

You can define a network based on several factors:

- Type

- Hardware

- Functionality

There are two general types of networks: peer-to-peer and client-server. A *peer-to-peer network* is one in which any client can also be a file server. Computers do not have to be dedicated to running the network operating system. Novell's Personal NetWare is a peer-to-peer network operating system product.

A *client-server* network is one in which one or more of the computers are used as dedicated file servers. There are three client-server network types, which follow:

- **LAN (Local Area Network).** Geographically located in the same area, such as a single office

- **MAN (Municipal Area Network).** Geographically located in a close area, such as several areas throughout a city

- **WAN (Wide Area Network).** Geographically located anywhere around the globe

Hardware Components

For information on the hardware and functionality that makes up a network, refer to Chapter 1, "Understanding NetWare 3.1x Functions and Services." The following 3.12 objectives provide more information on this topic:

- Describe the basic function and services of a network

- Describe the function of a server, its interface, and its communication with the network

Software Components

NetWare 2.2 still takes advantage of the benefits of *Open DataLink Interface* (ODI), but does not take advantage of 3.12's NetWare DOS Requester. Instead, 2.2 relies on the NetWare shell.

Choosing and Loading IPX and the Shell

The NetWare shell consists of two parts. The first part is IPX.COM, which is also used in NetWare 3.12, except that 3.12 uses an ODI version of IPX called IPXODI.COM.

 IPXODI.COM can be used in place of IPX.COM. Therefore, if you are working in a mixed NetWare OS environment, you can use IPXODI.COM on your workstation and still access a NetWare 2.2 file server. If you are using IPXODI.COM, however, you should also be using the NetWare DOS Requester (VLM.EXE and associated VLM files) instead of NETx.COM.

The second part of the NetWare memory shell is NETx.COM or one of its versions. You use the shell instead of the NetWare DOS Requester (VLM.EXE and associated VLM files) in the NetWare 2.2 environment.

The three versions of the NetWare memory shell are the following:

- The NetWare expanded memory shell (EMSNETx.EXE)

- The NetWare extended memory shell (XMSNETx.EXE

- The NetWare standard memory shell (NETx.EXE)

The shell that you use determines where in the computer's memory the shell files are to be loaded. The standard memory shell loads into your computer's conventional memory. The other two load into either expanded memory (XMSNETx.EXE) or extended memory (EMSNETx.EXE). The extended memory shell requires that your computer have extended memory in addition to the 1 MB maximum of conventional memory, as well as a LIM EMS v2.0 or compatible memory manager.

To load the IPX and the shell, load the following files in the specified order:

1. IPX

2. EMSNETx (or other version of the shell)

3. F: (to change to the first network drive)

The Best Option for Expanding Your Network

If you have NetWare 2.2 file servers on your network, you might want to make some changes to expand your network. If you need to accommodate new users, more applications, or connections to other networks, you can expand your 2.2 network by adding some or all of the following:

- File servers

- Hard disk and other data storage options

- Workstations

- Peripheral devices, such as printers and modems

- Routers, gateways, or both

- File server memory

The Distributed Processing Environment

After you load the appropriate communication files (IPX and the shell), you can run application programs from the file server. Starting an application program loads a copy of the required files into RAM on your workstation. From that point on, you access the application program files from your own workstation memory. This is known as *distributed processing*. Setting up a NetWare network and sharing application software on that network creates a distributed processing *environment*.

The NetWare 2.2 Menu System

As with NetWare 3.12, you can customize the user's environment by creating menus. This lets you design a system that several users can access.

To create a menu, you must first create the menu option file. This file, created using any text editor, is the main file from which the menu is created. When you create the menu option file, you must follow established guidelines.

When you create a menu in NetWare 2.2, you must create the menu with the following rules in mind:

- All menu and submenu names must start with a percent sign (%) followed by the menu name (without a space between) and must be left-justified to the margin

- Options to be displayed on a menu must be left-justified

- The names of all executable files must be on their own lines and indented one or more spaces

■ When calling (starting) a submenu, the submenu name must be indented and begin with a percent sign

■ Specify the position and color of the menu using the following format:

%MENUNAME,ROW#,COLUMN#, COLOR#

Replace ROW# with a number from 1–24

Replace COLUMN# with a number from 1–80

Replace COLOR# with a palate number from 0–4

> **Note** If you choose, you can define your own color palette using the COLORPAL utility, which is not part of the NetWare 2.2 System Manager course—therefore, it is not discussed in this chapter.

Figure 15.2 shows a sample menu option file.

```
C>type c:\usermenu.txt
%USERMENU,1,3,3
A. Word Processing
   s:
   wp
B. FILER
   z:
   FILER
C>
```

Figure 15.2
A sample menu option file.

You create a custom menu by using a DOS text editor and following the rules previously explained. After you create the menu option file using a text editor, you must save that file using these guidelines:

■ Create the file using any text editor or application from which the file can be saved as an ASCII text file

■ Give the file an MNU extension

■ Give the file a different extension, but you must use the complete name, including the non-MNU extension, when running the menu file

The sample menu shown in figure 15.2 would result in a menu such as the one shown in figure 15.3.

Figure 15.3
A custom menu.

The third step in creating custom menus is to run the menu and verify that it functions properly.

To run a menu, type **MENU** *menu_filename* at the DOS prompt and press Enter.

You can also run a menu from a login script by adding the MENU *menu file_name* command to a batch file that calls the menu, then calling that batch file from the login script using the EXIT command. If you create a menu called Usermenu, for example, you can create a batch file called USERMENU.BAT. Then, place the following command in the login script:

`EXIT USERMENU`

You can also run a menu from a login script by using the # call command, as shown in the following example:

`#MENU USERMENU`

 Running menus from a login script keeps the login script open from the file server until you close the menu. Menus also require additional workstation memory and reduce available application memory.

The NetWare 2.2 Backup and Restore Software

NetWare 3.12 provides SBACKUP as its backup and restore software. NetWare 2.2 provides NBACKUP for backing up and restoring network files.

With NBACKUP, you can do the following:

- Back up file server bindery files
- Back up directories and their files
- View the error and backup logs
- Restore files backed up with the NBACKUP utility

To use NBACKUP, you must use DOS read-and-write devices.

 DOS read-and-write devices include such things as disks, workstation or file server hard disks, and optical drives using a DOS device driver.

In addition, you need to have **R**ead and **F**ile Scan rights to the directories and files to be backed up, and **W**rite, **C**reate, **F**ile Scan, **E**rase, and **M**odify rights when restoring files and directories that have been backed up.

With NBACKUP, you can back up and restore both DOS and Macintosh files.

You must be a user with Supervisor rights to back up the entire NetWare file server. Regular users can, however, use NBACKUP to back up and restore directories and files to which they have the rights.

When using NBACKUP, you must do the following:

- Run it from a workstation on your network
- Restore using the same system type (such as local hard drive to local hard drive) from which it was backed up
- Use a DOS read-write device
- Use the correct file type names, such as DOS or Macintosh

To back up a NetWare file server, complete the following steps:

1. Login to the file server.
2. Run NBACKUP.
3. Choose the device type—DOS Devices if using the hard disk or floppy disks to perform the backup.
4. Choose Backup options from the Main menu.
5. Choose Select Working Directory from the Backup Menu and provide the path where the log files are to be stored (see fig. 15.4).

```
┌─────────────────────────────┐
│        Backup Menu          │
├─────────────────────────────┤
│  Select Working directory   │
│  Backup File Server         │
│  Backup Bindery             │
│  Backup By directory        │
│  View Backup Log            │
│  View Error Log             │
└─────────────────────────────┘
```

Figure 15.4

The NBACKUP Backup Menu.

6. Choose one of the following to back up:

   ■ Backup File Server

   ■ Backup Bindery

   ■ Backup By Directory

7. Provide information in the fields of the Backup Options window, as needed, then save the changes you made.

8. Choose Start Backup Now from the Start Backup window.

   If you prefer, you can choose to run the backup at a later time by choosing Start Backup Later and filling in the requested information.

9. Press Escape to exit NBACKUP when you have finished the backup.

Files that you backed up using NBACKUP can later be restored, also by using the NBACKUP utility. Files backed up using NBACKUP cannot be restored with other backup utilities because they are not compatible.

To restore a backup, complete the following steps:

1. Login to the file server.

2. Run NBACKUP.

3. Choose the device type—DOS Devices if using the hard disk or floppy disks to perform the backup.

4. Choose Restore options from the Main Menu.

5. Choose Select Working Directory and provide the path where the log files for the session to be backed up were stored when the backup was performed.

6. Choose Restore Session from the Restore Menu (see fig. 15.5).

```
┌─────────────────────────────┐
│        Restore Menu         │
├─────────────────────────────┤
│  Select Working directory   │
│  Restore Session            │
│  View Backup Log            │
│  View Error Log             │
└─────────────────────────────┘
```

Figure 15.5

The NBACKUP Restore Menu.

7. Choose the backup session to be restored.

8. Provide information in the fields of the Restore Options window, as needed, and then save the changes you made.

9. Choose Yes to Start Restore.

Using the NBACKUP utility to back up and restore network files also accomplishes another NetWare 2.2 System Manager objective—to use NBACKUP to protect your data.

Questions

1. Which TWO of the following are responsibilities of a system manager?

   ☐ A. Understand NetWare

   ☐ B. Run network cabling

   ☐ C. Keep up-to-date on networking technology

   ☐ D. Perform SYSOP duties

2. Of the following, which item is NOT normally recorded on a network log?

   ○ A. File server purchase date

   ○ B. Names of applications loaded on file servers

   ○ C. Name of the backup system manager

   ○ D. The NetWare Operating System version

3. The resource provided by Novell that lets you access software updates and modifications is called _____.

   ○ A. product documentation

   ○ B. NetWire

   ○ C. NetWare Buyer's Guide

   ○ D. online help

4. When planning your networking budget for the upcoming year, you might find Novell's _____ resource to be helpful.

   ○ A. product documentation

   ○ B. NetWire

   ○ C. NetWare Buyer's Guide

   ○ D. online help

5. Which of the following is NOT a factor that you can use to define a network?

   ○ A. Type

   ○ B. Hardware

   ○ C. Functionality

   ○ D. Application software

6. The EMSNETx.EXE, XMSNETx.EXE, and NETx.EXE files are all part of the _____.

   ○ A. NetWare DOS Requester

   ○ B. IPXODI

   ○ C. shell

   ○ D. VLM

7. Which of the following statements is true?

   ○ A. Options on a menu must be indented.

   ○ B. All menu names must start with a percent sign.

   ○ C. You only have six color palette numbers to choose from when creating a menu.

   ○ D. All executable files are listed on the Options line.

8. Use the _____ command to run a custom menu.

   ○ A. RUN

   ○ B. LOAD

   ○ C. INSTALL

   ○ D. MENU

9. You can back up _____ using NBACKUP.

   ○   A.   workstation files

   ○   B.   Unix files

   ○   C.   NetWare bindery files

   ○   D.   NetWare 4.*x* databases

10. You need _____ and _____ rights to backup directories and files using NBACKUP.

    ☐   A.   Create

    ☐   B.   Read

    ☐   C.   File Scan

    ☐   D.   Write

Answers

1. A C

2. C

3. B

4. C

5. D

6. C

7. B

8. D

9. C

10. B C

Networking Technologies

16   Computer Network Concepts 233

17   Network Services 239

18   The OSI Layered Protocol Model 255

19   Transmission Media 261

20   Transmission Media Connections 291

21   OSI Physical Layer Concepts 311

22   OSI Data Link Layer Concepts 329

23   OSI Network Layer Concepts 345

24   OSI Transport Layer Concepts 355

25   OSI Session Layer Concepts 359

26   OSI Presentation Layer Concepts 363

27   OSI Application Layer Concepts 369

28   Protocol Suites 377

29   Other Protocols and Standards 413

30   Tasks of Network Administrators 429

Computer Network Concepts

Computer networks enable computers to communicate directly in order to exchange information and services. Because computers are all different, are used in different ways, and might be located at different distances from each other, the task of enabling them to communicate can get quite involved, drawing on a wide variety of technologies.

As you study for the Networking Technologies test, you will be delving into some fundamental networking concepts. This chapter will ensure that you have a basic understanding of those concepts before you plunge into the details. Here you will learn a working definition of a computer network, along with definitions of the types of networks and their components.

Upon completing this chapter, you will be able to do the following:

■ Define computer networking

■ Describe the following models of network computing: centralized, distributed, and collaborative

■ Describe the characteristics of local, metropolitan, and wide area networks.

■ Describe the essential elements of a computer network

■ Describe servers, clients, and peers as they relate to computer networking

These skills will prepare you to understand the technologies that are examined in greater detail later in this section.

Models of Network Computing

Novell defines *networking* as the sharing of information and services. By this definition, people are networking when they are exchanging information. This course, however, is specifically concerned with computer networking, which has evolved under several different models to respond to different needs. These models are centralized, distributed, and collaborative.

Centralized Computing

The earliest computers were large, difficult to manage, and expensive. Originally, these large *mainframe* computers were not networked in the sense you are familiar with today. Jobs were entered into the system by reading commands from card decks.

The computer would execute one job at a time and generate a printout when the job was complete. Terminals, which enabled users to interact with the centralized computer, were a much later development.

In the computing environment of the mainframe world, all the processing and data storage are centralized in the mainframe computer. *Terminals* are simple devices that display characters on screens and accept typed input. Because terminals are simply input/output devices and do not process or store data, by Novell's definition of networking, no sharing of information is involved and no networking is taking place in a terminal-host environment. Networks developed when it became necessary for mainframe computers to share information and services.

In summary, the *centralized computing* model involves the following:

■ All processing in the central, mainframe computer

■ Terminals are connected to the central computer as input/output devices

■ Networks may be employed to interconnect two or more mainframe computers

Distributed Computing

As personal computers were introduced to organizations, a new model of distributed computing emerged. Instead of concentrating computing in a central device, PCs made it possible to give each worker an individual computer. Each PC can process and store data independently.

Under the distributed computing model, networking has evolved to enable the many distributed computers to exchange data and share resources and services.

In summary, *distributed computing* involves the following:

■ Multiple computers capable of operating independently

■ Tasks that are split up among the various computers

■ Networks that enable the computers to exchange data and services

Collaborative Computing

Also called cooperative computing, collaborative computing enables computers in a distributed computing environment to share processing power in addition to data, resources, and services. In a collaborative computing environment, computers might "borrow" processing power by running programs on other computers on the network, or processes might be designed so they will run on two or more computers. Obviously, collaborative computing cannot take place without a network to enable the various computers to communicate.

In summary, *collaborative computing* involves the following:

■ Multiple computers

■ Networks that enable the computers to exchange data and services

■ Multiple computers that may cooperate to perform a task

Local, Metropolitan, and Wide Area Networks

Computer networks may be classified according to their size characteristics. The most commonly used categories are the following:

■ *Local Area Networks* (LANs), which are confined to a relatively small area, typically limited to a few tens of kilometers in size. LANs typically employ a single transmission medium and are generally defined within a particular building or campus of buildings.

■ *Metropolitan Area Networks* (MANs) may grow in size to that of a metropolitan area, up to about 100 kilometers in scope. To be able to transmit data longer distances, MANs typically require different transmission media and network hardware.

■ *Wide Area Networks* (WANs) can cross the boundaries of states, countries, or even continents, and can be truly worldwide in scope.

An organization with computer operations at several widely separated sites may employ an *enterprise* WAN to interconnect the sites. An enterprise WAN can use a combination of private and commercial network services, but is dedicated to the needs of a particular organization.

Some WANs can be considered *global* in scope because they cross continental boundaries. An example is the Internet, which interconnects thousands of computers on all continents.

Of the three categories of network sizes, LANs and WANs are those most frequently encountered.

Components of Computer Networks

Until now, the definition of a computer network has been simply "something" that enables computers to exchange information. The time has come for a more thorough definition. Novell's definition of a network includes three components, as follows:

■ Two entities that have information to share. On a computer network, computers share *network services.*

■ A pathway by which the entities can contact each other. The pathway through which computers contact each other is called the *transmission media.*

■ Rules that establish orderly procedures for communication. The rules that govern computer communication are called *protocols.*

Each of these three components is discussed later in further detail.

> **Note** Merely having a transmission pathway does not produce communication. When two entities communicate, they do not merely exchange data, but they understand the data they receive from each other. The goal of computer networking is not merely to exchange data, but to be able to understand and use data received from other entities on the network.

Network Services

Networks enable computers to share their resources by offering *services* to other computers. Novell uses the term *service providers* to describe computers (or other entities) that share their capabilities with others. A service provider consists of the hardware and software that provides a specific network service.

Service providers share their capabilities with other entities on the network. A waiter in a restaurant is an example of a human service provider. Examples of network services include the following:

■ File services

■ Print services

■ Communication services

■ Electronic mail

Service requesters are entities that utilize network services. A customer ordering lunch in a restaurant is a human example of a service requester.

Service providers will advertise the services they can make available. Service requesters examine the lists of services and request the services they require.

> **Note** Service providers offer services to service requesters.

In this course, remember that the definition of networking is extremely generic. Any entities (human or machine) that are exchanging information are networking. Any entity (human or machine) on a network can become a service provider or a service requester.

Computer networks consist of three types of service providers and service requesters, as follows:

■ *Servers* function only as service providers.

■ *Clients* function only as service requesters and do not provide services for other computers.

■ *Peers* may concurrently provide and request services. In a peer network, a given computer might be requesting file services from one computer, while at the same time providing print services to another.

Whether a computer functions as a server, client, or peer depends on the software the computer is running. Examples from the NetWare world include the following:

- NetWare 3.12, which turns a PC into a file and print server

- NetWare client software (the NetWare Shell or Requester), which turns a PC into a client

- Personal NetWare, which enables a computer to function as a peer, both requesting and providing services

Networks that enable any computer to both provide and request network services (any entity can function as a peer) are frequently called *peer-to-peer* networks.

Many networks are configured so a given computer will function as either a service provider or a service requester, but not both. With this approach, a server is at the logical center of the network and provides all network services. Therefore, this is frequently called a *server-centric approach*. NetWare 3.12 and 4.1 are the most popular software for configuring server-centric networks.

You will learn more about network services in Chapter 17, "Network Services."

Transmission Media

Entities on networks communicate through some media. Human entities may communicate through telephone wires or sound waves in the air. Computers can communicate through cables, light, and radio waves.

Transmission media enable computers to send and receive messages, but do not guarantee that the messages will be understood.

You will learn more about transmission media in Chapter 19, "Transmission Media" and in Chapter 20, "Transmission Media Connections."

Protocols

Rules are necessary to ensure that messages are understood. The rules of English enable two English-speaking people to understand each others' messages.

The rules that govern computer communication are called protocols. A *protocol* is one or more standards that enable two devices to communicate.

Protocols of many types are utilized on networks. Chapter 19 will introduce you to the model that you can use to organize your understanding of protocols. The majority of this section, starting in Chapter 21, "OSI Physical Layer Concepts," will be devoted to expanding your knowledge of network protocols.

Questions

1. Which model of network computing does not take advantage of the processing capability of a user's desktop computer?

   ○ A.   Centralize

   ○ B.   Distributed

   ○ C.   Collaborative

   ○ D.   All of the above utilize the processing capabilities of personal PCs

2. In which model do user's personal computers process information independently from each other?

   ○ A.   Centralized

   ○ B.   Distributed

   ○ C.   Collaborative

   ○ D.   None of the above

3. In which model of network computing do computers share each others' processing capabilities?

   ○ A.   Centralized

   ○ B.   Distributed

   ○ C.   Collaborative

   ○ D.   Departmental

4. Which type of network is most likely confined to a building or a campus?

   ○ A.   Local-area

   ○ B.   Metropolitan

   ○ C.   Wide-area

   ○ D.   Departmental

5. What are the size limits of a wide area network?

   ○ A.   100 kilometers

   ○ B.   1,000 kilometers

   ○ C.   10,000 kilometers

   ○ D.   Worldwide

6. Which TWO entities can share services on a network?

   ☐ A.   Servers

   ☐ B.   Clients

   ☐ C.   Peers

   ☐ D.   Requesters

7. Which TWO entities can utilize services on a network?

   ☐ A.   Servers

   ☐ B.   Clients

   ☐ C.   Peers

   ☐ D.   Communicators

Answers

1. A

2. B

3. C

4. A

5. D

6. A D

7. B C

Network Services

*N*etwork services are the first components of the
network model. Network services are the resources that
servers share with clients, enabling clients to leverage the
computing power of other computers on the network.

An operating system *(OS) is the computer program
that directly manages the resources in a computer,
including memory, disk drives, printing, and input/
output functions. This course regards DOS, OS/2, and
Unix as* local *or* desktop *operating systems—operating
systems that are confined to a single computer. A
network operating system (NOS) such as NetWare
can be distributed on several computers on a network.*

It is possible to build network services as add-ons to local operating systems. Although DOS PCs can be made to network with some add-on programs, the result seldom has the robust, high-level of performance of an operating system that is made for networking. Network operating systems generally include built-in support for file, printing, and other services. Building networking into the NOS improves both performance and reliability, and has the added benefit of being easier to manage than a lot of add-ons.

Services such as file and printer sharing were the earliest incentives for networking computers, but many new network services are now becoming commonplace. In this chapter, you will learn about many network services and how they are managed on NetWare LANs.

When you complete this chapter, you will be able to do the following:

- Describe a variety of network services

- Identify appropriate network services to match organizational needs

- Determine how network services are implemented in centralized and distributed computing environments

In addition, you will examine how the following services function on a network:

- File services

- Print services

- Message services

- Application services

- Database services

File Services

File services enable networked computers to share each others' files. This capability was perhaps the primary reason it became so desirable to network personal computers. Users needed to exchange files, a problem that could be solved, if inconveniently, simply by trading files on disks. More importantly, users needed to share data in common database files, something that can only be done with a network.

The working definition for this course is that file services consist of all network applications that store, retrieve, or move data files. A feature of file services is access control. File services enable users to read, write, and manage files and data, but they should also restrict users to authorized file operations so that files are not accidentally overwritten or deleted.

This section examines the following file services:

- File transfer

- File storage

- File archiving

- Data migration

- File update synchronization

File Transfer

Without a network, the options for transferring files between computers are limited. You can, of course, exchange files on floppy disks, a process that came to be called "sneaker-net" because it consisted of networking by actually running around. Or you could use communication software to dial another computer and transfer files via a modem or a direct serial connection.

Note Although Novell course materials mention this file service first, NetWare 3.x and 4.x do not excel at file transfer between workstations. It is possible to copy files directly from one server to another, but not directly from one client to another. File transfer with NetWare 3.x and 4.x is most easily achieved by storing files to be shared on the NetWare server.

It is possible to add file transfer capability to clients using products, such as Novell's Personal NetWare, which enable clients to transfer files directly using peer-to-peer networking techniques.

NetWare 3.x and 4.x do support file transfer between servers and between clients and servers, but not directly from client to client.

When users are transferring files, the need for security arises. It might be necessary to limit file transfers to authorized users using password-controlled security systems, to assign file attributes that restrict the operations that may be performed with a file, or to encrypt files so they may be read only by authorized users.

File Storage

Most networks have at least some centralized file storage. All NetWare file servers are capable of storing vast amounts of data, sharing it with users, and controlling access to a high degree of precision.

For many years, most storage consisted of *online* storage—storage on hard disks that was always accessible immediately on demand. The files that could be accessed on a server were limited to the amount of hard drive space that was available. Hard drives are fast, but the cost to store a megabyte of data is fairly high. Hard drives have another

disadvantage: Generally speaking, they cannot be removed for off-site storage, exchange, or simply to build a library of files that is seldom required, but must be fairly readily available.

Almost all companies have large amounts of data that is used infrequently. There is no need to keep all of the financial reports available from the previous year, for example, but they had better be available in case of an audit.

One approach is *offline* storage, which consists of removable media that are managed manually. The most popular media used are data tapes or optical disks. Once data is written to a tape or optical disk, the disk can be removed from the server and shelved. Users who require offline data might need to know which tape or optical disk to request. Some systems provide indexes or other aids that make requesting the proper offline storage element automatic. A system operator still has to retrieve the tape or disk and mount it on the server, however.

When the slow response of offline storage is unacceptable, a near-line storage approach may be selected. *Near-line* storage employs a machine, often called a *jukebox*, to manage large numbers of tapes or optical disks automatically. The proper tape or disk is retrieved and mounted by the jukebox without the need for human intervention. With near-line storage, huge amounts of data can be available with only slight delays, but at a much lower cost than would be required to store the data on hard drives.

Data migration is a technology that automatically moves less-used data from online storage to near-line or offline storage. The criteria for moving files can depend on when the files were last used, the owner of the files, file size, or a variety of other criteria. An efficient data migration facility makes it easy for users to locate migrated files. Figure 17.1 illustrates one approach to data migration.

Figure 17.1
Data migration.

Files used within 60 days

Files older than 60 days

Files older than 180 days

Hard Drive

Optical Jukebox

Tape Autoloader

Novell supports the following standards for file storage and migration:

- ▪ *Real-Time Data Migration* (RTDM)

- ▪ *High Capacity Storage System* (HCSS) provides support for optical jukeboxes

- ▪ *Mass Storage Services* (MSS) schedules and maintains distributed hierarchical storage

File Archiving

File archiving (or backup) is basically offline storage that is primarily geared to creating duplicate copies of online files. These backup copies serve as insurance against minor or major system failures.

Networks enable file archiving to be centralized. It is possible, for example, for a single site to back up all the servers on a network. Many current backup systems also have the capability of backing up various client workstations, making it feasible to archive all files on the network to a central facility, whether the files are located on network servers or clients

File-Update Synchronization

In its simplest form, *file-update synchronization* is a means of ensuring that all users have the latest copy of a file. File-update synchronization services can manage files by monitoring the date and time

stamps on files to determine which were saved most recently. By tracking the users who access the file, along with the data and time stamps, the service can update all the copies of the file with the most recent version.

File-update synchronization, however, can be considerably more involved. In a modern computing environment, it is not always feasible for all users to access all files in real time. A salesman, for example, might be carrying a notebook computer on which to enter orders. It would be impractical to dial the central LAN every time an order was to be entered, so the salesman would enter orders offline (while disconnected from the network) and store them in the laptop. That evening, he would call the central LAN, log in, and transmit all of the day's orders at one time.

During this process, files on the LAN must be updated to reflect new data in the salesman's portable computer. In addition, the salesman's PC might need some updating, with order confirmations or new pricing information, for example. The process of bringing the local and remote files into agreement is known as file-update synchronization.

File-update synchronization becomes considerably more challenging when additional users are sharing the data files simultaneously. Complex mechanisms must be in place to ensure that users do not accidentally overwrite each others' data. In some cases, the system simply flags files that have multiple, conflicting updates and requires a human to reconcile the differences.

Print Services

Network printing was the second big incentive to install LANs. Among the advantages of printing on a network are the following:

■ Many users can share the same printers, which is especially useful with expensive devices, such as color printers and plotters.

■ Printers can be located anywhere, not just next to a user's PC.

■ Queue-based network printing is more efficient than direct printing because the workstation can get back to work as soon as a job is queued to the network.

■ Modern printing services are available that enable users to send facsimile (fax) transmissions through the network to a fax server.

In this course, *print services* are defined as network applications that control and manage access to printers, network fax, and other similar devices. The print service functions discussed in this course are as follows:

■ Providing multiple access

■ Servicing simultaneous print requests

■ Operating without distance limitations

■ Managing specialized equipment types

■ Providing facsimile (fax) service

Providing Multiple Access

A typical printer has a limited number of available connecting points, such as parallel or serial interface ports. In fact, many printers can have only a single active port, which means that a limited number of users' PCs can be connected to ports on a given printer. Without a network, this might mean that a printer is required for each PC.

Networks break the relationship of one PC to a port. Any user on the network can print to any network printer simply by printing through the network print service. In most organizations, this means that the number of printers can be reduced, even to a single printer for a department.

Servicing Simultaneous Print Requests

When each printer is servicing several users, print services must have an organized means of achieving two goals, as follows:

■ Enabling any user to print at any time

■ Printing all of the users' jobs in an orderly fashion

Print services manage these complex tasks by employing a technique known as *queuing*. A queue is a line where things wait to be serviced—theater patrons wait in a queue until a ticket clerk can service their ticket requests, for example.

Network print queuing works as shown in figure 17.2. In the figure, you can see how print jobs from several users are collected in the queue. While printing to a queue, the users' PCs are fooled into thinking that they are printing to a directly attached printer. Network printing services reroute printed data to the queue instead of to the PC's printer port.

Figure 17.2
*How print services use
print queues.*

Once the jobs are in queues, the print jobs are sent one-by-one to a printer. Even though a printer can print only one thing at a time, the appearance to the users is that they can print freely, even when the printer is busy.

Interestingly, print queuing usually services print requests more rapidly than printers that are connected directly to users' PCs. A network queue can collect print data at network speeds, which are generally much faster than printers can actually put the data on paper. After the print data is safely stored in a queue, the user can go on about his or her work knowing that the job will be printed as soon as the printer becomes available.

Operating without Distance Limitations

When a printer is connected directly to a PC, it can never be very far from the PC itself. Fifteen to fifty feet is the extreme limit of most printer cables.

Printers on a network, however, can be located anywhere. Any user can use any printer, whether the printer is nearby, in the next building, or across the country. This enables organizations to place printers where they are needed, not just where a user's PC is found.

Managing Specialized Equipment Types

Although many printer types have decreased in cost considerably, some types of printers remain so expensive that they must be shared if owning them is to make sense. Some examples are the following:

■ **High-speed printers.** Do you really want to print that 1,000 page report to your personal four-page-per-minute laser?

■ **Quality color.** The best color printers, such as thermal transfer, cost many thousands of dollars.

■ **Large format printers and plotters.** When 8 ½×11 is not large enough, it might be nice to have an 11×17 printer or a plotter available.

Providing Facsimile (Fax) Service

A standard fax machine uses a scanner to read the image on a printed form, render that image in electronic signals, and transmit the signals to another fax machine where the original paper image is reconstructed. Fax machines have become so popular that long lines are often encountered by users and much paper is wasted.

A new class of print service directs printed images to a device that can transmit the images as facsimiles. A network fax service enables any user to send a fax directly from a network application, such as a word processor, without needing to print the document and hand-carry it to the public fax machine. The fax service uses queuing so that many users can generate faxes simultaneously. Then the fax service takes care of transmitting the images in an orderly manner.

Moreover, a network fax server can receive faxes and route them electronically to users without generating a printout. Users can view faxes on their PCs, print them if desired, or store them as data files for future use.

Message Services

File services can pass data between users when the data comes in file form. Today, however, many new types of data are available, including audio, video, and graphics. Text data can be simple text, or it can come in exotic forms such as hypertext, which contains electronic links to other text, documents, images, sounds, or other types of data.

Message services consist of a wide variety of services that go beyond simple file sharing to store, transfer, and access text, binary, graphic, video, and audio data.

This course examines four types of message services, as follows:

- Electronic mail
- Integrated electronic mail and voice mail
- Object-oriented applications
- Workgroup applications

Electronic Mail

E-mail is the new reason to install a LAN. In fact, a LAN is an excellent platform for electronic mail because it provides reliable, high-speed service and is low in cost. E-mail is a technology for electronically transferring messages between networked computers.

E-mail systems can service anything from a local workgroup, to a corporation, to the world. By installing e-mail routing devices, mail can be transferred smoothly and efficiently among several LANs. Perhaps the most gargantuan e-mail system is found on the Internet, which enables users in dozens of countries throughout the world to exchange electronic messages more easily than mailing a paper letter.

Early text-based e-mail has given way to elaborate systems that supported embedded sound, graphics, and even video data. Modern e-mail systems also enable traveling clients to "call in" to send and receive mail.

Integrated Electronic Mail and Voice Mail

New messaging technologies are leading to closer interoperation of e-mail and voice mail systems. Voice mail can be more than a simple telephone answering system. Because voice-mail systems are themselves based on computers, they can be connected to networks, and voice data can be managed by messaging services. Eventually, this will enable various voice and e-mail systems to interoperate and freely exchange data.

A traveling user might direct that her e-mail messages should be forwarded to her voice mail. She then could call in and have the messages read electronically by a text-recognition system. Alternatively, speech recognition devices might be used to read a user's voice mail and convert it to a text-based e-mail message.

 Novell's Groupware division has produced a product called GroupWise that has some of these features.

Object-Oriented Applications

Objects are building blocks (consisting of abstract data types and program code) that can be combined to construct large, more complex, object-oriented applications.

Messaging services can be used as intermediaries that enable objects on the network to communicate. Messaging service applications achieve this by acting as agents for the objects. The object simply delivers data to an agent, which is then responsible for delivering the data to the destination object. This eliminates the need for objects to have the capability of communicating with all other objects on the network.

Workgroup Applications

Workgroup applications use network services to improve communication in workgroups. Two types of workgroup applications are discussed in this course: workflow management and linked-object documents.

Workflow Management Applications

Workflow management applications route electronic forms and documents among workgroup users. When reliable electronic signatures are added to the process, it becomes possible to replace numerous processes that are traditionally paper-bound. An electronic purchase order system might function like this:

1. The requester fills in an electronic form.

2. The form is routed to the requesters supervisor for an approval signature which is added electronically.

3. The signed form is routed to a budget manager who ensures that funds are available. Funding verification might even take place automatically before the form is brought to the budget manager's attention.

4. The approved purchase request is used to generate a paper purchase order that can be faxed to the vendor.

You can see how users along the way can add information to the form. The pioneering example of a workflow management application is Lotus Notes. Novell provides an automated forms management package called InForms.

Linked-Object Documents

Documents need no longer be regarded simply as files containing text. Modern documents can consist of many different types of objects, including text, graphics, sound, voice, spreadsheet data, and video. Various types of objects can be assembled to build documents.

Objects are more than just data. An object also has a degree of "intelligence" that enables it to pass messages to documents where they are integrated. Some sense of this operation can be had by experimenting with OLE in Microsoft Windows.

Directory Services

Until recently, most services on a network were operated fairly independently. Suppose that a network consisted of two file servers and an e-mail server. The network administrator would need to manage user accounts on all three servers independently. The larger the network, the more difficult network administration becomes.

Directory services can greatly simplify other network tasks as well. A *directory service* integrates all the information about objects on the network into an overall directory structure. Objects on the network can consult the directory to identify other objects and to enable objects to exchange messages. The objects themselves do not need to know the address, location, or messaging formats required to communicate—all of this information is provided by the directory service.

The directory structure hides the physical structure of the network from applications and from users. A print server is simply a part of the network—it is not a service being offered by a particular computer.

The actual directory, however, is stored in files that physically reside on one or more server. When information in the directory is duplicated on several servers, a *directory synchronization* process is needed to keep all copies of the directory up-to-date.

NetWare Directory Services is a directory service that has been integrated into NetWare 4.*x*.

Application Services

Application services enable applications to leverage the computing power and specialized capabilities of other computers on the network.

For example, business applications often must perform complex statistical calculations that are beyond the scope of most desktop PCs. Statistical software with the required capabilities might need to run on a mainframe computer or on a Unix minicomputer. The statistical package, however, can make its capabilities available to applications on users' PCs by providing an application service.

The client PC would send the request for a calculation to the statistics application server. After the results become available, they would be returned to the client. In this way, only one computer in an organization requires the expensive software license and processing power required to produce the statistics, but all client PCs can benefit.

Application services enable organizations to install servers that are specialized for specific functions. The most common application servers currently are database servers, discussed in the next section. Other application services, however, are beginning to emerge.

Application servers are an effective strategy for making a network more scaleable. New application servers can be added as new types of application needs emerge. If more power is needed for the application, only the application server needs to be upgraded. A database server, for example, might grow from a PC to a multiprocessor RISC system running Unix without requiring many or even any changes to the client PCs.

Each application service does not necessarily need to be hosted on a separate computer. Along with file and print services, NetWare servers can provide e-mail, database, and communication services.

If demand for services loads the server down and hurts performance, it is easy to move an application service to its own computer. This scaleability is one of the advantages of a LAN architecture.

Database Services

Database services are the most common examples of application servers. Because database servers enable applications to be designed in separate client and server components, they are frequently called *client-server databases.*

With a client-server database, the client and server applications are designed to take advantage of specialized capabilities of the client and database systems, as follows:

■ The client application manages data input from the user, generation of screen displays, some of the reporting, and generating data retrieval requests that are sent to the database server.

■ The database server manages the database files; adds, deletes, and modifies records in the database; queries the database and generates the result required by the client; and transmits results back to the client. The database server can service requests for multiple clients more or less at the same time.

Database services relieve clients of most responsibilities for managing data. A modern database server is a sophisticated piece of software that can do the following:

■ Provide database security

■ Optimize the performance of database operations

■ Determine optimal locations for storing data without requiring clients to know where the data is located

■ Service large numbers of clients by reducing the time any one client is accessing the database

■ Distribute data across multiple database servers

Distributed databases are becoming increasingly popular. They enable portions of databases to be stored on separate server computers, which may be in different geographic locations. This technique, known as *distributed data,* looks like a single logical database to users, but places the data users need in the most accessible location. East Coast sales data, for example, might be located on a database server in Boston, while West Coast sales data is on a server in San Diego. Special database mechanisms must be in place to keep the data in the copies of the database synchronized.

More simply, databases can simply be replicated; complete copies of the database can be stored in various locations. This provides a redundancy factor because disaster is unlikely to strike all copies at once. Additionally, database replication improves application response time because users can access the database locally rather than through a relatively slow wide area network.

As shown in figure 17.3, the most popular strategies for replication databases are the following:

■ Master server updates, where a single master server receives all updates and, in turn, updates all replicas

■ Locally driven updates, where any local server can receive an update and is responsible for distributing the change to other replicas

Implementing Services in Centralized and Distributed Environments

Just as networks may be organized according to centralized or distributed models, the services offered on networks can be centralized or distributed.

A *centralized* service may be located entirely on a mainframe computer or on a LAN server that uses a server-centric NOS. On networks that employ a peer-to-peer NOS, services may be centralized or may be *distributed* on two or more computers.

 A server-centric NOS does not imply a client-server relationship between workstations and the server. When a workstation is configured to function only by requesting services from the network server, network services then are centralized, but do not adhere to a client-server model.

A client-server model implies that the client is an intelligent device that cooperates with the server to manage data.

The remainder of this section discusses issues related to implementing network services.

Figure 17.3

Master-driven and locally driven database replication.

Control of Resources

The centralized approach follows the adage "Put all your eggs in one basket and watch that basket very carefully." When hardware and software are concentrated, they can be maintained by experts and closely monitored with management tools. This does not necessarily mean that all devices are physically located in the same area, only that they are grouped for efficient and effective management.

The centralized approach is also logically simpler, and fewer disruptive events are likely to jeopardize data. When resources are distributed through a network, it can be difficult to isolate the causes of problems.

The most important resources that are being controlled on any network are *files* which contain the organization's critical data. In most cases, organizations will choose to store the most critical files on a centralized file server from which all users will access and share the files. This approach is called *server-centric, client-server,* or *dedicated server file service.* It is important to understand the advantages and disadvantages of the centralized and distributed approaches.

Centralized File Services

Dedicated file servers have the following benefits:

- Files are in a specific place where they can be reliably archived.

- Central file servers can be managed more efficiently.

- Central file servers can contain expensive, high-performance hardware that expedites file services and makes the file servers more reliable.

- The cost of specialized file server technology is shared by a large number of users.

A few issues, however, should be considered with regard to central file services, as follows:

- When all data is stored on a single server, a single point of failure exists. If the server fails, all data becomes unavailable. This makes proper design and management of the server essential.

- Because all clients are contending for file services from a single source, average file access times might be slower with a centralized file server than when files are stored on individual, local hard drives.

Centralized file services are generally chosen for organizations that want to achieve the highest levels of protection for their data files.

Distributed File Services

In a peer-to-peer environment, any computer can share its files and applications with any other computer. The sharing of services must be established for each individual computer, and each user must have the skills required to manage the networking services on his or her PC. Because services are provided by many different computers, users must become aware of which computers are providing which services. Clearly, the skills and responsibility required of users is higher than for centralized file services.

Some advantages of distributed file storage include the following:

- No single point of failure. When a computer fails, only the files stored on that computer become unavailable.

- Individuals typically experience faster access for files located on local hard drives than for files on centralized file servers.

- No specialized server hardware is required. File services can be provided with standard PCs.

Some issues related to distributed file storage include the following:

■ It is more difficult to manage the file service and to protect the integrity of files. File backup is more difficult when files are distributed across many PCs.

■ Individual PCs generally do not have high-reliability hardware, including uninterruptible power supplies, disk mirroring, and so forth.

■ However, file services provided by peers are typically not as fast as file services provided by a central file server that is specifically designed for the purpose.

■ When higher performance is required, rather than upgrading one central file server, each computer must be upgraded.

Organizations tend to choose peer-to-peer networking for two primary reasons. One is a desire to network with their current stock of PCs without the expense of a centralized server. Another is that peer-to-peer is an informal networking approach that fits the working style of many organizations.

Server Specialization

Humans often specialize so that they become very good at one type of task. This approach has benefits for network servers as well. By dedicating each server computer to providing a specific set of services, it becomes possible to carefully tailor the computer to the requirements for that service. This results in optimal performance, simpler troubleshooting, and enhanced scaleability. Server specialization implies that the network is being organized using a centralized approach.

Selecting Network Operating Systems (NOS)

When vendors develop network operating systems, designers will choose whether to use a centralized or a distributed model. Some network operating systems are clearly designed to implement LANs based on centralized models, including the following:

■ Novell NetWare

■ Banyan VINES

■ OpenVMS

■ IBM OS/2 LAN Server

■ Microsoft Windows NT Server

On the other hand, many products are designed to implement peer-to-peer networking models, including the following:

■ Novell Personal NetWare

■ Microsoft Windows for Workgroups and Windows NT

■ AppleTalk (the networking system for Apple Macintosh computers)

■ Artisoft LANtastic

Many peer-to-peer products can be added to networks that are primarily managed by centralized servers. You can, for example, install Personal NetWare on networked PCs, enabling them to interact with each either using a peer-to-peer approach. The PCs, however, retain the capability of accessing the main NetWare servers to utilize centralized services.

Questions

1. Which of the following is a network operating systems?

   ○ A. OS/2

   ○ B. NetWare

   ○ C. Unix

   ○ D. MS-DOS

2. Which TWO of the following are offline file storage media?

   ☐ A. Tape data cartridges

   ☐ B. Removable disks

   ☐ C. Hard disk drives

   ☐ D. Optical jukebox

3. Which of the following is a near-line file storage media?

   ○ A. Optical jukebox

   ○ B. Hard disk drive

   ○ C. Floppy disks

   ○ D. Removable hard drives

4. Which file service is responsible for creating duplicate copies of files to protect against file damage?

   ○ A File transfer

   ○ B. File-update synchronization

   ○ C. File archiving

   ○ D. Remote file access

5. Which TWO of the following are file services?

   ☐ A. Archiving

   ☐ B. Remote file access

   ☐ C. Update synchronization

   ☐ D. Data integrity

6. What is the most important feature that enables networks to support printing from many users?

   ○ A. Networkable printers

   ○ B. Printer priorities

   ○ C. Queuing

   ○ D. Print servers

7. Which THREE types of information can be processed by a message service?

   ☐ A. Text

   ☐ B. Audio

   ☐ C. Interactive

   ☐ D. Video

8. Which THREE statements are true regarding directory services?

   ☐ A. Directory services enable users to determine physical locations of services.

   ☐ B. Directory services manage resources on multiple servers from a central point.

   ☐ C. Directory services enable users to access network services on multiple servers.

   ☐ D. The directory may be stored on more than one server.

9. Which THREE statements are true regarding application services?

☐ A. Clients request services.

☐ B. Application services lack scaleability.

☐ C. Application servers can be optimized to specialize in a service.

☐ D. Multiple services can be offered by the same server PC.

10. Which THREE statements are true regarding database services?

☐ A. A database server improves data security.

☐ B. All data must be located on the main database server.

☐ C. Database performance may be optimized.

☐ D. Database services enable multiple clients to share a database.

11. Which THREE are advantages of a centralized approach to providing file services?

☐ A. Centralized files may be readily archived.

☐ B. It provides the best possible performance.

☐ C. Management is efficient.

☐ D. The cost of high-performance, high-reliability servers can be spread across many users.

12. Which TWO are advantages of a distributed approach to providing file services?

☐ A. There is no central point of failure.

☐ B. It is less difficult to manage than a complex, centralized server.

☐ C. It is easily scaled to improve performance for all users.

☐ D. Specialized equipment is not required.

Answers

1. B
2. A B
3. A
4. C
5. A C
6. C
7. A B D
8. B C D
9. A C D
10. A C D
11. A C D
12. A D

The OSI Layered Protocol Model

If servers are to provide services to clients, the two parties must be able to communicate. Besides the cables that you see, numerous processes run behind the scenes to keep things running smoothly. These processes are called protocols. As Chapter 16 explains, protocols, along with services and transmission media, make up the three components of a network according to the course model.

After reading this chapter, you will be able to perform the following tasks:

- *Explain the place of rules in the communication process*
- *Describe the seven-layer OSI Reference Model*
- *Discuss how network protocols form protocol stacks*
- *Explain how protocols at given layers interact with peer layers in the protocol stacks of other devices*

Rules and the Communication Process

Networks rely on a great many rules to manage information interchange. Some of the problems that must be solved include the following:

■ The procedures used to initiate and end an interaction

■ The signals used to represent data on the media

■ How to direct a message to the intended destination

■ Procedures used to control the rate of data flow

■ Methods that enable different computer types to communicate

■ How to ensure that messages are received correctly

The process of enabling computers to communicate is an extremely complex one, often too complex to solve all at once with just one set of rules. Instead, the industry has chosen to solve parts of the problem so that the solutions can be put together like pieces of a puzzle. This puzzle comes together a different way each time to build a complete communication approach for any given situation.

The OSI Reference Model

To best understand how the pieces fit together, it is useful to have a model in mind. The most commonly used model is the *Open Systems Interconnection* (OSI) Reference Model, defined by the *International Organization for Standardization* (ISO).

The OSI model organizes communication protocols into seven layers. Each layer addresses a narrow portion of the communication process. The layers of the OSI model are shown in figure 18.1.

Each of these layers are examined in detail, starting with Chapter 21, "OSI Physical Layer Concepts." This chapter, however, introduces only the general characteristics of the model.

Layer 1, the physical layer, consists of protocols that control communication on the network media. Layer 7, the application layer, interfaces the network services with the applications in use on the computer. Between are five other layers that perform intermediate communication tasks.

 You need to know the names and order of the seven layers. Two phrases follow that will help you remember the first letters of the layers:

All **P**eople **S**eem **T**o **N**eed **D**ata **P**rocessing

Please **D**o **N**ot **T**hrow **S**ausage **P**izza **A**way

Choose one, depending on whether you are most comfortable working from the top of the model down or from the bottom up.

 The network media itself is not part of the model, which only deals with protocols. Protocols represent software constructions, whereas cabling is hardware. Networking cannot exist, however, without communication media. Sometimes, you will hear the medium referred to informally as "Layer Zero" of the OSI model.

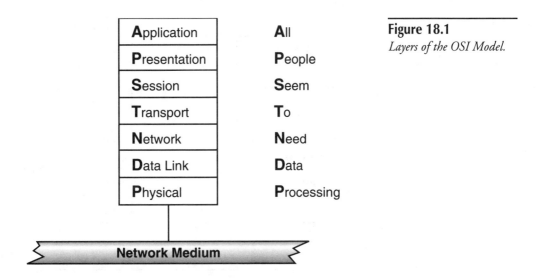

Application	**A**ll
Presentation	**P**eople
Session	**S**eem
Transport	**T**o
Network	**N**eed
Data Link	**D**ata
Physical	**P**rocessing

Network Medium

Figure 18.1
Layers of the OSI Model.

Figure 18.1 illustrates the origin of the term "protocol stack." The OSI model breaks the communication process into layers. At each layer, different protocols are selected to solve the needs of a particular communication environment. These protocols are "stacked" one on top of the other until the communication capability is complete. A protocol stack, then, is a set of compatible, layered protocols that have been implemented on a particular computer. Two common examples of protocol stacks are IPX/SPX, the standard NetWare protocols, and TCP/IP, the most widely implemented protocol stack in the computer industry.

A *protocol stack* is a hierarchical set of protocols that coordinate to perform a complete communication process. Each layer makes use of the services provided by the layer below it; and each layer provides services to the layer above it. Formally, layer N services layer $N+1$, and layer N is serviced by layer N-1.

Two computers must be running the same protocol stacks if they are to communicate; each layer in one computer's protocol stack must interact with a corresponding layer in the other computer's protocol stack (see fig. 18.2). The figure originates the path of a message starting in the transport layer. The message travels down the protocol stack, through the network medium, and up the protocol stack of the receiving computer. If the transport layer in the receiving computer understands the protocols used in the transport layer that originated the message, the message can be delivered.

Provided the protocol stacks on two computers are compatible, it is possible for different computer types to communicate. TCP/IP, for example, is available for almost any computer and operation system currently being made. If a Macintosh and a Unix workstation are both running TCP/IP, it is possible for the Mac to access files on the Unix workstation.

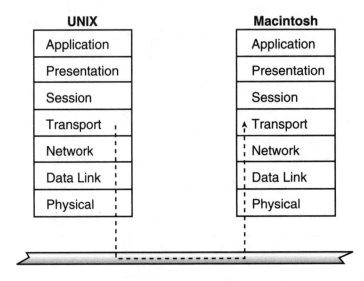

Figure 18.2

Peer communication between protocol stacks.

How Peer Layers Communicate

To communicate with its peer layer in another computer, each protocol layer adds its personal information to the message being sent. This information takes the form of a header added to the beginning of the message (see fig. 18.3).

Headers are added as the message is prepared for transmission, and headers are removed (*stripped*) by the receiver after the information in the header has been utilized.

Notice that the data for each layer consists of the header and data of the next higher layer. Because the data format is different at each layer, different

Figure 18.3

Adding headers to messages.

H_p = Presentation Header
H_t = Transport Header
H_s = Session Header
H_n = Network Header
H_d = Data Link Header

terms are commonly used to name the data package at each level. Table 18.1 summarizes these terms by layer.

Note The physical layer does not append a header because it is concerned with sending and receiving information on the individual bit level. The bits are assembled into longer message units in the data link layer.

Table 18.1
Data package names and
the OSI reference model.

Layer	Data Package Names
Application	Message (and packet)
Presentation	Packet
Session	Packet
Transport	Datagram, segment (and packet)
Network	Datagram (and packet)
Data Link	Frame (and packet)
Physical	Bit (and packet)

As you can see in the table, *packet* is a generic term applicable to all layers. It is the term, therefore, to be used for non-layer-specific discussion in later chapters.

Questions

1. The layers of the OSI model (in order) are included in which of the following choices?

   ○ A. Physical, data link, network, transport, system, presentation, application

   ○ B. Physical, data link, network, transport, session, presentation, application

   ○ C. Physical, data link, network, transform, session, presentation, application

   ○ D. Presentation, data link, network, transport, session, physical, application

2. In the OSI model, what is the relationship of a layer (N) to the layer above it (layer $N+1$)?

   ○ A. Layer N provides services for layer $N+1$.

   ○ B. Layer $N+1$ adds a header to information received from layer N.

   ○ C. Layer N utilizes services provided by layer $N+1$.

   ○ D. Layer N has no effect on layer $N+1$.

3. Which THREE of the following statements regarding protocol stacks are true?

   ☐ A. A given protocol stack can run on only one computer type.

   ☐ B. Layers add headers to packets received from higher layers in the protocol stack.

   ☐ C. A protocol stack is a hierarchical set of protocols.

   ☐ D. Each layer provides services for the next highest layer.

4. Which TWO of the following terms are used to describe data units at the network layer?

   ☐ A. Datagram

   ☐ B. Message

   ☐ C. Frame

   ☐ D. Packet

5. Which TWO of the following terms are used to describe data units at the data link layer?

   ☐ A. Datagram

   ☐ B. Message

   ☐ C. Frame

   ☐ D. Packet

Answers

1. D

2. A

3. B C D

4. A D

5. C D

Transmission Media

*N*etwork clients must have a channel through which they can communicate with network servers. The channel that carries messages between clients and servers *is called the* transmission media.

The media for local area networks usually consist of one of the following:

- *Cable (coaxial, twisted-pair, or fiber-optic)*
- *Wireless (radio, infrared, microwave)*

With wide area networks, you don't deal with media so much as you deal with services. You buy wide area network services from a commercial provider or connect to an existing network such as the Internet. In its course through a wide area network, a packet may pass through many types of media, but you as a network administrator need not be concerned with the media being employed. Two networks that provide wide area network support are examined in this chapter:

■ The public telephone network

■ The Internet

In this chapter, you will learn about the following:

■ What transmission media are

■ Common transmission media and their characteristics

■ Public network services that provide wide-area networking support

Network Transmission Media

Transmission media make it possible for the electronic signals in one computer to be transmitted to another computer. These electronic signals express data values in the form of binary (on-off) impulses. The signals are transmitted through the network using a combination of electronic devices (network boards, hubs, and so on) and transmission media (cables, radio, and so on) until they reach the desired destination computer where they again are converted into data signals inside the receiving computer.

All signals transmitted between computers consist of some form of *electromagnetic* (EM) waveform, ranging from radio frequencies, up through microwave, and infrared light. Depending on the frequency of the EM waveform being used, different media are used to transmit the signals. Figure 19.1 illustrates the range of electromagnetic waveforms, known as the *electromagnetic spectrum*, along with their associated frequencies.

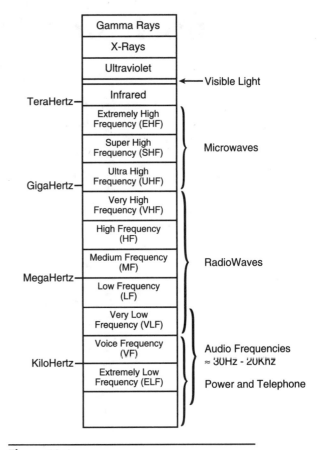

Figure 19.1

The electromagnetic spectrum.

Radio frequency waves are often used for LAN signaling. Radio frequencies can be transmitted using electrical cables (twisted-pair or coaxial) or using radio broadcast transmission.

Microwave transmissions can be used for tightly focused transmissions between two points. Microwaves are used to communicate between Earth stations and satellites. They also are used for line-of-sight transmissions on the Earth's surface. Microwaves also can be used in low-power forms to broadcast signals from a transmitter to many receivers. Cellular phone networks are examples of systems that use low-power microwave signals to broadcast signals.

Infrared light is ideal for many types of network communications. Infrared light can be transmitted relatively short distances and can either be beamed between two points or broadcast from one point to many receivers. Infrared and higher frequencies of light also can be transmitted through fiber-optic cables.

The next sections examine examples of network transmission media, and describe the advantages and disadvantages of each media type.

Characteristics of Transmission Media

Each media type has special characteristics that suit it to a specific type of service. You should be familiar with these characteristics:

- Cost

- Installation requirements

- Bandwidth

- Attenuation

- Immunity from electromagnetic interference

The last three characteristics require some explanation.

Bandwidth

Bandwidth is the measure of the capacity of a medium to transmit data. A medium that has a high capacity has a high bandwidth. A medium that has limited capacity has a low bandwidth. The term bandwidth comes about because it is a measure of the range of frequencies that the medium can carry.

Bandwidth can be understood through an analogy to water hoses. A half-inch garden hose that can carry waterflow from a trickle up to 2 gallons per minute might be said to have a bandwidth of 2 gallons per minute. A 4-inch firehose, however, might have a bandwidth of over 100 gallons per minute.

Transmission media have a lower frequency limit and an upper frequency limit. Frequencies are measured in *Hertz* (Hz), or cycles per second. The bandwidth of a voice telephone line is 400–4,000 Hz, meaning that the line can transmit signals with frequencies ranging from 400–4,000 cycles per second.

Data transmission rates frequently are stated in terms of the bits that can be transmitted per second. An Ethernet LAN theoretically can transmit 10 million bits per second and has a bandwidth of 10 megabits per second (Mbps).

The bandwidth that a cable can accommodate is determined in part by the cable's length. A short cable can generally accommodate greater bandwidth than a longer cable. This is one reason all cable designs specify maximum lengths for cable runs. Beyond those limits, the highest frequency signals can deteriorate and errors might be introduced into data signals.

Attenuation

Attenuation is a measure of how much a signal weakens as it travels through a medium. This course does not discuss attenuation in formal terms, but with regard to the impact of attenuation on performance.

Attenuation is a second reason cable designs must specify limits in the lengths of cable runs. When signal strength falls below certain limits, it might be difficult for the electronic equipment that receives the signal to isolate the original signal from the noise that is present in all electronic transmissions. The effect is exactly like trying to tune in distant radio signals. Even if you are able to lock into the signal on your radio, the sound produced generally contains more noise than the sound produced for a local radio station.

Electromagnetic Interference

Electromagnetic interference (EMI) consists of outside electromagnetic noise that distorts the signal in a medium. When you listen to an AM radio, you often hear noise caused by nearby motors or lightning. This is an example of EMI. Some network media are more susceptible to EMI than others.

Cable Media

Three types of cable media are discussed in this section:

■ Coaxial

■ Twisted-pair

■ Fiber-optic

Coaxial Cable

Coaxial cables were the first cable types used in LANs. Shown in figure 19.2, coaxial cable gets its name because two conductors share a common axis; the cable is most frequently referred to as *coax*. The components of a coaxial cable are as follows:

■ A center conductor, which is usually solid copper wire (although stranded wire can be used)

■ An outer conductor that forms a tube surrounding the center conductor. This conductor can consist of braided wires, metallic foil, or both. Because this conductor also protects the inner conductor from EMI, it is most frequently called the *shield*.

■ An insulation layer that also keeps the outer conductor spaced evenly from the inner conductor

■ A plastic encasement (jacket) that protects the cable from damage

Types of Coaxial Cable

All coax cables have a characteristic measurement called *impedance*, which is given in ohms. It is important to use a cable with the proper impedance in any given situation. Here are some types of coaxial cable frequently used on LANs:

■ RG-8 and RG-ll, 50-ohm cables used with thick Ethernet

■ RG-58, a 50-ohm cable used with thin Ethernet

■ RG-59, a 75-ohm cable used for cable TV

■ RG-62, a 93-ohm cable used with ARCnet

Figure 19.2
The structure of coaxial cable.

Characteristics

You will want to be familiar with the following characteristics of coaxial cable.

Installation

Coaxial cable typically is installed in two configurations: daisy-chained from device to device (Ethernet) and stars (ARCnet). Both are shown in figure 19.3.

You will learn the details of Ethernet cabling in Chapter 20, "Transmission Media Connections."

The Ethernet cabling shown in the figure is an example of thin Ethernet, which uses RG-58 type cable. Devices connect to the cable by means of T-connectors. Cables are used to provide connections between T-connectors. One characteristic of this type of cabling is that the ends of the cable run

Figure 19.3
Coaxial cable wiring configurations.

must be terminated by a special connector called a terminator. The *terminator* contains a resistor that is matched to the characteristics of the cable. The resistor prevents signals that reach the end of the cable from bouncing back and causing interference.

Coaxial cable is reasonably easy to install. The cable is robust and difficult to damage, and connectors can be installed with inexpensive tools and a bit of practice. The device-to-device cabling approach can be difficult to reconfigure, however, when new devices cannot be installed near an existing cabling path.

Cost

The coaxial cable used for thin Ethernet falls at the low end of the cost spectrum, whereas thick Ethernet is among the more costly options. Detailed cost comparisons are made after the remaining cable types have been introduced.

Bandwidth

LANs that employ coaxial cable typically have a bandwidth ranging from 2.5 Mbps (ARCnet) to 10 Mbps (Ethernet). Thicker coaxial cables have higher bandwidth, and the potential bandwidth of coax is much higher than 10 Mbps. This potential, however, is not taken advantage of by current LAN technologies.

Attenuation

All media suffer from attenuation, but coax has better attenuation characteristics than other copper cables such as twisted-pair. LANs employing co-axial cable are limited to a few thousand meters in length.

EMI Characteristics

All copper media are sensitive to EMI, although the shield in coax makes the cable fairly resistant to EMI. Coaxial cables, however, do radiate a portion of their signal, and this radiated signal can be detected by electronic eavesdropping equipment.

Twisted-Pair Cables

Twisted-pair cable has become the dominant cable type for all new network designs that employ copper cable. Several reasons account for the popularity of twisted-pair cable, with the most significant being low cost. Twisted-pair cable is inexpensive to install and has the lowest cost-per-foot of any cable type.

Figure 19.4 shows a basic twisted-pair cable, which consists of two strands of copper wire twisted together. The twists are an important part of the characteristics of twisted-pair cable. Twisting reduces the sensitivity of the cable to EMI and also reduces the tendency of the cable to radiate radio frequency noise that interferes with nearby cables and electronic components. The radiated signals from the twisted wires tend to cancel each other out. (Antennas, which are purposely designed to radiate radio-frequency signals, consist of parallel, not twisted, wires.)

Figure 19.4
A twisted-pair cable.

Insulating
Jackets

Conductors

Twisting also controls the tendency of the wires in the pair to cause EMI in each other. Whenever two wires are in close proximity, there is a tendency for the signals in each wire to produce noise in the other. Noise caused in this way is called *crosstalk*. Twisting the wires in the pair reduces crosstalk in much the same way that twisting reduces the tendency of the wires to radiate EMI.

Two types of twisted-pair cable are used in LANs: shielded and unshielded.

Shielded Twisted-Pair (STP) Cable

The first twisted-pair cables used in LANs were shielded twisted-pair, similar to the cable shown in figure 19.5, which shows IBM Type 1 cable, the first cable type used with IBM Token Ring. Early LAN designers employed shielded twisted-pair cable because the shield further reduces the tendency of the cable to radiate EMI and reduces the cable's sensitivity to outside interference.

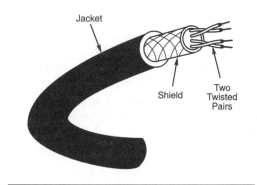

Figure 19.5
A shielded twisted-pair cable.

Coaxial and STP cables use shields for the same purpose. The *shield* is connected to the ground portion of the electronic device to which the cable is connected. A *ground* is a portion of the device, serves

as an electrical reference point, and usually is literally connected to a metal stake that is driven into the ground. A properly grounded shield tends to prevent signals from getting into or out of the cable.

The IBM Type 1 cable shown in figure 19.5 includes two twisted-pairs of wire within a single shield. Various types of STP cable exist, with some shielding each pair individually and others shielding several pairs. The exact configuration used is chosen by the engineers who design the cabling system. IBM designates several twisted-pair cable types for use with their Token-Ring network design, and each cable type is appropriate for a given kind of installation. A completely different type of STP is the standard cable for Apple's AppleTalk network.

Because so many different types of STP cable exist, it is difficult to state precise characteristics. Here, however, are some general guidelines.

Cost

STP cable costs more than thin coaxial or unshielded twisted-pair cables. STP is less costly, however, than thick coax or fiber-optic cable.

Installation

Different network types have different installation requirements. One major difference is the connector used. Apple LocalTalk connectors generally must be soldered during installation, requiring some practice and skill on the part of the installer. IBM Token Ring uses a so-called *unisex* data connector (the connectors are both male and female), which can be installed with common tools such as a knife, wire stripper, and a large pliers.

In many cases, installation can be greatly simplified by using pre-wired cables. You need to learn to install the required connectors, however, whenever your installation requires use of bulk cable.

Most connectors require two connector types to complete a connection. The traditional designation for connector types is male and female. The male connector is the connector with pins, and the female connector has receptacles into which the pins insert. In a standard AC wall outlet, the outlet itself is female and the plug on the line cord is male.

These designations originated when electrical installation was a male province, and the terms male and female gradually are being replaced. A commonly used alternative is "pins and sockets."

The IBM data connector is called a unisex connector because the connector has both pins and sockets. Any IBM data connector can connect to any other IBM data connector.

STP cable tends to be rather bulky. IBM Type 1 cable is approximately $1^{1}/_{2}$ inches in diameter. Therefore, it can take little time to fill up cable paths with STP cables.

Capacity

STP cable has a theoretical capacity of 500 Mbps, although few implementations exceed 155 Mbps with 100-meter cable runs. The most common data rate for STP cable is 16 Mbps, the top data rate for token-ring networks.

Attenuation

All varieties of twisted-pair cable have attenuation characteristics that limit the length of cable runs to a few hundred meters, although a 100-meter limit is most common.

EMI Characteristics

The shield in STP cable results in good EMI characteristics for copper cable, comparable to the EMI characteristics of coaxial cable. This is one reason STP might be preferred to unshielded

twisted-pair cable in some situations. Like all copper cables, STP is sensitive to interference and is vulnerable to electronic eavesdropping.

Unshielded Twisted-Pair Cable

Unshielded twisted-pair (UTP) cable does not incorporate a braided shield. The characteristics of UTP are similar in many ways to STP, differing primarily in attenuation and EMI characteristics. As shown in figure 19.6, several twisted pairs can be bundled together in a single cable. These pairs are typically color coded to distinguish the pairs.

Figure 19.6
A multi-pair UTP cable.

UTP cable is a latecomer to high-performance LANs because engineers only recently solved the problems of managing radiated noise and susceptibility to EMI. Now, however, a clear trend toward UTP is in operation, and all new copper-based cabling schemes are based on use of UTP.

UTP cable is available in the following five grades or categories:

- Categories 1 and 2 are voice-grade cables, suitable only for voice and for low data rates (below 4 Mbps). At one time, Category 1 was the standard voice-grade cable for telephone systems. The growing need for data-ready cabling systems, however, has caused Category 1 and 2 cable to be supplanted by Category 3 for new installations.

■ Category 3 is the lowest data grade cable and is generally suited for data rates up to 16 Mbps. Some innovative schemes, however, make it possible to support data rates up to 100 Mbps with Category 3 cable. Category 3 is now the standard cable used for most telephone installations.

■ Category 4 is a data-grade cable suitable for data rates up to 20 Mbps.

■ Category 5 is a data-grade cable suitable for data rates up to 100 Mbps. Most new cabling systems for 100 Mbps data rates are designed around Category 5 cable.

 In a UTP cabling system, the cable is only one component. All connecting devices also are graded, and the overall cabling system only supports the data rates permitted by the lowest grade of component in the system. In other words, if you require a Category 5 cabling system, it is essential to ensure that all connectors and connecting devices are designed for Category 5 operation.

Category 5 cable also requires more stringent installation procedures than the lower cable categories. Installers of Category 5 cable require special training and skills to understand these more rigorous requirements.

UTP cable offers an excellent balance of cost and performance characteristics.

Cost

UTP cable has the lowest cost of any cable type, although properly installed Category 5 tends to be fairly high in cost. In some cases, existing cable in buildings can be used for LANs, although it is important to verify the category of the cable and

also to know the length of the cable in the walls. Distance limits for voice cabling are much less stringent than for data-grade cabling.

Installation

UTP cable is easy to install. Some specialized equipment might be required, but the equipment is low in cost and can be mastered with a bit of practice. Properly designed UTP cabling systems easily can be reconfigured to meet changing requirements.

As noted earlier, however, Category 5 cable has stricter installation requirements than lower categories of UTP. Special training is recommended.

Capacity

The data rates possible with UTP have pushed upward from 1 Mbps, past 4 and 16 Mbps, and to the point where 100 Mbps data rates are now common. In fact, all new copper-based standards provide at least the option of using UTP cable.

Attenuation

UTP cable shares similar attenuation characteristics with other copper cables. UTP cable runs are limited to a few hundred meters, with 100 meters the most frequent limit.

EMI Characteristics

Lacking a shield, UTP cable is more sensitive to EMI than coaxial or STP cables. The latest technologies make it possible to use UTP in the vast majority of situations, provided reasonable care is taken to avoid electrically noisy devices such as motors and fluorescent lights. Nevertheless, UTP might not be suitable for noisy environments such as factories. Crosstalk between nearby unshielded pairs limits the maximum length of cable runs.

Fiber-Optic Cable

In almost every way, fiber-optic cable is the ideal cable for data transmission. Bandwidths are extremely high, there are no problems with EMI, cables are durable, and cable runs can be several kilometers long. The two disadvantages of fiber optic are cost and more difficult installation.

Figure 19.7 shows two types of fiber-optic cable. In each case, the center conductor is a fiber consisting of highly refined glass or plastic designed to transmit light signals with little loss. The fiber is coated with a cladding that reflects signals back into the fiber to reduce signal loss. A plastic sheath protects the fiber.

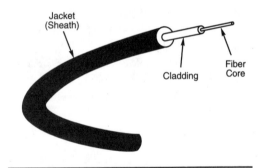

Figure 19.7
A fiber-optic cable.

Loose and tight cable configurations are available. Loose configurations incorporate a space between the fiber sheath and the outer plastic encasement; this space is filled with a gel or other material. Tight configurations include strength wires between the conductor and the outer plastic encasement. In both cases, it is the job of the plastic encasement to supply the strength of the cable. The gel layer or strength wires protect the delicate fiber from mechanical damage.

Although the figure shows cables with single fibers, it is common to bundle multiple fibers into cables. A small-diameter cable can incorporate an astonishing number of optical fibers, making fiber-optic cable ideal for cabling when cable paths are clogged.

Optical fiber cables do not transmit electrical signals. Instead, the data signals must be converted to light signals. Light sources include lasers and *light-emitting diodes* (LEDs). LEDs are inexpensive, but produce a fairly poor quality of light that is suitable for less-stringent applications.

A laser is a light source that produces an especially pure light that is monochromatic (one color) and coherent (all waves are parallel). The most commonly used source of laser light in LAN devices is called an *injection laser diode* (ILD). The purity of laser light makes lasers ideally suited to data transmissions because long distances and high bandwidths are possible. Lasers, however, are expensive light sources and are used only when their special characteristics are required.

The end of the cable that receives the light signal must convert the signal back to an electrical form. Several types of solid-state components can perform this service. The most common are types of photodiodes.

Optical fibers have several characteristics:

■ **Mode.** Single-mode cables support a single light path and are commonly used with lasers. Multi-mode cables support multiple light paths and are best suited to lower-quality light sources such as LEDs. At a much higher cost, single-mode cables with laser light sources support the longest cable runs and the greatest bandwidth. Figure 19.8 illustrates the difference between single- and multi-mode cables.

■ **Core diameter.** The cores of fiber-optic cables are small enough to be measured in microns (millionths of a meter). The symbol for micron is μ.

■ **Cladding diameter.** This dimension also is given in microns.

Figure 19.8
Modes of fiber-optic cables.

The following are common types of fiber-optic cables:

■ 8.3 micron core/125 micron cladding/ single-mode

■ 62.5 micron core/125 micron cladding/ multi-mode

■ 50 micron core/125 micron cladding/ multi-mode

■ 100 micron core/140 micron cladding/ multi-mode

Note the small core diameters of these cables. One of the significant difficulties of installing fiber-optic cable arises when two cables must be joined. The small cores of the two cables must be lined up with extreme precision to prevent excessive signal loss.

Fiber-Optic Characteristics

Like all cable types, fiber-optic cables constitute a blend of advantages and disadvantages.

Cost

The cost of the cable and connectors has fallen significantly in recent years. The electronic devices required are significantly more expensive than comparable devices for copper cable. An Ethernet network board for UTP cable now can cost less than $100. Network boards for use with fiber-optic cables, however, frequently cost in excess of $1,000 each. Fiber-optic cable is also the most expensive cable type to install.

Installation

Greater skill is required to install fiber-optic cable than is needed for most copper cables. Improved tools and techniques, however, have reduced the training required. Still, greater care is required because fiber-optic cables must be treated fairly gently during installation. Every cable has a minimum bend radius, for example, and fibers are damaged if the cables are bent too sharply. It also is important not to stretch the cable during installation.

Capacity

Bandwidths for fiber-optic cables can range as high as 2 Gbps (billion bps). Fiber-optic cable can support high data rates even with long cable runs. UTP cable runs are limited to less than 100 meters with 100 Mbps data rates. Fiber-optic cables can transmit 100 Mbps signals for several kilometers.

Attenuation

Attenuation in fiber-optic cables is much lower than in copper cables. Fiber-optic cables are capable of carrying signals for several kilometers.

EMI Characteristics

Because fiber-optic cables do not use electrical signals to transmit data, they are totally immune to electromagnetic interference. They also are immune to a variety of electrical effects that must be taken into account when designing copper cabling systems.

When electrical cables are connected between two buildings, a common problem to be dealt with is differences between the ground potentials (voltages) between the two buildings. When a difference exists (as it frequently does), current flows through the grounding conductor of the cable, even though the ground is supposed to be electrically neutral and no current should flow. When current flows through the ground conductor of a cable, the condition is called a *ground loop*. The results of ground loops are electrical instability and various types of anomalies.

Because fiber-optic cable is immune to electrical effects, the best way to connect networks in different buildings is by putting in a fiber-optic link segment.

Because they are not electrical in nature, the signals in fiber-optic cables cannot be detected by electronic eavesdropping equipment that detect electromagnetic radiation. Fiber-optic cable is, therefore, the perfect choice for high-security networks.

Summary of Cable Characteristics

Table 19.1 summarizes the characteristics of the four cable types discussed in this chapter.

Table 19.1
Comparison of Cable Media

Cable Type	Cost	Installation	Capacity	Attenuation	EMI
Coaxial	Medium < Cat 5 UTP > Cat 3 UTP Thin<STP Thick>STP <Fiber	Inexpensive/ Easy. May be difficult to reconfigure	10 Mbps typical	Less than STP or UTP. Limited to range of few kilometers	Less sensitive than UTP, but still subject to EMI and eavesdropping
Shielded Twisted-Pair	Medium >UTP =Thin coax <Thick coax <Fiber	Moderate cost/ Fairly easy. More difficult than UTP and coax	16 Mbps typical. Up to 500 Mbps	Limits range to several hundred meters	Less sensitive than UTP, but still subject to EMI and eavesdropping
Unshielded Twisted-Pair	Lowest	Inexpensive/ Easy	1-100 Mbps with 100-meter runs	Limits range to several hundred meters	Most sensitive to EMI and eavesdropping
Fiber-Optic	Highest	Expensive/ Difficult	10 Mbps to 2 Gbps. 100 Mbps typical	Lowest. Range of 10s of kilometers	Insensitive to EMI and eavesdropping

When comparing cabling types, it's important to remember that the characteristics you observe are highly dependent on the implementations. At one time, it was argued that UTP cable would never reliably support data rates above 4 Mbps, but 100 Mbps data rates are now commonplace with UTP.

Some comparisons are fairly involved. Although fiber-optic cable is costly on a per-foot basis, it is possible to construct a fiber-optic cable that is many kilometers in length. To build a copper cable that length, you would need to install repeaters at several points along the cable to amplify the signal. These repeaters could easily exceed the cost of a fiber-optic cable run.

Wireless Media

Cable lends itself to fixed installations and moderate distances. When end points are widely separated or when they are moving, it might be desirable to investigate wireless media. Several wireless media are available, of which the following will be considered:

- Radio

- Microwave

- Infrared

Radio

The radio portion of the electromagnetic spectrum extends from 10 KHz to 1 GHz. Within this range are numerous bands, or ranges of frequencies that are designated for specific purposes. The following are frequency bands with which you are probably familiar:

- Shortwave

- VHF (Very High Frequency): television and FM radio

- UHF (Ultra High Frequency): television

Within the United States, the use of radio frequencies is controlled by the Federal Communications Commission (FCC). The majority of frequency allocations are licensed; an organization is granted an exclusive license to use a particular range of frequencies within a certain limited geographic area. Thus, there only can be one television Channel 5 within an area. Channel 5 allocations are spread out so that they do not interfere with each other. A licensed frequency allocation guarantees the license owner a clear, low-interference communication channel.

A few frequency ranges are unlicensed, meaning that they can be used freely for the purpose specified for those frequencies. The FCC has designated three unlicensed frequency bands: 902–928 MHz, 2.4 GHz, and 5.72–5.85 GHz. The 902 MHz range has been available the longest and has been used for everything from cordless telephones to model airplane remote control. Because the 902 MHz range is quite crowded, many vendors are pushing development of devices for the less crowded 2.4 GHz band. Equipment for the 5.72 GHz remains expensive and is used infrequently.

Use of an unlicensed frequency is done at the user's risk, and a clear communication channel is not guaranteed. Equipment used in these frequency bands, however, must operate at a regulated power level to limit range and reduce the potential for interference.

Radio transmissions can be omnidirectional or directional. A radio station typically transmits an omnidirectional (all-directional) signal that can be received by all radios within the broadcast area. In some circumstances, a directional transmission might be used to direct all of the transmission power toward a specific reception point.

Various types of antennas are used depending on the desired transmission and reception characteristics. Several antenna types are shown in figure 19.9.

■ Broadcast towers generally are omnidirectional, although the specific radiation pattern can be adjusted to match the FCC restrictions for a particular licensee.

■ Dipole antennas receive a fairly broad range of frequencies and are moderately directional.

■ A random-length wire can be used for transmission or reception. *Random-length* means that the antenna length is not specifically chosen for the frequency being transmitted or received. The antenna on a typical AM/FM radio is a random-length wire.

■ A beam antenna uses multiple elements to tune the antenna for a specific frequency range and directiveness. A common antenna design is called the *Yagi*. A beam antenna is used to produce a fairly focused beam that can be aimed at a specific reception point (although the effect is not completely directional, and some signal leaks in all directions).

Characteristics of Radio Transmission

The characteristics of radio transmissions change dramatically with frequency. Low-frequency radio supports limited data rates, but has a significant advantage in that it can frequently communicate past the horizon. Shortwave operators are familiar with this phenomenon, and it is common for them to be able to monitor transmissions from the other side of the Earth.

As frequency increases, transmissions become increasingly line-of-site. AM radio broadcast frequencies range from the KHz to the low MHz range. You might have had the experience of picking up an AM radio station that is several states away, particularly late at night. This can occur because AM radio transmissions can bounce off some phenomena in the atmosphere. Some transmissions can bounce a considerable distance.

FM transmissions, however, seldom can be received past the horizon. You will seldom clearly receive an FM broadcast beyond a range of 100 miles. This is partly a function of power, but the primary cause of the range limitation is the inability of FM frequencies to go beyond the horizon.

Figure 19.9

Representative antenna types.

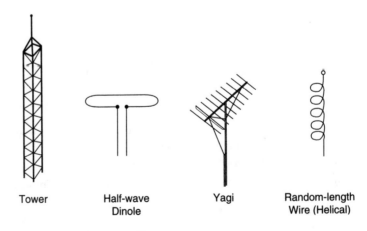

Tower   Half-wave Dinole   Yagi   Random-length Wire (Helical)

On a line-of-sight basis, however, high-frequency transmissions attenuate less rapidly than low-frequency transmissions.

Lower-frequency radio waves can penetrate solid materials to a greater degree than higher frequencies. Very low radio frequencies can be used to communicate with submerged submarines, although the data rates are extremely slow. Penetration capability is also a function of power. Higher-power transmissions penetrate building walls more effectively than lower-power transmissions.

As you can see, designing a radio system to have the ideal characteristics for an application requires a lot of design tradeoffs.

Three classes of radio frequency transmission are discussed in this chapter:

- Low-power, single frequency
- High-power, single frequency
- Spread spectrum

Low-Power, Single-Frequency Radio

Low-power systems are chosen to limit the interference between nearby radio systems. Transmission ranges might be as short as 20 to 30 meters. This approach resembles cellular telephone technology, which divides geographic areas into isolated, low-power cells, enabling frequencies to be reused in nearby cells.

Although low-frequency radio can penetrate building walls, the low power used with this radio class typically requires transmitters and receivers to have a line-of-sight path. The data rates possible with low-frequency radio do not support the data rates required for LANs.

It is theoretically possible to implement mobile stations with this radio class, although walls and low power limit the mobility that is possible.

Frequency Range

Any radio frequency can be used, but higher frequencies, typically in the GHz, generally are chosen to support higher data rates.

Cost

Cost depends on design, but can be low compared to other wireless media. As with most media, higher data rates come at a higher cost.

Ease of Installation

This characteristic is also dependent on design. Some single-frequency systems use licensed frequencies, and a license application must be filed with the FCC. In at least one case, however, a prominent vendor has obtained licenses in many major markets and handles the FCC paperwork for the customer.

Some single-frequency systems use unlicensed frequencies. Some troubleshooting might be needed to prevent interference from other nearby devices that use the same frequencies.

Capacity

Although the theoretical bandwidth of radio LANs is high, currently available products range from 1 to 10 Mbps.

Attenuation

Attenuation is high due to the low power levels used, but proper design turns this into an advantage by creating large numbers of independent areas that do not interfere with each other.

EMI Characteristics

EMI resistance is low, particularly in the 902 MHz band that is shared with other unlicensed devices. All radio LANs are vulnerable to electronic eavesdropping, although the low powers used typically reduce the range at which eavesdropping can occur to the confines of the building in which the LAN is housed.

High-Power Single-Frequency Radio

High-power radio has data capacity similar to low-power radio, but it can cover much larger areas. Transmissions can be line-of-sight or can be extended by bouncing signals off the atmosphere. Because power can be higher, this approach can result in practical mobile networking and can service stations on motor or marine vehicles.

Frequency Range

As with low-power radio, any part of the radio spectrum can be used. Frequencies in the GHz range are generally chosen to achieve high data rates.

Cost

High-power transmission equipment is considerably more expensive. Signal repeaters might be needed to extend the coverage area. Costs for high-power radio can be moderate to high.

Ease of Installation

High-power radio equipment must be operated under an FCC license by licensed personnel. Equipment must be maintained in proper order to remain within the terms of the license. Improperly installed and maintained equipment might function poorly and interfere with nearby radio services.

Bandwidth

Capacity can be high but typically falls between 1 and 10 Mbps.

Attenuation

Attenuation rates for high-power radio are fairly low. Signal repeaters can be employed to extend transmission range.

EMI Characteristics

Immunity to EMI is low, and the potential for eavesdropping is high. Signals might be easily intercepted anywhere within the broadcast area.

Spread Spectrum Radio

Spread spectrum is a technique originally developed by the military to solve several communication problems. Spread spectrum improves reliability, reduces sensitivity to interference and jamming, and is less vulnerable to eavesdropping than single-frequency radio.

Spread spectrum transmission uses multiple frequencies to transmit messages. Two techniques employed are direct sequence modulation and frequency hopping.

Direct sequence modulation breaks original messages into parts called *chips* (see fig. 19.10), which are transmitted on separate frequencies. To confuse eavesdroppers, decoy data also can be transmitted on other frequencies. The intended receiver knows which frequencies are valid, and can isolate the chips and reassemble the message. Eavesdropping is difficult because the correct frequencies are not known, and the eavesdropper cannot isolate the frequencies carrying true data. This technique can operate in environments with other transmission activity since different sets of frequencies can be selected. Direct sequence modulation systems operating at 900 MHz support bandwidths of 2–6 Mbps.

Figure 19.10
Direct sequence modulation.

Frequency hopping switches transmissions among several available frequencies. (See fig. 19.11.) Transmitter and receiver must remain synchronized for this technique to work. Some systems transmit on multiple frequencies simultaneously to increase bandwidth.

Frequency Range

Spread spectrum systems typically operate in unlicensed frequency ranges. 900 MHz devices are common, but 2.4 GHz devices are becoming available.

Costs

Costs are moderate compared to other wireless media.

Ease of Installation

This depends on the system design and the frequencies used. Installation complexity ranges from simple to somewhat complex.

Capacity

All 900 MHz systems support bandwidth capacities of 2–6 MHz. Newer systems operating in GHz frequencies can be expected to offer higher data rates.

Attenuation

This is determined by the frequency and power of the transmitted signals. Spread spectrum LANs typically operate at low power and exhibit high attenuation characteristics.

Figure 19.11
Frequency hopping.

Frequency A

Frequency B

Frequency C

Data to transmit

1 1 1 0 0 0 1 1 0 0 1 0

EMI Characteristics

Although individual frequencies are susceptible to EMI, the system can seek out clear frequencies on which to transmit. Overall resistance to EMI is, therefore, fairly high. Resistance to eavesdropping is high for the reasons cited earlier.

Microwave

As shown in figure 19.12, microwave communication can take two forms: terrestrial (ground links) and satellite links. The frequencies and technologies employed by these two forms are similar, but distinct differences exist between them.

Terrestrial Microwave

Terrestrial microwave communication employs Earth-based transmitters and receivers. The frequencies used are in the low-gigahertz range, limiting all communications to line-of-sight. You have probably seen terrestrial microwave equipment in the form of telephone relay towers, which are placed every few miles to relay telephone signals cross country.

Microwave transmissions are typically made using a parabolic antenna that produces a narrow, highly directional signal. A similar antenna at the receiving site is sensitive to signals only within a narrow focus. Since both the transmitter and receiver are highly focused, they must be carefully adjusted so that the transmitted signal is aligned with the receiver.

Microwave is frequently used as a means of transmitting signals where it would be impractical to run cables. If you need to connect two networks that are separated by a public road, you might find that you are not permitted to run cables above or below the road. In such a case, a microwave link is an ideal solution.

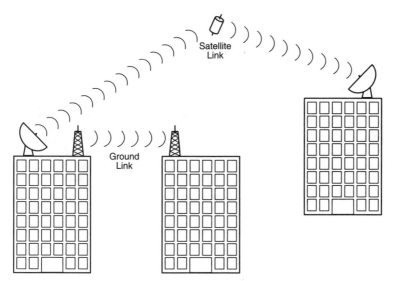

Figure 19.12
Terrestrial and satellite microwave links.

Some LANs operate at microwave frequencies, operate at low power, and use non-directional transmitters and receivers. Network hubs can be placed strategically throughout an organization, and workstations can be mobile or fixed. This approach is one way of enabling workstations to be mobile in an office setting.

In many cases, terrestrial microwave uses licensed frequencies. A license must be obtained from the FCC, and equipment must be installed and maintained by licensed technicians.

Frequency Range

Terrestrial microwave systems operate in the low-gigahertz range, typically at 4–6 GHz and 21–23 GHz.

Cost

Costs are highly variable depending on requirements.

Long-distance microwave systems can be quite expensive, but might be less costly than alternatives. A leased telephone circuit represents a costly monthly expense. When line-of-sight transmission is possible, a microwave link is a one-time expense that can offer greater bandwidth than a leased circuit.

Costs are decreasing for low-power microwave systems for the office. Although these systems do not compete directly in cost with cabled networks, when equipment must be frequently moved, microwave can be a cost-effective technology.

Installation

Licensing usually is required. Many equipment providers take care of licensing along with installation. Installation is a skilled operation generally requiring licensed technicians. Setup of transmitter and receiver sites can be difficult because antennas must be precisely aligned.

The requirement for a line-of-sight communication path might require purchase of access to suitable transmitter sites.

Bandwidth

Capacity can be extremely high, but most data communication systems operate at data rates between 1 and 10 Mbps.

Attenuation

Attenuation characteristics are determined by transmitter power, frequency, and antenna size. Properly designed systems are not affected by attenuation under normal operational conditions. Rain and fog, however, can cause attenuation of higher frequencies.

EMI Characteristics

Microwave systems are highly susceptible to atmospheric interference. They also might be vulnerable to electronic eavesdropping, and signals transmitted through microwave are frequently encrypted.

Satellite Microwave

Satellite microwave systems relay transmissions through communication satellites that operate in geosynchronous orbits 22,300 miles above the Earth. Satellites orbiting at this distance remain located above a fixed point on the Earth.

Earth stations use parabolic antennas (satellite dishes) to communicate with the satellites. Satellites can retransmit signals in broad or in narrow beams depending on which locations are to receive the signals. When the destination is on the opposite side of the Earth, the first satellite cannot transmit directly to the receiver and must relay the signal through another satellite.

Because no cables are required, satellite microwave communication is possible with most remote sites and with mobile devices, including ships at sea and motor vehicles.

The distances involved in satellite communication result in an interesting phenomenon: Because all signals must travel 22,300 miles to the satellite and 22,300 miles when returning to a receiver, the time required to transmit a signal is independent of distance. It takes as long to transmit a signal to a receiver in the same state as it does to a receiver a third of the way around the world. The time required for a signal to arrive at its destination is called *propagation delay*. The delays encountered with satellite transmissions range from 0.5 to 5 seconds.

Unfortunately, satellite communication is extremely expensive. Building and launching a satellite easily can cost in excess of a billion dollars. In most cases, organizations share these costs, or they purchase services from a commercial provider. AT&T, Hughes Network Services, and Scientific-Atlanta are among the firms that sell satellite-based communication services.

Frequency Range

Satellite links operate in the low-gigahertz range, typically at 11–14 MHz.

Cost

Costs are extremely high and are usually amortized across many users by selling communication services.

Ease of Installation

Earth stations can be installed by numerous commercial providers. Transmitters operate on licensed frequencies and require an FCC license.

Bandwidth

Bandwidth is related to cost, and firms can purchase almost any required bandwidth. Typical data rates are 1–10 Mbps.

Attenuation

Attenuation characteristics depend on frequency, power, and atmospheric conditions. Properly designed systems take attenuation into account. Rain and atmospheric conditions might attenuate higher frequencies.

EMI Characteristics

Microwave signals are sensitive to EMI and electronic eavesdropping. Signals transmitted through microwave frequently are encrypted.

Infrared Systems

You use an infrared communication system every time you control your television with a remote control. The remote control transmits pulses of infrared light that carry coded instructions to a receiver on the TV. This technology can be adapted to network communication.

Two methods of infrared networking are in use: point-to-point and broadcast.

Point-to-Point Infrared

Point-to-point networks operate by relaying infrared signals from one device to the next. An example of an infrared LAN is shown in figure 19.13. Transmissions are focused in a narrow beam, and the transmitter and receiver must be aligned carefully. Because the devices must be carefully placed and set up, point-to-point infrared is not suitable for use with devices that move frequently.

High-powered laser transmitters can be used to transmit data for several thousand yards when line-of-sight communication is possible. Lasers can be used in many of the same situations as microwave links, without the requirement of an FCC license. Consider infrared lasers for connections between buildings, particularly when they are separated by public rights of way.

Frequency Range

Infrared light falls in a range below visible light and has a frequency range of approximately 100 GHz to 1,000 THz.

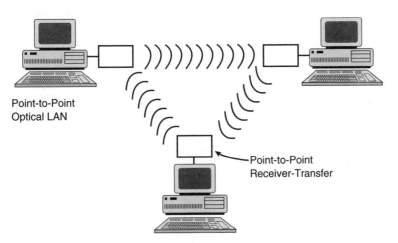

Figure 19.13
Point-to-point infrared networking.

Point-to-Point Optical LAN

Point-to-Point Receiver-Transfer

Cost

The cost of point-to-point infrared equipment is higher than the cost for a comparable cabled network. Most systems use transmitters based on LED technology, and the hardware cost is moderate. Long-distance systems use high-powered laser transmitters, which can be quite costly.

Ease of Installation

Installation requires careful alignment of the transmitters and receivers. Lasers used in high-powered transmitters can be hazardous and can burn or damage eyes.

Bandwidth

Bandwidth ranges from about 100 Kbps to 16 Mbps.

Attenuation

Attenuation characteristics are determined by the quality of the transmission, by presence of obstructions, and by atmospheric conditions.

EMI Characteristics

Infrared devices are insensitive to radio-frequency interference but reception can be degraded by bright light. Because transmissions are tightly focused, they are fairly immune to electronic eavesdropping.

Broadcast Infrared

Instead of focusing transmissions in tight beams, broadcast infrared disperses transmissions so that they are visible to several receivers. At least two approaches are possible, as shown in figure 19.14. One approach is to locate an active transmitter at a high point so that it can transmit to all devices.

Another is to place a reflective material on the ceiling; devices transmit toward the ceiling where the light signals are dispersed to other devices in the room.

Frequency Range

Infrared light falls in a range below visible light and has a frequency range of approximately 100 GHz to 1000 THz.

Cost

The cost of point-to-point infrared equipment is higher than the cost for a comparable cabled network. Because lasers produce a tightly focused beam, they are not very suitable to broadcast-type networks.

Ease of Installation

Installation is fairly simple because device alignment is not critical. It is essential that each device has clear transmission and reception pathways. Because these devices are sensitive to light interference, the control of ambient light is a significant installation concern.

Capacity

Typical bandwidths are less than 1 Mbps, although higher bandwidths are theoretically possible.

Attenuation

Attenuation characteristics are determined by the quality of the transmission, by presence of obstructions, and by atmospheric conditions. Typical ranges are limited to tens of meters.

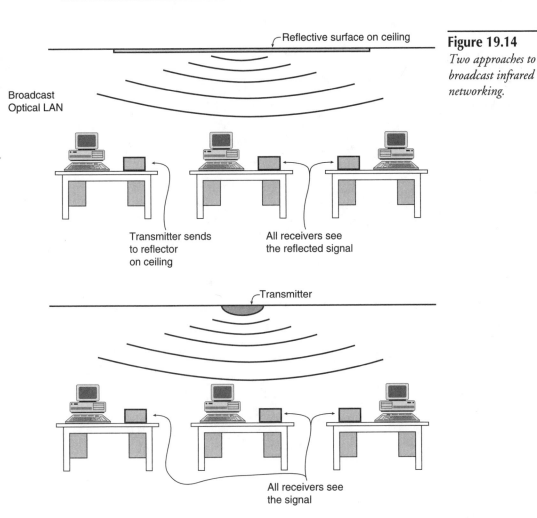

Figure 19.14
Two approaches to broadcast infrared networking.

EMI Characteristics

Infrared devices are insensitive to radio-frequency interference, but reception can be degraded by bright light. Because transmissions are tightly focused, they are fairly immune to electronic eavesdropping.

Summary of Wireless Media

Table 19.2 summarizes the characteristics of the wireless media discussed in this section.

Table 19.2
Comparison of Wireless Media

Media Type	Frequency Range	Cost
Low-power single frequency	All radio frequencies. Frequencies in the low GHz range are most common.	Moderate for wireless but higher than cabled devices
High-power single frequency	All radio frequencies. Frequencies in the low GHz range are most common.	More expensive than low-power
Spread spectrum	All radio frequencies. 902-928 MHz common in the US. 2.4 GHz most common worldwide.	Moderate
Terrestrial microwave	Usually low GHz, with 6 or 21–23 GHz most common.	Moderate to high but cost effective in many situations
Satellite microwave	Low GHz. 11–14 GHz most common.	High
Point-to-point infrared	100 GHz to 1000 THz	Low to moderate
Broadcast infrared	100 GHz to 1000 THz	Low for wireless, higher than cables systems

Public and Private Network Services

Communication must take place between distant points, but few organizations can justify the costs required to construct a private wide area network. Fortunately, a variety of commercial options are available that enable organizations to pay only for the level of service that they require. One option is the public telephone network. Another is to utilize a public network service, of which the Internet is an example.

The Public Telephone Network

Public telephone networks offer two general types of service:

- Switched services, which the customer pays for on a per-use basis

- Leased dedicated services, to which the customer is granted exclusive access

Switched services operate on the *Public Switched Telephone Network* (PSTN), which we know as the telephone system. Voice grade services have evolved

Installation	Capacity	Attenuation	EMI Sensitivity
Low difficulty	Below 1 Mbps to 10 Mbps	High	High EMI sensitivity. Vulnerable to eavesdropping.
High difficulty	Below 1 Mbps to 10 Mbps	Low	High EMI sensitivity. Vulnerable to eavesdropping.
Moderately difficult	2 to 6 Mbps	High	Some EMI sensitivity. Low eavesdropping vulnerability.
Difficult	Below 1 Mbps to 10 Mbps with higher rates possible	Depends on strength and atmospheric conditions	Low EMI sensitivity. Some eavesdropping vulnerability.
Very difficult	Below 1 Mbps to 10 Mbps with higher rates possible	Depends on frequency, signal strength, and atmospheric conditions	Low EMI sensitivity. Moderate eavesdropping vulnerability.
Moderately difficult	Below 1 Mbps to 16 Mbps	Depends on light purity and intensity as well as environmental conditions	Sensitive to intense light. Low eavesdropping vulnerability.
Low difficulty	Up to 1 Mbps	High	Sensitive to intense light. Low eavesdropping vulnerability.

to high levels of sophistication and can be adapted to providing many data services by using devices such as modems. Newer switched options are providing higher levels of service while retaining the advantages of switched access.

On a switched network, subscribers do not have exclusive access to a particular data path. The PSTN maintains large numbers of paths, but not nearly enough to service all customers simultaneously. When a customer requests service, a path is switched in to service the customer's needs. When the customer hangs up, the path is reused for

other customers. In situations when the customer does not need full-time network access, switched service is extremely cost-effective.

In the United States, the following terms are used to describe components of the PSTN (see fig. 19.15):

■ The *demarcation point,* or *demarc,* is the point at which outside wiring enters the customer's premises. The demarc is a specific point in the building at which customer wiring connects to the wiring of the local loop.

■ *Subscriber wiring and equipment* consists of all wiring and equipment on the customer side of the demarc. These items are owned by the customer, and the customer is responsible for operation and maintenance.

■ *Local loops* connect the demarc to a central office. The local loop can consist of unshielded twisted-pair wiring, fiber-optic cable, or a combination of the two.

■ The *central office* (CO) switches connections between customer sites. It also supplies reliable, filtered power for the local loop.

Central offices are interconnected by high capacity trunk lines.

Central offices rely on long-distance carriers to communicate with COs that are outside of the local service area. Long-distance carriers use various combinations of fiber-optic, copper, and microwave media to provide high-capacity long-distance service.

When customers require full-time access to a communication path, one option is a dedicated, leased line. Several levels of service are available. Common options are T-1 (1.544 Mbps) and T-3 (44.736 Mbps). Leased lines enable a customer to lease a specified bandwidth between two specified points.

Many organizations need to communicate among several points. Leasing a line between each pair of

Figure 19.15

Elements of the Public Switched Telephone Service.

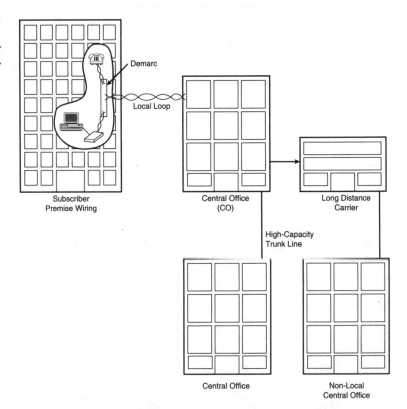

points can prove too costly. Many services now are available that route packets between different sites. Among the services available are X.25, Frame Relay, SONET (Synchronous Optical Network), and ATM. Each of these services has characteristics that suit it to particular uses, and all are available on a leased basis from service providers. An organization that needs to communicate among many sites simply pays to connect each site to the service, and the service takes on the responsibility of routing packets. The expense of operating the network is shared among all of the network subscribers. Because the exact switching process is concealed from the subscriber, these networks are frequently depicted as a communication cloud, as shown in figure 19.16.

Table 19.3 lists common network services and their associated bandwidths.

Table 19.3
Bandwidths of Network Services

Service	Bandwidth
Dedicated 56 KB (DDS)	56 Kbps
Switched 56	56 Kbps
X.25	56 Kbps
T1	1.544 Mbps
Switched T1	1.544 Mbps
Frame Relay	1.544 Mbps
SMDS	1.544 Mbps
ISDN	1.544 Mbps
E1 (Europe)	2.048 Mbps
T3	44.736 Mbps
ATM	≥44.736 Mbps

Figure 19.16
An example of a public network service.

These data rates can be compared to common LAN services such as Ethernet (10 Mbps) and token ring (4–16 Mbps).

The Internet

The Internet is a cooperative venture in which huge numbers of government agencies, educational institutions, and businesses have agreed to provide shared network services. Each organization on the Internet provides some amount of communication and computing capability that is freely shared with other network users. As a result of this cooperation, the Internet has grown to encompass computers in over 100 countries on all continents.

The United States has begun to encourage development of a national information infrastructure, popularly called the Information Superhighway. Research is underway to develop practical methods of establishing high-capacity media (>3 Gbps) with the capability of interconnecting large numbers of public and private networks.

Questions

1. Which of the following cable types supports the greatest cable lengths?

   ○ A. Unshielded twisted-pair

   ○ B. Shielded twisted-pair

   ○ C. Large coaxial cable

   ○ D. Small coaxial cable

2. Which TWO are advantages of UTP cable?

   ☐ A. Low cost

   ☐ B. Easy installation

   ☐ C. High resistance to EMI due to twists in cable

   ☐ D. Cables up to 500 meters

3. Which THREE are advantages of coaxial cable?

   ☐ A. Low cost

   ☐ B. Easy installation

   ☐ C. Good resistance to EMI

   ☐ D. Easy to reconfigure

4. Which TWO are disadvantages of fiber-optic cable?

   ☐ A. Sensitive to EMI

   ☐ B. Expensive hardware

   ☐ C. High installation cost

   ☐ D. Low bandwidth

5. Which of the following THREE cable types should be regarded as mature, well-proven technologies?

   ☐ A. Level 3 UTP

   ☐ B. STP

   ☐ C. Fiber-optic

   ☐ D. Level 5 UTP

6. Which of the following is a true statement?

   ○ A. Telephone wiring can be reliably used for most UTP networks.

   ○ B. Thin coaxial networks are easy to install and reconfigure.

   ○ C. Fiber-optic cable supports cable runs of tens of kilometers.

   ○ D. STP cable is insensitive to EMI.

7. Which cable type should be used to connect between two buildings?

   ○ A. UTP

   ○ B. STP

   ○ C. Coax

   ○ D. Fiber-optic

8. Which of the following cable types has the greatest data capacity?

   ○ A. Category 5 UTP

   ○ B. Thick coax

   ○ C. Single-mode fiber-optic

   ○ D. Multi-mode fiber-optic

9. Which statement is true of unlicensed radio frequencies?

   ○ A. Anyone may use them.

   ○ B. 902 MHz and 2.4 GHz are unlicensed frequency bands.

   ○ C. The FCC prevents users from interfering.

   ○ D. They are relatively uncrowded.

10. Which THREE of the following are antenna types?

    ☐ A. Beam

    ☐ B. Duplex

    ☐ C. Dipole

    ☐ D. Random-length wire

11. Which of the following radio transmissions is typically line-of-sight?

    ○ A. AM

    ○ B. FM

    ○ C. Microwave

    ○ D. None of the above

12. Which THREE of the following statements are true:

    ☐ A. Attenuation of radio waves is less with high-power signals.

    ☐ B. High-frequency radio LANs can penetrate office walls.

    ☐ C. Radio-frequency LANs have high bandwidth.

    ☐ D. Spread-spectrum technology reduces sensitivity to EMI.

13. Which TWO wireless technologies would be good choices for connecting two buildings on opposite sides of a highway?

    ☐ A. Satellite microwave

    ☐ B. High-power single-frequency

    ☐ C. Terrestrial microwave

    ☐ D. Broadcast infrared

14. Which TWO wireless technologies are sensitive to radio-frequency interference:

    ☐ A. Microwave

    ☐ B. Spread-spectrum

    ☐ C. Infrared

    ☐ D. High-power, single frequency

15. Which TWO statements are true of the public telephone network?

    ☐ A. Switched services enable customers to pay on a per-use basis.

    ☐ B. The demarc is the place at the Central Office where a user's connection attaches to the network.

    ☐ C. Local loops connect subscriber wiring to the demarc.

    ☐ D. Central offices switch calls between customer sites.

Answers

1. C	9. C
2. A B	10. A C D
3. A B C	11. A
4. B C	12. A C D
5. A B C	13. B C
6. C	14. B C
7. D	15. A D
8. C	

Transmission Media Connections

This chapter covers a wide variety of devices that are used to connect networks. The devices discussed range from the lowly connector to exotic units, such as routers and CSU/DSUs. Novell divides these devices into two categories, describing them either as network or internetwork devices.

This course defines a network as "a single, independent network." What does this mean? By this definition, a network consists of a single, local cabling system. Any device on the network can directly communicate with any other device on the same network. A network by this definition does not have any connections to other, remote networks.

According to the course definition, an *internetwork* consists of multiple independent networks that are connected together and can share remote resources. It is said that internetworks consist of "logically separate but physically connected networks" that can be dissimilar in type. The device that connects the independent networks together must have a degree of "intelligence" because it must determine when packets will stay on the local network or when they will be forwarded to another remote network.

Connectivity devices perform the following functions:

- Attaching devices to media

- Connecting media segments together

- Utilizing media capacity effectively

- Connecting remote (logically separate) networks

Listed below are the devices to be examined:

- Network connectivity devices:

   Connectors

   Network interface boards

   Hubs

   Repeaters

   Bridges

   Multiplexors

   Modems

- Internetwork connectivity devices:

   Routers

   Brouters

   CSU/DSUs

When you complete this chapter, you will be able to do the following:

- Identify connecting hardware used in computer networking

- Identify connecting hardware used to connect internetworks

- Select connectivity devices to meet specific requirements

Connecting Hardware

Each connection type will specify connectors to be used. Several are discussed in this section.

Connectors for Multi-Wire Cable

A variety of physical layer standards require cables with large numbers of wires. The RS-232 serial interface commonly used for modems can utilize as many as 25 wires (although seldom are all wires actually implemented).

Several types of connectors are used for these types of connections, three of which are shown in figure 20.1. A wide variety of D-type connectors are available, of which the DB-25 and the DB-9 are shown. The number reflects the number of pins or sockets that the connector can accommodate. You will encounter DB-9 connectors in several places. Token-ring network cards are frequently equipped with DB-9 connectors.

The DIX connector is similar to a DB-15 connector, and is used to connect devices with thickwire Ethernet. The DIX connector differs from a standard DB-15 because the DIX is secured to the mating connector with a sliding clip instead of screws. The sliding clip is installed on the connector that has sockets, which is not shown in the figure. The connector shown in figure 20.1 is equipped with pins and with studs that mate with the sliding clip.

The fourth connector shown in figure 20.1 is a DIN connector. DIN connectors are available in various configurations, with different pin counts and pin arrangements. In networking, you are most likely to encounter DIN connectors when cabling Macintoshes into AppleTalk networks.

Figure 20.1
Connectors used with multi-wire cables.

Connectors for Twisted-Pair Cables

The most common connector used with UTP cables is the RJ-45 connector, shown in figure 20.2. These connectors are easy to install on cables and are extremely easy to connect and disconnect. The RJ-45 connector has eight pins. You also will occasionally encounter the RJ-11 connector, which resembles the RJ-45, but has only four pins.

Figure 20.2
A RJ-45 connector.

Although AppleTalk and token-ring networks can both be cabled with UTP cable and RJ-45 connectors, both originated as STP cabling systems. For STP cable, AppleTalk employs a DIN-type connector, shown in figure 20.3. IBM uses the IBM Data Connector, also shown in the figure.

Figure 20.3
Connectors used with STP cable.

The IBM Data Connector is unusual because it does not come in two gender configurations. Any IBM Data Connector may be snapped to any other IBM Data Connector.

Most networking connections for STP token ring are made using IBM Data Connectors. The connection to the workstation, however, is made with a DB-15 connector. Figure 20.4 shows a PC that is set up to connect to a token-ring network.

Connectors for Coaxial Cable

Two types of connectors are commonly used with coaxial cable. The most common connector is the *BayoNette Connector* (BNC) connector, shown in figure 20.5. This figure shows several characteristics of thin Ethernet cabling, as follows:

■ A T-connector is used to connect the network board in the PC to the network. The T- connector attaches directly to the network board, and a cable is never used at this point.

■ BNC connectors attach cable segments to the T-connectors.

■ Both ends of the cable must be terminated. A *terminator* is a special connector that includes a resistor that is carefully matched to the characteristics of the cable system.

■ One of the terminators must be grounded. A wire from the connector is attached to a grounded point, such as the center screw of a grounded electrical outlet.

Thick Ethernet uses N-connectors, which screw on instead of using a twist-lock (bayonette) fitting (see fig. 20.6). As with thin Ethernet, both ends of the cable must be terminated and one end must be grounded.

Figure 20.4

PC ready to connect to a token-ring network.

- DB-9 Connector
- Shielded Twisted-Pair Cable
- IBM Data Connector

Figure 20.5

Connectors and cabling for thin Ethernet.

Workstations do not connect directly to the cable with thick Ethernet. The cable attachment is made with a *transceiver* (also called a *medium attachment unit* or MAU), which connects to the workstation with a cable called an *AUI cable*. Transceivers can connect to cables in the following two ways:

■ They can connect by cutting the cable and using N-connectors and a T-connector on the transceiver. This, the original method, is now used infrequently.

■ The more common approach is to use a clamp-on transceiver, which has pins that penetrate the cable without the need for cutting it. Because clamp-on transceivers force sharp teeth into the cable, they are frequently referred to as *vampire taps.*

Connectors for Fiber-Optic Cable

A variety of connectors are used with fiber-optic cable. The most common is the ST-connector, shown in figure 20.7. If two devices are to engage in two-way data exchange, two fibers are required, and you will frequently encounter fiber-optic cables with connectors in pairs.

When fiber-optic cable bundles must be interfaced to individual cables, a connection center will be used. Within the splice center, the individual fibers in the cable bundle can be connected to individual connectors that are used to connect to devices. Figure 20.8 illustrates a cabling system based on a splice center.

Figure 20.6

Connectors and cabling for thick Ethernet

Figure 20.7
An ST connector used for fiber optic cable.

Network Connectivity Devices

This section defines a variety of devices as "network connectivity devices." This definition focuses on the roles of these devices in local networks as opposed to internetworks.

Network Interface Boards

Each workstation must be equipped with hardware that enables the workstation to connect to the network. This course calls all such devices *network interface boards*, although they might not be boards at all:

■ A *network interface card* (NIC) may be installed in one of the computer's expansion slots.

■ The network interface circuitry may be built into the computer's main board. In this case, the connector is built into the computer's case.

■ A transmission media adapter may be used.

Several types of transmission media adapters are in common use, including the following:

■ Ethernet LANs use transceivers to connect DIX connectors on devices to network media. Transceivers are always used with thick coaxial cable and may be used with thin coax or

Figure 20.8
Fiber-optic cable.

Multi-fiber cable

Hub

Fiber-attached station

UTP. NICs for thin and UTP Ethernet usually have the transceivers built in so that an external transceiver is not required.

■ When UTP cable is used with token-ring networks, a media filter might be required when operating at 16 Mbps. The media filter prevents noise from getting out onto the LAN. Many token-ring NICs designed for 16 Mbps operation incorporate the media filter on the card.

Transceivers

Regardless of the form of the device, it will include a transceiver of some kind. A transceiver functions as both a *trans*mitter and a re*ceiver*.

The transmitter component translates the computer's internal signals to the signals required for the network. If the network uses UTP cable, the transceiver will supply the proper electrical signals to the proper type of connector. If the network uses fiber-optic cable, the transceiver will translate the computer's electrical signals into the light signals required for the network.

The receiver component performs the opposite service when signals are received from the network, translating them back to a form that matches the computer's internal requirements.

Network Interface Cards (NIC)

Also called an NIC, a *network interface card* is a network board that can be installed in a computer's expansion slot. NICs are the devices most commonly used to connect computers to networks.

NICs incorporate a transceiver, which can service several types of connectors. With the exception of thick Ethernet, NICs are available to connect directly to all types of networks.

Ethernet NICs are equipped with one, two, or possibly all three of the following:

■ RJ-45 connector for UTP Ethernet

■ BNC connector for thin Ethernet

■ AUI connector for thick Ethernet

Token-ring NICs are equipped with one or both of the following:

■ DB-15 connector for STP

■ RJ-45 connector for UTP

Transmission Media Adapters

Novell uses the term *transmission media adapter* to describe a device that adapts one type of connector on the computer to a different type of connector that is required for the network. Several types of devices can be classified as transmission media adapters, including the following:

■ **Transceivers (or MAUs).** Used to connect computers to thick coax Ethernets

■ **Media filters.** Adapt a DB-15 token-ring connector to connect to a UTP network with an RJ-45 connector

■ **Parallel port adapters.** Enable laptop computers to network by communicating through their parallel ports

■ **SCSI port adapters.** Enable computers to connect to networks through a SCSI interface

Hubs

Coaxial cable Ethernet is the only LAN standard that does not use hubs to bring wiring together in a central location, as shown in figure 20.9. Hubs are also called *wiring concentrators*. You will encounter three types of hubs, as follows:

- Passive
- Active
- Intelligent

Passive Hubs

This type of hub is called passive because it does not contain any electronic components and does not process the data signal in any way. The only purpose of a passive hub is to combine the signals from several network cable segments. All devices attached to a passive hub see all the packets that pass through the hub.

Because the hub does not clean up or amplify the signals (in fact, the hub absorbs a small part of the signal), the distance between a computer and the hub can be no more than half of the maximum permissible distance between two computers on the network. If the network design limits the distance between two computers to 200 meters, the maximum distance between a computer and the hub is 100 meters.

ARCnet networks commonly use passive hubs.

Token-ring networks also can use passive hubs, although the industry trend is to utilize active hubs to obtain the advantages cited in the following.

Active Hubs

Active hubs incorporate electronic components that can amplify and clean up the electronic signals that flow between devices on the network. The process of cleaning up the signals is called *signal regeneration*. There are two benefits of signal regeneration: the network is more robust and less sensitive to errors, and distances between devices can be increased. These advantages generally outweigh the fact that active hubs cost considerably more than passive hubs.

Later in the chapter, you will learn about *repeaters*, which are also devices that amplify and regenerate network signals. Because active hubs function in part as repeaters, they are occasionally called *multiport repeaters*.

Intelligent Hubs

Intelligent hubs are active hubs that include something more. Several functions can add intelligence to a hub, as follows:

Figure 20.9

Network wiring with a hub.

■ **Hub management.** Many hubs now support network management protocols that enable the hub to send packets to a central network console. They also enable the console to control the hub, ordering, for example, a hub to shut down a connection that is generating network errors.

■ **Switching hubs.** The latest development in hubs is the *switching hub*, which includes circuitry that very quickly routes signals between ports on the hub. Instead of repeating a packet to all ports on the hub, a switching hub repeats it only to the port that connects to the destination computer for the packet. Many switching hubs have the capability of switching packets to the fastest of several alternative paths. Switching hubs are replacing bridges and routers on many networks.

Repeaters

As you learned in Chapter 18, "The OSI Layered Protocol Model," all media attenuate the signals that they carry. Each media type, therefore, has a maximum range that it can reliably carry data. Figure 20.10 shows the use of a repeater to connect two Ethernet cable segments. The result of adding the repeater is that the potential length of the overall network is doubled.

Some repeaters simply amplify signals. Although this increases the strength of the data signal, it amplifies any noise on the network as well. Also, if the original signal has been distorted in any way, an amplifying repeater cannot clean up the distortion.

More advanced repeaters can extend the range of network media by both amplifying and regenerating the signals. Signal regenerating repeaters, for example, identify the data in the signal they receive and use the data to regenerate the original signal. This amplifies the strength of the desired signal while reducing noise, and clears up any distortion that might be present. The output of a regenerating repeater duplicates the original data signal.

It would be nice if repeaters could be used to extend networks indefinitely, but all network designs limit the size of the network. The most important reason for this limit is signal propagation. Networks need to work with reasonable expectations about the maximum time a signal might be in transit. This is known as *propagation delay*—the time it takes for a signal to reach the furthest point on the network. If this maximum propagation delay interval expires and no signals are encountered, a network error condition is assumed. Given the maximum allowed propagation delay, it is possible to calculate the maximum permissible cable length for the

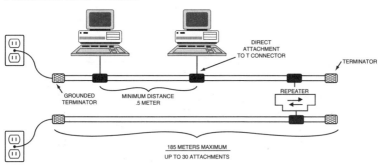

Figure 20.10

Using a repeater to extend an Ethernet LAN.

network. Even though repeaters enable signals to travel farther, the maximum propagation delay still sets a limit to the maximum size of the network.

Bridges

Bridges, on the other hand, are capable of extending the maximum size of a network. Although the bridged network in figure 20.11 looks much like the earlier example of a network with a repeater, the bridge is a much more flexible device.

A repeater passes on all signals that it receives. A bridge, on the other hand, is more selective and only passes on the signals that are targeted for a computer that is on the other side. A bridge can make this determination because a device on the network is identified by a unique address, and each packet that is transmitted bears the address of the device to which it should be delivered. The process works like this:

1. The bridge receives every packet on LAN A and LAN B.

2. The bridge learns from the packets which device addresses are located on LAN A and which are on LAN B. A table is built with this information.

3. Packets on LAN A that are addressed to devices on LAN A are discarded. So are packets on LAN B that are addressed to devices on LAN B. These packets can be delivered without the help of the bridge.

4. Packets on LAN A that are addressed to devices on LAN B are retransmitted to LAN B for delivery. Similarly, the appropriate packets on LAN B are retransmitted to LAN A.

Figure 20.11

Extending a network with a bridge.

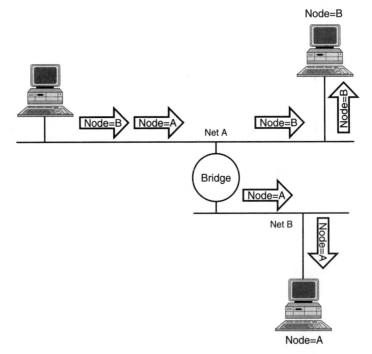

The address tables on older bridges needed to be manually configured by the network administrator. Newer bridges are called learning bridges— they function as described in step 2. *Learning bridges* automatically update their address tables as devices are added to or removed from the network.

Bridges accomplish several things. First, they divide busy networks into smaller segments. If the network is designed so that most packets can be delivered without crossing a bridge, traffic on the individual network segments can be reduced. If the Accounting and Sales departments are overloading the LAN, you might choose to divide the network so that Accounting is on one segment and Sales is on another. Only when Accounting and Sales need to exchange packets will a packet need to cross the bridge between the segments.

Bridges can also extend the physical size of a network. Although the individual segments are still restricted by the maximum size imposed by the network design limits, bridges enable network designers to stretch the distances between segments and extend the overall size of the network.

Bridges, however, cannot join dissimilar types of LANs. Bridges are dependent on the physical addresses of devices. Physical device addresses are functions of the data link layer, and different data link layer protocols are used for each type of network. A bridge, therefore, cannot be used to join an Ethernet segment to a token ring segment.

 Note Device addresses are functions of the OSI data link layer, which is discussed in greater detail in Chapter 22, "OSI Data Link Layer Concepts." Therefore, bridges are said to function at the data link layer.

Multiplexors

Multiplexors solve a different type of connectivity problem. What if you have several signals to transmit, but only one path that the signals must share? A *multiplexor* is a device that combines several signals so that they can be transmitted together, and then enables the original signals to be extracted at the other end of the transmission. (The process of recovering the original signals is called *demultiplexing*.) Figure 20.12 shows how the process works.

Modems

Standard telephone lines can transmit only analog signals. Computers, however, store and transmit data digitally. *Modems* are capable of transmitting digital computer signals over telephone lines by converting them to analog form.

The process of converting one signal form to another (digital to analog in this case) is called *modulation*. The reverse process of recovering the original signal is called *demodulation*. The term modem is derived from this *mo*dulation/*dem*odulation process.

Modems can be used to connect computer devices or entire networks that are at distant locations. (Before digital telephone lines became available, modems were about the only way of linking distant devices.) Some modems operate constantly over dedicated phone lines. Others use standard *public switched-telephone network* (PSTN) dial-up lines and make a connection only when one is required.

Common uses for modems on LANs include the following:

Figure 20.12
Multiplexing and demultiplexing a signal.

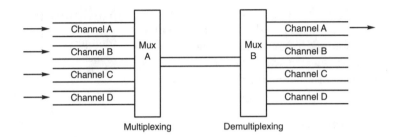

Enabling users to call in and access the LAN

Exchanging electronic mail between mail servers

Transmitting and receiving faxes with a fax server

Enabling LANs to exchange data on demand

Modems enable networks to exchange e-mail and to perform limited data transfers, but the connectivity made possible is extremely limited. By themselves, modems do not enable remote networks to connect to each other and directly exchange data. In other words, a modem is not an internetwork device. Nevertheless, modems may be used in conjunction with an internetwork device, such as a router, to connect remote networks through the PSTN, or an analog service, such as a 56 KB line.

The point is that a modem cannot enable remote networks to internetwork freely without the assistance of routers or brouters to manage the connection between the networks.

 Modems do not necessarily need to connect through the PSTN. *Short-haul modems* are even frequently used to connect devices in the same building. A standard serial connection is limited to 50 feet, but short-haul modems can be used to extend the range of a serial connection to any required distance.

Many devices are designed to assume that modems will be used. When you want to connect such devices without using modems, you can use a *null modem cable,* which connects the transmitter of one device to the receiver of the other device.

 A modem translates digital signals for transmission on analog phone lines. A codec (*co*der/*dec*oder) provides a similar service when analog signals are to be transmitted over digital phone lines, translating analog signals into digital form.

Internetwork Connectivity Devices

An *internetwork* consists of two or more independent networks that are physically connected, enabling them to communicate. The networks that make up an internetwork may be of quite different types. An internetwork might include Ethernet and token-ring networks, for example.

Earlier, you saw how bridges can be used to interconnect similar networks. When things get more complex, however, more advanced technologies might be required. This section discusses three such technologies: routers, brouters, and CSU/DSUs.

Routers

Recall that bridges subdivide networks by building tables that list which device addresses can be reached from a particular port on the router. This is a suitable strategy in relatively simple networks, but has shortcomings when networks become more complex.

Consider the network shown in figure 20.13. Let's examine why bridges are unsuitable for interconnecting the network segments in this manner.

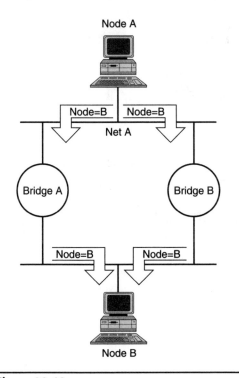

Node A

Node=B   Node=B
Net A

Bridge A   Bridge B

Node=B   Node=B

Node B

Figure 20.13
A complex network with bridges.

Both bridges are aware of the existence of Node B, and both will pick up the packet from Net A and forward it. At the very least, this means that the same packet will arrive twice at Node B.

A worse case, however, is that these relatively unintelligent bridges will start passing packets around in loops. This results in an ever-increasing number of packets that are circulating on the network and are never reaching their destinations. Ultimately, this activity will saturate the network.

So one restriction of bridges is that the network cannot include redundant paths. However, redundant paths are desirable because they enable the network to continue functioning when one path goes down.

 An algorithm called the *spanning tree algorithm* enables complex Ethernets to use bridges while redundant routes exist. The algorithm enables the bridges to communicate and to construct a logical network that does not contain redundant paths. The logical network is reconfigured if one of the paths fails.

Another problem is that the bridges cannot analyze the network and determine the fastest route over which to forward a packet. When multiple routes exist, this is a desirable capability, particularly in *wide area networks* (WANs) where some routes can be considerably slower than others.

Routers organize the large network in terms of logical network segments. Each network segment is assigned an address so that every packet has both a destination network address and a destination device address. Figure 20.14 shows a complex network based on routers.

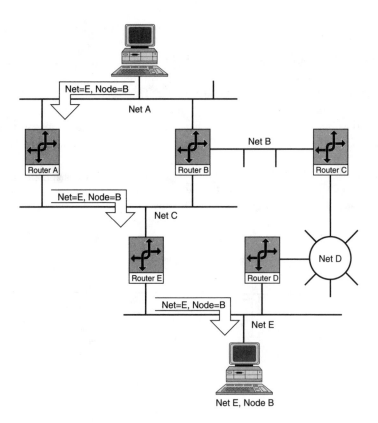

Figure 20.14

An internetwork with routers.

Net=E, Node=B
Net A
Router A
Net B
Router B
Router C
Net=E, Node=B
Net C
Router E
Router D
Net D
Net=E, Node=B
Net E
Net E, Node B

Note Recall the section definition of an internetwork is that which consists of two or more logically separate, but physically connected, networks. By this definition, any network that is segment with routers is an internetwork.

Routers are more "intelligent" than bridges. Not only do they build tables of where networks are located, but they also use algorithms to determine the most efficient path for sending a packet to any given network. Even though a particular network segment might not be directly attached to the router, the router will know the best way to send a packet to a device on that network. Therefore, Router A knows that the most efficient step is to send the packet to Router C, not Router B.

Notice that Router B presents a redundant path to the path provided by Router A. Routers can cope with this situation Because they exchange routing information that ensures that packet loops will not occur. In figure 20.14, if Router A fails, Router B provides a backup message path, making this network more robust.

Routers can be used to divide large, busy LANs into smaller segments, much as bridges can be used. But that is not the only reason for selecting a router.

Routers are also capable of connecting different network types. Notice that the network in figure 20.14 includes a token-ring segment with the Ethernet segments. On such networks, a router is the device of choice.

Because they can determine route efficiencies, routers are usually employed to connect a LAN to a wide area network. WANs are frequently designed with multiple paths, and routers can ensure that the various paths are used most efficiently.

 Device addresses are functions of the OSI network layer, which will be discussed in greater detail in Chapter 23, "OSI Network Layer Concepts." Routers, therefore, are said to function at the network layer.

The network layer functions independently of the physical cabling system and the cabling system protocols—independently, that is, of the physical and data link layers. This is the reason that routers can easily translate packets between different cabling systems. Bridges cannot because they function at the data link layer, which is closely tied to a given set of physical layer specifications.

Brouters

A *brouter* is a router that can also bridge. A brouter attempts to deliver packets based on network protocol information. If a particular network layer protocol is not supported, the brouter bridges the packet using device addresses.

CSU/DSUs

When LANs are connected into wide area networks, the connection is frequently by means of the public telephone network. Connecting to some telephone media requires the use of a *channel service network/digital service unit* (CSU/DSU).

Network service providers design their media for a particular type of signal, and may require use of a

CSU/DSU to translate the LAN signals to the signal format required. A CSU/DSU also isolates the local network from the public network to protect each network from noise and voltage fluctuations of the other.

Important Terms from This Chapter

A *network*, according to Novell study materials, is a "single independent network." On such a network, any device can communicate with any other device directly, without the need for a connection to a remote network. Under this definition, network connectivity devices are involved only in local network connectivity.

An *internetwork*, according to Novell study materials, consists of multiple independent networks that are connected together and can share remote resources. Internetwork connectivity devices facilitate connectivity between remote networks.

It is important to realize that "remote" does not necessarily mean "distant." An internetwork can be located entirely within a single building. The important distinction is whether the networks are logically separate, and actually has to do with protocol levels, which you will examine in greater detail in later sections. The crucial level is the network layer, which assigns an address to each network that makes up an internetwork. The following are ways to determine how a message was delivered:

■ If a message can arrive at its destination using information that is available at the data link layer of the OSI model, then the message is being delivered by a network.

■ If delivery requires use of the network address information that is available at the network layer, the message is being delivered through an internetwork.

Network connectivity devices, therefore, do not use network address information. Internetwork connectivity devices are capable of using network address information to assist in the efficient delivery of messages. The process of using network address information to deliver messages is called *routing*. The common feature that unites internetwork connectivity devices (routers and brouters) is that they can perform routing.

This distinction will become clearer to you as you progress through the rest of this section. Because each network in an internetwork is assigned an address, each network can be considered to be *logically separate*—that is, each network functions independently of other networks on the internetwork.

 For the purposes of this section, CSU/DSUs are considered internetwork devices, but this is not strictly correct. The primary purpose of a CSU/DSU is to interface the network to a public data network. A given device may perform routing or it may depend on a separate router, depending on the vendor's hardware design.

Questions

1. Which TWO of the following are characteristic features of internetworks?

   □ A. Multiple networks can be interconnected with bridges to form an internetwork.

   □ B. Devices can communicate with devices on the local network.

   □ C. Devices can communicate with devices on remote networks.

   □ D. An internetwork can consist of segments that utilize different network protocols.

2. Which TWO of the following are characteristics of networks?

   □ A. Devices can communicate with devices on the local network.

   □ B. Devices can communicate with devices on remote networks.

   □ C. Routers extend the range of a network.

   □ D. A network can include network segments that utilize different protocols.

3. Which TWO of the following are functions of network connectivity devices?

   □ A. Enabling devices to interface with media

   □ B. Converting protocols between network segments

   □ C. Connecting media segments together

   □ D. Fully utilizing media capacity

4. Which TWO of the following are functions of internetwork connectivity devices?

   □ A. Connecting remote networks

   □ B. Enabling networks with different protocols to communicate

   □ C. Attaching devices to media

   □ D. Extending the range of network segments

5. The DB-15 connector is commonly used with _____.

   ○ A. fiber-optic cable

   ○ B. token-ring connections to NICs

   ○ C. coaxial cable

   ○ D. RS-232 serial interfaces

6. Which TWO connectors are frequently used with STP cable?

   □ A. T-connectors

   □ B. RJ-45 connectors

   □ C. IBM unisex connectors

   □ D. AppleTalk DIN connectors

7. Which TWO connectors are commonly used with coaxial cable?

   □ A. DB-25 connectors

   □ B. N-connectors

   □ C. ST-connectors

   □ D. BNC connectors

8. Which THREE are some advantages of active hubs?

☐ A. They can regenerate network signals.

☐ B. LANs ranges can be extended.

☐ C. They are inexpensive.

☐ D. They function as repeaters.

9. Which TWO networks can use passive hubs?

☐ A. Ethernet

☐ B. ARCnet

☐ C. Token ring

☐ D. All of the above

10. Which TWO statements are true of repeaters?

☐ A. Repeaters amplify signals.

☐ B. Repeaters extend network distances.

☐ C. Repeaters regenerate signals.

☐ D. Repeaters can be used to extend the range of a network indefinitely.

11. Which THREE statements are true of bridges?

☐ A. Bridges amplify and regenerate signals.

☐ B. Bridges can connect logically separate networks.

☐ C. Bridges use device address tables to route messages.

☐ D. Bridges divide networks into smaller segments.

12. Modems can be used for which THREE of the following purposes?

☐ A. To connect remote networks

☐ B. To enable users to call in and access a LAN

☐ C. To transmit and receive faxes

☐ D. To extend the range of a serial interface

13. Which THREE features of routers are not features of bridges?

☐ A. Regenerating signals

☐ B. Connecting logically separate networks

☐ C. Connecting networks using different protocols

☐ D. Maintaining tables of network addresses

14. Which TWO of the following are functions of CSU/DSUs?

☐ A. Connecting networks with different protocols

☐ B. Connecting a network to some types of public telephone networks

☐ C. Routing signals between logical networks

☐ D. Isolating the local network from the public network

Answers

1. B C

2. A B

3. A C

4. A B

5. B

6. C D

7. B D

8. A B D

9. B C

10. A B

11. A C D

12. B C D

13. B C D

14. B D

OSI Physical Layer Concepts

*A*lthough the OSI physical layer does not define the media
used, the physical layer is concerned with all aspects of
transmitting and receiving data on the network media.
Specifically, the physical layer is concerned with
transmitting and receiving bits. This layer defines
several key characteristics of the physical network,
including the following:

- Physical structure of the network

- Mechanical and electrical specifications for using
  the medium (not the medium itself!)

- Bit transmission encoding and timing

Although the physical layer does not define the medium, it defines clear requirements that the medium must meet, and physical layer specifications will differ depending on the physical medium to be used. Ethernet for UTP will have different physical layer specifications than Ethernet for coax, for example.

When you complete this chapter, you will understand the following:

- The purpose of the OSI physical layer
- Types of network connections
- Physical topologies
- Analog and digital signaling
- Bit synchronization
- Bandwidth use
- Multiplexing

Connection Types

All network connections consist of two types of building blocks:

- Multipoint connections
- Point-to-point connections

A *multipoint connection* enables one device to communicate with two or more devices. An example is shown in figure 21.1. All the devices attached using a multipoint connection share the same network transmission medium.

A *point-to-point connection* enables one device to communicate with one other device (see fig. 21.2). When two devices are connected through a point-to-point link, they have exclusive use of the data capacity of the link.

Larger networks can be constructed by adding point-to-point links. In this case, devices rely on other devices to relay their messages. Point-to-point links can even come full circle to form a ring, enabling messages to be passed from any device to any other device on the ring.

Physical Topologies

The physical topology of a network describes the layout of the network media. Different physical topologies have different characteristics in terms of performance, ease of installation, troubleshooting, and reconfiguration.

Physical Topologies Based on Multipoint Connections

In fact, only one topology is based on multipoint connections—the bus, shown in figure 21.3. Notice that all devices are connected to a common transmission media. In some cases, the common media is referred to as a *backbone network*.

Figure 21.1

Examples of multipoint connections.

Figure 21.2
Point-to-point connections.

Figure 21.3
A bus physical topology.

Bus Characteristics

Chapters 19 and 20 discussed the cabling and connectors used for bus topologies. Recall that the ends of the cable must be terminated and that devices may be connected along the length of the cable. Connections are performed with T-connectors or with taps (transceivers) that attach directly to the cable and use a drop cable to connect to the workstation.

Typically, signals on a bus network are broadcast in both directions on the backbone cable, enabling all devices to directly receive the signal. With some unidirectional buses, however, signals travel in one direction only and can reach only downstream devices. In this case, the cable must be terminated in such a way that signals are reflected back on the cable and can reach other devices.

Installation

Bus installation is relatively simple and requires only basic tools and skill. Cable runs are generally fairly short because it is not necessary to run a separate cable to a central hub for each device on the network.

Bus networks such as Ethernet have carefully defined rules that must be adhered to for best network performance. Stations on a thick Ethernet cable, for example, should be attached at intervals that are multiples of $2 \frac{1}{2}$ meters. All network media have attenuation characteristics that limit the lengths of cables and the number of devices that can be attached.

Reconfiguration

Bus networks can be difficult to reconfigure. If the main cable does not run close to the new device, it might need to be rerouted. Adding new devices often involves cutting the main cable to add a T-connector, which requires the network to be shut down. In the process, it is important to adhere to rules regarding maximum number of devices and distances at which taps are to be spaced.

Troubleshooting

Bus networks can be difficult to troubleshoot because a single fault can render the entire bus inoperative. A broken cable, for example, is the same as having two unterminated cables. Without termination, signals can reflect back into both cable segments interfering with transmissions and making the system inoperable. (In addition, of course, devices cannot communicate with devices that are on the opposite side of the break.) Because all devices are affected by a cable break, it can be difficult to isolate a break to the cable that falls between two devices.

Physical Topologies Based on Point-to-Point Connections

As shown in figure 21.4, several different topologies can be based on point-to-point connections, as follows:

■ *Star topologies* utilize a point-to-point link (a "drop cable") to connect each device to a central hub.

■ *Mesh networks* establish a point-to-point link between each pair of computers on the network. Because the number of required links rises rapidly as the number of computers increases, large mesh networks are not frequently used.

■ *Hybrid mesh networks* are commonly used in wide-area networks. No attempt is made to provide a link between each possible pair of computers. Extra links, however, are installed to provide more direct paths, extra bandwidth, and some redundancy in case links fail.

■ *Ring networks* utilize point-to-point links to connect devices together in a ring. Messages are forwarded around the ring and can reach any station in this way.

■ *Cellular topologies* divide geographic areas into overlapping cells that are serviced by transmitter/receivers. Point-to-point radio links are established between a cellular data device and the transmitter in a cell. These point-to-point links are constantly reconfigured as the data device moves through the cellular network. (Multipoint links may also be established under appropriate circumstances.)

Each of these topologies is examined in greater detail in the next sections.

The Ring Topology

The ring topology is circular, and signals typically travel around the ring in one direction only. Each device incorporates a receiver and a transmitter and serves as a repeater that passes the signal on to the next device in the ring. Because the signal is regenerated at each device, signal degeneration is low.

Installation

Installation is fairly simple, but the amount of cable required can go higher than with a bus. As with all networks, it is essential to stay within network design restrictions regarding cable lengths between devices, total ring length, and number of devices.

Reconfiguration

Rings can be difficult to reconfigure, particularly when devices are located at large distances.

Troubleshooting

The repeating function makes it fairly easy to isolate cabling faults. When a break is present in the cable, devices will still be able to transmit to downstream devices on the near side of the break. Fault isolation becomes a matter of determining which device is not receiving signals from its immediate upstream neighbor.

Some rings incorporate redundant paths that can be switched in when a cable break occurs. The redundant path takes the form of a second ring that transmits signals in opposite directions from the main ring. When a break occurs in the main ring, the counter-rotating ring can be used to route signals around the break.

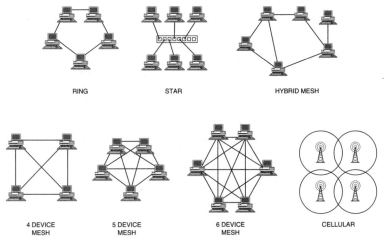

RING   STAR   HYBRID MESH

4 DEVICE   5 DEVICE   6 DEVICE   CELLULAR
MESH   MESH   MESH

Figure 21.4
Physical topologies based on point-to-point connections.

The Star Topology

A star topology networks each device with a cable that connects it to a central hub. The hub receives signals from network devices and routes the signals to the proper destination. Star hubs can be interconnected to form tree or hierarchical network topologies.

Installation

The major installation difficulty is that a separate cable must be run to connect each device to a hub. Cabling requirements are generally considerably higher than for bus or ring physical topologies.

A significant concern with star topologies is that cable lengths between hubs and devices are limited, typically to 100 meters. Therefore, it is necessary to ensure that a hub is located within 100 meters of every potential device location

Reconfiguration

The payoff for cabling to a central hub is that networks are easy to reconfigure. Most adds and moves can be accomplished by simply moving a plug to a new hub port.

Troubleshooting

It is easier to troubleshoot stars than buses and, generally speaking, than rings. It is easy to build troubleshooting features into hubs, which can be monitored centrally.

When the cable to a device fails, it generally affects that device only. In cases where a device cable causes problems for the entire network, it is simple to disconnect the cable from the hub. Many managed hubs will automatically disconnect devices that are producing network errors.

Star topologies are subject to a single point of failure. If the hub fails, all devices are affected.

Mesh Topologies

Mesh networks consist of a point-to-point link between each pair of devices on the network. In most cases, the number of connections required limits the use of true mesh networks to a few stations. A five-device mesh network requires 24 ($4 \times 3 \times 2$) connections, but a six-device mesh requires 120 ($5 \times 4 \times 3 \times 2$)!

Two advantages can be stated for a mesh topology. The first is that every device has a guaranteed communication channel capacity with every other device. The other is a high level of fault tolerance. Even multiple media failures will probably leave the network capable of delivering messages to all devices.

More common is the hybrid network, which contains some redundant links, particularly to the most important devices or where the greatest capacity is needed. When it is essential that the network never go down, redundant links are a good form of insurance.

Installation

Mesh networks are difficult to install, with the difficulty increasing rapidly as the number of devices increases.

Hybrid mesh networks are most commonly in wide area networks, where the links consist primarily of leased communication services. Installation is primarily a matter of setting up routers, CSU/DSUs, and so on. WAN connections of this sort can get involved to install and manage.

Reconfiguration

Mesh networks can be extremely difficult to reconfigure.

Troubleshooting

Mesh networks are easy to troubleshoot because each device keeps track of every other device.

Hybrid mesh networks introduce concerns about how signals are routed through the network. This is a skilled task that calls for sophisticated diagnostic and management systems to ensure that the network operates smoothly.

Mesh networks are extremely robust because redundant links abound. They are, therefore, seldom subject to single points of failure. Performance can degrade, however, if failure of one link causes traffic on other links to rise to unacceptable levels.

Cellular Topology

Cellular networks divide the area being serviced into cells, each of which is serviced by a central station. Devices use radio signals to communicate with the central station, and the central station routes messages to other devices. Cellular data networks can be implemented on an office level or in large geographic areas.

Installation

Installation of office-based cellular LANs is quite different from installation of cable-based LANs. Much depends on the degree to which the office building supports the requirements of the cellular system that has been chosen. Transmitters are of limited power and cannot penetrate walls, so some building types are unsuitable. If hubs can be located so they can communicate clearly with devices, installation is relatively simple.

Reconfiguration

Within the area serviced by a hub, devices can be located and relocated easily. Hubs are often con-

nected to other hubs using cable, however, and relocation of hubs can be more involved.

Troubleshooting

Troubleshooting depends on the network design. If hubs maintain a point-to-point link with devices, troubleshooting is simplified.

When a hub fails, all devices serviced by the hub lose service. Because devices are mobile, they can be relocated to a working area to restore service.

Digital and Analog Signaling

Signaling is the process of communicating information. The information being communicated can take one of two forms: analog or digital. Frequently, information in one form must be converted to the other. This frequently involves the use of some encoding scheme that enables the original information to be recovered from a signal after the signal has been received.

When an analog or digital signal is altered so that it contains information to be communicated, the process is called *modulation* or *encoding*. AM radio transmits information by modulating the radio signal, increasing or decreasing the amplitude (signal strength) depending on the information content. Many similar schemes are used to communicate information through different types of signals.

■ *Analog information* is information that changes continuously and can take on many different values. The hands on an analog clock move constantly, displaying time on a continuous scale.

■ *Digital information* is characterized by discrete states. A lightbulb is on or off, for example. A digital clock represents the time in one minute intervals and doesn't change its numbers again until the next minute. A digital clock can represent exact minutes, but nothing in between.

Figure 21.5 illustrates the difference between analog and digital signals. The analog signal is constantly changing and takes on values throughout the range of possible values. The digital signal takes on only two (or a few) specific states.

Digital Signaling Techniques

Computer data is inherently digital, and the majority of networks use digital signaling. This chapter examines two methods of modulating a digital signal to encode digital data, as follows:

■ Current state

■ State transition

Current State Encoding

This encoding technique assigns specific signal states to represent each possible data value. The signal is monitored periodically to determine its current state, from which a data value may be determined. A voltage of +5 might represent a binary 1 and a voltage of -5 might represent a binary 0, for example. Many different signal variations could be used. The important characteristic is that a given state represents one and only one data value. In figure 21.6, a high voltage represents a binary 0, while a low voltage represents a binary 1.

The following encoding schemes make use of current state encoding, although discussion of their specific characteristics is beyond the scope of this chapter:

■ Unipolar

■ Bipolar

■ Return-to-Zero (NRZ)

■ Biphase

State Transition Encoding

This encoding technique uses transitions in the digital signal to represent data. Following are a couple of ways this could be done:

■ A transition from high to low voltage always represents a 1, and a transition from low to high voltage always represents a 0.

Figure 21.5
Analog and digital signals.

ANALOG SIGNAL

DIGITAL SIGNAL

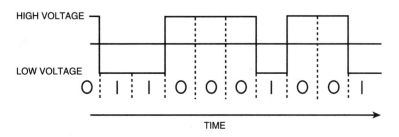

Figure 21.6
Current state encoding.

■ Any transition always represents a 1, and the absence of an expected transition represents a 0. This scheme is depicted in figure 21.7.

The following encoding schemes make use of state transition encoding, although discussion of their specific characteristics is beyond the scope of this chapter:

■ Bipolar-Alternate Mark Inversion (AMI)

■ Non-Return-to-Zero (NRZ)

■ Manchester

■ Differential Manchester

■ Biphase Space (FM-O)

 The terms "current state" and "state transition" were invented by Novell for use in this course and are not standard terms in the industry.

The common industry term for current state is *level triggered* because recognition of a given state is triggered (initiated) by a specific signal level.

The common industry term for state transition is *edge triggered,* since either the leading or trailing edge of a signal transition (the edge of the signal transition) is used to signal that a state change has taken place.

Analog Signaling

Analog signals are constantly varying in one or more values. These changes in values can be used to represent data.

Analog wave forms frequently take the form of sine waves. The sine wave in figure 21.8 illustrates two characteristics that define an analog wave form, as follows:

■ **Frequency.** Indicates the rate at which the waveform is changing. Frequency is associated with the wavelength of the waveform, which is a measure of the distance between two similar peaks on adjacent waves. Frequency is generally measured in Hertz (Hz), which indicates the frequency in cycles per second. Frequency is illustrated in figure 21.8.

Figure 21.7
State transition encoding.

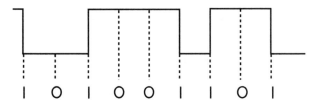

Figure 21.8

*Two analog waveforms
differing in frequency.*

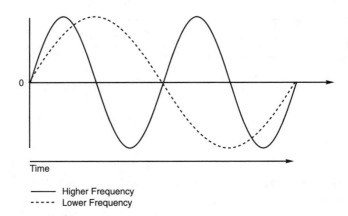

■ **Amplitude.** The measure of the strength of the waveform. Amplitude is illustrated in figure 21.9.

A third characteristic, *phase*, can also be defined. Figure 21.10 illustrates waveforms that differ in phase. These waveforms have identical frequency and amplitude, but they do not begin their transitions at the same time.

■ In figure 21.10, WAVE B begins to rise from the reference line at the same time that Wave A is peaking. Therefore, Wave B is ¹/₄

of a wave behind Wave A. If a complete wave is represented as having 360 degrees, Wave B lags behind Wave A by 90 degrees.

■ In figure 21.11, notice that Wave B is a mirror image of Wave A. Because Wave B is ¹/₂ of a wave behind Wave A, Wave B lags behind Wave A by 180 degrees. Wave C is ¹/₃ of a wave behind A and lags behind Wave A by 120 degrees.

Each of these characteristics, frequency, amplitude, and phase can be used to encode data.

Figure 21.9

*Two analog waveforms
differing in amplitude.*

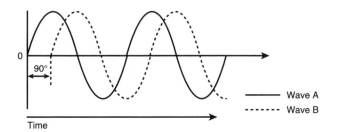

Figure 21.10
Two analog waveforms differing in phase.

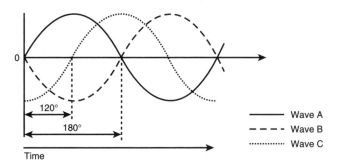

Figure 21.11
Three analog waveforms differing in phase by different amounts.

Amplitude Shift Keying

This is a current state method of modulation in that specific signal amplitudes are assigned specific data values. A high-amplitude signal, for example, might be assigned a value of 1, while a low-amplitude signal is assigned a value of 0. The first example in figure 21.12 illustrates amplitude shift keying.

Frequency Shift Keying

Frequency shift keying is also a current state modulation method. Specific frequency values are assigned specific data values. A high frequency, for example, might represent 0, while a lower frequency might represent 1. The second example in Figure 21.12 illustrates frequency shift keying.

Phase Shift Keying

Phase shift keying is a transition state modulation method. For example, a reference phase might represent 0, while a 180-degree phase shift would represent a 1 value. The process is illustrated in the third example of figure 21.12.

Bit Synchronization

With both current state and transition state modulation methods, the receiving device monitors the signal, looking for an expected characteristic. Timing is important because the receiver needs to know when it should check the incoming signal. If the check is made at the wrong time, erroneous data might be extracted.

Figure 21.12

Keying methods for amplitude waveforms.

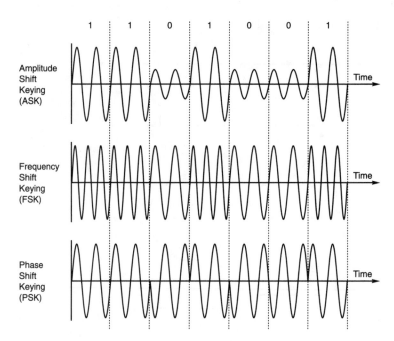

Two methods of coordinating signal timing follow:

- Asynchronous communication
- Synchronous communication

The methods differ primarily in the way they adjust the clocks of the sending and receiving devices.

Asynchronous Communication

Although the sender and receiver have internal clocks, these clocks are not directly synchronized. Each message begins with a start bit that enables the receiver to synchronize its internal clock with the timing of the message. Messages are kept short so the receiver's clock will not drift out of synchronization for the duration of the message. A *stop bit* signals that the message is complete. Asynchronous techniques are primarily used to transmit character data, and the message part of the transmission is limited to 7 or 8 bits.

To make the system work, the sender and receiver must reach a general agreement on the speed at which data is to be transmitted. You are probably familiar with the process of setting the data rate for modems. Even though the sending and receiving clocks are not directly synchronized, if they agree to transmit at, say 9,600 bits per second, their clocks can remain sufficiently synchronized to enable a single short transmission to be completed.

One characteristic to note is that the signals are intermittent and the transmission media is idle except when a transmission is actually taking place. No clock signals are transmitted to keep the receiver's clock synchronized with the sender's clock.

Synchronous Communication

Synchronous communication employs a clocking mechanism to ensure that the sending and receiving devices remain synchronized. Three techniques will be discussed, as follows:

- Guaranteed State Change
- Separate Clock Signals
- Oversampling

Guaranteed State Change

Some encoding techniques are designed to ensure that state changes occur at regular intervals. The receiving device adjusts its internal clock to match the frequencies of the state changes.

Signals of this type are called *self-clocking* because the clocking information is embedded in the signal itself and no other clocking mechanism is required.

Separate Clock Signals

The separate clock signal approach utilizes a separate communication channel to carry clocking information. The common RS-232 serial interface uses this approach. One of the wires in the cable carries clocking signals that enable the sending device to tell the receiver when it should monitor the incoming data.

This approach is useful over short distances, but becomes problematic with longer cables. Signals can travel through different wires in the cable at different rates, and at some point the clocking signal will no longer be synchronized with the signals on the data wires. RS-232 connections, for example, are typically limited to a maximum length of 50 feet for this reason.

Oversampling

With this technique, the receiver samples incoming data at a higher rate than the rate at which the data is being transmitted. If the receiver monitors at ten times the rate at which signal transitions are occurring, it is easy to determine when transitions

have taken place. The extra samples also enable the receiver to determine when its clock is drifting and needs to be resynchronized.

Baseband and Broadband Transmissions

There are two ways to allocate the capacity of transmission media, as follows:

- **Baseband.** Devotes the entire capacity of the medium to one communication channel

- **Broadband.** Enables two or more communication channels to share the bandwidth of the communications medium

Baseband is the most common mode of operation. Most LANs function in baseband mode, for example. Baseband signaling can be accomplished with both analog and digital signals.

You have a great deal of experience with broadband transmissions, however, whether you know it or not. The TV cable coming into your house from an antenna or a cable provider is a broadband medium. Many television signals can share the bandwidth of the cable because each signal is modulated using a separately assigned frequency. You can choose the channel you want to watch by selecting its frequency with the television tuner. This technique of dividing bandwidth into frequency bands is called *frequency-division multiplexing* (FDM) and works only with analog signals. Another technique called *time-division multiplexing* (TDM) supports digital signals and will be described in the next section.

Figure 21.13 contrasts the difference between baseband and broadband modes of operation.

Figure 21.13
Baseband and broadband transmission modes.

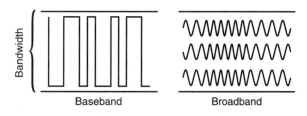

Baseband   Broadband

Multiplexing

Multiplexing is the technique that enables broadband media to support multiple data channels. There are several times when multiplexing makes sense, as follows:

■ **When media bandwidth is costly.** A high-speed leased line, such as a T-1 or T-3, is expensive to lease. Providing the leased line has sufficient bandwidth, multiplexing can enable the same line to carry mainframe, LAN, voice, video conferencing, and various other data types.

■ **When bandwidth is idle.** Many organizations have installed fiber-optic cable that is being used only to partial capacity. With the proper equipment, a single fiber can support hundreds of megabits or even a gigabit or more of data capacity.

■ **When large amounts of data need to be transmitted through low-capacity channels.** Multiplexing techniques can divide the original data stream into several lower-bandwidth channels, each of which can be transmitted through a lower capacity medium. The signals can be recombined at the receiving end.

Multiplexing is the process of combining multiple data channels for transmission on a common medium. *Demultiplexing* is the process of recovering the original separate channels from a multiplexed signal.

Multiplexing and demultiplexing are performed by a *multiplexor*, which usually has both capabilities. A multiplexor is sometimes called a *mux*.

The following two techniques are used to multiplex signals:

■ Frequency-division multiplexing

■ Time-division multiplexing

Frequency-Division Multiplexing

Figure 21.14 illustrates *frequency-division multiplexing*. The technique works by converting all data channels to analog form. Each of these analog signals can be modulated by a separate frequency (called a *carrier frequency*) that makes it possible to recover that signal during the demultiplexing process. At the receiving end, the demultiplexor can select the desired carrier signal and use it to extract the data signal for that channel.

FDM can be used in broadband LANs (a standard for Ethernet exists). One advantage of FDM is that it supports bi-directional signaling on the same cable.

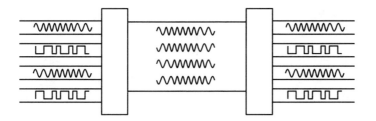

Figure 21.14
Frequency-division multiplexing.

Time-Division Multiplexing

Time-division multiplexing (TDM) divides a channel into time slots that are allocated to the data streams to be transmitted. Figure 21.15 illustrates the process. Provided that the sender and receiver agree on the time slot assignments, the receiver can easily recover and reconstruct the original data streams.

TDM transmits the multiplexed signal in baseband mode. Interestingly, this makes it possible to multiplex a TDM multiplexed signal as one of the data channels on an FDM system.

Conventional TDM equipment utilizes fixed time divisions and allocates time to a channel regardless of how busy that channel is. If a channel is not busy, its time slot is not being fully utilized. Because the time divisions are programmed into the configurations of the multiplexors, this technique often is referred to as *synchronous TDM*.

If it is important to use the capacity of the data medium more efficiently, a more sophisticated technique called *statistical time-division multiplexing* (StatTDM) may be used. A stat-mux uses the time-slot technique, but allocates time slots based on the traffic demand on the individual channels. Figure 21.16 illustrates the process. Notice that Channel B is allocated more time slots than Channel A, while Channel C is allocated the fewest time slots. Channel D is idle and no slots are allocated to it. To make this procedure work, the data transmitted for each time slot includes a control field that identifies to which channel the data in the time slot should be assigned.

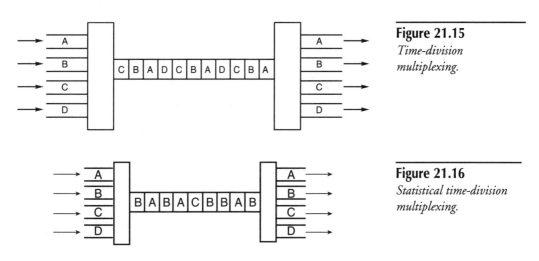

Figure 21.15
Time-division multiplexing.

Figure 21.16
Statistical time-division multiplexing.

Questions

1. Which THREE of the following are functions of the OSI physical layer?

   ☐ A. Mechanical and electrical specifications for using the medium

   ☐ B. Generating electrical signals on the medium

   ☐ C. Network topology

   ☐ D. Bit transmission encoding and timing

2. Which THREE of these network topologies consist of point-to-point links?

   ☐ A. Bus

   ☐ B. Ring

   ☐ C. Star

   ☐ D. Mesh

3. Which network topologies are subject to a single point of failure (that is, one failure can stop all network communication)?

   ○ A. Mesh

   ○ B. Bus

   ○ C. Star

   ○ D. Ring

4. Which THREE are advantages of star topologies?

   ☐ A. Reconfiguration is simplified

   ☐ B. Cable costs are minimized

   ☐ C. Active hubs can regenerate signals

   ☐ D. They are easy to troubleshoot

5. Which TWO are advantages of bus topologies?

   ☐ A. Long cable runs are possible without signal regeneration.

   ☐ B. They often require least amounts of cable.

   ☐ C. They are well-proven technology.

   ☐ D. They are easy to troubleshoot.

6. Which TWO are examples of analog data?

   ☐ A. Light from a switched electric light

   ☐ B. Sound from a radio

   ☐ C. Morse code

   ☐ D. A sine wave

7. Which TWO of the following are analog modulation techniques?

   ☐ A. Phase shift keying

   ☐ B. Binary modulation

   ☐ C. State transition encoding

   ☐ D. ASK

8. Which TWO of the following characteristics of an analog waveform are directly related?

   ☐ A. Amplitude

   ☐ B. Wavelength

   ☐ C. Frequency

   ☐ D. Phase

9. Which bit synchronization techniques can operate without a single-channel medium, such as a single pair of wires?

☐ A. Guaranteed state change

☐ B. Asynchronous

☐ C. Oversampling

☐ D. Separate clock signals

10. Which TWO techniques encode data in digital form for transmission on the media?

☐ A. Time-division multiplexing

☐ B. Frequency-division multiplexing

☐ C. Phase shift keying

☐ D. Current state encoding

Answers

1.	A C D
2.	B C D
3.	C
4.	A C D
5.	B C
6.	B D
7.	A D
8.	B C
9.	A B C
10.	A D

OSI Data Link Layer Concepts

Recall from the previous chapter that the OSI physical layer is concerned only with transmitting and receiving bits. Network communication, however, is considerably more involved than moving bits from one device to another. In fact, dozens of steps must be performed to complete the task of transporting a message from one device to another. This chapter examines the tasks performed by the data link layer.

Real messages consist not of single bits but of meaningful groups of bits. The data link layer receives messages called frames from upper layers (recall the description of OSI layer-to-layer communication in Chapter 18, "The OSI Layered Protocol Model"). A primary function of the data link layer is to disassemble these frames into bits for transmission and then to reconstruct frames from bits that are received.

The data link layer has other functions as well (although all functions may not be performed by a given network protocol stack). This layer performs the following tasks:

- Identifies devices on the network

- Controls (and possibly corrects) errors

- Controls access to the network medium

- Defines the logical topology of the network

- Controls data flow

 The data link layer is conventionally divided into two sublayers:

- *Media access control* (MAC). This sublayer controls the means by which multiple devices share the same media channel.

- *Logical link control* (LLC). This sublayer establishes and maintains links between communicating devices.

This chapter covers the following data link layer topics:

- Logical topologies

- Media access control

- Addressing

- Transmission synchronization

- Connection services

Logical Topologies

Chapter 21, "OSI Physical Layer Concepts," introduces physical topologies, which describe how the media are physically arranged to build a network.

Besides having a physical topology, a network has a logical topology that describes the path that a signal follows on a network. The logical and physical topologies of a network may be the same or different.

Token ring is the most dramatic example of a network having different physical and logical topologies. Figure 22.1 illustrates how computers are connected on a token ring. Each computer transmits signals to the receiver on the next computer. In this way, signals travel through each station on the cabling system, eventually completing a trip back to the station that originated them. Recall that a logical topology describes the manner in which signals travel on the network. It is easy to see why token ring networks have a *ring* logical topology.

T = TRANSMIT
R = RECEIVE

Figure 22.1
Logical topology of a token-ring network.

Token-ring networks, however, are never physically wired in rings. Hubs are used instead, and each computer is cabled to the hub by a drop cable. Figure 22.2 shows how the computers and cables are arranged. Notice the way the cables are connected within the hub so that the transmitter side of one computer connects to the receiver of the next computer. This is exactly the same logical relationship we saw in Figure 22.1, and the logical topology is still a ring.

Due to the manner in which each computer is cabled individually to a hub, however, the physical topology of a token ring is a star.

Coax Ethernet is an example of a bus network where every station is connected to every other station in a multi-point physical topology. Also, every Ethernet station broadcasts signals to every other station, resulting in a bus logical topology as well. Ethernet, therefore, has a physical bus topology and a logical bus topology (see fig. 22.3).

A 10BASE-T Ethernet uses UTP cable and hub-based wiring, but it remains a logical bus because devices continue to communicate using multi-point communication. A 10BASE-T Ethernet, therefore, is a physical star but a logical bus.

 The following are some rules of thumb for distinguishing between physical and logical:

■ If you can see it or touch it, it is physical.

■ If you can't see it or touch it, it is logical.

The following are rules of thumb for distinguishing between bus and ring networks:

■ If signals from each computer are received by every other computer, the network is a bus.

■ If each computer receives signals from only one other computer, the network is a ring.

T = TRANSMIT
R = RECEIVE

Figure 22.2
A logical ring is configured as a physical star.

Figure 22.3
Ethernet is both a physical and a logical bus.

Media Access Control

Any given media channel can support only one signal at a time. If two computers transmit on the channel at the same time, their signals will interfere with each other, much as voices interfere when two people speak at the same time. Media access control is the process of controlling access to the media so that interference cannot take place.

This section discusses three forms of media access control:

- Contention
- Token passing
- Polling

Contention

With contention-based access control, any computer can transmit at any time. This system breaks down when two computers attempt to transmit at the same time, in which case a collision occurs (see fig. 22.4). Eventually, when a network gets busy enough, most attempts to transmit result in collisions and little effective communication can take place.

Mechanisms, therefore, are usually put into place to minimize the effects of collisions. One mechanism is *carrier sensing*, in which each computer listens to the network before attempting to

transmit. If the network is busy, the computer refrains from transmitting until the network is quiet. This simple "listen before talking" strategy can significantly reduce collisions.

Another mechanism is *carrier detection*. With this strategy, computers continue to listen to the network as they are transmitting. If a computer detects another signal that interferes with the signal it is sending, it will stop transmitting. Both computers then wait a random amount of time and attempt to retransmit. Unless the network is extremely busy, carrier detection along with carrier sensing can manage a large volume of transmissions.

Both of these mechanisms used together form the protocol used in all types of Ethernet, which is called *Carrier Sense Multiple Access with Collision Detection* (CSMA/CD).

Apple's LocalTalk networks uses the protocol *Carrier Sense Multiple Access with Collision Avoidance* (CSMA/CA). *Collision Avoidance* uses additional techniques to further reduce the likelihood of collisions.

Note According to the course definitions, contention is an access-control *method*. CSMA/CD and CSMA/CA are *protocols* that incorporate contention-access methods.

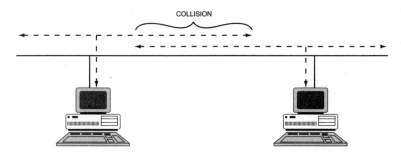

Figure 22.4

A collision on a contention-based network.

The following summarizes the characteristics of contention-access controls:

■ Pure contention systems permit all stations to transmit whenever they want (although mechanisms are virtually always in place to limit transmission).

■ Collisions always occur at some level on contention-based networks, with the number increasing geometrically as transmissions increase.

■ CSMA/CD and CSMA/CA are two protocols that reduce the damage caused by collisions.

Although it sounds as if contention methods are unworkable due to the damage caused by collisions, contention (in particular CSMA/CD) is the most popular media access control method on LANs in the form of Ethernet. (In fact, no currently employed LAN standards utilize pure contention access control without adding some mechanism to reduce the incidence of collisions.)

Contention is a simple protocol that can be managed with simple software and hardware. Unless traffic levels exceed about 30 percent of bandwidth, contention works quite well. Contention-based networks offer excellent performance at low cost.

Because collisions occur at unpredictable intervals, however, no computer is guaranteed the capability

to transmit at any given time. Contention-based networks are called "probabalistic" because a computer's chance of being permitted to transmit cannot be predicted.

Collisions increase in frequency as more computers use the network. When the number of computers on the network climbs to an unmanageable amount, collisions dominate network traffic and few frames are transmitted without error.

All computers on a contention-based network are equal. Consequently, it is not possible to assign certain computers higher priorities and therefore greater access to the network.

 This course recommends contention access control for networks that experience bursty traffic—that is, large intermittent file transfers—and have relatively few computers.

Token Passing

Token passing utilizes a frame called a *token,* which circulates around the network. A computer that needs to transmit must wait until it receives the token frame, at which time it is permitted to transmit. When the computer is finished transmitting, it passes the token frame to the next station on the network. Figure 22.5 shows how token passing is implemented on a token-ring network.

Figure 22.5
Token passing.

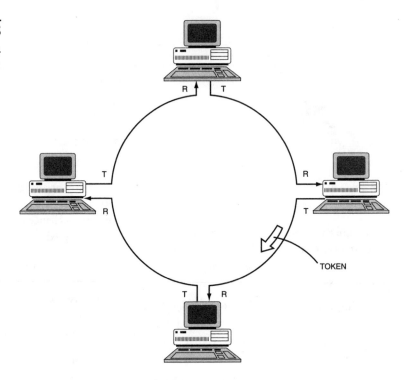

Several network standards employ token passing access control:

■ The most common is token ring, defined by IEEE standard 802.5.

■ IEEE standard 802.4 defines a bus network that also employs token passing. This standard is implemented only infrequently.

■ FDDI is a 100 Mbps fiber-optic network standard that uses token passing and rings in much the same manner as 802.5 Token Ring.

Token passing methods can use station priorities and other methods to prevent any one station from monopolizing the network. Because each computer has a chance to transmit each time the token travels around the network, each station is guaranteed a chance to transmit at some minimum time interval.

 Token passing is more appropriate than contention under the following conditions:

■ When the network is carrying time-critical data. Because token passing results in more predictable delivery, token passing is called deterministic.

■ When the network experiences heavy utilization. Performance typically falls off more gracefully with a token passing network than with a contention-based network. Token passing networks cannot become gridlocked due to excessive numbers of collisions.

■ When some stations should have higher priority than others. Some token passing schemes support priority assignments.

Comparing Contention and Token Passing

As an access control mechanism, token passing appears to be clearly superior to contention. You will find, however, that Ethernet, by far the dominant LAN standard, has achieved its prominence while firmly wedded to contention access control.

Token passing requires a variety of complex control mechanisms to make it work well. The hardware required is considerably more expensive than the hardware required to implement the much simpler contention mechanisms. The higher cost of token passing networks is difficult to justify unless the special features are required.

Because token passing networks are designed for high reliability, it is common to build network diagnostic and troubleshooting capabilities into the network hardware. This further increases the costs of token passing networks. Organizations must decide whether this additional reliability is worth the extra cost.

Conversely, though token passing networks perform better than contention-based networks when traffic levels are high, contention networks have superior performance under lighter loading conditions. The process of passing the token around (and other maintenance operations) eats into the available bandwidth. As a result, a 10 Mbps Ethernet and a 16 Mbps token ring perform comparably under light loading conditions, but the Ethernet costs considerably less. Figure 22.6 illustrates the performance characteristics you can expect from each access control method. (This figure reproduces the graph used for the course, and implies that token passing throughput will eventually reach a zero level, which cannot, in fact, happen, regardless of the loading conditions. Although a station's access to the network may be limited, access is guaranteed with each circuit of the token.)

 The course materials emphasize that the comparisons being stated consider only pure contention-based networks, not networks that employ collision reduction schemes such as Ethernet. As noted, however, no current LAN standards employ contention as a media access control method without adding collision reduction techniques.

Polling

Polling is an access control method that employs a central device to regulate all access to the network. Polling is the most common access control method employed with mainframe computer networks.

The central device, called a *primary*, requests data from devices on the network, called *secondaries*. After it is *polled*, a secondary can transmit an amount of data that is determined by the protocols employed on the network. A secondary device cannot transmit unless it is polled by the primary.

Polling guarantees each device fair access to the network, and is suitable for use with time-critical data. In fact, polling has many of the advantages of token passing:

- Access times are predictable. Access is, therefore, deterministic.

- Priorities can be assigned.

- Collisions are eliminated.

A significant difference between polling and token passing is that polling centralizes control. This centralization can be an advantage from a management standpoint, but introduces a single point of failure. If the central control mechanism fails, the network stops functioning. Token passing uses more distributed control functions that are less subject to single points of failure.

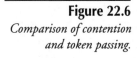

Figure 22.6
Comparison of contention and token passing.

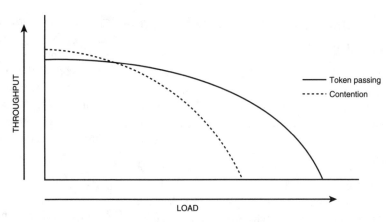

Because polling centralizes control, secondary devices cannot communicate directly with other secondary devices. Rather, they must use the primary as an intermediary.

Furthermore, because the primary must poll each secondary—whether or not the secondary has data to transmit—polling wastes large amounts of network bandwidth. This can result in excessive delays as some secondaries wait while others are polled.

Summary of Access Control Methods

Access control method	*Advantages*	*Considerations*
Contention	Simple software.	Access is probalistic (not guaranteed).
	Once access is gained, device has complete control of the medium.	No priority mechanism.
		Collisions increase geometrically with demand.
Token passing	Each device is guaranteed media access (deterministic).	More complex software and hardware.
	Priorities might be assigned.	Might require a central control device.
	Collisions are eliminated.	
	High throughput under heavy load.	

Access control method	Advantages	Considerations
Polling	Each device is guaranteed media access (deterministic).	Polling uses significant portion of network bandwidth.
	Priorities might be assigned.	Polling requires bandwidth overhead, even for devices that have nothing to transmit.
	Collisions are eliminated.	

Addressing

The data link layer maintains device addresses that enable messages to be sent to a particular device. The addresses used are called *physical device addresses*, which are unique addresses associated with the networking hardware in the computer. In most cases (for example, Ethernet and token ring) the physical device address is burned into the network interface card at the time the card is manufactured.

The standards that apply to a particular network determine the format of the address. Because the address format is associated with the media access control method being used, physical device addresses are frequently referred to as *MAC addresses*.

The device address is not actually used to route a message to a specific device. Frames on LANs are typically transmitted so that they are available to all devices on the network. Each device reads each frame far enough to determine the device address to which the frame is addressed. If the frame's destination address matches the device's own physical address, the rest of the frame will be received. If the addresses do not match, the remainder of the frame is ignored.

As Chapter 20, "Transmission Media Connections," explains, bridges can be used to divide large networks into several smaller ones. Bridges use physical device addresses to determine which frames should remain on the current network segment and which should be forwarded to devices on other network segments. Some bridges must be programmed with the device addresses for each attached network segment, but transparent or learning bridges can learn addresses by analyzing network traffic.

Because bridges utilize physical device addresses to manage frame routing, they function at the level of the data link layer and are data link layer connectivity devices.

Transmission Synchronization

Chapter 21 introduces the need to synchronize bit transmissions between sending and receiving devices. The data link layer, however, operates on data after the bits have been assembled to form characters, frames, or other data groups. At the data link layer, it is also necessary to synchronize frame transmissions. This section discusses three mechanisms:

■ Asynchronous

■ Synchronous

■ Isochronous

Asynchronous Transmission

Asynchronous transmission does not use a clocking mechanism to keep the sending and receiving devices synchronized. Instead, bit synchronization is used to synchronize the devices for each frame that is transmitted.

Each frame begins with a start bit that enables the receiving device to adjust to the timing of the transmitted signal. Messages are kept short so that the sending and receiving devices do not drift out of synchronization for the duration of the message. Asynchronous transmission is most frequently used to transmit character data and is ideally suited to environments where characters are transmitted at irregular intervals, such as when users are typing in character data.

Figure 22.7 illustrates the structure of a typical frame used to transmit character data. This frame has four components:

■ **A start bit.** Signals that a frame is starting and enables the receiving device to synchronize itself with the message.

■ **Data bits.** Consist of 7 or 8 bits when character data is being transmitted.

■ **A parity bit.** Optionally used as a crude method of detecting transmission errors.

■ **A stop bit or bits.** Signal the end of the data frame.

Error detection in asynchronous transmission makes use of the parity bit. Several schemes are available for using the parity bit. The most common include the following:

■ **Even parity.** The parity bit is set to ensure that an even number of 1 bits are sent. If the data field has three 1's, the parity bit will be set to 1 to produce a total of four 1 bits.

■ **Odd parity.** The parity bit is set to ensure that an odd number of 1 bits are sent. If the data field has three 1's, the parity bit will be set to 0 to produce a total of three 0 bits.

Parity techniques can detect errors that affect one bit. They might, however, be unable to detect errors that affect two or more bits.

Asynchronous transmission is a simple, inexpensive technology ideally suited for transmitting small frames at irregular intervals.

Because start, stop, and parity bits must be added to each character to be transmitted, however, overhead for asynchronous transmission is high, in the neighborhood of 20 to 30 percent. This wastes bandwidth and makes asynchronous transmission undesirable for transmitting large amounts of data.

Asynchronous transmission is frequently used for PC-to-PC and terminal-to-host communication. Data in these environments is often of the bursty, character-oriented nature that is ideal for asynchronous communication. In both cases, it is also generally desirable to reduce costs of communication hardware, which is best achieved with asynchronous transmission.

Figure 22.7
Structure of an asynchronous frame.

Synchronous Transmission

Communication can be made more efficient if the clocks on the transmitting and receiving devices are synchronized. This synchronization is accomplished in two ways:

■ By transmitting synchronization signals with data. Some data encoding techniques, by guaranteeing a signal transition with each bit transmitted, are inherently self-clocking.

■ By using a separate communication channel to carry clock signals, a technique that can function with any signal encoding technique.

Figure 22.8 illustrates two possible structures of messages associated with synchronous trans mission.

Both transmissions begin with a series of *synch signals*, which notify the receiver of the beginning of a frame. Synch signals generally utilize a bit pattern that cannot appear elsewhere in messages, ensuring that they will always be distinct and easy for the receiver to recognize.

A wide variety of data types can be transmitted. Figure 22.8 illustrates both character-oriented and

bit-oriented data. Notice that multiple characters or long series of bits can be transmitted in a single data frame. Because the transmitter and receiver remain in synchronization for the duration of the transmission, frames may be of great length.

When frames are longer, parity is no longer a suitable method of detecting error. If errors are occurring, it is more likely that multiple bits will be affected and that parity techniques will not report an error properly. The technique used with synchronous transmission is the *cyclic redundancy check* (CRC). The transmitter uses an algorithm to calculate a CRC value that summarizes the entire value of the data bits. This CRC value is appended to the data frame. The receiver uses the same algorithm, recalculates the CRC, and compares the CRC in the frame to the value it has calculated. If the values match, it is virtually certain that the frame was transmitted without error.

An *end bit pattern* unambiguously indicates the end of a frame. As with the synch bits, the end bit pattern is frequently a pattern that cannot appear in the body of the data frame, eliminating confusion on the part of the receiver.

SYNCH	SYNCH	CHARACTER	• • •	CHARACTER	CRC	END

Figure 22.8
Structures of synchronous transmissions.

SYNCH	SYNCH	BINARY DATA	CRC	END	FILL BITS	SYNCH	SYNCH	DATA	CRC	END

When synchronous transmission links are idle, it is common to transmit *fill bits* that keep the devices synchronized, eliminating the need to resynchronize devices when a new frame is transmitted.

Synchronous transmission has many advantages over asynchronous transmission. Overhead bits (synch, CRC, and end) are a smaller proportion of the overall data frame, making synchronous transmission far more efficient in its use of bandwidth. Synchronization enables the systems to utilize higher speeds and to improve error detection.

The disadvantage of synchronous transmission is primarily higher cost due to the more complex circuitry required. Consequently, synchronous transmission is employed primarily when high volumes of data must be transmitted.

Synchronous transmission is frequently used in mainframe-to-mainframe communication, and is also used to achieve high efficiency levels on LANs. Both Ethernet and token ring, for example, utilize self-clocking signals.

Isochronous Transmission

Isochronous transmission employs a common device that supplies a clocking signal shared by all devices on the network. The clocking device creates time slots. Devices with data to transmit monitor the network and insert data into open time slots as they become available. A given time slot can be filled to capacity with multiple frames.

Isochronous transmission guarantees transmission rates, is deterministic, and has low overhead. The technique, however, introduces a single point of failure; it is necessary to ensure that the clocking device is fault-tolerant.

Connection Services

Network connection services provide a variety of functions:

■ Flow control determines the amount of data that can be transmitted in a given time period. Flow control prevents the transmitting device from overwhelming the receiver. Flow control can take place at several protocol levels, including the LLC sublayer.

■ Error control detects errors in received frames and requests retransmission of frames. Error control is a function of the LLC sublayer.

■ Sequence control enables receivers to reassemble data frames into their original order. Frame size is limited, and packet fragmentation and reassembly is necessary to transmit large messages. Sequence control is a function of the network layer.

Three types of connection services provide different combinations of the above services:

■ **Unacknowledged connectionless services.** Provide no flow, error, or sequence control. When required, these services must be provided by higher protocol layers. Unacknowledge connectionless service provides high performance when network communication can be safely assumed to be reliable (as on most LANs).

■ **Connection-oriented services.** Provide flow, error, and sequence control through use of acknowledgments. Connection-oriented services have higher overhead, reducing performance but improving reliability when network reliability is in question (as on most WANs).

■ **Acknowledged connectionless services.** Use acknowledgments to provide flow and error control on point-to-point connections.

Flow Control at the LLC Sublayer

Flow control prevents receiving devices from being overwhelmed by faster transmitting devices. Two common techniques of flow control are guaranteed rate flow control and window flow control.

Guaranteed Rate Flow Control

With *guaranteed rate flow control*, the sending and receiving devices negotiate a mutually acceptable transmission rate. Typically, this transmission rate holds constant for the duration of a communication session.

To ensure that frames are received without error, some protocols require the receiver to acknowledge each frame as it is processed. If no error is detected, an acknowledgment frame is returned to the transmitter, instructing it to send the next frame. If errors are detected, the receiver does one of two things: it sends a retransmission request, or it simply waits until the transmitter times out and retransmits the frame.

Essentially, guaranteed rate flow control assumes that the receiver processes one message unit (bit or frame) for each unit transmitted. This rather inflexible approach often fails to make the most efficient use of transmitter, receiver, and media channel capacities.

Window Flow Control

Buffering is a technique that enables transmitters and receivers to operate with more flexibility. Buffers consist of memory that can receive data from the network and hold it until the receiver can process the data and acknowledge that it has been received.

Windowing is a technique that enables the transmitter to send several data frames prior to receiving

acknowledgment from the receiver. Several frames may be buffered in the receiver as they are processed. The number of frames a transmitter can send without receiving an acknowledgment is known as a *window*.

Static window flow control limits the window size to a specific number of frames, usually defined by the number of frames that can fit in the receiver's input buffer. If the window size is 7, the transmitter can have as many as seven outstanding frames. An eighth frame cannot be transmitted, however, until one of the outstanding frames is acknowledged (see fig. 22.9).

Dynamic window flow control improves efficiency by enabling the communicating devices to adjust the window size. Other terms for this technique are *floating* or *sliding* windows. One dynamic window technique enables the receiver to send out a *choke frame* when its input buffer is nearing capacity. This choke frame signals the transmitter to slow down. After the transmitter adjusts its transmission rate downward, it will slowly increase its transmission rate until it receives another choke frame. In this way, bandwidth utilization is optimized.

Error Control

Two LLC error conditions can exist:

■ When CRC errors are detected

■ When expected acknowledgments are not received

Recall from earlier in this chapter that synchronous data frames incorporate a *cyclic redundancy check* (CRC) field that can be used to detect transmission errors. When a receiving device detects a CRC error, it can transmit a *negative acknowledgment* (NAK) that requests retransmission of the frame.

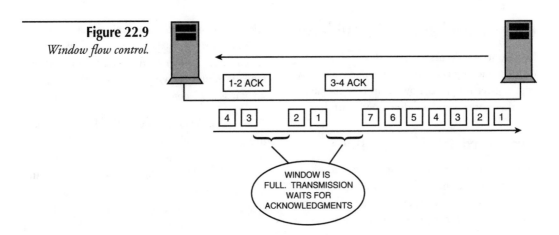

Figure 22.9
Window flow control.

When acknowledged services are employed, the transmitter expects *acknowledgment* (ACK) frames from the receiver for each frame (or a group of frames in a windowed protocol). When a specified interval of time expires without an acknowledgment, the transmitter assumes that the frame was lost and retransmits it.

Questions

1. Which of the following statements is true?

   ○ A. Logical topologies are determined by the cabling system.

   ○ B. A physical bus network may be a logical ring.

   ○ C. A physical star network can be a logical ring.

   ○ D. Contention can be used as an access control medium on a physical ring.

2. Which protocol layer enables multiple devices to share the transmission medium?

   ○ A. Physical

   ○ B. MAC

   ○ C. LLC

   ○ D. Network

3. Which of the following is an error control mechanism?

   ○ A. Contention

   ○ B. Synchronous transmission

   ○ C. CRC

   ○ D. LLC

4. Which of the following layers establishes and maintains a link between communicating devices?

   ○ A. Physical

   ○ B. MAC

   ○ C. LLC

   ○ D. Network

5. Which of the following techniques uses network bandwidth most efficiently?

   ○ A. Static window flow control

   ○ B. Guaranteed rate flow control

   ○ C. Dynamic rate flow control

   ○ D. Dynamic window flow control

6. Which of the following access methods is centrally managed?

   ○ A. Contention

   ○ B. Token passing

   ○ C. Polling

   ○ D. Collision detection

7. Which TWO of the following services provides flow control?

   ☐ A. Acknowledged connectionless

   ☐ B. Unacknowledged connectionless

   ☐ C. Unacknowledged connection-oriented

   ☐ D. Connection-oriented

8. Which of the following access control methods is probabalistic?

   ○ A. Polling

   ○ B. Contention

   ○ C. Token passing

   ○ D. Sliding window

9. Which of the following methods relies on the internal clocks of transmitting and receiving devices?

   ○ A. Synchronous

   ○ B. Isochronous

   ○ C. Asynchronous

   ○ D. Nonsynchronous

10. Which of the following connectivity devices functions at the data link layer?

   ○ A. Repeater

   ○ B. Router

   ○ C. Hub

   ○ D. Bridge

Answers

1. C	6. C
2. B	7. A D
3. C	8. B
4. C	9. C
5. D	10. D

OSI Network Layer Concepts

The data link layer deals with communication between devices on the same network. Physical device addresses are used to identify data frames, and it is the responsibility of each device to monitor the network and receive frames that are addressed to that device.

The network layer involves communication with devices on logically separate networks that are connected to form internetworks. Because internetworks can be large and can be built of different types of networks, the network layer utilizes routing algorithms that can be used to guide packets from their source to their destination networks.

A key element of the network layer is that each network in the internetwork is assigned a network address that can be used to route packets. The nature of those addresses and how they are used to route packets defines the majority of topics in this chapter, which include the following:

- Addressing

- Switching

- Routing algorithms

- Connection services

- Gateway services

Addressing

You have already encountered the use of physical device addresses, which uniquely identify each device on a network. The network layer makes use of two additional address types, as follows:

- *Logical network addresses*, which are used to route packets to specific networks on the internetwork

- *Services addresses*, which route packets to specific processes running on the destination device

Logical Network Addresses

Logical network addresses are assigned when the networks are configured. If you have installed NetWare servers, you are familiar with the process of assigning a logical network address to each LAN that is attached to the server. One of the tasks a network installer must accomplish is to make sure that each network address is unique on a given

internetwork. Network addresses enable routers to forward frames through the internetwork to the appropriate networks.

Service Addresses

The operating systems on most computers are capable of running several processes at once. When a packet arrives, it is necessary to determine which process on the computer should receive the data in the packet. This is achieved by assigning service addresses, which identify upper-layer processes and protocols. These service addresses are included with the physical and logical network addresses in the data frame. (Some protocols refer to service addresses as *sockets* or *ports*.)

Some service addresses, called *well-known addresses*, are universally defined for a given type of network. Other service addresses are defined by the vendors of network products.

Addressing Summary

A possible format of the address information for a packet is shown in figure 23.1. Three address components appear, as follows:

- *Physical (MAC) network addresses* identify a particular device as the source or destination of a frame.

- *Logical network addresses* identify a particular network on the internetwork as the source or destination of a packet.

- *Service addresses* identify a process or protocol on the computer that is the source or destination of a packet.

Figure 23.1
Address information showing physical and logical network addresses with a service address.

Switching

Many internetworks include redundant data paths that may be used to route messages. The following switching techniques may be used to route messages:

- Circuit switching

- Message switching

- Packet switching

Circuit Switching

As shown in figure 23.2, *circuit switching* establishes a path that remains fixed for the duration of a connection. Much as telephone switching equipment establishes a route between your telephone on the East Coast and a telephone you dial on the West Coast, circuit switching networks establish a path through the internetwork when the devices initiate a conversation.

Circuit switching provides devices with a dedicated path and a well-defined bandwidth.

Circuit switching is not without disadvantages, however. The process of establishing a connection between devices may be time-consuming. Because other traffic cannot share the dedicated media path, bandwidth may be inefficiently utilized. Because circuit switching networks must have a surplus of bandwidth, they tend to be expensive to construct.

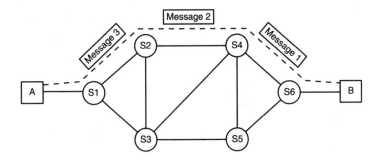

Figure 23.2
Circuit switching.

Message Switching

Message switching treats each message as an independent entity. Each message carries address information that describes the message's destination. This information is used at each switch to transfer the message to the next switch in its route. Message switches are programmed with information concerning other switches in the network that can be used to forward messages to their destinations. They may also be programmed with information about the most efficient routes. Depending on network conditions, different messages may be sent through the network by different routes, as shown in figure 23.3.

Message switching transfers the complete message from one switch to the next switch, where the message is stored before it is forwarded another time. Because each message is stored before it is sent on to the next switch, this type of network is frequently called a *store-and-forward* network. The message switches are often general-purpose computers. They must be equipped with sufficient storage (usually hard drives) to enable them to store messages until it is possible to forward them.

Electronic mail is a common application for message switching. Some delay is permissible when

delivering mail, unlike the requirements when two computers are exchanging data in real time. Message switching uses relatively low-cost devices to forward messages and can function well with relatively slow communication channels. Other applications for message switching include group applications such as workflow, calendaring, and groupware.

Message switching has several advantages, as follows:

■ Data channels are shared among communicating devices, improving the efficiency of using available bandwidth.

■ Message switches can store messages until a channel becomes available, reducing sensitivity to network congestion.

■ Message priorities may be used to manage network traffic.

■ Broadcast addressing uses network bandwidth more efficiently by delivering messages to multiple destinations.

The chief disadvantage of message switching is that it is unsuitable to real-time applications, including data communication, video, and audio.

Figure 23.3

Message switching.

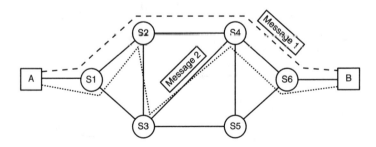

Packet Switching

In *package switching*, messages are divided into smaller packets. Each packet includes source and destination address information so that individual packets can be routed through the internetwork independently. As you can see in figure 23.4, the packets that make up a message may take very different routes through the internetwork.

So far, this looks a lot like message switching. The distinguishing characteristic is that packets are restricted to a size that enables the switching devices to manage the packet data entirely in memory, without the need to store the data temporarily on disk. Packet switching, therefore, routes packets through the network much more rapidly and efficiently than is possible with message switching.

Several methods of packet switching exist. The following two are discussed in this course:

■ Datagram

■ Virtual circuit

Datagram Packet Switching

Datagram services treat each packet as an independent message. Each packet is routed through the internetwork independently, and each switch node decides which network segment should be used for the next step in the packet's route. This capability enables switches to bypass busy segments and take other steps to speed packets through the internetwork. This is the specific approach that was shown in figure 23.4.

Datagrams are frequently used on LANs. Network layer protocols are responsible for delivering the frame to the appropriate network. Then, because each datagram includes destination address information, devices on the local network can recognize and receive datagrams that they are intended to receive.

 Packet switching matches the need to transmit large messages with the fairly small frame size that can be accommodated by the physical layer. The network layer is responsible for fragmenting messages from upper layers into smaller datagrams that are appropriate for the physical layer. The network layer is also responsible for reconstructing messages from datagrams as they are received.

Figure 23.4
Packet switching.

Virtual Circuit Packet Switching

Virtual circuits operate by establishing a formal connection between two devices that are in communication. When devices begin a session, they negotiate communication parameters, such as maximum message size, communication windows, network paths, and so forth. This negotiation establishes a *virtual circuit*, a well-defined path through the internetwork through which the devices communicate. This virtual circuit generally remains in effect until the devices stop communicating.

Virtual circuits are distinguished by the establishment of a logical connection. *Virtual* means that the network behaves as though a dedicated physical circuit has been established between the devices that are communicating. Even though no such physical circuit exists, the network presents the appearance of a physical connection so far as the devices at the ends of the circuit are concerned.

Virtual circuits are frequently employed in conjunction with connection-oriented services, which are discussed later in this chapter.

Advantages of Packet Switching

Packet switching optimizes the use of bandwidth by enabling many devices to route packets through the same network channels. At any given time, a switch may be routing packets to several different destination devices, adjusting the routes as required to achieve the best efficiency possible at the present time.

Because entire messages are not stored at the switches prior to forwarding, transmission delays are significantly less than delays encountered with message switching.

Although the switching devices do not need to be equipped with large amounts of hard drive capacity, they might need a significant amount of real-time memory. Also, they must have sufficient processing power to run the more complex routing protocols that are required for packet switching. Among the new complexities is the need to recognize when packets have been lost so that retransmission can be requested.

Routing Algorithms

Routing is the process of forwarding messages through switching networks. In some cases, routing information is programmed into switching devices. However, preprogrammed switches cannot adjust to changing network conditions. Most routing devices, therefore, have the capability of discovering routes through the internetwork and storing the route information in route tables.

Route tables do not store only path information. They also store estimates of the time taken to send a message through a given route. This time estimate is known as the *cost* of a particular path. There are several methods of estimating routing costs, as follows:

- *Hop count* describes the number of routers that a message would cross before it reaches its destination. If all hops are assumed to take the same amount of time, the optimum path is the path with the smallest hop count.

- *Tic count* is an actual time estimate, where a *tic* is a time unit that is defined by the routing implementation.

- *Relative expense* is any defined measure of the cost (including the monetary cost) to use a given link.

After costs are established, routers can select routes either statically or dynamically, as follows:

■ *Static route selection* uses routes that have been programmed in by the network administrator.

■ *Dynamic route selection* uses routing cost information to select the most cost-effective route for a given packet. As network conditions change and are reflected in routing tables, the router can select different paths to maintain low costs.

Two methods of route discovery are discussed in this course: distance vector and link-state.

Distance Vector Routing

Distance vector routers advertise their presence to other routers on the network. Periodically, each router on the network will broadcast the information in its routing table. This information can be used by other routers to update their own router tables.

Figure 23.5 illustrates how the process works. In the figure, server S3 learns that server S2 can reach server S1 in three hops. Because Server S3 knows that Server S2 is one hop away, Server S3 knows that its cost to reach Server S1 through Server S2 is two hops.

Distance vector routing is an effective algorithm, but can be fairly inefficient. Because changes must ripple through the network from router to router, it might take a while for a change to become known to all routers on the network. In addition, the frequent broadcasts of routing information produce high levels of network traffic that can hurt performance on larger networks.

 Distance vector routing is the standard routing algorithm for NetWare and is used by the NetWare *Routing Information Protocol* (RIP). You can observe routing information including hop counts by typing **TRACK ON** at a NetWare 3.*x* or 4.*x* server console. Type **TRACK OFF** to cancel the display of routing information.

Figure 23.5
Distance vector routing.

Link-State Routing

Link-state routing reduces the network traffic required to update routing tables. Routers that are newly attached to the network can request routing information from a nearby router.

After routers have exchanged routing information about the network, routers broadcast messages only when something has changed. These messages contain information about the state of each link the router has with other routers on the network. Because routers keep each other updated, complete network routing updates are needed infrequently.

 Link-state routing is employed by Novell's recently introduced *Network Link-State Protocol* (NLSP), which may be substituted for RIP on NetWare 3.*x* and 4.*x* servers.

Connection Services

In Chapter 22, you were introduced to three types of connection services, as follows:

■ *Unacknowledged connectionless services,* which provide no flow control, error detection, or packet sequence control

■ *Connection-oriented services,* which provide flow control and error detection with acknowledgments

■ *Acknowledged connectionless services,* which use acknowledgments to provide flow and error control

The network layer also provides connection-oriented services, including flow control, error

detection, and acknowledgments. Network acknowledgments are employed to provide flow control, error detection, and packet sequence control.

Network Layer Flow Control

The data link layer manages flow control based on the capacities of the devices that are in communication.

The network layer manages flow control to avoid congestion on the network. As you learned in the discussion about routing, the network layer determines the number of packets that will be sent through a given route. By routing packets around busy links, available network bandwidth is used more effectively and congestion is reduced. For this reason, network flow control is often referred to as *congestion control.*

Network layer flow control can permit devices to negotiate a guaranteed data rate. Static and dynamic windows may also be employed.

Receiving devices can control congestion by delaying before sending acknowledgments. Under these circumstances, the sender may assume that the packet was lost and retransmit it. To prevent unnecessary retransmission, some protocols define packets that signal congestion and enable receiving devices to explicitly request delays in transmission.

Network Layer Error Control

A variety of error conditions may be detected at the network layer.

Errors in data are typically detected using CRC algorithms. Because packet header information changes at each hop (addresses change), CRC values must be recalculated by each router.

Although the network layer can implement detection of lost and duplicate packets, these functions are typically handled by the transport layer.

Packet Sequence Control

Recall that packet switching networks may route packets by varying routes. As a result, the packets for a message might arrive at their final destination out of order. This can be the case for both datagram and connection-oriented services.

The network layer may be configured to handle packet sequence control, although that function is generally handled at the transport layer.

Gateway Services

Routers can handle interconnection of networks whose protocols function in similar ways. When the rules are sufficiently different on the two networks, however, a more powerful device is required.

A *gateway* is a device that can reconcile the different rules that are used on two different networks. Gateways are commonly required to connect LANs into mainframe networks, which have completely different protocol architectures than LANs. Mainframe networks, such as IBM's SNA, for example, do not use the same device address schemes as LANs employ (they differ in many other ways as well). It is necessary to "fool" the mainframe network into thinking that mainframe devices are on the LAN, and it is also necessary to make the mainframe look like a LAN, so far as devices on the LAN are concerned.

 Gateways may be implemented at the network layer or at higher layers in the OSI model, depending on where the protocol translation is required.

Questions

Because the material is so intertwined, study questions for this chapter can be found at the end of Chapter 27.

OSI Transport Layer Concepts

The transport layer is the next layer of the OSI model. Lower layer protocols are concerned with delivering messages between devices. The transport layer, however, is concerned with delivering messages between processes running on those devices. Whenever a device is using a multitasking operating system, and multiple processes might be running on the device, it becomes essential that messages be delivered from one process on the transmitting device to the correct process on the receiving device.

The transport layer can implement procedures to ensure the reliable delivery of those segments to their destination devices. The term "reliable" does not mean that errors cannot occur, only that if errors occur, they will be detected. If errors such as lost data are detected, the transport layer either requests retransmission or notifies upper layer protocols so that they can take corrective action.

The transport layer enables upper layer protocols to interface with the network, but hides the complexities of network operation from them. Among it's functions, the transport layer breaks large messages into segments that are suitable for network delivery.

The following transport layer topics are covered in this chapter:

- Addressing
- Address/name resolution
- Segment development
- Connection services

Addressing

Transport layer addressing is concerned with delivering messages from a specific process on one computer to the correct process running on the destination computer. Messages can be identified in two ways: connection identifiers and transaction identifiers.

Connection Identifiers

A connection identifier (connection ID) might also be called a socket or a port depending on the specific protocol implementation. The *connection identifier* labels each conversation and enables a process to communicate with processes running on other devices. A numeric identifier is assigned to each conversation. A service, running at higher OSI levels, identifies communications with a connection ID number that enables the transport layer to direct lower layer addressing and deliver the messages as required.

Transaction Identifiers

Connection identifiers are used when two devices are engaged in multiple exchanges of data. Transaction identifiers are used when the exchange is a one-time event consisting of a request and a response. Only this simple exchange is tracked, no multiple-message conversations that might be occurring between the devices are tracked.

Address/Name Resolution

Network addresses are always binary numbers, which are often 32 bits in length. These numbers can be expressed in decimal or hexadecimal notation to make them easier for humans to identify. Long decimal and hex numbers, however, are not as recognizable as words. For that reason, some network protocols implement a scheme of logical alphanumeric names that humans use when specifying network devices. These names are translated into numeric network addresses by a service on the network. This translation can be performed by individual network devices or by a central name server.

Service-Requester-Initiated Address/Name Resolution

With this method, a device that requires address information broadcasts a packet requesting the information for a given name, address, or service. The device that corresponds to the name, address, or service responds with the required information.

Service-Provider-Initiated Address/Name Resolution

This method employs a central directory server (also called a name server) that collects information which is broadcast by devices on the network. Devices that require name or address information can request it from the directory server.

Segment Development

When messages from higher-level protocols exceed the size allowed by a protocol stack for a segment, the transport layer divides outbound messages into segments of a suitable size. The transport layer also recombines incoming segments into message formats required by upper layers.

The transport layer also can combine multiple small messages into a single segment to improve network efficiency. As shown in figure 24.1, each message component is identified by a connection identifier (CID). The CID enables the transport layer of the receiving device to deliver each message to the proper process.

Connection Services

Some services can be performed at more than one layer of the OSI model. In addition to the data link and network layers, the transport layer can have some responsibility for connection services.

Segment Sequencing

One connection-oriented service provided by the transport layer is segment sequencing. When large messages are divided into segments for transport, the transport layer must resequence the segments when they are received prior to reassembling the original message.

Error Control

When segments are lost in transmission, or when segments have duplicate segment IDs, the transport layer must initiate error recovery. The following strategies are available:

■ Unique segment sequence numbers

■ Virtual circuits, permitting only one virtual circuit per session

■ Timeouts removed from the network segments that have been misrouted and have remained on the network past a specified time

ADDRESS
INFORMATION

MULTIPLE MESSAGES
COMBINED INTO A
SINGLE SEGMENT

Figure 24.1
Identification of messages at transport layer.

The transport layer also detects corrupted segments by managing end-to-end error control using techniques such as checksums.

End-to-End Flow control

The transport layer uses acknowledgments to manage end-to-end flow control between two connected devices.

Besides negative acknowledgments, some transport layer protocols can request the retransmission of the most recent segments. These acknowledgments are called *go back n* or *selective repeat* acknowledgments.

Go back *n* acknowledgments request retransmission of the last *n* packets. Selective repeat acknowledgments can request retransmission of specific packets.

This approach is useful when the receiving device's buffers overflowed before it was able to warn the transmitting device to cease transmission.

Questions

You will find study questions for this chapter at the end of Chapter 27, "OSI Application Layer Concepts."

OSI Session Layer Concepts

he session layer manages dialogs between two computers by establishing, managing, and terminating communications.

The following two session layer topics are discussed in this chapter:

- *Dialog control*
- *Session administration*

Dialog Control

As illustrated in figure 25.1, dialogs can take three forms:

■ **Simplex dialogs.** Involve one-way data transfers. An example is a fire alarm, which sends an alarm message to the fire station, but cannot (and does not need to) receive messages from the fire station.

■ **Half-duplex dialogs.** Involve two-way data transfers in which the data flows in only one direction at a time. When one device has completed a transmission, it must "turn over" the medium to the other device so that it has a turn to transmit.

CB radio operators, for example, converse on the same communication channel. When one operator is through transmitting he must release his transmit key so that the other operator may send a response.

■ **Full-duplex dialogs.** Permit two-way simultaneous data transfers by providing each device with a separate communication channel. Voice telephones are full-duplex devices, and either party to a conversation may talk at any time. Most computer modems are capable of operating in full-duplex mode.

Costs rise for half- and full-duplex operation because the more complex the dialog technology is, the more expensive it is. Designers of communica-

tions systems, therefore, generally use the simplest dialog mode that satisfies the communication requirements.

Half-duplex communication can result in wasted bandwidth during the intervals when communication is being turned around. On the other hand, full-duplex communication generally requires a greater bandwidth than half-duplex communication.

 The Novell course materials associate simplex transmission with broadcast transmission, and therefore imply that simplex transmission is used with multiple receivers. This implication is incorrect, as the above-mentioned example of the fire alarm shows.

Simplex transmission may indeed be implemented as a broadcast technology. Commercial radio is an example of broadcast simplex transmission.

A CB radio is, however, an example of half-duplex communication that also operates in a broadcast mode. Many operators may listen in to CB radio communications. Many operators may also reply to transmissions by waiting for a break in the dialog and pressing the transmit key.

For the purposes of this course, simplex transmissions are defined as providing broad area coverage with the potential for reaching large target audiences.

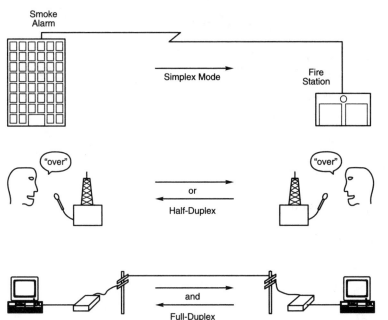

Figure 25.1
*Simplex and duplex
communication modes.*

Session Administration

A *session* is a formal dialog between a service requester and a service provider. Sessions have at least three phases:

■ **Connection establishment.** A service requester requests initiation of a service. During the setup process, communication is established and rules are agreed upon.

■ **Data transfer.** Because of the rules agreed upon during setup, each party to the dialog knows what to expect. Communication is efficient and errors are easy to detect.

■ **Connection release.** When the session is completed, the dialog is terminated in an orderly fashion.

Connection Establishment

Several tasks can be performed at the time a session is initiated:

■ Specification of services that are required

■ User login authentication and other security procedures

■ Negotiation of protocols and protocol parameters

■ Notification of connection IDs

■ Establishment of dialog control, as well as acknowledgment of numbering, and retransmission procedures

Data Transfer

Once the connection has been established, the devices involved can initiate a dialog. Besides exchanging data, these devices exchange acknowledgments and other control data that manage the dialog.

The session layer can also incorporate protocols to resume dialogs that are interrupted. After a formal dialog has been established, devices recognize a lost connection whenever the connection has not been formally released. A device, therefore, realizes that a connection has been lost when it fails to receive an expected acknowledgment or data transmission.

Within a certain time period, two devices can reenter the session that was interrupted but not released.

Connection Release

This is an orderly process that shuts down communication and releases resources on the service provider.

Session Layer Topics and Methods

Dialog control	Simplex
	Half-duplex
	Full-Duplex
Session administration	Connection establishment
	Data transfer
	Connection release

Questions

Study questions for this chapter can be found at the end of Chapter 27.

OSI Presentation Layer Concepts

The presentation layer deals with the syntax, or grammatical rules, needed when communicating between two computers.

This chapter discusses two major services performed at the presentation layer:

■ *Translation of data from one form to another*

■ *Encryption/decryption of data*

The name *presentation layer* has caused considerable confusion in the industry because some people mistakenly believe that this layer presents data to the user. However, the name has nothing to do with displaying data, which is performed instead by applications that are running above the application layer.

The presentation layer is so named because it presents a uniform data format to the application layer. As a matter of fact, this layer is not commonly implemented because most presentation layer functions are typically performed by applications.

Data Translation

An important goal to strive for when designing networks is to enable different types of computers to interchange data. Although this goal is seldom met completely, effective use of data translation techniques can make it possible for many types of computers to communicate.

The following discussion covers four forms of data translation: bit order, byte order, character code, and file syntax.

Bit Order

When binary numbers are transmitted through a network, they are sent one bit at a time. Consider the binary number 11110000. The transmitting computer could start at either end of the number:

■ It could start at the *most-significant digit* (the MSD, which is the highest value digit) and send a 1 first.

■ It could start at the *least-significant digit* (the LSD, which is the lowest value digit) and send a 0 first.

Unless the sending and receiving devices agree on bit-order conventions, they will change the values of the binary numbers that are being transmitted.

Byte Order Translation

A similar logic applies to byte orders. Complex values generally must be represented by more than one byte, but different computers use different conventions as to which byte should be transmitted first:

■ Intel microprocessors start with the least-significant byte. Because they start at the small end, they are called *little endian.*

■ Motorola microprocessors start with the most-significant byte and are called *big endian.*

Byte order translation might be needed to reconcile these differences.

Character Code Translation

Most computers use one of the following binary numbering schemes to represent character sets:

■ ASCII, the *American Standard Code for Information Interchange*, used to represent English characters on all microcomputers and most minicomputers (see fig. 26.1)

■ EBCDIC, the *Extended Binary Coded Decimal Interchange Code*, used to represent English characters on IBM mainframes (see fig. 26.2)

■ Shift-JIS, used to represent Japanese characters

Figure 26.1

The ASCII character code.

 Note Novell and other vendors are beginning to incorporate Unicode in their products. *Unicode*, a 16-bit code that can represent 65,536 characters in English and other languages, is organized into code pages devoted to the characters required for a given language, improving portability of products between different language environments.

File Syntax Translation

When file formats differ between computers, they require translation. Some situations that might require file format translation include:

■ Copying files between a Macintosh and a DOS PC. Macintosh files actually consist of two related files called a *data fork* and a *resource fork*. PC files, on the other hand, consist of single file.

■ Copying files between DOS PCs and Unix workstations.

Properly done, these translations can be completely transparent. NetWare, for example, enables DOS, Macintosh, and Unix users to share the same files on a NetWare server by using a feature called *name space support.*

Encryption

It is often desirable to ensure that data on a LAN is absolutely secure. Even if an eavesdropper were successful in listening in, sensitive data can be encrypted so that it is unusable.

Encryption techniques employ a form of reversible data scrambling that renders data unreadable without a key. A *key* is a code word or number that allows the encryption/decryption software to scramble and unscramble the data.

Given time, every encryption can be broken. High-speed computers make it feasible to crack many codes by simply trying different key values until the right one is found. A great deal of effort, therefore, has gone into creating powerful encryption algorithms boasting a low probability of failure.

Figure 26.2

The EBCDIC character code.

8765 \ 4321	0000	0001	0010	0011	0100	0101	0110	0111	1000	1001	1010	1011	1100	1101	1110	1111
1111	0	1	2	3	4	5	6	7	8	9						
1110			S	T	U	V	W	X	Y	Z						
1101		J	K	L	M	N	O	P	Q	R						
1100		A	B	C	D	E	F	G	H	I						
1011																
1010			s	t	u	v	w	x	y	z						
1001		j	k	l	m	n	o	p	q	r						
1000		a	b	c	d	e	f	g	h	i						
0111											:	#	@	'	=	"
0110	-	/									¦	,	%	_	>	?
0101	&										!	$	*	)	;	¬
0100	SP										¢	.	<	(	+	|
0011		SYN			PN	RS	UC	EOT					DC4	NAK		SUB
0010	DS	SOS	FS		BYP	LF	EOB	PRE			SM			ENQ	ACK	BEL
0001	DLE	DC1	DC2	DC3	RES	NL	BS	IL	CAN	EM	CC		IFS	IGS	IRS	IUS
0000	NUL	SOH	STX	ETX	PF	HT	LC	DEL			SMM	VT	FF	CR	SO	SI

Two common techniques are the following:

- Private keys
- Public keys

Private Keys

Private keys use the same key to encrypt and decrypt the message. This has several disadvantages. The sender and receiver must be sure to inform each other of the key. If the key is intercepted, the message becomes vulnerable. Each time the key is changed, and private keys are changed often in case they are compromised, the new key must be communicated and is vulnerable to discovery.

Public Keys

A *public key* is used to encrypt messages, whereas a *private key* is used for decryption. The public key is created by a user by applying an algorithm to a private key, which is known only to the intended receiver of the message.

The sender of the message uses the public key to encrypt a message and does not know or need to know the private key. In fact, anyone who has a person's public key can encrypt a message for that person.

The receiver decrypts the message by combining the public key with the private key, known only to him- or herself.

The algorithms used for public key encryption are extremely complex and make it unlikely that even a super computer will stumble on the correct key within a reasonable period of time (your lifetime, for example). Nevertheless, the code makers are never far ahead of the code breakers, and more sophisticated encryption techniques are always under development.

Questions

Study questions for this chapter may be found at the end of Chapter 27, "OSI Application Layer Concepts."

OSI Application Layer Concepts

The application layer is concerned with providing services on the network. These services include file services, print services, database services, and the other services discussed in Chapter 17, "Network Services."

A common misunderstanding is that the application layer is responsible for running user applications such as word processors. This is not the case. The application layer, however, does provide an interface whereby applications can communicate with the network.

The application layer performs two functions related to the utilization of services on the network. One function involves the advertisement of available services. Another function involves the use of the services.

Advertising Services

To inform clients of services that are available, the application layer advertises the services to the network. You encountered the use of service addresses when the network layer was discussed in Chapter 23, "OSI Network Layer Concepts." These service addresses provide the mechanism that enables clients to communicate with services.

The application layer can employ *active* and *passive* methods of advertising services.

Active Service Advertisement

When servers actively advertise their services, they broadcast messages announcing the services they offer. Most protocols consider these service advertisements to be valid for a limited time. Unless the information is refreshed within a specified time, clients remove the information from their service tables.

Clients also can transmit messages that request specific services. Servers respond with a list of services they support.

NetWare employs an active service advertisement protocol called the *Service Advertisement Protocol* (SAP).

Passive Service Advertisement

Servers also can list their services and addresses with a central service registry. Clients query the directory to determine which services are available and how to access them—this is called *passive service advertisement.*

Service Use Methods

Clients can access services using three methods:

- OS call interruption
- Remote operation
- Collaboration

OS Call Interruption

Applications on client systems request services by placing service calls to their local operating systems. A *service call* is a formal procedure set up by the designers of an operating system that provides an interface with the programs the operating system supports. Normally, these service calls invoke services on the local client PC.

When a client is configured for network operation, OS call interruption intercepts service requests. Service calls that request local resources are forwarded to the client's OS. Service calls that request network resources are transferred to the network, where they are forwarded to the appropriate server. The process is shown in figure 27.1.

OS call interruption enables a client to utilize network services even when OS has no inherent networking capability.

This is the service access method used by NetWare requesters for DOS and OS/2, as well as for other operating systems supported for NetWare such as Macintosh.

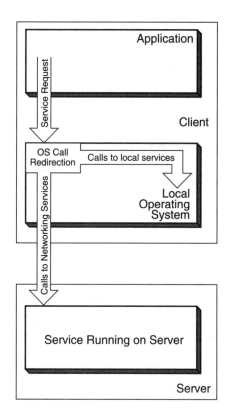

Figure 27.1
OS call interruption.

Remote Operation

When the client OS has network capability built-in, it can access the server by remote operation. The client OS interfaces directly with the network. Requests from the client OS appear to the server to be the same as requests from the server's own systems. In other words, the server is not directly aware of the separate existence of client systems.

Collaborative Computing

Some server and client operating systems are so advanced that the border between them blurs. The operating systems work together to coordinate the use of resources on the two respective computers. Recall from Chapter 16 the discussion of collaborative computing, which consists of far more than computers simply accessing each other's services. Indeed, computers participating in collaborative computing pool all of their resources. One computer can start a process on another, for example, to take advantage of some free processing cycles. This requires the participating operating systems to be capable of a high level of cooperation.

The following table summarizes the topics discussed in this chapter along with the associated methods.

Application Layer Topics and Methods

Topic	*Method*
Service advertisement	Active
	Passive
Service use	OS call interception
	Remote operation
	Collaborative processing

Questions

Here are some sample questions to help you evaluate your understanding of Chapters 23 through 27.

1. Which TWO address types are associated with individual devices?

   ☐ A. Service

   ☐ B. Network

   ☐ C. Physical

   ☐ D. Virtual

2. Which switching method employs virtual circuits?

   ○ A. Message

   ○ B. Circuit

   ○ C. Packet

   ○ D. All of the above

3. Which network layer is concerned with data encryption?

   ○ A. Network

   ○ B. Transport

   ○ C. Session

   ○ D. Presentation

4. Which network layer is concerned with delivering messages between processes on devices?

   ○ A. Network

   ○ B. Transport

   ○ C. Session

   ○ D. Presentation

5. Which network layer is concerned with address/name resolution?

   ○ A. Network

   ○ B. Transport

   ○ C. Session

   ○ D. Presentation

6. Which switching method makes the most efficient use of network bandwidth?

   ○ A. Message

   ○ B. Circuit

   ○ C. Packet

   ○ D. Methods are about equal

7. Which TWO connection services perform flow-control?

   ☐ A. Unacknowledged connectionless services

   ☐ B. Connection-oriented services

   ☐ C. Acknowledged connectionless services

   ☐ D. Unacknowledged connection-oriented services

8. What is another name for a message switching network?

   ○ A. Connectionless

   ○ B. Datagram

   ○ C. Store-and-forward

   ○ D. Virtual circuit

9. Which is the most common network switching method?

    ○   A.   Message

    ○   B.   Packet

    ○   C.   Circuit

    ○   D.   Virtual

10. Which TWO statements about virtual circuits are true?

    ☐   A.   They usually are associated with connection oriented services.

    ☐   B.   A virtual circuit represents a specific path through the network.

    ☐   C.   A virtual circuit appears to the connected devices as a dedicated network path.

    ☐   D.   Virtual circuits dedicate a communication channel to a single conversation.

11. Which of the following statements is true?

    ○   A.   Hop count is a measure of routing cost.

    ○   B.   Distance vector routing methods are technically simple and make efficient use of network bandwidth.

    ○   C.   Link-state routing protocols rely on tick counts to make routing determinations.

    ○   D.   Link-state routing protocols transmit routing information at regular intervals.

12. Which THREE of the following terms are related?

    ☐   A.   Port

    ☐   B.   Connection ID

    ☐   C.   Socket

    ☐   D.   Service address

13. Which switching method fragments messages into small units which are routed through independent paths?

    ○   A.   Message

    ○   B.   Packet

    ○   C.   Circuit

    ○   D.   Virtual

14. Which activity involves the use of connection IDs?

    ○   A.   Packet switching

    ○   B.   Routing

    ○   C.   Segment development

    ○   D.   End-to-end flow control

15. Which TWO of the following are transport layer error control strategies?

    ☐   A.   Using datagram packet switching

    ☐   B.   Utilizing unique segment sequencing numbers

    ☐   C.   Using time-outs to drop packets that have remained on the network too long

    ☐   D.   Using parity checking to detect errors

16. Which TWO of the following statements are true?

☐   A.   The data link layer deals with device-to-device traffic.

☐   B.   The network layer deals with traffic between upper layer processes.

☐   C.   The transport layer deals with traffic between end-nodes.

☐   D.   All of the above are true.

17. Which of the following methods of dialog control provides two-way communication?

☐   A.   Simple duplex

☐   B.   Simplex

☐   C.   Half-duplex

☐   D.   Full-duplex

18. Dialog control is a function of which layer of the OSI Reference Model?

○   A.   Network

○   B.   Transport

○   C.   Session

○   D.   Presentation

19. Which THREE of the following are functions of session administration?

☐   A.   Connection establishment

☐   B.   Checksum error detection

☐   C.   Data transfer

☐   D.   Connection release

20. Which TWO of the following are functions of connection establishment?

☐   A.   Resumption of interrupted communication

☐   B.   Login name and password verification

☐   C.   Determining required services

☐   D.   Acknowledgment of data receipt

21. Which TWO of the following are possible functions of the presentation layer?

☐   A.   Data encryption

☐   B.   Presentation of data on display devices

☐   C.   Data translation

☐   D.   Display format conversion

22. Which TWO statements are true about public key data encryption?

☐   A.   Encoded data is vulnerable should the public key become known.

☐   B.   A public key is generated from a secret key.

☐   C.   Public key encryption is less secure than private key encryption.

☐   D.   The public key is used to encrypt messages, and a separate key is used to decrypt messages.

23. Which THREE of the following are possible functions of the application layer?

☐   A.   Network printing service

☐   B.   End-user applications

☐   C.   Client access to network services

☐   D.   Service advertisement

24. Which of the following methods is used by the NetWare requester to access network services?

   ○ A. Collaborative

   ○ B. OS call interception

   ○ C. Remote operation

   ○ D. Peer-to-peer communication

Answers

1. A C	13. B
2. C	14. C
3. D	15. B C
4. B	16. A C
5. B	17. C D
6. C	18. C
7. B C	19. A C D
8. C	20. B C
9. C	21. A C
10. A C	22. B D
11. A	23. A C D
12. A C D	24. B

Protocol Suites

In the preceding chapters, you have seen how the process of designing network protocols is usually done in pieces, with each piece solving a small part of the overall problem. By convention, these protocols are regarded as layers of an overall set of protocols called a protocol suite or a protocol stack.

You have seen one approach to defining the layers of a protocol stack. The OSI Reference Model is useful as a conceptual tool for understanding protocol layering. Although protocols have been designed in strict conformance with the OSI Reference Model, the OSI protocol suite has not become popular. The main influence of the Reference Model is as a conceptual framework in which to understand the process of network communication and in which to compare various types of protocols.

Protocols are real implementations, in program code and hardware, of the conceptual rules defined in the Reference Model. The tasks described in the Reference Model can be performed in various ways, depending on the goals of the network designers, and various protocol suites are in common use. Some protocols and protocol suites existed before the OSI Reference Model was published and can be matched only loosely to the seven-layer model.

In this chapter, you will get down to the task of examining a variety of actual protocols. In the process, you will apply what you have learned about the OSI Reference Model to several of the most popular protocol stacks.

This chapter examines the following protocol stacks:

- NetWare IPX/SPX
- Internet Protocols (TCP/IP)
- AppleTalk
- Digital Network Architecture (DNA)
- Systems Network Architecture (SNA)

Models and Protocols

Three stages take place before a protocol goes to work:

1. A model describes the general function of the protocol.

2. The protocol itself is defined in complete detail.

3. The protocol must be realized by software and hardware designers in real products.

Consider the process of designing a building. The architect first produces sketches that describe the general nature of the building. Then the architect, possibly working with a specialist in particular building trades, develops blueprints that describe every detail of the building. Finally, an actual building is constructed.

Protocols are the blueprints of networking. They are highly-detailed descriptions of all the functions at a given communication layer. Until the protocol is expressed in hardware and software, however, it cannot go to work.

The act of translating a protocol into hardware and software can be a difficult one, and different designers often have difficulty getting their equipment to interact without some tweaking, particularly in the early life stages of a protocol. Eventually, implementation of a protocol becomes fairly routine, but it always is advisable to inquire into the compatibility testing that has been performed on a new piece of equipment.

Because many problems are encountered when attempting to interconnect devices running different protocols, many organizations have pushed for *open systems* (sets of hardware and software standards that could be generally applied throughout the industry to ease communication difficulties).

The OSI Reference Model has been used as one strategy for developing open systems, and some vendors have redesigned existing protocol suites to make them more compliant with the OSI model. Others—a good example is the TCP/IP community—have argued that they already have a highly-functional set of protocols that are, in fact, open in the sense that they are freely available to everyone in the industry. As a result, the impact of the OSI model has been limited to the products of some manufacturers.

Figure 28.1 illustrates how the protocol suites discussed in this chapter relate to the layers of the OSI Reference Model.

NetWare IPX/SPX

The protocols utilized with NetWare are summarized in figure 28.2. The NetWare protocols have been designed with a high degree of modularity, making it easy to adapt to different hardware and to incorporate other protocols into the configuration. The discussion of NetWare protocols in this course is fairly brief considering the importance of these protocols to NetWare engineers. For a more detailed description, you might want to consult *NetWare: The Professional Reference, Fourth Edition* from New Riders Publishing.

Each of the protocols in figure 28.2 is discussed later in this chapter. Many of the features of the protocols are summarized in table 28.1.

Multiple Link Interface Driver (MLID)

MLIDs implement the *medium access control* (MAC) sublayer of the OSI data link layer. Practically speaking, MLID is Novell's name for the software that drives a network interface board. The specifi-

cations for writing MLIDs are defined by Novell's *Open DataLink Interface* (ODI) specification, which describes Novell's overall architecture for network protocols. An MLID must be written for each board design.

As such, the specific methods incorporated into a specific MLID depend on the underlying physical layer architecture. An MLID written for an Ethernet card uses contention access control, whereas an MLID written for a token-ring card uses token access.

The MLID is implemented in a software driver that usually takes its name from the model number of the network board being supported. An MLID for the Novell/Eagle NE2000 card, for example, is packaged in a file named NE2000.COM.

MLIDs are not dependent on any specific upper layer protocols. One feature of the ODI specification is that multiple protocols can access the same network interface board by linking to the same MLID.

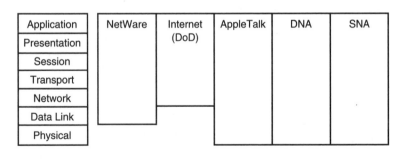

Figure 28.1

A comparison of various protocol suites to the OSI Reference Model.

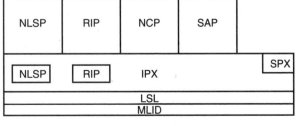

Figure 28.2

The NetWare protocol suite.

Multiple Link Interface Driver (MLID) Topics And Methods

OSI Layer	Topics	Methods
Data link (MAC sublayer)	Medium access	Contention Token passing Polling (Underlying physical layer defines MAC headers)

Link Support Layer (LSL)

The LSL implements the *logical link support* (LLC) sublayer of the OSI data link layer and functions as the interface between the MLID and the upper layer protocols.

When multiple upper layer protocol stacks are being used, the LSL software is responsible for passing packets to the appropriate protocol stack.

On NetWare DOS clients, the LSL sublayer is implemented in a file named LSL.COM.

Link Support Layer (LSL) Topics And Methods

OSI Layer	Topics	Methods
Data link (LLC sublayer)	Protocol specific	Interfaces MLID to upper layer protocols

Internetwork Packet Exchange Protocol (IPX)

IPX is a network layer protocol that provides connectionless (datagram) service. (IPX was developed from the XNS protocol originated by Xerox). As a network layer protocol, IPX is responsible for internetwork routing and for maintaining network logical addresses. Routing uses the RIP protocol (described below) to make route selections.

IPX relies on hardware physical addresses found at lower layers to provide network device addressing. It also makes use of *sockets*, upper-layer service addresses, to deliver packets to their ultimate destinations.

On the client, IPX support is provided as a component of the older DOS shell and the current DOS NetWare requester.

Internetwork Packet Exchange Protocol (IPX) Topics And Methods

OSI Layer	Topics	Methods
Network	Addressing	Logical network service
	Route selection	Dynamic
	Connection services	Connectionless

Router Information Protocol (RIP)

RIP uses the distance-vector route discover method to determine hop counts to other devices. Like IPX,

RIP was developed from a similar protocol in the XNS protocol suite. RIP is implemented as an upper-layer service and is assigned a socket (service address). RIP is based directly on IPX and performs network layer functions.

Router Information Protocol (RIP) Topics and Methods

OSI Layer	Topics	Methods
Network	Route discovery	Distance vector

Network Link Services Protocol (NLSP)

NLSP is a link-state routing protocol derived from an ISO protocol named IS-IS (intermediate system-to-intermediate system). NLSP supports fault-tolerant mesh and hybrid mesh networks with a high level of fault tolerance.

(This protocol is mistakenly named the NetWare Link Services Protocol in the course materials.)

Network Link State Protocol (NLSP) Topics And Methods

OSI Layer	Topics	Methods
Network	Route discovery	Link-state

Note Due to the frequency of messages required to advertise routing information, RIP has been a traditional bottleneck in NetWare performance, particularly

with large internetworks that include slower wide-area links. NLSP is a newer protocol that can greatly improve performance of NetWare internetworks. It is shipped with 4.1 and is available as an upgrade for other NetWare implementations such as 3.*x* and earlier versions of 4.*x*.

Sequenced Packet Exchange (SPX)

SPX is a transport layer protocol that extends IPX to provide connection-oriented service with reliable delivery. Reliable delivery is ensured by retransmitting packets in the event of error. SPX is derived from a similar SPX protocol in the XNS network protocol suite.

SPX establishes virtual circuits called *connections*. The connection ID for each connection appears in the SPX header. A given upper-layer process can be associated with multiple connection IDs.

On the client, SPX support is provided as a component of the older DOS shell and of the current NetWare requester.

Sequenced Packet Exchange Protocol (SPX) Topics And Methods

OSI Layer	Topics	Methods
Transport	Addressing	Connection ID
	Segment development	Division and combination
	Connection services	Segment sequencing
		Error control
		End-to-end flow control

NetWare Core Protocols (NCP)

NCP provides numerous function calls that support network services such as file service, printing, name management, file locking, and synchronization. NetWare client software interfaces with NCP to access NetWare services.

It is interesting to note that most NetWare services do not rely on a transport layer protocol such as SPX. In almost all cases, NCP provides the upper layer protocol structure that provides services, connection management, and reliable delivery. In most cases, SPX is not required and can even be left out of the client configuration.

NetWare Core Protocols (NCP) Topics And Methods

OSI Layer	Topics	Methods
Transport	Connection services	Segment sequencing
		Error control
		End-to-end flow control
Session	Session administration	Data transfer
Presentation	Translation	Character code
		File syntax
Application	Service use	OS redirector or Collaborative (depending on client)

Service Advertising Protocol (SAP)

SAP is used by NetWare servers to advertise their services to the network. Each server identifies itself once a minute by transmitting a SAP packet. SAP users also can request service information by transmitting a service query packet. SAP implementations obtain service address information from IPX header information.

Service Advertising Protocol (SAP) Topics And Methods

OSI Layer	Topics	Methods
Session	Session administration	File transfer
Application	Service advertisement	Active

Internet Protocols

The Internet protocol suite (also commonly called the TCP/IP protocol suite) was originally developed by the United States Department of Defense (DoD) to provide robust service on large internetworks that incorporate a variety of computer types. In recent years, the Internet protocols have become increasingly popular and constitute the most popular network protocols now in use. If you want more detailed information about the Internet protocols than that provided in this course, you can consult *NetWare TCP/IP and NFS* from New Riders Publishing.

One reason for this popularity is that the Internet protocols are not owned by any one vendor, unlike the NetWare, DNA, SNA, AppleTalk, and various other protocols. The protocol suite evolves in response to input from a wide variety of industry sources. As such, the Internet protocol suite is the most open of the protocol suites and is supported by the widest variety of vendors. Virtually every brand of computing equipment now supports the Internet protocols.

Much of the popularity of the TCP/IP protocols comes from their early availability on Unix. The protocols were built into the Berkeley Standard Distribution (BSD) Unix implementation. Since then, TCP/IP has achieved universal acceptance in the Unix community and is a standard feature on all versions of Unix.

Figure 28.3 illustrates the relationship of the protocols in the Internet suite to the layers of the OSI Reference Model. Notice that the suite does not include protocols for the data link or physical layers. TCP/IP was designed to work over established standards such as Ethernet. Over time, TCP/IP has been interfaced to the majority of data link and physical layer technologies.

It should be noted that the Internet protocols do not map cleanly to the OSI Reference Model. The DoD model was, after all, developed long before the OSI model was defined. The model for the Internet protocol suite has four layers, which are also shown in figure 28.3. From this, you can see the approximate relationships of the layers of the two models. The functions of the layers of the DoD model are as follows:

- The *network access* layer corresponds to the bottom two layers of the OSI model. As previously mentioned, this was deliberately done to enable the DoD protocols to coexist with existing data link and physical layer standards.

- The *internet* layer corresponds roughly to the OSI network layer. Protocols at this layer are concerned with moving data between devices on networks.

- The *host-to-host* layer can be compared to the OSI transport layer. Host-to-host protocols enable peer communication between hosts on the internetwork. (At the time these protocols were designed, personal computers and workstations did not exist and all network computers were host computers. As a result, devices on TCP/IP networks are typically referred to as *hosts*. The concept of a client/server relationship did not exist, and all communicating hosts were assumed to be peers.)

- The *process/application* layer embraces functions of the OSI session, presentation, and application layers. Protocols at this layer provide network services.

A large number of protocols are associated with the Internet protocol suite.

Figure 28.3
The Internet protocol suite.

Internet Protocol (IP)

IP is a connectionless protocol that provides datagram service, and IP packets are most commonly referred to as IP datagrams. IP is a packet-switching protocol that performs addressing and route selection. An IP header is appended to packets, which are transmitted as frames by lower level protocols. IP routes packets through internetworks by utilizing dynamic routing tables that are referenced at each hop. Routing determinations are made by consulting logical and physical network device information, as provided by the *Address Resolution Protocol* (ARP).

IP performs packet disassembly and reassembly as required by packet size limitations defined for the data link and physical layers being implemented. IP also performs error checking on the header data using a checksum, although data from upper layers is not error-checked. The following table shows IP topics and methods.

Internet Protocol (IP) Topics And Methods

OSI Layer	Topics	Methods
Network	Addressing	Logical network
	Switching	Packet
	Route selection	Dynamic
	Connection services	Error control

Internet Control Message Protocol (ICMP)

ICMP enhances the error control provided by IP. Connectionless protocols such as IP cannot detect internetwork errors such as congestion or path failures. ICMP can detect such errors and notify IP and upper layer protocols.

Internet Control Message Protocol (ICMP) Topics And Methods

OSI Layer	Topics	Methods
Network	Connection services	Error control
		Network-layer flow control

Routing Information Protocol (RIP)

RIP in the Internet protocol suite is not the same protocol as RIP in the NetWare suite, although the two serve similar functions. Internet RIP performs route discovery using a distance vector method, calculating the number of hops that must be crossed to route a packet by a particular path. A *hop* is defined as crossing a single router.

While it works well in localized networks, RIP has many weaknesses that limit its utility on wide-area internetworks. These weaknesses are similar to those of NetWare RIP and are causing RIP to be replaced gradually by the OSPF link-state protocol.

**Routing Information Protocol (RIP)
Topics And Methods**

OSI Layer	Topics	Methods
Network	Route discovery	Distance vector

Open Shortest Path First (OSPF)

OSPF is a link-state route discovery protocol that is designed to overcome the limitations of RIP. On large internetworks, OSPF can identify the internetwork topology and improve performance by implementing load balancing and class-of-service routing.

Open Shortest Path First (OSPF) Topics And Methods

OSI Layer	Topics	Methods
Network	Route discovery	Link-state

Transmission Control Protocol (TCP)

TCP is an internetwork protocol that corresponds to the OSI transport layer. TCP provides full-duplex, connection-oriented transport. When the overhead of a connection-oriented transport is not required, the *User Datagram Protocol* (UDP) can be substituted for TCP at the transport (host-to-host) level.

TCP also provides message fragmentation and reassembly, and can accept messages of any length from upper layer protocols. TCP fragments message streams into segments that can be handled by

IP. When used with IP, TCP adds connection-oriented service and performs segment synchronization, adding sequence numbers at the byte level.

In addition to message fragmentation, TCP can maintain multiple conversations with upper layer protocols and can improve use of network bandwidth by combining multiple messages into the same segment. Each virtual-circuit connection is assigned a connection identifier called a *port*, which identifies the datagrams associated with that connection.

**Transmission Control Protocol (TCP)
Topics And Methods**

OSI Layer	Topics	Methods
Network	Addressing	Service
Transport	Addressing	Connection identifier
	Segment development	Division and recombination
	Connection services	Segment sequencing
		Error control
		End-to-end flow control

User Datagram Protocol (UDP)

UDP is a connectionless transport (host-to-host) layer protocol. UDP does not provide message acknowledgments, it simply transports datagrams.

Like TCP, UDP utilizes port addresses to deliver datagrams. These port addresses, however, are not associated with virtual circuits and merely identify local host processes. UDP is preferred over TCP when high performance or low network overhead is more critical than reliable delivery. Because UDP does not need to establish, maintain, and close connections, or control data flow, it generally outperforms TCP.

UDP is the transport layer protocol used with the *Simple Network Management Protocol* (SNMP), which is the standard network management protocol used with TCP/IP networks. UDP enables SNMP to provide network management with a minimum of network overhead.

User Datagram Protocol (UDP) Topics And Methods

OSI Layer	Topics	Methods
Transport	Addressing	Connection identifier
	Segment development	Combination
	Connection services	Connectionless (datagram)

Address Resolution Protocol (ARP)

The following three types of address information are used on TCP/IP internetworks:

■ Physical addresses used by the data link and physical layers.

■ IP addresses, which provide logical network and host IDs. IP addresses consist of four numbers typically expressed in "dotted-decimal" form. An example of an IP address is 134.135.100.13.

■ Logical node names, which identify specific hosts with alphanumeric identifiers. These are easier for humans to recall than the numeric IP addresses. An example of a logical node name is MYHOST.COM.

Given a logical node name, ARP can determine the IP address associated with that name. ARP maintains tables of address resolution data and can broadcast packets to discover addresses on the internetwork. The IP addresses discovered by ARP can be provided to data link layer protocols.

Address Resolution Protocol (ARP) Topics And Methods

OSI Layer	Topics	Methods
Network	Address resolution	Matches logical (IP) and physical device addresses

Domain Name System (DNS)

DNS provides name/address resolution as a service to client applications. DNS servers enable humans to use logical node names to access network resources.

Domain Name System (DNS) Topics And Methods

OSI Layer	Topics	Methods
Transport	Address/name resolution	Service-provider initiated

File Transfer Protocol (FTP)

FTP is a protocol for sharing files between networked hosts. FTP enables users to log onto remote hosts. Logged-on users can inspect directories, manipulate files, execute commands, and perform other commands on the host. FTP also has the capability of transferring files between dissimilar hosts by supporting a file request structure that is independent of specific operating systems.

 Note NetWare users should note that FTP is more than simply a remote file access protocol. Users are not limited to reading and writing files unlike when they are logged into a NetWare server. FTP is a peer-to-peer protocol that enables users to initiate processes on the remote host.

File Transfer Protocol (FTP) Topics And Methods

OSI Layer	Topics	Methods
Session	Session administration	Connection establishment
	File transfer	Connection release
Presentation	Translation	Machine-independent file syntax
Application	Network services	File services
	Service use	Collaborative

Simple Mail Transfer Protocol (SMTP)

SMTP is a protocol for routing mail through internetworks, and it makes use of the TCP and IP protocols. SNMP does not provide a mail interface for the user. Creation, management, and delivery of messages to end users must be performed by an e-mail application. (The most popular e-mail application on the Internet is named Eudora.)

SMTP is implemented by NetWare messaging gateways. SMTP also is provided with UnixWare.

Simple Mail Transfer Protocol (SMTP) Topics And Methods

OSI Layer	Topics	Methods
Application	Network services	Message services

Remote Terminal Emulation (TELNET)

TELNET enables PCs and workstations to function as dumb terminals in session with hosts on internetworks. TELNET implementations are available for most end-user platforms including Unix (of course), DOS, Windows, and Macintosh OS.

TELNET is provided as a part of NetWare XCONSOLE, NetWare NFS, FlexIP, and NetWareIP through UNICON. TELNET also is provided with UnixWare.

Remote Terminal Emulation (TELNET) Topics And Methods

OSI Layer	Topics	Methods
Session	Dialog control	Half-duplex
	Session administration	Connection establishment
		File transfer
		Connection release
Presentation	Translation	Byte order Character code
Application	Service use	Remote operation

Network File System (NFS)

NFS, developed by Sun Microsystems, is a family of file access protocols that are a considerable advancement over FTP and TELNET. Since Sun made the NFS specifications available for public use, NFS has achieved a high level of popularity. NFS consists of the following protocols:

■ eXternal Data Representation (XDR) supports encoding of data in a machine-independent format. C programmers use XDR library routines to describe data structures that are portable between machine environments.

■ Remote Procedure Calls (RPC) function as a service request redirector that determines whether function calls can be satisfied locally or

must be redirected to a remote host. Calls to remote hosts are packaged for network delivery and transmitted to RPC servers, which generally have the capability of servicing many remote service requests. RPC servers process the service requests and generate response packets that are returned to the service requester.

Network File System (NFS) Topics And Methods

OSI Layer	Topics	Methods
Application	Network services	File services
	Service use	Remote operation

Remote Procedure Call (RPC) Topics And Methods

OSI Layer	Topics	Methods
Session	Session administration	Connection establishment
		File transfer Connection release

External Data Representation (XDR) Topics And Methods

OSI Layer	Topics	Methods
Presentation	Translation	Byte order
		Character code
		File syntax

AppleTalk

AppleTalk is the computing architecture developed by Apple Computer for the Macintosh family of personal computers. Although AppleTalk originally supported only Apple's proprietary LocalTalk cabling system, the suite has been expanded to incorporate both Ethernet and token ring physical layers.

AppleTalk originally supported networks of limited scope. The AppleTalk Phase 2 specification issued in 1989, however, extended the scope of AppleTalk to enterprise networks. The Phase 2 specification also enabled AppleTalk to coexist on networks with other protocol suites. Table 28.1 summarizes the differences between AppleTalk Phases 1 and 2.

Table 28.1
Comparison of AppleTalk Phases 1 and 2

Characteristic	Phase 1	Phase 2
Maximum zones on a network segment	1	255
Maximum nodes per network	254	About 16 million
Dynamic addressing based on	Node ID	Network+Node ID
supported link access protocols	LocalTalk Ethernet	LocalTalk IEEE 802.2 IEEE 802.5
Split-horizon routing	No	Yes

AppleTalk Phase 1 protocols do not support internetworks because addressing is limited to a unique node ID. This approach is called a *nonextended network* under Phase 2 terminology. Phase 2 also supports extended networks in which addressing is determined by a combination of a network and a node ID, and can make use of the hardware-based device IDs that are coded into Ethernet and token ring cards.

Figure 28.4 presents a layered perspective of the AppleTalk protocols. Each of these protocols is described in this chapter. Each AppleTalk protocol is briefly discussed below.

LocalTalk, EtherTalk, and TokenTalk Link Access Protocols (LLAP, ELAP, and TLAP)

These are link access protocols that integrate AppleTalk upper layer protocols with the LocalTalk, Ethernet, and token ring environments.

LLAP is a protocol developed by Apple for operation with the LocalTalk cabling system, a system based on shielded twisted-pair cabling. LocalTalk is suitable primarily for small, low performance networks. The maximum data rate is 230.4 Kbps (compared to 10 Mbps for Ethernet), and cable segments are limited to 300 meters in length and a maximum of 32 devices.

LLAP uses addresses called AppleTalk addresses that are developed dynamically on the network. LLAP is ideally suited to Apple's "plug and play" Macintosh philosophy because a Macintosh can discover a unique physical address when it connects to the network without the need for any configuration.

Figure 28.4
The AppleTalk protocol suite.

LocalTalk *Topics And Methods*

OSI Layer	Topics	Methods
Physical	Connection types	Multipoint
	Physical topology	Bus
	Digital signaling	State transition
	Bit synchronization	Synchronous
	Bandwidth use	Baseband
Data Link (MAC)	Logical topology	Bus
	Media access	Contention
	Addressing	Physical device
Data Link (LLC)	Transmission synchronization	Synchronous
	Connection services	LLC flow control
		Error control

AppleTalk Address Resolution (AARP)

Both Ethernet and token ring make use of physical device addresses that are built into the interfaces when they are manufactured. AARP maps AppleTalk addresses to Ethernet and token ring physical addresses, enabling upper AppleTalk protocols to interface with the Ethernet and token ring physical layers.

AppleTalk Address Resolution Protocol (AARP) Topics And Methods

OSI Layer	Topics	Methods
Network/ Data Link	Address resolution	Matches logical names with physical device addresses

Datagram Delivery Protocol (DDP)

DDP is a network-layer protocol that provides connectionless service between two sockets. A *socket* is the AppleTalk term for a service address. A combination of a device address, network address, and socket uniquely identifies each process.

DDP performs network routing and consults routing tables maintained by RTMP to determine routing. Packet delivery is performed by the data link protocol operating on a given destination network.

Datagram Delivery Protocol (DDP) Topics And Methods

OSI Layer	Topics	Methods
Network	Addressing	Logical network service
	Route selection	Dynamic
	Interoperability	Network layer translation

Routing Table Maintenance Protocol (RTMP)

RTMP provides DDP with routing information based on a distance vector method similar to RIP.

Routing Table Maintenance Protocol (RTMP) Topics And Methods

OSI Layer	Topics	Methods
Network	Route discovery	Distance vector

Zone Information Protocol (ZIP)

ZIP organizes devices into zones, which organize service providers into logically named groups. Zones reduce the complexity of a network by limiting users network views to the devices they need.

ZIP functions with routers to organize service providers into zones and to resolve zone and network names.

Zone Information Protocol (ZIP) Topics And Methods

OSI Layer	Topics	Methods
Session	Protocol-specific	Organization of service providers into zones

Name Binding Protocol (NBP)

AppleTalk enables devices to have logical names in addition to their addresses. These names hide lower-layer addresses from users and from upper-layer processes.

NBP enables an application to match a logical name with it's associated address. Recall that AppleTalk addresses are dynamic and can change from session-to-session. NBP obtains up-to-date information that enables devices to use a logical name to determine address information even though the address varies.

Name Binding Protocol (NBP) Topics And Methods

OSI Layer	Topics	Methods
Transport	Address resolution	Service requestor initiated

AppleTalk Transaction Protocol (ATP)

ATP is a connectionless transport layer protocol. Reliable service is provided through a system of acknowledgments and retransmissions. Retransmissions automatically are initiated if an acknowledgment is not received within a specified time interval.

ATP reliability is based on transactions. A transaction consists of a request followed by a reply.

ATP is responsible for segment development and performs fragmentation and reassembly of packets that exceed the specifications for lower layer protocols. Packets include sequence numbers that enable message reassembly and retransmission of lost packets. Only damaged or lost packets are retransmitted.

AppleTalk Transaction Protocol (ATP)
Topics And Methods

OSI Layer	Topics	Methods
Transport	Addressing	Transaction identifier
	Segment development	Division and combination
	Connection services	Error control

AppleTalk Session Protocol (ASP)

ASP is a session layer protocol that establishes, maintains, and releases sessions between service requesters and service providers. The focus of ASP is on providing file services. ASP works with ATP to provide a complete transport service. ATP messages are limited to eight packets, each with a maximum size of 578 bytes. ASP can generate multiple ATP transactions as required to control message overhead on large data transfers.

Multiple sessions can be maintained between service requesters and providers. Sessions can be requested by service requesters, but not by service providers.

AppleTalk Session Protocol (ASP) Topics
And Methods

OSI Layer	Topics	Methods
Transport	Connection services	Segment sequencing
		End-to-end flow control
Session	Session administration	Connection establishment
		Data transfer
		Connection release

Printer Access Protocol (PAP)

PAP is a session layer protocol similar to ASP. As the name implies, the protocol provides printing services, but it also supports other types of connections between service requesters and providers.

PAP permits sessions to be initiated by both service requesters and service providers.

Printer Access Protocol (PAP) Topics And
Methods

OSI Layer	Topics	Methods
Session	Session administration	Connection establishment
		Data transfer
		Connection release

AppleTalk Data Stream Protocol (ADSP)

Notice in figure 28.4 that ADSP provides a protocol stack that is an alternative to protocols that are layered onto ATP.

ADSP performs services associated with several network layers. It is considered a transport layer protocol in that it establishes, maintains, and releases sessions between sockets. At the session layer, ADSP substitutes for ASP and PAP.

ADSP replaces ATP at the transport layer and incorporates segment sequencing and sliding window flow-control. The service provided is full-duplex.

ADSP is not transaction-based like ATP. Instead ADSP uses a connection identifier and byte streams. ADSP provides better performance on lower-bandwidth channels than does ATP working with ASP or PAP.

AppleTalk Data Stream Protocol (ADSP) Topics And Methods

OSI Layer	Topics	Methods
Transport	Addressing	Connection identifier
	Segment development	Division and combination
	Connection establishment	Error control
		End-to-end flow control
		Segment sequencing

OSI Layer	Topics	Methods
Session	Session administration	Connection establishment
		Data transfer
		Connection release

AppleTalk Filing Protocol (AFP)

AFP provides file services and is responsible for translating local file service requests into formats required for network file services. AFP directly translates command syntax and enables applications to perform file format translations.

AFP is responsible for file system security, and verifies and encrypts login names and passwords during connection setup.

AppleTalk Filing Protocol (AARP) Topics And Methods

OSI Layer	Topics	Methods
Session	Session administration	Data transfer
Presentation	Translation	File syntax
	Encryption	Public key

AppleShare (ASP)

AppleShare provides the following three primary application services:

■ The AppleShare File Server uses AFP to enable users to store and access files on the network. It logs in users and associates them with network volumes and directories.

■ The AppleShare Print Server uses NBP and PAP to support network printing. NBP provides name/address information that enables PAP to connect to printers. The AppleShare Print Server performs print spooling and manages printing on networked printers.

■ The AppleShare PC enables PCs running MS-DOS to access AppleShare services by running an AppleShare PC program.

AppleShare Topics And Methods

OSI Layer	Topics	Methods
Application	Network services	File service
		Print service
	Service advertisement	Active
	Service use	Collaborative

Digital Network Architecture

Since it's introduction in 1974, the Digital Network Architecture (DNA) has evolved several times. It's current generation is called Phase V. DECnet is Digital's family of products that implement the DNA architecture.

As DNA has evolved, Digital has placed a strong emphasis on use of standards-based protocols and on achieving close conformance with the OSI Reference Model. A variety of ISO standards are incorporated into the DNA protocol suite.

Prior to DNA Phase V, DNA relied heavily on Digital proprietary protocols above the network layer. This stack—which includes Digital's NSP, Naming Service, Session Control, and other protocols—is still supported for the purpose of backward compatibility. Other pre-Phase V protocols also are supported at the lower network levels.

DNA Phase V introduced an alternative protocol stack based on ISO standards.

Figure 28.5 illustrates the layers of the DNA protocol suite. DNA is based on several physical and data link standards that are discussed in Chapter 29, "Other Protocols and Standards," including IEEE 802.X, FDDI, and X.25/LAPB.

Figure 28.5

Protocols in the Digital Network Architecture.

Application				MAILbus	NVTS	Naming Service
Presentation	ASN.1				Session Control	
Session	ISO 8327					
Transport	ISO 8073		NSP		Naming Service	
Network	CLNS			CONS		
Data Link	Ethernet Version 2	HDLC	DDCMP	Other Protocol		
Physical						

Ethernet Version 2

Digital was joined by Intel and Xerox to develop the first version of Ethernet, physical and data link protocol. Since that time, the standard has been updated, and the current version is Ethernet Version 2.

Ethernet has the following characteristics:

■ 10 Mbps signaling over coaxial cable.

■ Media access control method is CARRIER-sense multiple access with collision detection (CSMA/CD).

■ Signaling uses Manchester encoding.

The IEEE 802.3 standard was developed with slight modifications from Ethernet Version 2. Among those changes was a modification to the frame format, which makes 802.3 frames incompatible with Ethernet Version 2.

 NetWare LANs can interface to DECnet networks using the NetWare for LAT product.

Ethernet Version 2 Topics And Methods

OSI Layer	Topics	Methods
Physical	Connection types	Multipoint
	Physical topology	Bus
	Digital signaling	State transition
	Bit synchronization	Synchronous

OSI Layer	Topics	Methods
	Bandwidth use	Baseband
Data Link (MAC sublayer)	Logical topology	Bus
	Media access	Contention
	Addressing	Physical device

Digital Data Communications Message Protocol (DDCMP)

DDCMP is a data link protocol that dates from the earliest DNA implementations and remains as an optional Phase V protocol. DDCMP has the following capabilities:

■ Asynchronous or synchronous service

■ Half- or full-duplex modes

■ Point-to-point or multipoint operation

■ Connection-oriented error control using commands and acknowledgments along with CRC-based error detection

■ LLC flow control and message sequencing (Digital uses the term *message* to describe data link level frames.)

 At the time the DNA protocols were being defined, all users interacted with central computers by means of computer terminals. Terminal support was provided by the Local Area Transport protocol (LAT), which enables terminal server devices to support multiple terminals and multiplex their traffic over a single channel. LAT does not conform to the OSI network layer, in that packets do not incorporate routing information and cannot be routed on wide area networks.

NetWare networks can interface with the DNA environment using the product NetWare for LAT.

Digital Data Communications Message Protocol (DDCMP) Topics And Methods

OSI Layer	Topics	Methods
Physical	Connection types	Point-to-point
		Multipoint
Data Link (LLC Sublayer)	Transmission synchronization	Asynchronous
		Synchronous
	Connection services	LLC-Level flow control
		Error control
		Message sequencing

High-Level Data Link Control (HDLC)

HDLC is a data link protocol that supports transmissions over physical layer modem communication protocols. HDLC has the following features:

■ Determines the data frame format and the frame transfer command syntax

■ Supports asynchronous and synchronous communication

■ Performs LLC flow control

High-Level Data Link Control (HDLC) Topics And Methods

OSI Layer	Topics	Methods
Physical	Connection types	Point-to-point
Data Link (LLC Sublayer)	Transmission synchronization	Asynchronous
		Synchronous
	Connection services	LLC-Level flow control

Connectionless-Mode Network Service (CLNS)

CLNS is a connectionless network layer service that incorporates the following three ISO protocols:

■ ISO 8473 is a connectionless-mode network service that manages communication between end systems.

■ ISO 9542 is a routing protocol that operates between *end systems* (devices) and *intermediate systems* (routers). This protocol, most frequently referred to as ES-IS, can be relatively simple because it does not need to perform internetwork routing.

■ ISO 10589 is a routing protocol that operates between intermediate systems. IS-IS is a more complex protocol than ES-IS because it must be capable of determining routes through complex internetworks. Figure 28.6 illustrates the relationships of the two routing protocols.

These connectionless protocols are used to perform route discovery and selection, addressing, and switching.

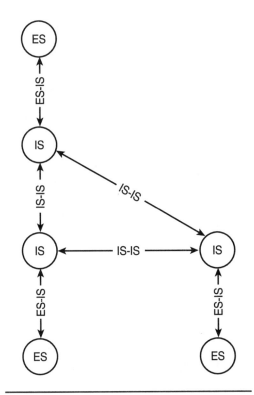

Figure 28.6
ES-IS and IS-IS routing protocols.

Connection-Mode Network Service (CONS)

CONS is a connection-oriented network layer service based on the following protocols:

■ ISO 8208 is an ISO version of the X.25 packet-switching protocol, which is discussed in Chapter 29.

■ ISO 8878 is an additional protocol that enables X.25 networks to provide connection-oriented services.

CLNS is employed more commonly than CONS to provide network layer services.

Connectionless Mode Network Service (CLNS) Topics And Methods

OSI Layer	Topics	Methods
Network	Addressing	Logical network
	Route discovery	Link-state
	Route selection	Dynamic

Connection-Mode Network Service (CONS) Topics And Methods

OSI Layer	Topics	Methods
Network	Addressing	Logical network
	Route discovery	Link-state
	Route selection	Dynamic
	Connection services	Network layer flow control
		Error control
		Packet
		Sequence control

Connection-Oriented Transport Protocol Specification (ISO 8073)

ISO 8073 is a transport layer protocol that provides five service classes, tailored to different requirements. Network implementations can select a service level based on required levels of flow, error, and packet sequencing.

Connection-Oriented Transport Protocol Specification Topics And Methods

OSI Layer	Topics	Methods
Transport	Addressing	Connection identifier
	Connection services	Segment sequencing
		Error control
		End-to-end flow control

Network Services Protocol (NSP)

NSP was incorporated in the original DNA protocol suite. NSP is a connection-oriented transport protocol that manages normal or expedited full-duplex subchannels. End-to-end flow control is performed in response to congestion messages from network layer protocols. Either windowing or guaranteed flow rates can be used to control data flow.

Network Services Protocol (NSP) Topics And Methods

OSI Layer	Topics	Methods
Transport	Addressing	Connection identifier
	Connection services	Segment sequencing
		Error control
		End-to-end flow control

Session Control

Session Control is a DNA protocol that performs session and presentation layer functions. Functions performed by Session Control include:

- Address/name resolution.
- Transport connection management.
- Connection identifier management.
- Selection of protocol stacks. When devices initiate a session, Session Control negotiates a protocol stack that is supported on both systems.

Session Control Topics And Methods

OSI Layer	Topics	Methods
Transport	Address/name resolution	Service-requestor initiated
	Addressing	Connection identifier

OSI Layer	Topics	Methods
Session	Session administration	Connection establishment
		Data transfer
		Connection release

Session Protocol Specification (ISO 8327)

ISO 8327 is a session layer protocol that implements the specification ISO 8326, Session Service Definition. OSI 8327 provides the following services:

■ Connection establishment, half-duplex data transfer, and connection release.

■ Support for multiple transport layer connections for each session.

■ Packet synchronization. The method uses tokens that can be used to request retransmission from any point.

ISO 8327 Session Protocol Specification Topics And Methods

OSI Layer	Topics	Methods
Session	Dialog control	half-duplex
	Session administration	Connection establishment
		Data transfer
		Connection release

Abstract Syntax Notation One with Basic Encoding Rules (ASN.1 with BER)

ASN.1 (ISO 8824) is a set of extensible syntax rules that establish data types and structures. The rules themselves are described in the Basic Encoding Rules. These protocols operate at the presentation DNA layer.

These standards are designed to facilitate data exchange between different systems by establishing a common set of data formats. These translations might include conversion between character sets, number representation systems, or other data types. The rules can be extended as required to embrace new data types.

Abstract Syntax Notation (ASN.1 with BER) Topics And Methods

OSI Layer	Topics	Methods
Presentation	Translation	Character code

File Transfer, Access, and Management (FTAM) and Data Access Protocol (DAP)

FTAM (ISO 8571) is an application layer file service protocol. The specification requires a certain set of document types and services, but permits vendors to create customized implementations of the protocol. Standard document types include binary, text, and hierarchical files. Standard services include file transfer and management.

Data Access Protocol (DAP)

DAP performs file services including file creation, deletion, storage, retrieval, and transfer.

File Transfer, Access, and Management (FTAM) and DAP Topics and Methods

OSI Layer	Topics	Methods
Application	Network service	File services

Network Virtual Terminal Service (NVTS)

This service enables multiple terminal types to access computer services. A virtual terminal is a conceptual representation of a computer display. Both the host and the terminal emulating device maintain a copy of this model, which serves as a common intermediate data representation that enables the host and device to exchange terminal data.

Network Virtual Terminal Services (NVTS) Topics And Methods

OSI Layer	Topics	Methods
Presentation	Translation	Character code (commands)
Application	Network service	Terminal service
	Service use	Remote operation

MAILbus and X.400 Message Handling System

These systems provide DNA electronic messaging services. The MAILbus family of products provides proprietary mail services and use the X.400 messaging specification to interface with other X.400-based systems.

MAILbus and X.400 Topics And Methods

OSI Layer	Topics	Methods
Application	Network service	Message service

Naming Service and X.500 Directory

Naming Service is an application-level naming service that provides address/name resolution. A *name service* enables humans to describe network services with logical, alphanumeric identifiers. These identifiers are translated to network addresses by the naming service.

X.500 is a standard for a naming service. Digital has stated that the DNA Naming Service will migrate toward conformance with X.500.

Naming Service and X.500 Topics And Methods

OSI Layer	Topics	Methods
Transport	Address/name resolution	Service-provider initiated
Application	Network service	Directory service

Systems Network Architecture (SNA)

Like DNA, IBM's Systems Network Architecture (SNA) evolved when terminals were the normal devices used to interact with centralized computers. SNA terminal networks are organized hierarchically, and when it was introduced in 1974, SNA supported only hierarchical networks. An example of an SNA network is shown in figure 28.7. The network hierarchy consists of a central control point (the host computer), controllers (communication controllers and cluster controllers), and terminals.

In 1984, SNA was updated to support distributed processing environments with a feature called *Advanced Peer-to-Peer Networking* (APPN). APPN can implement a distributed processing environment that can leverage the processing capabilities of mainframe hosts, minicomputers, and personal computers.

The next refinement of SNA, the Systems Application Architecture (SAA), was announced in 1987 and represents IBM's strategic direction.

SNA and the OSI Reference Model

SNA was not developed from a preconceived, carefully thought-out model from which protocols were developed. IBM literally was pioneering the development of computer networking, and new protocols were added to meet new needs and design criteria. One result of this is that multiple protocols

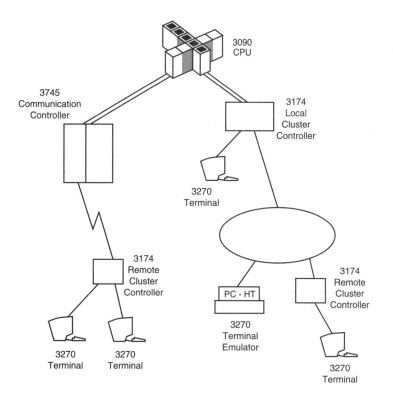

Figure 28.7
An example of an SNA network.

3090
CPU

3745
Communication
Controller

3174
Local
Cluster
Controller

3270
Terminal

3174
Remote
Cluster
Controller

PC - HT

3270
Terminal
Emulator

3174
Remote
Cluster
Controller

3270
Terminal

3270
Terminal

3270
Terminal

can be present at any given layer. Each protocol serves a somewhat different purpose in the overall scheme of SNA. As such, SNA does not consist of a protocol stack so much as it consists of multiple protocols that work together in different combinations to meet different needs.

SNA was a mature model by the time formulation of the OSI Reference Model was undertaken, and the SNA architecture had a significant influence on the definition of the OSI model. For that reason, this course includes a comparison of the two models.

In addition to showing the organization of the SNA protocols, figure 28.8 compares the layers of the OSI Reference Model to the layers of the SNA model.

The layers of the SNA model and their features are as follows:

■ **Physical control** covers the same functions as the OSI physical layer. Both are concerned with the electrical, mechanical, interface, and control characteristics of the physical medium. IBM developed the Token Ring physical layer standard for this layer, but market forces have pushed IBM to extend SNA to embrace other popular physical layer standards such as Ethernet (IEEE 802.3).

■ **Data link control** includes many functions of the OSI data link layer. The *Synchronous Data Link Control* (SDLC) protocol is the SNA data link protocol and is responsible for communication between master/primary nodes and slave/secondary nodes.

■ **Path control** incorporates functions from two OSI layers. Path control is responsible for flow control, a data link layer function. Path control also is responsible for the routing and packet disassembly/assembly functions of the network layer.

■ **Transmission control** is analogous to the OSI transport layer and provides end-to-end connection services. This layer also performs encryption/decryption, services OSI provides at the presentation layer.

■ **Data flow control**, like the OSI session layer, controls dialogs.

■ **Presentation services** perform data translation services similar to the OSI presentation layer, but also are responsible for sharing resources and synchronizing operations.

■ **Transaction services** provide application services, supporting distributed processing and management services. *SNA Distributed Services* (SNADS) is an example of a distributed service.

Figure 28.8

SNA protocols and the OSI Reference Model.

SNA	OSI	SNA Protocols				
Transaction Services	Application	DIA	SNADS	DPM		User Applications
Presentation Services	Presentation	APPC	CICS	IMS	TSO	DB2
	Session					
Data Flow Control	Transport	APPN	VTAM			
Transmission Control	Network	NCP				
Path Control						
Data Link Control	Data Link	Token Ring	SDLC		X.25	
Physical Control	Physical		V.35	RS-232C		

Network Addressable Units

SNA networks are organized hierarchically and consist of *network addressable units* (NAUs). An NAU is a hardware device or a program (or a combination of hardware and software) that can be addressed on the network. Two types of NAUs can be found: physical units and logical units.

A *physical unit* (PU) is a device consisting of the hardware, firmware, and software required to manage node communication. Communication controllers and cluster controllers are examples of physical units.

 Note By definition under SNA terminology, a node is, by definition, a physical unit (PU). Terminals, printers, and other peripherals are not regarded as nodes.

Logical units (LUs) are the end points of network communication. (The course definition calls LUs "the 'entities' of the network.") Examples of LUs are peripherals such as terminals, printers, and programs that communicate by means of SNA.

SNA defines several types of PUs and LUs, some of which are illustrated in figure 28.9. The types of each are discussed next.

Until the 1980s, virtually all devices on SNA networks operated in a master/slave relationship under which a master device, the control point, controls all network communication. Terminals, printers, and other peripheral devices function as slaves controlled by the master device, which uses polling to manage communication.

Figure 28.9
PUs and LUs in an SNA network.

During the 1980s, IBM introduced Advanced Program-to-Program Networking (APPN), which enabled LUs to communicate in a peer-to-peer fashion. LU Type 6.2 and PU Type 2.1 were introduced to support APPN.

Physical Units

SNA defines the following three types of physical units:

■ **PU type 5** nodes are host nodes. A *host node* is the control point that manages networking in a domain. A *domain* consists of all the PUs, LUs, and other network resources that a given host can control. Domains can be divided into subareas. On SNA networks consisting of multiple hosts, terminals can be configured to access applications on more than one host.

The host node runs a program called *Virtual Terminal Access Method* (VTAM), which provides the *System Services Control Point* (SSCP) service that controls all connection requests and network flow. All SNA network hierarchies are organized around an SSCP.

■ **PU type 4** nodes are communication controllers. A *communication controller* is a device that runs a *Network Control Program* (NCP) and serves as a communication front-end for the host node. (For this reason, this device typically is called a front end processor.) A communication controller relieves the host node of the responsibility for directly supervising remote communication resources. The IBM 3745 is a type of communication controller.

■ **PU Type 2** nodes are peripheral nodes. Typically, *peripheral nodes* are *cluster controllers*, devices that enable printers, terminals, and other devices to connect to the network. The IBM 3174 is a type of communication controller.

 Note The course materials state that terminals and printers are also examples of PU Type 2 devices. Terminals and printers, however, are more typically defined as logical units, which are discussed in the next section.

Logical units are the network end-points between which communication occurs. Quite often an LU consists of a software process that is running on a type 2 node (a cluster controller). This process in turn services data input and output for a particular terminal, printer, or other peripheral.

The most important thing about PUs and LUs is the *function*, not the hardware in which the function is performed. A terminal, for example, must be serviced by a PU Type 2 function as well as an LU Type 2 function. These two functions typically are performed by the hardware and software operating in a cluster controller.

Some SNA printers might be equipped with hardware that enables them to network as PU Type 2 devices, enabling them to network without a cluster controller. These printers, however, must still include the LU function as well as the PU function.

For purposes of this course, some types of terminals and printers might be considered to be Type 2 PUs.

The course also lists a PU Type 1—a type no longer in use—which is a type of terminal node.

All communication of PU Type 2 nodes is managed by the central control point, the SSCP. Two type 2 devices, therefore, cannot directly communicate.

PU Type 2.1 is a new subclass of PU Type 2 that enables the device to provide a control point. This control point enables type 2.1 PUs to engage in peer-to-peer communication.

 Note In summary, control points manage data communication on the network. Control points are found on type 5 PUs and type 2.1 PUs only.

Logical Units

Logical units are the endpoints of SNA communication and consist of physical devices (terminals, printers, etc.) and programs. The various LU types are summarized in table 28.2.

Table 28.2
Logical Unit Types

LU	Communication Endpoints	Description
0	Program-to-program	An older LU type supporting program-to-program communication. Replaced by LU type 6.2.
1	Program-to-device	Master/slave. SNA character-stream data on printers, card readers, and hard copy terminals.
2	Program-to-device	Master/slave. Supports terminals using the 3270 protocol.
3	Program-to-device	Master/slave. Supports printers using the 3270 protocol.
4	Program-to-program	Master/slave, peer-to-peer, or program-to-device SNA character stream to printers.
6&6.1	Program-to-program	Peer-to-peer interprogram communication. (Such as CICS-CICS, IMS-IMS, CICS-IMS.)
6.2	Program-to-program	Peer-to-peer Advanced Program-to-Program Communication (APPC).
7	Program-to-device	Communication using 5250 data streams, such as terminals on AS/400, System 36, and System 38.

Key SNA Protocols

The following are brief descriptions of common SNA protocols.

Token Ring

Token Ring is IBM's specification for a token-access LAN based on a ring logical topology. This specification was used as the basis for developing the IEEE 802.5 token ring standard. IBM Token Ring originally operated at 4 Mbps but has been extended to function at 16 Mbps data rates. The Token Ring specification describes various cable types, connectors, hubs, and wiring specifications.

Token Ring Topics And Methods

OSI Layer	Topics	Methods
Physical	Connection types	Point-to-point
	Physical topology	Star
	Digital signaling	State transition
	Bit synchronization	Synchronous
	Bandwidth use	Baseband
Data Link (MAC sublayer)	Logical topology	Ring
	Media access	Token passing
	Addressing	Physical device

Synchronous Data Link Control (SDLC)

SDLC is a high-performance data link protocol developed to support communication between computers and to function with dedicated or dial-up lines. SDLC supports point-to-point and multipoint communication in half- and full-duplex modes. SDLC frame types can be used to communicate data or to perform control functions.

Synchronous Data Link Control (SDLC) Topics And Methods

OSI Layer	Topics	Methods
Data Link (MAC sublayer)	Media access	Polling
	Addressing	Physical device
Data Link (LLC sublayer)	Transmission synchronization	Synchronous Synchronous
	Connection services	Flow control
		Error control

Network Control Program (NCP)

NCP is the protocol that manages network communication on front end processors. NCP functions at the data link and network layers and supports routing and gateway functions.

Network Control Program (NCP) Topics And Methods

OSI Layer	Topics	Methods
Data Link (MAC sublayer)	Media access	Polling
	Addressing	Physical device
Data Link (LLC sublayer)	Connection services	Flow control
Network	Addressing	Logical network
	Route selection	Static
	Gateway services	Network layer translation

Virtual Telecommunications Access Method (VTAM)

VTAM operates on the host control node and provides the *System Services Control Point* (SSCP) function for the network. The SSCP controls the network hierarchy and works in conjunction with NCPs running on front end processors. VTAM can manage single or multiple domains and supports interconnections between networks.

Virtual Telecommunications Access Method (VTAM) Topics And Methods

OSI Layer	Topics	Methods
Transport	Addressing	Connection identifier
	Segment development	Division and combination

OSI Layer	Topics	Methods
	Connection services	End-to-end flow control
Session	Dialog control	Half-duplex
	Session administration	Connection establishment
		Data transfer
		Connection release

Advanced Peer-to-Peer Networking (APPN)

APPN is the SNA architecture for network peer-to-peer communication. Any PU Type 2.1 can communicate with other PU type 2.1 devices directly, without the need for an SSCP control node. Thus APPN supports networking without the requirement for a mainframe computer. APPN provides directory services, route discover, and window-based flow control.

Advanced Peer-to-Peer Networking (APPN) Topics And Methods

OSI Layer	Topics	Methods
Network	Addressing	Logical network
	Route discovery	
Transport	Connection services	Segment sequencing
		End-to-end flow control

Customer Information Control System (CICS)

CICS is a transaction processing environment used to build applications. Transaction processing is intended for critical applications, and CICS provides the security, transaction tracking, error recovery, transaction backout, and restart capabilities that are required in such demanding environments as banking and stocks trading.

Customer Information Control System (CICS) Topics And Methods

OSI Layer	Topics	Methods
Session	Dialog control	Half-duplex
	Session administration	Connection establishment
		Data transfer
		Connection release
Presentation	Translation	File syntax

Information Management System (IMS)

IMS is another application processing environment, and it supports both database and transaction management. The IMS Database Manager is a powerful hierarchical database that can operate under CICS or under the IMS Transaction Manager. IMS databases can be shared among various applications, with IMS scheduling activities and switching messages.

Information Management System (IMS) Topics And Methods

OSI Layer	Topics	Methods
Session	Dialog control	Half-duplex
	Session administration	Connection establishment
		Data transfer
		Connection release
Presentation	Translation	File syntax

Advanced Program-to-Program Communication (APPC)

APPC is the IBM specification that defines LU Type 6.2.

Advanced Program-to-Program Communication (APPC) Topics And Methods

OSI Layer	Topics	Methods
Transport	Addressing	Connection identifier
	Connection services	Segment sequencing
		End-to-end flow control
Session	Dialog control	Half-duplex
	Session	Connection establishment
		Data transfer
		Connection release

Distributed Data Management (DDM)

DDM uses an OS call redirection approach to provide remote file access to SNA applications. DDM receives service requests and executes them locally or directs them to a DDM server elsewhere on the network as appropriate.

**Distributed Data Management (DDM)
Topics And Methods**

OSI Layer	Topics	Methods
Application	Network services	File
	Service use	OS call interception

SNA Distributed Services (SNADS)

SNADS provides asynchronous distribution by implementing a store-and-forward distribution service. This service complements the synchronous delivery supported by SNA session capabilities and is useful for distribution of messages and documents. Among its functions, SNADS provides an infrastructure for distribution of e-mail.

**SNA Distribution Services (SNADS)
Topics And Methods**

OSI Layer	Topics	Methods
Application	Network services	File Message

Document Interchange Architecture (DIA)

DIA defines standards for data interchange between dissimilar computer systems, and coordinates storage, transfer, and retrieval of files.

**Document Interchange Architecture (DIA)
Topics And Methods**

OSI Layer	Topics	Methods
Application	Network services	File

Questions

1. Which TWO protocols are designed to provide reliable delivery?

   ☐ A. IPX

   ☐ B. TCP

   ☐ C. UDP

   ☐ D. SPX

2. Which protocol enables clients to identify available NetWare servers?

   ○ A. IPX

   ○ B. NLSP

   ○ C. SAP

   ○ D. RIP

3. Which THREE protocols translate logical device names into device addresses?

   ☐ A. DNS

   ☐ B. NBP

   ☐ C. SAP

   ☐ D. X.500

4. If your network includes large numbers of NetWare servers, connected via a wide area network, which protocol should you evaluate as a means of reducing network traffic overhead?

   ○ A. SPX

   ○ B. SAP

   ○ C. NLSP

   ○ D. RIP

5. Which of the following protocols are most similar?

   ○ A. NetWare IPX and Internet TCP

   ○ B. NetWare NLSP and AppleTalk RTMP

   ○ C. NetWare NLSP and DNA CLNS

   ○ D. NetWare RIP and Internet OSPF

6. Which Novell protocol usually provides transport-layer functions?

   ○ A. SPX

   ○ B. IPX

   ○ C. NLSP

   ○ D. NCP

7. Which protocol suite provides the standards with the broadest industry support?

   ○ A. AppleTalk

   ○ B. Internet

   ○ C. NetWare

   ○ D. SNA

8. Which types of addresses are used on LocalTalk networks?

   ○ A. Physical node numbers

   ○ B. Static logical IDs

   ○ C. Dynamic logical IDs

   ○ D. Logical device names

9. Which protocol enables Ethernet and token ring networks to interface with AppleTalk protocols?

   ○ A. RTMP

   ○ B. AARP

○ C. LLAP

○ D. ZIP

10. Which protocol is responsible for matching user's logical device names with AppleTalk addresses?

○ A. AARP

○ B. ZIP

○ C. NBP

○ D. ATP

11. Which THREE AppleTalk protocols provide session-level services?

☐ A. ASP

☐ B. PAP

☐ C. ADSP

☐ D. AFP

12. Which TWO components are required to enable a NetWare LAN to communicate with a Digital computer?

☐ A. Ethernet v.2 support

☐ B. IEEE 802.3 Ethernet support

☐ C. TCP/IP

☐ D. NetWare for LAT

13. Which TWO of these DNA protocols are regarded as presentation layer protocols?

☐ A. ASN.1

☐ B. NVTS

☐ C. FTAM

☐ D. MAILbus

14. Which THREE of the following statements are true regarding SNA network addressable units?

☐ A. A PU type 2 is a communication controller

☐ B. An LU 6.2 device is capable of program-to-program communication

☐ C. A PU consists of the hardware and software required to manage the resources of nodes.

☐ D. Control points are found on Type 5 and Type 2.1 PUs.

15. Which SNA protocols are required to implement peer-to-peer communication?

○ A. DDM

○ B. SNADS

○ C. APPN and APPC

○ D. NCP

Answers

1. B D	9. B
2. C	10. C
3. A B D	11. A B D
4. C	12. A D
5. C	13. A B
6. D	14. B C D
7. B	15. C
8. C	

Other Protocols and Standards

This chapter discusses a variety of network protocols that you are likely to encounter. The following protocols are covered:

- ■ *The IEEE 802 family*
- ■ *Fiber Distributed Data Interface (FDDI)*
- ■ *Serial Line Internet Protocol (SLIP) and Point-to-Point Protocol (PPP)*
- ■ *CCITT/ITU X.25*
- ■ *Frame Relay*
- ■ *Integrated Service Digital Network (ISDN) and Broadband ISDN (B-ISDN)*
- ■ *Asynchronous Transfer Mode (ATM)*
- ■ *Synchronous Optical Network (SONET) and the Synchronous Digital Hierarchy (SDH)*
- ■ *Switched Multimegabit Digital Service (SMDS)*

More information about many of these protocols can be found in NRP's NetWare: The Professional Reference, Fourth Edition.

The IEEE 802 Family

The *Institute of Electrical and Electronic Engineers* (IEEE) is the largest professional organization in the world and is extremely influential with regard to setting standards. The 802 committee of the IEEE has developed a series of standards for *local area networks* (LANs), *metropolitan area networks* (MANs), and *wide area networks* (WANs). These standards have been recognized and reissued by the *International Organization for Standardization* (ISO) as the ISO 8802 standards.

Twelve subcommittees oversee the 802 standards. (A thirteenth committee has been proposed for the developing 100-BASE-X standard.) Figure 29.1 illustrates the position each standard occupies in the OSI Reference Model. The following table summarizes the topics and methods associated with each standard.

802.2 Topics and Methods

Layer	Topics	Methods
Data link	Protocol specific	Identification of upper-layer protocols
LLC sublayer		

IEEE 802.2

The IEEE 802.2 standard defines an LLC sublayer that is utilized by other lower-layer protocols. Because a single LLC protocol layer is used by lower-layer protocols, network layer protocols can be designed independently of the network's physical layer and MAC sublayer implementations.

The LLC appends a header to packets that identifies which upper-layer protocols are associated with the frame. The header also declares which processes are the source and destination of each packet.

IEEE 802.3

The IEEE 802.3 standard defines a network derived from the Ethernet network originally developed by Digital, Intel, and Xerox. This standard defines characteristics related to the MAC sublayer of the data link layer and to the OSI physical layer. With one minor distinction—frame type—IEEE 802.3 Ethernet functions identically to DIX Ethernet v.2. The two standards can even coexist on the same cabling system, although devices using one standard cannot communicate directly with devices using the other. The following table about 802.3 summarizes the topics and methods associated with each layer.

Figure 29.1

The relationship between the IEEE 802 standards and the OSI Reference Model.

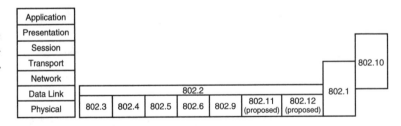

802.3 Topics and Methods

Layer	Topics	Methods
Physical	Physical topology	1BASE5 star
		10BASE5 bus
		10BASE2 bus
		10BROAD36 bus
		10BASE-F star
		10BASE-T star
	Connection types	Multipoint
	Digital signaling	State transition
	Bit synchro-nization	Synchronous
	Bandwidth use	Baseband (except 10BROAD36 broadband)
Data link (MAC sublayer)	Logical topology	Bus
	Media access	Contention
	Addressing	Physical device address

The MAC sublayer uses a variety of contention access called *Carrier Sense Multiple Access with Collision Detection* (CSMA/CD). This technique reduces the incidence of collision by having each device listen to the network to determine if it is quiet ("carrier sensing"); a device only attempts to transmit when the network is quiescent. This reduces but does not eliminate collisions because signals take some time to propagate through the network. As devices transmit, they continue to listen so they can detect a collision should it occur. When a collision occurs, all devices cease transmitting and send a "jamming" signal that notifies all stations of the collision. Then, each device waits a random amount of time before again attempting to transmit. This combination of safeguards significantly reduces collisions on all but the busiest networks.

The physical layer definition describes signaling methods (both baseband and broadband are available), data rates, media, and topologies. Several physical layer variants have been defined. Each is named following a convention that states the signaling rate (1 or 10) in Mbps, baseband (BASE) or broadband (BROAD) mode, and a designation of the media characteristics. The following are the 802.3 variants:

■ **1BASE5** is a 1 Mbps network that utilizes UTP cable with a signal range up to 500 meters (250 meters per segment). A star physical topology is used.

■ **10BASE5** uses a large diameter (10mm) "thick" coaxial cable with a 50-ohm impedance. A data rate of 10 Mbps is supported with a signaling range of 500 meters per cable segment on a physical bus topology. This variant is typically called *Thick Ethernet* or *Thicknet.*

■ **10BASE2** is similar to Thicknet, but uses a thinner coaxial cable that can support cable runs of 185 meters. (In this case, the 2 only approximately indicates the cable range.) The transmission rate remains 10 Mbps and the physical topology is a bus. This variant is typically called *Thin Ethernet* or *Thinnet.*

■ **10BASE-F** uses fiber-optic cables to support 10 Mbps signaling with a range of 4 kilometers. Three subcategories include 10BASE-FL (fiber link), 10BASE-FB (fiber backbone), and 10BASE-FP (fiber passive).

■ **10BROAD36** is a broadband standard that supports channel signal rates of 10 Mbps. 75-ohm coaxial cable supports cable runs of 1,800 meters (up to 3,600 meters in a dual-cable configuration) using a physical bus topology.

■ **10BASE-T** uses UTP cable in a star physical topology. The signaling rate remains at 10 Mbps. Devices might be up to 100 meters from a wiring hub.

■ **100BASE-X** is a proposed standard that is similar to 10BASE-T but supports 100 Mbps data rates.

> **Note** The industry is not in accord regarding the proper use of the name Ethernet. Xerox has placed the name Ethernet in the public domain, therefore no one can claim authority over it. Purists often claim that Ethernet refers only to the original Digital-Intel-Xerox standard. More frequently, however, the term is used to designate any network based on CSMA/CD access control methods.

It is usually necessary to be specific about the standard that applies to a given network configuration. The original standard is called Ethernet version 2 (the older version 1 is still in occasional use) or Ethernet-II. The IEEE standard is distinguished by its committee title as 802.3.

The distinction is important because Ethernet version 2 and 802.3 Ethernet use incompatible frame types. Devices using one frame type cannot communicate with devices using the other frame type. Fortunately, NetWare is conversant with both frame types on both servers and clients.

IEEE 802.4

The 802.4 standard describes a network with a bus physical topology that controls media access with a token mechanism. The standard was designed to meet the needs of industrial automation systems but has gained little popularity. Both baseband and broadband (using 75-ohm coaxial cable) configurations are available.

802.4 Topics and Methods

Layer	*Topics*	*Methods*
Physical	Physical topology	Bus
	Connection types	Multipoint
	Digital signaling	State transition
	Bit synchronization	Synchronous
	Bandwidth use	Baseband
Data link (MAC sublayer)	Logical topology	Ring
	Media access	Token passing
	Addressing	Physical device address

IEEE 802.5

The IEEE 802.5 standard was derived from IBM's Token-Ring network, which employs a ring logical topology and token-based media access control. Data rates of 1, 4, and 16 Mbps have been defined. The IEEE 802.5 standard does not describe a cabling system. Most implementations are based on the IBM cabling system, which uses twisted-pair cable wired in a physical star.

802.5 Topics and Methods

Layer	Topics	Methods
Physical	Physical topology	Star/Ring
	Connection types	Point-to-point
	Digital signaling	State transition
	Bit synchro-nization	Synchronous
	Bandwidth use	Baseband
Data link (MAC sublayer)	Logical topology	Ring
	Media access Addressing	Token passing Physical device address

IEEE 802.6

The IEEE 802.6 standard describes a MAN standard called *Distributed Queue Dual Bus* (DQDB). Much more than a data network technology, DQDB is suited to data, voice, and video transmissions. The network is based on fiber-optic cable in a dual-bus topology. Traffic on each bus is unidirectional. When operated in pairs, the two buses provide a fault-tolerant configuration. Bandwidth is allocated using time slots, and both synchronous and asynchronous modes are supported.

802.6 Topics and Methods

Layer	Topics	Methods
Physical	Physical topology	Ring
	Connection types	Point-to-point
	Bandwidth use	Baseband
Data link (MAC sublayer)	Logical topology	Ring

IEEE 802.9

The IEEE 802.9 standard supports a 10 Mbps asynchronous channel along with 96 64-Kbps (6 Mbps total bandwidth) channels that can be dedicated to specific data streams. The total bandwidth is 16 Mbps. This standard is called *Isochronous Ethernet* (IsoEnet) and is designed for settings that have a mix of bursty and time-critical traffic.

IEEE 802.11

IEEE 802.11 is a standard for wireless LANs, currently under development. A CSMA/CD method has been approved, but the final standard is pending.

802.11 (Proposed) Topics and Methods

Layer	Topics	Methods
Data link (MAC sublayer)	Media access	Contention

IEEE 802.12

The IEEE 802.12 standard is based on a 100 Mbps proposal promoted by AT&T, IBM, and Hewlett-Packard. Called 100VG-AnyLAN, the network is based on a star wiring topology and a contention-based access method whereby devices signal the wiring hub of a need to transmit data. Devices can transmit only when granted permission by the hub. This standard is intended to provide a high-speed network that can operate in mixed Ethernet and Token Ring environments by supporting both frame types.

802.12 (Proposed) Topics and Methods

Layer	Topics	Methods
Physical	Physical topology	Star
	Connection types	Multipoint
	Bandwidth use	Baseband
Data link (MAC sublayer)	Logical topology	Bus
	Media access	Contention

Fiber Distributed Data Interface

Fiber Distributed Data Interface (FDDI) is a standard for fiber-based networks that was developed by the X3T9.5 committee of the *American National Standards Institute* (ANSI). The ISO has adopted FDDI as standard 9314. FDDI was developed for WANs but has been used in MANs and LANs as well.

As shown in figure 29.2, FDDI covers the physical layer and the MAC sublayer of the OSI Reference Model. Most frequently, the IEEE 802.2 standard is employed for the LLC sublayer.

Figure 29.2
The relationship of FDDI to the OSI Reference Model.

FDDI is a 100 Mbps network that functions similarly to 802.5 Token Ring, and is based on token-passing access control and a ring topology. Originally developed for optical fiber cable, the standard has been extended so that it can be supported with copper UTP. Use of optical fiber cable enables FDDI to support physically large networks.

Although FDDI networks can be cabled as physical stars, stars might be impractical with larger networks, and FDDI networks are then typically cabled in physical rings. Stations can be attached in two ways as shown in figures 29.3A and 29.3B. Stations on a single ring configuration are called *single-attached stations*. On a single ring, failure of the medium at any point causes the network to fail.

To provide greater fault tolerance, FDDI is typically cabled with *dual-attached stations* (DASs) using two counter-rotating rings. As figure 29.3B shows, if the cable fails at any one point, the two

rings are automatically reconfigured to maintain a complete ring transmission path. (Note that a failed link between single-attached stations cannot be corrected in this manner.) Under normal operation, both rings can be used for data and traffic can be balanced between rings. It is desirable, however, to design the network to half its dual-ring capacity and to half its size limit. If a ring failure occurs under these conditions, the total length of the two rings will be within specifications and the traffic will be manageable with only a single active ring.

Figure 29.3A
Normal operation of an FDDI network with single- and dual-attached stations.

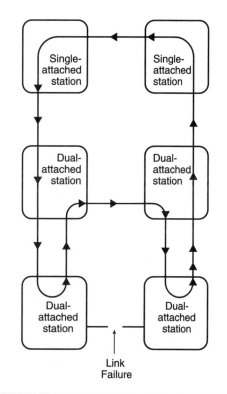

Figure 29.3B
Dual-attached FDDI stations correcting for a failed link.

FDDI Topics and Methods

Layer	Topics	Methods
Physical	Physical topology	Star or ring
	Connection types	Point-to-point
	Bandwidth use	Baseband
Data link (MAC sublayer)	Logical topology	Ring
	Media access	Token passing

Serial Line Internet Protocol and Point-to-Point Protocol

The *Serial Line Internet Protocol* (SLIP) and *Point-to-Point Protocol* (PPP) were designed to support dial-up access to networks based on the Internet protocols. SLIP is a simple protocol that functions at the physical layer, whereas PPP is a considerably enhanced protocol that provides physical layer and data link layer functionality. The relationship of both to the OSI model is shown in figure 29.4.

SLIP was developed to provide dial-up IP connections. It is an extremely rudimentary protocol that suffers from a lack of rigid standardization such that different implementations might not interoperate.

SLIP Topics and Methods

Layer	Topics	Methods
Physical	Connection type	Point-to-point

PPP was defined by the *Internet Engineering Task Force* (IETF) to improve on SLIP by providing the following features:

- Security using password login

- Simultaneous support for multiple protocols on the same link

- Dynamic IP addressing

- Error control

Different PPP implementations might offer different levels of service and can negotiate service levels when connections are made.

Figure 29.4

The relationship of SLIP and PPP to the OSI Reference Model.

PPP Topics and Methods

Layer	Topics	Methods
Physical	Connection type	Point-to-point
Data link (MAC sublayer)	Addressing	Physical device
Data link (LLC sublayer)	Connection services	Error control

Application
Presentation
Session
Transport

Network		X.25
Data Link		LAPB
Physical		X.21, etc.

Figure 29.5
The relationship of X.25 to the OSI Reference Model.

CCITT/ITU X.25

X.25 is a packet-switching network standard developed by the *International Telegraph and Telephone Consultative Committee* (CCITT), which has been renamed the *International Telecommunications Union* (ITU). The standard, referred to as Recommendation X.25, was introduced in 1974, and is most commonly implemented in WANs.

As shown in figure 29.5, X.25 is one level of a three-level stack that spans the network, data link, and physical layers.

Physical layer connectivity is provided by a variety of standards including X.21, X.21bis, and V.32.

X.21 Topics and Methods

Layer	Topics	Methods
Physical	Connection type	Point-to-point
	Physical topology	Hybrid mesh
	Bit synchronization	Synchronous

Link Access Procedures-Balanced (LAPB) is a bit-oriented, full-duplex, synchronous data link layer LLC protocol.

LAPB Topics and Methods

Layer	Topics	Methods
Data link control (LLC sublayer)	Connection services	LLC flow
		Error control

X.25 packet-switching networks provide the options of permanent or switched virtual circuits. Although a datagram (unreliable) protocol was supported until 1984, X.25 is now required to provide reliable service and end-to-end flow control. Because each device on a network can operate more than one virtual circuit, X.25 must provide error and flow control for each virtual circuit.

X.25 networks are typically implemented with line speeds up to 64 Kbps. These speeds are suitable for the file transfer and terminal activity that comprised the bulk of network traffic when X.25 was defined. Such speeds, however, are inadequate to provide LAN-speed services, which generally require speeds of 1 Mbps or better. X.25 networks are, therefore, poor choices for providing LAN application services in a WAN environment.

Recommendation X.25 Topics and Methods

Layer	Topics	Methods
Network	Addressing	Channel (logical address maintained for each connection)
	Switching	Packet (virtual circuit)
	Connection services	Network layer flow control
		Error control

Frame Relay

Frame relay was designed to support the *Broadband Integrated Services Digital Network* (B-ISDN), which is discussed in the following section, "ISDN and B-ISDN." The specifications for frame relay address some of the limitations of X.25. Like X.25, frame relay is a packet-switching network service. Frame relay is standardized by ANSI and ITU (CCITT).

Unlike X.25, frame relay assumes a more reliable network. This enables frame relay to eliminate much of the X.25 overhead required to provide reliable service on less reliable networks. Frame relay relies on higher-level protocol layers to provide flow and error control.

Frame relay typically is implemented as a public data network and is, therefore, regarded as a WAN protocol. The relationship of frame relay to the OSI model is shown in figure 29.6. Notice that the scope of frame relay is limited to the physical and data link layers.

Frame relay provides switched and permanent virtual circuits. Frame relay services are typically implemented at line speeds of 56 Kbps up to 1.544 Mbps (T1).

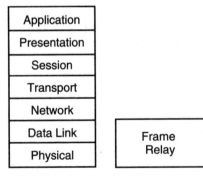

Figure 29.6
The relationship of Frame Relay to the OSI Reference Model.

Customers typically purchase access to a specific amount of bandwidth on a frame relay service. This bandwidth is called the *committed information rate* (CIR), a data rate for which the customer is guaranteed access. Customers may be permitted to access higher data rates on a pay-per-use, temporary basis. This arrangement enables customers to tailor their network access costs based on their bandwidth requirements.

Frame Relay Topics and Methods

Layer	Topics	Methods
Physical	Connection type	Point-to-point
	Physical topology	Hybrid mesh
	Switching	Packet (virtual circuit)
Data link	Connection services	LLC-level flow control (LLC sublayer)
		Error control (detection but not recovery)

ISDN and B-ISDN

Integrated Services Digital Network (ISDN) is a group of ITU (CCITT) standards designed to provide voice, video, and data transmission services on digital telephone networks. ISDN uses multiplexing to support multiple channels on high-bandwidth circuits. The relationship of the ISDN protocols to the OSI Reference Model is shown in figure 29.7.

Figure 29.7
The relationship of ISDN protocols to the OSI Reference Model.

A variety of ISDN channel types are defined. These channel types, often called *bit pipes*, provide different types and levels of service. The various channels are described in the following list:

■ A channel provides 4 kHz analog telephone service.

■ D channels support 64 Kbps digital data.

■ C channels support 8 or 16 Kbps digital data, generally for out-of-band signaling.

■ D channels support 16 or 64 Kbps digital data, also for out-of-band signaling. D channels support the following subchannels:

  ■ p subchannels support low-bandwidth packet data.

  ■ s subchannels are used for signaling (such as call setup).

  ■ t subchannels support telemetry data (such as utility meters).

■ E channels provide 64 Kbps service used for internal ISDN signaling.

■ H channels provide 384, 1,536, or 1,920 digital service.

The following three standard channel combinations have been defined:

- *Basic rate* includes two B channels and one D channel.

- *Primary rate* includes one D channel, 23 B channels (in the U.S. and Japan), or 30 B channels (in Europe and Australia).

- *Hybrid* provides one A channel and one C channel.

ISDN functions as a data transmission service only. Acknowledged, connectionless, full-duplex service is provided at the data link layer by the LAPD protocol, which operates on the D channel.

ISDN Topics and Methods

Layer	Topics	Methods
Physical	Multiplexing	Time-division multiplexing
Network	Switching	Packet
		Circuit

LAPD Topics and Methods

Layer	Topics	Methods
Data link (MAC sublayer)	Addressing	Physical device
Data link (LLC sublayer)	Connection services	LLC flow control
		Frame sequencing

Broadband ISDN is a refinement of ISDN that is defined to support higher bandwidth applications such as video, imaging, and multimedia. Physical layer support for B-ISDN is provided by *Asynchronous Transfer Mode* (ATM) and the *Synchronous Optical Network* (SONET). SONET is discussed further in the following section. Typical B-ISDN data rates are 51 Mbps, 155 Mbps, and 622 Mbps over fiber-optic media.

Synchronous Optical Network and the Synchronous Digital Hierarchy

Bell Communications Research developed SONET, which has been accepted as an ANSI standard. SONET is regarded as a WAN standard.

A similar set of standards, published by the ITU (CCITT), is called the *Synchronous Digital Hierarchy* (SDH). Regional variations of SDH, including SDH-Europe, SDH-SONET (North America), and SDH-Japan, have been defined to accommodate local differences. Figure 29.8 illustrates the relationship of the SONET/SDH standards to the OSI Reference Model.

Data rates for SONET are organized in a hierarchy based on the *Optical Carrier* (OC) speed and the corresponding *Synchronous Transport Signals* (STS) employed. The basic OC and STS data rate is 51.84 Mbps. Higher data rates are provided in multiples of the basic rate. Thus OC-48 is 48×51.84 Mbps = 2488.32 Mbps.

| Application |
| Presentation |
| Session |
| Transport |
| Network |
| Data Link |
| Physical |

| SONET/SDH |

Figure 29.8

The relationship of SONET/SD to the OSI Reference Model.

SDH data rates begin at 155.52 Mbps and are calculated in multiples of that rate. Thus an SDH-16 has a data rate of 2488.32 Mbps, equivalent to the SONET STS-48 data rate.

SONET/SDH Topics and Methods

Layer	Topics	Methods
Physical	Connection type	Point-to-point
	Physical topology	Mesh
		Ring
	Multiplexing	Time-division

Asynchronous Transfer Mode (ATM)

ATM is a high-bandwidth switching technology developed by the ITU *Telecommunications Standards Sector* (ITU-TSS). An organization called the *ATM Forum* is responsible for defining ATM implementation characteristics. ATM can be layered on other physical layer technologies such as FDDI and SONET. The relationships of these protocols to the OSI model are shown in figure 29.9.

| Application |
| Presentation |
| Session |
| Transport |
| Network |
| Data Link |
| Physical |

| ATM |
| SONET/SDH, FDDI, etc. |

Figure 29.9

The relationship of ATM to the OSI Reference Model.

ATM has several characteristics that distinguish it from other switching technologies discussed in this course. ATM is based on fixed-length, 53-byte cells, whereas other technologies employ frames that vary in length to accommodate different amounts of data. Because ATM cells are uniform in length, switching mechanisms can operate with a high level of efficiency.

The unit of transmission for ATM is called a *cell*. All cells are 53 bytes in length and consist of a 5-byte header and 48 bytes of data. The 48-byte data size was arrived at by the standards committee as a compromise between the needs of audio and data transmission. Audio information must be delivered with little latency (delay) to maintain a smooth flow of sound. Audio engineers preferred a small cell so that cells would be more readily available when needed. For data, however, large cells reduce the overhead required to deliver a byte of information.

Asynchronous delivery is another distinguishing feature of ATM. *Asynchronous* refers to the characteristic of ATM whereby transmission time slots do not occur periodically, but are granted at irregular intervals. ATM uses a technique called *label multiplexing*, which allocates time slots on demand. Traffic that is time critical, such as voice or video, can be given priority over data traffic that can be delayed slightly with no ill effect. Channels are identified by cell labels, not by specific time slots. A high-priority transmission need not be held until its next time slot allocation. It might only be required to wait until the current 53-byte cell has been transmitted.

Other multichannel technologies utilize time-division techniques to allocate bandwidth to channels. A T1 (1.544 Mbps) line, for example, might be time-division multiplexed to provide 24 voice channels. With this technique, each channel is assigned a specific time slot in the transmission schedule. The disadvantage of this technique is that an idle channel does not yield its bandwidth for the creation of other channels.

Devices communicate on ATM networks by establishing a virtual path, which is identified by a *virtual path identifier* (VPI). Within this virtual path, virtual circuits can be established, which are in turn associated with *virtual circuit identifiers* (VCIs). The VPI and VCI together make up a three-byte field that is included in the cell header.

Other networks, such as a routed Ethernet, require a six-byte physical address as well as a network address to uniquely identify each device on an internetwork. ATM can switch cells with three-byte identifiers because VPIs and VCIs apply only to a given device-to-device link. Each ATM switch can assign different VPIs and VCIs for each link. Up to 16 million circuits can be configured for any given device-to-device link.

The following three characteristics define the classes of ATM service:

■ **Time relation between source and destination.** Some data types require a precise time relationship between transmission and reception of cells.

■ **Bit rate.** Constant and variable bit rates are available. Many audio and video signaling techniques require constant bit rates. Newer techniques based on data compression might have the capability to function on variable-rate services.

■ **Connection mode.** Connection-oriented and connectionless services are available.

Using these characteristics, the following service classes have been defined:

■ **Class A.** Timing required, constant bit rate, connection-oriented.

■ **Class B.** Timing required, variable bit rate, connection-oriented. Data for this class must be delivered with a constant delay.

■ **Class C.** No timing, variable bit rate, connection-oriented.

■ **Class D.** No timing, variable bit rate, connectionless.

■ **Class X.** Unrestricted, variable bit rate, connection-oriented or connectionless.

Although ATM was developed primarily as a WAN technology, it has many characteristics of value for high-performance LANs. An interesting advantage is that ATM makes it possible to use the same technology for both LANs and WANs.

ATM Topics and Methods

Layer	Topics	Methods
Data link	Transmission synchronization	Isochronous
	Connection services	Error control
Network	Switching Route selection	Cell switching Static

Switched Multimegabit Digital Service (SMDS)

Switched Multimegabit Digital Service (SMDS) is a technology developed by Bell Communications Research in 1991. SMDS is related to ATM in that it transports data in 53-byte cells. SMDS supports cell switching at data rates of 1.544–45 Mbps.

SMDS is a connectionless data link layer service. IEEE 802.6 (DQDB metropolitan area network) is the primary physical layer standard employed with SMDS, although other physical layer standards are supported as well. Figure 29.10 illustrates the relationships of these protocols in the context of the OSI model.

Figure 29.10
The relationship of SMDS to the OSI Reference Model.

SMDS Topics and Methods

Layer	Topics	Methods
Data link (LLC sublayer)	Transmission synchronization	Isochronous
Network	Switching	Cell switching

Questions

1. Which TWO of the following are regarded as WAN protocols?

   ☐ A. Frame relay

   ☐ B. SLIP

   ☐ C. IEEE 802.6

   ☐ D. X.25

2. Which protocols are commonly used with IEEE 802.2?

   ○ A. IEEE 802.3

   ○ B. IEEE 802.5

   ○ C. IEEE 802.6

   ○ D. All of the above

3. What is the primary characteristic that distinguishes a cell from a packet?

   ○ A. Cells are generally smaller than packets.

   ○ B. Cells do not incorporate physical addresses.

   ○ C. All cells have the same fixed length.

   ○ D. Packets cannot be switched.

4 What are the primary differences between Ethernet version 2 and IEEE 802.3 Ethernet?

   ○ A. They require different network hardware.

   ○ B. IEEE 802.3 Ethernet functions at a higher data rate.

   ○ C. They use different frame formats.

   ○ D. Ethernet version 2 does not use CSMA/CD media access control.

5. Which TWO of these protocols are intended primarily for use on fiber-optic cable?

   ☐ A. Frame relay

   ☐ B. FDDI

   ☐ C. SONET

   ☐ D. X.25

6. Which TWO of these standards use token passing for media access control?

   ☐ A. IEEE 802.4

   ☐ B. IEEE 802.6

   ☐ C. Frame relay

   ☐ D. FDDI

7. Which TWO of these standards are designed to support audio data?

   ☐ A. IEEE 802.10

   ☐ B. ISDN

   ☐ C. ATM

   ☐ D. Frame relay

8. Which TWO of these network standards are well suited to delivering time-critical data?

   ☐ A. X.25

   ☐ B. IEEE 802.5

   ☐ C. Frame Relay

   ☐ D. ATM

Answers

1. A D
2. D
3. C
4. C

5. B C
6. A D
7. B C
8. B D

Tasks of Network Administrators

The job of network managers involves a wide variety of responsibilities, the basic concepts for some of which this chapter discusses, including the following topics:

- *Configuration management*
- *Fault management*
- *Performance management*
- *Security management*
- *Accounting management*

This book assumes you have had some experience as a network administrator, so discussion is brief and to-the-point, and no review questions follow.

Configuration Management

Configuration management is a process of tracking the components of a network and the configurations of those components. A detailed history of changes to the network is a tremendous aid for troubleshooting. When a problem occurs, the first thing you want to know is, "What's changed?" A configuration management database can tell you.

Following are just a few of the things your configuration management procedures should track:

■ All hardware that has vital data, such as firmware (ROM) revisions, when installed (for example, a design change without a new model number), and configuration details, such as interrupts, addresses, and so forth

■ Workstation configuration files, such as CONFIG.SYS and AUTOEXEC.BAT, to which many problems trace owing to users making changes

■ Network software, such as NetWare shell and Requester versions

■ Software licenses, to ensure that your network operates within the bounds of the license terms

■ Problems encountered and related solutions; history tends to repeat itself, so the solutions to many problems might already be known and recorded

You can manage proper configuration most easily if you use software designed for that purpose. Novell offers the *NetWare Management System* (NMS). Commercial NetWare configuration management products include Bindview and Cheyenne Monitrix.

Fault Management

Fault management involves using tools and procedures that anticipate network problems and help correct them when they occur.

When failures do occur, having the proper tools can improve the rapidity with which you can isolate and diagnose the fault. Many of these tools have evolved to the point that they report events that are not apparent as problems but that betray a degradation in the network. If a network card generates increasing numbers of damaged packets that must be retransmitted, the right tools report the condition before the NIC fails or generates so many errors that it degrades overall network performance.

Fault management includes some of the following practices:

■ **Data archiving and backup.** Properly speaking, archiving and backup are not part of fault management procedure, other than that a good set of backup tapes, properly stored, ensures against catastrophic data loss. Novell's standard for data archiving and backup is the *Storage Management Services* (SMS).

■ **Fault-tolerant design.** You can configure many network components in a fault-tolerant configuration such that one hardware failure cannot halt the network. NetWare provides the following three levels of server fault tolerance:

■ **SFT I (hot fix).** Enables servers to recover from minor failure in hard drive media

■ **SFT II (disk mirroring and duplexing).** Enables hard drives to operate in parallel so that a single hard drive failure does not cause data loss or service interruption

■ **SFT III (server duplexing).** Enables pairs of servers to operate in parallel so that even complete failure of a single server does not cause data loss or service interruption

You can achieve network fault-tolerance by designing in redundant data paths, fault-tolerant hubs, uninterruptible power supplies, and other such features.

■ **Network management systems.** Protocols for network management include the *Simple Network Management Protocol* (SNMP—a protocol in the TCP/IP suite that is *the* dominant network management protocol) and *Common Management Information Protocol* (CMIP). Devices that run these protocols (such as routers, hubs, switches, managed NICs, and so on) can generate network management messages that are directed to a network management console that analyzes incoming management information and generates network performance statistics and alerts. The console also can possess the capability to remotely manage network devices. On managed network hubs, for example, the console might automatically shut down a hub port that generates high numbers of errors. Novell's NetWare Management System is an SNMP management console for which you can use "snap-in" accessory products to extend its capabilities.

■ **Protocol analyzers receive all packets on the network and decode them for analysis.** Many network problems betray themselves in the form of abnormal packets. Network managers can capture packets from the network data stream and examine them for abnormalities. The latest versions of protocol analyzers perform much of the analysis automatically and assist with the rest. Some even incorporate expert systems that can intelligently diagnose network problems. Novell offers a software-based protocol analyzer, called LANalyzer for Windows.

■ **Cable testers are available at many levels of sophistication.** The best cable testers isolate faults to a specific area of a cable and even inform you when a cable is operating, but not performing up to specification.

Performance Management

Performance management is the proactive companion to fault management. Monitoring the performance of a network provides "baseline" data that is a snapshot of the network performing well under normal conditions, which proves valuable for identifying deteriorating network performance and as a standard of comparison when network failures occur.

You might monitor the following paramaters:

■ **Response time.**

■ **Throughput.**

■ **Network load.** A measure of network traffic as a percentage of total performance capacity.

■ **Errors.** All networks display some errors, but rising error levels are a clear indication of an impending problem.

Performance management enables you to plan future network enhancements, in addition to helping you anticipate problems. As network demand rises, you can add capacity before users become aware of problems.

Security Management

Anyone who has managed NetWare has dealt with *security management.* One of your tasks is to anticipate security threats and install safeguards. You might consider selecting some of the following security provisions:

- Establishing user and group security

- Restricting internal and external access to data

- Conducting security risk assessments

- Establishing security policies

- Protecting the network from viruses

- Auditing the network to detect security breaches

NetWare 4 provides for auditing the network, by supporting the establishment of network auditors who can function independently of network administrators. NetWare 4 network auditors can monitor all network operations to detect security breaches, including those that supervisors perform.

Accounting Management

Accounting management involves assessing the costs of using network resources. Some organizations use this information to charge departments for network use. These charges can be used to provide incentives for using LAN resources intelligently. User demand for additional LAN storage capacity and performance tends to rise rapidly if not controlled.

Other organizations simply use accounting information to control costs and plan improvements. When network enhancements are anticipated, accounting data can aid in assessing the cost/performance ratio of various options.

PART

Service and Support

31 *Troubleshooting the Network* *435*

32 *Using Research Tools in Troubleshooting* *443*

33 *Working with Network Adapter Cards and Cabling* *457*

34 *Troubleshooting Network Storage Devices* *491*

35 *Troubleshooting the DOS Workstation* 523

36 *Troubleshooting Network Printing* 535

37 *Network Optimization and Disaster Recovery* *541*

Troubleshooting the Network

It is wonderful when everything works as it should, but there is a finite life to everything. This means that no matter how well your network might be operating today, it is only a matter of time before there is a failure in cards, cabling, or any other component from which the network is built.

This chapter explores the following two components of network management:

- *Preventing problems*
- *Troubleshooting*

Regardless of how well you do the first, an occasion will come when you will have to do the second. This chapter places primary emphasis on details that can easily become test fodder. Your purpose for reading this chapter is that you want to be able to answer questions on the Novell tests. Aside from that, the material is presented in as practical a manner as possible, and lends itself well to use in the real world.

Problem Prevention

Preventing problems after a network is up and running is one of the primary jobs of an administrator. Because there are so many different types of problems that can occur, one cannot plan for all eventualities. The possibilities, however, can be divided into the following four categories:

- Physical
- Electrical
- Security
- Viruses

The following sections examine each of these.

Physical Problems

Temperature is one of the most critical environmental components affecting a computer's operation—whether a server or a workstation. Ambient temperature figures in, but more importantly is the temperature inside the computer. There can be as much as a 40 degree difference between the inside and outside of a computer due to the heat generated by the components. One reason for leaving computers turned on all the time is to prevent the internal temperature from fluctuating too greatly.

 Note When new equipment arrives, you should allow it to adjust to room temperature before using it. This assures that there will not be undue thermal strain on the components, should they have been bouncing around in a frozen FedEx truck for three days.

It is critical that a server have adequate ventilation to keep from overheating, otherwise "chip creep" can occur wherein integrated circuits lose their seating and contact with the socket. It is equally important that ambient air, which is sucked into the machine, be filtered and be of as high a quality as possible. A consistent temperature in the room should be maintained, and particles such as smoke and dust should be filtered out as much as possible with appropriate filtration devices.

Electrical Problems

Whereas physical problems can deteriorate a server or other computer slowly, electrical problems tend to do it immediately. They can destroy components, trash data, and make you wonder why you didn't keep the job at ChemLawn.

The four types of electrical problems are as follows:

- **Crosstalk.** Crosstalk is when two wires interfere with the magnetic fields of each other. The best solution is to use proper cable shielding and to avoid physical proximity between cables.

- **Static.** It is not the build up that wreaks damage, it is the sudden discharge. What makes it dangerous is that it can build to phenomenal levels before discharging all at once. Also known as *Electro-Static Discharge* (ESD), it must be beyond 3,000 volts for you to even feel it, but charges of 20 and 30 volts can damage equipment. The best solution to avoiding ESD is to use static discharge equipment and ground cords.

You should always ground yourself and any equipment on which you will be working. Never directly touch any electrical leads and always use antistatic bags to store components. You also can control static by keeping ambient humidity low.

 Note　Styrofoam is a common carrier of static buildup. It is highly recommended that Styrofoam cups not be left near servers or workstations.

■ **Transients.** Transients are sudden, high voltage bursts of current. Also known as spikes, transients usually occur randomly and last for less than one second. The randomness makes them hard to isolate, and they can often be associated with trouble farther down a power line, such as a blackout or lightning strike. Suppressor diodes are the best line of defense, as well as putting computers on their own circuit with isolated grounds.

■ **Line noise.** Low in voltage and low in current, noise usually occurs in an observable pattern. Most of the time, the culprit is another electrical device such as a microwave oven, a motor, or even the ballast of a fluorescent lamp. The best solution is to properly ground equipment and avoid running cable near other sources of interference.

 Note　When discussing noise, there are two acronyms commonly used. *Radio Frequency Interference* (RFI) is caused by microwaves, ovens, and appliances. *Electromagnetic Interference* (EMI) is caused by lights, radar, and industrial tools.

Security

Network security, and the implementation thereof, is the responsibility of the system administrator. *Electronic Data Processing* (EDP) Environmental Security entails thoroughly thinking through all the risks in your installation and creating a plan for dealing with them.

The following are four types of threats:

1. Destruction

2. Corruption

3. Disclosure

4. Interruption

To deal with the possibility of these threats, the administrator should think about each network segment and evaluate what potential risks there are. Next, he should evaluate and implement steps to minimize those risks effectively.

Some examples of security that can be implemented include the following:

■ Restricting login times to business hours

■ Requiring regular password changes

■ Requiring unique passwords

■ Turning off modems after working hours

■ Building RAID and redundancy into the server

Encryption also can be used to keep an intruder from understanding data that he intercepts. Beginning with NetWare 3.11, encryption is now standard, providing the SET command has ALLOW UNENCRYPTED PASSWORDS set to OFF.

Viruses

In simple terms, *viruses* are programs that interfere with the normal flow of processing. Viruses interfere by changing files and configurations, or by attaching themselves to everything they come in contact with and growing exponentially.

Viruses, by nature, require some action to activate them, and so they attach themselves to executable files. Those files are usually denoted by their extension, which can be BAT, EXE, or COM. Overlays, OVL files, provide other opportunities, however, as do FAT tables and boot sectors.

Very rarely have there been occurrences of viruses shipping with retail software. Most of the time, viruses enter the workplace through pirated software, downloaded shareware, or other suspect software. In a perfect world, the best solution is to prevent anyone other than the system administrator from installing software on the network. In this sense, "network" refers to all things physically attached—not only the server, but all workstations, too.

Given that there is no perfect world, and that you often cannot prevent installation of software on an individual's workstation, you must contend with the possibility of a virus attack. To do so, you should perform the following:

- Regularly back up the server and workstations

- Routinely scan for viruses with third-party software

- Flag EXE and COM files as Read-Only and Execute-Only

- In the PUBLIC and LOGIN directories, grant only Read and File Scan rights

- Check every disk for viruses before you install

- Discourage the downloading of BBS software

- Be prepared for action

Bear in mind that NetWare includes some safeguards against virus attacks. For one thing, the NetWare FAT table is different from that of workstations and cannot be attacked. Therefore, NetWare viruses are not as common as DOS viruses, and most virus attacks occur on workstations, as opposed to the server.

Troubleshooting

After a problem has occurred, prevention is a meaningless word and troubleshooting comes into play. The overall goal of troubleshooting is to restore service in a timely manner. The following are the four steps to the basic troubleshooting model:

1. Gather information.

2. Develop an attack plan.

3. Isolate the problem and execute the plan.

4. Document what was done.

By following these four steps, you can successfully restore a network to its fully operational state in the most efficient time possible. The importance of the fourth step cannot be overstated; it is easy to see where an experienced administrator has an advantage over an inexperienced one.

There are several questions you should ask when someone first reports a problem (and before you ever arrive on site). As rudimentary as these questions might seem, taking the time to ask them will save you an enormous amount of time in the long run.

■ **Has it ever worked?** Quite often, when a user calls to complain about something that doesn't work, it might be because she just installed it or has made some other major change that she does not want to mention without prodding.

■ **When did it work last?** If the accounting clerk is calling to complain about a printer that is not printing checks, it can be worth knowing that the printer in question has been offline for the last year and a half.

■ **What has changed since then?** You should consider, for example, whether you have moved from one building to another, or rearranged your offices? Did you pull your own cable through the ceiling?

The four step troubleshooting model discussed earlier suggests the following steps to solving workstation problems:

1. Rule out any possibility of user error.

2. Check the physical site to verify that all is as it should be. Make certain that an electrical cord or printer cable did not come unplugged.

3. Power everything down and then back up.

4. Back up data if there is a question of storage media (a hard drive or drives).

5. Eliminate as much overhead as you can. If the problem is with a workstation, reduce the CONFIG.SYS and AUTOEXEC.BAT files to the bare minimum and try the process again. Be certain that all *terminate-and-stay-resident* (TSR) programs that do not need to boot to get on the network are commented out of the AUTOEXEC.BAT file.

Whether solving problems on a workstation or server, you should always think in terms of dollars. During the hypothesis stage, consider what all the possibilities are and try those that cost the least first. Keep in mind that dollars are associated not only with any components that might need replacement, but also with downtime and the time of the administrator.

Documents and Records

As mentioned earlier, the importance of documentation cannot be overstated. The importance of *good* documentation can never be surpassed by any other tool. Even on the smallest of networks, time and money can be saved by documenting problems and keeping good records.

You should maintain three types of records—those relating to the LAN system, the history surrounding it, and the resources available.

For the LAN system, there should be a detailed map identifying the location of users, and all tangible components: printers, routers, bridges, and so forth. You also should keep an inventory of the components and documentation on cabling and the workstations.

The history of the LAN should include user profiles, what the purpose of the LAN is, a log of past problems, and usage information. Not only can this come in handy when an administrator is trying to diagnose a problem, but also when said administrator meets a bus somewhere other than the bus stop. Should a change in administrators take place, there is no better way to keep a business on its feet than to have its network thoroughly documented.

The documentation regarding available resources should include information about the protocols and routing in use, as well as the LAN architecture. The most important resource of all, however, is people. You should have a chart of people and phone numbers readily available for when problems become too difficult for the administrator. VAR numbers, manager numbers, and any other emergency personnel numbers should be kept in an easy to find location.

Diagnostic Software

Third-party, diagnostic software is used to provide information about hardware. That hardware can be virtually anything from the server to a workstation to a cable. A considerable number of packages are available at a variety of prices. The most important consideration should be that they offer information that is useful to you.

Check It PRO is one program that can give quick facts about your hardware and operating system. It can also benchmark the components and show information about the interrupts.

There are a variety of programs with similar features. The following shows an example of output generated at a workstation with System Information—one of the tools available in Norton Utilities:

```
       Computer Name: IBM AT
     Operating System: DOS 6.20
   Built-in BIOS dated: Friday, January 15, 1988
        Main Processor: Intel 80386              Serial Ports: 2
          Co-Processor: Intel 80387            Parallel Ports: 3
 Video Display Adapter: Video Graphics Array (VGA)
    Current Video Mode: Text, 80 x 25 Color
  Available Disk Drives: 13, A: - C:, F: - I:, P:, S:, V:, X: - Z:

DOS reports 639 K-bytes of memory:
   254 K-bytes used by DOS and resident programs
   385 K-bytes available for application programs
A search for active memory finds:
   640 K-bytes main memory     (at hex 0000-A000)
   128 K-bytes display memory  (at hex A000-C000)
   128 K-bytes extra memory    (at hex C000-E000)
 1,024 K-bytes expanded memory
ROM-BIOS Extensions are found at hex paragraphs: C000

  Computing Index (CI), relative to IBM/XT: Testing...                      73.0
       Disk Index (DI), relative to IBM/XT: Not computed. No drive specified.

Performance Index (PI), relative to IBM/XT: Not computed.
```

Much of the same workstation information can be achieved with newer versions of DOS and MSD

utility. The following is an excerpt from a report run on the same machine with this utility:

```
Microsoft Diagnostics version 2.01    1/24/95    7:44pm    Page   1
============================================================================

----------------------- Summary Information --------------------------


            Computer: Gateway/Phoenix, 486DX
              Memory: 640K, 15104K Ext, 1024K EMS, 1024K XMS
               Video: VGA, ATI , Ultra
             Network: Novell, Shell 4.10.00
          OS Version: MS-DOS Version 6.20, Windows 3.10
               Mouse: Serial Mouse 7.05
      Other Adapters: Game Adapter
         Disk Drives: A: B: C: F: G: H: I: P:
           LPT Ports: 3
           COM Ports: 2


---------------------------- Computer ----------------------------


       Computer Name: Gateway
   BIOS Manufacturer: Phoenix
        BIOS Version: 680486 ROM BIOS PLUS Version 0.10 G21-2
       BIOS Category: Phoenix PC/AT Compatible BIOS
      BIOS ID Bytes: FC 81 00
           BIOS Date: 01/15/88
           Processor: 486DX
     Math Coprocessor: Internal
            Keyboard: Enhanced
            Bus Type: ISA/AT/Classic Bus
      DMA Controller: Yes
       Cascaded IRQ2: Yes
   BIOS Data Segment: None


---------------------------- Network ----------------------------


           Network Detected: Yes
               Network Name: Novell
   MS-DOS Network Functions: Not Supported
            NetBIOS Present: No
              Shell Version: 4.10.00
                   Shell OS: MS-DOS
           Shell OS Version: V6.20
              Hardware Type: IBM_PC
             Station Number: 3
    Physical Station Number: 0060:8C84:A8DD
              IPX Installed: Yes
              SPX Installed: Yes
          ODI/LSL Installed: Yes
```

Regardless of which utility you use, you should run reports regularly and store them in a place where they are easily accessible. When problems arise, immediately run the utility again and look for any discrepancies that signal problems.

Questions

1. To reduce problems with static electricity, _____.

    ○ A. place a humidifier in the computer room

    ○ B. use proper antistatic protection such as grounded hardware

    ○ C. keep Styrofoam cups away from computers

    ○ D. All of the Above

2. Which of the following is not a type of electrical problem?

    ○ A. Electro-Static Discharge

    ○ B. Crosstalk

    ○ C. Ephemeral

    ○ D. Transients

3. EMI includes all of the following except _____.

    ○ A. appliances

    ○ B. radar

    ○ C. power tools

    ○ D. ignition systems

4. Noise is _____.

    ○ A. low voltage, low current

    ○ B. low voltage, high current

    ○ C. high voltage, low current

    ○ D. high voltage, high current

5. Encrypted passwords _____.

    ○ A. are the default with NetWare 3.1x

    ○ B. can be turned on starting with NetWare 3.12

    ○ C. can be implemented with Check It PRO

    ○ D. couldn't keep my big brother out

Answers

1. D
2. C
3. A
4. A
5. A

Using Research Tools in Troubleshooting

*A*nyone who has ever dealt with computers and computer
networks knows that increasing the number of computers arithmetically increases the number of problems
logarithmically. The number of computer components
and peripherals on the market today makes it impossible
for network administrators to go without updated
research tools at their fingertips. These factors have in
no small part influenced Novell's decision to include the
knowledge of three basic research tools into their
certification curriculum and testing procedures.

This section covers in-depth the tools that Novell has suggested NetWare network administrators use to manage a NetWare network. This chapter reviews Novell's *Network Support Encyclopedia* (NSEPro), Novell's online NetWare assistance database (NetWire), and the Micro House Technical Library, an invaluable hardware reference tool. Each of these products are *query specific* (the data that the program returns depends directly on user input), so the examples that show how the programs work use realistic scenarios.

Any network administrator who uses these three products can shorten the time required to get a system into an operational status. Testing of this portion of the Service and Support CNE examination is three hours, during which you have available a CD-ROM that has NSEPro and the Micro House Technical Library. You need to reference material on these disks much as you would in a real-world situation.

 All NSEPro available is Windows-based. At the same time, when taking the Service & Support test, the machines use a DOS-based version.

NSEPro

Novell's Network Support Encyclopedia is designed to be your front line against outdated software and driver revisions, as well as an answer source for frequently asked NetWare-related questions. Novell distributes it to subscribers monthly on compact disk (and you should install it as soon as you get it).

NSEPro was basically reserved for NetWare and network-related subjects, until February of 1995, when Novell decided to include WordPerfect and QuattroPro in it. Although the move makes sense from Novell's standpoint—and you should peruse

these capabilities for future reference—you should not expect questions on WordPerfect or QuattroPro on the CNE exam.

Installing NSEPro

Installing NSEPro is similar to installing other CD distributed software. If your hard drive is large enough (presently over 170 MB), and you use NSEPro frequently, Novell suggests that you copy all of the data and *Folio* (the database application software) onto your nonremovable media. Should you want to install only NSEPro but not the downloadable files, you only need 100 MB. And if you have next to no available drive space for the NSEPro data, you can select to install only the Windows files necessary to launch NSEPro from your CD. Either of the first two instances not only obviously speeds program access over running applications directly from compact disks, but you then can store your CD in a safe place until a time when your NSEPro data might become corrupted.

If you know how to install software into Windows, you know how to install NSEPro. You can select File, New, Item, Browse, and so on, to install the different modules, or you can use the Windows File Manager application to install the package (the preferred method). To use File Manager to install NSEPro, first open File Manager and select the drive letter that corresponds to your CD-ROM device. Run SETUP.EXE, and you are prompted for which of the three installations you want to use. That's it. One warm or cold system reboot and you can access your NSEPro infobase.

To install NSEPro in a DOS-only environment, simply move over to your CD-ROM device and type **INSTALL** *<drive_letter>* **[DFILES/NODFILES]**. You want to modify your path environment to include your working NSEPro directory, or move to the NSEPro directory when you want to run the Network Support Encyclopedia.

Using NSEPro

Invoking NSEPro in DOS is as simple as typing **NSEPRO**. If you install NSEPro onto a network, you need a minimum of write rights for the encyclopedia directory. If not, you cannot create a swap file for your graphics and other data. When you initiate NSEPro, you initially are taken to the main menu from which you can select the manual you want.

As with most DOS- and Windows- compatible applications, the MS Windows version is much more user-friendly and less keyboard intensive. After you install NSEPro into your Windows environment, you have an NSEPro program group that consists of your different NSEPro modules. Simply point to the application you want to invoke, double-click the mouse, and navigate the infobase as you please (see fig. 32.1).

Running Queries

Because the NSEPro infobase includes such a vast amount of data, you really do need to familiarize yourself with NSEPro search methods. The most basic form is to search in binary, in which you want to use the "and" and "or" operands. Using generic terminology returns a large number of finds or "hits."

As shown in figure 32.2, if you were to perform a simple search on "ne2000" (a network interface card), the infobase would return 4,996 hits. Nobody really wants to wade through almost five thousand documents, so you might narrow the search by "anding" the ne2000 parameter with the vendor's eagle or smc (which would be 727 and 4,213 hits total in the infobase, respectively), which would drop the number to a slightly (but only marginally) more manageable 3,604. To further

Figure 32.1

The NSEPro Windows program group allows direct access to the different applications.

reduce the number and limit the search, you might "and" the outcome from the previous search concatenation with the term "ethernet," which would bring the outcome to a much more manageable 273. If you were to find 273 acceptable, you would select OK and review the query table of contents.

By focusing the search, the NE2000 NIC example was reduced from almost 5,000 to a much more manageable number. Whether you are in What's New, Service and Support, File Updates, or any of the other NSEPro databases, you have the same basic search and management toolbelt. If you run NSEPro from within MS Windows, you have eight different buttons across your screen. The various buttons enable you to do the following tasks:

■ **Query.** Enables you to search the database by selecting combinations of search parameters and keywords

■ **Clear Query.** Enables you to clear your previous query criteria so you can easily initiate a new search

■ **Next (hit).** When you run a query that returns multiple matches, you can move from one instance to the next by selecting the next button

■ **Previous (hit).** Opposite of the next button; you can move back up to the previously matched search criteria instance

■ **Backtrack.** Enables you to back through your searches and links so that you can modify your criteria

■ **Trail.** Enables you to see the trail you've created with your links and queries and select any part of your trail to move directly to that point

■ **Contents.** Enables you to switch from the actual document and the table of contents

■ **Print.** Enables you to open your Windows print dialog box and print your search results

You also can run NSEPro from within a DOS environment. The selections in DOS follow the basic MS DOS format; that is, you can select from File, Edit, View, Search, Window, and Help. The display is less graphical than the Windows counterpart, but you basically have a similar representation of the manuals included in the Windows counterpart (see fig. 32.3).

Figure 32.2

The Query dialog box used to search the NSEPro infobase.

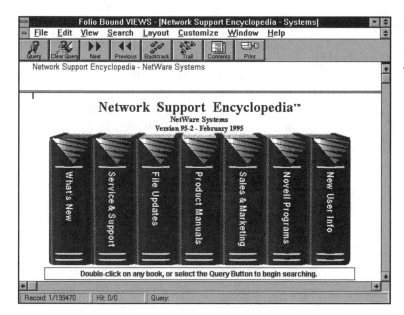

Figure 32.3
*Double-click on the spine
for the manual you want.*

What's New

Anything new or added to NSEPro is covered in this section. Review this section for changes in format for data presentation, as well as any other noteworthy program or driver modifications.

NetWare Support Encyclopedia Modules

As NetWare grows and interfaces with new and different platforms, operating systems, and peripherals, this area will afford you information on various NetWare-related modules.

Service and Support

The Service and Support section is arguably the most used and important section of the CD. It contains the following subsections:

■ **Technical Information Documents.** Technical documents and FYI documents written by Novell engineers and technicians

■ **Files, Patches, and Fixes.** Names of files available to download from the NetWire BBS, including descriptions of the file names, upload dates, locations, and briefly what the files do

■ **Third Party Files.** Items like network interface drivers or "requesters" for various operating systems

■ **NetWare Application Notes.** Electronic version of the AppNotes published monthly by Novell, covering new NetWare technologies, implementations, and fine-tuning (for example, NFS and TCP/IP installation and tuning parameters)

■ **Novell Professional Developer Bullets.** Another periodical, but more directed toward NetWare-specific application development than addressing the needs of NetWare network administration

■ **Novell Lab Bulletins.** Reflect the status of NetWare-compatible third-party products that Novell is testing for compatibility. NetWare compatibility as confirmed by Novell helps network administrators increase the probability of products purchased for certain applications functioning properly

■ **Training-Related Information.** Included in the Service and Support section of NSEPro and includes many typical questions and answers regarding training, classes, and other training-related issues

■ **Service Providers Guide.** Geographical representation of third-party support providers and the number of Novell certified personnel on their staffs

■ **Top Issues.** Most frequently asked questions and answers, particularly useful for newly released products or product versions

■ **Printing Decision Trees.** Enables you to methodically address many NetWare-related problems, beginning from the most logical starting point (as determined by Novell after extensive problem analysis), through a multitude of analytic decisions, drawing conclusions depending on your previous answers; useful for most NetWare problem solving

File Updates

The File Updates section of NSEPro is designed to ensure that critical NetWare and Novell network-related files are up-to-date for a network administrator. Because the number of support are as vast as they are varied, they have been clustered into logical groups for review and download. This issue of NSEPro has fifteen different categories (see fig. 32.4).

Figure 32.4

As Novell network-related products enter and leave the market, the File Updates main menu changes accordingly.

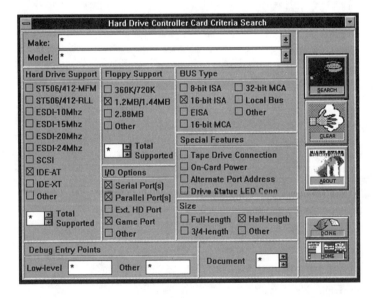

Product Manuals

You can find literally dozens of NetWare and Novell product manuals in electronic form in this area. Granted, NetWare literature has shrunk significantly since version 2.*x*, but having manuals available on one thin media is a vast improvement over even the most concise of documentation.

Sales and Marketing

Network administrators frequently underuse the Sales and Marketing tool. Although the terms "sales" and "marketing" basically go 180 degrees against network administration and engineering, the *NetWare Buyer's Guide* is a tool that you simply cannot overuse. Network administrators have no major use for the sales tools themselves, but the buyer's guide provides an invaluable list that has brief descriptions of all Novell-developed products.

Novell Programs

This section contains information about Novell Education Certification Programs such as CNE, NPA, and NUI.

New User Information

New User Information is a great place to start when you first use NSEPro, because it has hints and tips on maximizing time in NSEPro.

NetWire

If you purchased this book, you are more than likely technically literate and familiar with modems

and bulletin board systems (BBSes). NetWire is Novell's bulletin board system developed so people who had NetWare network technical questions had an expedient way to get answers to their questions around the clock. The foundation of the NetWire user interface is the CompuServe Information Manager for Windows and DOS (WINCIM), which provides user-friendly access to NetWire via CompuServe.

When you use WINCIM to access NetWire, a user-friendly graphical interface greets you. If you decide to connect to the NetWire system, WINCIM dials the specified CompuServe account and automatically logs you in to the NetWire forum. The main menu for NetWire closely resembles the modules in NSEPro.

Although many people believe BBSes are frivolous and nothing more than an extension of the corporate coffee pot (where people sit and chat), you can use NetWire to do things like ask questions in a variety of forums to perform database searches. Take a look at figure 32.5.

Micro House Technical Library (MHTL)

If you have ever worked with computer hardware, you know that even when you limit the manufacturers and products you use in your network, that versions, as well as form factors, change frequently. And each change basically forces you to relearn how to configure the product, set the jumpers, set the BIOS settings, and on and on. MHTL is included with this book.

Figure 32.5

By focusing your search criteria, you can travel both up and down your threaded path.

Even the likes of Stephen Hawking could not memorize all the settings and parameters for the products on the market. Micro House Technical Library to the rescue. The MHTL ships on a compact disk and contains information on almost every product that you might encounter while working with computer hardware. Included on the CD are such items as the following:

■ BIOS settings for IDE drives

■ Jumper settings for popular drives, network interface cards, and other peripheral boards

■ A diagnostic program that determines the BIOS settings of your computer

The easiest way to learn how to use the Micro House Technical Library tool would be to follow a couple of examples step-by-step. You can go in one of three basic directions after you boot the MHTL

program (see fig. 32.6). The first route you might follow is the Hard Drive Encyclopedia.

Imagine that you have acquired a computer that has lost its CMOS battery and that you must reenter the BIOS information. You can tell by looking that the hard drive is a Seagate ST251-1. You need only click on the Hard Drive Encyclopedia button from the MHTL main menu, click on the Hard Drives button from the Hard Drive submenu, then enter what information you know about the drive into the appropriate fields (see fig. 32.7). After you enter the appropriate information, click on the Search button and the MHTL program searches its database for a search map. If you have entered the information correctly, the odds are that MHTL has the information and you soon see a list of the hard drive settings as suggested by the drive's manufacturer.

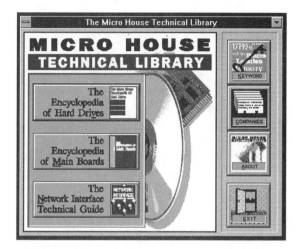

Figure 32.6
The Micro House Technical Library is widely recognized as the resource guide for network hardware configuration.

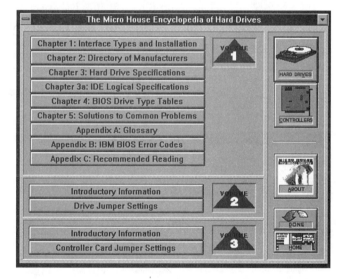

Figure 32.7
The Hard Drive Encyclopedia submenu enables you to access various aspects of hard drive specifications and related data.

Now, assume that your BIOS was actually wiped out due to a surge in your power source, and that your IDE controller was smoked, too. You need to find a controller to replace the one that has passed away and you want MHTL to help.

Buckets and buckets of hard drive controllers are available, so you want to narrow your focus as much as possible. First, open the Hard Drive

Encyclopedia module by selecting the Like button from the main menu. Then, select the **C**ontrollers button (refer to fig. 32.7) rather than the Hard Dri**v**es button as in the last example. The Hard Drive Controller Card Criteria Search menu appears.

Here, you select the specific parameters you want the product to match; suppose you need a 16-bit ISA IDE-AT half-length card. Further, you want the card to have a 1.2 MB/1.44 MB controller, a serial port, a parallel port, and a game port. After you select the appropriate boxes, you would press the Search button.

Search results show that twenty-two products meet the search criteria (see fig. 32.8). Now you review each product to see whether you like or dislike any additional features before you buy. Suppose you're familiar with Acculogic products and have liked them in the past.

To see the configuration settings for the Acculogics IDE-4/PLUS board, you would simply double-click on the respective Acculogic line on your display. MHTL really shines here in most network administrators' eyes. You are then presented with a series of spreadsheets that display all the possible switch settings, jumper configurations, and additional specifications (see fig. 32.9). If you want to see what the board physically looks like, use your cursor to select the See Diagram #1 button.

Pressing the See Diagram #1 button brings up a physical representation of the board and any switch, jumper, accessory chip, and connectors locations (see fig. 32.10). The different locations are cross-referenced with the text mentioned in the last paragraph. With this information on CD, most frustration of many network administrators goes the way of the 8-track cassette tape. And if you do not have a photographic memory, you can print the different pages in a variety of sizes and alignments.

Now let's say that not only was the BIOS lost and the IDE controller toasted, but that your motherboard is dysfunctional, and what the heck, as long as the case is open, you want a new network interface card, too. You already have seen basic searching in the hard drive section of the MHTL application. Now, you would select the Main Boards Encyclopedia and Network Interface Technical Guide buttons respectively rather than the Hard Drive Encyclopedia button from the main menu.

Figure 32.8

Our search for a 16-bit ISA IDE controller with additional criteria has resulted in a list of twenty-two products.

Figure 32.9
The text associated with the various products in the MHTL is as extensive as many expensive hardware encyclopedias.

Figure 32.10
Being able to see a representation of the motherboard and match the references to a text chart is invaluable to any network administrator.

The motherboard section of the program enables you to select your criteria much as you did in the hard drive example, but you can select the type of processor, the bus clock speed, the number and type of slots, and other motherboard-related criteria.

You decide you want a 80386/80486/Pentium-compatible board that can handle up to sixty-six MHz. After you narrow your choices, you scrutinize the resulting list and decide you want a TMC Research Corporation PAT34PV board, which can support 32 MB of RAM, a 256 KB cache, and uses AMI BIOS. Good enough, but what is the form factor? As in the drive and controller example, you would double-click on the PAT34PV line, which would bring up the board specifications and chip/connector/jumper location text, and the Diagram button. Click on the Diagram button to bring up a visual layout drawing of the motherboard (refer to fig. 32.10).

In the spirit of avoiding too many redundant details, selecting a network interface card is very much the same. Suffice it to say that having drawings of the different boards, as well as the specifications, is more than just a luxury. Most network environments use few combinations of hardware to ease the support burden. When one comes out, make the new one look the same as the old one, and put the new one in. But what happens when a product you use moves from one vendor to another (which happens frequently)? You know what the board looks like and you usually know a few of the specifications. But do you now know the model number or the manufacturer?

If not, you can enter as much information as you know and then take a look at the board to confirm that you're ordering the right product. For this example, suppose you know that the board is an Ethernet board with 10BASE-T, 10BASE2, and an AUI port. It also has a status LED and is a 10-bit card. You would first enter the proper information into the Network Interface Card Criteria Search menu (see fig. 32.11) and review the listing that results from the MHTL search (see figure 32.12). Fortunately, the second NIC on the list matches the NIC you removed from the computer (except the labels have changed). Figure 32.13 displays the network interface card, which helps an administrator configure the NIC.

After you master searching the MHTL database for one type of product, you should pretty much know how to search for other products. And as for the ways you can use Micro House Technical Library to maximize your computer skill productivity, you can confidently purchase and support virtually any type of desktop computer on the market today.

Figure 32.11

The Network Interface Card Criteria Search menu enables you to select many different hardware/topology/protocol combinations for your search.

Figure 32.12

The network interface card Hit List affords you enough initial data to drastically narrow your search.

Figure 32.13

The network interface card display helps the network administrator determine how to configure his or her NIC.

Questions

1. Which is not a spine title that appears in NSEPro?

   ○   A.   What's New

   ○   B.   Sales & Marketing

   ○   C.   Patches

   ○   D.   Product Manuals

2. The best source of information on network hardware configuration is _____.

   ○   1.   Micro House Technical Library

   ○   2.   NetWire

   ○   3.   NSEPro

   ○   4.   NetWare documentation

3. What is the required hard drive space needed to copy all of NSEPro onto your hard drive?

   ○   1.   150 MB

   ○   2.   170 MB

   ○   3.   190 MB

   ○   4.   210 MB

Answers

   1.   C

   2.   A

   3.   B

Working with Network Adapter Cards and Cabling

*I*n this chapter, you learn about several of the network
interface components used when configuring a NetWare
LAN. Proper planning, research, and verification of
certified NetWare-compatible components is an integral
part of building an efficient network. The items
discussed in this chapter include the following:

■ ARCnet board settings, cabling, and troubleshooting

■ Ethernet board settings, cabling, frame types, and
troubleshooting

■ Token Ring board settings, cabling, and
troubleshooting

■ FDDI cabling, advantages, disadvantages, and
troubleshooting

During the planning phase of a network implementation project, many hardware choices are available. The verification of component compatibility and confirmation of Novell certification of all hardware and software to be integrated is obtained from several sources. Vendor documentation, FAXBACK phone numbers, technical support lines, and peers are good sources for verification. Novell provides a technical support desk that can be reached by dialing 1-800-NETWARE. Access to the technical bulletins in a NetWare Support Encyclopedia can provide some of the information needed.

Without verification that the hardware you want to use has been tested thoroughly using NetWare, you do not know what compatibility problems may occur. If you do not choose hardware that has been verified at the Novell Labs, you will have a much more difficult time troubleshooting problems. You also will not have Novell support to help fix problems. Spending some time at this phase saves you money in the long run. Novell also offers a service called FAXBACK where you can have certain documents sent to your fax. A master document containing all the titles of the documents on FAXBACK helps you choose which item will provide the information you need. In the U.S. or Canada, call 1-800-233-3382 or 1-801-429-5363.

 Diagnose and correct incompatibilities between the network adapter card and the CPU data bus.

After you have obtained the equipment to build your network, you must configure the hardware to avoid conflicts. Conflicts among different pieces of hardware occur when their settings match or overlap. Unless the hardware has special features to avoid conflicts, you must be aware of the areas where conflicts are most likely to occur. The following list contains the most common conflicts that occur when configuring a PC adapter card:

- Interrupt conflicts

- Base I/O and memory address conflicts

- Page memory range conflicts

- DMA channel conflicts

- Node address conflicts

Keep in mind that conflicts are internal to the individual PC. A common misconception is that all network boards on the same network must share the same settings. This is not true and is impractical to enforce unless all your machines are identical in their components. Look at each client individually for configuration information.

Interrupts are dedicated to certain resources. It is possible to use a dedicated interrupt by disabling an unneeded resource. For example, if you do not need a second COM port, you can disable COM2 by using the PC's configuration program, setting switches or jumpers on the system board, or removing the board that supports COM2. This frees up INT 3 for use with a LAN card.

The following is a list of additional items to research as part of the planning process:

- Cabling specifications and requirements

- Hard drive specifications and requirements

- Software drivers to ensure that they are certified with the version of operating system to be used

Now that you have an idea of what needs to be verified, the next section details information about ARCnet, Ethernet, and Token Ring specifications.

Note Differentiate among media types and physical media protocols.

Exploring ARCnet Specifications

ARCnet is an acronym for Attached Resource Computer NETwork, which was founded by the Datapoint Corporation. Novell uses the term RX-Net to denote its form of this architecture and TRX-Net for the Turbo version. ARCnet uses a token-bus packet passing scheme.

Note A Turbo version is an updated RX-Net version that hands packets off to the communications buffers rather than attempting to place the *NetWare Core Protocol* (NCP) packets in a *File Server Process* (FSP) buffer.

ARCnet operates at 2.5 Mbps throughput and can be connected using RG-62/U coax cable or *unshielded twisted-pair* (UTP) wiring. Although ARCnet can support up to 255 node numbers on a single network, systems of this size are not practical.

Figure 33.1 shows the components of a typical ARCnet card. This card is configured for use with twisted-pair wiring. ARCnet cards for use with coax cable have a *Bayonet Navy Connector* (BNC) twist-on connector. You will find jumpers or DIP (Dual In-line Package) switches for setting the following characteristics:

■ Node number

■ Base I/O address

■ Memory address

■ Interrupt

■ Network timeout

The node number and network timeout are unique to ARCnet and are described later in this chapter.

Each *network interface card* (NIC) on an ARCnet network is assigned a node number. This number must be unique on each network and in the range of 1 to 255.

ARCnet manages network access with a token mechanism. The token is passed from the lowest number node to higher number nodes in ascending order. Lower numbered addresses get the token before the higher numbered addresses.

Traffic is controlled by assigning sequential numbers to nodes using the same order in which they are cabled. Choosing random numbers can create a situation in which a node numbered 23 can be a whole building away from the next number, 46, but in the same room as numbers 112 and 142. The token has to travel in a haphazard manner that is less effective than if you numbered the three clients in the same office sequentially, 46, 47, and 48, and the client in the other building 112. With this configuration, the packet stays within the office before venturing on to other stations.

ARCnet was one of the topologies used early on in networking and is rarely used as the topology of choice in current LAN environments. ARCnet, however, still is a functional and cost-effective means of networking.

Figure 33.1

Example of an ARCnet NIC.

ARCnet Board Settings

Depending on the vendor design specifications of your ARCnet card, most base I/O addresses, node addresses, and memory addresses are set by DIP switches. These addresses are set using a binary mode calculation with an on or off setting in the required switch block. Interrupt settings are made by jumper combinations at marked locations on the network interface card. Many types and brands of ARCnet cards are on the market today. Refer to the MicroHouse Technical Library, the documentation for the NIC or, as a last resort, call the technical support group for the specific vendor of the component.

Most ARCnet cards require a shared memory address. Many manufacturers use the area of D000:0 to DFFF:0 as the default. Standard DOS memory is limited to the first 640 KB of a PC's memory.

However, extended or expanded memory managers can be used to make memory above 640 KB available for use by DOS programs. If memory above the 640 KB line (above hex address A000:0) is used for network boards, however, the memory becomes unavailable for use by a memory manager. This makes it difficult to optimize a PC's upper memory area. If a network card requires a memory area such as D000:0-DFFF:0, the memory available for use by DOS memory managers is reduced by 64 KB.

ARCnet Cabling

The ARCnet topology uses coax, twisted-pair, or fiber-optic cabling to connect network devices. An ARCnet network is used primarily with either coax or twisted-pair cable. Coax is an RG-62/U type cable and is terminated with 93-ohm terminators.

Twisted pair uses stranded 24- or 26-gauge wire or solid core 22-, 24-, or 26-gauge type cable and is terminated with 100-ohm terminators. Many ARCnet networks use a mix of both coax and UTP cabling. UTP cable is simple to install and provides a reliable connection to the clients, whereas coax provides a means to span longer distances.

ARCnet can run off a linear bus topology using coax or twisted-pair as long as the cards support BUS. The most popular installations of ARCnet run off two types of hubs:

■ *Active hubs* have active electronic signals that amplify signals and split them to multiple ports. The number of ports on an active hub varies with the manufacturer, but eight is typical. A port on an active hub can be connected to a port on another active device (such as another active hub or an NIC) or to a passive hub.

■ *Passive hubs* cannot amplify signals. Each hub has four connectors. Because of the characteristics of passive hubs, unused ports must be equipped with a *terminator*, a connector containing a resistor that matches the ARCnet cabling characteristics. A port on a passive hub can connect only to an active device (an active hub or an NIC). Passive hubs can never be connected to passive hubs.

One of the greatest flexibilities of ARCnet is that you can integrate connections from active hubs to a linear bus connection as long as you terminate at the last connection point.

A maximum time limit of 31 microseconds is allotted for an ARCnet signal. This is also called a time-out setting. Signals on an ARCnet can travel up to 20,000 feet during the 31-microsecond default time-out period. You can sometimes extend the range of an ARCnet by increasing the time-out value. However, 20,000 feet is the distance at which ARCnet signals begin to seriously degrade. Extending the network beyond that distance can result in unreliable or failed communication. Therefore, the time-out parameter and cabling distance recommendations should be increased only with great caution.

The maximum cable distances between individual components in an ARCnet network are dependent on how the components are connected (see table 33.1).

In cabling ARCnet networks with coax cable, you must follow several rules:

■ Never connect a passive hub to another passive hub directly

■ Passive hubs should never be used to connect two active hubs

■ Passive hubs are only used to connect an active hub and a node

■ Unused connectors on active hubs do not need to be terminated

■ Unused connectors on passive hubs must be terminated using a 93-ohm terminator

Figure 33.2 shows an ARCnet configuration using active and passive hubs. Active hubs are required to extend the network for long distances and to configure networks that have more than four nodes. Passive hubs are used as an economical means of splitting a port on an active hub to support three devices.

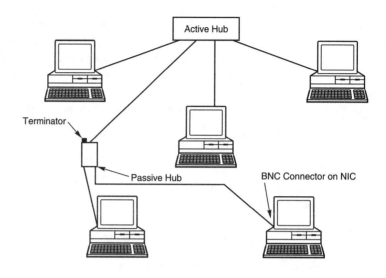

Figure 33.2

Example of an ARCnet topology using active and passive hubs and coax cable.

Table 33.1
Maximum ARCnet Cable Distances

Maximum Distance	From	To
2,000 feet	Network node	Active hub
2,000 feet	Active hub	Active hub
100 feet	Active hub	Passive hub
Not supported	Passive hub	Passive hub
100 feet	Network node	Passive hub
2,000 feet	Network node	Network node
20,000 feet	Farthest node	Farthest node

ARCnet Troubleshooting

Note Troubleshoot common problems with cards, cables, and related hardware for the three most common networking topologies.

Common sources of problems on ARCnet networks are as follows:

■ No more than one node can have a given node address on the same network. If two or more nodes share an address, one of the two clients will either lose its network connection or will not be able to find a network.

■ Missing terminators might not present visible problems on a small network. Missing terminators cause data retransmits on smaller systems, eventually appearing as transmit time-out errors or network errors.

■ Using a terminator with an incorrect ohm rating. Coax uses 93 ohm; twisted-pair uses 100 ohm. A terminator's value in ohms depends on the impedance of the cable. The cable's impedance and the terminator's value should always match.

■ The ARCnet bus using NICs that do not use the same impedance level. Signals will become attenuated and/or reflected, causing interference with other signals on the wire.

■ Failed NICs.

■ Failed active hubs (or a port on that hub).

■ Cable lengths that exceed specifications (refer to table 33.1). Twisted-pair, cabled in a bus rather than a star, cannot have more than ten NICs per segment. This number varies with different manufacturers. ARCnet UTP installed in a bus configuration is generally used only in very small networks of six nodes or less. This configuration has the major drawback of halting the network if a single cable is disconnected. In an ARCnet bus configuration, the network must be brought down to make any changes or service to the ARCnet cards.

■ Coax connectors not built or crimped correctly. Twist-on connectors are responsible for more intermittent errors on a network than most other failures because of their design.

Twist-on coax connectors became popular in the IBM 3XXX systems. These systems used RG-62 coax cable and operated at 1.5 Mbps throughput.

The twist-on connectors are not recommended for use on any modern LAN cable system because of the higher data rates employed.

The primary characteristics of ARCnet are as follows:

■ The maximum time it takes for the ARCnet signal to travel the length of the network is 31 microseconds.

■ The maximum distance an ARCnet signal can travel between the two nodes farthest away from each other is 20,000 feet.

■ The absolute maximum number of ARCnet nodes that can occupy a given network segment is 255. An ARCnet segment consists of all cabling and nodes that share a given network address.

Understanding Ethernet Specifications

Ethernet was originally developed by the Xerox Corporation, Digital Corporation, and the Intel Corporation in the early 1970s. Ethernet is also known as a *spanning tree topology* because the networks expand by branching in tree structures that do not allow redundant paths between nodes. Ethernet uses the *Carrier Sense Multiple Access/ Collision Detection* (CSMA/CD) media contention access method and supports a maximum throughput of 10 Mbps. The Ethernet and 802.3 protocols are described in the Ethernet Frame Types section of this chapter, as well as in Part IV of the book.

The origins of Ethernet are commemorated in the initials DIX, which is a 15-pin connector used to interface Ethernet components. The acronym DIX is derived from the combination of leading letters of the founding Ethernet vendors: Digital, Intel, and Xerox.

The term Ethernet commonly refers to original Ethernet (which has been updated to Ethernet II) as well as the IEEE 802.3 standards. However, Ethernet and the 802.3 standards differ in ways significant enough to make standards incompatible in terms of packet formats. At the physical layer, Ethernet and 802.3 are generally compatible in terms of cables, connectors, and electronic devices.

Today, NetWare 3.11 uses the IEEE 802.3 frame format as a default on its networks. However, a variety of other Ethernet frame formats are supported. NetWare 3.12 and 4.x use the IEEE 802.2 frame format as the Ethernet frame type default. To change this default, change the frame type in the NET.CFG file. Add this frame type if you need to communicate with networks using older Ethernet frame types.

Ethernet is generally used on light-to-medium traffic networks, and performs best when a network's data traffic is sent in short bursts. Ethernet is the most popular network standard. It has become especially popular in many university and government installations.

Ethernet Board Settings

Most older versions of Ethernet NICs are configured using jumpers to set addresses and interrupts.

Current models of NICs can be configured using a diagnostic program that enables changing of interrupt and memory address settings stored in a special memory chip on the NIC.

An example of an Ethernet NIC is shown in figure 33.3. Some of the features of these cards are as follows:

■ Shared memory selection; most Ethernet cards do not require the use of shared memory

■ I/O address

■ Interrupt

■ Connectors

■ Active connector selection jumpers

■ Socket for a remote boot PROM

Ethernet cards can have one, two, or possibly all three of the following connectors:

■ BNC connectors support coax cabling

■ RJ-45 connectors support 10BASE-T (UTP) cabling

■ DIX connectors are used to connect to external transceivers

With some cards, DIP switches or blocks of jumpers are used to select the active connector. In many cases, however, the active connector can be selected with configuration software.

A limitation of 1,024 nodes (physical addresses) per network address exists on an Ethernet network. Addresses are assigned by IEEE to the vendor for the first three bytes of a six-byte address. The vendor is responsible for assigning the rest of the address and ensuring unique IDs.

Figure 33.3
Features of an Ethernet NIC.

As with the Token Ring cards, the card's manufacturer "burns" a unique node address into ROM on each NIC. Unless you override the burned-in address, address conflicts cannot occur on an Ethernet. Vendors sometimes label their cards with the node address. If the address is not visible, use the diagnostic disk supplied by the vendor.

Ethernet Cabling

A variety of cables can be used to implement Ethernet networks. Traditionally, Ethernet networks have been cabled with coaxial cables of several different types. Fiber-optic cables are now frequently employed to extend the geographic range of Ethernet networks.

The contemporary interest in using twisted-pair wiring has resulted in a scheme for cabling using unshielded twisted-pair. The 10BASE-T cabling standard, which uses UTP in a star topology, is described later.

Ethernet remains closely associated with coaxial cable, however. Two types of coaxial cable still used in small and large environments are thin net (also known as cheapernet) and thick net. The Ethernet networks have different limitations based on thin net and thick net cable specifications. The best way to remember the requirements is to use the 5-4-3 rule of thumb for each cable type.

The 5-4-3 Rule

The 5-4-3 rule states that the following can appear between any two nodes in the Ethernet network:

■ Up to five segments in a series

■ Up to four concentrators or repeaters

■ Three segments of (coax only) cable that contain nodes

10BASE2

The 10BASE2 cabling topology, also referred to as thin net, generally uses the on-board transceiver of the network interface card to translate the signals to and from the rest of the network. Thin net cabling can use RG-58A/U or RG-58C/U coaxial type cable, 50 ohm terminators, and T-connectors that directly attach to the BNC connector on the NIC.

A grounded terminator must be used on one end of the network segment.

 Note A *transceiver* is a device that takes the digital signal from the node and translates it to communicate on a baseband cabling system. NICs that support thin net or 10BASE-T cable generally have built-in transceivers. External transceivers are used for thick Ethernet although they may be used for thin net and UTP as well.

Use RG-58A/U cable for Ethernet topology, not RG-58U, which is for use with cable TV setups.

Advantages of 10BASE2

The main advantage of using 10BASE2 in your network is cost. When any given cable segment on the network does not have to be run further than 185 meters, 10BASE2 is often the cheapest network cabling option.

10BASE2 is also relatively simple to connect. Each network node is connected directly to the network cable using a T-connector attached to the NIC.

Troubleshooting 10BASE2

The first step in troubleshooting a 10BASE2 network is to ensure that you have met the rules for using 10BASE2. Several additional rules must be adhered to in 10BASE2 Ethernet environments, including the following:

■ The minimum cable distance between clients must be 1.5 feet, or 0.5 meters.

■ Pig tails, also known as drop cables, from T-connectors should not be used to connect to the BNC connector on the NIC. The T-connector must be connected directly to the NIC.

■ You may not go beyond the maximum network segment limitation of 607 feet, or 185 meters.

Figure 33.4

Two segments using 10BASE2 cabling.

Ground Wire

Terminator with Ground

Transceiver Cable

Transceiver

Repeater

■ The entire network cabling scheme cannot exceed 3,035 feet, or 925 meters.

■ The maximum number of nodes per network segment is 30 (this includes clients and repeaters).

■ A 50-ohm terminator must be used on each end of the bus with only one of the terminators having either a grounding strap or a grounding wire that attaches it to the screw holding an electrical outlet cover in place.

■ You may not have more than five segments on a network. These segments may be connected with a maximum of four repeaters, and only three of the five segments may have network nodes.

Additional troubleshooting tips are found in the Ethernet Troubleshooting section of this chapter.

As mentioned previously, the IEEE 802.3 standard for Thinnet is 10BASE2. This standard describes a 10 Mbps baseband network with a maximum segment length of approximately 200 meters (the actual limit, as stated previously, is 185 meters). Figure 33.4 shows two segments using 10BASE2 cabling.

10BASE5

The 10BASE5 cabling topology, also referred to as thick net, uses an external transceiver to attach to the network interface card (see Fig. 33.5). The NIC attaches to the external transceiver by an *Attachment Universal Interface* (AUI) cable to the DIX connector on the back of the card. The external transceiver clamps to the thick net cable. As with thin net, each network segment must be terminated at both ends, with one end using a grounded terminator. The components of a thick net network are shown in figure 33.6.

Figure 33.5

Two segments using 10BASE5 cabling.

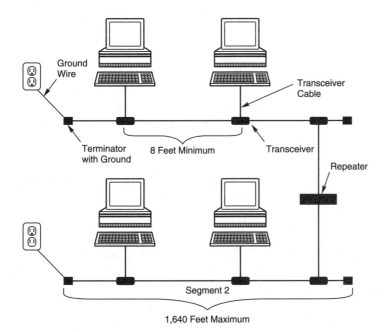

Figure 33.6
*Components of a thick
Ethernet.*

 RG-11 is a 75-ohm cable. 10BASE5 requires 50 ohms.

Advantages of 10BASE5

The primary advantage of 10BASE5 is its ability to exceed the cable lengths to which 10BASE2 is restricted. However, it does have restrictions of its own that should be considered when installing or troubleshooting a 10BASE5 network.

Troubleshooting a 10BASE5 Network

As with 10BASE2 networks, the first consideration when troubleshooting a 10BASE5 network should be the cabling rules and guidelines that have been established. Several additional guidelines, along with the 5-4-3 rule, must be followed in thick Ethernet networks:

■ The minimum cable distance between transceivers is 8 feet, or 2.5 meters.

■ You may not go beyond the maximum network segment length of 1,640 feet, or 500 meters.

■ The entire network cabling scheme cannot exceed 8,200 feet, or 2,500 meters.

■ One end of the terminated network segment must be grounded.

■ Drop cables can be as short as required, but cannot be longer than 50 meters from transceiver to NIC.

■ Cable segments that are cut and connected using a "Vampire Tap" should come from the same cable spool to ensure that each connected piece carries the identical electrical cabling to the other.

■ The maximum number of nodes per network segment is 100. (This includes all repeaters.)

Additional troubleshooting tips are found in the Ethernet Troubleshooting section of this chapter.

The IEEE 802.3 standard that describes thick net is 10BASE5. This standard describes a 10 Mbps baseband network that can have segments up to 500 meters long. Figure 33.7 shows two segments using thick net and the appropriate hardware.

Thin net and thick net cable can be combined to extend the distance of an Ethernet network topology. The following formula can be used to define the maximum amount of thin net cable that can be used in one network segment combination:

Maximum length of = 1,640 feet
thin net that can   (Length of new
be used   network segment to
                                  be added)

 Note A linear bus topology is more economical than wire because it is not necessary to have a separate cable run for each client. However, some local problems on a linear bus have the capability of bringing the entire network down.

If a break is in the cable or a streaming NIC is in the channel, the entire network can go down. Streaming is more frequently referred to as a broadcast storm. This occurs when a network card fails, and the transmitter floods the cable with traffic, just like a faucet that is stuck open. At this point, the network becomes unusable.

10BASE-T

The trend in wiring Ethernet networks is to use *unshielded twisted-pair* (UTP) cable. UTP or 10BASE-T cable is one of the three most popular implementations for Ethernet. It is based on the IEEE 802.3 standard.

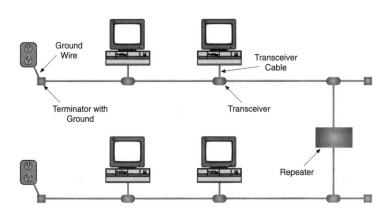

Figure 33.7
Example of thick net Ethernet cabling.

10BASE-T cabling is wired in a star topology. However, it functions logically like a linear bus. The cable uses RJ-45 connectors, and the network interface card can have RJ-45 jacks built into the back of the cards. External transceivers attached to a DIX connector found in combination with RJ-45 or BNC connectors on the NIC can be used to connect standard Ethernet cards into a twisted-pair topology. Figure 33.8 shows Ethernet cabling using twisted-pair cabling and a hub, also called a concentrator.

Advantages of 10BASE-T

The star wiring of 10BASE-T provides several advantages, particularly in larger networks. First, the network is more reliable and easier to manage because 10BASE-T networks use a concentrator (a centralized wiring hub). These hubs are "intelligent" in that they can route network traffic around a bad cable segment, and they can detect defective cable segments. This makes it easier for you to locate and repair bad cable segments.

10BASE-T enables you to design and build your LAN one segment at a time, growing as your network needs grow. This makes 10BASE-T more flexible than other LAN cabling options.

10BASE-T is also relatively inexpensive to use compared to other cabling options. In some cases where a data-grade phone system has already been used in an existing building, this cabling can be used for the LAN.

 Note Networks with star wiring topologies can be significantly easier to troubleshoot and repair than bus wired networks. With a star network, a problem node can be isolated from the rest of the network by simply disconnecting the cable and directly connecting it to the cable hub. If the hub is considered "intelligent," management software developed for that hub type, as well as the hub itself, can disconnect the suspect port.

Figure 33.8
Example of twisted-pair Ethernet cabling.

Twisted-Pair Ethernet Cabling

Troubleshooting 10BASE-T

The first step in troubleshooting a 10BASE-T network is to ensure that your network meets the rules for using 10BASE-T. The rules for a 10BASE-T network are as follows:

■ The maximum number of network segments is 1,024.

■ The cabling used should be 22, 24, or 26 *American Wire Gauge* (AWG), and be rated for an impedance of 85 to 115 ohms at 10 MHz.

 Note Unshielded twisted-pair uses a terminator resistance level of 100-200 ohms; shielded twisted-pair uses 150 ohms.

■ The maximum number of nodes is 512, and they may be connected on any three segments, with five being the maximum number of available line segments.

■ The maximum unshielded cable segment length is 328 feet, or 100 meters.

 Note You should be able to translate cable segment lengths from feet to meters, or from meters to feet. A meter is equivalent to 39.37 inches.

Additional troubleshooting tips are found in the Ethernet Troubleshooting section of this chapter.

 Note 10BASE-T requires that the UTP cable system be compliant with the Level IV standard. Level IV is cable-certified to operate at 10 Mbps throughput.

Ethernet Frame Types

In order for information to be transmitted successfully across an Ethernet network, the sending and receiving network nodes must agree in advance on the structure of the information being transmitted. The sending node must organize the information in an orderly and predictable manner so that the receiving node can find and interpret the transmitted information. This orderly arrangement of information traveling across an Ethernet network is known as an *Ethernet frame*. Different Ethernet frame types describe different standards that specify the protocol structure (configuration of the media).

There are four possible Ethernet frame types. The same Ethernet frame type must be loaded at both the server and accessing clients in order for proper communication to take place. The four available frame types are ETHERNET 802.3 (also known as raw ETHERNET), ETHERNET 802.2, ETHERNET SNAP, and ETHERNET II.

Raw ETHERNET (802.3) was developed before the IEEE 802.3 standard was completed and released. Therefore, ETHERNET 802.3 is not in complete compliance with the IEEE standard. ETHERNET 802.3 is used only on IPX/SPX Novell networks. ETHERNET 802.3 does not contain a field to specify which protocols may be contained within the packet. The lack of this field is one feature of ETHERNET 802.3 that makes it almost exclusively unique to Novell's NetWare 2.2 and NetWare 3.*x* Operating Systems.

Common features of the ETHERNET 802.3 standard include the following:

■ A frame size between 64 and 1,518 bytes

■ A preamble in the first line of the header (it contains alternating ones and zeroes to synchronize the communicating stations)

■ A one-byte *Start Frame Delimiter* (SFD) field that follows the preamble and designates the beginning of the frame

■ A six-byte field that specifies the address of the station to which the packet is being sent

■ An originating address indicating the client, server, or router from where the packet was last sent

■ A two-byte field that specifies the length of the data portion of the packet, and which must not have a length greater than 1,500 bytes to be considered valid

■ A data field which must be no shorter than 46 bytes and no longer than 1,500 bytes

■ A four-byte *Cyclical Redundancy Check* (CRC) or Frame Check Sequence that helps to ensure that the transmitted data is valid

ETHERNET 802.2 is fully compliant with the IEEE 802.3 standard. ETHERNET 802.2 is the default frame type used in NetWare 3.12 and NetWare 4.*x* networks. Common features of the ETHERNET 802.2 standard include the following:

■ All of the same fields as the 802.3 specification

■ Three additional *Logical Link Control* (LLC) fields, one byte long, that act much like an 802.3 header

■ A frame size between 64 and 1,518 bytes

ETHERNET SNAP (SubNetwork Address Protocol) is fully compliant with ETHERNET 802.2

and is actually considered an enhancement to the 802.2 specification. Common features of the ETHERNET SNAP standard include the following:

■ Two of the LLC fields, which contain fixed data indicating that this is a SNAP packet

■ A type field as the third of the LLC fields, which enables the packet to carry other high-level protocols within the frame structure, thus ensuring compatibility and making it possible for network operating systems to carry protocols over other types of media, such as Token Ring

ETHERNET II frame types support TCP/IP for NetWare 3.11. Common features of the ETHERNET II frame type include the following:

■ A packet type field located immediately after the source address field, which is the location of the packet length field in other ETHERNET frame types

■ A combined preamble and Start Frame Delimiter field that are referred to jointly as the preamble

Although four ETHERNET frame types are available, load only the frame type that you need to use on your network server. If it is necessary in order to support multiple upper-layer protocols, you can load more than one frame type on a server.

Each LAN NIC in the server must have at least one protocol bound to it. To bind a protocol to a NIC, first LOAD the NIC drivers, then bind the protocol to the NIC as in the following:

```
LOAD NE2000 port=320 int=5
frame=ETHERNET_802.3    NAME=ENE5
BIND IPX TO ENE5 NET=BAC1234
```

Ethernet Troubleshooting

Trend measurement and analysis can be applied to all network types. The use of a sophisticated protocol analyzer, such as LANalyzer for WINDOWS and simpler tools, along with your own experience and knowledge, are two other effective troubleshooting techniques for Ethernet networks. This section covers the latter option.

When troubleshooting an Ethernet network, begin with the more obvious physical problems. For example, check to make certain that all connectors are tight and properly connected. Make certain that ground wires and terminators are used when required. Also, be certain that manufacturer's specifications are met, and that cable lengths, maximum number of nodes, and so on, are correct.

Consider the following when troubleshooting Ethernet networks:

■ With 10BASE-T, make sure that the cable used has the correct number of twists to meet the data grade specifications.

■ Check for electrical interference. Electrical interference can be caused by tying the network cable together with monitor and power cords. Outside interference also can be caused by fluorescent lights, electric motors, and other electrical devices.

■ Make sure that connectors are pinned properly and crimped tightly.

■ Check the cable lengths to make sure that distance specifications are not exceeded.

■ If excess shielding on coax cable is exposed, make sure it is not grounding out the connector.

■ Make sure that coax cables are not coiled tightly together.

■ Check the grade of the cable being used. For 10BASE2, RG-58/U is required. All 10BASE5 cable must meet Ethernet specifications.

■ If using a linear bus setup, make sure that the topology rules are followed.

■ Check for missing terminator or terminators with improper impedance ratings.

■ Check for malfunctioning hardware, such as a bad NIC, transceiver, concentrator, T-connector, or terminator. Check to make certain that connectors have not been mixed up, such as ARCnet connectors being used on an Ethernet network.

■ Test the continuity of the cable, using various physical testing devices, such as an Optical Time Domain Reflectometer, or software, such as Novell's COMCHECK utility.

■ If the Fileserver not found error message appears, check for a mismatch in the Ethernet frame type between the server and the client.

■ Verify that the LAN card is working properly. Clean the connector fingers (do not use an eraser because it leaves grit on the card); pull the card and replace it with one that you know is in working order; or run the NIC's diagnostics software.

■ If NIC resource conflicts seem to be a potential cause of network problems, remove all cards except the file server NICs, then replace them one at a time until the conflicting card is found. Then correct the NIC settings and continue checking NICs one at a time. If you are installing new NICs, avoid using the common COM port interrupts of 3 and 4 to prevent potential Ethernet card conflicts.

■ Make sure that all the component cables in a segment are connected together. A user who moves his client and removes the T-connector incorrectly can cause a broken segment.

Understanding Token Ring Specifications

Token Ring uses a token-passing architecture that adheres to the IEEE 802.5 standard. The topology is physically a star, but logically uses a ring to pass the token from station to station. Each node must be attached to a concentrator called a *multistation access unit* (MSAU or MAU).

Token Ring network interface cards can run at 4 Mbps or 16 Mbps. 4 Mbps cards can run only at that data rate. However, 16 Mbps cards can be configured to run at 4 or 16 Mbps. All cards on a given network ring must be running at the same rate.

As shown in figure 33.9, each node acts as a repeater that receives token and data frames from its *nearest active upstream neighbor* (NAUN). After a frame is

processed by the node, the frame is passed downstream to the next attached node. Each token makes at least one trip around the entire ring. It then returns to the originating node. Workstations that indicate problems send a "beacon" to identify an address of the potential failure. You will learn more about this topic later in this chapter.

 To find out if any beacon messages have been sent on your Token Ring network, review your System Error Log, found in SYSCON through Supervisor Options.

Token Ring Board Settings

As with the Ethernet cards, the node address on each NIC is burned in at the manufacturer and is unique to each card. The node address in some cases can be overridden by vendor-specified software instructions. (Check with the vendor of the component.) A maximum of two Token Ring cards can be installed in any node, with each card being defined as the primary or alternate Token Ring card in the machine. A typical Token Ring card is shown in figure 33.10.

Figure 33.9

Operation of a Token Ring.

Figure 33.10
Features of a Token Ring NIC.

Off Is Up
1 2 3 4 5 6 7 8 9 10 11 12
DIP Switch Settings

9 Pin Female Connector
(Male connector on type
3 filter uses pins 1, 5, 6, and 9)

The following are features of a Token Ring NIC:

- DIP switches (see table 33.2)

- 9-pin female connector

- Remote boot PROM socket

 When loading two Token Ring NICs in a NetWare file server, make sure that you configure the primary card at port address of A20. The alternate card must be set at A24. For v3.1x or v4.x, in the AUTOEXEC.NCF file or at the file server console, use the following example commands:

```
LOAD TOKEN PORT=A20 INT=2 MEM=CC000
NAME=CARD1

LOAD TOKEN PORT=A24 INT=3 MEM=DC000
NAME=CARD2
```

The interrupt and base memory address on each Token Ring NIC must be set to avoid conflicts with all other components. Table 33.2 defines the

proper DIP switch settings for an IBM 16/4 Token Ring card.

Each Token Ring card comes with a diagnostic disk that provides testing for the adapter. Refer to the appropriate documentation for your card for more detailed instructions.

Token Ring Cabling

Traditional Token-Ring networks used shielded twisted-pair cable. The following are standard IBM cable types for Token Ring:

- **Type 1.** A braided shield surrounds two twisted pairs of solid copper wire. Type 1 is used to connect terminals and distribution panels, or to connect between different wiring closets that are located in the same building. Type 1 uses two STPs of solid-core 22 AWG wire for long, high data grade transmissions within the building's walls.

Table 33.2
IBM 16/4 Token-Ring Switch Settings

Switch Blk (Off is Up, On is Down)	1	2	3	4	5	6	7	8	9	10	11	12
ADDRESS												
CC000	Off	On	On	Off	Off	On						
DC000	Off	On	Off	Off	Off	On						
INTERRUPT												
2							Off	Off				
3							On	Off				
6							Off	On				
7							Off	Off				
PRIMARY									Off			
ALTERNATE									On			
SHARED RAM												
8 KB										On	On	
16 KB										Off	On	
32 KB										On	Off	
64 KB										Off	Off	
DATA RATE												
16 Mbps												Off
4 Mbps												On

■ **Type 2.** Type 2 uses a total of six twisted pairs; two are STPs (for networking), four are UTPs (for telephone systems). Additionally, this cable type incorporates two unshielded twisted pairs that can be used for voice circuits. This cable is used for the same purposes as Type 1, but enables both voice and data cables to be included in a single cable run.

■ **Type 3.** Type 3 has unshielded twisted-pair copper with a minimum of two twists per inch, used as an alternative to Type 1 and Type 2 cable because of its reduced cost. It has four UTPs of 24 AWG solid-core wire for networks or tele-

phone systems. Type 3 cannot be used for 16 Mbps Token-Ring networks. It is used primarily for long, low data-grade transmissions within walls. Signals will not travel as fast as with Type 1 cable because Type 3 does not have the shielding used by Type 1.

■ **Type 5.** With Type 5, fiber-optic cable is used only on the main ring. Type 5 can use two 100-um or 140-um optical fibers in one fiber jacket.

■ **Type 6.** A braided shield surrounds two twisted pairs of stranded copper wire. It is made up of two 26 AWG stranded-core STPs. This cable supports shorter cable runs than Type 1, but is more flexible due to the stranded conductors. Type 6 is the IBM standard for patch cables and extension cables, used also in wiring closets.

■ **Type 8.** Type 8 uses a single 26 AWG stranded-core STP and is especially designed for use under carpet.

■ **Type 9.** Type 9 is the same as Type 6 cable except that it is designed to be fire-resistant for use in plenum installations. It uses two STPs of solid-core 26 AWG wire and is used for long runs within the walls of a building.

Token ring cabling is used to connect clients to the MSAU, or to connect one MSAU to another. Cables that connect between MSAUs are called patch cables. Patch cables may also be made of IBM Type 6 cable.

 Novell defines Token-Ring cabling in terms of two types of systems:

■ Small movable

■ Large non-movable

The small movable system supports up to 96 clients and file servers and 12 MSAUs. It uses Type 6 cable to attach clients and servers to IBM Model 8228 MSAUs. Type 6 cable is a shielded twisted-pair cable with stranded conductors. This cable is flexible, but has limited distance capabilities. The characteristics of this cable make it suitable for small networks and for patch cords.

The large non-movable system supports up to 260 clients and file servers, with up to 33 MSAUs. This network configuration uses IBM Type 1 or Type 2 cable. These are shielded twisted-pair cables with solid-wire conductors suitable for carrying signals greater distances

than are possible with Type 6. The large nonmovable system also involves other wiring needs such as punch panels or distribution panels, equipment racks for MSAUs, and wiring closets to contain the previously listed components.

The MSAU is the central cabling component for IBM Token-Ring networks. The 8228 MSAU was the original wiring hub developed by IBM for Token-Ring networks. Figure 33.11 shows 8228 MSAUs. Each 8228 has ten connectors, eight of which accept cables to clients or servers. The other connectors are labeled RI (ring in) and RO (ring out). The RI and RO connectors are used to connect multiple 8228s to form larger networks.

8228s are mechanical devices that consist of relays and connectors. Their purpose is to switch clients in and out of the network. Each port is controlled by a relay powered by a voltage sent to the MSAU from the client. When an 8228 is first set up, each of these relays must be initialized with a setup tool shipped with the unit. The setup tool is inserted into each port and held there until a light indicates that the port is properly initialized.

IBM Token Ring networks use two types of connectors. NICs are equipped with a nine-pin D-connector. MSAUs, repeaters, and most other equipment use a special IBM data connector. Two types of cables are employed:

■ *Patch cables* have IBM data connectors at both ends. These cables interconnect MSAUs, repeaters, and most other Token-Ring components.

■ *Token Ring adapter cables* have an IBM data connector at one end and a nine-pin connector at the other. Adapter cables connect client and server NICs to other network components that use IBM data connectors.

Figure 33.11 shows an example of a network cabling several clients and MSAUs. The distances noted in the figure are based on the rules for the small movable cabling system.

When you are connecting a Token-Ring network, make sure that you do the following:

1. Initialize each port in the 8228 MSAU by using the setup tool shipped with the MSAU (wait for the click) before connecting a cable.

2. If using more than one MSAU, connect the RO port of each MSAU with the RI port of the next MSAU in the loop. This must physically complete a circle or ring.

A variety of rules must be observed when configuring Token Rings. The following rules apply to small, movable Token-Ring networks:

■ The minimum patch cable distance between two MSAUs is eight feet.

■ The maximum patch cable distance between two MSAUs is 150 feet. Patch cables come in standard lengths of 8, 30, 75, and 150 feet for Type 6.

■ The maximum patch cable distance connecting all MSAUs is 400 feet.

■ The maximum adapter cable distance between an MSAU and a node is 150 feet.

A small movable IBM cable system consists of the following:

■ Maximum 96 nodes

■ Maximum 12 MSAUs

■ Uses Type 6 cable

A large non-movable IBM cable system consists of the following:

■ Maximum 260 nodes

■ Maximum 33 MSAUs

■ Uses Type 1 or Type 2 cable

 Token-Ring networks also can be cabled using UTP cabling, which IBM calls Type 3 cable. The IEEE 802.5 standard describes 4 Mbps Token Ring using UTP cable. However, level 5 UTP is currently used for 16 Mbps Token Ring.

When using UTP wiring, a media filter must be installed between the NIC and the UTP cable. Some newer Token Ring NICs have built-in media filters and RJ-45 jacks ready to interface with UTP wiring.

Token Ring Troubleshooting

When troubleshooting a Token-Ring network, as with troubleshooting other types of networks, begin with the more obvious physical problems, checking such things as connectors to see if they are tight and properly connected. You also should check to see that manufacturer's specifications are met, and that cable lengths, maximum number of nodes, and so on, are correct.

When troubleshooting Token-Ring networks, you also should look for the following:

■ Any base I/O, DMA shared memory, or interrupt conflicts with other boards.

■ The version of the client or server software driver, to make sure that its revision level is compatible with your NIC (drivers are different for file servers and clients).

150 Feet Maximum

8 Feet Minimum

Patch Cable

RI   RO   RI   RO

Adapter Cable

Token-Ring Cabling

Figure 33.11
An example of Token-Ring cabling using MSAUs.

■ Proper connections of MSAUs, with ring out ports connecting to ring in ports throughout the ring. In troubleshooting problems that you have first isolated to a particular area of the network, if you suspect the MSAU, isolate it by changing the ring in and ring out cables to bypass the MSAU. If the ring is now functional again, consider replacing the MSAU. You may also find that if your network has MSAUs from more than one manufacturer, they are not wholly compatible. Impedance and other electrical characteristics may show slight differences between manufacturers, causing intermittent network problems.

■ Other MSAU problems. Some MSAUs other than the 8228 are active and require a power supply. These MSAUs fail if they have a blown fuse or a bad power source.

■ Correct attachments of patch cables and the adapter cable. Remember, patch cables connect MSAUs together, and the adapter cable connects the NIC to the MSAU. Patch cables, adapter cables, and MSAUs are common sources of problems. Isolating the problem is easier to do if you have a current log of your network's physical design. Once you have narrowed down the problem, you can isolate potential problem areas on the network from the rest of the network, and then use a cable tester to find the actual problem.

■ A failed NIC. Try substituting another one known to work properly. NICs that have failure rates that exceed a preset tolerance level may actually remove themselves from the network.

■ A bad MSAU or MSAU port. Ports may need to be reinitialized with the setup tool. Removing drop cables and reinitializing each MSAU port is a "quick fix" that is useful on relatively small Token-Ring networks.

■ Incorrect card speeds; for example, a 16 Mbps card is inserted into a 4 Mbps ring or vice versa. Neither situation is correct. The speed of the NIC is displayed when the Token-Ring driver is loaded at the client.

■ The wrong type of cable for the speed of the network.

■ Bent or broken pins on the adapter cable.

■ Duplicate node addresses. If you are overriding the burned-in network addresses, it is possible that duplicate node addresses may be set.

■ The Type 3 media filter, if connecting to a 4 Mbps twisted-pair network.

One of the advantages of a Token-Ring network is its built-in ability to monitor itself. This process provides electronic troubleshooting and, when possible, repair processes. When it is not possible for the Token-Ring network to make its own repairs, a process called *beaconing* is helpful. Beaconing narrows down the portion of the ring where the problem is most likely to exist. This potential problem area is referred to as the *fault domain*.

The Beaconing Process

The design of the Token Ring network itself contributes greatly to the ability of the beaconing process to troubleshoot its own network. The design includes two types of network stations known as Active Monitors and Standby Monitors. Only one Active Monitor can exist on a network at a time. All other stations are Standby Monitors.

Generally, the first station that is powered-up and becomes part of the network is automatically the Active Monitor station. The responsibility of the Active Monitor station is to announce itself to the next active downstream station as the Active Monitor station, and request that station to announce itself to its next active downstream station. The Active Monitor station sends out this beacon announcement every seven seconds.

Once each station has announced itself to its next active downstream neighbor, the announcing station becomes the nearest active upstream neighbor (NAUN) to the downstream station. Each station on a Token-Ring network has an upstream neighbor as well as a downstream neighbor.

Once each station is aware of its NAUN, the beaconing process continues every seven seconds. If for some reason a station does not receive one of its expected seven-second beaconed announcements from its upstream neighbor, it attempts to notify the network of its lack of contact from the upstream neighbor. It sends a message out onto the network ring, which includes the following:

■ The sending station's network address

■ The receiving NAUN's network address

■ The beacon type

From this information, the ring can determine which station may be having a problem and attempt to fix the problem without disrupting the entire network. This problem fix is known as *autoreconfiguration*. If the autoreconfiguration is unsuccessful, manual correction is required. Figure 33.12 shows a Token-Ring network utilizing the beaconing process.

The preceding section detailed common characteristics of ARCnet, Ethernet, and Token Ring. Other components also must be examined for conflicts and proper configuration. The next section describes these items.

Figure 33.12

Token Ring beaconing.

Understanding FDDI

Fiber Distributed Data Interface is a LAN standard that, like Token Ring, follows the IEEE 802.5 standard for accessing the network. FDDI carries both LED and laser-generated LAN communications through fiber-optic cables.

 Note Decide when it is appropriate to consider the installation of FDDI.

Fiber optic cable is primarily made of pure glass that is pulled into very thin wires or fibers. Many of these fibers are bundled together to form a core. This core is surrounded by another layer of glass called *cladding*. The LED sends the signals through the core of this cable, and the cladding contains these signals to the core. The signal on each fiber can go in only one direction at a time. The bundle of fibers enables the LED to send multiples of signals at a time.

Unlike Token Ring and its related network interface cards that transfer data across the network at speeds of 4 or 16 Mbps, FDDI transfers information at a rate of 100 Mbps. In addition, FDDI is structured to take advantage of two rings, rather than one. This Dual Counter Rotating Rings structure enables FDDI to transfer data across one ring while it performs backup and other services on the second ring.

In addition, FDDI uses multiple tokens and has the ability to bypass network stations designated as low priority, so it can provide faster service to high-priority network stations.

Like a Token-Ring LAN, FDDI uses a token to transfer data frames around the network. After the data frame is processed by the correct network station, the token is passed on to the next attached network node.

The second ring in the FDDI network rotates in the opposite direction of the first ring. This counter-rotation enables the network to compensate for a break in the fiber. If one ring in the network becomes broken due to a problem at one of the network stations, those stations located on either side of the break can isolate the break in the fiber by forming a single ring (wrapping) from their own ports, as shown in figure 33.13.

Each network station can be attached to either one ring or to both rings, depending on the class of the connected station. There are two types of station classes: Class A and Class B.

Class A stations, also called *Single Attached Stations* (SAS), can be attached to only one ring at a time. Only Class B stations, or Dual attached Stations (DAS), can be connected to both rings simultaneously. This designation of station classes helps to keep unstable network devices from breaking both network rings.

Another method of isolating faulty nodes in the network is through the use of wiring concentrators. Wiring concentrators function in theory much like the Token-Ring MSAU. They act as centralized cabling connection devices for network stations. Unlike MSAUs, however, wiring concentrators are capable of communicating with stations and verifying the integrity of the station-to-concentrator connection.

Advantages of Using FDDI

The ability to isolate a break in the cable and continue network communication makes FDDI an extremely reliable cabling option. FDDI has several other advantages.

FDDI overcomes some of the performance problems experienced by traditional Token-Ring networks. It accomplishes this by implementing a standard that provides fair and timely access to the network.

Increased reliability is another advantage of using FDDI. That reliability comes in several forms, including the following:

■ **Information security.** Fiber-optic cable is difficult to wiretap.

■ **Physical security.** Fiber-optic cable is more resistant to cable breakage than are other types of cabling.

■ **Electrical security.** Fiber-optic cable is not susceptible to electrical interference and does not conduct electricity.

FDDI also can transmit network packets over its cable for distances that are significantly longer than other types of cabling. For example, on a fiber-optic cable with no cable bends or breaks that would otherwise reduce the integrity of the transmission, information theoretically can travel hundreds of miles.

FDDI also has built-in management of three aspects of the network, including the following:

■ **Ring Management (RMT)** is responsible for finding and resolving faults in the network ring.

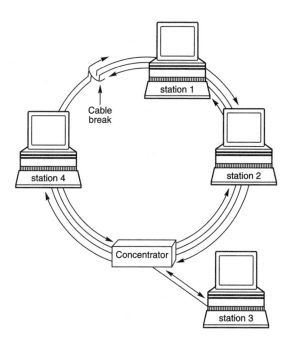

Figure 33.13
Isolated cable break in an FDDI network.

■ **Connection Management (CMT)** is responsible for controlling stations that are inserting themselves into the network, or removing themselves from the network.

■ **Station Management (SMT)** makes it possible for special high-level programs to monitor the ring.

As noted earlier, FDDI networks are substantially faster than Token-Ring networks, capable of communicating at a rate of 100 Mbps. They accomplish this speed not only as a result of the type of cable (fiber optic) that they use, but also as a result of their use of multiple tokens and their ability to service only the high-priority network stations, bypassing the low-priority stations whenever necessary.

A fiber-optic cable is also significantly lighter in weight than is, for example, twisted-pair cabling with an equivalent bandwidth.

 Don't look directly at fiber-optic cable without eye protection. To check to see whether a fiber-optic port is transmitting, darken the room and place a piece of paper in front of the port. If it is transmitting, a light will be reflected onto the paper.

Disadvantages of Using FDDI

There are two primary disadvantages of using FDDI in your network. First, because of the complexity and newness of FDDI technology, you need a great deal of expertise to install and subsequently maintain an FDDI network.

Second, although the cost of the cable itself is comparable to that of unshielded twisted-pair (UTP) cabling, the concentrators and LAN adapters are relatively expensive. For example, a typical FDDI concentrator runs between $1,000 and $1,500 per network node. Therefore, the overall cost of an FDDI network for a LAN of any size can quickly become quite costly.

FDDI Cabling

Various types and wavelengths of fiber-optic cables are available. A typical fiber-optic cable consists of a core made from silica, surrounded by a primary and secondary buffer, and then enclosed in a jacket. Kevlar may be added to provide strength.

The important thing to remember about choosing a fiber-optic cable is to select one based on its intended use, and to match the cable to its appropriate connectors. Figure 33.14 shows a typical duplex fiber-optic cable.

FDDI Troubleshooting

As with troubleshooting all types of networks, begin by looking for the obvious problems, such as loose connectors, damaged cables, and so on. After ruling out these types of problems, consider other possible causes. Look first at those problems considered typical of FDDI networks:

■ Incorrect cable type for actual distance between nodes. On an FDDI network where network information must travel thousands of feet, Multimode Fiber should be used. When distances between nodes begin to reach tens of thousands of feet, or exceed distances of two kilometers, Single-Mode Fiber is necessary.

■ Problems with communicating between network nodes. Even small breaks in a fiber-optic cable can result in network communication problems. There are several ways to detect cable problems, except for one that requires special equipment. If a break in a segment of the cable

is a complete break, you can detect the break using a flashlight. Otherwise, you can use an optical power meter and a source of light energy to test the cable. If either of these methods is insufficient, you can use the most expensive method, an *Optical Time Domain Reflectometer* (OTDR).

■ Dirt on connectors is another cause of communication problems between network nodes. Data is transmitted through fiber-optic cables using light. Therefore, it is important that you keep connectors free from dust and dirt. You can clean connectors using any type of lint-free cloth dampened with alcohol. Do not use water or any type of cleaning fluids other than alcohol.

■ Communication problems also can be caused by bad connectors or by a segment of the cable that is open (incorrectly terminated). A loss of optical power that exceeds 13.0 decibels is an indication that cable problems of this nature may exist. To correct these problems, replace faulty connectors and properly close any open cable segment.

■ A delay of up to four milliseconds in communication is not unusual for fiber-optic cable. If communication delays are a problem, consider using NetWare's Packet Burst Protocol to send multiple rather than single frames across the network, thus reducing transmission delay.

■ When the network does not efficiently handle transmissions across cable that exceeds 50 meters, or which requires 10 Mbps or more throughput, this problem may be directly related to the type of fiber-optic cable. If you are using plastic fiber-optic cable in your network, consider replacing all or at least some of this cable with glass cable. Speed can be affected by the type of fiber-optic cable used.

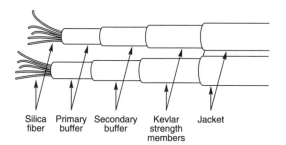

Silica   Primary   Secondary   Kevlar   Jacket
fiber   buffer   buffer   strength
                                    members

Figure 33.14
Fiber-optic duplex cable assembly.

■ The path that network information must travel should be the most efficient. If you are using bridges instead of routers in your network, consider switching to network routers. NetWare network routers, or routers such as CI500 and Wellfleet that are certified by Novell, can choose the best path for any given packet. They are somewhat slower than bridges, however, because of the increased processing that they perform. The design of FDDI translation bridges makes routers the preferred choice for FDDI networks running NetWare.

Which Topology Should I Use?

As a network administrator or support engineer, you have to make some tough decisions on the best type of topology to incorporate into your network environment. It is similar to choosing what type of vehicle and size of engine you need to drive your loads on local streets, freeways, or highways. You need to consider using Token Ring (4 Mbps or 16 Mbps) or Ethernet (10 Mbps). You also need to consider which type of cabling system you need for your network.

The factors that are involved in your choice include the following:

■ Type of applications and their percentage of overall use

■ Flexibility of setup

■ Cost

■ Knowledge level of your support or vendor source

■ Availabilty of replacement or add-on components

No one topology is better than another. Your choice is dependent on how the factors affect your network environment.

Choose the Ethernet topology for those types of networks with a light-to-medium workload. If you are using standard applications, such as word processing, spreadsheets, gateway host sessions, electronic mail, and calendaring packages, Ethernet will work efficiently.

Ethernet has a maximum throughput of 10 Mbps. (Standard loads usually are working around 8-9.1 Mbps.) The cost is nominal, and interchangeable components are readily available. Clients can attempt to transmit more quickly rather than waiting their turn, as is done with the Token Ring topology.

The disadvantage of Ethernet is that the size of the data frames in the packets may require more traffic to pass along the data files on the media. Also, the collision-oriented system can be degraded with the heavy use of database, imaging, multimedia, or CAD/CAM applications.

Token Ring topology is a choice for networks that tend toward heavy workloads. The size of the data frame in the packet is larger than in Ethernet. Token Ring can handle large file transfers, such as database, CAD/CAM, and multiple accesses to imaging files, more easily. Token Ring runs at 4 Mbps or 16 Mbps on many types of media. Some applications of 16 Mbps Token Ring speed are not always as efficient as using the 4 Mbps or the Ethernet 10 Mbps.

Token Ring is more reliable because no collisions occur with the token passing scheme. The disadvantages of Token Ring are cost, station transmission capabilities, and the overhead for management of the token scheme. Also, the more clients you add to a ring, the more that performance can be degraded. Consider splitting the ring into smaller rings with fewer clients attached.

Use your best judgment on your network setup. Where your applications reside, the location of your workloads, and the availability of your network components will determine whether you should use one topology or perhaps mix them.

Questions

1. Which is the least important when configuring a client?

   ○ A. Avoiding conflicts

   ○ B. How other clients are configured

   ○ C. Checking that cables meet specifications for their intended topology

   ○ D. Matching drivers to operating system revisions

2. Which statement about ARCnet is false?

   ○ A. ARCnet can be cabled in star or bus.

   ○ B. ARCnet uses RG-62/U for coax.

   ○ C. ARCnet has the unique feature time-out setting of 31 microseconds.

   ○ D. ARCnet can span a distance of 25,000 feet.

3. Which combination is not supported?

   ○ A. Passive hub to passive hub

   ○ B. Active hub to passive hub to active hub

   ○ C. Active hub to passive hub

   ○ D. Network node to passive hub

4. Which is not a feature of an Ethernet board?

   ○ A. Ethernet boards usually have DIX connectors.

   ○ B. Ethernet boards can have thick (DIX), thin (BNC), or twisted-pair (RJ-45) connectors.

   ○ C. Ethernet boards have internal transceivers for thin net.

   ○ D. Ethernet boards have a time-out setting.

5. Which level cable is correct for 10BASE-T?

   ○ A. Level I

   ○ B. Level II

   ○ C. Level IV

   ○ D. Level VI

6. Which statement about Token Ring cabling is true?

   ○ A. Small, movable systems support up to 96 clients and 12 MSAUs. Token Ring networks cannot use UTP cabling.

   ○ B. The maximum patch cable distance between two MSAUs is 75 feet.

   ○ C. The minimum patch cable distance is 2.5 feet.

   ○ D. Token-Ring uses Type 2, Type 4, and Type 6 cabling.

7. Which TWO of the following statements regarding FDDI are true?

   ☐ A. It follows the IEEE 802.5 standard.

   ☐ B. Like Token Ring, it uses only a single token.

   ☐ C. FDDI can transfer data at speeds of 100 Mbps.

   ☐ D. Stations must attach to the cable by a concentrator.

8. FDDI stands for _____.

○ A. Fiber-based Data Distribution Interface

○ B. Fiber Distributed Data Interface

○ C. Fiber Optic Data Distributed Interface

○ D. Fiber Data Distribution Interface

9. Plastic and glass fiber-optic cables can be used equally well in all situations except _____.

○ A. when the cable distance is less than 50 meters

○ B. when the cable has an open condition

○ C. when stations are attached using a concentrator

○ D. when throughput of 10 Mbps or greater is required

10. Which of the following is one advantage that FDDI has over Token Ring?

○ A. Fiber optic cable is difficult to wiretap.

○ B. FDDI is capable of isolating cable breaks.

○ C. FDDI provides fair and timely access to the network.

○ D. FDDI has built-in ring management.

11. What is the main advantage of using 10BASE2 when network segments do not have to exceed 185 meters?

○ A. It is relatively simple to connect.

○ B. Drop cables can be used, making it easier to troubleshoot.

○ C. Each node connects directly to the cable.

○ D. It is the least expensive of the cabling options.

12. Which TWO of the Ethernet cabling options requires that each end of the bus be terminated?

☐ A. 10BASE2

☐ B. 10BASE5

☐ C. 10BASE-T

☐ D. Thin net

13. Which of the cabling options is considered the trend for wiring Ethernet networks?

○ A. 10BASE2

○ B. 10BASE5

○ C. 10BASE-T

○ D. Thick net

14. Which of the following is not an advantage in using 10BASE-T for cabling a network?

○ A. It is easier and more reliable to manage.

○ B. Centralized hubs make it easier to detect bad cable segments.

○ C. Beaconing helps to isolate cable breaks.

○ D. It is relatively inexpensive to use.

15. Which of the following Ethernet frame types
    is designated as raw Ethernet?

    ○   A.   ETHERNET_802.2

    ○   B.   ETHERNET_802.3

    ○   C.   ETHERNET_SNAP

    ○   D.   ETHERNET_II

Answers

1. B

2. D

3. A

4. D

5. C

6. C

7. A C

8. B

9. B

10. A

11. D

12. B A

13. C

14. C

15. B

Troubleshooting Network Storage Devices

In this chapter, you will learn about the advantages and disadvantages of different types of storage devices that can be used on the network. There are many storage devices that have evolved throughout the history of the computer industry. Understanding how these devices operate and what their limitations are is an important function of a network administrator's job. The following are the types of storage devices that will be discussed in this chapter:

- *Hard drives*

- *CD-ROM players*

- *Magneto-optical drives*

Hard Drives

The hard drive is perhaps the most important storage device on your network. Great care and attention must be given to the hard drive because it is the core of the file server. The operating system that gives a network its functionality must reside on that core drive. If that core drive fails, the entire network will go down. A network administrator is responsible for developing a design for fault tolerance in protecting the core of the network. You also must be able to diagnose potential failure points and be proactive in preventative maintenance. An experienced network administrator must be able to do capacity planning and know how to react in a contingency management mode.

The terminology in the computer industry uses the term *fixed disk* to mean *hard disk*. The fixed disk or the *platters* are contained in the hard drive casing, as opposed to inserting a removable disk in the floppy drive (see fig. 34.1). The technology of a hard drive enables it to provide speed, reliability, and a lot of storage in a small space in one location.

The device that enables the communication between the hard drive and the CPU is called the *disk controller card*. The disk controller card can be built into the motherboard, as part of the drive or as a separate component. The controller interprets the commands from the CPU and sends the interpreted signals to either seek, read, or write data to the hard drive.

 The drive casing is sealed by the manufacturer in a dust- and moisture-free environment. Do not open this drive casing for any reason—dust particles can scratch your platters. They can become inoperable and you could lose valuable data.

The hard drive is made up of many components that work in unison and can be described as an electronic wonder. The drive contains a spindle motor that rotates the platters inside the drive casing. The voice coil actuator moves the read/write heads to the needed position on the disk platter. The time it takes for the read/write heads to find the correct track is called *seek time*.

After the track has been located, the amount of time it takes for the needed piece of data to rotate under the read/write head is called *drive latency*. The combination of seek time and drive latency (the total amount of time it takes to get to the data on the platter) is called *access time*. To "settle" a drive is the time it takes for the head to stabilize above the track after the process or the motion for seeking data has stopped.

The *data transfer rate* is the speed at which data is moved from the disk to the electronic "brains" of the CPU. The amount of data moved is measured in megabytes per second. All these timing features in a hard drive are important to how quickly data can be accessed on the network.

 A cluster is the minimum unit of space for the storage of a file allocated by DOS. A block is the minimum unit of space (usually 4 KB) for the storage of file information by NetWare.

Types of Hard Drive Interfaces

There are several types of hard drive interfaces and encoding schemes used with these interfaces in the networking environment. As a network administrator or support engineer, you should become familiar with each type because of the varied install base that still exists. An early example of a type of

Figure 34.1
Internal components of a hard drive.

a hard drive is an ST-506 model manufactured by Seagate. The ST-506 originally was built for 5MB size drives. The *Run Length Limited* (RLL) or the *Modified Frequency Modulation* (MFM) encoding scheme is used for the larger ST-506 drives.

 MFM is referred to as double-density recording and is used as a coding system to pack more information on hard disks. MFM is still used today on floppy disks and small hard drives.

RLL has increased data density capabilities over MFM by the way it manipulates electronic flux transitions. Fluxes are defined as the way the magnetic field handles the 0s and 1s of digital information. The RLL handles a higher data throughput over the MFM encoding scheme.

Integrated Drive Electronics (IDE) Drives

The Integrated Drive Electronics drive uses the mechanics of having the controller interface integrated with the electronic controls of the hard drive. The IDE terminology often is identified as an AT-type interface with the cable connector for the controller built into the CPU's motherboard. The IDE drive is a cost-effective solution that uses the RLL encoding scheme. Even though the IDE solution has widely replaced the ST-506 drives, there are some limitations on using IDE drives with NetWare:

■ Unless a special nonstandard BIOS is used, there is a maximum drive capacity of 528MB.

■ IDE does not support drive command overlapping, nor can it multitask I/O. If you are mixing IDE drives in a file server with other types of drives, the network operating system must wait for the IDE to complete any

commands issued before the network operating system can issue any commands to any other drives.

■ IDE does not support any optical or tape drives (the SCSI interface does).

■ IDE does not support bus-mastering.

 It is recommended that you never do a low-level format on an IDE drive. If you do this repair task, you could erase the manufacturer's bad block information that is written in a special format on the IDE drive.

Enhanced Small Device Interface (ESDI) Drives

The Enhanced Small Device Interface uses one cable for floppy control, one for hard drive control, and one for data. The ST-506 drive uses the same cabling system, but it is not interchangeable with the ESDI drive. The ESDI drive became more popular than the ST-506 because of its capability of having a higher performance level and using a larger storage capacity. The ESDI also can store information about bad tracks onto the disk, and the interface is designed to work with tape systems. The popularity of ESDI was fairly short-lived, however, and SCSI drive systems have replaced ESDI as the drives of choice on network servers.

Older ESDI drives are supported by the computer's BIOS. Newer drives that have 1,024 or more cylinders do not work well in older ESDI machines. Drives that have more than 1,023 cylinders and 33 sectors per track are not likely to be supported by DOS versions before v3.3. The controllers of XTs, ATs, and Western Digital WD1002 controllers cannot recognize the cylinder count above 1,023 in larger drives.

Note If you are using PS/2 CPUs as file servers (older ones came with ESDI drives) and early versions of NetWare, be careful in updating disk information with the reference disk after NetWare has been loaded. The older operating systems wrote the Cold Boot Loader to part of the track 0 on the ESDI drive.

When the reference disk updates drive information, it writes to track 0 and it will write on top of the cold boot loader. You will have to use your backup copy of the NET$OS.EXE file and boot from a floppy drive to get the server back up. If you want to boot from the hard drive again, you have to rebuild the file server from scratch.

Small Computer Systems Interface (SCSI) Drives

The Small Computer Systems Interface provides an expansion bus architecture that allows up to seven SCSI-type devices (hard drives, CD-ROM, tape units). These can all be the same tape device, be used in combination, or be only one device on one bus slot (see fig. 34.2). These devices are attached to the cable chain that is attached to the SCSI controller card installed in a server or a client.

The devices that are installed internally in the CPU use ribbon cables designed for SCSI. External devices attach by cables that are built with the appropriate connectors for each of the devices attached to the SCSI chain.

The SCSI arbitration scheme allows a faster data transfer rate among the devices attached to each bus slot chain. The advantage in using SCSI is that the CPU does not have to intervene with the processing on the chain in order for the SCSI devices to complete their operations. The SCSI controller has its own BIOS that will run in the upper memory area of the CPU. It also uses hardware port addresses, memory addresses, and DMA channels to ensure compatibility with other components in the CPU.

Each SCSI address can support a controller that provides access to one or two hard drives. An *advanced SCSI programming interface* (ASPI) device driver is provided by the manufacturer and is needed to coordinate communications between

Figure 34.2
SCSI drive device addressing.

different types of devices. There are SCSI controllers that are available with connector ports for use with floppy disk drives. If you want to use the floppy controller already built into your CPU, you can disable the floppy controller on the SCSI board.

The SCSI bus must be terminated at both ends (see fig. 34.3). A SCSI device driver cannot interpret the difference between the original signals or returned signals as an Ethernet bus does. To prevent confusion caused by reflected signals, terminators are used to absorb or prevent signals from becoming unstable. Each SCSI device connected to this terminated bus must have a unique address. This unique address is called a *Logical Unit Number* (LUN).

The American National Standards Institute (ANSI) X3T9.2 committee sets the standards for the SCSI interface. The newest SCSI standard, SCSI-2, defines the protocols, hardware, and command set to run devices other than hard disks. The older SCSI standard could not reliably control the devices beyond the hard drive setup. It is not recommended that you mix SCSI-1 and SCSI-2 standards in the same host, unless the SCSI adapter provides a method of handling both standards. The ISA bus has a transfer data rate maximum of 2 MB per second, whereas the SCSI-2 can transfer data at 4 MB, and, during the FAST operation, can transfer data up to 10 MB per second. You should use the EISA, MCA, or PCI bus with the appropriate SCSI interface cards for the FAST SCSI-2 operation to work efficiently.

There is an implementation of SCSI called WIDE SCSI-2 that is not used as much as the FAST SCSI-2 standard, as WIDE SCSI-2 is fairly new. WIDE SCSI-2 uses a second data path that offers the capability of 20 MB per second data transfer

rate. The WIDE SCSI-2 controller integrates the 68-pin SCSI cable and the differential signaling process. Standard SCSI devices use a 50-pin cable and the single-ended signaling process. There are SCSI host adapters that have a combination of connection slots for a SCSI internal bus with both 68-pin and 50-pin cables. These combination type adapters use either the differential or single-ended signaling process, but not both.

You cannot mix the differential and single-ended devices on the same SCSI bus—they are electronically incompatible. If you have both types of SCSI devices, use one adapter for WIDE SCSI using differential signaling, and another adapter that uses the single-ended devices. Future implementations for the WIDE SCSI devices will develop enhancements for using single-ended signaling.

Tips for Working with SCSI Devices

The use of SCSI devices is rapidly becoming an industry standard. These devices are flexible, affordable, and are relatively easy to install. As a network administrator or support engineer, you should use the following tips in setting up a SCSI environment:

■ When selecting your hardware and software, make sure the revision levels are current and that each can work within the same bus with the other devices.

■ Use all SCSI-2 devices when designing a network. Older SCSI-1 hard disks will mix with SCSI-2 equipment if you have to use available resources.

■ Use SCSI host adapters that use a software setup for jumper and termination settings. Then you do not have to remove the card from the CPU each time you need to change the settings.

Internal SCSI Setup

SCSI Host
(Terminators used)
Adapter

Ribbon Cable

Master Drive
(Terminators Removed)

Slave Drive

Internal Terminators

Figure 34.3

*Termination of SCSI
internal/external setups.*

Internal/External SCSI Setup

SCSI

Host Adapter
(No Termination)

Terminated
Externally

Internal Ribbon
Cable

Terminated
Here

External
Ribbon
Cable

External
SCSI Device

External SCSI Setup

SCSI Host
Adapter

Terminated
Externally

Terminated
Internally

External
Ribbon
Cable

External
SCSI Device

■ Make sure that you use the proper pin number and connector size for the SCSI host adapter and the devices attached to complete the bus. Watch for cables with FAST SCSI-2 adapter connections attaching to the standard Centronics connector on the external SCSI devices. Unfortunately, the proper SCSI connector cables are not always shipped to meet the needs in your environment.

■ Always confirm that each SCSI bus is properly terminated and that the cables are fitting snugly into the connector slots. The maximum length for a SCSI bus is 19 feet, 10 inches. Make sure that the external disk subsystems are using cables that match the proper impedance level.

■ The SCSI bus requires a stable current for the signals to operate properly. Verify that your host adapter and other SCSI devices are supplying the necessary terminating power.

■ Make sure your SCSI host adapter's BIOS, port address, IRQ, and DMA channel addresses do not conflict with other components in the CPU.

■ Make sure that each SCSI device has a unique identifier number (LUN). Each SCSI adapter has a default address of 7 set by the manufac-

turer. The first bootable hard disk must have a SCSI LUN of 0. Other standard SCSI devices on the bus should be numbered 1-6 in the sequential order that the devices are located in the SCSI chain. Some Hewlett-Packard and IBM PS/2 CPUs use a SCSI adapter with an ID of 7 and the devices on the bus start at LUN 6; then each device is numbered sequentially downward to 0.

■ It is best not to mix models of SCSI adapters if they are being used in the same computer. The ASPI software manager that is used by the adapter is written uniquely for that card. Mixing ASPI managers—even by the same manufacturer but different models—can cause operating conflicts.

■ SCSI host adapters can coexist with other types of hard disks and their controllers. Still, it is best to keep device models consistent in the computer.

 There are many third-party software utilities that can be used to determine what drive interface is used in a client or file server. Tools such as CHECKIT PRO, as shown in figure 34.4, can assist a network administrator in determining the needed details.

Figure 34.4
CHECKIT PRO Hard Drive information screen example.

Disk Coprocessor Boards (DCBs)

Disk Coprocessor Boards are controller cards that offload the I/O from the CPU onto the DCB's own coprocessor chip. This frees up the CPU's processor to assist in improving network performance. DCBs also are referred to as *Host Bus Adapters* (HBAs) in Novell literature.

A file server can handle up to four DCB channels. A *disk channel* is a DCB and its disk subsystems. Each DCB can handle a maximum of eight SCSI controllers, with each controller supporting up to two disk drives. SCSI external disk subsystems can be daisy-chained off the DCB port on the end of the card (see fig. 34.5). DCBs are developed for the ISA (AT bus), EISA, and Micro-channel architecture. Development of DCBs today is done by third-party vendors.

Figure 34.5
Disk Coprocessor Board configuration.

The original DCBs were developed by Novell and had an 80188 on-board processor. The DCB also served as a UPS monitor that could gracefully down a server in the event of a UPS "battery low" condition. DCBs also were used as a keycard for serialization of early versions of NetWare 2.*x.* The DISKSET utility is required for using Novell's DCBs to send disk and drive configuration information to the EEPROM on the DCB. Any physical adds or deletions to the controller or disk drive setup required the use of DISKSET. Current DCBs by third parties use the utilities provided by the

vendor. Most extended channel disk subsystems or internal multiple drives today use internal SCSI cards in the file server instead of DCBs.

Although the DCB was at one time the preferred method for constructing high-performance disk storage systems, many current SCSI controllers offer much higher performance.

■ A file server can handle up to 4 DCB channels.

■ A disk channel consists of a DCB and the disk subsystems that attach to it.

■ Each DCB can handle a maximum of eight SCSI controllers.

Proper integration of hardware components in a network is integral for efficient LAN performance. Verification from vendors and Novell Technical Support can help in your network planning. You must pay attention to potential conflicts for interrupts, memory addresses, and node addresses. Cabling limitations, hard drive requirements, addressing and termination, and certified software drivers also must be considered. If you do the proper homework and planning, you will reduce the chances of cost overruns and unplanned down time.

Setting Up Hard Drives

The hard disk is the most important device in a file server for storing both data and the applications that provide the glue for the network to function. The speed, the capacity, and the reliability of the hard disk can make or break your everyday operations (and maybe your sanity!). Understanding the hard disk, using the proper setup features, and performing proactive maintenance is an important function of a network administrator.

Working with Jumpers on the Hard Drive

When the hard drive arrives from the manufacturer and is unpacked from the box, all the jumpers on the drive are set at default options. These settings may or may not work in your computer. As a network administrator or support engineer, you must confirm that the settings on the drive will work for the interface type and encoding scheme required for that computer. Depending on your drive type, the following jumpers might need to be set directly on the drive:

■ **ACT.** Set primarily on IDE and SCSI drives, and lights an external LED to indicate that the drive is active.

■ **Drive Select.** Used primarily by ESDI, MFM, and RLL drives, depending on the number of drives and if you are using a flat or twisted cable.

■ **C/D or DS.** Used by IDE to determine if the drive is to be a C or a D drive.

■ **SCSI Address.** A unique address set by three jumpers that define a binary number. The manufacturer sets this address at 0. Check your drive documentation for all SCSI drives—this setting can vary with different vendors.

■ **DSP.** Used by IDE to designate when a cable is being shared or which one of the drives is the master drive.

The controller card (if used by the drive) might need to have the following jumpers set:

■ **Controller Interrupt.** You also might need to establish this setting in the STARTUP.NCF file on your file server when the DSK file is loading. Usually, this setting is made by the manufacturer and should be left at this default setting.

■ **Base I/O.** This should not conflict with any other device in the computer. This is set as a default from the manufacturer and rarely is changed unless there is a conflict.

■ **DMA Channel.** NetWare does not recommend sharing a DMA channel between two devices. There are some ESDI and SCSI controllers that may need to have this setting verified.

■ **Base BIOS Address.** Some controller cards use ROM BIOS and may need to have this set. Addresses over E000h may not be supported by some motherboards. Conflicts may arise with this setting and network interface cards or VGA cards.

Types of Cables Used with Hard Drives

The cable setup is important; it should be installed so that the pins in the connectors on the cable can receive and transmit the proper signals for data transfer. As a network administrator or support engineer, you must be aware of different cable types and proper installation of these cables. Improper installation can cause the loss of data and the potential destruction of drive components. Use the following recommendations when working with drive cables:

■ Make sure that the colored stripe (usually red) is attached to Pin 1 on the controller card and to the hard drive (see figure 34.6).

■ In an AT standard computer, the floppy and hard drive cables have different twists and cannot be interchanged.

Figure 34.6

Proper connection of Pin 1 between a hard drive and a disk controller card.

 Practical TIP MFM and RLL hard drive cables have five twisted lines, and a floppy cable has seven twisted lines.

Floppy cables have the twists in the lower pin numbers.

■ Small-numbered wires: twisted, smaller drive (that is, floppy disk drive).

■ High-numbered wires: twisted, larger drive (that is, hard drive).

■ A SCSI cable may have 25 or 50 pins on the connector, and the bus it is attached to must

have exactly two terminated ends. Terminators may be found near the connector slot on the SCSI device in packs of three resistors.

■ An IDE cable must not be longer than 18 inches, and it uses a 40-pin cable.

■ You need three cables to connect two RLL or MFM drives to one controller: two data cables and one control cable. The control cable regulates the way the disk functions. If you are using two drives, remove the terminator that is on the drive in the middle of the chain (see fig. 34.7).

Figure 34.7
Types of drive cables.

Formatting the Hard Drive

Physical installation of a hard drive into a computer, setting the jumpers, and connecting the cables are the initial necessary tasks in preparing the drive for network use. When you receive a new hard drive or are reusing an existing drive, you must prepare these drives in the required format so that data can be stored on them.

There are four important steps in preparing a hard drive to operate as it is designed:

1. Low-level formatting

2. Entering CMOS setup information

3. Establishing partitions

4. Performing a high-level DOS format

Low-Level Formatting

Low-level formatting usually is done by the manufacturer of the drive at the factory. It is a destructive process and should only be done as the last resort in attempting to repair a drive. A low-level format is the process of defining sectors and the bad spots on the hard drive. Sectors provide the marking points (or indexes such as in a phone book) where information can be read, retrieved, or written.

There are third-party programs such as CKLLFMT in the CheckIt PRO software package. Some versions of DOS or the advanced drive diagnostics disk for the drive include low-level format utilities. You should check with the manufacturer of your drive for the proper procedure and program to do a low-level format.

A low-level format not only establishes sector IDs, it marks off bad sectors, tests the disks by performing a surface analysis, temporarily fills each sector, and sets the interleave ratio entered. Besides using a low-level format to give a new hard drive the directions on getting started, a low-level format can be done to remark the sectors of a drive that have been previously used, make an attempt at repairing a drive that is exhibiting a large number of errors, or change the interleave ratio.

 If for some reason you have to low-level format a drive, make sure you format the drive in the same temperature and in the same position it will be used—flat or sideways. The temperature and gravity environment are very important to disk drives.

Setting the Interleave Ratio

Establishing the interleave ratio helps the drive to manage the flow of information between the computer and the disk better. Setting the interleave factor is not as necessary a concern for newer drives. Older drives used to be faster than what the CPU's microprocessor could handle; therefore, the interleave factor was developed to slow the drive down but still make it functional. The interleave ratio can help prevent bottlenecks if it is set properly.

 Technology has enabled newer drives to set sector sparring, which is similar to NetWare's hot fix. This new feature will reserve one sector on every track for the remapping of bad sectors. This reduces the capacity of your new drive and should only be used if there are a lot of problems with the drive.

The physical sector arrangement and the logical arrangement of how the sectors are numbered in a track determines the interleave ratio (see fig. 34.8). An interleave factor is chosen by setting a ratio for the computer to use in determining how it is to read disk information. A ratio is defined as the length of a sector and the distance between two logical sectors. One sector is used as the starting point for measuring the length of an interleave. Setting an interleave factor too low or high can impede performance.

 IDE drives use cache and really have no need for an interleave setting. Some SCSI drives and all MFM encoded drives can manage interleave ratios. The following interleave ratios are recommended:

continues

Figure 34.8

Sector reading by a hard drive set at a 2:1 interleave ratio.

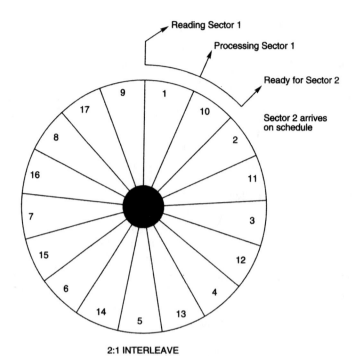

Reading Sector 1

Processing Sector 1

Ready for Sector 2

Sector 2 arrives on schedule

2:1 INTERLEAVE

■ 1:1 for machines running NetWare that are 10 Mhz or faster, using 286 or 386 system boards. DOS machines at 20 Mhz or faster using 286 or 386 motherboards use this interleave. All 486 machines use 1:1.

■ 2:1 for machines running DOS that are 10–16 Mhz and are using 286 or 386 motherboards.

■ 3:1 for 6–8 Mhz AT class computers and for XT type machines running DOS applications.

■ 4:1 for all 4.77 Mhz XT class machines.

Establishing Partitions

The hard drive must be partitioned after a low-level format has been completed. Modern drives that are new out of the box are already low-level formatted and ready to be partitioned. The operating system must be compatible with the format of the logical structure of the hard disk. The logical structure is set up with a DOS program called FDISK (see fig. 34.9). FDISK sets the partitions needed on a hard drive.

• Note

For NetWare 3.*x* and above file servers, a DOS partition of only 10 MB is recommended. DOS must be installed in a Primary DOS partition, which must be configured as the drive's Active partition. This can be done with an FDISK program.

```
    Current fixed disk drive: 1

    Choose one of the following:

    1. Create DOS partition or Logical DOS Drive
    2. Set active partition
    3. Delete partition or Logical DOS Drive
    4. Display partition information

    Enter choice: [1]

Press Esc to exit FDISK
```

Figure 34.9

Opening screen using an FDISK program to partition hard drives.

The DOS operating system recognizes the rest of the NetWare-ready hard drive as a non-DOS partition. After the NetWare operating system is loaded, NetWare identifies the DOS partition as *Physical partition #0* and the NetWare partition as *Physical partition #1*.

 The low-level format utility that is shipped with a SCSI drive is the best program to use if you need to perform the low-level format process. Generic-type low-level format utilities usually will not work with the SCSI drives.

Entering CMOS Setup Information

The *Complementary Metal-Oxide Semiconductor* (CMOS) is a battery-operated chip that is found on the motherboard of the computer. The CMOS chip is an important microprocessor found primarily in the newer generation of personal computers. This chip is important to the operation of the computer because it is responsible for telling the electronics of the PC what is contained in the CPU and the location of these components in the scheme of being able to operate together. The CMOS chip provides the electronic current management for

the positive and negative electrons that provide the flow of electrical signals to the components.

 If your computer shows unexplained erratic behavior or is losing the date or time, replace the battery with a new one that meets the same voltage requirements. This voltage number is printed or stamped on the battery.

The CMOS must be told what type of components the computer has and where they are located. The information about the hard drive is an important setup requirement in CMOS. You can get to CMOS with most computers during the power-up process by pressing Ctrl+Alt+Esc. You also can view CMOS information through third-party utilities such as CheckIt PRO, as shown in figure 34.10. The CMOS setup characteristics require the TYPE number of the drive, which is found marked on the drive or in the manufacturer's documentation. The type information includes the number of cylinders, heads, sectors, and the size of the hard drive. If the drive requires write precompensation information, the CMOS asks for this detail also.

Figure 34.10
*CMOS Setup Information
found by CHECKIT
PRO.*

The drive you install does not have to match one of the CMOS drive types perfectly. IBM's CMOS Type 1 is used for most ESDI drives. The Type 1 represents a 10 MB drive, and at power-up the BIOS from the ESDI controller card overwrites this information to what is needed for ESDI operations. SCSI drives use the Type 0 or Not Installed parameter. The MicroHouse Technical Library has an extensive listing of drive types from which to find a type that closely represents your drive. Choose a type that has the cylinder count that is equal to or less than the number of cylinders available on your drive. Do not use a type that exceeds the megabyte size or the number of heads on your physical drive.

 Note   Write precompensation is used primarily by older drives. This process manages the timing of retrieval of information from the platters as the sectors get closer together toward the center of the drive. The magnetic field that is passed to the read/write heads on a hard drive is made stronger to handle the changes in the geometric division of the drive as the read/write heads move to the center of the disk. As a default, write precompensation is determined by taking the

maximum number of cylinders on that individual drive and dividing that number by two.

High-Level DOS Format

The fourth part in setting up a hard drive is performing a high-level format. The DOS program FORMAT accomplishes this task on a new or used drive. The high-level format can be used to erase all the files in an entire DOS partition.

For a file server to have a bootable partition, you must format the primary DOS partition with the following command:

FORMAT /S

The /S parameter places the hidden DOS system information files and the COMMAND.COM in the DOS partition. The format process also accomplishes the following tasks:

■ Creates a blank root directory (except when using the /S parameter)

■ Creates a DOS boot sector and a DOS *file allocation table* (FAT)

■ Scans the disk and notes the bad sectors

It is a benefit to have a DOS bootable partition on a NetWare 3.*x* and above file server. The server boots up faster from the hard disk. You can set the necessary statements to remotely reboot a server. You also can load a communication package on the DOS partition, down the server, then have an on-site person set the server as a host. Then you could dial in to copy updated files, such as DSK or NLM drivers, or maybe run CheckIt PRO to investigate server details.

Before you format a used drive that already contains data, make sure you back up all the files you need to protect. Low-level formats never allow the data to be recovered by an unformatted utility. There are some third-party utilities that can recover high-level formats, provided the hard drive has not been written to since the format was performed. Professional data recovery services such as On-Track can assist in recovering data from a destroyed drive. As a network administrator or support engineer, you should be aware that most disks have bad sectors—don't panic if you see a few. A manufacturer considers a hard drive to be acceptable to be shipped if the bad sectors are less than 1 percent of the total size of the drive.

NetWare Drive Information

NetWare calculates a unique device code for each device on the bus or for each hard drive. System error messages use this code to display failure messages. As an example, the device code 20010 refers to the first drive (0) on the second controller (1) on the first host bus adapter (0) on the first instance the ISADISK.DSK driver (20) is found. NetWare uses the ISADISK device driver for ST-506 drives using RLL or MFM encoding schemes. These types of drives have the disk controller and the host bus adapter on the same physical drive. The controller digit found in the device code always is zero. The IDE type drives can use the

ISADISK.DSK file or preferably the IDE.DSK device drivers. The SCSI drivers are provided by the manufacturer of the host adapter card. The device code for SCSI is always set to 0.

 The device drivers that come in the core package of a new 3.11 operating system box are slightly outdated. Although they are operational, enhanced ISADISK and IDE drivers are available on NetWire or on NSEPRO.

When a 3.*x* server is setting up the operating system, it establishes the hot fix redirection area first. NetWare considers the location from the beginning of the NetWare data area to the end of the NetWare data area as a *logical partition*. A NetWare logical partition holds the NetWare operating system files and the data that is loaded to be accessed by the network users. Each logical partition has its own identifying number. A NetWare logical partition can be made up of more than one physical partition, contiguous with a physical partition, or be made as part of a physical partition. NetWare uses physical partition numbers for housekeeping tasks performed by the operating system. Logical partition numbers are used for mirrored drive designation.

After you set up NetWare partitions through the INSTALL.NLM, you also must establish volume information. NetWare 3.*x*(20) enables volumes to be spanned across multiple hard drives. Volume segments are made up of the same volume information on different hard disks. There can be up to 8 segments on a hard drive and 32 segments per volume. Performance can be improved by spanning volumes. The disadvantage to spanning is that the loss of one drive and its partial volume segment can cause the loss of access to the entire volume. RAID, mirroring, or duplexing can help prevent the loss of an entire volume from happening.

Working with RAID Drives

The network environment of today has evolved from having only a file server, a printer, and a few client stations, to having large enterprise designs requiring unlimited availability. The critical nature of data accessibility requires that network administrators or support engineers provide the best storage and recovery solutions as cost effectively as possible. The reliability of the network is not required for just the file server, but for the client also. The early history of the computer environment lacked the flexibility of the PC world, and the critical data needed was kept on a mainframe machine. Data manipulation on a mainframe requires many lines of code and cooperation from several differently skilled computer technicians. With the flexibility of the PC environment, extra precautions must be made in protecting against human or mechanical error.

The *Redundant Array of Inexpensive Drives* (RAID) can work with NetWare's *System Fault Tolerance* (SFT) features to protect data in a network environment. The use of RAID enables you to set up the best disk array design to protect your system. RAID is defined in detail as the architecture of combining two or more disks to create a large virtual disk structure to develop a source for redundancy of data. In a disk array, the drives are coordinated into different levels of RAID to which the controller card distributes the data as it is designed to do.

RAID uses a format of splitting data among drives at the bit, byte, or block level. The term *data striping* refers to the capability of arranging data in different sequences across drives. An example demonstration of this data splitting is shown in figure 34.11.

Your input in designing the most reliable drive setup for your network is an important responsibility. You must choose the best RAID implementation level that will meet your users' requirements in data integrity and cost. There are seven levels of RAID available on the market today. The numbers that represent RAID levels are 0, 1, 2, 3, 4, 5, and 10. A higher number does not necessarily mean that it is a better choice than the lower number. You must select the best for your environment. The following paragraphs present a brief discussion of each of the seven available levels.

RAID 0

Level 0 uses data striping and block interleaving. This level distributes the data block-by-block across the disk array in the same location across each drive. Data can be read or written to these same sectors from either drive, improving performance. The failure of a single drive can bring down the system. Redundancy of data is not provided.

RAID 1

Drives are paired or mirrored with each byte of information being written to each identical drive. You can duplex these devices by adding a separate host adapter for each drive. Mirroring provides a better performance benefit than that of RAID 0. If one drive in the pair fails, the other drive can continue to operate. This level can get expensive with the cost of drives to meet your needs for capacity. You will need to make sure your power source has enough wattage to handle the additional devices.

RAID 2

This level uses data striping with bit interleave. This means that data is written across each drive in succession, one bit at a time. Faulty bits are isolated

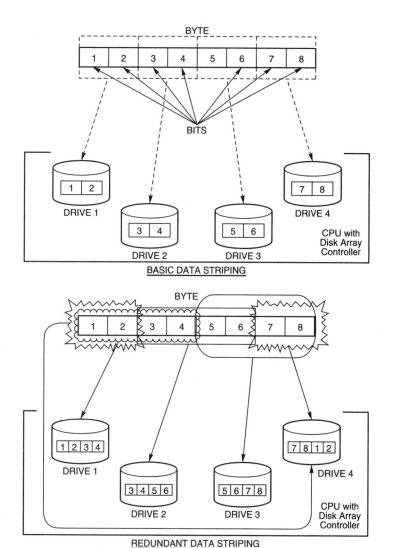

Figure 34.11
Examples of data striping.

by using checksum-capable drives. This level does not require total data redundancy. RAID 2 drives are transmitting in a parallel mode, enabling a faster data transfer rate. The write mode can be slower because each drive is working on every write attempt. The data used for checksum information is redundant. This level is not effective or cost-efficient for use in personal computers.

RAID 3

This level uses bit interleave data striping with parity checking capabilities. Data striping is done across the drives, one byte at a time. There usually are four or five drives at this level, with one drive dedicated for parity information to ensure the integrity of the data. RAID 3 has a very high data transfer rate and can handle long data transfers. This level is more reliable than RAID 2. Parity maintenance can be an overhead problem and cause the write performance to slow because the parity drive must be accessed for every write. There also could be major system problems if any two drives fail. The failure of a single drive will not affect the availability of data; the array controller will use the parity drive to reconstruct the contents of the failed disk. RAID 3 is not ideal for NetWare 3.*x*. As a default, NetWare accesses data in 4 KB blocks, which is not considered a long transfer rate.

RAID 4

This level uses block interleave data striping with parity checking. This means that this level uses a single parity drive, as does RAID 3, and uses block data striping, as does RAID 0. The drives in this RAID level function individually, with an individual drive reading a block of data. The combination of multiple drives has the ability to do multiple simultaneous reads. The block-level striping process is more efficient than RAID 3 byte-level striping. The downfalls of this level are the same as RAID 3, with the addition of the parity drive not being used to store data. If the array controller fails, the entire array cannot function.

RAID 5

This level uses block interleaved data striping with distributed check-data on all drives in the array. RAID 5 is efficient in handling small blocks and has quicker transfer rates because reads and writes can happen in parallel mode. The capability of virtual redundancy at an inexpensive cost is a benefit of RAID 5. This level is not as fast as RAID 0 or RAID 1 because it distributes parity information across all drives. Large file transfers are done in blocks and can be slower than RAID 3, which uses parallel

bytes. RAID 5 efficiency goes up as the number of disks in the array increases. You can use hot spares mounted in the array cabinet. These extra drives can be picked up by the array automatically, replacing the failed drive. The data will be rebuilt to the added drive to function in sequence with the rest of the array as if nothing happened. This failed drive can then be replaced on the fly.

RAID 10

This level is defined as data that is duplicated across two identical RAID 0 arrays or hard disk drives. All data that is contained on a physical drive in one array is mirrored on a drive in the second array. RAID 10 uses the similar concept that NetWare's SFT III mirrored file servers use.

When you are choosing RAID for the customer, consider the following factors to make the best selection:

- The importance of the applications and data to the cost of downtime and lost business
- The number of users and the amount of drive capacity needed
- The size of the data blocks and whether they require direct or sequential access on the drives
- The proportion of reads to writes to the I/O activity, and the maximum transfer rate needed

There are many vendors that offer RAID solutions. Some examples of these vendors include AST, Compaq, Dell, IBM, and Storage Dimensions. Dell Computer offers a reliable high-end file server that uses RAID 10, PCI bus architecture, a Pentium processor, and FAST SCSI-2 host adapters. This combination can be used for the mission-critical environment using NetWare.

Understanding Disk Mirroring and Disk Duplexing

Disk mirroring and disk duplexing are two important system fault tolerance features added in SFT II to protect information in the event of hardware failure.

Disk Mirroring

Disk mirroring is defined as two hard drives—one primary and one secondary—using the same disk channel (controller cards and cable). The process is illustrated in figure 34.12. Disk mirroring is most commonly configured using disk drives contained in the server. You soon see that duplexing enables you to configure a more robust hardware environment.

All changes to the primary disk are duplicated on the secondary so that the secondary is a mirror image of the primary. In the event that the primary drive fails, users can access data on the secondary drive as if nothing happened. Disk mirroring can be done internally in a file server if enough drive and card slots are available. A DCB can be used to provide access to an external disk subsystem. Disk drives must be the same logical size, terminated properly, and addressed correctly.

Disk Duplexing

In the event of a disk channel failure (controller card or cable), access to all data on the channel is stopped. A message is displayed on the file server console screen (if your users do not let you know about it first). Even though drives can be mirrored, if they are connected to the same disk controller, all disk activity on the mirrored pair ceases.

Disk duplexing performs the function of simultaneously writing data to disks located on different channels. As figure 34.13 illustrates, each hard disk in a duplexed pair is connected to a separate hard disk controller. This figure shows a configuration in which the drives are housed in separate disk subsystems. Each subsystem has a separate power supply. This is a more reliable setup than is possible with mirroring, because a failure of one disk drive power supply does not disable the server, which continues to work with the system that remains under power.

A duplex configuration has two disk channels. In this example, each channel has two disks. NetWare identifies the drives by their channel and drive numbers, as shown in figure 34.13.

Duplexing enables NetWare to perform split seeks, in which NetWare seeks with both drives of a duplexed pair and retrieves data from the first drive on which the data is found. Split seeks are a distinct advantage of duplexing when compared to mirroring and can significantly improve a server's file access time.

Working on the same channel is analogous to going to a baseball game when only one gate is open to the stadium. You can enter or exit through only one gate (channel) at the stadium (file server), and the crowd (data) can get backed up on both sides. If more than one gate (another channel) is open, the crowd (data) does not get backed up on both sides of the fence (file server or workstation).

 Duplexing protects information at the hardware level with duplicate channels (controller cards and cables) and duplicate hard drives (refer to fig. 34.12).

continues

Mirroring uses one controller card and two hard drives (refer to fig. 34.13). The point of failure for this setup is primarily the controller card or the cable connecting the drives to the controller card. Disk duplexing uses two controller cards and a minimum of one drive per controller card. The point of contention for failure is reduced with duplicate hardware.

Figure 34.12
How disk duplexing works.

DRIVE 0
(DATA IS WRITTEN AND
READ HERE FIRST)

DRIVE 1
(DATA IS WRITTEN AND
READ HERE SECOND)

DISK
CONTROLLER
(CHANNEL 0)

Disk Mirroring or Duplexing in Version 3.*x*

Use the INSTALL.NLM to mirror or duplex in 3.*x*. The following example is done on a network drive after the original operating system installation was completed. The following steps must be completed to install a disk pair as mirrored or duplexed:

1. Install the hardware components with the correct termination and hardware addresses. Document the model of the controller card and drives.

2. Bring the server up and at the file server console (or through RCONSOLE) load the

Figure 34.13

How disk mirroring works.

INSTALL.NLM. From the Installation Options menu, select Disk Options. The screen shown in figure 34.14 displays the Available Disk Options menu.

3. Select Mirroring and press Enter. The Partition Mirroring Status screen appears as shown in figure 34.15. This screen contains the status of all the drives in the 3.*x* file server

to be edited. Select the drive designated as Logical Partition #1 to be the primary drive and press Enter.

4. The screen displays the Mirrored NetWare Partitions menu as shown in figure 34.16. Press Insert to add another partition to the Mirrored NetWare Partitions screen. The menu screen shown in figure 34.17 then displays the Available Partitions from which to choose.

Figure 34.14
The Available Disk Options menu in INSTALL.

Figure 34.15
The Partition Mirroring Status display in INSTALL.

Figure 34.16
The Mirrored NetWare Partitions display in INSTALL.

Figure 34.17

Display of partitions available for assignment as mirrors.

Highlight an available partition and press Enter. The Device numbers come from the addressing and termination of the SCSI drive installation.

5. The Mirrored NetWare Partitions screen menu (see fig. 34.18) displays the In Sync status of the primary mirrored partition. In Sync means that the designated partition is unmirrored and has no data problems. The Partition 2 shows an Out Of Sync status. Within ten seconds, the Partition 2 drive begins synchronizing with Partition 1.

To check the status of the remirroring process, press Alt+Esc to get to the colon prompt. The message Remirroring partition # appears, indicating that the process has begun.

The synchronization process takes several minutes, depending on the size of the drive being mirrored.

6. The Partition Mirroring Status menu screen (see fig. 34.19) then shows confirmation of the logical partition as being mirrored when the synchronization process from step 5 is completed. The partitions are now mirrored and in operation.

Figure 34.18

The Mirrored NetWare Partitions box displaying information about an out-of-sync mirrored pair.

Figure 34.19
Mirrored drives in process of synchronization.

```
NetWare 386 Installation  V1.56              NetWare 386 Loadable Module

      Installation Options
       Disk Options
       Vo
       Sy  Ava      Partition Mirroring Status
       Pr
       Ex  Fo   Not Mirrored: Logical Partition #1
           Pa   Not Mirrored: Logical Partition #2
           Mi
           Su
           Re


       Highlight a partition and press <ENTER> to view / modify the
       associated mirror set.  Press <MODIFY> (F3) to restore an "Out
       Of Sync" partition.  Press <ESCAPE> to return to previous menu.
```

Press Esc until you exit from the INSTALL.NLM. You now can continue to do normal processing.

Note The mirroring process should be performed during nonproduction hours, and all user logins should be disabled.

Tips for Working with Mirrored/ Duplexed Drives

As a network administrator or support engineer, you must plan appropriately the use of mirrored/ duplexed drives in your file server. Improper setup or lack of monitoring these types of hard drive setups can cause loss of data and destruction of hardware. As part of your maintenance process, use the following recommendations in your planning design:

■ Mirroring and duplexing should not take the place of backups—keep doing them on a regular basis.

■ Always load the disk drivers in the same order—the internal controllers should be loaded first, in the order they are to be addressed.

■ NetWare does not differentiate between mirroring or duplexing in its system messages.

■ Periodically check the status of your mirrored or duplexed drives to see if they are still "in synch." Check the physical and the logical window using the INSTALL.NLM on the file server.

■ As part of your network documentation, keep a record of the device codes of your hard drives. This could help you troubleshoot the load order of your disk drivers using system messages.

■ IDE drives should not be used as duplexed drives because of how the built-in controllers piggyback each other in a master/slave relationship. If the primary drive goes down, the second drive will also. Exceptions to this rule are the use of a motherboard that has dual IDE ports or the use of paddle boards.

Working with CD-ROM Drives

CD-ROM players can enhance your network environment by adding flexibility to your resources for multitudes of information. You can have a CD-ROM player attached as a device on your SCSI bus that is connected to your file server. A CD-ROM drive can be found that has multiple drive bays, with each bay recognized as a volume on the server. For 3.1x, software packages such as SCSI-Express and Corel SCSI can do this volume setup. NetWare 3.12 has a CDROM.NLM that enables the CD-ROM to be seen as a built-in volume. The client can use a locally attached CD-ROM player with the proper MSCDEX driver extensions and parameters loaded in the CONFIG.SYS and AUTOEXEC.BAT files. The CD-ROM unit in the NetWare environment must be ISO-9660-compliant.

The following are the advantages of a CD-ROM player in a networked environment:

■ The file formats are standardized and can be accessed easily.

■ There is access to more volumes of information. Keyword searches on some applications increase data resources in one setting.

■ Media is lightweight, can be stored easily, and costs for duplication are low.

The following are the disadvantages of a CD-ROM player:

■ CD-ROM players can get expensive, but continually are coming down in price.

■ CD-ROM players are slower than hard disks. Modern hard drives are 20 times faster than the 200–300-millisecond seek rate of the CD-ROM. Newer CD-ROM players coming to the market that are available for networks will have 3X and 4X speed capabilities.

Tips for Working with CD-ROM Players

CD-ROM players can be an enhancement to any network. A network administrator or support engineer must be knowledgeable in this hardware arena. As with any other device included in your network environment, improper planning can cause expensive data recovery and troubleshooting delays. Use the following tips when using CD-ROM players in your network:

■ Check for incompatibilities by having the CD-ROM player and the hard drive on the same SCSI controller. Review the manufacturer's documentation and check the software vendor's requirements.

■ Some CD-ROM players require a "caddie" box for the CD-ROM platter to be placed in before it can be inserted into the player. Make sure your users know about this—failure to properly use a caddie box can result in severe damage to your CD. (*Please* read your documentation before using the player!)

■ Do not install a CD-ROM player in a drive bay in the CPU that is located directly above a hard drive in the CPU casing. The magnetic fields created by the CD-ROM unit can erase data from the hard drive.

■ The error message Invalid drive specification means that the MSCDEX file is loaded too low in your AUTOEXEC.BAT file. The error message Disc not High Sierra Format means you need to upgrade the version of your currently installed MSCDEX extension drivers to work with the newer ISO-9660 CD-ROM format.

Working with Magneto-Optical Drives

Magneto-optical Drives (M-O) are used to capture text, audio, video, and other types of integrated media in a combined format on the optical platter. M-O drives are used as a compromise between *digital access tape* (DAT) drives which are an inexpensive, slower medium, and hard drives which are expensive, yet faster in speed. M-O drives are faster than tape and more expensive than hard drives.

The use of optical drives can replace the standard tape and hard drives for backup, archiving (which is the best use for M-O), and storage of data-intensive applications such as CAD/CAM type programs. The setup of M-O drives is similar to tape backup units; they can be jukeboxes, external, or internal devices. M-O should not be confused with *Write Once Read Many* (WORM) systems because WORM drives cannot have the data changed on the optical-type disk after it has been written.

A magneto-optical drive operates with the use of laser beams and magnetism. An M-O disk is coated with layers on which spiral grooves have been molded. To write data, a polarized laser beam is reflected onto the surface of the M-O platter. The reflection is measured for its rotation on the plane of the disk that has been polarized magnetically.

The data is then interpreted from how the rotation is magnetically oriented. Reverting the magnetic orientation to the way it was directed prior to the M-O disk being written to will erase data.

The following are the advantages of magneto-optical disks:

■ **Removable Media.** Disks can be removed and are capable of being changed with another M-O disk.

■ **Capacity.** M-O can handle capacities from 650 MB to 1,000 GB and can be loaded into jukeboxes for increased capacity of data accessibility.

■ **Random Access.** M-O supports many read/write operations, unlike streaming tape cartridges.

■ **Durability.** Head crashes are impossible because of the use of laser beams.

■ **Backup.** It can be used for large unattended backups and archiving of data.

The following are the disadvantages of magneto-optical disks:

■ **Cost.** Very expensive currently. Drive prices range from $3,500 to $5,000, and the optical disk platter ranges in price from $180 to $300.

■ **Speed.** Magneto-optical drives are not as fast as SCSI drives. M-O drives need a double pass to the platter to write any data.

■ **Size.** These drives are too big to fit inside laptops. This may interfere with the requirements for the mobile network of today.

Questions

1. The most important storage device on the network is _____.

   ○ A. fixed disk

   ○ B. CD-ROM

   ○ C. magneto-optical disk

   ○ D. floppy disk

2. Communication between the hard drive and the CPU is handled by which device?

   ○ A. NIC

   ○ B. Fixed disk cable

   ○ C. Disk controller card

   ○ D. Floppy drive cable

3. The time it takes for the read/write heads to find the correct track on a fixed disk is known as _____.

   ○ A. access time

   ○ B. transfer rate

   ○ C. megabytes per second

   ○ D. seek time

4. Which of the following is NOT one of the components of a hard drive?

   ○ A. Spindle motor

   ○ B. Voice coil actuator

   ○ C. Platter

   ○ D. Cluster block

5. Which of the following is NOT a limitation of an Integrated Drive Electronics (IDE) drive?

   ○ A. It cannot multitask I/O.

   ○ B. It has a maximum drive capacity of 528M even when a special non-standard BIOS is used.

   ○ C. It does not support any optical or tape drives, as does the SCSI interface.

   ○ D. It does not support bus-mastering.

6. The main reason that you should never do a low-level format on an IDE drive is that _____.

   ○ A. you might erase the manufacturer's bad block information

   ○ B. you might be unable to access the IDE drive again to reestablish it

   ○ C. it removes the drive's ability to support overlapping and multitasking of I/O

   ○ D. electronic flux transitions of the drive might be reversed

7. Which TWO of the following are cited as reasons why ESDI drives have become more popular than ST-506 drives that use the same cabling system?

   ☐ A. ESDI drives are interchangeable with ST-506 drives.

   ☐ B. ESDI drives are capable of performing at higher levels.

   ☐ C. ESDI drives allow the Cold Boot Loader to be written to track 0, freeing disk space for data storage.

☐ D. ESDI drives have a larger storage capacity.

8. Which drive type provides an expansion bus that allows up to seven types of devices to be connected?

○ A. IDE

○ B. ESDI

○ C. SCSI

○ D. ASPI

9. Which of the following is NOT true of the WIDE SCSI-2 implementation of SCSI?

○ A. It uses a 50-pin cable and the single-ended signaling process.

○ B. It uses a second data path offering up to 20 MB per second data transfer rate.

○ C. It implements a 68-pin SCSI cable with the differential signaling process.

○ D. It is not used as much as the FAST SCSI-2 standard.

10. Which drive device is rapidly becoming the industry standard?

○ A. ASPI

○ B. ESDI

○ C. SCSI

○ D. IDE

11. If you do not want to remove the SCSI host adapter each time you need to change its settings, you should do which of the following?

○ A. Make sure that the same cabling is used for all SCSI devices on the network.

○ B. Make sure that you use a SCSI host adapter that uses software for setup of jumpers and termination settings.

○ C. Make sure that each SCSI device has a unique identifier number.

○ D. Make sure that all SCSI devices are the same, using either all SCSI-1 or all SCSI-2 devices.

12. The SCSI LUN required for the first bootable hard disk on all except for some HP and PS/2 machines is _____.

○ A. 0

○ B. 1

○ C. 6

○ D. 7

13. One primary use of the third-party tool called CHECKIT PRO is _____.

○ A. to set up hard drives for storage

○ B. to modify jumpers on the drive

○ C. to enable you to mix SCSI devices

○ D. to determine a workstation's drive interface

14. Which of the following is not a jumper that might have to be set on the hard disk?

○ A. ACT

○ B. IDE

○ C. DS

○ D. DSP

15. Although usually set for the controller card by the manufacturer, you might need to put which setting into the STARTUP.NCF file of a network server?

   ○ A. Controller interrupt

   ○ B. Base I/O

   ○ C. DMA channel

   ○ D. Base BIOS address

Answers

1.	A	9.	A
2.	C	10.	C
3.	D	11.	B
4.	D	12.	A
5.	B	13.	D
6.	A	14.	B
7.	B D	15.	A
8.	C		

Troubleshooting the DOS Workstation

*S*everal versions of DOS are installed in the workplace today. Many businesses, either for economic reasons or because they have never seen a need to upgrade, are still running version 3.3. If upgrade decisions are made on a departmental basis, then it is possible that one LAN administrator could be supporting PCs running versions 3.3, 4.x, 5.0, and 6.x.

Not only do all of these Microsoft versions exist, but there are also DOS versions from IBM and Novell. Novell's DOS was acquired in a purchase of Digital Research. DR DOS 5.0 gave way to DR DOS 6.0, which in turn gave way to Novell DOS 7. All of these combine together to make a fine stew for the administrator to stay on top of.

The majority of problems arise when one resource is accessed by more than one entity, for example, memory. This chapter examines these problems as well as the following topics:

- Working with IPX/NETX
- Working with ODI
- Working with the DOS Requester
- Working with Remote Boot
- Troubleshooting with TRACK
- Diagnosing conflicts
- Conflict resolution
- PC memory
- DR DOS

Working with IPX/NETX

Figure 35.1 depicts the *Internetwork Packet Exchange* (IPX) architecture and shows how the components work together. NCP is the NetWare Core Protocol going to the server, while the NetWare shell is going to the workstation. The LAN driver could be Ethernet, ARCnet, Token Ring, or any other.

With NetWare, as with any client/server system, one station interacts with another as the client makes requests of the server. The IPX.COM and the NetWare shell carry out this interaction between the two components.

 The command IPX I shows information about the version of IPX running on your workstation.

The purpose of IPX is to function as a go-between for the NIC card and communication link. This is

described in the Administration sections of this book, and it is strongly encouraged that you review the specific coverage there. Here, suffice it to say that IPX is responsible for communication functions and management of the sockets used in the workstation. It also is responsible for ascertaining the address of the network segment to which the workstation is connected, the network number, and the node address.

Figure 35.1
The IPX architecture for a DOS workstation.

The NetWare Core Protocol regulates how connection control information is passed. Every server packet must have the connection number and a sequence number assigned to it. The only purpose for the sequence number is to ascertain when a packet is lost.

What To Do If You Cannot Connect to the Server

The following steps should be followed if a workstation cannot connect to the server:

1. Verify proper seating of the NIC and connection of the cables.

2. Verify that the NIC is set to the same configuration as the IPX.COM.

3. Look for conflicts in interrupts, memory, and hardware addresses.

4. Verify that the server LAN driver is bound to IPX.

The Watchdog

When users leave a workstation, they should log out from the server to clear their connection and free resources. The Watchdog process, running at the server, routinely sends a poll to workstations to verify if they are active or not. If they are not active for a specified period of time, they automatically are cleared.

Working with ODI

ODI is nothing more than a specification of how the data link layer works in the OSI model. Developed by Novell and Apple in 1989, it provides support for multiple protocols on the same network with one driver. Up to four network cards can be active in the same machine, and drivers can be unloaded as easily as they were loaded. This means that IPX and TCP/IP can live in network harmony, and ODI drivers have replaced IPX.COM in the workplace.

The components of ODI, as discussed in the Administration sections, include:

■ LSL.COM

■ The LAN driver

■ IPXODI.COM (which includes SPX)

The *Multiple Link Interface Driver* (MLID) is a part of the LAN driver specification, which controls communication between the board and the LSL. Figure 35.2 illustrates the interaction between the components.

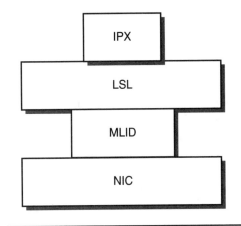

Figure 35.2
The ODI architecture.

Protocol stacks figure into the equation as they receive packets from the LSL. They operate independently of the board type and remove the header information that is pertinent only to them. Protocol stacks include TCP/IP, AppleTalk, OSI, and IPX/SPX.

Troubleshooting ODI

The first step when trying to diagnose ODI workstations is to check the board and cabling to make certain there are no obvious physical problems. Next, check that you have an ODI LAN driver for the board. Following that, boot with a bare-bones AUTOEXEC.BAT and CONFIG.SYS—loading no drivers of any kind. When booted, load LSL, the LAN driver, IPXODI, and the NETX.

Any of the four networking components can be unloaded in the opposite order they were loaded by following their command with a *U*:

NETX U

IPXODI U

{LAN driver} U

LSL U

If problems persist, turn your attention to the NET.CFG file. Within that file, main headings must be left-justified, with other entries indented by a tab or space. Headings must precede each section and end with a carriage return, but case sensitivity does not apply. The following is an example of a NET.CFG file:

```
Link Driver NE2000
        INT 5
        PORT 340
        MEM D0000
        FRAME ETHERNET 802.2
NETWARE DOS REQUESTER
        FIRST NETWORK DRIVE=F
```

INT must match the IRQ set on the board, while PORT gives the I/O address. MEM shows the memory range used by the board, and FRAME is used with boards that support multiple types. Other entries that can be present, or needed, include the following:

■ **DMA.** Allows the DMA channels to be configured

■ **NODE ADDRESS.** Used to override hard coded board addresses

■ **SLOT.** Makes the driver see a specific board first

■ **PROTOCOL.** Signifies that existing LAN drivers can handle new protocols

Working with DOS Requester

The DOS Requester replaces NETX and all the variants that Novell traditionally shipped with successive versions of NetWare. Providing complete backward compatibility, it uses a modular approach to anticipate future enhancements.

Within DOS, the COMMAND.COM file serves as the shell. It accepts commands and determines whether the request can be handled internally, or if a search of the PATH statement directories is necessary to find an executable file to carry out the command. When NetWare is installed, the DOS Requester encompasses the DOS shell and intercepts commands before they get there. It then decides whether the command typed in is a NetWare command—in which case it directs it appropriately—or a DOS command—in which case it passes it through to the DOS shell for regular processing. Figure 35.3 symbolizes the relationship between these two shells.

The Requester actually is more than one entity; it is composed of a number of VLM files. Each VLM (Virtual Loadable Module) is a TSR program that can be loaded and unloaded by VLM.EXE as needed. These are stored, by default, in the NWCLIENT subdirectory on the workstation, and are loaded and unloaded by the manager (VLM.EXE). If the VLMs are in another directory, there must be a VLM= line in NET.CFG to point to the appropriate path.

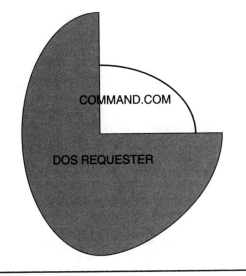

Figure 35.3
The relationship between the DOS Requester and the DOS shell.

Installing the DOS Requester

The steps to installing on a client machine are as follows:

1. Run INSTALL.EXE. This creates the NWCLIENT directories and copies in the VLMs.

2. Give the Windows path when prompted, if you are using Windows.

3. Give the configuration information when prompted—this is used to build the NET.CFG file.

The files you should see are shown in the following table.

VLM File	Function
AUTO.VLM	Automatic reconnect
BIND.VLM	Protocol bindery service
CONN.VLM	Connection table manager
FIO.VLM	File input\output
GENERAL.VLM	Miscellaneous NETX functions
IPXNCP.VLM	Transport protocol using IPX
NETX.VLM	Shell compatibility
NWP.VLM	Protocol multiplexer
PRINT.VLM	Print redirector
REDIR.VLM	DOS redirector
RSA.VLM	Encryption
TRAN.VLM	Transport protocol multiplexer

Working with Remote Boot

With diskless workstations, there is a read-only memory chip on the NIC. The code within that chip is executed on boot-up and is responsible for contacting the server and getting the necessary information to establish a communication link. Typically, the ROM size is 8 KB.

DOSGEN is the utility used to create the remote image the workstation communicates with on the server. Reasons for using diskless workstations include the following:

■ Cost

■ Convenience

- Security
- Speed

The created image appears to the workstation as a virtual drive, and the workstation functions as if there were a drive installed within it. To the workstation, the image is seen as a floppy from which it is booting, thus it needs files such as the following:

- CONFIG.SYS
- AUTOEXEC.BAT
- IPX
- NETX

It also needs the necessary command to get to the LOGIN routine (this can be within the AUTOEXEC.BAT file).

The file NET$DOS.SYS is created and placed in the working directory; it must be flagged as sharable to properly function.

 Note Remote booting DOS 5 requires RPLFIX run against the existing NET$DOS.SYS. The sole purpose of this utility is to change parameters since COMMAND.COM is larger in 5.0 than other DOS versions.

Troubleshooting with TRACK

TRACK is a console command used to diagnose router and server problems. It shows the network, server, and connection request information on a Router Tracking Screen. Information is depicted as it comes in and goes out. TRACK ON turns the monitor screen on, while TRACK OFF removes it.

The two requests to keep in mind are *Router Information Protocols* (RIP) and *Service Advertising Protocols* (SAP). RIPs are transmitted from routers to servers to advertise their presence, and SAPs are sent by print servers, gateways, and all servers to denote their presence.

A file server is seen by a workstation when it is "SAPing." Thus, the workstation knows it is there and attempts to connect to it—preferably the one within the nearest proximity. If a file server is not SAPing, there can be a problem with IPX not being bound to the card, or volumes not being mounted.

When a workstation shell loads, TRACK should report the following three things on the console if all is working as it should:

1. Get Nearest Server
2. Give Nearest Server *server_name*
3. Route Request

SLIST can be detrimental in isolating problems if a message of Unknown file server appears when the user tries to log in at the workstation.

Diagnosing Conflicts

Interrupt Request Channels (IRQ) conflicts can take a long time to diagnose. This is because the connection might work properly for a considerable amount of time, then die off at unexpected moments. IRQ conflicts do not happen until two devices attempt to access the same IRQ at the same time.

IRQs are directly tied to hardware components such as modems and printers. When a call is made to their device, the CPU puts other jobs on a wait status and processes the request made of that interrupt—in essence, they are interrupting other processing. A number of utilities can be used to diagnose IRQ problems, and Check It PRO is one worth noting. On DOS machines running version 6.*x*, MSD can offer similar information. The following listing depicts an example of an MSD report.

Normally, COM1 and COM3 use IRQ4, while COM2 and COM4 use IRQ3. It also is worth noting that early machines (XTs) have only eight interrupts, and newer ones have sixteen (numbered 0-15).

The I/O address gives the memory range reserved by the CPU. These are areas set aside specifically for each interrupt. If more than one device is using the same address, conflicts occur. The range of CA000 to DFFFF is safe for network adapter configurations.

Conflict Resolution

System configuration, once the domain of dip switches, now resides in CMOS memory. Usually, you can access CMOS during bootup by pressing a key sequence, which can be anything from the Esc key to Ctrl+Alt+Ins. The necessary key sequence is determined by the hardware manufacturer, and there is no standard throughout the industry.

The EISA Configuration Utility is a menu-driven approach to configuring EISA boards and solving conflicts. It reads the CFG file that comes with the board, and Verification Mode can be used to automatically check to see if conflicts can occur with other devices.

```
Microsoft Diagnostics version 2.01    1/24/95    7:44pm   Page  6
   ========================================================================


   ---------------------------- IRQ Status ----------------------------

   IRQ  Address   Description      Detected             Handled By
   --   --------  ---------------  ------------------   ----------------
    0   2AB6:0000 Timer Click      Yes                  win386.exe
    1   0A79:1923 Keyboard         Yes                  Block Device
    2   08B4:0057 Second 8259A     Yes                  Default Handlers
    3   08B4:006F COM2: COM4:      COM2:                Default Handlers
    4   0364:02C2 COM1: COM3:      COM1: Serial Mouse   MS$MOUSE
    5   08B4:009F LPT2:            Yes                  Default Handlers
    6   08B4:00B7 Floppy Disk      Yes                  Default Handlers
    7   0070:06F4 LPT1:            Yes                  System Area
    8   08B4:0052 Real-Time Clock  Yes                  Default Handlers
    9   F000:9C54 Redirected IRQ2  Yes                  BIOS
   10   166A:01D4 (Reserved)                            3C509
   11   08B4:00E7 (Reserved)                            Default Handlers
   12   08B4:00FF (Reserved)                            Default Handlers
   13   F000:9C45 Math Coprocessor Yes                  BIOS
   14   08B4:0117 Fixed Disk       Yes                  Default Handlers
   15   F000:FF53 (Reserved)                            BIOS
```

Working with PC Memory

The following list shows the memory detail displayed with DOS 6's MSD utility.

When the 8088 CPU was first designed, it divided the 1 MB address space into several areas, including 640 KB for application usage. To maintain compatibility, subsequent CPUs have kept the same scheme. Memory optimizers, such as MEMMAKER (MS DOS) and OPTIMIZE (QEMM), enable you to avoid manual memory tuning and automatically configure your system for optimal memory performance.

Real Mode is the term used to indicate the backward compatibility between subsequent models of CPU boards and the 8088. All x86 machines, when running in real mode, act as if they were running an 8086 chip.

Protected mode is the native mode for all CPUs from 80286 on up. Protected mode refers to the fact that memory is not used without first requesting it from the operating system.

```
------------------------- Memory -------------------------------

    Legend:  Available " "  RAM "##"  ROM "RR"  Possibly Available ".."
       EMS Page Frame "PP"  Used UMBs "UU"  Free UMBs "FF"
     1024K FC00 RRRRRRRRRRRRRRRR FFFF  Conventional Memory
          F800 RRRRRRRRRRRRRRRR FBFF                   Total: 640K
          F400 RRRRRRRRRRRRRRRR F7FF               Available: 442K
      960K F000 RRRRRRRRRRRRRRRR F3FF                         452976 bytes
          EC00                  EFFF
          E800                  EBFF  Extended Memory
          E400                  E7FF                   Total: 15104K
      896K E000                  E3FF
          DC00 PPPPPPPPPPPPPPPP DFFF  MS-DOS Upper Memory Blocks
          D800 PPPPPPPPPPPPPPPP DBFF              Total UMBs: 28K
          D400 PPPPPPPPPPPPPPPP D7FF         Total Free UMBs: 0K
      832K D000 PPPPPPPPPPPPPPPP D3FF       Largest Free Block: 0K
          CC00 UUUUUUUUUUUUUUUU CFFF
          C800 ...UUUUUUUUUUUUU CBFF  Expanded Memory (EMS)
          C400 RRRRRRRRRRRRRRRR C7FF             LIM Version: 4.00
      768K C000 RRRRRRRRRRRRRRRR C3FF     Page Frame Address: D000H
          BC00 ................ BFFF                   Total: 1024K
          B800 ................ BBFF               Available: 1024K
          B400 ................ B7FF
      704K B000 ................ B3FF  XMS Information
          AC00 ................ AFFF             XMS Version: 2.00
          A800 ................ ABFF          Driver Version: 2.05
          A400 ................ A7FF      A20 Address Line: Enabled
      640K A000 ................ A3FF       High Memory Area: In use
                                               Available: 1024K
                                     Largest Free Block: 1024K
```

Memory Types

Conventional memory, also known as base memory, is everything within the first 640 KB that is available to DOS applications. The following 384 KB is known as upper memory and is used by adapter cards, video, and serial ports. This completes the first 1 MB, or 1,024 KB of memory. Expanded memory is nothing more than pages of memory that can be swapped in and out of the upper memory space.

Extended memory comes next, and it is everything above the 1 MB space. High memory is a subset of extended memory and comprises the first 64 KB of extended memory. Within the range of 1,024 KB to 1,088 KB, it is available to DOS applications with an XMS memory manager.

Figure 35.4 illustrates this concept.

Loading LAN drivers into high memory can free up more of the lower 640 KB for applications. This is accomplished by placing lines in CONFIG.SYS similar to the following:

```
DEVICE=C:\DOS\HIMEM.SYS
DEVICE=C:\DOS\EMM386.SYS NOEMS
DOS=HIGH,UMB
```

This is followed up in the AUTOEXEC.BAT file with this:

```
LH LSL
LH 3C509 (or your card type)
LH IPXODI
LH NETX
```

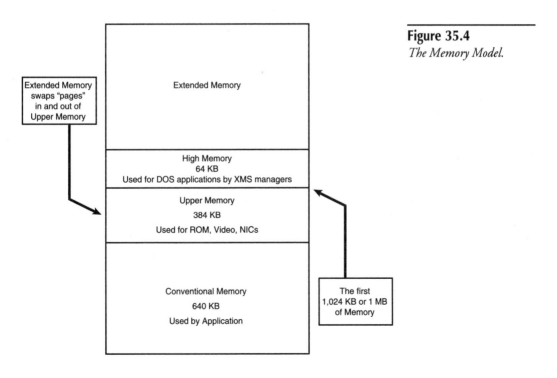

Figure 35.4
The Memory Model.

DR DOS

DR (Digital Research) DOS, from Novell, is a workstation operating system fully compatible with Microsoft's DOS. It features data compression, disk defragmentation utilities, a read/write cache, task switching, and enhanced memory management.

Enhancements have been made to the following external DOS commands:

- CHKDSK

- DISKCOPY

- HELP

- MEM

- REPLACE

- TREE

- UNDELETE

- XCOPY

Typing any command and following it with /H or /? displays all the options available. The following are additional features DR DOS offers over other products:

- DISKMAX is the set of compression utilities.

- DOSBOOK offers online documentation of the available commands.

- HIDOS.SYS is a driver for configuring memory on 80286 and earlier machines.

- HIDOS=ON, HIBUFFERS=xx are used in conjunction to move the operating system out of base memory.

- LOCK is used to lock the keyboard and keep anyone from using it without entering the password. This provides additional security at the workstation level.

- SETUP is a full screen menu used to configure any of the DOS features, including TASKMAX, MEMMAX, and DISKMAX.

- TASKMAX is the task switcher, enabling you to move between DOS programs in much the same manner as Windows does.

Questions

1. Which of the following is a connectionless protocol?

   ○ A. SPX

   ○ B. IPX

   ○ C. NCP

   ○ D. NetBios

2. The utility used to generate workstation files on the local drive is _____.

   ○ A. WSUPDATE

   ○ B. DOSGEN

   ○ C. IPXODI

   ○ D. WSGEN

3. Which THREE of the following are network communication protocols:

   ☐ A. TCP

   ☐ B. SPX

   ☐ C. NFS

   ☐ D. IPX

4. Unloading drivers is accomplished by _____ and _____.

   ☐ A. using the U option

   ☐ B. running the command a second time

   ☐ C. specifying the drivers in reverse order of their load

   ☐ D. using a memory management utility to remove the TSRs

5. Features of the DOS Requester do not include _____.

   ○ A. backward compatibility

   ○ B. modular design

   ○ C. architecture independent protocol support

   ○ D. the use of current technology

6. The Protocol Mulitplexer is loaded with which VLM?

   ○ A. NWP.VLM

   ○ B. MULTI.VLM

   ○ C. NDS.VLM

   ○ D. RSA.VLM

7. How many interrupts do XT machines have?

   ○ A. 2

   ○ B. 4

   ○ C. 8

   ○ D. 16

8. How many interrupts do current machines have?

   ○ A. 2

   ○ B. 4

   ○ C. 8

   ○ D. 16

Answers

1. B
2. D
3. A B D
4. A C
5. C
6. A
7. C
8. D

Troubleshooting Network Printing

Network printing is one of the most difficult processes to install and maintain. Because the process is so mechanical in nature, a series of problems can occur. When they do occur, the cause is not always visible. This chapter explores the issue from two sides:

- Preventing problems
- Troubleshooting

Before you consider taking the certification test, you should review the administrative topics pertinent to printing that are covered in the book's two administration course sections. The following topics are of particular interest:

- PCONSOLE
- PRINTCON
- PRINTDEF
- PSERVER
- RPRINTER

You should know how to create a print server and print queue; assign print servers to file servers; configure ports and printers; and manage queue and spool assignments.

Preventing Problems

Most of the steps used to prevent printer problems can be thought of as common sense precautions. They include cleaning paper and ribbon paths on a regular basis and vacuuming paper particles from inside the unit.

Temperature ranges and humidity should be kept as constant as possible, and there should be adequate space for ambient air to circulate around the printers. Laser printers should never be pointed directly at anyone, for the thermal radiation they give off can be harmful.

Troubleshooting

Printer problems can be broken into the following subcategories:

- Physical problems
- Print queues

- Print servers
- Remote printers
- Printer configuration
- Printer utilities
- PostScript printers

When diagnosing a problem, check the obvious components first. Make certain the electrical cord and printer cord are firmly attached and connected to the appropriate place. If there are any lights on the printer that indicate the power is on, check that they are lit. Also check to be sure that any switch boxes, electrical or A/B type, are working properly.

After you are convinced that the connections are functioning as they should be, turn the printer off and on again, and try sending your print job once more. If this attempt is unsuccessful, run a self-test on the printer and verify that it is working properly as a stand-alone. If it is, try printing to it again with a different application, such as a print screen, to see if the application is the culprit.

Physical Problems

Physical problems are the easiest problems to verify, and the first for which you should check. You should begin by checking the cables, as mentioned already. Next, make sure that the paper is not jammed, and that there is a ribbon or toner cartridge in working condition in the unit. If the ribbon is damaged or the toner cartridge is empty, replace the faulty component and try again.

 Parallel printing is four to six times faster than serial printing, and the faster the machine's CPU, the more obvious this becomes. Novell recommends that parallel printers be used as often as possible. The maximum standard cable length for parallel printers is 10 feet (150 by some manufacturers) compared to the standard of 50 for serial printers (500 by some manufacturers).

Parallel printers are, moreover, universally compatible, although serial printers are not. Only limited error checking is available on parallel printers; serial printers have parity checking, which slows printing speed by 10 percent.

Print Queues

The print queue's physical representation is the directory on the file server where the print jobs wait until they are printed by the print server. Problems can occur if you run out of hard drive space, or if the queue has become corrupted. You can monitor job entries with PCONSOLE to show their status.

 If problems occur when using NPRINT, check for older versions of IPX and update them.

One of the first things you should do when a user complains that a job won't print is use PCONSOLE to verify that the job is still in the queue. If it is not in the queue, the application might not be net-work-aware. Check to see that CAPTURE is active on the workstation before going further.

Print Servers

If the job is still in the queue, and all the physical checks appear correct, re-enable the server's capa-bility to service queues. Verify that the latest ver-sion of PSERVER.NLM is running; then, using PCONSOLE, take the print server down and bring it back up again.

 PSERVER needs 512 KB of memory. An additional 10 KB is needed for every extra printer added to the server.

When using PSERVER.EXE (as opposed to PSERVER.NLM), make sure that your SPX CON-NECTIONS are set to at least 60.

 NETERR.ZIP is a file of utilities useful for problem solving with print servers and a variety of other hardware devices. It is highly recommended that this file be downloaded from NOVLIB on NetWire or taken from NSEPro and extracted for use.

Remote Printers

Remote serial printers demand constant attention. If the error message Not Connected appears, RPRINTER has not yet been run to activate the defined printer.

If RPRINTER has been run, and there are still problems, the problems might be attributed to a lack of memory, older versions of the software, or an incompatible PC clone.

Many times, conflicts can occur between RPRINTER and the NIC card installed in the machine. If such is the case, change the interrupt setting on the card to solve the problem.

Routers between RPRINTER workstations and print servers can cause problems and cause the remote printer to periodically hang. If such is the case, increase the NET.CFG parameters for the following two fields:

- SPX ABORT TIMEOUT
- IPX RETRY COUNT

Printer Configuration

PRINTDEF and PRINTCON are utilities used to create printer and job definitions. It is imperative that the printer definitions be correct in order for the print jobs to function as efficiently and error-free as possible. Often, a slight problem in the configuration means that short jobs will print without any errors, but large graphics jobs will fail.

Printer Utilities

You can solve many printing problems by upgrading older printer utilities, such as PSERVER.EXE and others, to the newest ones available. The latest utilities can be found on NSEPro or on the NOVLIB forum of NetWire.

Incorrect buffer sizes can cause characters to get lost on a printout. If such is the case, use PCONSOLE to increase the buffer size.

You can use PRINTCON when files are printing with improper page breaks. Redefine the configuration and change the Timeout Count.

PostScript Printers

PostScript is a printer language created by Adobe that provides a method of interfacing with a printer to create high-end, high-quality graphics. A great many PostScript problems can be solved by updating application drivers to the latest available.

It is important to verify that any cartridges used on the printer to generate PostScript are properly inserted and seated. It is also highly recommended

that when printing in PostScript, you use the following settings:

- **/NB.** No banner
- **/NT.** No tabs
- **/NFF.** No form feed

Questions

1. The standard maximum length of a serial cable is _____.

   ○ A.　10 feet

   ○ B.　30 feet

   ○ C.　50 feet

   ○ D.　500 feet

2. The Print Server does which of the following THREE tasks?

   ☐ A.　Stores print jobs in the queue

   ☐ B.　Sends data to a remote printer

   ☐ C.　Accepts data from the queue

   ☐ D.　Polls the queue for print jobs

3. Parity checking is used with print jobs sent _____.

   ○ A.　to a remote printer

   ○ B.　to a serial printer

   ○ C.　to a parallel printer

   ○ D.　to any printer

4. When unloading PSERVER.NLM because of a problem, you should _____.

   ○ A.　reboot the print server

   ○ B.　unload the NLMs in an orderly manner

   ○ C.　use PRINTCON to stop incoming jobs

   ○ D.　laugh like a pirate

5. RPRINTER is _____.

   ○ A.　used to define remote print jobs

   ○ B.　the main utility for establishing network printing

   ○ C.　a loadable server module for remote printing

   ○ D.　a utility used at a workstation to activate remote printing

Answers

1. C

2. B C D

3. B

4. B

5. D

Network Optimization and Disaster Recovery

Let's think about the two most basic needs of network administrators—how to best utilize the software and hardware resources on hand, and how to best ensure that your precious data will be there when you need it. This section of the Service and Support test is arguably by far the most important aspect of administering any network.

The SET Parameter

NetWare is generally quite good at optimizing the SET parameters. You can degrade system performance drastically by altering memory SET parameters incorrectly. If the alterations are performed correctly, however, your system and peripherals will function optimally.

On the other hand, as with any popular network operating system, you must know how to change these parameters. With NetWare you can alter communications, memory, file caching, directory caching, file system, locks, transaction tracking, disk, and miscellaneous parameters by adding the necessary SET commands into the appropriate STARTUP.NCF or SYS:SYSTEM\AUTOEXEC.NCF files.

 Unless you have a full understanding of the ramifications involved in changing the various SET commands, do not change them. Although the system should remain intact after you make the changes, the potential exists for devastating results.

Communications Parameters

The following paragraphs give explanations for the parameters and their defaults and options.

Console Display Watchdog Logouts: OFF [ON, OFF]

If this parameter is set to ON, a message is displayed at the console when a connection is cleared.

New Packet Receive Buffer Wait Time: 0.1 Seconds [0.1 to 20]

This parameter determines how long the system will wait after receiving a request for another packet. If you have an EISA NIC in your server, you should not have to worry about your system granting too many receive buffers during high usage periods.

Maximum Physical Receive Packet Size: 1130 [618 to 4202]

As indicated by the name, this parameter establishes the maximum size of the packets that a system can receive. The parameter is configured in the STARTUP.NCF. The default is 1 KB (with packet header). If you have a NIC that can transmit packets larger than 512 bytes, you should increase this number to equal the largest packet size supported by your NIC.

Maximum Packet Receive Buffers: 100 [50 to 2000]

Use MONITOR to establish the number of service processes and packet receive buffers that your system is currently using. Increase the number in increments of 10 until you have 5 buffers per EISA or microchannel board, or until each workstation has 10.

Number of Watchdog Packets: 10 [5 to 100]

This value represents the number of watchdog packets that your server will send without receiving a reply before it disconnects the workstation.

Delay between Watchdog Packets: 59.3 Seconds [1 to 626.2]

Simply put, this is the amount of time that exists between sending the watchdog packets if the system receives no reply.

Delay before First Watchdog Packet: 240 Seconds [15.7 to 172.3]

This is the amount of time that a system will wait without receiving a request from a workstation before the system sends a watchdog packet to that workstation.

Memory Parameters

The following paragraphs give explanations for the parameters and their defaults and options.

Cache Buffer Size: 4096 Bytes [4096, 8192, or 16384]

If your block allocation size is smaller than 4096, increasing this value will diminish your system performance. If, however, your block allocation sizes are larger than 4096, system performance will increase if you increase this value.

Maximum Alloc Short-Term Memory: 2097152 [50000 to 16777216]

This critical memory pool stores drive mappings, loadable module tables, queued broadcast messages, open and locked files, service request buffers, and user connection information. The default 2 MB should be sufficient for 250 users with 26 drive mappings apiece.

Auto Register Memory above 16 Megabytes: ON [ON, OFF]

Care should be taken when altering this variable. If you install a NIC or disk controller that uses 24-bit address lines, only 16 MB of memory can be accessed properly. If your server can address more than 16 MB and you have installed one of the aforementioned EISA boards, only low memory will be addressed (in lieu of high), and the low memory that is being used by the NOS may become corrupted.

File Caching Parameters

The following paragraphs give explanations for the parameters and their defaults and options.

Maximum Concurrent Disk Cache Writes: 50 [10 to 100]

Increasing this variable increases the efficiency of write requests. Decreasing, on the other hand, increases read efficiency. If your dirty cache buffers rises above 70 percent of the total cache buffers, you should increase this number.

Dirty Disk Cache Delay Time: 3.3 Seconds [0.1 to 10]

This parameter sets the duration that your NOS will hold a write request before writing the data to the disk. This parameter is best left at the default.

Minimum File Cache Report Threshold: 20 [0 to 1000]

Your server will warn you when it has allocated some number greater than the minimum. Although changeable, this variable should be left at default in the vast majority of installations.

Minimum File Cache Buffers: 20 [20 to 1000]

As named, this variable sets the minimum number of file cache buffers that can be allocated at any given point in time. Increasing this number too high decreases resources available for other server processes.

Directory Caching Parameters

The following paragraphs give explanations for the parameters and their defaults and options.

Dirty Directory Cache Delay Time: 0.5 Seconds [0 to 10]

This parameter determines the amount of time that the system will wait until a directory table write request is written to disk. Increasing this parameter increases both system performance and the possibility of directory table corruption.

Maximum Concurrent Directory Cache Writes: 10 [5 to 50]

In a manner similar to the previous Maximum Concurrent Disk Cache Writes, when you increase this variable, you increase write efficiency at the cost of cache reads. The converse is also correct.

Directory Cache Allocation Wait Time: 2.2 Seconds [0.5 to 120]

How long will the operating system wait between allocating allocation buffers? Here is where this value is determined. If you notice that when you run DIR or NDIR the response time is lagging, try reducing this parameter.

Directory Cache Buffer Nonreferenced Delay: 5.5 Seconds [1 to 120]

Logically, some time must pass before your NOS can overwrite a nonreferenced directory entry with another. Increasing this value will increase allocated directory cache buffers and increase performance.

Maximum Directory Cache Buffers: 500 [20 to 4000]

This value is permanent until a server is rebooted and determines how large the directory cache is. Increase this number if directory searches are sluggish.

Minimum Directory Cache Buffers: 20 [10 to 2000]

This parameter is inverse parameter to the previous Maximum Directory Cache Buffers. For obvious reasons, don't set the Minimum Directory Cache Buffers greater than the Maximum Directory Cache Buffers.

File System Parameters

The following paragraphs give explanations for the parameters and their defaults and options.

Maximum Extended Attributes per File or Path: 32 [4 to 512]

This variable establishes the number of extended attributes that a file or path can have. This applies to all volumes on the server.

Immediate Purge of Deleted Files: OFF [ON, OFF]

If this self-explained variable is set to ON, no SALVAGE features will be able to recover deleted files. If set to OFF, deleted files are salvageable.

Maximum Subdirectory Tree Depth: 25 [10 to 100]

This variable determines how deep your deepest directory tree can be. Increasing this variable requires more system memory.

Volume Low Warn All Users: ON [ON, OFF]

If you value the data on your system and are not one to check your system variables regularly, you will want to leave this option ON so you are alerted if your drives approach full. If you change this option to OFF, you should run VOLINFO or CHKVOL daily.

Volume Low Warning Reset Threshold: 256 [0 to 100,000]

After you receive an initial warning that your volume is getting low (as set in Volume Low Warning Threshold), space is freed up by deleting files. Volume Low Warning Reset Threshold determines the amount of threshold space that must be exceeded for a second volume low warning.

Volume Low Warning Threshold: 256 [0 to 1,000,000]

Because this value is in blocks rather than bytes, you will first need to establish your system's block size (determined when you set up your volume during installation). If you want your system to warn you when your volume has only 5 MB left, you need to

divide your desired volume-free size by your block size to establish the number of blocks that will trigger the warning. If your volume block size is 4 KB, then you would select 1280 blocks to be warned at 5 MB.

Turbo FAT Re-Use Wait Time: 329.6 Seconds [0.3 to 1 Hour 5 Minutes 54.6 Seconds]

If a program randomly accesses a file containing greater than 64 FAT entries, a turbo FAT index is automatically built. These builds take time, so a re-build wait time is implemented so your NOS doesn't immediately rebuild the index every time a file is closed.

Minimum File Delete Wait Time: 65.9 Seconds [0 to 7 days]

This is an extremely valuable variable in environments where people delete files by accident. Since this situation could happen in just about every network in existence, increase this value if you have the resources. Realize, however, that this value is absolute, and that deleted files will not be purged until this time limit has been met (even if the volume is full and users are not able to create new files).

File Delete Wait Time: 329.6 Seconds [0 to 7 days]

Similar to the Minimum File Delete Wait Time, this value lets the system know when a deleted file may be marked as purgeable. Because NetWare tries to keep a minimum of $1/32$ of the total volume for new files, if your free space drops below $1/32$ and files are marked as purgeable, they will automatically be purged. At this point the file is history and can not be salvaged.

NCP File Commit: ON [ON, OFF]

Files can typically flush all pending file writes to disk.

Don't mess with this parameter unless you know what you are doing or a Novell representative instructs you to do so.

Maximum Percent of Volume Used by Directory: 13 [5 to 50]

How much of a volume may be used as directory space? This parameter provides the answer.

Maximum Percent of Volume Space Allowed for Extended Attributes: 10 [5 to 50]

This value is typically fine at the default setting, and is addressed only when the volume is being mounted.

Lock Parameters

The following paragraphs give explanations for the parameters and their defaults and options.

Maximum Record Locks per Connection: 500 [10 to 10,000]

A setting of 500 is usually more than sufficient in non-SQL environments (and even when you are in one). This parameter enables you to determine how many records each connection can establish. You might need to increase the value if you have a system-to-system *pipeline* in which multiple users will use one connection.

Maximum File Locks per Connection: 250 [10 to 1000]

If you have one connection that needs more than 250 files locked at one time, you have a unique environment! Suffice it to say that the default value should be fine.

Maximum Record Locks: 20,000 [100 to 200,000]

See the aforementioned Maximum Record Locks Per Connection, and take it to the server level. Changing this parameter is pretty straightforward.

Maximum File Locks: 10,000 [100 to 100,000]

This parameter enables you to set the number of files you can lock per connection.

Transaction Tracking Parameters

The following paragraphs give explanations for the parameters and their defaults and options.

Auto TTS Backout Flag: OFF [ON, OFF]

Although the default is OFF, if it is more important for your system to automatically boot after crashing, you might want to consider changing this value to ON. This enables your system to automatically back out of any incomplete transactions without asking you if it may do so.

TTS Abort Dump Flag: OFF [ON, OFF]

If you change the Auto TTS Backout Flag to ON, you will probably want to change this value to ON as well. If you do so, the system will create a log file that reflects what data has been backed out of the TTS.

Maximum Transactions: 10,000 [100 to 10,000]

Simply put, this parameter controls the number of transactions that can be performed at any given time on the system.

TTS Unwritten Cache Wait Time: 65.9 Seconds [11 to 659.1]

Certain transactional blocks are more courteous than others and for other blocks to be written to disk before they go. This value is the maximum time that any TTS block may wait in memory before being written to disk.

TTS Backout File Truncation Wait Time: 59 Minutes 19.2 Seconds [65.9 Seconds to 1 Day 2 Hours 21 Minutes 51.3 Seconds]

This parameter controls how long allocated blocks are available to the TTS backout file.

Miscellaneous Parameters

The following paragraphs give explanations for the parameters and their defaults and options.

Enable Disk Read After Write Verify: ON [ON, OFF]

If your media is "raided" or mirrored, then you may want to consider turning off this variable to increase performance. If not, or if you want to have a backup failsafe procedure in place, let your system verify that what it has just written to disk is the same as what was just in memory (default setting).

Maximum Outstanding NCP Searches: 51 [10 to 1000]

Normally your network will have only one NetWare Core Protocol directory search going on at any time. Ten searches are probably more than you will ever need, but if your network environment involves software that makes multiple NCP calls concurrently, you might need to increase this value. If your software needs this, it will let you know up front. Make any changes accordingly.

Allow Unencrypted Passwords: OFF [ON, OFF]

If you are running NetWare 3.0 or later, leave this OFF. Setting the variable to ON allows your passwords to be sent across your wire unencrypted.

New Service Process Wait Time: 2.2 Seconds [0.3 to 20]

This variable assigns how long the NOS waits after receiving a request for a new service before it actually allocates the new process.

Pseudo Preemption Time: 2000 [1000 to 10,000]

Certain types of software (NLMs) are CPU time-sensitive. Change this parameter only if your software suggests.

Display Spurious Interrupt Alerts: ON [ON, OFF]

This value should not be altered, because it reflects whether you have a hardware interrupt conflict in your file server. If this alarm is displayed at the system console, remove all unnecessary add-on boards and begin troubleshooting.

Display Lost Interrupt Alerts: ON [ON, OFF]

Again, this value should not be altered from the default value. An alarm will appear on the system console if a hardware interrupt call is made, but lost before the CPU can respond.

Display Disk Device Alerts: OFF [ON, OFF]

This is not a bad variable to change in any environment. Novell suggests turning this ON if you are experiencing hard drive problems.

Display Relinquish Control Alerts: OFF [ON, OFF]

This is a CPU watchdog control. If an NLM holds the CPU for more than 0.4 seconds, an alarm is displayed on the system console if this variable is turned ON.

Display Old API Names: OFF [ON, OFF]

This variable can be changed periodically to verify that new APIs are being used. Old APIs should still function, but they do so more slowly and should be updated.

Maximum Service Processes: 20 [5 to 40]

Increase this number only if you have sufficient resources (memory), and MONITOR reflects that you are using the number that is currently allocated.

Performance Modifications and Considerations

If your system requires that data be stored on the NetWare server in various file system formats, it is best that you do not mix file systems and name spaces on one volume. If you do require multiple name services on one volume, increase the Minimum Directory Cache Buffers setting, and the volume will mount more rapidly.

If you are going to implement more than one name space on a volume, install all name spaces on the volume when it is initially installed. If you are not able to do so and are adding a name space after your server has been running for some period of time, consider backing your system, re-installing the drive, adding all of the required name spaces, and then restoring the data. This will make efficient use of the Disk Directory Entry Table Blocks.

Monitoring with MONITOR

Whoever was on the development team of MONITOR.NLM is a friend to every network administrator. With MONITOR you have the ability to monitor various aspects of your network in real time, including various system utilizations, cache memory, network connections, drives, volumes, network drivers, modules, open file status, and memory usage.

When you invoke MONITOR.NLM, your initial screen will display information about the basic health of your system. Some information, such as file server up time, is nifty, but it is usually nothing more than a basis of bragging rights between network administrators. The remainder of the information is very pertinent indeed. The Utilization number reflects what percentage of your overall resources are being used. If this number is consistently over seventy, add memory and tune how these resources are being used. The Cache buffers numbers are also critical. If your Dirty Cache Buffers are close to or match your Total Cache Buffers, you have a bottleneck somewhere, and unless you find the source (that is, faulty cabling), your system will hang and need to be rebooted. Lastly, Current Disk Requests are transactions that are waiting for the disk to become available. Again, if your transactions get too stacked, your system will hang and need to be rebooted.

Connection Information

This section provides various information you need concerning connections.

List Active Connections

Displays connection time, network address, requests, kilobytes read, kilobytes written, semaphores, logical record locks, and open files for the user that is highlighted.

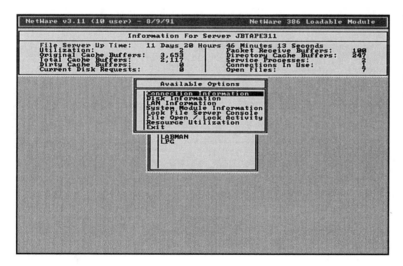

Figure 37.1

The MONITOR.NLM is an invaluable tool for anyone needing to tune a NetWare network.

List Physical Record Locks for a User

Show the beginning and ending offsets for locked files, how the record is locked, and the status of the file.

Clear a Connection

You can clear a connection using this section of the MONITOR program. Simply select the connection you want cleared, press Delete, and answer Yes when prompted to clear the connection. If you want to clear multiple connections, press F5 to select multiple connections before pressing the Delete key.

List Open Files

Lists the open files for the user that is highlighted. See figure 37.2.

Disk Information

This section discusses things you'll need to know about disks and other memory devices.

List System Hard Disks

This option enables you to view information about all system volumes. Select the desired drive from the drive list, and you will see a variety of information about the drive. Included is the driver for the disk, the disk size, partitions, mirror status, hot fix status, partition blocks, data blocks, redirection blocks, redirected blocks, and reserved blocks.

List Volume Segments per Hard Disk

This option displays basic information about a hard drive's volume segments.

Change the "Read After Write Verify" Status of the Hard Disk

Can change the read after write status between software level verify, hardware level verify, and disable verify events.

Flash the Hard Disk Light

Flashes the drive light.

Figure 37.2

The Connection Information screen.

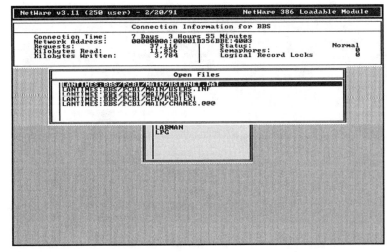

Activate/Deactivate a Hard Disk

Can switch a system drive between active and inactive.

Mount/Dismount a Removable Media Device

Makes it possible to mount and dismount devices such as magnetic optical or compact disk devices before they are removed. You can also view the status of the various removable devices from this utility (see fig. 37.3).

Lock/Unlock a Removable Media Device

It is good practice to lock a removable device prior to mounting it as a NetWare volume. This renders most eject buttons on removable media devices useless. Figure 37.3 shows the Drive Status screen.

LAN Information

This section covers information concerning details about local area networks.

LAN Drivers and Statistics

Displays information about the various network interface devices and connect points (see fig. 37.4). Included in the information is the driver name, version, node address, protocols, network address, total packets sent, total packets received, no ECB available count, send packet too big count, send packet too small count, receive packet overflow count, receive packet too big count, receive packet too small count, send packet miscellaneous errors, receive packet miscellaneous errors, send packet retry count, checksum errors, and hardware receive mismatch count.

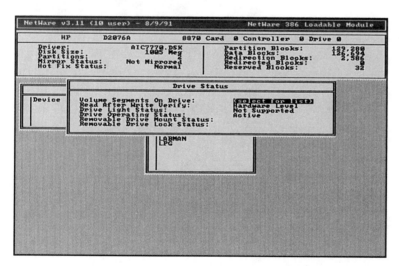

Figure 37.3

The Drive Status screen shows you pertinent information about your various hard drive media.

System Module Information

■ List system modules (see fig. 37.5)

■ List resources used by system modules

Lock File Server Console

■ Lock the file server console

■ Unlock the file server console

File Open/Lock Activity

■ Check the status of a file

■ View mounted volumes

Figure 37.6 shows the File Open/Lock Activity screen.

Figure 37.4

The LAN Information screen is your first reference point when using the MONITOR.NLM program.

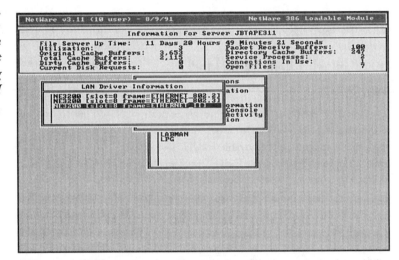

Figure 37.5

The System Modules screen affords you detailed information about your server status.

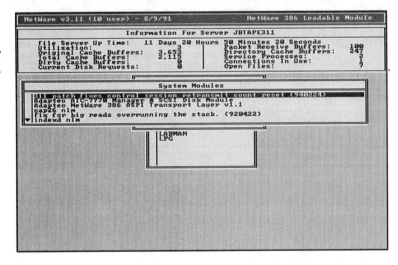

Resource Utilization

■ View memory statistics

■ View tracked resources

Figure 37.7 shows the Resource Utilization screen.

PATCHMAN

PATCHMAN is a utility available on NetWire and NSEPro that enables administrators to ensure that network modules are current and up to date. This is performed by means of the PATCHMAN.NLM that tracks and manages all official patches for

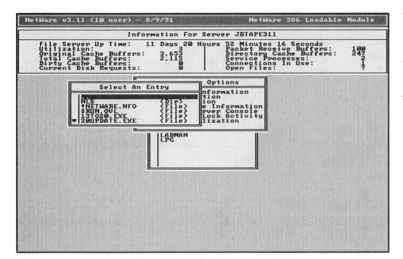

Figure 37.6

The File Open/Lock Activity screen lets you see at a glance what files a person presently has held open.

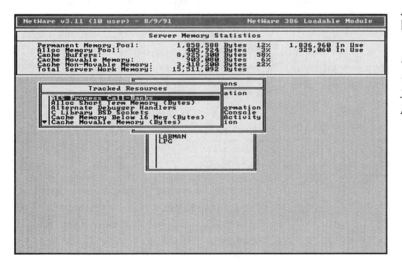

Figure 37.7

The Resource Utilization screen can give you detailed information about how your network resources are presently being used.

NetWare 3.11. The following list presents three basic types of patches for NetWare:

■ **Dynamic.** Patches that can be loaded and unloaded at will. They are called *dynamic* because the server need not be powered down to have the changes take effect.

■ **Semi-Static.** These semi-static patches can be loaded while the server is running (similar to dynamic patches), but cannot be unloaded unless you power down the server.

■ **Static.** A *static* patch literally alters the SERVER.EXE file. It is good practice to back up your original SERVER.EXE prior to implementing any static patches.

Following is the PATCHMAN, dynamic, and semi-static patch installation procedure:

1. PATCHMAN is installed by first running the self-extracting file UPD311.EXE. This uncrunches the PATCHMAN.NLM that needs to be placed into the SYS:\SYSTEM directory.

2. Rename any patches that are currently on the system so that any new patches that have the same name as the current will not overwrite the old (in case you want to return the system to the pre-patch state).

3. Copy the new patches into the SYS:\SYSTEM directory.

4. Put LOAD PATCHMAN into the same script that holds your other system boot loadable modules.

To modify your SERVER.EXE file using a static patch, do the following steps:

1. Back your existing SERVER.EXE somewhere safe.

2. Copy the static patches into the directory that holds your existing SERVER.EXE file.

3. Patch your SERVER.EXE by typing the patch name followed by SERVER.EXE.

In the same way that you type MODULES to display the modules that are currently running on your server, you can type PATCHES to display what patches are currently in place in your server's memory. The patches will be grouped with regard to whether they are dynamic, semi-dynamic, or static.

Bridges, Routers, and Hubs

If your channel utilization exceeds 60 to 70 percent, split the channel with the bridge or router. The answer to the question of how much data should flow locally versus over bridges and routers, 80 percent should be local with a maximum of 20 percent over the bridge or router.

Bridges and routers do not always play well together. Routers cannot properly route packages when bridges are involved, and there is a possibility of data getting "trapped" in a segment of the topology.

Remember that no more than four repeaters can be included in any local topology. This includes many hubs that amplify the incoming signal prior to shipping it back out.

Speed should always be an issue. Realize that since routers need to make decisions as to how to route the packet, they typically take substantially longer to receive the packet and then send it along its merry way.

Protocol Analyzers

There is nothing quite like having a good protocol analyzer on your side when troubleshooting a network wire problem. If you have ever spent hours trying to find out where the intermittent break or short in a 10BASE2 cable is, even on a relatively small network, you can appreciate why so many administrators have sent buckets of money in the direction of the Hair Club for Men.

Spend just one evening, weekend, or holiday searching for cable gremlins, and you know that you can put almost no dollar value on a device that not only tells you how far and in what direction a problem exists, but what the problem actually is!

Realize that many protocol analyzers perform such intricate tasks such as capturing the packets and disseminating the information for you to review, but for the CNE exam you only need to know how to start an analyzer, stop the capture, and what data will help you analyze your problem.

Novell uses LANalyzer for Windows as its example for the CNE exam. This product is commercially available and is simple to use. It is not the most extensive network-monitoring package on the market today, but with it you can monitor real-time activity, identify trends, create reports, and troubleshoot your system.

When you use LANalyzer for Windows, you can monitor real-time activity either graphically or in text form. The main graphical dashboard display shows you in real time the packets per second, utilization percentage, errors per second, and the size of your capture buffer for your network, server, or router. These easy-to-read dials move accordingly with the respective network/server/router activity.

Identifying trends is an important aspect of troubleshooting any network. If you have a network card that is going bad and is "chattering" on your network, you will notice a network speed degradation that could possibly bring that segment to a halt. LANalyzer for Windows has a variety of charts that enable you to track trends. For the chattering NIC, the station monitor display would probably be most useful. If you were monitoring the station monitor screen while a NIC was merrily sending garbage away, you would probably notice an inordinate amount of data being generated from one station. Couple this discovery with minimal to no activity on the other stations and an increase in the error count, and your first action might be to swap out the NIC in the suspect machine to see if this rectifies your problem. Realize that just because one workstation is much more active than the others does not necessarily mean that the NIC is faulty. You might just have one workstation that is more communication-intensive than the others.

If you decide to frequent your LANalyzer for Windows program, you will undoubtedly want to set some thresholds for alarms within the program. "Settable" parameters include packets per second, utilization percentage, broadcasts per second, fragments per second, CRC errors per second, and server overload per minute. These parameters are self-explanatory, but unless you intend to scrutinize every aspect of your LANalyzer program every time you turn it on, take a moment to set your defaults so that you are alerted to any potential network problems.

Third-Party Disaster Recovery Products

Nowadays, when everybody seems to be coming out with backup and restoral products, it is important to take a look at a product's certified compliance. In the NetWare realm of backup products, the most popular certified compliance is *Storage Management System* (SMS) compliance. This standard began years ago with Novell's SBACKUP, but Novell has since released the standard to a standards committee in hopes that SMS will become the industry standard.

Without a standard, the backup and restore industry was becoming segmented. Segmentation is not necessarily a bad thing in the free-enterprise system; in this case, however, the end-user was frequently the loser. Frequently network administrators purchased "whiz-bang" backup utilities only to realize the utilities' shortcomings after a year or two. Upon attempting to contact the vendor to inquire about an upgrade path, network administrators frequently discovered that, in the cut-throat tape backup industry, their vendors had either gone away or merged with other companies. Often the vendors changed their formats (which were frequently not readable by other backup products anyway), which meant that if an administrator decided to purchase and use a new version (or merged product), past backups were history.

It cannot be stressed enough how important system backups are. Here are a few guidelines to follow when handling your backup procedures:

1. If a backup product does not allow for you to verify-after-write, don't buy it. You should always have this feature turned on.

2. Test the data that you back up. Ideally, you should have a mirror server identical to your online server. You can test that your backed-up data is valid by restoring it to your mirrored server. Realistically, you will only have a small area into which you can restore a small portion of your backup to ensure that the backup was valid.

3. Take an electronic look at your backup to verify that the data that you want to be backed up actually is. With many products, there is a log file that displays the names of all of the files that are backed to tape.

4. Obvious but necessary—do not ever overwrite your most recent tape.

Novell suggests that you verify that your data is indeed corrupted prior to restoring your server from tape. There are a couple of tools that can assist you in performing these tasks. The first is INSTALL.NLM. If you are having problems with drives or data, INSTALL displays useful information about the status of your drive and volume.

VREPAIR.NLM can be an invaluable tool when dealing with a suspect drive or volume. As invaluable as it is, however, if your hardware is damaged, there is nothing that you can do about it with software.

Burst Mode Advantages and Drawbacks

Normally, when a workstation makes a request to a server, the server responds with an acknowledgement that it has received a request. On smaller networks this is of little concern, but as your network grows, every little bit of optimization helps to keep the users from complaining about how slow their system is running. By enabling packet burst mode, you can increase performance on a larger LAN or WAN by expanding the size of the packet to over 512 bytes, as well as by allowing more than one packet to be included to the server before an acknowledgement is sent.

Although it might sound like enabling packet burst mode is a feature that should be implemented from the get go, by doing so you increase the possibility of damaging packets because of the congestion that will result in having to resend. This is where the argument for virtual loadable modules rather than NETX comes into play. NETX (or NET4, NET5, NET6, and so forth) is quite literal and will take packet sizes and order as law. VLMs, on the other hand, are more intelligent than NETX, and can dynamically adjust the packet window on the fly for both performance and speed. Although NETX's packet burst increases performance by an average of 38 percent, the VLM version displays an efficiency increase of 82 percent. Learn your VLMs and you will be happy that you did.

Questions

1. SET parameters can be changed _____.

   ○ A.   in AUTOEXEC.NCF

   ○ B.   in STARTUP.NCF

   ○ C.   All of the Above

   ○ D.   None of the Above

2. SET can be used to alter parameters for all except _____.

   ○ A.   file caching

   ○ B.   communications

   ○ C.   palette colors

   ○ D.   memory

3. Dirty Directory Cache Delay Time is used to determine the amount of time _____.

   ○ A.   the system will wait until a directory table write request is written to disk

   ○ B.   directory contents are stored in read-ahead buffers

   ○ C.   the system will hold corrupted (dirty) data before discarding it

   ○ D.   a user must wait before a response is given to their DIR request

4. By default, NetWare 3.0 and later use encrypted passwords.

   ○ A.   True

   ○ B.   False

Answers

1.   C

2.   C

3.   A

4.   A

NetWare 3.1x Installation

38   *Preparing for a NetWare Installation* *561*

39   *Installation and Configuration* *567*

40   *Migrating a 3.11 Server to a 3.12 Server* *583*

41   *Installing Client Software* *593*

42   *Tuning for Performance* *607*

Preparing for a NetWare
Installation

This section of the book is designed to provide you with the knowledge and skills necessary to complete the NetWare 3.1x Installation and Configuration Workshop portion of Novell's CNE program. It is intended for experienced network administrators who have a basic understanding of general NetWare principles and procedures. In this section, you learn how to plan a NetWare 3.1x installation, as well as perform all necessary installation steps.

This section does NOT discuss the administrative commands and utilities such as SYSCON. As a CNE candidate, you do need to have a thorough knowledge of these utilities and commands; this chapter focuses on the installation of NetWare. The administrative commands are thoroughly documented in the administrative sections of this book.

This section should help you accomplish the following objectives:

■ Understand the terms used for NetWare 3.1*x* operating system installation

■ Demonstrate the ability to find third-party software drivers required for NetWare 3.1*x* operating systems installation

■ Identify the software needed to install NetWare 3.1*x* operating systems

■ Describe the hardware needed to install NetWare 3.1*x* operating systems

■ Describe the various methods available for installing NetWare 3.1*x*

Terms and Files

Novell's operating systems for NetWare 3.1*x* and above have the distinguishing factor of being able to be dynamically configured. In earlier NetWare versions and with other network operating systems, object modules selected during installation have to be "bound" together to form the operating system. This procedure is known as *static linking*, or *generating*. Through static linking, the operating system is configured to operate with a particular hardware configuration. In NetWare 3.1*x*, however, the ability to dynamically link operating system modules enables the module to be added to the operating system as it is loaded into memory—on-the-fly.

The reverse is also true—that is, modules can be unloaded and thus dynamically removed from the operating system. These software modules are referred to as *NetWare Loadable Modules* (NLMs)—a group of cooperating software tasks or engines that enable NetWare to be dynamically configured to operate with almost any hardware configuration.

 NetWare's dynamic linking is similar to the *Dynamic Link Libraries* (DLLs) found in Windows and OS/2. The difference between NetWare's NLMs and other forms of Dynamic linking is NetWare NLMs are linked at load time, rather than at execution.

NLMs are activated from the server's console with NetWare's LOAD command, as in the following line:

```
LOAD MONITOR
```

NLMs are deactivated by simply unloading the NLM. You can unload an NLM by using NetWare's UNLOAD command, as follows:

```
UNLOAD MONITOR
```

NLMs can be loaded or unloaded whenever the network administrator desires.

The flexibility of NLMs enables third-party hardware and software providers to take advantage of being a part of the operating system. Certain NLMs, such as network card drivers and disk controller drivers, can be added to the operating system at any time. These specialty NLMs can also be designed to accept command-line parameters, which enable the driver behavior to be modified, as in the following line:

```
LOAD NE2000 port=300 int=3
➥frame=Ethernet_802.2 Net=38823
```

In this situation, the command-line parameters enable the NetWare administrator to load the driver at the correct port, interrupt, frame type, and network segment.

 NLMs written specifically for a network card will have a file extension of LAN. NLMs written for a disk driver will have a file extension of DSK.

NetWare has the capability to be dynamically configured because it is based on a software bus-like architecture. This *bus* allows services to be loaded or attached to the operating system so that it can communicate with the device that is providing the service. The server cannot communicate with the hard disk without first loading the disk driver (*.DSK), for example, nor can it communicate with the network board without first loading the appropriate LAN driver (*.LAN). Likewise, other services can be loaded into the software bus, as shown in figure 38.1.

Because of NetWare's dynamic configuration properties, there are a lot of installation parameters that are not automatically set during installation. For this reason, you must be aware of the correct configuration information, especially for the network card and disk driver. If these settings are not correct, NetWare will not properly function.

Finding Third-Party Drivers and NLMs

Knowing you have the correct drivers for your particular hardware is crucial to a successful NetWare installation. Thus, you will need to know where you can find the drivers for the LAN card, as well as the driver for the disk controller.

NetWare ships with several different LAN and DSK drivers. The third-party drivers that ship with NetWare can be found in the System directory of the System-2 and System-3 floppy disks. After NetWare is installed, all of the third-party NLMs are located in the System directory on the SYS volume.

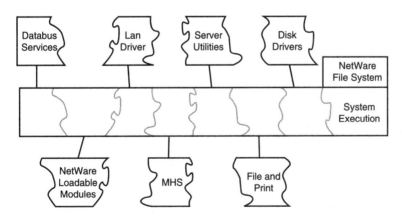

Figure 38.1
NetWares Dynamically configurable bus-like architecure.

If you are installing NetWare 3.12 from CD-ROM, the disk and network card drivers can be found in either of the following directories:

```
Disk drivers <CD-ROM drive letter>
➥\NetWare.312_____\diskdrv

LAN drivers <CD-ROM drive letter>
➥\NetWare.312_____\landrv
```

Most vendors ship NetWare drivers with their cards. Never assume that the drivers with the card or the drivers that come with NetWare are the latest version, however. The only way to be absolutely sure which driver is the latest is to contact your hardware manufacturer.

Contacting the manufacturer does not necessarily mean via phone. Most manufacturers have bulletin boards, forums on a public network such as CompuServe, or even fax-back services. Most of these services will inform you of the latest driver release dates.

Required Software

Besides having all of the necessary hardware drivers (disk driver and LAN driver), you will also need a copy of NetWare and a copy of DOS version 3.3 or later.

DOS is required because NetWare first needs to boot to DOS. After booting to DOS, you will be able to store the NetWare boot files, such as SERVER.EXE, on the DOS device. SERVER.EXE is the primary NetWare operating system file and makes the machine a NetWare 3.1*x* file server.

 Note During the initial server installation, you need to copy the SERVER.EXE file to the hard drive. Doing this enables you to load the file from the hard drive, instead of from a floppy.

With NetWare 3.12, the SERVER.EXE file, along with all the other necessary boot files, is copied to the SERVER.312 directory on the DOS partition of the hard drive. With 3.11, however, it is left up to you to copy the SERVER.EXE and other boot files to the hard drive.

After SERVER.EXE is executed, it loads the NetWare file system and takes over the operation of the computer. Because NetWare does not use the services of any other operating system (including DOS), it is important to verify that no memory managers or other device drivers are loaded prior to executing NetWare.

Required Hardware

As client software becomes increasingly resource intensive, the lines between client and server hardware continue to gray; it is the function of the machine that determines if it is a client or a server, not the hardware configuration. However, it is common for the file server to have more memory, disk space, and other enhancements than a workstation. Again, the differentiation comes when NetWare is loaded because once it is loaded it will provide services to all the network users, manage the file system, provide security, and control communication services for clients and other devices.

Even though a server uses many of the same hardware components as a PC or a client workstation, there are some minimal server hardware requirements that must be met before you can install NetWare 3.12. They are as follows:

- 386 or better Intel-based processor

- Minimum of 6 MB of memory

- Network card with LAN driver

18

- A hard disk with at least 10 MB of free space

- Disk controller with disk driver

- Floppy drive

- (Optimal) CD-ROM drive

NetWare is a multitasking operating system, and therefore requires at least a 386-based processor. Each server must also contain at least 6 MB of memory, although 8 MB or more is recommended. Actually, the amount of RAM your server needs for its optimal operation depends on the overall hardware configuration—the more disk space you have, the more memory you need.

A NetWare 3.1*x* server must have a bare minimum of 10 MB of free disk space. Again, this is the bare minimum, which will only enable you to load the NetWare files.

When preparing for your NetWare installation, you will need to know your disk channel configuration as well as your disk space requirements. This knowledge will help you in planning for future disk expansion, and in determining the appropriate initial server configuration.

For example, if you do not plan to grow, you might be able to get along with a single, internal drive. If growth is probable, you might want to consider using an internal drive for your boot partition, and use external drives as your main storage area. This concept can be seen in figure 38.2.

As you plan your disk configuration you will also want to keep in mind NetWare's hot fix area. This is an area of the drive that is reserved for storing data in the event a drive encounters any bad blocks (areas of the drive not stable enough to accept data). To prevent data loss, NetWare automatically redirects data to the reserved section or hot fix area of the drive. By default, approximately two percent of the drive is reserved for the hot fix area.

Figure 38.2

NetWare supports internal as well as external drives.

Questions

1. What group of software components is required before installing NetWare?

   ○ A. Third-party drivers (LAN and disk channel), NetWare, and DOS

   ○ B. DOS, OS/II, and Windows NT

   ○ C. NetWare loadable moudles, disk drivers, and LAN drivers

   ○ D. DOS, STARTUP.NCF file, and NetWare

2. An NLM is loaded from which of the following?

   ○ A. Workstation

   ○ B. Windows System Directory

   ○ C. DOS prompt

   ○ D. NetWare Console

3. What extension is found on a NetWare NLM that provides the interface between a disk controller card and the NetWare operating system?

   ○ A. NCF

   ○ B. DSK

   ○ C. NLM

   ○ D. LAN

4. What extension is found on a NetWare NLM that provides the interface between a network card and the NetWare operating system?

   ○ A. NCF

   ○ B. DSK

   ○ C. NLM

   ○ D. LAN

5. What is the minimal amount of memory required to load NetWare 3.12?

   ○ A. 10 MB

   ○ B. 6 MB

   ○ C. 4 MB

   ○ D. 12 MB

Answers

1. A

2. D

3. B

4. D

5. B

Installation and Configuration

*his chapter offers two methods of installation. First, it
provides a quick guide, or list of steps, that must be
performed during the installation process. It then
provides a more detailed version, discussing in depth—
and illustrating—several of the NetWare 3.12 installation steps.*

*After reading this chapter, you should be able to list, in
order, all the steps required for installing NetWare. You
should also understand why each step is necessary.*

The following lists the steps required to install a NetWare 3.1*x* file server. Each step is necessary and must be completed in the proper order.

1. Partition the hard disk for DOS.

2. Format the hard disk with DOS.

3. Load and boot to DOS.

4. Load INSTALL.BAT.

5. Enter a server name.

6. Assign a unique internal IPX number.

7. Enter the source and destination paths.

8. Select the locale configuration settings.

9. Select the file format.

10. Specify any special startup set commands.

11. Elect to have the AUTOEXEC.BAT file load SERVER.EXE.

After you have completed the steps listed above, you will also need to complete the following:

1. Load the HBA driver.

2. Load INSTALL.NLM.

3. Create a NetWare partition.

4. Create a NetWare volume.

5. Mount volume SYS.

6. Copy public and system files to the file server.

7. Load the LAN driver.

8. Create   AUTOEXEC.NCF   and STARTUP.NCF files.

 Note Performing each step in order is not absolutely necessary, but following this sequence ensures that nothing is forgotten.

If you are not familiar with all of the above steps, read on. The following section discusses each of the individual installation steps.

Performing a NetWare 3.12 Installation

This section discusses all the steps required to install a NetWare file server successfully.

Partitioning the Hard Disk for DOS

When a NetWare server boots, it must first load DOS, which means a server has to boot either from a floppy drive or from a small DOS partition located on the active, primary partition of the hard drive.

There are several advantages to creating a DOS partition over booting from a floppy drive. The most obvious advantage is simply speed. Other advantages include: a place to store necessary startup files, convenience, security, and so forth.

Older *Host Bus Adapters* (HBAs) known as *Disk Controller Boards* (DCBs) do not support the use of a DOS partition.

Formatting the Hard Disk with DOS

The NetWare installation utility requires a DOS partition on your hard disk in order to install the NetWare operating system. NetWare's installation utility creates a DOS partition using Novell DOS. If you do not want NetWare's installation to create this partition for you, exit and manually create the partition using DOS's FDISK and FORMAT commands.

By default, most setup routines use the entire drive for DOS, leaving no room for NetWare. When the DOS installation routine asks if you want to use the entire drive for DOS, answer No. A 10 or 20 MB DOS partition should suffice.

 Note NetWare's installation routine requires a DOS partition; however, the NetWare operating system does not. If you do not want a DOS partition on your server's hard drive, you will have to install NetWare manually.

Creating the DOS partition to store NetWare files is no different for a server than it is for a typical PC.

Most versions of DOS provide an automatic installation routine or setup program. These installation aids automatically partition the drive, assign the first partition on the drive as the active partition, format the drive, and install DOS on the active partition.

 Note To boot from the partition, the partition must be a primary DOS partition and be designated as the active partition. Most DOS setup routines automatically create a partition and set it active. If you are using a SCSI controller, however, you often have to set the partition active manually.

You can also let NetWare's installation routine guide you through the creation of the DOS partition. This process uses Novell DOS's FDISK command to create the primary boot partition. After creating the partition, you will have to reboot the server and reload the INSTALL.BAT file.

After restarting the INSTALL.BAT file, the installation routine recognizes that a partition now exists, but that the partition has not yet been formatted. It prompts for your permission to format the new partition.

Creating a partition and formatting the drive deletes all the information on the drive.

 Note After formatting the partition, the server must once again be rebooted. Your server should now have a DOS partition and be freshly booted. Start the INSTALL.BAT file again. After starting the installation routine, the Disk Partition Options screen reflecting the newly created and formatted DOS partition will appear.

NetWare's installation routine, as mentioned previously, formats the server so it can be booted. This formatting requires that the DOS system files be transferred to the computers boot sector. It also means that the COMMAND.COM file needs to be located on the hard drive. It does not, however, mean that a complete copy of DOS will be installed on the server boot partition.

NetWare does not require any of the DOS files; however, some of the DOS files, especially utility type files that are used for maintenance, such as EDIT, XCOPY, DELTREE, and so on, are very handy to have on the partition. If you do not mind using the disk space, you might want to go ahead and install a complete copy of DOS onto the boot partition. You need to be sure, though, that none of the DOS memory managers are loaded.

 Note If you are installing 3.11, you will want to manually copy supporting startup files—such as VREPAIR.NLM, a volume repair utility necessary if the NetWare partition is inaccessible—to the DOS partition of the hard drive. You also should keep your LAN drives on the DOS partition.

Entering a Server Name

After loading INSTALL.BAT, you are prompted to enter a server name which can be 2 to 47 characters long. It should be used to bring meaning to the server, yet be as short as possible. Give the server a name that indicates its primary function or who is using it. This scheme is easier for users to remember, and the shorter the server name, the easier it is to type. Also, the name must be unique from any other servers on the network.

 The server name can be any length of characters from 2 to 47 long. It can contain any alphanumeric character (letters A–Z, numbers 0–9). It can even contain some special characters such as a hyphen or an underscore; it cannot, however, contain spaces or periods.

Assigning a Unique Internal IPX Number

After entering a server name, you assign an internal IPX number, which is an internal two to eight-digit hexadecimal number (using numbers 0 through 9 and letters A through F). The Internal IPX number is a "logical" network number used by NetWare to identify each server on the network. Because it is used as a unique identifier, you must ensure that no two servers have duplicate IPX numbers. The uniqueness of the internal IPX number is very important—so important that large sites will devise a scheme of assigning internal IPX numbers in an attempt to guard against accidental duplications.

The NetWare 3.12 installation routine creates a NETWARE.312 directory on the DOS partition of the hard drive. After you assign a unique name and Internal IPX number to the server, the routine transfers all the necessary startup files from the source (CD-ROM, floppy disks, or another server) to the target directory on the server's boot drive.

The transferred files include SERVER.EXE, VREPAIR.EXE, disk drivers, LAN drivers, and other necessary startup files.

A bar graph shows the progress of the file copy. If you are installing from floppy disks, you are prompted to change disks during the copy procedure.

Entering Local Support Codes

NetWare supports several different languages (French, English, German, Spanish, and so on). To ensure that the correct message files are displayed, the installation routine prompts you to enter the correct Country Code, Code Page, and keyboard mapping.

Selecting the File Name Format

NetWare shells prior to NetWare 3.12's Requester technology supported file names that included extended characters and lowercase letters. To continue this support, you must use the shells (NETX.EXE) rather than the requesters (VLM.EXE). To avoid confusion and problems, you should simply select the DOS file format, which maps lowercase characters to uppercase file names.

After choosing your local settings, the installation prompts you for any special commands that you would like to have stored in the STARTUP.NCF or AUTOEXEC.NCF files, which are much like batch files in DOS; that is, they store a list or *batch* of commands that are automatically execute when the file is launched. Furthermore, these files are much like the CONFIG.SYS and AUTOEXEC.BAT files in that they are automatically executed when the server is started.

Additions to these files can be made at anytime using INSTALL.NLM.

Like with DOS batch files, you can also create a file with an NCF extension and have the file process the commands when the file is processed. If, for example, you want to load MONITOR, INSTALL, RCONSOLE, and so forth, you could store the load commands in an NCF file called START.NCF. Typing **START** at the file server's console would then launch the batch of commands.

After you have entered any special startup commands, the install utility automatically loads SERVER.EXE. Once SERVER.EXE is loaded, DOS commands will no longer function. NetWare is now loaded, and the install utility returns you to a colon prompt, which is known as the *NetWare console* prompt.

Loading the Disk Driver

The disk drivers provide the communication interface between the controller, the drive, and NetWare. In addition to loading the driver, you need to provide the disk controller settings. These settings usually include the appropriate interrupt (INT) and I/O address.

If you are using an EISA machine, enter the slot where the controller is located.

If you are using an ISA-based machine, enter the correct interrupt and I/O address.

Although NetWare ships with several SCSI disk controller drivers, it is good practice to use the very latest driver. This driver will usually whip the SCSI controller; however, you should check with the controller's manufacturer to verify that you have the most current driver.

If you are using an MFM controller and hard disk combination, use the drivers (ISADISK.DSK) that ship with NetWare.

If you are using an IDE disk controller, use the IDE.DSK file that ships with NetWare, or, if the manufacturer of the IDE controller ships a NetWare drive, use it.

After the disk drivers are loaded, NetWare can access the hard drives, which enables you to define NetWare disk partitions.

Loading INSTALL.NLM

INSTALL.NLM is the Install utility that creates NetWare disk partitions and volumes. INSTALL.NLM is loaded at the server console by typing:

LOAD INSTALL

The INSTALL utility is used for the initial installation of NetWare, plus much more. It manages disk drives, performing such tasks as formatting, partitioning, mirroring, and surface testing. INSTALL provides information concerning your NetWare volumes, such as volume name, block size, and disk size. It indicates whether or not a particular volume is mounted. Moreover, it is the easiest place in NetWare to create, edit, and save crucial startup files, such as the AUTOEXEC.NCF and STARTUP.NCF files.

Creating a NetWare Partition

With the Install utility, you can divide the drive into logical sections called partitions. A NetWare *partition* consists of a data area, which should be the largest portion of the drive, and a hot fix redirect area, which should be about two percent of the drive.

To partition a server's drive, select Create NetWare Partition from the partition table menu. After indicating a partition size for NetWare, press Enter. A partition verification screen appears, where you can complete the following tasks:

- Change hot fix

- Create a NetWare partition

- Delete any partition

After selecting the Partition Tables option, a partition options menu appears. If your drive does not contain any partitions, the Partition Type area of the box indicates that the drive has free space, or contains no partitions. If your drive is partitioned, the Partition Type indicator specifies the type of partitions installed on the drive, as seen in figure 39.1.

Creating a partition in NetWare is similar to performing a low level format and running FDISK on a DOS drive. You can only have one NetWare partition on a drive. Likewise, every drive in the server, if it is to be accessed by NetWare, has to have a NetWare partition.

Creating a NetWare Volume

After creating a partition, you must create a NetWare volume. Creating a NetWare volume is like formatting a DOS drive, in that it allows NetWare to store files on the drive's surface. With NetWare you can have more than one volume on a single drive. You can also have a single volume span multiple drives.

To create a NetWare volume, select Volume Options from INSTALL's main menu. These options enable you to create, delete, rename, or expand a volume. If your server currently has volumes created, selecting this menu item initiates a list of those volumes. To view the configuration or to modify a volume, highlight the volume and press Enter.

To create the very first NetWare volume on your server, press Insert, and the screen in figure 39.2 appears.

The first volume on your NetWare server must be named SYS. Consequently, when you create the first volume, the Volume Name box is automatically filled in with "SYS." You can, however, change the first volume's (SYS) block size and volume size.

Figure 39.1
NetWare's partition creation screen.

Figure 39.2
NetWare 3.12's create volume screen.

If the volume you want to create is not the first on the server, enter its name and press Enter. Press Esc and type **Y** at the Create Volume prompt, then specify the block size and volume size.

In the volume information screen, you have the option of changing the block size of the volume. The smaller the block size, the more memory your server needs. The larger the block size, the more sequential the storage and the better the data retrieval time; the drive, however, holds less data (that is, if the volume block size is set to 64 KB, then a 2 KB file consumes an entire 64 KB block).

Mount Volume SYS

After creating the volumes, you are ready to mount them. Mounting a volume enables you to copy the necessary NetWare files onto the drive.

You can mount a volume using INSTALL.NLM's Volume Options, or you can press Alt+Esc, switching from the INSTALL utility back to the server's console prompt. At the console, type the following:

MOUNT SYS

After pressing Enter, a message appears indicating that the volume is in the process of mounting.

Copying Public and System Files

Before continuing you should have first completed the following tasks: loaded SERVER.EXE, assigned a name and IPX number to the server, loaded INSTALL, defined a NetWare partition, created a volume SYS, and mounted volume SYS. After performing these initial installation steps, you are ready to install the NetWare files to the file server.

From Install's main menu, select System Options, as seen in figure 39.3.

 Remember the SYS volume must be mounted before the operations in this menu selection can be used.

If the volume is not mounted and one of these items is selected, a dialog box appears asking if you would like to mount volume SYS. To mount the volume, simply select the YES option.

Selecting System options provides access to the operations.

Figure 39.3

The System Files option of Install's main menu.

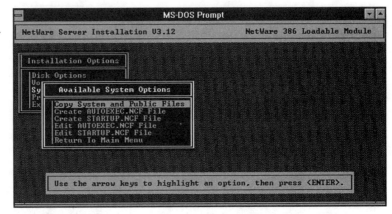

To install NetWare's operating system files and utility files, select Copy System and Public Files. You are then given the option either to insert the NetWare disks in the A drive, or to press F6 to change the location of the source drive.

 In NetWare 3.11 you have to load INSTALL with a /J parameter to be able to change the location of the source drive.

With either version, the source drive does not necessarily have to be a floppy drive; it can be a CD-ROM, a NetWare mapped drive, or even a DOS partition on the same drive.

Loading the LAN Driver

Much like disk drivers, LAN card drivers are an integral part of the network installation. They enable the server to communicate with other network stations (workstations and servers). NetWare 4 ships with several LAN drivers; but they, like disk drivers, are the responsibility of the card manufacturer. Again, contact the manufacturer to obtain the most current drivers.

Before installing a network card driver, you need to perform the following tasks:

- Select the correct interrupt
- Verify the I/O port and memory addresses
- Choose your network's frame type
- Bind the LAN driver to a network address

An IRQ is an Interrupt Request Line that enables the computer to interrupt whatever the processor is doing so some other "important" job can be completed, such as receiving a packet coming across the Ethernet card.

Unfortunately, confusion explodes when more than one device is using the same interrupt (IRQ); even more unfortunate is the difficulty of determining what devices are using what interrupts. The scarcity of interrupts and the confusion caused by not understanding which device uses which interrupt, makes resolving interrupt conflicts one of the most difficult network workstation problems.

If, for example, the addition of a sound card or modem to a network workstation—a workstation that has been functioning properly—causes problems, most likely you have placed a new device at the same interrupt as an existing device.

Each card in the computer's bus must use a different IRQ setting, including the Ethernet, Token Ring, or ARCNET card that hooks your computer to the network cable.

If two cards, or devices, are using the same IRQ setting, a conflict occurs: either the machine hangs up or one of the cards is completely ignored. The best way to determine the current setting is to use a software diagnostic utility or consult your PC documentation.

An Ethernet or other network board driver could load when the wrong interrupt is specified, causing a tremendous amount of confusion. The entire installation might appear to have gone smoothly, yet no stations are able to connect to the server.

After the actual loading of the LAN driver, you need to specify the frame type(s) your network is currently running. You also need to bind the driver to a specific network address.

You should have already loaded the LAN card, selected an interrupt, selected an I/O port, and chosen a memory address. After completing these steps, continue loading the network card driver by performing the following steps:

■ At the server's console, type **BIND** *IPX* **to** *NE2000. IPX* is the protocol you are using, and *NE2000* is the name of the driver you previously loaded.

■ Enter the appropriate network address.

The BIND command is one of the final steps in the LAN driver loading process. It's the step that links the LAN driver to a communication protocol and to a specific network board in the NetWare server. Unless you link a communication protocol to the board, the board cannot process packets.

NetWare 3.1*x* allows protocols other than IPX to function on the network. The following steps use

IPX as an example protocol to bind each LAN driver to the file server.

To bind IPX to each LAN driver, type the following:

```
BIND IPX to LAN_driver
```

 It is only necessary to use the BIND command the first time you load a LAN driver, or if you have not previously saved the BIND command in the AUTOEXEC.NCF file. If you let the INSTALL utility create an AUTOEXEC.NCF file for you, the BIND command and the correct parameters are added to the AUTOEXEC.NCF file, and thus, loaded each time the server is brought up.

This binds only to IPX. For other protocols, you must edit the AUTOEXEC.NCF file, or manually enter additional bind commands.

It is also important to note that you can link more than one frame type to the same network board. If you want an Ethernet card to run both 802.2 and 802.3 frame types, for example, simply load the network card driver again. You are then given the following message:

```
Do you want to add another frame type for a
previously loaded board?
```

If you do, press **Y**.

NetWare displays a message (see fig. 39.5) indicating all available frame types for that particular network board (ones that are not currently loaded) (see fig. 39.4).

To load an additional frame type, enter the number to the left of the listed frame type.

Each LAN driver must be assigned the correct network address; that is, it must be assigned the network address that correctly identifies the cabling system on which it resides. In other words, the same network address must be assigned to all the network cars needed to communicate with similar LAN drivers on the network.

If this is the first server on the network, any random network address will work.

If this is not the first server on the network, you need to know the correct network address of the LAN segment to which the server is attached, as executed in the following command:

```
BIND IPX to LAN_driver NET=A
```

 The network address is not the same as the internal IPX network number that you assigned to the file server.

If you are using multiple frame types on a single LAN, you must assign a different network address for each of the loaded and bound frame types on any given segment or card.

The network address is an eight-digit hexadecimal number that uniquely identifies a server's network boards and cable segments. A network address identifies a network cabling scheme, much like a node number identifies a network station along the cable. Each packet on a network is stamped with a source and destination address, which consists of a network address and a node number.

A network, therefore, is a single cabling scheme identified by a unique address to which one or more stations are attached, each of which are identified by numbers unique along the network.

 There is no set convention for assigning network numbers—they are arbitrary (unless your company has a set policy for network numbering/naming conventions).

Figure 39.5 shows a multiserver network, along with the network numbers and node addresses.

Multiple servers on one network have the capability to route packets back and forth. This connection means the clients hooked to this segment (wire) will be able to see all the servers on the same network segment. It also means that all the servers on this segment must be using the same network number (if they are using the same frame type).

Further, with NetWare, a server can internally route between different network segments. If server A, for example, is using a different protocol (perhaps ARCNET) than server D (using Ethernet), you can use server B to route packets between the two different protocols (see fig. 39.6).

By having one of the network servers internally route between different protocols, the users on each segment are able to access both of the servers. In other words, users on the ARCNET segment are able to access the server using Ethernet, even though their workstations do not have Ethernet cards.

Figure 39.4

Available frame type screen.

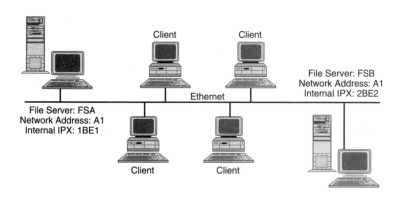

Figure 39.5
A multiserver network.

The first time you load a network card, the driver automatically loads a frame type. The default frame type for NetWare 3.12 is 802.2; the default frame type for NetWare 3.11 is 802.3. Consequently, if you want the two servers to communicate, you need to change the frame types to be the same or load both frame types on all the servers.

Loading both frame types on all the servers increases the amount of packets each server has to look at. Thus, performance is affected—the slower the server, the more it is affected.

Creating AUTOEXEC.NCF and STARTUP.NCF Files

After SERVER.EXE is loaded, the STARTUP.NCF and AUTOEXEC.NCF files are automatically loaded. These files contain the necessary information to bring up the server. The files are usually created with the INSTALL utility during the installation procedure.

The STARTUP.NCF file is loaded first. It contains those settings that must be present before NetWare actually loads (it can be compared to DOS's CONFIG.SYS file). It holds the disk controllers

NetWare driver commands, for example, which must be loaded before you can access any NetWare drives.

The AUTOEXEC.NCF file stores the server name and internal network number, loads the LAN drivers and setting for the network boards, and binds the protocols to the installed network drivers. Just as with DOS's AUTOEXEC.BAT file, you can also launch other programs or utilities, such as MONITOR, or INSTALL.

 Note An NCF file can be used just as a DOS batch file. If you have a list of commands that you load on a regular basis but do not want to include them in your AUTOEXEC.NCF file, you can simply create an NCF file using any text editor. The only requirement is that you use the NCF extension, just as you have to use the BAT extension when naming a DOS batch file.

The AUTOEXEC.NCF is located on the SYS volume in the system directory. Remember, the AUTOEXEC.NCF is used to load modules and to set the NetWare operation system's configuration. It stores items such as the server's name, internal IPX number, and other configuration options.

Figure 39.6
Internal routing.

To create an AUTOEXEC.NCF or STARTUP.NCF file, select System Options from Install's main menu. The Available System Options screen appears. From this menu you can select one of the following options:

- Copy Public and System Files
- Create AUTOEXEC.NCF File
- Create STARTUP.NCF File
- Edit AUTOEXEC.NCF File
- Edit STARTUP.NCF File
- Return to Main Menu

After making one of the above NCF file selections, an editing screen appears. If you do not currently have an AUTOEXEC.NCF file, the screen displays the files that have been manually loaded at the server's console since the server was last loaded. If you do have an AUTOEXEC.NCF file, select the EDIT option; the editing screen then displays the commands currently in the AUTOEXEC.NCF file. Add or delete the commands you want. Press Esc to save the changes.

Remember, commands loaded by the STARTUP.NCF are the first files loaded by the NetWare operating system; so the STARTUP.NCF file contains such commands as disk drivers, namespace option, and various SET parameters. Because these options have to be loaded before a volume is mounted, the STARTUP.NCF file is located on your boot device.

After choosing the Create STARTUP.NCF File option, an editing screen appears. This screen displays the commands loaded when you first brought up the server. If the commands listed are sufficient, simply press Esc and type **Y** to save the changes. If the commands need editing, make the necessary changes and then press Esc.

Changes made to the STARTUP.NCF do not take effect until the server is downed and brought back up. The STARTUP.NCF file needs to be located on the boot device (DOS partition).

Differences between a NetWare 3.11 and NetWare 3.12 Installation

One the biggest differences between NetWare 3.11 and 3.12 is that 3.12 can be installed from a CD-ROM drive.

The steps are the same when installing from disk, but some of the default settings have changed. The default frame type for NetWare 3.11 is 802.3, for example, and the default frame type for NetWare 3.12 is 802.2.

CD-ROM Installation Issues

Because NetWare 3.12 can be installed from a CD-ROM drive, you should become familiar with CD-ROM drive installation issues; they are covered in this next section.

The steps you need to complete to gain access to your CD-ROM device depend on the type of CD-ROM you are using. CD-ROM devices are available in several different interfaces. These different interface styles are usually determined by the type of controller providing a link between the CD-ROM drive and the computer. The Five most popular CD-ROM interface types are CD-ROMs that use a proprietary interface controller; CD-ROM drives that hook to a Sound Blaster controller interface; CD-ROM drives that hook to a computer's parallel port; CD-ROMS that use the IDE channel; and CD-ROM drives that use the SCSI interface. Each of these is capable of installing NetWare, but if you want to have NetWare access the CD-ROM device after the operating system is installed, you want a SCSI type CD-ROM device. SCSI CD-ROM drives also usually provide the best throughput and access times (that is, they are faster).

A SCSI CD-ROM hooks to a SCSI controller, which provides the CD-ROM device access to the computer's bus. After having gained access to the computer's bus, you need to make sure that the drive and controller "hook into" the operating system. This connection between the operating systems and the CD-ROM is usually accomplished by loading operating specific drivers. You need a driver for DOS and a driver for NetWare. The driver for DOS enables you to access the CD-ROM device as a DOS drive.

Gaining access to a SCSI CD-ROM device from DOS usually consists of several steps. First, you need SCSI software for DOS, obtainable from the manufacturer of the SCSI controller or from a third-party software developer. You also need a DOS device driver, which usually ships with your version of DOS. MS DOS 6.O, for example, ships with a Microsoft CD-ROM extension driver called MSCDEX.EXE. This file needs to be loaded and is usually found in your AUTOEXEC.BAT file. The Microsoft CD-ROM extension file often ships with your CD-ROM configuration. You must be certain, however, that the MSCDEX.EXE file matches the version of DOS you are using.

If your CD-ROM extension does not match your DOS version, an error message appears, informing you that an incorrect version of DOS is being used. If this happens, either find the correct version of the MSCDEX.EXE file, or add this file and the correct DOS version to DOS's SETVER.EXE file listing. Also, add the SETVER.EXE command to your CONFIG.SYS file. (See your DOS manual for further instructions on how to add a file to the SETVER.EXE listing as well as how to load device drivers from your CONFIG.SYS file).

After gaining access from DOS to the CD-ROM device, most of the battle is over.

NetWare 3.12's INSTALL.BAT File

NetWare 3.12 has an install batch file utility. When this utility is launched, it starts an automatic installation routine, which simplifies the installation process by automatically loading SERVER.EXE. It then provides the following prompts:

- Create and format a DOS partition

- Create DOS partition (optional)

- Prompt for a server name

- Assign an IPX internal number

- Copy the NetWare 3.12 server boot files to the server 3.12 directory on the DOS partition

- Set code page information

- Select DOS filename format

- Create an AUTOEXEC.BAT file

- Load SERVER.EXE

NetWare 3.12 ships with the necessary portions of DOS to create and format a DOS partition. If you have a DOS partition already created and you start the INSTALL.BAT file, you are asked if you want to retain or create new DOS partition information.

If you select to create new DOS partition information, all current information on the DOS partition is lost.

In NetWare 3.12, you are prompted for each of these steps. After completing them, you must complete the following tasks (just as in NetWare 3.11).

1. Load INSTALL.NLM.

2. Create a NetWare partition.

3. Create a NetWare volume.

4. Mount volume SYS.

5. Copy public and system files to the file server.

6. Load the LAN driver.

7. Edit AUTOEXEC.NCF and STARTUP.NCF files.

For information regarding any of the individual steps, see the "Installing NetWare 3.11" section of this chapter.

The Automatically Installed File System

During the previous steps, you will have copied the public and system file to your new NetWare file server. Most of the files are copied into one of two directories: the Public directory or the System directory.

The files that need to be accessed by the majority of—or by all—the NetWare users are located in the Public directory (that is, the SYS:PUBLIC directory). This general-access directory is created automatically and is also flagged as being read-only. Files located in the directory cannot be erased without changing the file's attributes.

NetWare utilities, help files, and some message and data files (such as the system log in script file and the NET$LOG.DAT) are public files to which all NetWare users have Read, Open, and Search rights.

The files accessed primarily by the network system's supervisor, or by the system itself, are copied into the SYS:SYSTEM directory.

Questions

1. Which of the following information is NOT needed when you are installing NetWare 3.12?

   ○ A. Server Name

   ○ B. Serial number

   ○ C. Disk Type

   ○ D. LAN Driver Type

2. Which of the following LAN card information is needed during a NetWare 3.12 installation?

   ☐ A. Frame Type(for Ethernet)

   ☐ B. LAN Driver Type

   ☐ C. I/O address

   ☐ D. Interrupt (for ISA bus)

3. Which of the following sequences best describes a NetWare 3.12 installation?

   ○ A. Load Disk driver, load DOS, load LAN driver, load NetWare

   ○ B. Load NetWare, load LAN driver, load disk driver, configure DOS

   ○ C. Load DOS, invoke SERVER.EXE, load disk driver, configure NetWare, copy NetWare files

   ○ D. Copy NetWare files, invoke DOS, load LAN driver, load disk driver, start SERVER.EXE

4. After loading the LAN driver, you must also complete which of the following steps?

   ○ A. Reentrantly load any other frame types

   ○ B. Bind communications by attaching the communication protocol to the correct LAN driver

   ○ C. Enter the correct network number for the cable that will be attached to the network adapter

   ○ D. All of the above

5. Which of the following file sequences is the most correct?

   ○ A. AUTOEXEC.NCF, STARTUP.NCF, SERVER.EXE, AUTOEXEC.BAT

   ○ B. AUTOEXEC.BAT, SERVER.EXE, STARTUP.NCF, AUTOEXEC.NCF

   ○ C. STARTUP.NCF, SERVER.EXE, AUTOEXEC.NCF, AUTOEXEC.BAT

   ○ D. SERVER.EXE, STARTUP.NCF, AUTOEXEC.BAT, AUTOEXEC.NCF

6. Which of the following names must be assigned to the first volume on a NetWare server.

   ○ A. VOL1

   ○ B. SYS

   ○ C. SERVER

   ○ D. PUBLIC

7. Which of the following directories is NOT created for you automatically?

   ○ A. Applications

   ○ B. Public

○ C. System

○ D. Mail

8. A file server name is automatically generated for you.

○ A. T

○ B. F

9. Each server on any given cable segment should have an identical internal IPX number.

○ A. T

○ B. F

10. During the protocol binding process, you must enter a network number for the server that is the same as all other servers on that particular wire segment.

○ A. T

○ B. F

11. Under normal operations, you will have to assign a network number for every LAN card in the server.

○ A. T

○ B. F

12. During installation, an internal IPX number is randomly generated for you. This number can be changed as long as it is unique from any other server on the network.

○ A. T

○ B. F

Answers

1.	B
2.	A B C D
3.	C
4.	D
5.	B
6.	B
7.	A
8.	F
9.	F
10.	T
11.	T
12.	T

Migrating a 3.11 Server to a 3.12 Server

*P*art of a NetWare administrator's job is to keep the
system up to date. This often requires that you upgrade
NetWare itself. Currently, there are several methods to
upgrade NetWare. The method you use will depend on
your current situation, as well as the hardware you will
have available. This section covers all the available
migration tools, as well as their options.

In this chapter, you'll learn about the utilities used for a
NetWare 3.11 to 3.12 migration, suggested prepara-
tions to perform prior to an upgrade, the procedures and
results of the NetWare 3.11 to 3.12 upgrade, and how
to upgrade a 3.11 server to a 3.12 server.

Overview

Before upgrading you should take the opportunity to "clean up" or perform some housekeeping tasks on your file server before actually starting the migration processes. The following list contains examples of "housecleaning tasks" that should be done before you begin a server migration:

1. Delete any outdated users or groups.

2. Verify all your user default settings (as you want them on the new server).

3. Eliminate unnecessary security equivalencies and workgroup or user account manager designations.

4. Verify the security of the system with the SECURITY.EXE file.

5. Run BINDFIX.

6. Remove unnecessary files from user directories and public areas.

7. Restrict the directory tree depth to 25 subdirectories.

8. Perform two complete system backups.

9. Verify that you have at least 6 MB of RAM on the server.

10. Verify that you have at least 25 MB of free space on your server's SYS volume.

11. Log out all user and print servers from the server.

12. Guard against users logging in during the upgrade (type DISABLE LOGIN at the console).

13. Verify that the frame types and other communication parameters are the same for both servers.

14. Bring down the server that is to be upgraded.

Besides performing some of the housekeeping tasks in the preceding list, you should make sure you are using the best possible migration utility. Table 40.1 lists the advantages and disadvantages of each migration option.

Table 40.1
NetWare Upgrade Advantages and Disadvantages

Upgrade from–to	Options	Advantages	Disadvantages
Upgrade 2.*x* to 3.12	Across-the-wire to an installed 3.1 server	No risk of data loss Can migrate many servers to one server Can choose what data you want to migrate Can direct data to specific volumes or directories	Need a 3.12 server installed

Upgrade from–to	Options	Advantages	Disadvantages
	Same-server migration	Can choose what data you want to migrate	Some risk of data loss Need a workstation (or tape backup) with enough disk space for data files
	In-place upgrade from 2.1x or 2.2 to 3.12	Need only one 2.1x server	Cannot upgrade from 2.0a Need 80386 or higher processor If upgrade fails, you may have to restore your 2.1x data from backup
NetWare 3.x to 3.12	Across-the-wire to an installed 3.12 server	No risk of data loss Can migrate many servers to one server Can choose what data you want to migrate Can direct data to specific volumes or directories	Need a 3.12 server installed
	Same-server migration	Can choose what data you want to migrate	Some risk of data loss Need a workstation or tape device capable of handling all your current data
	In-place upgrade from 3.x to 3.12	Just need one 3.x server—no additional hardware is needed	Cannot upgrade from 3.0 If upgrade fails, you will have to use a backup to restore the server to its original state

Note Regardless of the migration method used, you want to have a solid, reliable, proven backup. It is good practice and recommended that you have at least two verified backups of your data and bindery information before starting any major work on the server, including a migration.

The following sections discuss each migration method in more detail.

Across-the-Wire Migration

Across-the-wire migration is a method of migrating your existing data and bindery files from a NetWare 3.1*x* file server to a 3.12 server (see fig. 40.1). Across-the-wire migration is a workstation-based utility that transfers your network information (files, users, print queues, and so on) to a working directory on the workstation's hard drive (the workstation from which you start the migration utility). The bindery and files are then translated into 3.12 format so that they can be transferred to the new server. After translation, the objects are placed in the 3.12 file server's bindery.

The across-the-wire method provides you the option of migrating your data from your old server to a new server that is attached to the same physical network. With across-the-wire migration utility you also can temporarily copy information from the old server to a workstation and then transfer it back to your original server, in the new format. This same-server approach is more risky, but does not require a second server. Migrating across-the-wire to a new server leaves the existing server and all of its information intact, and is much safer (you can always go back to the old server).

The following list contains information that should be migrated during a system upgrade.

- User information:

    Login scripts

    Account restrictions

    Station restrictions

    Time restrictions

    Security equivalencies

Figure 40.1

Across-the-wire migration.

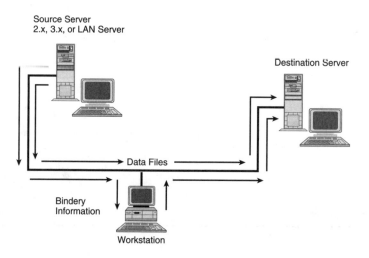

■ Printing information:

    Print queues

    Print queue users and operators

    Print servers

    Print server users and operators

    Print server control files

■ Information about groups:

    Group rights

    Group members

■ Default account restrictions

■ Accounting information

The following information should not be migrated:

■ Data files

■ Passwords

■ Volume restrictions

The following list explains some key points on data and server migration when the across-the-wire method is used:

■ NetWare 3.1*x* file server system files are not migrated.

■ A file on the source server will not be copied if the file name already exists on the destination server (an error will be listed in the error log).

■ The system login script is not migrated.

■ User login scripts are migrated.

■ If the destination server contains a directory with the same name as a directory on the source server, then the files in both directories will be merged.

■ During a server consolidation, if users with the same user name exist on more than one file server, the user accounts will be merged.

The Same-Server Method

The same-server migration takes the bindery information on an existing 3.11 server, copies it to a working directory on a workstation, upgrades (translates) the bindery information into a 3.12 format, then migrates it from the workstation back to the server.

The MIGRATE.EXE utility is located on the NetWare 3.12 CD-ROM in the following directory:

    D:\CLIENT_____\MIGRATE\ENGLISH

There are two options with the MIGRATE.EXE utility: Custom migration and Standard migration. The Custom option, as its name implies, enables you to select from a list the information that you want migrated. This selection process enables you to create a custom destination server.

Although the Standard migration option is less flexible and therefore easier to use, it migrates all information from the source server, across the network, to the destination server. You cannot select specific information to migrate; all data files and LAN information are automatically migrated.

The same-server upgrade uses a DOS client station to manage the migration process and uses the same computer as both the source and the destination device (see fig. 40.1). This method does not migrate data, so you must back up your data files and restore them to the server after NetWare 3.12 is completely installed.

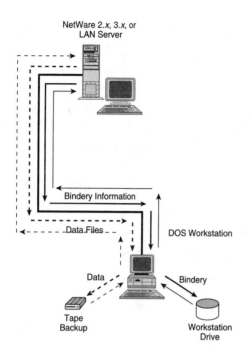

Figure 40.2

Same-server migration.

The in-place upgrade method involves the following four phases:

- Analysis of the file system
- Analysis of the disk drives
- Modification of the disk drives
- Creation of a NetWare 3.12 bindery

Phase one, the analysis of the file system, takes inventory of the disk drives and attempts to determine how much memory is required to complete the upgrade process.

Phase two, the disk analysis, locates the Hot Fix area, File Allocation Tables, and Directory Entry Tables. It then re-creates such areas on the new NetWare 3.12 server. The Directory Entry Tables and File Allocation Tables are translated, and directory file attributes are upgraded.

 Macintosh files also are migrated. Be sure to load the Macintosh Name Space on any volumes that contain Macintosh files, however.

After creating a backup, you use the MIGRATE.EXE utility to migrate the bindery information to the working directory of the client. Now the server is ready to have NetWare 3.12 installed as a new installation. Restore the data from the tape backup and then execute the migration utility to migrate the bindery information to the new NetWare 3.12 server.

Phase two also verifies that you have enough memory to complete the upgrade process. If you do not have enough memory, the procedure will halt. You can restart it again after more memory is added.

Phase three is the phase in which modification of data on the disk actually occurs—the partition table is upgraded and the system files are written to the system area (track zero).

If the upgrade process fails or is stopped during phase three of the upgrade, you have to restore the old NetWare 2.*x* file server to its original state and start the migration process again.

 Passwords are not migrated to the NetWare 3.12 server. The utility assigns either random passwords or no passwords. If you choose to have random passwords assigned, a file (NEW.PWD) is created in the SYS: SYSTEM directory. This file contains a list of all the users' passwords.

Phase four, creation of a NetWare 3.12 bindery, upgrades the 2.1*x* bindery to a 3.1*x* bindery. As with the MIGRATE.EXE, you have the option to have the system generate random passwords, or you can perform the migration without passwords (passwords are not migrated).

Performing the 3.11 to 3.12 Upgrade Steps

This section provides you with the steps necessary to perform an upgrade from a NetWare 3.11 to a 3.12 file server:

1. Start the INSTALL.BAT file from the 3.12 server CD-ROM by changing to the <*CD-ROM Drive*>:\NETWARE\ENGLISH directory and typing **INSTALL.BAT**.

2. Access the upgrade portion of the NetWare 3.12 installation utility (see fig. 40.3).

3. Copy files to the DOS partition.

At this point you are given some information about drivers that were not copied to the new server. It is important that you verify that none of these drivers need to be used.

4. Assign locale information—country code, code page, and keyboard mappings—and file format. The DOS file format is almost always recommended.

5. Decide whether to invoke the existing STARTUP.NCF file.

   Usually you will not invoke the STARTUP.NCF file unless all the disk controller drivers and other startup paramaters are identical. If these files are not identical and the STARTUP.NCF is used, errors occur and the boot process is halted. Thus, it is better to skip the STARTUP.NCF file and load the drivers manually (unless you have settings that have to be loaded from the STARTUP.NCF file—for example, memory settings).

Figure 40.3

Selecting to upgrade an existing NetWare 3.1x server.

Perform the following steps if you did not invoke the STARTUP.NCF file:

1. Assign a server name.

2. Start SERVER.EXE.

3. Assign an IPX internal network number.

4. Load the disk driver.

5. Mount all volumes (load name spaces).

6. Load the INSTALL.NLM from the DOS partition.

7. Install system and public files to the SYS volume (see fig. 40.4).

8. Load and bind the LAN driver.

9. Verify that the AUTOEXEC.NCF and STARTUP.NCF files contain the appropriate changes.

10. Reboot the server using the newly created AUTOEXEC and STARTUP files.

11. Log in to the NetWare 3.12 server as a user that existed on the old server, to verify the migration.

Post-Migration Procedures

After you finish the migration process, perform the following tasks before you count the migration as complete:

1. Update user login scripts.

2. Check system login scripts.

3. Check user restrictions and accounting change rates.

4. Check printing services.

5. Test your applications.

6. Check data integrity.

After all these procedures are complete you should make a backup of the new server.

Figure 40.4

Copying the public and system files.

Questions

1. What information is needed prior to upgrading 3.11 to 3.12?

   ○ A. Country code information

   ○ B. Code page information

   ○ C. Keyboard mapping type

   ○ D. All of the above

2. What is the default frame type for NetWare 3.12?

   ○ A. Ethernet 802.3

   ○ B. Ethernet 802.2

   ○ C. Ethernet_SNAP

   ○ D. TCP/IP

3. Which TWO of the following are valid file name formats for a NetWare server?

   ☐ A. DOS

   ☐ B. HPFS

   ☐ C. NT Advanced server

   ☐ D. NetWare

4. Which TWO of the following are valid migration methods?

   ☐ A. Across-the-wire

   ☐ B. Same server

   ☐ C. Backup and restore

   ☐ D. Restore

5. During a migration, you have the opportunity not to use the STARTUP.NCF file. Which of the following is a reason not to invoke the STARTUP.NCF file?

   ○ A. Country code information has changed.

   ○ B. The default frametype has changed.

   ○ C. The LAN card is different.

   ○ D. The Disk controller drive is different.

6. When performing a 3.11 to 3.12 migration, which of the following are true?

   ☐ A. NetWare system files are not migrated.

   ☐ B. Code page information must be entered.

   ☐ C. AUTOEXEC.NCF files must be changed to reflect the default frametype changes.

   ☐ D. Passwords will not be migrated.

7. Starting the NetWare 3.12 INSTALL.BAT file will give you access to which TWO of the following migration utilities?

   ☐ A. Custom migration

   ☐ B. Standard migration

   ☐ C. 2XUPDATE.NLM

   ☐ D. All of the above

Answers

1. D	5. D
2. B	6. A B C D
3. A D	7. A B
4. A B	

Installing Client Software

This chapter provides you with much more than the basic steps for installing a NetWare client. It also provides you with an understanding of the basic differences between the shell style client and the new requester technology, and, in addition, covers the enhancements to the client in the NetWare 3.12 software.

After you finish this section, you should be able to identify the different types of client technology and explain how to use and configure them. You also should be able to install a NetWare requester client and name the installation steps.

Client Support in NetWare 3.12

NetWare supports all the popular client platforms. This section informs you of the types of clients NetWare supports, as well as some of the software required for each particular client technology. NetWare 3.1*x* supports the following types of clients:

- Macintosh
- OS/2, 2.1 and above
- Unix
- DOS (Windows)

Macintosh

NetWare 3.12 now includes a five-user version of NetWare for Macintosh version 3.12. It also is backward compatible with 3.11, and incorporates software fixes and the management utilities necessary for some of the system administrator functions to be completed from a Macintosh client.

If you need to support more than five Macintosh clients, you can buy a separate 200-user license.

OS/2

NetWare 3.1*x* supports OS/2 2.1 and above.

OS/2 remote printing support uses NPRINTER.EXE rather than RPRINTER.EXE. NPRINTER.EXE is the same remote printing file used in NetWare 4.*x*.

Unix

For Unix support, NetWare includes routing services for TCP/IP connections. The necessary files are placed in the SYS:ETC and SYS:SYSTEM directories of the automatically installed file system.

To support a Unix client on a NetWare 3.12 server, use version 1.2b of NetWare for NFS.

DOS

NetWare also obviously supports DOS-based machines (with or without Windows).

The DOS support includes the following software components:

- Open Data LINK interface (ODI)
- NetWare DOS Requester
- NetWare DOS *Virtual Loadable Module* (VLM)

All your clients should run the latest version of the DOS requester. If you run the latest version of the requester, you provide your DOS clients with the most stable and feature-rich network client support.

Open Data-Link Interface (ODI) provides flexibility by supporting multiple transport protocols for a single network board. Before ODI, multiple-protocol support required that you install multiple network boards in each of the client stations, not to mention reset the workstation whenever the board or transport method was needed. The ODI client drivers include the following files:

- LSL.COM (Link Support Layer)

- LAN driver file (Multiple Link interface driver or MLID)

- IPXODI.COM (Communication protocol)

These three files replace the older, dedicated IPX.COM file that was generated using WSGEN.EXE or SHELLGEN.EXE. The older IPX.COM driver was incapable of simultaneously supporting multiple protocols.

Furthermore, DOS technologies have been updated from shell to requester. The DOS Requester is required to use NetWare 4.*x* as well as to get all of the functionality from 3.12. The new requester technology, for instance, provides a NetWare DOS client the following functionality:

- Memory swapping technology and DOS redirection capabilities

- Faster client speeds and response times with Packet Burst

- Enhanced MS windows client support

- Backward compatibility with NETX.EXE

Furthermore, the new client design incorporates modularity, which ensures that the Requester is equipped for future functionality.

Differences between the Shell and Requester

In the NetWare 3.*x* shell, NETX.EXE acts as a front end for DOS, intercepting user and application requests before they reach NetWare. Any commands heading for the workstation operating system are intercepted, interpreted, and then passed

to the appropriate location—DOS or NetWare. So, if the request is not for the network, the shell passes the instructions on to DOS. If the request is for the network, the instructions are passed to NetWare.

The DOS requester has the following two components:

- The Manager (VLM.EXE)

- Virtual Loadable Modules (VLMs)

The manager component, or VLM.EXE, loads and subsequently manages the VLMs. Its major responsibilities include the following:

- Handling requests from applications and routing them to the proper VLM

- Managing communication between modules

- Controlling memory services, allocation, and management

The Virtual Loadable Modules are composed of small pieces of code, which are files that have a VLM extension.

Each VLM provides a specific function. For instance, the PRINT.VLM controls printing functions. VLMs can be one of two types:

- Child VLMs

- Multiplexer (Parent VLMs)

The VLM manager transparently loads a *child VLM* into the workstation's memory. You also can specify which VLMs the VLM manager loads by placing or removing them from the NET.CFG (network configuration) file. If you choose to specify the load files, know that you must load child VLMs before their associated multiplexers.

In the past, Novell has used the Shell, however, they are moving to a requester style client for several technical reasons.

The files that compose the VLM technology can be arranged into the three following layers, as seen in figure 41.1:

■ **DOS Redirection Layer.** Provides all the DOS file services through the DOS redirecter (REDIR.VLM).

■ **Service Protocol Layer.** Contains several parallel services, such as NWP.VLM, RSA. VLM, FIO.VLM, and PRINT.VLM, each of which contains several other "child" VLMs.

  ■ NWP.VLM

  ■ RSA.VLM

  ■ FIO.VLM

  ■ PRINT.VLM

■ **Transport Protocol Layer.** Mechanism responsible for maintaining the connections, providing packet transmissions between connections and performing other transport-specific functions.

The requester performs the same functions as a shell—passes information from the client to the network operating system—but does so differently. The NetWare shell had to retain its own set of internal resource tables for network file and print services. In contrast, the more tightly integrated DOS Requester can actually share resource tables with DOS, thereby eliminating the need to maintain redundant tables and decreasing memory requirements for the DOS Requester.

If DOS receives a request it cannot service, it uses the interrupt to call a redirected service (REDIR.VLM). When an application makes a request to DOS, for example, DOS first attempts to qualify the request to determine ownership of the requested resource, such as a drive letter, a file handle, or a print device. If DOS determines that it does not own the resource, DOS polls the redirecters to allow them to determine ownership. If a redirecter claims ownership, DOS then makes the appropriate calls to that redirecter so that it can complete the request.

As part of the Requester technology, Novell has made it possible for workstations running applications that use the old DOS shell calls to be compatible with the new Requester technology.

Figure 41.1

Novell's client arcitecture.

Owing to the different methods they use to manage resources, the NetWare shell (NETX.EXE) and the DOS Requester (VLM.EXE) cannot coexist, meaning that you cannot load them together. After you install the VLM client kit for Windows, in fact, you have to use the VLMs.

The architecture of the Requester technology is much more modular than its Shell counterpart, enabling you to set up the VLMs in a variety of memory configurations. You can load them into extended memory, expanded memory, or conventional memory. You even can make the VLMs use the upper memory blocks, if any exist. When you load VLM.EXE, it relocates its startup code at the top of conventional memory, which enables it to load and unload modules as needed, so memory is not unnecessarily waited. In a sense, the VLM.EXE file is its own memory manager; when you load the VLM.EXE, it temporarily loads each of the VLM modules specified by the NET.CFG file for loading. After it loads each module, it reports its ID, memory requirements, and global transient information.

This temporary loading procedure causes a series of dots to appear on-screen. During this initialization stage, each VLM module executes its initialization code, including initializing internal variables, hooking interrupts, notifying other VLMs of its presence, and detecting the presence of other dependent VLMs.

Because VLM.EXE now knows the amount of memory each module can use, it can calculate the total memory requirement for the overall configuration. It then sets aside enough memory for the transient portions and the global portions for each requester module.

The global portion contains the global segments of each VLM's code. After initialization, the global segment is stored in conventional memory or, if available, the upper memory blocks. This code often must remain in conventional memory for compatibility or backward compatibility issues.

VLM.EXE automatically detects and selects the type of memory that is available. After it determines the available memory, it allocates its use. It tries to use the best possible configuration by using extended memory first, expanded memory second, and conventional memory last. If you do not have a memory manager loaded, VLM.EXE must reserve space in conventional memory for both the global and transient portions of VLM module code, which can quickly consume memory.

To determine where the VLMs transient portions are loaded, use the following command-line commands: /mx, /me, and, /mc (extended, expanded, and conventional).

The transient portion is often called the Swap block. It consists of the sections of requester code that do not always have to be loaded into memory, and thus are swapped in and out of memory. The transient swap block is roughly the size of the largest VLM module at initialization, but afterward is reduced to match the largest transient segment of the largest VLM module.

VLM Functions fall into one of the following three service categories:

- DOS Redirection
- Service Protocol
- Transport Protocol

You use REDIR.VLM to manage DOS redirection services. The Service protocols portion of the VLM technology handles requests for very specific services, such as connection establishment, broadcast messages, file reads and writes, and print redirection, whereas the Transport protocol portion of the VLMs handles maintaining server connections and providing packet transmissions and other transport-related services.

NET.CFG File

The VLM-Requester technology is modular and uses the NET.CFG file or its configuration. The following section provides you with some examples of different configurations optimized for different situations. You use entries in the NET.CFG file to change the workstations network environment or configuration. For example, you might want to change the configuration for the following reasons:

■ You changed the default hardware setting on your network board.

■ You use Novell's LAN Workplace.

■ You use multiple protocols on the same network board.

■ You want to optimize your workstation's configuration.

As a rule of thumb, NET.CFG file should be located in the same directory as the rest of the VLM files.

Several different types of configuration options are set in the NET.CFG file, including the network interface card settings, protocol settings, and so on. The NET.CFG file is created during installation of the client software and can be edited with any text editor.

 The NET.CFG file is similar to the old SHELL.CFG file, as well as the NET.CFG file used with the ODI drivers.

You must follow certain rules when you work with a NET.CFG file, such as the following:

■ You must begin each option section at the very left of the file (flush left).

■ You can list only one option per line.

An *option section* is a line that performs a function, such as the following:

LINK DRIVER NE2000

■ Each option section can have several parameters, such as the following:

■ INT 4

■ PORT 340

■ Frame Ethernet_802.2

■ You must indent each parameter line (at least one space) and locate the line beneath its respective option section (only one parameter per line).

■ You must place a hard return at the end of each parameter setting in each line (including the last line of the file).

■ You can remark out a text or comment line by placing REM or a semicolon in front of the line.

 The NET.CFG file is not case-sensitive.

Because the VLMS is so easy to configure, you can optimize a client for several different purposes; you can configure the client for the best possible performance, memory optimization, or even for specific configuration that combines performance and memory optimization.

This section includes three sample NET.CFG files. The first grants higher performance but sacrifices memory. The second conserves memory at the expense of performance. The third and final example attempts to find a common ground at which you do not sacrifice performance for memory, nor memory for performance. In each of these example NET.CFG files, the boldface entries are by default set for a specific purpose (performance or memory). For simplicity, the options that have no relevance are omitted.

Performance

When you optimize VLMs for performance, you use about 100 KB of conventional memory.

```
CACHE WRITES = ON
CHECKSUM = 0 (only use with 802.2)
LARGE INTERNET PACKETS = ON
LOAD LOW CONN = ON
LOAD LOW IPXNCP = ON
MINIMUM TIME TO NET = ON
NETWARE PROTOCOL = NDS, BIND, PNW (only use
necessary options e.g. NDS, BIND - BIND -
PNW)
PB BUFFERS = 0
PRINT BUFFER SIZE = 256
SIGNATURE LEVEL = 0
TRUE COMMIT = OFF
```

If you are optimizing for memory, you will want to make some of the following changes in your NET.CFG file.

```
AUTO LARGE TABLE = OFF
AUTO RECONNECT = OFF
CACHE BUFFERS = 0 (PERFORMANCE HIT
AVERAGE NAME LENGTH = CALCULATED VALUE, (48-
DEFAULT)
CONNECTIONS = CALCULATED VALUE, (8 DEFAULT)
LOAD LOW CONN = OFF
LOAD LOW IPXNCP = OFF
EXCLUDE VLM = <VLM>
NETWORK PRINTERS = 0
PB BUFFERS = 0 (0 SETS PACKET BURST OFF)
PRINT HEADER = 0
PRINT TAIL = 0
SIGNATURE LEVEL = 0
```

When you optimize for memory, be sure not to load the VLMs that you don't need. The following is a list of the optional VLMs:

- AUTO.VLM_
- PRINT.VLM_
- SECURITY.VLM_
- NDS.VLM_
- BIND.VLM_
- PNW.VLM_
- NETX.VLM_
- RSA.VLM_
- WSSNMP.VLM_
- WSREG.VLM_
- WSTRAP.VLM_
- MIB2IF.VLM_
- MIN2PROT.VLM_
- NMR.VLM_

 Disabling VLMs means also disabling its respective functions. For example, disabling the last seven VLMs in the preceding list effects SNMP services. Disabling PRINT.VLM, for example, means you can't print. Disabling NDS.VLM means you can't access NetWare 4 Directory Services. Disabling BIND.VLM means you can't connect to a NetWare 3.x server.

You can disable, or not load, specific VLMs in three ways:

- Delete the VLM

- Rename the VLM file to a different name, using an extension other than VLM

■ Include the line `Exclude VLM = <VLM name>` under the NetWare DOS requester section of the NET.CFG file

VLMs come with default configurations for optimizing both memory and performance. The default values are as follows:

```
AUTO LARGE TABLE = OFF
AUTO RECONNECT = ON
AVERAGE NAME LENGTH = 48
CACHE BUFFERS = 5
CACHE BUFFER SIZE = <MAX MEDIA SIZE>
CACHE WRITES = ON
CHECKSUM = 1
CONNECTIONS = 8
LARGE INTERNET PACKET = ON
LOAD LOW CONN = ON
LOAD LOW IPXNCP = ON
MINIMUM TIME TO NET = 0
NETWARE PROTOCOL = NDS BIND PNW
NETWARE PRINTERS = 3
PB BUFFERS = 3
PRINT BUFFER SIZE = 64
PRINT HEADER = 64
PRINT TAIL = 16
SIGNATURE LEVEL = 1
TRUE COMMIT = OFF
```

The NetWare DOS requester is the preferred workstation, or client software. Some applications, however, might use specific *Application Program Interfaces* (API) that employ calls that can't be redirected, in which case you might need to use NETX.EXE (shells). Novell includes all the files necessary to use the older shell workstation software.

These files, NETX.EXE (and the extended and expanded memory versions), are automatically copied into the SYS:LOGIN directory during a NetWare file server installation. These files can also be retrieved from the installation disks, specifically the SYSTEM_3 disk from the LOGIN subdirectory.

The DOS requester architecture offers the following advantages:

■ Provides a modular architecture that has advantages for current and future applications

■ Takes advantage of memory-swapping technology and DOS redirection capabilities

■ Includes Packet Burst and *Large Internet Packet* (LIP) support

■ Provides backward compatibility with NETX.EXE

Performing Workstation Installation Steps

During the workstation software installation, you must know some specific information regarding your network boards and client configuration. The following list can help prepare you for the questions you have to answer during the installation process.

■ Interrupt your network board uses

■ Base I/O address your network board uses

■ Frame type your network uses

■ Other settings your card might use

You can usually get this information from the network boards documentation.

After you obtain the preceding information for your configuration, you need to make sure that you have the following disks:

WSDOS_1

WSWIN_1

WSDRV_1

WSDRV_2

If you install an OS/2 client, you also need the following disks:

WSOS2_1

WSOS_2

WSDRV_1

Besides these NetWare client disks, you also need to be sure to have a recent third-party driver for your network board. Because both the network cards, as well as NetWare itself, might have been sitting on a vendor's shelf, you want to verify that you are installing the latest drivers; never assume the drivers that came with the card or drivers that came with NetWare are the latest.

Installation Methods

Installing workstation software varies, depending on the type of network card you use, as well as the version of NetWare drivers you try to load. This section assumes that you use an Ethernet card and the drivers that come with NetWare (opposed to the ones that ship with your network card).

Currently three methods are available for installing the NetWare client software: from disk, from the CD-ROM, or off the server.

Installing the client software directly from the NetWare Operating System CD-ROM is simple and quick. You must, however, have a CD-ROM drive in every workstation.

When you install the NetWare server, you can create and install the client software. You always should install the client software to the server, even if it is not your preferred choice of client installation, because having the software on the server enables you to

update any client software from the server if the clients are currently connected. This method of installing client software assumes that you already have client-to-file server connection, and is the best in situations where you are upgrading.

Creating Client Disks

Creating a set of client disks is absolutely necessary if all your workstations do not have CD-ROMs or if you do not currently have a client-to-server connection (and you should do so even if one or both of the above conditions are met). Creating a set of client disks requires that you have several preformatted disks before you begin duplication.

Before you can create installation disks from a NetWare 3.12 operating system CD, you must have the CD-ROM as a DOS volume or as a Network volume. After you gain access to the CD-ROM, you need to complete the following steps:

1. Use the DOS FORMAT command to format five high-density disks.

2. Change to one of the following subdirectories in the client directory of the CD-ROM:

   ■ DOSWIN

   ■ OS/2

3. Set the NWLANGUAGE environment variable by typing the following at the command line:

   `Set NWLANGUAGE=Language`

4. Type the following command:

   `MAKEDISK drive_letter`

After you enter the MAKEDISK command, you are prompted to insert the blank disk in the selected target drive. If anything at all interrupts the MAKEDISK routine, you must start over from the beginning.

 The disk creation procedure simply copies the client files off the CD-ROM to disk. Thus, you really need to use blank disks. If the disks are not blank, the copy procedure returns an error indicating the disk does not have enough room, in which case, you must start all over again, regardless of the progress already made. In other words, if the last disk that you attempt to make is not blank, you must re-create the first four.

After you begin the copy procedure, a message appears indicating that the copy is in progress. After the first disk is completed, the copy routine informs you to label the disk and to insert the next disk. After all of the disks in the set are created, you are returned to the DOS prompt.

Installing from a File Server or Network Directory

To install the client software from network directory you must have all the client installation prerequisites, as well as having the client connected to the server with a previous version of the network workstation software. You must also have a complete copy of the workstation software loaded on the server.

To install the software from a file server, complete the following steps:

1. Log in to the file server.

2. Map a drive to the directory on which the client software resides.

The next section covers the basic tasks that you must do, regardless of client installation method, to successfully install the NetWare client software for a DOS workstation.

Installation Steps

DOS and MS Windows workstation share the same DOS-based installation routine. To start the client install process, type **INSTALL.**

 Be sure you are completely out of Windows and not in a DOS box because the install procedure needs to modify some of the Windows files.

After you type **INSTALL**, a screen appears (see fig. 41.2).

During installation, a directory is created in the root of the drive from which you boot DOS (with the default name of \NWCLIENT). All workstation files for DOS and Windows are copied to this newly created directory, including the NetWare user tools for DOS and Windows, VLM program files, VLM manager files, Network board drivers, and Unicode tables with their corresponding code pages, numbers, and country codes.

Also, during the installation a Windows group file is automatically created. This group file contains a User tools icon.

In the first installation screen, you are asked to verify several installation options. Most of these options, such as whether you want to install MS Windows support, or whether to use the default client directory, are pretty straightforward. However, you also must identify the correct hardware

Figure 41.2
Workstation installation screen.

and hardware settings for your network card at this installation screen.

To select a network card, move the cursor to step four and press Enter. The screen shown in figure 41.3 then appears, from which you can select the appropriate network card.

If you currently have an older version of network software loaded, the installation routine recognizes the settings in use and simply uses the same driver and card settings. So, if you are upgrading, loading the client drivers and then installing the new client software is your best option.

If the correct network card driver can't be found, an error message appears, informing you that you have two options:

■ Copy the driver to the current directory and start the install routine over

■ Modify the LINK DRIVER section of your NET.CFG to load the appropriate driver file after the installation is completed

After you select the driver that matches your network card, you must specify the correct settings (if you have changed the card from its default

Figure 41.3
Select the appropriate network card.

settings). To specify the correct settings, select option five, and the screen shown in figure 41.4 appears.

To change the settings of your network board, highlight the location you want and press Enter. A dialog screen appears, from which you can make your selection. If you select the Hardware interrupt line, for instance, you receive the options similar to the one shown in figure 41.5.

The options box lists all of the interrupts your card supports. To select an interrupt, move the highlight bar to the correct setting and press Enter.

If you're installing from floppies, you are informed which disks you need to use. If you're installing from one of the other methods, the installation begins to copy the client files to your workstation's boot drive.

Figure 41.4

Selecting the correct network card settings.

Figure 41.5

The Hardware Interrupt options box.

Questions

1. Which THREE of the following methods are valid client installation methods?

   ☐ A. From CD-ROM

   ☐ B. From disk

   ☐ C. From the server

   ☐ D. From the router

2. Which part of the VLM drive acts as a memory manager?

   ○ A. CONN.VLM

   ○ B. NWP.VLM

   ○ C. VLM.EXE

   ○ D. REDIR.VLM

3. Which file is used to determine the configuration of the VLMs?

   ○ A. VLM.EXE

   ○ B. AUTOEXEC.NCF

   ○ C. NET.CFG

   ○ D. AUTOEXEC.BAT

4. When using the VLM client, which of the following changes must be made to the CONFIG.SYS file?

   ○ A. LASTDRIVE=Z

   ○ B. SET NWLANGUAGE=ENGLISH

   ○ C. LASTDRIVE=F

   ○ D. BUFFERS=100

5. Which of the following are main sections of the NET.CFG file?

   ☐ A. Link Driver

   ☐ B. Link Support

   ☐ C. Protocol IPX

   ☐ D. NetWare DOS Requester

Answers

1. A B C

2. C

3. C

4. A

5. A B C D

Tuning for Performance

The NetWare 3.1x operating system is a set of dynamically linked collections of components and software subsystems. Each component can directly or indirectly affect the performance of the entire NetWare operating system. This chapter looks at how you can optimize the following NetWare components:

- *Server memory*
- *File system and cache*
- *Communications subsystem*
- *System processor*

This chapter also teaches you how to use the NetWare set commands to "tweak" NetWare for your particular environment.

Only network administrators who understand how changing one portion of the operating system can affect each operating system component should use these "fine tuning tips." These configuration changes should be tested in a nonproduction environment before being implemented.

NetWare 3.1*x* has a modular design that lends it the capability to automatically allocate and deallocate memory and other resources as needed by the operating system. You can use the tunable SET parameters to manually configure these dynamic allocating features to create a very efficient, customized implementation, but little information is available on how you use them. Therefore, the server usually is simply left with the default parameters.

NetWare is a specialized networking operating system designed and coded to give optimum speed and performance to most configurations. Changing a default setting can actually result in a performance loss.

The most vital factor when you tweak the NetWare operating system is realizing that any tweaking of a NetWare server is not an exact science, and that any performance tuning must be based on the characteristics of the server's actual production workloads.

NetWare 3.11 Server Components

Server hardware tuning is the most critical factor in the optimization of NetWare systems. However, after you tune and balance the server's hardware, you can effectively optimize NetWare.

To optimize NetWare, you need to understand each of the subsystems and the characteristics of those subsystems, including the following:

■ **Memory.** Because NetWare uses file caching extensively, it is extremely memory oriented. You need to have a basic understanding of how the server allocates memory because you must consider the memory impact of each tuning parameter.

■ **Communications system or server LAN I/O channel.** The communications system can affect performance in a number of ways: packet size, communication buffers, Burst Mode protocol, SAP traffic, and network interface cards. Because each of these components affect the overall network performance, you can tweak them to enhance overall network response times.

■ **File system.** The NetWare file system is very cache oriented; any change in available memory for cache directly affects overall performance. A bottleneck in the physical disk channel also directly degrades overall network performance.

■ **System processor.** The system processor typically is a subsystem that requires a lot of attention; NetWare is very rarely processor bound. The processor, however, is tied directly to the server's bus, which is the most common bottleneck. Because of the relationship of the processor and the bus, these components are discussed together.

Memory Pools

Memory allocation refers to reserving specific memory locations in RAM for processes, instructions, and data. NetWare 3.12 uses memory pools to manage RAM. These memory pools are designed to be allocated and optimized based on whether they are to have long-term or short-term usage.

Short-term memory is used to perform such activities as mapping drives, providing user-connection information, locking files, and so on. *Long-term memory* is used for the servers's communication buffers, directory cache buffers, and so on.

Figure 42.1 illustrates NetWare 3.12's use of memory. Table 42.1 represents how these memory pools are used.

After memory resources are released from the file cache buffer pool to the permanent memory pool or to the allocated short-term memory pool, they cannot be returned to the main memory pool until after the server is brought down and the primary memory segment is reestablished.

Frequent loading and unloading of NLMs causes fragmentation of your file server's memory, so it might not have enough contiguous RAM to actually service all requests of memory.

You can optimize your file server's memory allocation in one of two ways:

■ Minimize loading and unloading of NLMs to prevent RAM fragmentation.

■ If the RAM becomes fragmented, bring down the server and start it back up. This eliminates fragmentation and makes contiguous memory available to NLMs.

The memory model for NetWare 3.12 is based on the use of 32-bit registers, which enables NetWare to provide access to one flat segment of RAM up to 4 GB.

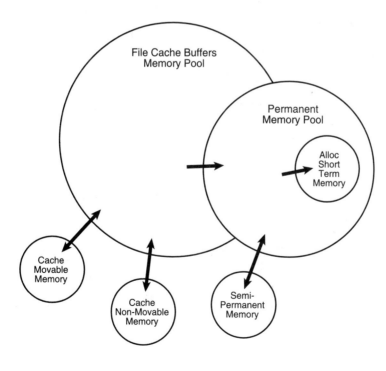

Figure 42.1

NetWare 3.12 memory pools.

Table 42.1
Memory Pool Utilization

Memory Pool or Subpool	Description and Use	Status
File Cache Buffer	Main memory pool; used for caching reads and writes	Primary memory segment
Cache Movable	Subpool used by NetWare; used for internal system tables that change size dynamically: Hash tables File allocation tables (FATs) Directory entry tables (DETs) No fragmentation Expandable	Returnable to file cache buffer in contiguous blocks
Cache Non-Movable	Subpool used by NLMs, including CLIB, when loaded Causes fragmentation Non-expandable	Returnable to file cache buffer in non-contiguous blocks
Permanent Memory	One-way allocation pool for long-term memory needs used for communication buffers and directory cache buffers	Not returnable to file cache buffer
Semi-Permanent	Subpool used by LAN and disk drivers	Returnable to permanent memory, but not to file cache buffer
Allocated Short-term	Pool used for small, short-term memory allocations such as drive mappings, SAP and RIP tables, Queue manager tables, and connection information	Not returnable to permanent memory or to file cache memory Unused allocated memory remains in the pool for other uses

Rather than allocating chunks of memory at the time of installation, most resources (such as memory for communication buffers and drive mappings) are allocated as needed.

Any preassigned values must be specified in the server's STARTUP.NCF and AUTOEXEC.NCF files.

NetWare 3.12 uses the same memory architecture as earlier versions of 3.11. In 3.12, however, Novell made some changes to the core operating systems. These changes require 3.12 to have a greater use of the alloc short term memory pool.

NetWare 3.12 commonly needs more than 2 MB in its ALLOC memory pool. Other demands—such as users not logging out, clients using MS-Windows and OS/2, and some disk drivers—cause the alloc short term memory pool to reach its maximum value quickly.

Therefore, the default value and the range of values available have been increased. The default value for the Alloc Short Term Memory pool has changed from 2 MB in NetWare 3.11 to 8 MB in 3.12. The maximum value of the Alloc Short Term memory pool has also been increased from 16 MB in 3.11 to 32 MB in 3.12.

To change the default value of the Alloc Short Term memory pool, use the following SET command:

```
SET MAXIMUM ALLOC SHORT TERM MEMORY = value
```

 The range of values is 50,000 to 33,554,432 bytes (32 MB).

You can view the Resource Utilization option in the Monitor utility, from the console screen, to verify the amount of memory the alloc short term memory pool is using.

The best policy for adjusting the alloc short term memory pool is to let the server *self-adjust*, that is, to let the server run under normal situations for about three or four days. During this period, the server uses the amount of memory it most likely needs. Then, if you want to manually change the alloc short term memory levels to always reflect your environment, you can enter the SET command manually.

You might want to adjust the alloc short term memory value based on the information found in the MONITOR.NLM. You might want to decrease the value, for instance, if your server does not use the allotted memory. Or, you might want to increase the value if the server issues warnings that an operation cannot be completed because this memory pool has reached its limit.

File System Adjustments

Optimizing the NetWare 3.12 caching mechanism includes adjusting parameters that affect *NetWare Core Protocol* (NCP) reads and writes, as well as adjusting the disk block size, buffer size, FATs, and directory entry tables.

The following list provides some common rules of thumb for adjusting the components of the NetWare file:

■ Increasing the amount of file cache buffers optimizes the file system. The default is to use all remaining memory for file cache buffers, under which circumstance adjustments made to other subsystems that require more memory can negatively affect performance.

■ The larger the disk block size, the more efficient the read-ahead cache, which equate to better performance (however disk space is sacrificed).

■ Modifying the cache block size adds efficiency to the file server by increasing response time between server and client.

■ Increasing the Turbo FAT reuse wait time ensures that Turbo FAT index structures are not flushed as often; that is, if the file is reused, the location of the file can be obtained from cache memory rather than from the hard drive.

■ Adding any extra name spaces to a volume requires multiple FATs and DETs to be cached, which decreases performance. If multiple name spaces are required, consider using separate volumes for each name space, which divides files that require name spaces, to help optimize NetWare file system performance. However, multiple volumes also chew up valuable RAM.

■ For optimal performance, consider using the SET parameters to turn read-after-write verification to OFF and Immediate Purge of files to ON, as follows:

```
SET ENABLE DISK READ AFTER WRITE VERIFY = OFF

SET IMMEDIATE PURGE OF DELETED FILES = ON
```

■ Using an intelligent controller—or in some RAID systems, an intelligent driver—often provides support for data retrieval and writing techniques, such as scattering, merging, queuing, mingling, and so on. These intelligent components help optimize disk I/O.

 Note For some controllers (such as those used with Compaq disk arrays), the hot fix verification is perceived as redundant and the hardware turns off the read-after-write and hot fix functionality.

Some SCSI controllers implement read-after-write verification, providing a redundant level of error checking.

Several enhancements were made to NetWare 3.12 (over 3.11), including the following:

■ Read-ahead cache

■ Enhanced extended attribute support for OS/2 2.1

■ Ability to mount a CD-ROM as a volume

Cache read-ahead allows the server to read more into the cache buffer when the server is performing a sequential file read, which allows for faster file access. You use the SET parameter to control cache read-ahead, as follows:

```
READ AHEAD ENABLED = ON    (default)
```

Communications Subsystems

You need to consider several factors you made to evaluate the performance of a network's communication channel. Most of these considerations deal with the actual design of the network, the amount of segments being used, the medium (Ethernet, token ring, and so on) being used, the type of hardware connecting the network segments (internal or external routing connections mechanisms), and the list goes on. Although these types of questions provide more insight to the overall tuning effort, this section concentrates on those items that the network administrator uses to tune the internal server communications channel, which includes the following components:

■ Packet size

■ Communication buffers

■ Burst Mode technology

■ SAP traffic filtering

Packet Size

The best advice for optimizing the communication channel is simply to use the largest packet size possible. The packet size is a function of the network card.

 Note The default packet receive buffer size for a NetWare 3.11 server is 1 KB (1,024 bytes).

To enable the server to use a packet size other than the default of 1 KB, you must modify a SET parameter in the server's STARTUP.NCF file, as follows:

`SET MAXIMUM PHYSICAL RECEIVE PACKET SIZE =`

The following table lists the most common packet sizes.

Drivers	Default	Packet Size
Token Ring	4 Mbps	2154 KB
Token Ring	16 Mbps	4202 KB
Ethernet		1130 KB
ARCnet		618 KB

 Note Although using the largest supported packet size is the best way to go, you should be aware that using an overly large packet size is about the worst configuration mistake you can make. If you choose a 4 KB packet size, for instance, you need only a 1 KB packet size, and the communication buffers needs to be 4 KB, too. Because communication buffers are allocated in permanent memory, it requires more memory to be permanently allocated out of file cache buffers, which slows disk access.

Communication Buffers

Communication buffers are allocated dynamically based on an aging algorithm in the OS. A minimum number of buffers can be allocated when the server boots, and a maximum number specified to prevent an out-of-control growth situation. A lack of packet receive buffers results in a No ECB Available Count error message.

NetWare's communication buffers support all protocols that the underlying network card drivers could possibly use. Any change to the size of these buffers reflects across all protocol stacks. Remember this when you set about to modify the buffer size.

You use a SET parameter in the STARTUP.NCF file to modify buffer size, as follows:

`SET MAXIMUM PHYSICAL RECEIVE PACKET SIZE =`

 Note The value for this parameter equals the size of the data portion plus the protocol overhead.

In NetWare 3.11, when a packet passes through an intermediate NetWare router, NetWare reduces the packet size to 512 bytes (to accommodate different topologies it must assume the least common denominator).

 Practical TIP To get around this 512-byte router packet size limitation in NetWare 3.11, you need to use LIPX.NLM.

The network administrator can use SET parameters in the STARTUP.NCF and AUTOEXEC.NCF files to control the increase in the number of communication buffers. Two SET parameters work to reconfigure or reallocate the number of buffers based on usage. The first SET parameter controls the minimum number of buffers that can ever be allocated:

```
SET MINIMUM PACKET RECEIVE BUFFERS =
```

The network administrator can use the MONITOR utility to compare the number of configured buffers versus the number currently in use. If the total number of communication buffers peaks at 100 after several months of continuous server operation, for example, the administrator can take advantage of the SET Minimum Packet Receive Buffers parameter to reallocate more than the default of 10 buffers the next time the server is rebooted.

The second SET parameter controls the maximum number of buffers that can ever be allocated:

```
SET MAXIMUM PACKET RECEIVE BUFFERS =
```

If occasional peaks in server usage cause the number of buffers to grow significantly, you might need to control this growth to control the impact on memory.

The administrator can set the maximum at 200 to prevent these peaks from causing unnecessary allocations into permanent memory.

A third SET parameter controls the amount of time the system waits before spawning a new buffer:

```
SET NEW PACKET RECEIVE BUFFER WAIT TIME =
```

You use this parameter in conjunction with the SET Maximum Packet Receive Buffers parameter, acting as a peak inhibitor.

All three of these SET parameters are very closely related and you should use them in a complementary fashion. However, you should use good judgment; these buffers are allocated out of permanent memory, so the memory they use is never returned to the main memory pool.

Burst Mode

Packet Burst is a protocol built on top of an IPX that expedites the transfer of multiple-packet NCP file reads and writes. In older versions of NetWare, for instance, when a NetWare client made an NCP request, a *one-request/one-response method of communication* was followed; that is, each packet of the request had to be followed by an individual acknowledgment—quite inefficient, especially when the requested data requires more than one packet.

Packet Burst is more efficient because it allows client read requests without acknowledgment. Thus, the server can return the requested data in a "burst."

Packet burst is now built into the NetWare 3.12 operating system code and enabled by default in the new client software.

 Note When Packet Burst is enabled at a server and is communicating with a client at which Packet Burst is not enabled, the server communicates with this client in the old one-request/one-response mode.

Service Advertising Protocol (SAP) Traffic

The *Service Advertising Protocol* is used by servers, print servers, gateways, and so forth, to advertise their respective services. Normally, SAP broadcast traffic is very efficient, except for in large Internet works, or WANs. In these situations SAP traffic can occasionally clog the lines.

To reduce this possibility of NetWare SAP traffic clogging the lines, use the new *NetWare Link Services Protocol* (NLSP).

Note NLSP replaces RIP and SAP, offering better performance, reliability, and management of NetWare traffic. Yet it retains compatibility with existing routers, enabling you to upgrade servers and routers on your network one at a time.

Novell's implementation of NLSP is offered as a NetWare Loadable Module (NLM). It will run on versions 3.11 and later on the NetWare operating system.

Large Internet Packet (LIP)

Large Internet Packet is another factor for enhancing the network environment. It works to increase the speed of data transmission of router communication.

LIP allows the client and server to negotiate the packet size used when communication occurs through a router. With LIP, the packets can be set to a maximum of 4,202 bytes. The negotiated packet size depends on the maximum physical packet size of the server.

Network administrators would want to take advantage of the NLSP for three main reasons:

- Reduce SAP traffic

- Prevent users from seeing specific servers

- Lower information coming from remote servers

Note Like Packet Burst, LIP is included in the operating system code of NetWare 3.12 and in the client connection software. LIP is enabled by default at both the server and the client. In some cases, packet size is hard-coded in the router. LIP is not effective in these instances.

Network Interface Card Issues

In NetWare 3.1x, a single network card can support multiple frame types (such as 802.3, Ethernet II, and Ethernet_SNAP) and multiple protocols (such as IPX/SPX, TCP/IP, and AppleTalk). Given this flexibility, configurations are often used where the NIC is simply saturated. Determining whether the network interface card and driver is a bottleneck, however, is not a simple endeavor.

NetWare's MONITOR utility does provide some useful information for determining the status of the network card.

Not every NIC's manufacturer will provide you with all the information you need.

There are basically two sets of NIC statistics: general error information and custom statistics.

The general error statistics, as its name implies, consists of general error entries. All network card manufacturers are urged to write its drivers such that these 15 different statistics are maintained. These include statistics such as total packets sent and received, packets dropped due to no available communication buffers, and so forth.

The optional statistics, which consist of another 15 to 20 additional statistics, provide custom driver information. Thus, and unfortunately, not all Ethernet cards will have the same set of custom statistics.

Some of this information can be extremely helpful. For instance, if the network card displays this level of information, you can use these statistic to determine if the network card is "keeping up."

The Enqueued Send Counts reports the number of packets the NIC had to buffer because the driver or card was too busy to send a packet that the processor had ready.

If this count increments regularly and reaches 1 to 2 percent of the total packets transmitted, it indicates that the NIC driver is having trouble keeping up with the server and is reaching or has reached its saturation point.

System Processor

The system processor is the last frontier for performance optimization. High server CPU utilization does not always mean the server lacks in system processor power. Many resources, including NLMs and NICs, contend for CPU time. Network administrators frequently make the mistake of assuming that 90 percent utilization means the CPU is saturated. Replacing the server with a new 80486 machine may not yield the expected performance gains. Typically, the other server subsystems must be optimized before the system processor emerges as a bottleneck.

Using the NetWare's MONITOR utility, you can evaluate your server's CPU utilization. To do so select the Processor utilization option. It will provide you with a list of processes by interrupt, which identifies inefficient or CPU-intensive resources in the server.

The regularity with which an interrupt is triggered is an indication of which hardware device is being accessed most frequently. For example, if a NIC configured for interrupt 3 is constantly servicing packets and utilizing a large percentage of CPU time, that NIC could be a possible bottleneck.

Managing the server's CPU utilization is often best accomplished by balancing the server's hardware. For example, using 32-bit disk controller technology in an EISA bus machine with a slower ISA bus network card will ultimately be a bottleneck. You should also use technologies such as Bus Mastering

cards. This technology allows the server to move data in and out of system memory and on to the card without interrupting the CPU.

Questions

1. Each of the server components can directly or indirectly affect the performance of the entire NetWare operating system.

   ○ T.

   ○ F.

2. Adding any extra name spaces to a volume requires multiple FATs and DET to be cached, which decrease performance.

   ○ T

   ○ F

3. Which of the following enhancements made to NetWare 3.12 (over 3.11) is most likely to effect performance?

   ○ A. Read-ahead cache

   ○ B. Enhanced extended attribute support for OS/2 2

   ○ C. Ability to mount a CD-ROM as a volume

   ○ D. None of the above

4. Network administrators would want to take advantage of the NLSP for which one of the following reasons?

   ○ A. To reduce SAP traffic

   ○ B. To prevent users from seeing specific servers

   ○ C. To lower information coming from remote servers

   ○ D. All of the above

5. Which of the following server subsystems is not a concern to overall network performance?

   ○ A. Server memory

   ○ B. File system and cache

   ○ C. Communications subsystem

   ○ D. None of the above

Answers

1. T

2. T

3. A

4. D

5. D

PART PART PART PART PART PART PART PART PART PART PART PART PART

DOS/Microcomputer Basics

43   *DOS Concepts for NetWare Administrators* *621*

44   *Microcomputer Concepts for NetWare Administrators* *641*

DOS Concepts for NetWare Administrators

*D*OS is software that runs on a PC and manages system resources. Tasks performed by DOS include the following:

- *Reading and writing data to and from floppy and hard disks*
- *Managing file systems on disks*
- *Displaying data on monitors*
- *Inputting characters from the keyboard*
- *Running applications*
- *Controlling how the computer operates*

The following three versions of DOS are available:

- *MS-DOS, from Microsoft*
- *PC-DOS, from IBM*
- *Novell DOS (DR-DOS), from Novell*

This course concentrates on information common to all of these versions.

DOS consists of the following types of files:

■ **System files.** MS-DOS names the files MSDOS.SYS and IO.SYS. PC-DOS names them IBMDOS.COM and IBMBIO.COM. These files are installed in the boot track (track 0) of the boot drive and are started by the BIOS at the end of the POST test procedure. *See Chapter 44, "Microcomputer Concepts for NetWare Administrators," for more information on the boot process.*

IBMBIO.COM (IO.SYS in MS-DOS) handles input/output functions for DOS, such as keyboard input and video display.

IBMDOS.COM (MSDOS.SYS in MS-DOS) is the core DOS component that coordinates communication among the components of the microcomputer.

■ **COMMAND.COM.** This file is the command processor that accepts commands from the user. Many common commands, called *internal commands*, are built into COMMAND.COM. When a user enters a command that does not match an internal command, COMMAND.COM searches for an auxiliary command file.

■ **Auxiliary commands.** Many DOS commands, such as FORMAT and DISKCOPY, are stored in separate files. These are called *external commands* because they are not built into the command processor.

The DOS File System

Data is stored in files. DOS files have some characteristics with which you should be familiar.

File Names

DOS file names follow the "eight-dot-three" convention: one to eight characters followed by a period, which is optionally followed by one to three characters. A period (called a "dot") separates the two parts.

The following characters can appear in the file name:

■ Alphanumeric characters (A–Z and 0–9)

■ ! @ # $ % ^ & ( ) ` [ ] ~ - _

■ Characters with ASCII values above 127 in the IBM character set

■ A single period ("dot"), separating the first and last parts of the file name

The following characters cannot appear in the file name:

■ # ? + = \ / ; : " , < > [ ]

■ Spaces

■ DOS-reserved names such as COM1, COM2, COM3, COM4, AUX, CON, LPT1, LPT2, LPT3, NUL, PRN, or CLOCKS

The following are examples of valid file names:

COMMAND.COM
HIMEM.SYS
MOUSE.EXE
TEMP.FIL
REPORT.XLS
1-5-95.DOC
$SALE$.DAT
95.3%
MY_MEMO.TXT

The following are examples of invalid file names:

MY MEMO.TXT (Spaces not allowed)
1994SALES.DAT (Too many characters)
REPORT.PRN (PRN is reserved)
SALES?.DAT (? is invalid)

Types of Files

Programs are instructions that are executed by the microprocessor to perform a task. Programs are stored in executable files, which end with the extensions EXE ("executable") or COM ("command"). The DOS XCOPY command, for example, is stored in the executable file XCOPY.EXE. When you enter a command, DOS locates the executable file that matches the command and executes the program in the file.

System files, ending with the SYS extension, are special executable files that must be executed from the CONFIG.SYS file when the PC boots.

Batch files also can be executed. These consist of text files that contain valid commands. All batch files end with a BAT extension. When you enter the name of a batch file, the commands in the file's text are executed.

Data files are not executable. Word processing documents, spreadsheets, and databases are examples of data files. The extension names for data files do not need to conform to any special rules. Some examples of common data file extensions are as follows:

- **DOC.** Document files
- **TXT.** Text files
- **OVL.** Program overlay files containing program segments that are loaded by other programs

- **DAT.** Data files
- **BAS.** Programs written in the programming language BASIC

File Attributes

Attributes can be assigned to DOS files to determine some characteristics of the files. The following list describes the DOS file attributes:

- **A.** Indicates that a file has been modified. After the file is backed up, the A attribute is removed.
- **H.** Causes files to be hidden from directory listings.
- **R.** Flags files as read-only. These files cannot be erased, renamed, or modified.
- **S.** Indicates system files that are both hidden and read-only. Some DOS files are flagged with the S attribute, but this attribute is not usually applied by users.

Booting DOS

DOS PCs can be cold or warm booted. A *cold boot* occurs when the PC is turned on or, on some PCs, after the reset button is pressed. A cold boot invokes the *Power On Self-Test* (POST), as described in Chapter 44. To cold boot a PC, perform the following steps:

1. Ensure that the hard drive is formatted as a system disk or that a bootable floppy is in the A drive.
2. Turn on the power or press the reset button.
3. Wait for the DOS prompt.

A *warm boot* can be used to restart a PC without turning off power and does not perform a POST test. A warm boot does clear memory and restart DOS, however, and can be used to recover from hung applications. To warm boot a PC, perform the following steps:

1. Ensure that the hard drive is formatted as a system disk or that a bootable floppy is in the A drive.

2. Press the Ctrl, Alt, and Del keys at the same time.

3. Wait for the DOS prompt.

Using DOS Commands

The DOS command interpreter (COMMAND.COM) receives command input and initiates command execution. When you see a DOS prompt (usually A>, C>, or another drive letter followed by a flashing cursor) the command interpreter is awaiting a command. Typing a command at the flashing cursor and pressing Enter causes the command to be executed.

DOS always has a current drive, the letter of which usually is displayed in the prompt. The *current drive* is the default drive from which DOS attempts to locate command files. These drive letters have the following meanings:

■ A is the first floppy drive.

■ B is the second floppy drive.

■ C is the first hard drive partition.

■ D through Z are additional hard drive partitions.

Some keys have special effects when they are entered in conjunction with commands. The following list describes these effects:

■ **Enter.** Completes the command and instructs DOS to execute it.

■ **Ctrl.** Along with a letter generates control codes, some of which have special functions in DOS. Ctrl+Z, for example, aborts some DOS processes.

■ **Alt.** Also is used in combination with other keys, but has no special DOS function except for the Ctrl+Alt+Del reboot key sequence.

■ **Cursor keys.** Can perform some elementary command-line editing.

■ **F1 through F12** are used by some utilities.

Internal Commands

Internal commands are commands that are stored in the COMMAND.COM command processor. DOS does not need to locate command files to execute these commands. Examples of internal commands are as follows:

■ **DIR.** Displays a listing of files along with their sizes, dates, and time stamps

■ **TYPE.** Shows the contents of a file on-screen

■ **COPY.** Duplicates a file

■ **DEL.** Removes a file (as does the ERASE command)

■ **REN.** Renames a file

■ **CLS.** Erases all data from the screen

External Commands

External commands are not found in COMMAND.COM. Instead, DOS must look for them in program files ending with COM or EXE file name extensions. Many DOS programs, and all applications, are programmed in command files.

Examples of DOS external commands are as follows:

- **FDISK.** Manages hard drive partitions

- **FORMAT.** Formats hard and floppy disks

- **BACKUP.** Backs up files to floppy disks

- **LABEL.** Adds an eleven-character label to a DOS disk

- **XCOPY.** Copies commands more efficiently than the internal COPY command

- **DISKCOPY.** Duplicates floppy disks

Command Parameters

Many commands require specification of parameters. You cannot rename a file without specifying the current and new file names, as in the following example:

```
REN ABC.DOC XYZ.DOC
```

Command Switches

The syntax of many commands specifies switches that affect the operation of the commands. Most DOS commands use a forward slash to designate a switch, followed by a switch letter. The /W switch in the following command line, for example, causes the DIR command to display directory entries in multiple columns:

```
DIR /W
```

Case Insensitivity

DOS does not distinguish between upper- and lowercase. Therefore you can enter commands in upper-, lower-, or mixed-case.

Error Messages

When DOS cannot interpret a command by finding a matching internal or external command, it produces an error message, as in the following example:

```
DRI *.*
Bad command or file name
```

When a command specifies the letter of a drive that is not available, DOS responds with a message like the following:

```
DIR B:
Not ready reading drive B
Abort, Retry, Fail?
```

You can use one of the following three options to recover from issuing a command that specifies an unavailable drive:

- Press **A** to cancel the process. DOS will attempt to restore a command prompt on a valid drive.

- Press **R** to reattempt the process, for example, after inserting a missing floppy disk.

- Press **F** to fail the operation. You will be asked to specify the drive letter of a valid drive to reestablish the environment of the command processor.

Procedures Used with Disks

The following sections describe some disk-related procedures with which you should be familiar. The following processes are covered:

- Formatting floppies
- DOS file storage
- Changing disk volume labels
- Creating boot disks
- Selecting a default disk
- Accessing files on non-default disks
- Copying disks

Formatting Floppy Disks

When a floppy disk matches the standard capacity of the disk drive, formatting it is simple. Just enter the FORMAT command, specifying the drive letter as follows:

FORMAT B:

DOS prompts you to insert a disk and press Enter. After the format is completed, DOS prompts you again as follows:

```
Volume label (11 characters, ENTER for none)?
```

This prompt gives you the opportunity to label the disk. After this step, FORMAT reports the capacity of the disk, as in the following example:

```
1457664 bytes total disk space
1457664 bytes available on disk

Format another (Y/N)?
```

Formatting Hard Disks

Hard disk drives are formatted in the same way, but DOS asks you a few more questions to ensure that you don't wipe out an entire hard disk accidentally. If you have specified a volume label, you need to enter the label as a safeguard when reformatting the hard disk.

When the floppy disk doesn't match the default capacity of the drive, switches are required. The following command formats a 5.25-inch double-density (360 KB) disk in a 5.25-inch high-density (1.2 MB) drive:

```
FORMAT A: /4
```

A 3.5-inch double-density (720 KB) disk is formatted in a high-density drive with the following command:

```
FORMAT A: /N:9/T:80
```

This command formats the disk with 80 tracks and 9 sectors per track.

DOS 5 and 6 support the /F switch, which enables you to directly specify the desired disk density. You can use the following command to format a 360 KB double-density disk in a high-density 5.25-inch drive:

```
FORMAT A: /F:360
```

A 720 MB double-density disk can be formatted with the following command:

```
FORMAT A:/F:720
```

DOS File Storage Methods

The process of storing a file involves several steps. These steps are explained in the following list:

■ Creating a directory entry that includes the file name and extensions, file attributes, data and time stamps, and the file size in bytes

■ Updating the *File Allocation Table* (FAT) to reserve the clusters occupied by the file

■ Recording the track and sector where the beginning of the file can be located

DOS begins writing files proceeding inward from the first available cluster starting from track one. As files are erased, gaps are created in the clusters, and new files can be stored in various clusters on many tracks. This process is called *file fragmentation*, and it can hurt system performance because more head seeks must be performed to retrieve the entire file than if the file were stored in contiguous clusters. Therefore, file storage efficiency can be improved by periodically using a utility to defragment the files on a disk.

Changing Disk Volume Labels

Each floppy and hard disk can be assigned a label of up to eleven characters. The following command assigns the label VOLUME_XYZ to the floppy in drive A:

`LABEL A: VOLUME_XYZ`

To view the label, type the label command without a label parameter as follows:

`LABEL A:`

The label is displayed, and you will have the option of changing it.

Creating Boot Disks

To make a disk bootable, it must contain the system files in Track 0 (the boot track) as well as

COMMAND.COM. These files can be installed in two ways: during formatting and by the SYS command on a previously formatted disk.

To install the system files during formatting, type the following command:

`FORMAT A: /S`

The /S parameter instructs FORMAT to copy the system files after a format.

The SYS command adds system files to a formatted disk. The system files can be installed only if no files are stored in track 0 of the target disk, which generally means that the disk must be newly formatted. Type the following to use the SYS command:

`SYS A:`

Selecting a Default Disk

DOS always assumes that commands refer to a default disk. After booting, the default disk is A or C, depending on the boot disk. To change the default disk, merely type the new disk letter at the command prompt. To default to disk B, for example, type `B:`.

Accessing Files on Non-Default Disks

Because COMMAND.COM is always running, internal commands are always available. Special steps are required to access files on disks other than the default disk, however.

To reference a file on a disk other than the default disk, include the disk letter in the file specification. To run an external command on another disk, add the disk letter to the command, as in the following example:

```
C:PRINT REPORT.DOC
```

You also can include the disk letter when the file name is a parameter, as in the following example:

```
PRINT A:REPORT.DOC
```

Copying Disks

DISKCOPY copies the entire contents of one disk to a target disk of the identical size and capacity. You cannot use DISKCOPY, for example, to copy from a 1.4 MB 3.5-inch disk to a 1.2 MB 5.25-inch disk.

If you have two drives of the same capacity, insert the disks and specify the source and destination disks as in the following command:

```
DISKCOPY A: B:
```

Drive A in this example is the source drive and drive B is the destination, also called the *target drive.*

You also can perform a same-drive copy by typing the command as follows:

```
DISKCOPY A: A:
```

In this case, DISKCOPY prompts you to swap disks periodically. Recent DOS versions require only one disk swap. Earlier versions might require several swaps.

Directories and Subdirectories

DOS organizes files into directories and subdirectories, much like files in drawers of a file cabinet.

Each disk starts with a single directory called the *root,* which is designated with a backslash \.

Directories can be added to the root directory. DOS external command files are generally installed in a directory named \DOS, where the starting \ indicates that DOS is a directory just below the root directory.

Directories can contain subdirectories, which can contain more subdirectories. The following example displays a series of subdirectories:

```
\DOCS
\DOCS\REPORTS
\DOCS\REPORTS\FY1994
```

A *directory path* shows all directories between the root and a specific subdirectory.

Creating Directories

You can use the MD command to create directories. Subdirectories must be created one level at a time.

To create a new directory, type MD followed by the new directory's name, as in the following example:

```
MD \DOCS
```

Then repeat the command, adding successive subdirectories, as follows:

```
MD \DOCS\REPORTS
MD \DOCS\REPORTS\FY1994
```

Deleting Directories

Similarly, the RD command can remove directories one level at a time:

```
RD \DOCS\REPORTS\FY1994
RD \DOCS\REPORTS
RD \DOCS
```

The Default Directory

Just as DOS always has a default disk, it always has a default directory in which it looks first for files. To make another directory the default directory, use the CD command. Type **CD** followed by the new default directory as in the following example:

CD \DOCS\REPORTS

You can specify files that are not in the default directory by including a directory path in the file specification as follows:

DIR \DOCS\REPORTS

A disk letter can be combined with a directory path to provide a complete path, as in the following example:

TYPE A:\ARCHIVE\SALES.RPT

Relative Directory Paths

The directory paths you have seen until now list all directories between the root directory and the subdirectory of interest. You can tell this is the case because these names all begin with a \ indicating the root directory, as in the following example:

\REPORTS\SALES\1994

You also can specify a relative path name—one that begins with the current (default) directory. If your current directory is \REPORTS, for example, you can TYPE a file in the 1994 subdirectory with the following command:

TYPE SALES\1994\SUMMARY.TXT

Because the path name omits a leading \, it is a relative path name that begins with the current directory.

Using a DOS Path

It is bad practice to put all executable files in the same directory. Unless you do, however, you need to change default directories or include path names to execute a file that is not in the current directory.

The DOS PATH enables you to specify a list of directories in which DOS is to search for command files. The PATH consists of directory names separated by semicolons. You do not have to include the drive letter, but it is often a good idea, especially if your PC has several disk drives and you might be changing your default drive. If a drive letter is not specified in the PATH, DOS looks for the directories in the path on the current disk drive.

Do not include floppy disk letters in the PATH. An Abort, Retry, Fail error message appears each time DOS checks a floppy drive that does not have a disk inserted.

To create a PATH, use a statement like the following:

PATH
C:\DOS;C:\WINDOWS;C:\WORDPERF;C:\123

When you enter a command, DOS searches each directory in the PATH, starting from the beginning, in an attempt to locate the associated command file.

To display the current PATH, simply type the PATH command alone.

How DOS Searches for Commands

First, DOS looks for a matching internal command.

Next, DOS looks for a matching COM, EXE, or BAT file (in that specific order) in the current directory.

Next, DOS looks for a matching COM, EXE, or BAT file in each directory in the PATH.

If a command file still cannot be located, a Bad command or file name error message is displayed.

File Management Procedures

The Novell DOS test expects you to be familiar with several file management procedures.

The DIR Command

DIR produces a listing of files in a directory. For example, typing **DIR** can produce the following lines:

```
Volume in drive C has no label
Volume Serial Number is 1D75-7355
Directory of C:\FILES

.            <DIR>        02-17-95   7:26p
..           <DIR>        02-17-95   7:26p
REPORT1  TXT          27  02-17-95   7:27p
REPORT2  TXT          71  02-17-95   7:28p
      4 file(s)             98 bytes
                   340,131,840 bytes free
```

Two files are displayed, along with their sizes and the dates and times they were last modified.

Also shown are two directories, indicated by <DIR>. The . directory is DOS shorthand for the current directory. The .. directory is shorthand for the parent directory, the directory that contains the current directory. Because the root directory has no parent directory, you do not see the . or .. entries

when you perform a directory listing on the root directory.

DIR accepts two switches—/P and /W—that make it easier to manage large directories. These two switches are described in the following list:

- ■ **/P** pauses the directory listing with each screenful of data.

- ■ **/W** lists directory names in columns, omitting the file size, date, and time stamp.

TYPE

To display the contents of a text file use the type command as follows:

TYPE C:\AUTOEXEC.BAT

Copying Files

To create a copy of a file with a new name, specify the old and new names:

COPY FILEA.TXT FILEB.TXT

To copy a file to a different directory, include the destination directory in the destination file specification. If you do not want the destination file to have a different name, the name can be omitted, as in the following example:

COPY FILEA.TXT \REPORTS\SALES

A disk also can be a destination. To copy files to a floppy, use a command like the following:

COPY FILEA.TXT A:

You can copy files from another directory to the current directory without specifying a destination. The following example copies all files from \REPORTS to the current directory:

COPY \REPORTS

Copying Input to a File

DOS recognizes many devices as if they were files. Among these are CON (the console or keyboard), LPT1-3, and COM1-4. You can use COPY to copy input or output with these devices.

Enter the following keystrokes to start a copy from CON to a file, enter some data, and end the process:

```
COPY CON TESTFILE.TXT<Enter>
This is text for the file.<Enter>
<F6><Enter>
```

After you execute the COPY CON command, everything you type is routed to the file TESTFILE.TXT. You terminate the copy command by pressing F6 followed by the Enter key. F6 inserts a Ctrl+Z character in the file, which is required at the end of every DOS text file.

DEL and ERASE

Both the DEL and ERASE commands erase files. Entering either of the following commands has the same effect:

```
DEL THISFILE.TXT
```

```
ERASE THISFILE.TXT
```

Wild Cards

Wild cards are symbols that you can use to represent the names of groups of files. The following two wild-card symbols are used:

■ * Matches any series of characters of any length

■ ? Matches any one character

You can include wild-card characters in the file name specifications for any DOS command. To display all the BAT files in a directory, you use the following command:

```
DIR *.BAT
```

To display all the files with an extension starting with WK (WKS, WK1, and so on) you use the following command:

```
DIR *.WK?
```

The command COPY REPORT?.DOC copies files named REPORT.DOC, REPORT1.DOC, and REPORTA.DOC. Because ? stands for one character only, however, the command does not copy REPORT11.DOC. Notice that REPORT.DOC is copied even though no character is in a position that matches the ?.

The wild card for all file names is *.*, often read as "star dot star." Although *.* makes it easy to manipulate all the files in a directory, *.* and all wild cards should be used with caution when deleting files.

Do not use the * at the beginning of a file name. The file specification *AB.* is equivalent to *.*. Files will be matched whether or not the name portion ends with AB.

ATTRIB

In the section "File Attributes" earlier in this chapter the four DOS file attributes—A, H, R, and S—are listed. The ATTRIB command is used to add, remove, and display these file attributes.

To add an attribute, in this case the H attribute, use the following format:

```
ATTRIB +H FILE1.TXT
```

Attaching the R (Read Only) attribute to a file provides insurance against accidental erasure of the file. The S (System) attribute is a combination of the R and H (Hidden) attributes. S is seldom applied by users, but several DOS files are marked with the S attribute.

To remove the attribute, replace the + with a – as follows:

```
ATTRIB -H FILE1.TXT
```

When removing attributes, you must first remove the S attribute if present. Next must come the R attribute. Finally, you can remove the H attribute. The A attribute is removed only when the file is archived with a backup program.

You can combine several attribute changes in a single command, as in the following example:

```
ATTRIB -H +R ABCD.EXE
```

To simply display attributes of files, use the ATTRIB command without parameters. For example, issuing **ATTRIB *.*** produces the following results:

```
A  H      C:\DOC\REPORT.DOC
          C:\DOC\SALES.DOC
A         C:\DOC\PLANS.DOC
```

Issuing the ATTRIB command is one way to see the system files DOS installs in the boot track. These files display in a manner similar to the following:

```
SHR       C:\IO.SYS
SHR       C:\MSDOS.SYS
```

XCOPY

XCOPY is a more recent version of the COPY command with the following improvements:

■ Copies groups of files at a time, whereas COPY completely copies one file at a time. XCOPY reads as much file information as it can buffer and writes all buffered information in a single operation. The result is a faster copy process.

■ Copies subdirectory structures and files in subdirectories.

■ Recognizes the A attribute and can be used to archive modified files.

For copying files, XCOPY is used with the same command syntax as COPY. When you specify destination directories, however, XCOPY operates differently. For example, type the following command, assuming that \DIR2 does not exist:

```
XCOPY C:\DIR1 C:\DIR2
```

XCOPY then asks you whether to create a directory or a file, as follows:

```
Does DIR2 specify a file name
or directory name on the target
(F = file, D = directory)
```

If you specify D, XCOPY creates the target directory and copies all files in DIR1 to DIR2.

If you include the /S switch, XCOPY creates and copies all subdirectories in the source directory as well.

The /M (modified) switch instructs XCOPY to copy only files that have the A attribute assigned. After the files are copied, the A attribute is cleared from the original and the copy of the file. The /M flag enables you to set up a file archive system whereby only modified files are copied to the archive media.

Utility Commands

You should be familiar with several DOS utility commands.

DATE and TIME

The DATE and TIME commands display the current DOS date and time and can be used to set the DOS clock. They do not, however, change the time and date in the system CMOS clock; the CMOS time and date are restored after the system is rebooted.

If you enter the DATE command, DOS responds similarly to the following:

```
Current date is Sat 02-18-1995
Enter new date (mm-dd-yy):
```

If you press Enter, the date does not change. If you enter a new date, the DOS date will be altered. Valid date formats can use / or - (hyphen) as separator characters, for example, 5-3-95 and 5/3/95 are both valid.

The TIME command works in much the same way. The time is represented using a 24-hour clock, whereby 18 represents 6 p.m.

VER

The VER command displays the version of DOS that was used to boot the PC. Simply type **VER** to display the version.

PROMPT

The PROMPT command enables you to customize the characters in the DOS prompt. The following command converts the DOS prompt to display the current directory path, followed by a greater-than sign (>):

```
PROMPT $P$G
```

The following special characters can appear in the PROMPT command parameters:

- **$B** A vertical bar character (|)
- **$D** The current date
- **$G** A greater-than sign (>)
- **$L** A less-than sign (<)
- **$N** The default drive letter
- **$P** The current drive and directory path
- **$Q** An equal sign (=)
- **$T** The current time
- **$$** A dollar sign ($)

You can combine text with PROMPT characters as in the following example:

```
PROMPT Current directory is $P. -$G
```

CLS

The CLS command clears the DOS screen.

PRINT

The PRINT command prints a text file to a printer port. To print a file named REPORT.TXT, you would use the following command:

```
PRINT REPORT.TXT
```

After you issue the PRINT command, you are asked to specify a printer port. The default port is PRN: (LPT1), and you specify it by pressing Enter. Specify another port to direct the printed output differently.

Redirection

The > character is the DOS *redirection operator*. It enables you to send the output of a command to a file or device. To send the results of a DIR command to a text file, you use a command like the following:

```
DIR *.* > FILES.TXT
```

You can then manipulate the file in a text editor, or use TYPE to display it on the screen.

Redirection can be used with devices as well. To print a directory, you can redirect DIR output to PRN as in the following example:

```
DIR *.EXE > PRN:
```

Use redirection with caution with commands that ask for user input. The prompt for input goes to the redirected file or device, not to the monitor, and the process might appear to hang when it is waiting for a keystroke.

Batch Files

Batch files are text files that contain executable commands. They are an effective means of repetitively performing multi-step procedures. The following example executes a word processing command by first switching to the appropriate directory:

```
CD \APPS\WORDPERF
WP
CD \
```

The final command CD \ does not execute until you exit the WP program. At that time, you are sent to the root directory.

If you store this batch file in a directory on your PATH, you do not need to include the application directory itself in the PATH.

Batch files can be created with the COPY CON technique discussed previously, or with any text editor such as the EDIT program included with recent versions of MS-DOS. A batch file can contain any command you can type at the keyboard.

Several special commands are provided to enhance batch files. Three are discussed in this chapter—REM, ECHO, and PAUSE.

REM

REM inserts remarks in the batch file. Remarks are not executable commands. They consist of text that explains the operation of the batch file. A file that starts the NetWare Requester might contain the following commands:

```
REM Start the NetWare Requester

CD \NWCLIENT

LSL

NE2000

IPXODI

VLM
```

ECHO

ECHO determines whether DOS displays the commands in batch files as they are executed. ECHO ON turns on command display (the default), and ECHO OFF turns off command display. After a new batch file has been tested, it is useful to add ECHO OFF as the first line to suppress command display and clean up file execution.

ECHO displays messages to users during batch file execution. The following example prompts a user to insert a floppy disk:

```
ECHO Insert a floppy disk in A:
XCOPY *.* A: /H
```

PAUSE

PAUSE temporarily halts batch file execution until a key is pressed. Here is an example of PAUSE in a batch file:

```
ECHO Insert a floppy disk in A:
PAUSE
XCOPY *.* A: /H
```

AUTOEXEC.BAT

As the last step of the boot process, a DOS PC attempts to execute a batch file named AUTOEXEC.BAT. This file can contain commands that are to be executed every time the PC boots. The following list contains such commands:

```
ECHO OFF

CLS

PROMPT $T $P $G

PATH C:\DOS;C:\WINDOWS

REM Start the NetWare Requester

CD \NWCLIENT

LSL

NE2000

IPXODI

VLM
```

```
F:

LOGIN
```

MS-DOS version 6.*x* recogizes two function keys that enable you to control the execution of CONFIG.SYS and AUTOEXEC.BAT. When DOS is booting, look for the message Starting MS-DOS.... While this message is displayed, you can take one of the following actions:

■ Press F5 to bypass CONFIG.SYS and AUTOEXEC.BAT completely.

■ Press F8 to execute CONFIG.SYS and AUTOEXEC.BAT one line at a time. You are asked to confirm whether each line should be executed.

Installing and Configuring DOS

The following steps are required to install DOS:

1. Partition the hard drive and set an active partition.

2. Format the active partition.

3. Install DOS in the active partition.

4. Configure the CONFIG.SYS and AUTOEXEC.BAT files.

These steps are covered in detail in the following sections.

Partitioning Hard Drives

A utility named FDISK is used to partition hard disk drives. To use FDISK with DOS, each hard disk must have one primary partition, which is formatted as drive C.

In addition, each drive can have one extended partition that can be organized into multiple logical DOS drives from D through Z.

A disk also can include non-DOS partitions, which are created by other operating systems such as Unix, NetWare, or OS/2.

The following listing shows the first menu screen from the MS-DOS FDISK utility:

```
               MS-DOS Version 6
           Fixed Disk Setup Program
   (C)Copyright Microsoft Corp. 1983 - 1993


               FDISK Options

Current fixed disk drive: 1

Choose one of the following:

1. Create DOS partition or Logical DOS Drive
2. Set active partition
3. Delete partition or Logical DOS Drive
4. Display partition information


Enter choice: [1]


Press Esc to exit FDISK
```

To create a primary partition, you first select option 1, Create DOS partition or Logical DOS Drive. The following menu then appears:

```
           Create DOS Partition or
              Logical DOS Drive

Current fixed disk drive: 1

Choose one of the following:

1. Create Primary DOS Partition
2. Create Extended DOS Partition
```

```
3. Create Logical DOS Drive(s) in the
   Extended DOS Partition


Enter choice: [1]


Press Esc to return to FDISK Options
```

From the menu, select option 1, Create Primary DOS Partition. You are then given the opportunity to specify the size of the DOS partition being created.

■ If the drive is to be used entirely for DOS, you can choose to create a partition that occupies all available space on the drive.

■ If the drive is being used on a NetWare 3.*x* or 4.*x* server, you should create a DOS partition of 5–10 MB, leaving the rest of the drive available for NetWare.

After you create the partition, you return to the FDISK Options menu. Choose option 2, Set Active Partition, to make the new partition active. Only an active primary partition can be used to boot the PC.

Formatting the DOS Partition

Next you need to boot the PC with a bootable floppy and format the new partition. To make the partition bootable, you use the /S parameter as follows:

FORMAT C: /S

Configuring CONFIG.SYS

While DOS is booting it looks for configuration information in a file named CONFIG.SYS. The actual commands differ significantly between different DOS versions, but here is an example using MS-DOS:

```
BUFFERS=30

FILES=20

LASTDRIVE=Z

DEVICE=C:\DOS\HIMEM.SYS

DEVICE=C:\DOS\EMM386.EXE
```

Following are brief explanations of the four keywords that appear in this file: BUFFERS. FILES, LASTDRIVE and DEVICE.

BUFFERS

DOS sets aside 512 KB buffers that are used to store data that is read from the disk. When DOS needs to read from the disk, it first checks the buffers for the information, which is faster than checking the disk itself. The default number of buffers is seldom enough for best performance, which is why the example shown in the preceding section allocates 30 buffers.

FILES

The number of files DOS can open at one time is determined by the FILES parameter. The default value of 8 files is seldom enough, particularly in a Windows environment in which many applications might be active. The example instructs DOS

to increase this limit to 20, which is probably a bare minimum for modern applications.

LASTDRIVE

The LASTDRIVE parameter establishes which drive letter is the last drive available for use by DOS. Normally, DOS allocates drive letters A through E for its use. The DOS Requester requires that the number of drives be increased to make additional drive letters available for network drives. The example sets LASTDRIVE to Z so that all 26 drive letters are available for use as network drives.

The older DOS Shell could use only drive letters above the LASTDRIVE value. Therefore LASTDRIVE=E was usually used so that drives F through Z could be used on the network.

DEVICE

This command loads device drivers. *Device drivers* are special programs, usually designated with a SYS extension but sometimes with EXE, that are installed during the DOS boot process.

The device drivers shown in the previous example of CONFIG.SYS commands are HIMEM.SYS and EMM386.EXE, which configure MS-DOS to use extended memory. Other types of drivers can be installed in CONFIG.SYS as well, including SCSI adapter drivers, CD-ROM drivers, special display adapters, and so on.

Questions

1. Which of the following extensions can legally be used with a DOS file name?

   ○ A. TX!

   ○ B. CON

   ○ C. NUL

   ○ D. EX%

2. Which of the following is NOT the extension of an executable file?

   ○ A. COM

   ○ B. SYS

   ○ C. EXE

   ○ D. BAT

3. Which TWO of the following file names are valid?

   ☐ A. ~REPORT.DA?

   ☐ B. SALES1995.TXT

   ☐ C. CONTROL.CON

   ☐ D. SALES$.$$$

4. Which THREE are the required characteristics of a bootable DOS partition?

   ☐ A. It must occupy the entire disk.

   ☐ B. It must be a primary partition.

   ☐ C. It must be active.

   ☐ D. It must be formatted with system files.

5. If your current directory is C:\DOS and the prompt command in your AUTOEXEC.BAT file is $P-$G, what will be the appearance of the prompt?

   ○ A. DOS\

   ○ B. C:\DOS>

   ○ C. C:\DOS->

   ○ D. C:\DOS

6. Which command formats a 720 MB 3.5-inch floppy disk in a 1.44 MB drive?

   ○ A. FORMAT A: /4

   ○ B. FORMAT A: /D

   ○ C. FORMAT A: /N:9/T:80

   ○ D. FORMAT A: /720

7. DOS looks for executable files in which order?

   ○ A. EXE, COM, BAT

   ○ B. EXE, BAT, COM

   ○ C. COM, EXE, BAT

   ○ D. BAT, COM, EXE

8. Which list describes the order in which DOS searches locations for files?

   ○ A. PATH, current directory, subdirectories, internal commands

   ○ B. Internal commands, current directory, PATH

   ○ C. Current directory, internal commands, PATH

   ○ D. Internal commands, current directory, subdirectories, PATH

9. After you type the command COPY FILE1.TXT FILE2.TXT, _____.

   ○ A. FILE2.TXT replaces FILE1.TXT

   ○ B. FILE2.TXT and FILE1.TXT exist in the same directory

   ○ C. the contents of FILE1.TXT and FILE2.TXT will be the same

   ○ D. the contents of FILE1.TXT will have moved to FILE2.TXT

10. Which files will be listed by the command DIR FILE?.TXT?

    ☐ A. FILE1.TXT

    ☐ B. FILEA.TXT

    ☐ C. FILE11.TXT

    ☐ D. FILE.TXT

11. Which files will be listed by the command DIR FILE*1.TXT?

    ☐ A. FILE1.TXT

    ☐ B. FILEA.TXT

    ☐ C. FILE11.TXT

    ☐ D. FILE.TXT

12. Which TWO of the following must be done to create a DOS bootable hard disk drive?

    ☐ A. Create a primary partition that occupies the entire hard drive

    ☐ B. Format the primary partition

    ☐ C. Copy the DOS system files to the hard drive

    ☐ D. Create an extended partition

13. Which TWO of the following commands can appear in AUTOEXEC.BAT?

    ☐ A. ECHO

    ☐ B. DEVICE

    ☐ C. COPY

    ☐ D. BUFFERS

14. Which TWO of the following commands can appear in CONFIG.SYS?

    ☐ A. DEVICE

    ☐ B. CD

    ☐ C. XCOPY

    ☐ D. LASTDRIVE

15. Which TWO attributes can you manage with the ATTRIB command?

    ☐ A. A

    ☐ B. H

    ☐ C. D

    ☐ D. S

Answers

1 A	9 C
2 B	10 A B D
3 A D	11 A B C D
4 B C D	12 B C
5 C	13 A C
6 C	14 A D
7 C	15 B D
8 B	

Microcomputer Concepts for NetWare Administrators

This chapter is intended to refresh your memory and round out your knowledge about PC hardware.

Basic Functions of a Computer

A computer performs the following five basic operations:

■ **Bootup.** Starting the computer

■ **Input.** Receiving data from an external source

■ **Processing.** Manipulation of data

■ **Storage.** Placement of data on permanent storage devices

■ **Output.** Transmission of data to an outside device

Microcomputer Hardware

Microcomputer systems typically consist of the following three major components:

■ A system unit, which houses the main circuit board and the *central processing unit* (CPU)

■ An input device, usually a keyboard

■ An output device, usually a video monitor

The system unit generally houses most of the computer system. A logical diagram in figure 44.1 illustrates the components.

The *motherboard*, or main circuit board in the system unit, supports the CPU, memory, and input/output interfaces. Typical components on the motherboard include the following:

■ A keyboard controller, which is almost always built into the motherboard.

■ An expansion bus, which consists of a series of connectors into which option cards can be installed.

■ Output ports, such as serial and parallel ports, which can operate from circuitry built into the motherboard or from expansion cards that are plugged into an expansion bus.

■ A central processing unit, which on microcomputers is contained in a single integrated circuit called a *microprocessor*.

■ Memory that is fast enough to support the high-speed processor. The cost to store a unit of data in memory is high, but memory is needed for its speed. The contents of most memory types disappear when the computer is powered off.

■ Inexpensive and relatively slow storage devices that store data for long periods of time. These can consist of hard disk drives or floppy disk drives.

Microprocessor Characteristics

A *microprocessor* is a "CPU on a chip," a single integrated circuit that performs all CPU functions. The CPU performs all of the actual processing (data manipulation) that occurs on the computer. CPUs have the following two major internal components:

■ A *control unit* (CU), which directs the operation of the CPU. The CU keeps track of and performs instructions contained in programs, and directly or indirectly controls all components of the microcomputer, including memory, input/output, and storage.

Figure 44.1

Major components of a microcomputer.

■ An *arithmetic/logic unit* (ALU), which, as directed by the CU, performs arithmetic (addition, subtraction, multiplication, division) and logical operations.

Microprocessors have a variety of characteristics that affect their capabilities and performance. Features discussed in this course include the following:

■ **The internal data bus size.** The number of bits that the microprocessor can move around within itself at one time. Bus sizes can range from 8 to 64 bits, with larger bus sizes offering better performance.

■ **The external data bus size.** The number of bits that the microprocessor can input or output from external devices in a single operation. The data bus is visible externally as a series of connectors on the motherboard into which expansion cards can be installed. External data bus sizes range from 8 to 64 bits, and again, more is better.

■ **Memory address size.** The larger the memory address size, the more main memory the microcomputer can support.

■ **Clock speed.** A clock determines how quickly the microprocessor handles instructions. Higher performance microcomputers operate at higher clock speeds. Clock speed is measured in millions of clock cycles per second using a unit. One million cycles per second is a measure called one *megahertz* (MHz).

Intel Microprocessors

The majority of microcomputers are based on the design of the IBM AT microcomputer and use microprocessors either manufactured by Intel or engineered to match Intel specifications. You should become familiar with the main characteristics of the various Intel microprocessors, as discussed in table 44.1.

Table 44.1
Features of Intel Microprocessors

	8086	8088	80286	80386DX	80386SX	80486DX	80486SX	Pentium
Register size (in bits)	16	16	16	32	32	32	32	64
Data bus size (in bits)	16	8	16	32	16	32	32	64
Address size (in bits)	20	20	24	32	32	32	32	32
Maximum memory	1 MB	1 MB	16 MB	4 GB	4 GB	4 GB	4 GB	4 GB
Virtual memory	none	none	1 GB	32 TB	32 TB	32 TB	32 TB	32 TB
Speed (in MHz)	4.77–10	4.77–10	6–20	16–33	16–20	25–33	20–25	60–100
Math coprocessor	extra	extra	extra	extra	extra	built-in	extra	built-in
Real mode	yes	yes	yes	yes	yes	yes	yes	yes
Virtual real mode	no	no	no	yes	yes	yes	yes	yes

The following discussion introduces the various types of Intel microprocessors.

8086

The 8086 had 16-bit internal and external data buses when most microprocessors had 8-bit designs. The 8086 uses 20-bit memory addresses, enabling it to address 1 MB of memory.

8088

The 8088 is identical internally to the 8086 but has an 8-bit external bus. IBM selected the 8088 for the first PC due to the high cost of 16-bit components. The original PC used an 8088 microprocessor that operated at a clock speed of 4.77 MHz.

80286

Introduced in 1984, the 80286 addresses many of the limitations of the 8086/8088. The 80286 has a 16-bit data bus and a 6 MHz clock, and was chosen for the IBM Advanced Technology (AT) computer, which was introduced in 1985.

The 80286 has two operational modes. *Real mode* mimics a "real" 8086 processor to ensure that software written for the 8086 will run on the 80286. Real mode is constrained by the 1 MB memory limitation of the 8086/8088 processors.

A new operational mode is *protected mode*, which on the 80286 can address 16 MB of memory and can use disk storage as *virtual memory* to extend memory up to 1 GB. Virtual memory enables hard drives to appear to the CPU like memory. Virtual memory operates much more slowly than semiconductor memory but has some value in memory-intensive applications. Protected mode enables the microprocessor to perform multitasking, a capability that was exploited in operating systems like OS/2 and NetWare 286.

80386

The 80386 is the first Intel microprocessor to have 32-bit internal and external data buses. The 80386 can address real memory of 4 GB and virtual memory of 32 TB (terabytes). The 80386 sets the basic application architecture for all later Intel microprocessors.

80386 processors have real and protected modes. They also are equipped with a "virtual real" or "virtual 8086" mode that enables the processor to emulate multiple 8086 processors simultaneously. Virtual real mode enables the processor to run multiple DOS processes at the same time.

80386SX

When the 80386 was introduced, few PCs supported 32-bit expansion devices. Therefore, Intel designed the 80386SX, which is identical to the 80386 internally, but uses a 16-bit external data bus. This approach reduces system costs but limits performance.

80486

The 80486 combines the capabilities of an 80386 processor with a built-in math coprocessor. A math coprocessor is capable of performing many mathematical operations, such as floating point arith-

metic, more efficiently than is possible with a standard microprocessor. Prior to the 80486, math coprocessors were add-in, extra cost items. Separate versions were required for the 8086, 80286, and 80386 processors.

The 80486 does not add any modes and is upwardly compatible with the 80386. The 80486 offers higher performance, however, due to some advanced features.

One new technology, a cache controller, uses high-speed memory in the CPU to buffer instructions being brought in from memory. This improves efficiency because the cache memory is considerably faster than system memory and the CPU does not wait while instructions are fetched from memory.

Intel has designed clock doubling chips for the 80486 processors. These overdrive chips enable a 25 MHz chip to operate at 50 MHz and a 33 MHz CPU to operate at 66 MHz. 80486 processors that have the overdrive feature built-in are called *80486DX2 processors*. Recent versions employ clock tripping to push 80486 processors up to 100 MHz operations. Clock-tripled versions are called *80486DX4 processors*.

80486SX

Because many users do not run software that requires a math coprocessor, Intel introduced a version of the 80486 in which the coprocessor is disabled. This version is called an 80486SX. Notice that the SX extension does not mean the same thing for the 80486SX as it did for the 80386SX.

Pentium

The Pentium is the microprocessor that follows the 80486. Although the Pentium retains a 32-bit address bus, the data bus width doubles to 64 bits.

The Pentium has two 8-bit caches compared to one on the 80486. Pentium processors currently operate at 60, 66, 90, and 100 MHz.

Pentiums also incorporate two data pipelines that enable them to process two instructions at once. This process is called *multithreading*, and it is the key to a new set of capabilities in operating systems and applications. In a standard multitasking environment, tasks share the CPU by switching processing between the tasks very rapidly. This gives the illusion that multiple things are happening at one time, but in reality only one task is being executed at a given time. Multithreading processors can actually execute two or more processes independently and at the same time. The result is like having two microprocessors.

Motorola Processors

Apple computers have always been based on Motorola microprocessors, and the Macintosh series has relied on a series of processors in the Motorola M68000 family. Recently, Power Macintoshes have been introduced that employ a new microprocessor called the *PowerPC*, which was jointly developed by IBM, Apple, and Motorola. The following discussion introduces you to the characteristics of these processors.

MC68000

The MC68000 has a 32-bit internal data bus and a 16-bit external bus. Its 24-bit address bus enables it to access 16 MB of memory. Models were released with clock speeds of 8–16 MHz. Early Macintoshes were based on the MC68000, although early Mac Portables used a version called the MC68HC000, a similar chip with lower power consumption. The following Macintosh models use the MC68000:

- Macintosh 128K
- Macintosh 512K
- Macintosh 512Ke
- Macintosh Plus
- Macintosh SE
- Macintosh Classic
- Macintosh Portable

MC68020

The MC68020 has 32-bit internal and external data buses and can address 4 GB of memory. A 256-byte instruction cache holds instructions pending execution. The MC68020 is used in the Macintosh II and the Macintosh LC. Clock speeds range from 12–16 MHz. Two models of Macintosh use the MC68020:

- Macintosh LC
- Macintosh II

MC68030

The MC68030 has a paged memory feature that enables it to take advantage of the virtual memory features of System 7. Virtual memory enables hard drives to appear to be RAM. Although the performance is not as fast as true RAM, virtual memory is an inexpensive way to support memory-hungry processes.

The MC68030 has two independent 32-bit address buses and two independent 32-bit data buses. These parallel buses allow the CPU to perform multiple tasks simultaneously. A 256-byte data cache is added to the 256-byte instruction cache that originated in the MC68020. Clock speeds range from 16–40 MHz.

The MC68030 is used in several Macintosh models:

- Macintoish SE/30

- Macintosh IIx

- Macintosh IIcx

- Macintosh IIci

- Macintosh IIsi

- Macintosh IIfx

MC68040

The MC68040 was first used in the Quadra product line. It has 4 KB caches for data and for instructions. It also incorporates a math coprocessor. A new *pipelining* capability allows the CPU to decode and execute several program instructions at a time.

Table 44.2 summarizes the characteristics of the Motorola microprocessors.

RISC Processors

A debate over microprocessors has long raged between advocates of *Complex Instruction Set Computer* (CISC) and *Reduced Instruction Set Computer* (RISC) processors.

CISC processors (such as the Intel 80*x*86 and the Motorola MC68*xxx* series) include a large number of complex instructions, enabling software to perform complicated tasks by sending a relatively small number of instructions to the CPU. In other words, the CPU is made to work harder so that programs can be made simpler. RISC advocates argue that CISC architectures are expensive to develop and manufacture, and that performance suffers because the CPU must perform so much work.

RISC processors are based on a relatively smaller number of simpler instructions. To perform complex tasks, the logic must be built into the software. Programs, particularly operating systems, are somewhat more complex to develop for this reason.

Table 44.2
Features of Motorola Microprocessors

	MC68000	*MC68020*	*MC68030*	*MC68049*
Register size	24 bit	32 bit	32 bit	32 bit
Data bus size	16 bit	32 bit	32 bit	32 bit
Address size	24 bit	32 bit	32 bit	32 bit
Maximum memory	16 MB	4 GB	4 GB	4 GB
Cache	No	No	Yes	Yes
Math Processer	No	Extra	Yes	Yes
Speed	16MHz	16MHz	40MHz	64MHz

CISC advocates feel that the performance of CISC processors can be made to match the performance of RISC processors, while at the same time greatly simplifying software design.

You can get an indication of who is winning the debate by examining the workstation market, a class that is generally designed for greatest performance. All workstations, which tend to be more expensive than typical personal computers, are based on RISC processors. *Processor Independent* (PI) NetWare is available to perform file service functions on several brands of RISC machines. The following are the most significant manufacturers of RISC systems:

- Sun Microsystems
- Hewlett-Packard
- IBM
- Digital Equipment
- Silicon Graphics
- Intergraf

A new RISC processor, jointly developed by IBM, Apple, and Motorola, is finding its way into personal computers. Newer Macintosh computers are based on the PowerPC, and IBM is gradually following suit. The PowerPC model 601 has the following characteristics:

- 16 KB cache
- 32-bit internal bus
- 64-bit external bus
- Clock speeds of 60 and 66 MHz

The Expansion Bus

In most microcomputers, the data bus of a microprocessor connects to an expansion bus into which optional accessories may be installed. The data bus serves to transfer data between the CPU and memory, and between the CPU and the expansion bus.

The data bus consists of printed-circuit wiring traces on the motherboard. If an expansion bus is present, the wiring traces on the motherboard attach to a series of connectors that support accessories. Because the expansion bus is the main point at which data enters and leaves the computer, design of the expansion bus is critical to performance of a computer.

Characteristics of Expansion Buses

To understand the characteristics of various expansion buses, you need to be familiar with several of their characteristics, including interrupts, data bus size, address bus size, and clock speed.

Interrupts

Interrupts enable peripherals to signal the microprocessor for attention. When an expansion card has data for the microprocessor, it will signal with an interrupt. This mechanism relieves the microprocessor of the need to continually check each device in the computer to see if it requires attention. The microprocessor lines that handle interrupts are often called *Interrupt Request* (IRQ) lines.

Memory Addresses

As mentioned earlier, the larger the size memory address a microprocessor can manage, the greater amount of memory it can access. A 32-bit address, for example, supports 4 GB of memory.

Data Bus Width

The width of the data bus determines how much data can be moved on the bus in a single operation. A 32-bit data bus can move four times as much data in one step as an 8-bit data bus.

Maximum Clock Speed

You have read about microprocessors with clock speeds up to 100 MHz. Unfortunately, most data buses are restricted to much lower speeds. Newer bus designs are pushing bus performance nearer to microprocessor clock speeds.

Buses Used in PC Compatibles

Several buses have been used in computers based on IBM PCs. The connectors used in these buses are depicted in figure 44.2. Table 44.3 summarizes the characteristics of these buses.

ISA Bus

The original IBM PC used a bus with an 8-bit data bus width. This severely limited bus performance, and the bus was expanded to a 16-bit data bus when the IBM AT computer was introduced in 1985. This 16-bit bus is widely used in the majority of IBM PC compatibles, and is now called the *Industry Standard Architecture* (ISA) bus. The 8-bit bus is no longer being used in new PCs.

The 8-bit card used a single connector with 62 pins. The 16-bit card added a second 36-pin connector. This feature allowed 16-bit expansion slots to accept older 8-bit cards.

The ISA bus is limited to clock rates no greater than 10 MHz, and is seldom operated above 8 MHz. Soon after the IBM AT was introduced, PCs based on 16 MHz 80386 processors began to appear, and the limitations of the ISA bus became clear. Several

proprietary bus designs, such as the Compaq Flex Architecture, were developed to get around these severe performance limitations.

Eight-bit ISA buses supported 8 interrupts numbered 0 through 7, of which 0 and 1 were reserved for the system. 16-bit ISA buses support interrupts numbered 0 through 15. Table 44.4 summarizes the common uses of these interrupts.

Figure 44.2
Connectors for PC compatible buses.

Table 44.3
Characteristics of IBM PC Buses

	8-Bit ISA	16-Bit ISA	Micro Channel	EISA	VL-Bus	PCI
Data bus width	8-bits	16 bits	32 bits	32 bits	32 bits	64 bits
Address bus width	20 bits	24 bits	32 bits	32 bits	32 bits	32 bits
Speeds	4.77 MHz	4.77–8 MHz	10+ MHz	8 MHz	33 MHz	60+ MHz
Bus mastering	No	No	Yes	Yes		
Configuration	Manual	Manual	Automatic	Automatic	Automatic	Plug-and-Play

Table 44.4
Interrupts of ISA buses

IRQ	8-bit	16-bit
0	Reserved	Reserved
1	Reserved	Reserved
2	EGA (generally available)	Cascade to IRQ 9
3	COM 2 (serial port 2)	COM 2
4	COM 1 (serial port 1)	COM 1
5	Hard disk controller	LPT 2
6	Floppy disk controller	Disk controller (hard and floppy)
7	LPT 1 (printer)	LPT 1
8		Real-time clock
9		Available
10		Available
11		Available
12		Available

IRQ	8-bit	16-bit
13		Coprocessor
14		Hard disk controller
15		Available

Many of these interrupts are available if the standard resources are not being used. If the PC does not have a printer port, for example, IRQ 7 is available.

Interrupts 2 and 9 on the 16-bit bus are unusual. IRQ 2 is the cascade interrupt that passes interrupt signals to the second set of eight IRQs by means of interrupt 9. Two things result from this: IRQ 2 and IRQ 9 are functionally the same, and some accessories cannot function properly when assigned these interrupts.

Interrupts are typically set with jumpers or with DIP (dual in-line pin) switches. Examples of both are shown in figure 44.3.

The features of the 16-bit bus that limit its usefulness are its speed limits (less than 10 MHz) and its 16-bit data path. The bus has a 24-bit address limit that is limited to supporting 16 MB of memory, which renders it unsuitable for use in file servers on the basis of both performance and memory capability.

Figure 44.3

Examples of jumpers and DIP switches.

IBM Micro Channel Architecture (MCA) Bus

IBM recognized the limitations of the ISA bus and introduced a new bus called the *Micro Channel Architecture* (MCA) in the PS/2 line of computers introduced in 1987. Two factors limited the acceptance of this bus. At first, IBM chose to charge a royalty for manufacturers who incorporated the bus in their equipment. Although the royalty requirement was later dropped, the damage was done, and other bus designs such as EISA had gained prominence. Another factor was that the Micro Channel bus used a different connector, obsoleting users' stocks of ISA cards. IBM chose not to include ISA slots for backward compatibility even though this would have made sense with many slower expansion devices.

The MCA bus has 32-bit data paths and 32-bit addressing, and can thus accommodate the bus and address sizes of the 80386 and 80486 processors. Early MCA buses operated at 10 MHz, but later implementations have been pushed to much higher speeds.

Micro Channel cards do not usually include jumpers or switches and are configured using an *automatic installation* configuration program.

Micro Channel Architecture introduced a feature called *bus mastering* or *multidevice handling*. Bus mastering allows expansion cards to seize control of the bus and to manage I/O and other operations without the intervention of the microprocessor. This feature is especially desirable in network file servers.

The Micro Channel bus was included only in high-end PS/2s, including the Models 50 and 60, which had 16-bit MCA buses, and the Models 70 and 80, which had 32-bit buses. The bottom of the line Models 25 and 30 still used the ISA bus. Since then,

IBM has introduced a wide variety of computers using various configurations of ISA, MCA, EISA, and PCI buses.

EISA Bus

The Micro Channel Architecture bus had everything users wanted except compatibility, and was regarded as a proprietary technology. Several vendors formed a consortium to develop a new bus and, in 1988, announced the *Enhanced Industry Standard Architecture* (EISA) bus.

The EISA bus connector has two rows of contacts. The top row is identical to the 16-bit ISA configuration. When an EISA card is inserted, it connects with both rows. An ISA card inserts into the expansion slot only far enough to engage the top row of contacts. Thus, the EISA connector supports both EISA and ISA expansion cards.

EISA supports 32-bit data paths and addressing. Because it was designed around the ISA slot, the EISA bus is limited by ISA speed limitations, and can operate only up to 10 MHz.

EISA has its own version of automatic configuration and incorporates bus mastering.

VESA Local Bus (VL-Bus)

Both ISA and EISA buses are subject to a 10 MHz maximum data rate, which is insufficient for today's faster processors and more demanding applications. The Micro Channel Architecture bus has higher performance limits, but has never become popular. In 1987, computer buyers were not ready to discard their option cards to switch to a new expansion bus standard.

A *local bus* is one that is attached directly to the microprocessor's circuitry without the intervention of large amounts of bus controller components. Such a bus can operate at the same speed as the processor. Several computer manufacturers have designed proprietary local buses, including Compaq, Hewlett-Packard, and Dell.

A non-proprietary approach was developed by the Video Electronic Standard Association (VESA). Video applications are among the most data intensive applications on a modern, graphic-oriented computer. ISA-based video cards are limited to data rates of about 600,000 pixels per second. The VL-Bus (also called the VESA Local Bus) developed by VESA can move 50–60 million pixels per second.

Bus connectors for VL-Bus consist of an extra connector that is placed in-line with existing ISA connectors, enabling a slot to support either ISA or VL-Bus cards. The configuration is shown in figure 44.4. The VL-Bus design is limited to two cards for a given microprocessor, although buffering can expand this capability to three cards.

1SA slots

VL-Bus slots

Motherboard

Figure 44.4
Slot placement for VL-Bus.

VL-Bus can perform 32-bit data transfers at rates as high as 132 MB per second. The bus was originally developed for video, but has been adapted to other purposes, such as hard drive controllers and LAN adapters. Still, the bus has widest acceptance supporting video.

Local buses must be designed for specific microprocessors, and VL-Bus was designed explicitly for the 80486. Consequently, VL-Bus has been slow to adapt to the new 64-bit Pentium processors. A second-generation bus has been developed, but VL-Bus is clearly losing momentum to the newer PCI bus.

Peripheral Component Interconnect (PCI) Bus

The Peripheral Component Interconnect bus, which was developed by Intel, is becoming the most popular performance bus on newly manufactured microcomputers. The bus has been designed with 32- and 64-bit data paths, and operates at clock rates matching current Intel processors. PCI also has a plug-and-play feature that will enable future operating systems to automatically configure expansion components without the need to manually set interrupts.

The PCI bus is described as a mezzanine bus because it is one hardware layer away from the microprocessor's bus. Buffer chips transfer data between the microprocessor and the bus, insulating the microprocessor from the bus. Other chips transfer signals to 16-bit ISA slots that are included in all current PCI-based computers. At present, the PCI design accommodates only three expansion slots, although means are being developed of doubling that number.

654   **Part VII:** DOS/Microcomputer Basics

PCI bus connectors are installed alongside ISA connectors. Most configurations have three PCI connectors and one ISA connector. One ISA connector and one PCI connector are paired such that either can be used, but not both. The slot arrangement is shown in figure 44.5.

Figure 44.5
Slot placement for PCI bus

Buses Used in Macintoshes

Macintoshes use two technologies to support plug-in expansion devices: Processor Direct Slot and NuBus.

Processor Direct Slot (PDS)

Processor Direct Slot, Apple's term for a local bus in the Macintosh environment, is a bus that is connected directly to the microprocessor. Because expansion devices have direct access to the microprocessor, devices on a PDS can operate at high speeds. Only one expansion device can be sup-

ported by a PDS, however. Also, a PDS and plug-in options are designed explicitly for a given model of microprocessor. Thus, a device designed for the PDS slot for an MC68030 cannot work in the PDS slot for an MC68040.

NuBus

NuBus was developed by engineers at MIT and has been standardized by the IEEE. NuBus, as implemented in Macintoshes, is entirely self-configuring; there is no need to manually set interrupts, addresses, or other hardware parameters. Each NuBus expansion card stores its configuration information in CMOS, from which it can be read during system startup.

Features of NuBus include the following:

- 32-bit address and data buses
- Self-configuring option boards
- 10 MHz operation
- Bus mastering

Microcomputer Memory

Memory in microcomputers can be broadly divided into the following two types:

- **Random-access memory (RAM).** RAM can be modified dynamically by programs running on the computer. "Random" means that any memory unit can be directly addressed without the need to step through series of memory units.

- **Read-only memory (ROM).** The contents of ROM cannot be modified (at least not easily). Because ROM contents cannot change, it is a good place to store basic programs that must be available when the computer starts up.

The following sections discuss several variations of RAM and ROM.

Dynamic RAM (DRAM)

Dynamic RAM memory locations function like miniature capacitors, which can store an electric charge for a brief period of time. When data is stored in a memory location, a charge is stored in the capacitor for that location. This charge can be detected to determine the value of the memory location.

DRAM is commonly used because it is inexpensive. It has two disadvantages, however. It is slow compared to SRAM (discussed in the following section). And, because the capacitors lose their charges fairly quickly, the charges must be reestablished by refreshing the memory.

Static RAM (SRAM)

The memory elements in static RAM function like switches. Once a memory location is set to a value, it remains with that value as long as power is applied. No refresh mechanism is required.

Although SRAM is faster than DRAM, it is used less frequently due to its considerably higher cost.

SRAM is frequently used in high-speed data caches with high performance processors. The processor can access data cached in SRAM more rapidly than it could retrieve data from DRAM main memory.

Complimentary Metal-Oxide Silicon (CMOS)

Complimentary Metal-Oxide Silicon memory is a type of static memory that can store its contents using very little power. A battery is capable of powering CMOS memory for a year or more. Some CMOS memory is included in most microcomputers to store configuration data when the machine is powered off.

Read-Only Memory (ROM)

ROM stores data permanently, even when power is not applied. In most cases, the data is burned into ROM memory when the chip is manufactured and cannot be erased. Other types of ROM can be programmed electrically. Some electrically programmable memory can be erased by exposing it to a high-intensity ultraviolet light, but this erases all memory contents.

ROM is useful for storing information when the computer is turned off and is most commonly used to store the BIOS (Basic Input/Output System) that controls the basic functions of a microcomputer, including the startup operation. BIOS ensures that the PC will be able to power on, test itself, initialize its circuitry, and access a hard drive to load an operating system. Macintosh system ROMs are another example of ROM memory.

Organization of a Data Byte

IBM PCs organize memory chips in groups of nine bits, as shown in figure 44.6. Eight bits represent a byte, the basic unit of memory. The ninth bit is used for parity, to detect errors. The parity bit is always set so that the total number of all bits in the nine-bit unit will be odd. If an error affects one bit in the byte, the bit count will no longer be odd and the system knows that an error has occurred. A parity error generally causes the system to lock up, on the theory that bad data is worse than no data at all. Macintosh computers do not implement parity checking and use only eight bits to implement a byte of storage.

Figure 44.6
*Organization of chips in
an IBM PC.*

Parity

8 Bits Data

Organization of Memory in a DOS PC

Early IBM PCs were designed around the 8088 processor, which can address a maximum of 1 MB of memory. DOS was designed around that limit and remains so to this day. Memory on the original PC was organized as shown in figure 44.7.

DOS memory is organized in four sections, as follows:

■ User memory, which extends from 0 to 640 KB. This memory stores user programs and system software. A portion of DOS runs in this area, and many expansion cards are allocated a few bytes of storage in the bottom of this area.

■ Video RAM, which extends from 640 to 786.

■ ROM BIOS, which extends from 960 to 1,024 KB. BIOS programs stored in ROM must be mapped into the 1 MB memory range so that they can be accessed by the microprocessor.

■ Upper memory is memory between video memory and the BIOS. This memory can be used to support some utilities if it is configured with a proper memory driver.

Expanded Memory (EMS)

Before long, larger software programs, such as Lotus 1-2-3, outgrew the 640 KB of memory that was set aside for DOS programs. Lotus, Intel, and Microsoft developed the "LIM" *expanded memory* specification to give programs access to additional memory.

The operation of LIM memory is shown in figure 44.8. A portion of upper memory is configured with 16 KB page frames. The LIM software drivers allow DOS programs to access memory in these page frames.

LIM software drivers can swap 16 MB chunks of memory in and out of separate expanded memory. The expanded memory is not directly accessible to programs. Because memory must be swapped into page frames, expanded memory performance is not particularly high, but it was the only option available to designers at the time.

Current versions of DOS have memory managers that can simulate expanded memory by using memory above the 1 MB line. Special expanded memory hardware is not required because processors starting with the 80286 can access memory above 1 MB and can perform the memory swapping. The expanded memory technique remains necessary for DOS programs, however, because they are still designed around the limitations of the 8088 and 8086 processors.

Figure 44.7
Organization of DOS memory.

Extended Memory (XMS)

Extended memory is memory above the 1 MB line, as depicted in figure 44.9. DOS alone cannot access extended memory, but many other operating systems can, such as NetWare, Unix, and OS/2. DOS can be given a limited capability to access extended memory by using programs, such as Microsoft Windows, which are not designed to the DOS 1 MB limit. Individual DOS programs running under Windows are limited to using 1 MB, but Windows itself can manage far more memory.

Extended memory differs from expanded memory in that it is no longer necessary to swap chunks of memory in and out of page frames. Extended memory is continuously addressable by a suitable CPU and operating system.

Memory Packaging

Memory is packaged in integrated circuits that are housed in DIP (dual in-line pin) packages. Early PCs used individual chips, and it was necessary to plug in nine individual chips for each bank of memory being added to the computer.

Memory chip configurations are identified by a width and a length. A 1×256 chip consists of bits organized 1 wide and 256 K bits long. Nine such chips implement 256 KB of memory organized in bytes with parity.

All PCs now use some form of memory module. The most common configuration is the *Single In-Line Memory Module* (SIMM). Each SIMM consists of a small circuit board on which memory chips are factory-installed. The SIMMs are plugged into special slots on the system board. A wide variety of SIMMs are available, and it is necessary to ensure that the width and length of the SIMMS match the specifications of the system board.

Memory chips are rated in terms of *access time,* which identifies the maximum speed at which data can be reliably read. The memory used must be at least as fast as the system board requires, but memory that is faster than specifications does not provide enhanced performance. Low-performance memory may have an access time of 100 nanoseconds. High-performance PCs require memory that is rated at 70 nanoseconds or better.

Figure 44.8
*Operation of expanded
memory.*

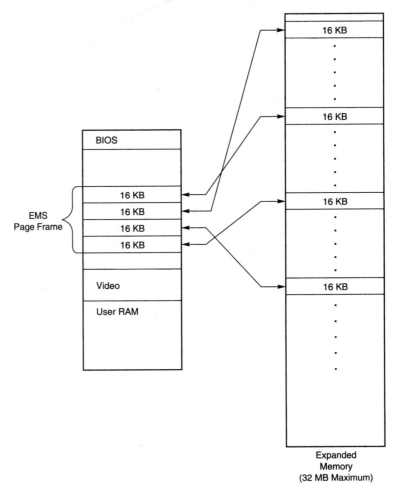

Disk Storage

Hard disk drives and floppy disk drives are used to store large amounts of data in non-volatile form. Data is stored in the form of magnetic fields on a magnetic surface that coats a hard or flexible disk.

Data on a disk is organized in two fundamental units, as shown in figure 44.10. The disk is divided into concentric *tracks* that pass under the recording head of the drive. Each track is divided into *sectors*, which usually store 512 bytes.

DOS views disk storage in terms of *clusters*, which consist of one or more sectors. A cluster can range in size from 512 to 8,096 bytes.

The following sections examine the types of floppy disks as well as the characteristics of hard disks.

Figure 44.9

Extended memory.

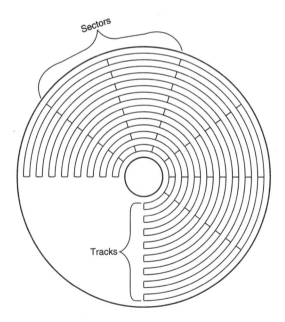

Figure 44.10

Tracks and sectors on a disk.

Types of Floppy Disks

Floppy disks received their names because the recording media consists of a metal oxide coating on a flexible plastic disk. Two sizes of floppy disks are in common use: 5.25 inch and 3.5 inch.

5.25-Inch Floppy Disks

A 5.25-inch floppy disk has the following features:

■ **Flexible jacket.** The entire disk and jacket combination is slightly flexible and can be bent and damaged.

■ **Drive hole.** This hole in the center is grasped by the drive mechanism to spin the disk.

■ **Read/write access hole.** This hole enables the read/write heads to contact the disk. One head is used for each side of the disk, except on very early single-sided drives.

■ **Write protect notch.** When this notch on the side of the jacket is covered with tape, the drive mechanism will not allow the read/write head to write new data to the disk.

5.25-inch disks are available in double-density (360 KB) and high-density (1.2 MB) capacities. The magnetic materials used are different, and a narrower read/write head is used with high-density drives. Consequently, high-density disks cannot be recorded or read in double-density drives. A high-density drive can read double-density disks but should not be used to write data because the disks cannot be read reliably by double-density drives.

5.25-inch disks have been largely superseded by 3.5-inch floppy disks.

3.5-Inch Disks

These disks are used in Macintoshes and are now the overwhelming favorites for IBM PC compatibles as well. 3.5-inch disks have the following features:

■ **Rigid plastic case.** Protects the flexible magnetic disk.

■ **Metal slide.** Covers the read/write access hole. This slide closes automatically when the disk is withdrawn to protect the magnetic material.

■ **Write protect hole (equipped with a slider).** When the slider covers the hole, data can be written to the disk. When the slider does not cover the hole, data cannot be written. No stick tape is required as with 5.25-inch disks.

■ **High-density sensor hole.** Notifies the drive whether the disk is double-density (no hole) or high-density (hole).

3.5-inch disks are designed for greater interchangability than 5.25-inch disks. Although a double-density drive can read and write only double-density disks, a high-density drive reads the high-density sensor hole and adapts its operation to read and write to either double- or high-density disks.

Macintoshes format double-density 3.5-inch disks to a 800 KB capacity. The number of sectors-per-track varies from 8 to 12, with more sectors being used on outer tracks that have larger diameters. A few older Macintoshes use single-sided 3.5-inch disks formatted to 400 KB. Macintoshes equipped with SuperDrives can also read and write 1.44 MB DOS-format disks.

DOS PCs format double-density 3.5-inch disks to 720 KB and high-density disks to 1.44 MB.

Calculating the Capacity of Disks

The capacity of a disk is calculated as follow:

capacity =   number of disk sides
              × number of tracks
              × number of sectors per track
              × sector size in bytes

The capacity of a 3.5-inch high-capacity DOS disk is derived from the following formula:

capacity = 2×80×18×512 = 1,474,560

The formatted capacity of a disk is somewhat less than the calculated capacity because a portion of the disk is reserved by DOS for information such as sector addresses, system files, file allocation tables, and directories.

Table 44.5 summarizes the unformatted and formatted capacities of various floppy disks.

Hard Disk Drives

Hard disk drives have multiple rigid platters arranged as shown in figure 44.11. These disks rotate much more quickly than floppy disks and can transfer data at higher rates, typically at speeds of 2,400–3,600 rpm. Higher capacities are possible because rigid platters can be manufactured to higher precision than flexible plastic. A separate read/write head is included for each side of each platter. As the platters spin, the read/write heads ride on an air cushion a microscopic distance from the disk surface.

Table 44.5
Capacities of Floppy Disks

Disk	Density	Tracks per Side	Sectors per Track	Total Sectors	Bytes per Sector	Sectors per Cluster	Unformatted Capacity	Formatted Capacity
5.25 DOS	Double	40	9	720	512	2	368,640	362,496
5.25 DOS	High	80	15	2,400	312	1	1,228,800	1,213,952
3.5 DOS	Double	80	9	1,440	512	2	737,280	730,112
3.5 DOS	High	80	18	2,880	512	1	1,474,560	1,457,664
3.5 Mac	Double	80	8-2	1,600	512	n/a	819,200	
3.5 Mac	High	80	18	2,880	512	n/a	1,474,560	

Figure 44.11
Components of a hard disk drive.

Hard disk drives, like floppy disk drives, organize disks into tracks and sectors. They also organize tracks into cylinders. A cylinder consists of all matching tracks on all platters.

Besides the speed of platter rotation, a good measure of the performance of a hard drive is *random access time*, which is an indication of the time required, on average, to position the read-write head at a given track.

Partitioning Hard Disk Drives

Before hard disk drives can be formatted for data storage, they must be partitioned. *Partitioning* reserves portions or all of the disk for use by an operating system.

DOS versions 3.30 and earlier are restricted to partition sizes of 32 MB. Larger hard drives are configured with multiple 32 MB partitions. After the partitions are formatted, DOS treats each partition as a separate drive with its own drive letter.

DOS versions 4, 5, and 6 can create partitions up to 2 GB. The BIOS in many older PCs, however, restricts this size to 512 MB.

Multiple operating systems can be supported by assigning each its own partition(s) on the hard drive. Thus, DOS and Unix partitions can coexist on a hard drive.

NetWare also partitions hard drives. NetWare 2.*x* partitions the entire hard drive as a NetWare partition. NetWare 3.*x* and 4.*x* are configured with a small DOS partition on the first hard drive. The remainder of the first hard drive, and all other hard drives, are partitioned as NetWare partitions.

Hard Disk Drive Interfaces

A variety of hard drive controller technologies have been used on IBM PC compatibles. The technology has gradually improved as the need for performance increased. Four interface technologies are discussed next: ST506/412, ESDI, IDE, and SCSI.

ST506/412

The original IBM PC used an interface developed by Seagate Technology that is commonly called the ST506 interface. Due to performance limitations, this technology is obsolete.

ST506 supports the following two data encoding techniques:

- *Modified Frequency Modulation* (MFM) enables data transfer rates up to 5 Mbps

- *Run Length Limited* (RLL) enables data transfers at 7.5 Mbps and increases drive capacity by 50 percent.

Both the controller and the disk drive must be engineered to support the same encoding technique.

Enhanced Small Device Interface (ESDI)

ESDI was first used on the IBM AT and is a standard of the American National Standards Institute (ANSI). ESDI is an improved ST506 interface that can transfer data at rates from 10–15 Mbps. Like ST506, ESDI is an obsolete technology.

Integrated Drive Electronics (IDE)

IDE is the current choice for most personal computers. IDE integrates Western Digital drive controller electronics into the hard drive package. Because the controller is closely matched to the hard drive, significant performance improvements are possible. Many PC motherboards are equipped with built-in connectors that support IDE drives. Expansion slot interfaces are also available.

IDE uses RLL encoding to support high data transfer rates and dense disk storage.

Small Computer System Interface (SCSI)

SCSI is the most common interface for high-performance computers and file servers. SCSI performs parallel, 8-bit file data transfers, whereas the other interfaces discussed perform serial, 1-bit-at-a-time transfers.

SCSI supports a variety of devices besides hard drives, including CD-ROMs and tape drives. SCSI is configured as a bus that can support up to seven devices from a single controller card. Each device is identified by a number ranging from 0 to 6.

SCSI is a system-level interface that hides the physical nature of the devices being controlled from the operating system. The computer simply requests certain data, while the SCSI controller hardware determines how to retrieve the data from storage.

Current SCSI devices use a technology called *embedded SCSI*, with which the controller circuitry is built into the peripheral. This combination reduces cabling complexity and enhances performance.

Many SCSI bus adapters are available for IBM PC compatibles. Macintoshes have built-in SCSI interfaces.

Ports

Ports are used to interface PCs to external devices (peripherals). Two port types are in common use: parallel ports and serial ports.

Parallel Ports

Printers are the most common devices supported by parallel ports, although other uses are emerging. Parallel ports generally require little or no configuration, making peripheral attachment easy and nearly foolproof.

Printer parallel ports generally use a Centronics connector, named after a printer manufacturer that was common in the early 1980s. At the PC end, a 25-pin D connector is used. Round, shielded cables are generally used to connect devices to parallel ports, because flat, unshielded cables tend to radiate electronic noise.

IBM PCs can support three parallel ports, labeled LPT1, LPT2, and LPT3.

Parallel ports transfer eight bits at a time (in "parallel") over eight data lines. Nine wires in the cable carry control signals. Table 44.6 summarizes the wiring configuration.

Table 44.6
Wire Configuration Summary

Wire	Function	Direction
1	Strobe	PC -> Printer
2	Data line 0	PC -> Printer
3	Data line 1	PC -> Printer
4	Data line 2	PC -> Printer
5	Data line 3	PC -> Printer
6	Data line 4	PC -> Printer
7	Data line 5	PC -> Printer
8	Data line 6	PC -> Printer
9	Data line 7	PC -> Printer
10	Acknowledge	PC <- Printer
11	Busy	PC <- Printer
12	Out of paper	PC <- Printer
13	Select	PC <- Printer
14	Auto feed	PC -> Printer
15	Error	PC <- Printer
16	Initialize	PC -> Printer
17	Select input	PC -> Printer
18–25	Ground	

The most significant limitation of parallel ports is that cables have a limited length. Ten feet is the generally recommended maximum, but 50-foot cables generally function reliably. When cables get too long, crosstalk and other distortion-causing effects can affect the integrity of the data signals.

Serial Ports

Serial ports divide data into individual bits that are transferred one at a time. Most serial ports conform to the RS-232 specification of the Electronics Industry Association (EIA).

IBM PCs support serial ports labeled COM1, COM2, COM3, and COM4.

Serial ports can transfer data in the following two modes:

■ *Synchronous mode* transmits a timing (clocking) signal on one of the interface lines that synchronizes the sending and receiving devices so that they agree when each bit starts. Synchronous transmission equipment is expensive because more lines are used, but transmission speeds are higher.

■ *Asynchronous mode* transmits data in small units. Start bits inform the receiver that data are arriving and allow the receiver to synchronize with the signal. Because no clocking signal is used, the receiver may drift out of synchronization. Consequently, transmissions are kept short so that drift does not become a problem. Asynchronous transmission is inexpensive because fewer lines are required, but does not offer the data transfer rates of synchronous transmission.

Chapter 21 of the Networking Technologies course section, "OSI Physical Layer Concepts," provides further discussion of synchronous and asynchronous communication.

Display Devices

Two dominant technologies are used for computer displays. Most desktop PCs use *cathode ray tubes* (CRTs). Portables generally have *liquid crystal displays* (LCD), which are easily adapted to the battery power available on portable PCs. Another type, the gas-plasma display, is seldomly used due to high power consumptions.

Screen resolution is measured in *pixels*, a term that is short for picture elements. A 640×480 resolution display can display 640 pixels on each of 480 horizontal lines.

Color Displays

Several types of color video monitors have been used with PCs.

Red, Green, Blue (RGB)

The first IBM displays were RGB monitors, which used digital signaling, and which separated the video signal into separate red, green, and blue signals. Each signal is transmitted on a separate cable. RGB video systems tend to be expensive.

Color Graphics Adapter (CGA)

The first color standard for the IBM PC was called Color Graphics Adapter. CGA can display 16-color text and graphics and can function with suitable monochrome monitors. Screen resolution is 320×240. When CGA is used to display 80 text characters on a line, the result is fuzzy and unusable for long periods of time. CGA can display four colors at a time, chosen from a palette of 16 colors.

The majority of early PCs were equipped with monochrome monitors due to the poor quality of CGA and its high cost. Text applications were then in the majority and monochrome monitors provided superior usability.

Enhanced Graphics Adapter (EGA)

The Enhanced Graphics Adapter improved resolution to 640×350 pixels for text and graphics. EGA became the first serious alternative to monochrome monitors.

EGA had to supplement the basic PC BIOS to display 16 colors from a 64-color palette. EGA adapters can also display text and graphics on monochrome monitors, and can display CGA graphics as well.

Video Graphics Array (VGA)

The Video Graphics Array was introduced with the IBM PS/2 line of computers and now represents the entry level for color monitors.

VGA uses analog signaling (earlier standards were digital) to increase the size of the color palette. At 320×200 resolution, VGA can display 256 colors from a palette of 262,144 colors. At 640×480 resolution, VGA can display 16 colors.

Many vendors support enhanced VGA modes. A common industry standard is Super VGA (SVGA), which can display 256 colors at 800×600 resolution. Much higher resolutions are becoming quite common, however.

Multiscanning Color Displays

Each display standard uses different techniques to generate video signals. At one time, you needed to match the monitor type to the signals being produced by the video controller. Multiscanning monitors were introduced that had the capability of automatically adjusting to different signal types. The NEC Multisync monitor is the best-known multiscanning monitor, but many other brands are now available.

Monochrome Displays

Monochrome displays were once the choice of serious computer users but are used less frequently now that high-quality color displays are available at a reasonable cost. Several monochrome display technologies have been used with IBM PCs.

Transistor-Transistor Logic (TTL)

Transistor-Transistor Logic monitors were used primarily to display high-quality text. Monitor displays were frequently green or amber in color.

Composite Monochrome

With composite monochrome, all monitor signals are transmitted through a single cable. This approach does not produce a high-quality display.

VGA Monochrome

The VGA standard enabled the same video adapter to drive color and monochrome displays. The adapter determines which monitor is present and adjusts its signals accordingly. Monochrome VGA transmits only the green signal with 64 shades of gray.

Multiscanning Monochrome

Multiscanning monitors are also available for monochrome video.

Configuration Issues for PCs

Before you can use a PC, you must configure it with information about its hardware. This information is stored in CMOS memory on the motherboard and is used by the system's ROM BIOS while the

PC boots. Common items included in setup information include the following:

■ Number and type of floppy and hard disk drives

■ Memory size

■ Time and data of the system clock

■ Presence of a math coprocessor

■ Primary monitor type

Configuring CMOS

Since the IBM AT, all PC compatibles have included CMOS memory to store system settings. A special program was used to determine the system's hardware features and store appropriate values in the CMOS. A battery enabled the CMOS memory to retain setup data when the PC was turned off.

Most new PCs have the system setup program built into the ROM BIOS. By hitting a special key combination during system booting, users can access the setup program. This arrangement eliminates the need to keep track of a special configuration disk.

Booting the Computer

After CMOS has been configured, it is possible to boot the computer. This takes place in several steps, as follows:

1. Execution of the ROM BIOS begins automatically when power is applied.

2. Power-on Self Test (POST). The POST is the first thing performed by the ROM BIOS, and tests the basic health of the PC hardware.

3. Locating the operating system. The BIOS then begins to look for operating system files, starting with drive A, then moving to drive B, and drive C. The operating system system files are always stored in a special track called the *boot track* (track 0) that the BIOS knows how to locate.

For MS-DOS, the system files are named MSDOS.SYS and IO.SYS. IBM's PC-DOS calls these files IBMBIO.COM and IBMDOS.COM. A bootable disk contains at least these two system files along with a file named COMMAND.COM. The files are placed on a disk in the proper location by executing a DOS SYS command or by formatting the disk with the /S option.

After DOS boots, two configuration steps take place.

1. First, commands in a file named CONFIG.SYS establish the basic DOS configuration.

2. Then commands in a file named AUTOEXEC.BAT are executed. Any valid DOS command can be placed in AUTOEXEC.BAT.

Please refer to Chapter 43, "DOS Concepts for NetWare Administrators," for a more detailed discussion of the CONFIG.SYS and AUTOEXEC.BAT files.

Questions

1. Which THREE of the following are computer functions?

   ☐ A. Processing

   ☐ B. Bootup

   ☐ C. Memorizing

   ☐ D. Output

2. Which TWO of the following are components of all microprocessors?

   ☐ A. CPU

   ☐ B. Arithmetic logic unit

   ☐ C. Memory

   ☐ D. Math coprocessor

3. Which features distinguish an 8086 from an 8088 microprocessor?

   ○ A. 8086 has a higher clock speed.

   ○ B. 8086 has a larger address bus.

   ○ C. 8086 has a larger external data bus.

   ○ D. 8086 has a math coprocessor.

4. Which feature(s) distinguish an 80386 from an 803SX processor?

   ○ A. 80386SX has a top clock rate of 33 MHz, versus 25 MHz for the 80386.

   ○ B. The 80386SX has a math coprocessor.

   ○ C. The 80386 has a 32-bit external bus. The 80386SX has a 16-bit external bus.

   ○ D. The 80386 has a 32-bit internal bus. The 80386SX has a 16-bit internal bus.

5. Which TWO are new features of a Pentium microprocessor?

   ☐ A. 64-bit address bus

   ☐ B. 64-bit data bus

   ☐ C. Built-in math coprocessor

   ☐ D. Multithreading

6. Which THREE Motorola processors have 32-bit external data buses?

   ☐ A. MC68000

   ☐ B. MC68020

   ☐ C. MC68030

   ☐ D. MC68040

7. Which of these buses is the best choice for use in a file server?

   ○ A. 8-bit ISA

   ○ B. 16-bit ISA

   ○ C. EISA

   ○ D. VL-Bus

8. Which THREE of these buses support 32-bit data paths?

   ☐ A. 16-bit ISA

   ☐ B. EISA

   ☐ C   Micro Channel Architecture

   ☐ D. PCI

9. Which THREE of these features are enhancements of the EISA bus?

    ☐ A. 16 MHz clocking

    ☐ B. Additional interrupts

    ☐ C. Jumperless configuration

    ☐ D. 32-bit data bus

10. Which of the following is an example of SRAM?

    ○ A. Microprocessor

    ○ B. High-speed cache

    ○ C. Main system memory

    ○ D. CMOS

11. Which statement is true?

    ○ A. Expanded memory outperforms extended memory.

    ○ B. Extended memory extends memory available to DOS.

    ○ C. 80486 processors cannot support expanded memory.

    ○ D. Extended memory can be used with an 80386 microprocessor.

12. Which statement is true?

    ○ A. Parity improves the performance of memory.

    ○ B. Parity detects one-bit memory errors.

    ○ C. Macintoshes and PCs both use parity.

    ○ D. Parity corrects the effects of bad data.

13. Which type of memory is used as extended memory?

    ○ A. CMOS

    ○ B. ROM

    ○ C. DRAM

    ○ D. SRAM

14. Which of the following hard drive controller technologies is best for servers?

    ○ A. ST506/412

    ○ B. ESDI

    ○ C. SCSI

    ○ D. IDE

15. Which term describes a section of a hard drive that is dedicated to an operating system?

    ○ A. Track

    ○ B. Cylinder

    ○ C. Partition

    ○ D. Fragment

16. Which TWO types of hard drive integrate the controller with the drive itself?

    ☐ A. ST506/412

    ☐ B. ESDI

    ☐ C. SCSI

    ☐ D. IDE

17. Which TWO of the following are character-
    istics of a VGA display?

    ☐ A. 640×350 pixel resolution

    ☐ B. Digital signaling

    ☐ C. Adapts to color or monochrome

    ☐ D. At 320×200 resolution, displays
            256 colors from one 262,144-color
            palette

18. Which was the first color technology to
    provide a viable alternative to monochrome
    displays?

    ○ A. CGA

    ○ B. TTL

    ○ C. EGA

    ○ D. XLS

Answers

1. A B D	10. C
2. A B	11. D
3. C	12. B
4. C	13. C
5. B D	14. C
6. B C D	15. C
7. C	16. C D
8. B C D	17. C D
9. B C D	18. C

INDEX

Symbols

login script command, 86
* (asterisk) wild card, 631
* login script command, 86
> redirection operator, 634
? (question mark) wild card, 631
10BASE-T cabling, *see* UTP cable
10BASE2 (thin net) cabling (Ethernet), 465-467
10BASE5 (thick net) cabling (Ethernet), 467-469
3.5-inch floppy disks, 660
5-4-3 rule (Ethernet), 465
5.25-inch floppy disks, 660
802.2 frame type, 119-120
802.2 standard (IEEE), 414
802.3 (Raw) frame type, 120
802.3 standard (IEEE), 414-416
802.4 standard (IEEE), 416
802.5 standard (IEEE), 417
802.6 standard (IEEE), 417
802.9 standard (IEEE), 417
802.11 standard (IEEE), 417-418
802.12 standard (IEEE), 418
80286 microcomputers (Intel), 644-645
80386 microcomputers (Intel), 645
80386SX microcomputers (Intel), 645
80486 microcomputers (Intel), 645
80486SX microcomputers (Intel), 645
8088 microcomputers (Intel), 644

A

AARP (AppleTalk Address Resolution) protocol, 390
ABORT REMIRROR console command, 117
Abstract Syntax Notation One with Basic Encoding Rules (ASN.1 with BER) (ISO 8824) protocol, 399
Access Control rights, 27
access time, 492, 657
accessing
    file servers from workstations, 61-63
    file systems, 43-44
    networks, 42
        NetWare 2.2, 209
account managers, 26
accounting management, 432
accounts
    group, setting up, 31-32
    user
        restrictions, 25-26
        setting up, 31-32
ACK (acknowledgment), 342
acknowledged connectionless services, 340

ACONSOLE utility, 34-35, 62-63

across-the-wire migration, 586-587

ACT jumper, 500

active hubs, 298

active service advertisement, 370

Address Resolution Protocol (ARP)
  protocol, 386

address/name resolution, 386
    transport OSI layer, 356-357

addresses
    logical network, 346
    memory, 643, 648
    NAUs (network addressable units), 403-405
    packet information format, 346
    physical device, 337
    resolution, 386, 390
    service, 346
    transport OSI layer message identifiers, 356

ADMIN utility, 93

ADSP (AppleTalk Data Stream Protocol)
  protocol, 393

Advanced Peer-to-Peer Networking (APPN)
  protocol, 407

Advanced Program-to-Program Communication (APPC) protocol, 408

advertising services to clients (application OSI
  layer), 370

AFP (AppleTalk Filing Protocol) protocol, 393

AFTER311 NLM, 122

alloc short term memory pool, 131

allocating file server memory, calculating
  amounts, 134-138

ALLOW utility, 34

Alt key, 624

ALUs (arithmetic/logic units), 643

amplitude, 320

amplitude shift keying, 321

analog signaling, 319-321

ANSI
    frame relay standard, 422-423
    SONET (Synchronous Optical Network)
      standard, 424-425

APPC (Advanced Program-to-Program
  Communication) protocol, 408

AppleShare (ASP) protocol, 393-394

AppleTalk Address Resolution Protocol
  (AARP), 390

AppleTalk Data Stream Protocol
  (ADSP), 393

AppleTalk Filing Protocol (AFP), 393

AppleTalk protocol stack, 389-394

AppleTalk Session Protocol (ASP), 392

AppleTalk Transaction Protocol
  (ATP), 391-392

application layer (OSI model), 149, 369
    advertising services to clients, 370
    service access methods, 370-371

application services, 247-248

application software, 84-85
    NetWare 2.2, 216
    object-oriented, 246
    User Tools for Windows, 74
    workgroup, 246-247

APPN (Advanced Peer-to-Peer Networking)
  protocol, 407

Archive needed attribute, 29

archiving, see backing up

ARCnet (Attached Resource Computer
  NETwork) specifications, 459-463

arithmetic/logic units (ALUs), 643

ARP (Address Resolution Protocol) protocol,
  386

ASCII (American Standard Code for
  Information Interchange), 364

ASN.1 with BER (Abstract Syntax Notation
  One with Basic Encoding Rules) (ISO 8824)
  protocol, 399

ASP (AppleShare) protocol, 393-394

ASP (AppleTalk Session Protocol)
  protocol, 392

asterisk (*) wild card, 631

asynchronous
    distribution, SNADS (SNA Distributed
      Services) protocol, 409
    transmissions
      bits (physical OSI layer), 322
      frames (data link OSI layer), 338

ATM (Asynchronous Transfer Mode) protocol,
  425-427

ATP (AppleTalk Transaction Protocol)
protocol, 391-392
ATTACH utility, 210
attenuation, 264
  broadcast infrared transmissions, 282
  coaxial cable, 266
  fiber-optic cable, 271
  high-power/single-frequency radio, 276
  low-power/single-frequency radio, 275
  point-to-point infrared transmissions, 282
  satellite microwave transmissions, 281
  spread spectrum radio, 277
  STP (shielded twisted-pair) cable, 268
  terrestrial microwave transmissions, 280
  UTP (unshielded twisted-pair) cable, 269
ATTRIB command, 631-632
attributes
  DOS files, 623, 631-632
  security, 29
AUTO VLM, 527
AUTOEXEC.BAT file, 41-42, 635
AUTOEXEC.NCF file, 117-118
  installing file servers, 577-579

B

B-ISDN (Broadband ISDN), 424
backing up, 102-104, 189, 198-201
  files, 242
  in NetWare 2.2, 227-228
  third-party products for, reliability, 556
bandwidth, 263
  broadcast infrared transmissions, 282
  coaxial cable, 266
  fiber-optic cable, 271
  high-power/single-frequency radio, 276
  low-power/single-frequency radio, 275
  point-to-point infrared transmissions, 282
  satellite microwave transmissions, 281
  spread spectrum radio, 277
  STP (shielded twisted-pair) cable, 268
  terrestrial microwave transmissions, 280
  UTP (unshielded twisted-pair) cable, 269

BAS file extension, 623
Base BIOS Address jumper, 500
Base I/O jumper, 500
base memory, 531
baseband signaling, 323
Basic Message Handling Service (MHS), 93-94
BAT file extension, 623
batch files, 634-635
  AUTOEXEC.BAT, 635
  INSTALL.BAT, 580
  on network file servers, 191
BayoNette Connector (BNC) connectors, 294
BBSes (bulletin board systems), NetWire, 449
beaconing process, 480
BIND console command, 55
BIND VLM, 527
bindery, 24
bindery files
  backing up, 199-200
  troubleshooting, 187
BINDFIX utility, 186-187
BINDREST utility, 186-187
bit order translation, 364
bits, 655
  transmission synchronization, 321-323
  types, 338
blocks, 492
BNC (BayoNette Connector) connectors, 294
boards, *see* network boards
bootable disks, 627
booting computers, 667
  DOS PCs, 623-624
  remote, DOS workstations, 527-528
BREAK login script command, 86
bridges, 300-301
  brouters, 305
  optimizing performance, 554-555
broadband
  multiplexing, 324-325
  signaling, 323
Broadband ISDN (B-ISDN), 424
BROADCAST console command, 56, 117
broadcast infrared transmissions, 282-284

brouters, 305
buffers (communication), optimizing
  performance, 613-614
BUFFERS parameter (CONFIG.SYS file), 637
bulletin board systems (BBSes), NetWire, 449
Burst mode, 556-557, 614
bus topology, 312-314, 331
buses, expansion, 648-654
byte order translation, 364
bytes, 655

C

C/D jumper, 500
cables
  ARCnet specifications, 460-461
  coaxial, 264-266
  comparing types, 272-273
  connections, 292-296
  Ethernet specifications, 465-471
  FDDI, 484
  fiber-optic, 270-272
  hard drives, 500-501
  protocol analyzers (troubleshooting
    tools), 555
  Token Ring specifications, 475-478
  twisted-pair, 266-269
cache buffers, 132-133, 137
cache movable memory pool, 132
cache non-movable memory pool, 132
caching, SET parameters, 543-544
capacity, calculating for floppy disks, 661
CAPTURE utility, 74
  print job settings, 166-169
carrier detection, 332
Carrier Sense Multiple Access with Collision
  Avoidance (CSMA/CA) protocol, 332
Carrier Sense Multiple Access with Collision
  Detection (CSMA/CD) protocol, 332
carrier sensing, 332
case sensitivity, DOS, 625
CCITT (International Telegraph and Telephone Consultative Committee), see ITU

CD MOUNT console command, 117
CD-ROM drives, 517-518
  installation issues, 579-580
  read-only, 159-160
cellular topology, 317
central processing units (CPUs), 642-648
centralized
  computing, 234
  network services versus distributed network
    services, 249-251
CGA (Color Graphics Adapter), 665
channel service network/digital service units
  (CSU/DSUs), 305-306
character code translation, 364-365
child software, 189
CHKVOL utility, 45
CICS (Customer Information Control System)
  protocol, 408
circuit switching, 347
CISC (Complex Instruction Set Computer)
  microprocessors, 647
CLEAR MESSAGE console command, 214
CLEAR STATION console command, 55
clearing
  connections (Watchdog process), 525
  DOS screen, 633
CLIB NLM, 122
client disks, creating, 601-602
client-server databases, 248
clients, 236-237
  accessing file servers, 61-63
  backing up, 200-201
  configuring, 40-42
  connecting to networks, 42
  diskless, 160
  installing, 40-42
  installing client workstation files, 151-153
  NET.CFG file, 598-600
  NetWare support, 594-595
  ODI (Open Data-Link Interface)
    environment, 148-150
  shells versus DOS Requester, 595-598
  updating client workstation files, 153-154

CLNS (Connectionless-Mode Network Service)
protocol, 396-397
clocks
DOS, displaying/setting date/time, 633
speeds, 643, 649
system, setting time/date, 189-190
CLS DOS command, 633
CLS console command, 56
clusters, 492, 658
CMOS (Complementary Metal-Oxide
Semiconductor)
configuring, 667
setup information, 505-506
CMOS (Complimentary Metal-Oxide Silicon)
memory, 655
CMT (Connection Management), 483
coaxial cable, 264-266
comparing with other cable types, 272-273
connections, 294-295
cold boots, 623
collaborative computing, 235, 371
Color Graphics Adapter (CGA), 665
color video monitors, 665-666
COM file extension, 623
command-line utilities, 17
COMMAND.COM file, 622
commands
ATTRIB, 631-632
CLS, 633
console, 54-56
MEMORY, 138
NetWare 2.2, 213-214
REGISTER MEMORY, 138-139
TRACK, 190-191, 528
Control (menus), 90-91
COPY, 46, 630-631
DATE, 633
DEL, 46, 631
DIR, 630
DISKCOPY, 628
displaying as executed, 634-635
DOS operating system, 624-625
ECHO, 634-635

ERASE, 631
external, 622, 625
FIRST NETWORK DRIVE=, 42
FLAG, 29
FLAGDIR, 29
FORMAT, 506, 626-627
INSTALL, 40
internal, 624
LABEL, 627-628
LASTDRIVE=Z, 41
LISTDIR, 46, 209
LOAD, 116-117, 562
login scripts, 86-88
MAIL, 94
MAP, 43-44
MD, 628
NDIR, 46, 209
NetWare 2.2, 211-214
NMENU, 92
Organizational (menus), 90
PATH, 629
PAUSE, 635
PRINT, 633
PRINTER, 215
PROMPT, 633
QUEUE, 215
RD, 628
REM, 634
REN, 46
RENDIR, 209
SET, 116-117
parameters, 140-142
SET TIME, 189-190
SET TIMEZONE, 189-190
SYS, 627
TIME, 633
TYPE, 629-630
UNLOAD, 562
VER, 633
VOLINFO, 45, 209
WSUPDATE, 153-154
XCOPY, 632
see also utilities

comments, 634
communications
  maintaining network performance, 178
  requirements, 9-11
  rules, 256
  transmission synchronization
    asynchronous, 322, 338
    isochronous, 340
    synchronous, 322-323, 339-340
communications channel, optimizing
  performance, 612-616
Communications Protocol, 11
communications protocols, NetWare Protocol
  Suite, 120-122
communications SET parameters, 542-543
comparing migration utilities, 584-586
Complementary Metal-Oxide Semiconductor
  (CMOS)
  configuring, 667
  setup information, 505-506
Complex Instruction Set Computer (CISC)
  microprocessors, 647
Complimentary Metal-Oxide Silicon (CMOS)
  memory, 655
composite monochrome monitors, 666
computers
  basic operations, 642
  components, 642-666
  configuring, 666-667
COMSPEC login script command, 86
CONFIG.SYS file, 41, 637
configuration console commands, 54
configuration files
  CONFIG.SYS file, 41, 637
  file servers, 115-118
  NET.CFG, 598-600
    *configuring NetWare DOS Requester,
    158-159*
    *configuring NetWare ODI
    environment, 157-158*
  Windows, 152-153
configuration management, 430

configurations
  clients, 40-42
  computers, 666-667
  print jobs, 75
    creating defaults, 166-169
    printing with defaults, 169
  print servers, 71
  printers, troubleshooting, 538
  reconfiguring
    bus topology, 314
    cellular topology, 317
    mesh topologies, 316
    ring topology, 315
    star topology, 316
  system, DOS workstations, 529
CONN VLM, 527
connection identifiers (transport OSI
  layer), 356
Connection Management (CMT), 483
Connection-Mode Network Service (CONS)
  protocol, 397
connection-oriented services, 340
connection-oriented transport
  ISO 8073 (Connection-Oriented Transport
    Protocol Specification) protocol, 398
  NSP (Network Services Protocol)
    protocol, 398
  TCP (Transmission Control Protocol)
    protocol, 385
connectionless (datagram) service, 380,
  384-386, 390-391
Connectionless-Mode Network Service (CLNS)
  protocol, 396-397
connections
  bridges, 300-301
  brouters, 305
  cable, 292-296
  clearing (Watchdog process), 525
  data link OSI layer services, 340-342
  DOS workstations to servers, troubleshoot-
    ing, 524-525
  establishing for sessions, 361
  gateways, 353

hubs, 297-299
modems, 301-302
monitoring, 549-550
multiplexors, 301
network boards, 296-297
network OSI layer services, 352-353
releasing sessions from, 362
reliable delivery, SPX (Sequenced Packet Exchange) protocol, 381
repeaters, 299-300
routers, 303-305
transport OSI layer services, 357-358
types, 312
workstations to networks, 42
CONS (Connection-Mode Network Service) protocol, 397
console commands, 54-56
NetWare 2.2, 213-214
see also commands
Console operator users, NetWare 2.2, 211
console security (file servers), 29-31
implementing, 34-35
contention-based media access control, 332-333
versus token passing media access control, 335
Control commands (menus), 90-91
control units (CUs), 642
Controller Interrupt jumper, 500
conventional memory, 531
converting, *see* upgrading
COPY command, 46, 630-631
Copy Inhibit attribute, 29
copying
disks, 628
files, 46-47, 630, 632
input/output to, 631
public/system, for file server installation, 573-574
cost
broadcast infrared transmissions, 282
coaxial cable, 266
fiber-optic cable, 271
high-power/single-frequency radio, 276

low-power/single-frequency radio, 275
point-to-point infrared transmissions, 282
routing, estimating, 350
satellite microwave transmissions, 280
spread spectrum radio, 277
STP (shielded twisted-pair) cable, 267
terrestrial microwave transmissions, 279
UTP (unshielded twisted-pair) cable, 269
CPUs (central processing units), 642-648
CRC (cyclic redundancy check), 341
Create rights, 27
crosstalk, 436
CSMA/CA (Carrier Sense Multiple Access with Collision Avoidance) protocol, 332
CSMA/CD (Carrier Sense Multiple Access with Collision Detection) protocol, 332
CSU/DSUs (channel service network/digital service units), 305-306
Ctrl key, 624
current state encoding, 318
Cursor keys, 624
CUs (control units), 642
Customer Information Control System (CICS) protocol, 408
cyclic redundancy check (CRC), 341

D

D-type connectors, 292
DAP (Data Access Protocol) protocol, 400
DAS (dual attached stations), 482
DAT file extension, 623
data bits, 338
data bus sizes, 643, 649
data flow control (SNA model), 402
data integrity
SFT (System Fault Tolerance), 100-101
SMS (Storage Management Services), 102-103
data link control (SNA model), 402
data link layer (OSI model), 149
connection services, 340-342
logical topologies, 330-331

media access control, 332-336

physical device addresses, 337

purpose, 329-330

transmission synchronization, 337-340

data link protocols

DDCMP (Digital Data Communications Message Protocol), 395-396

HDLC (High-Level Data Link Control), 396

SDLC (Synchronous Data Link Control), 406

data migration, 241

data transfer rate, 492

data translation (presentation OSI layer), 364-365

data types, establishing, 399

database processing, 408

database services, 248-249

databases, backing up/restoring, 189, 198-201

datagram (connectionless) service, 380, 384-386, 390-391

Datagram Delivery Protocol (DDP), 390-391

datagram packet switching, 349

DATE command, 633

dates

DOS clock, setting/displaying, 633

system clock, setting, 189-190

DCBs (Disk Coprocessor Boards), 499

DCONFIG command, 213

DDCMP (Digital Data Communications Message Protocol) protocol, 395-396

DDM (Distributed Data Management) protocol, 409

DDP (Datagram Delivery Protocol) protocol, 390-391

dedicated telephone services, leased, 286-288

default

directories, 629

disks (DOS), 627

login scripts, 85

print job settings

creating, 166-169

printing with, 169

DEL command, 46, 631

Delete Inhibit attribute, 29

deleted files

purging, 50

recovering, 48

DELETED.SAV directory, 16

deleting

directories, 628

files, 631

name space support from volumes, 188

DETs (Directory Entry Tables), duplicate, 101

DEVICE parameter (CONFIG.SYS file), 637

DIA (Document Interchange Architecture) protocol, 409

diagnostic software, 440-441

dial-up access to networks, 420-421

dialog control (session OSI layer), 360

differential backups, 103

Digital Data Communications Message Protocol (DDCMP) protocol, 395-396

Digital Network Architecture (DNA) protocol stack, 394-400

digital signaling, 318-319

DIN connectors, 293

DIP (dual in-line pin) packages, 657

DIR command, 630

directional radio signals, 273

directories, 13-16

attributes, 29

components, 628

contents, listing, 630

creating, 628

default, 629

deleting, 628

information about, listing, 46

managing, 47-48

network, installing client software from, 602

Public, 580

System, 580

directory cache buffers, 133, 138

directory caching SET parameters, 544

directory paths, 628

relative, 629

directory services, 247
directory structures (NetWare 2.2), 208-209
directory table blocks, 134
directory tables, 133-134
dirty cache buffers, 137
DISABLE LOGIN console command, 55
DISABLE TRANSACTIONS console
  command, 214
disk allocation blocks, 134
disk blocks, 134
disk channels, 499
disk controller cards, 492
Disk Coprocessor Boards (DCBs), 499
disk driver NLMs, 57, 112-114
disk drivers, loading at file server
  installation, 571
disk duplexing, 101, 511-516
disk mirroring, 101, 511-516
DISKCOPY command, 628
diskless clients, 160
disks
    bootable, 627
    client, creating, 601-602
    copying, 628
    DOS, default, 627
    floppy
        formatting, 626
        types, 660
    hard, *see* hard drives
    volume labels, 627
display devices, 665
DISPLAY login script command, 86
DISPLAY NETWORKS console
  command, 214
DISPLAY SERVERS console command, 117
distance vector routing, 351
distributed
    databases, 248
    computing, 234-235
    network services versus centralized network
        services, 249-251
    processing (NetWare 2.2), 225
Distributed Data Management (DDM)
  protocol, 409

DIX connectors, 292-293
DMA Channel jumper, 500
DNA (Digital Network Architecture) protocol
  stack, 394-400
DNS (Domain Name System) protocol, 386
DOC directory, 16
DOC file extension, 623
Document Interchange Architecture (DIA)
  protocol, 409
documentation, 439-440
    ElectroText electronic (Novell), 17-18
    MHTL (Micro House Technical Library),
        449-454
    NetWare 2.2, 223
    NetWire BBS, 449
    NSEPro (Network Support Encyclopedia),
        444-449
documents, linked-object, 246-247
DoD (United States Department of Defense)
  model, 382-383
Domain Name System (DNS) protocol, 386
DOS
    > redirection operator, 634
    booting PCs, 623-624
    client support, 594-595
    clock, displaying/setting date/time, 633
    commands, 624-625
    directories, 628-630
        listing contents, 630
    disks
        bootable, 627
        copying, 628
        default, 627
        formatting, 626
        volume labels, 627
    files
        accessing on non-default disks, 627-628
        attributes, 623, 631-632
        AUTOEXEC.BAT, 635
        batch, 634-635
        copying, 630, 632
        deleting, 631
        listing contents, 630
        names, 622-623

printing, 633
storing, 626-627
types, 622-623
    formatting hard drives with, 568-569
    installing, 635-637
    partitioning hard drives for, 568
    screen, clearing, 633
    versions, displaying, 633
DOS prompt, 624
    customizing, 633
DOS redirection VLMs, 155
DOS Requester, 11
    DOS workstations, 526-527
    versus shells, 595-598
DOS text utilities, 16
    accessing help, 17
DOS workstations
    DOS Requester, 526-527
    DR (Digital Research) DOS (Novell), 532
    IPX (Internetwork Packet Exchange)
      architecture, 524-525
    IRQ (Interrupt Request Channels) conflicts,
      528-529
    memory, 530-531
    ODI, 525-526
    remote booting, 527-528
    system configurations, 529
    tracking routers, 528
DOSGEN utility, 527
DOWN console command, 55
DR (Digital Research) DOS (Novell), 532
DRAM (Dynamic RAM), 655
drive latency, 492
drive letters, 624
DRIVE login script command, 86
Drive Select jumper, 500
drivers
    disk, loading at file server installation, 571
    finding for NetWare installation, 563-564
    LAN, 10-11, 42, 114-115
      loading at file server installation, 574-577
    MLID (Multiple Link Interface Driver),
      150, 379-380

drives
    CD-ROM, 517-518
      installation issues, 579-580
    hard, *see* hard drives
    magneto-optical (M-O), 518
    mapping, 43-44
    monitoring, 550-551
    network (regular), 43
    search, 43-44
DS jumper, 500
DSK file extension, 112, 563
DSP jumper, 500
dual attached stations (DAS), 482
dual in-line pin (DIP) packages, 657
dumb terminal emulation, 387-388
duplexing hard drives, 511-516
dynamic patches, 554
Dynamic RAM (DRAM), 655

E

e-mail (electronic mail), 245
    Basic Message Handling Service (MHS),
      93-94
    integrating with voice mail, 245-246
    transferring, 387
EBCDIC (Extended Binary Coded Decimal
    Interchange Code), 364
ECHO command, 634-635
EDIT NLM, 118
effective rights, 28-29
    viewing, 33
EGA (Enhanced Graphics Adapter), 666
EISA (Enhanced Industry Standard
    Architecture) bus, 652
ELAP (EtherTalk Link Access Protocol)
    protocol, 389-390
electrical problems, prevention, 436-437
ElectroText electronic documentation (Novell),
    17-18
EM (electromagnetic) waveform, 262
EMI (electromagnetic interference), 264, 437
    broadcast infrared transmissions, 283

coaxial cable, 266
fiber-optic cable, 271-272
high-power/single-frequency radio, 276
low-power/single-frequency radio, 276
point-to-point infrared transmissions, 282
satellite microwave transmissions, 281
spread spectrum radio, 278
STP (shielded twisted-pair) cable, 268
terrestrial microwave transmissions, 280
UTP (unshielded twisted-pair) cable, 269
EMS (Expanded Memory), 531, 656
ENABLE LOGIN console command, 55-56
ENABLE TRANSACTIONS console
  command, 214
encryption (presentation OSI layer), 365-367
END login script command, 86
end-to-end flow control, 358
Enhanced Graphics Adapter (EGA), 666
Enhanced Industry Standard Architecture
  (EISA) bus, 652
Enhanced Small Device Interface (ESDI) drives,
  494-495, 663
enhancement and management utility NLMs,
  58-60
Enter key, 624
environment, maintaining network
  performance, 178
ERASE command, 631
Erase rights, 27
error control, 340
    data link OSI layer, 341-342
    ICMP (Internet Control Message Protocol)
      protocol, 384
    network OSI layer, 352-353
    transport OSI layer, 357-358
error messages, DOS, 625
ESDI (Enhanced Small Device Interface) drives,
  494-495, 663
ET.INI file, 151
ETC directory, 15
Ethernet
    frame types, 119-120, 472
    specifications, 463-474

ETHERNET 802.2 frame type, 472
ETHERNET II frame type, 119, 472
ETHERNET SNAP (SubNetwork Address
  Protocol) frame type, 472
Ethernet Version 2 protocol, 395
EtherTalk Link Access Protocol (ELAP),
  389-390
even parity, 338
EXE file extension, 623
EXEC menu command, 90
Execute Only attribute, 29
EXIT console command, 56
Expanded Memory (EMS), 531, 656
expanding networks (NetWare 2.2), 225
expansion buses, 642, 648-654
Extended Memory (XMS), 531, 657
external commands, 622, 625
External Data Representation (XDR)
  protocol, 388

F

FATs (File Allocation Tables), duplicate, 101
fault domain, 480
fault management, 430-431
fault-tolerant mesh topologies, NLSP (Network
  Link Services Protocol) protocol, 381
fax servers, 245
FAXBACK, 458
FCC (Federal Communications
  Commission), 273
FCONSOLE operators, 26
FDDI (Fiber Distributed Data Interface)
  standard, 418-420
    specifications, 481-485
FDISK utility, 635-636
FDISPLAY login script command, 86
Federal Communications Commission
  (FCC), 273
Fiber Distributed Data Interface (FDDI)
  standard, 418-420
    specifications, 481-485

fiber-optic cable, 270-272
   comparing with other cable types, 272-273
   connections, 295-296
file cache buffers, 133
   memory pool, 131
file caching SET parameters, 543-544
File Scan rights, 28
file server consoles
   monitoring, 552
   security, 29-31
     implementing, 34-35
file servers
   accessing from workstations, 61-63
   batch files, 191
   bindery files, backing up, 199-200
   components, 110-115
   configuration files, 115-118
   configuring, 54
   hard drives, monitoring status, 185-186
   information about, listing, 45-46, 59
   installing, 55, 58-59
     assigning internal IPX numbers, 570
     copying public/system files, 573-574
     creating partitions, 571-572
     creating volumes, 572-573
     formatting hard drives with DOS,
      568-569
     loading disk drivers, 571
     loading LAN drivers, 574-577
     local support codes, 570
     mounting volumes, 573
     naming servers, 569-570
     NetWare 3.11 versus 3.12, 579-580
     partitioning hard drives for DOS, 568
     required steps, 568
     selecting file name formats, 570-571
     STARTUP.NCF and AUTOEXEC.NCF
      files, 577-579
   installing client software from, 602
   LIP (Large Internet Packet) protocol, 142
   listing, 14-15
   maintaining, 55-56

managing, 47-48
memory
   calculating allocation amounts, 134-138
   components, 132-134
   information about, viewing, 138
   monitoring statistics, 184-185
   pools, 130-132
   registering additional, 138-139
   SET parameters, 140-142
multiple to print servers, setup and management design, 165
NetWare features, 8-9
Packet Burst protocol, 143
starting, 123
storing files with non-DOS naming
   conventions, 118-122
file services, 240-243
   AFP (AppleTalk Filing Protocol)
   protocol, 393
file syntax translation, 365
file system SET parameters, 544-546
file systems, 11
   accessing, 43-44
   NetWare 2.2, 208-209
   optimizing performance, 611-612
   security, implementing, 32-34
File Transfer, Access, and Management
   (FTAM) (ISO 8571) protocol, 399-400
File Transfer Protocol (FTP), 387
FILER utility, 32, 47-48
files
   accessing, 388
   attributes, 29
   AUTOEXEC.BAT, 41-42, 635
   AUTOEXEC.NCF, 117-118
     installing file servers, 577-579
   backing up, 102-104, 189, 198-201, 242
     in NetWare 2.2, 227-228
   batch, on network file servers, 191
   bindery
     backing up, 199-200
     troubleshooting, 187

client workstation
installing, 151-153
updating, 153-154
CONFIG.SYS, 41, 637
copying, 46-47
deleted
purging, 50
recovering, 48
DOS
accessing on non-default disks, 627-628
attributes, 623, 631-632
batch, 634-635
copying, 630, 632
copying to, 631
deleting, 631
names, 622-623
printing, 633
storing, 626-627
types, 622-623
DOS Requester, 527
extensions
BAS, 623
BAT, 623
COM, 623
DAT, 623
DOC, 623
DSK, 112, 563
EXE, 623
LAN, 563
NCF, 191
NLM, 112
OVL, 623
SYS, 623
TXT, 623
VLM, 155
INSTALL.BAT, 580
IPX.COM, 224-225
IPXODI.COM, 10, 42
listing, 630
listing contents, 630
LOGIN.EXE, 15
LSL.COM, 10, 42
managing, 47-48

monitoring, 552
NET.CFG, 41-42, 598-600
configuring NetWare DOS Requester,
158-159
configuring NetWare ODI environment,
157-158
NETx.COM, 224-225
non-DOS naming conventions, storing files
with, 118-122
public/system, copying for file server
installation, 573-574
restoring, 189, 198-201
in NetWare 2.2, 227-228
SERVER.EXE, 112
SLIST.EXE, 14-15
STARTUP.NCF, 116-117
installing file servers, 577-579
storing, 241-242
transferring, 240-241, 387
TSA_SMS.COM, 104
updating, file-update synchronization,
242-243
VLM.EXE (VLM Manager), 10-11, 42
Windows configuration, 152-153
see also NLMs; VLMs
FILES parameter (CONFIG.SYS file), 637
finding drivers/NLMs for NetWare installation,
563-564
FIO VLM, 527
FIRE PHASERS login script command, 86
First Mail utility, 94
FIRST NETWORK DRIVE= command, 42
fixed disks, *see* hard drives
FLAG command, 29
FLAGDIR command, 29
floppy disks
formatting, 626
types, 660
see also disks
flow control, 340
data link OSI layer, 341
end-to-end (transport OSI layer), 358
network OSI layer, 352

FORMAT command, 506, 626-627
formatting
    floppy disks, 626
    hard drives, 502-507, 626
       with DOS, 568-569
    partitions, 636
forms
    definitions for printing, 78
    mounting, 170-171
frame relay standard, 422-423
frame types, 42, 119-122
    Ethernet specifications, 471-472
frames, synchronizing transmissions, 337-340
frequency, 319
frequency shift keying, 321
frequency-division multiplexing, 324
FTAM (File Transfer, Access, and Management) (ISO 8571) protocol, 399-400
FTP (File Transfer Protocol) protocol, 387
full backups, 102
full-duplex dialogs, 360
function keys, 624

G

gateways, 353
GENERAL VLM, 527
generating modules, 562
GETO menu command, 91
GETP menu command, 91
GETR menu command, 91
GRANT utility, 34
graphical utilities, 17
    accessing help, 17
GREETING_TIME login script command, 86
group accounts, setting up, 31-32
groups, removing from trustee lists, 34
guaranteed rate flow control (data link OSI layer), 341
guaranteed state changes, 323

H

half-duplex dialogs, 360
hard drives, 111-112, 661-663
    cables, 500-501
    components, 492
    disk duplexing, 511-516
    disk mirroring, 511-516
    file servers, monitoring status, 185-186
    formatting, 502-507, 626
       with DOS, 568-569
    interface types, 492-499
    jumpers, 500
    monitoring, 550-551
    partitions
       creating, 635-636
       for DOS, 568
       formatting, 636
    RAID (Redundant Array of Inexpensive Drives), 508-510
hardware
    communications, requirements, 9-10
    computer components, 642-666
    connections, 292-296
    file server components, 110-112
    maintaining network performance, 178
    MHTL (Micro House Technical Library), 449-454
    NetWare 2.2 components, 224
    NetWare installation requirements, 564-565
HCSS (High-Capacity Storage System), 242
HDLC (High-Level Data Link Control) protocol, 396
help
    accessing from within NetWare utilities, 17
    ElectroText electronic documentation (Novell), 17-18
    NetWare's Online Help System (NetWare 2.2), 223
    product documentation (NetWare 2.2), 223
hertz (Hz), 263
Hidden attribute, 29
High Capacity Storage System (HCSS), 242

high memory, 531
High-Level Data Link Control (HDLC)
    protocol, 396
high-level formatting, 506-507
high-power/single-frequency radio, 276-278
    comparing with other wireless media,
        283-284
HOLDOFF command, 213
HOLDON command, 213
hop counts, 350
    determining, 380-381, 384-385
host-to-host layer (DoD model), 383
hosts, 103
hot fixes, 101
HOUR24 login script command, 87
hubs, 297-299
    optimizing performance, 554-555
Hz (hertz), 263

I

IBM Data Connectors, 293-294
IBMBIO.COM file, 622
IBMDOS.COM file, 622
ICMP (Internet Control Message Protocol)
    protocol, 384
IDE (Integrated Drive Electronics) drives,
    494, 663
IEEE (Institute of Electrical and Electronic
    Engineers) 802 family of standards, 414-418
IF...THEN...ELSE login script command, 87
IMS (Information Management System)
    protocol, 408
INCLUDE login script command, 87
incremental backups, 102
Industry Standard Architecture (ISA) bus,
    649-651
Information Management System (IMS)
    protocol, 408
infrared transmissions, 263, 281-283
    comparing with other wireless media,
        283-284
Inherited Rights Masks (IRMs), 28

input devices, 642
INSTALL command, 40
INSTALL NLM, 58-59, 117-118
    disk duplexing/mirroring, 512-516
    loading, 571
INSTALL.BAT file, 580
installation console commands, 55
installing
    Basic MHS, 93
    broadcast infrared transmissions, 282
    bus topology, 314
    cellular topology, 317
    client workstation files, 151-153
    clients, 40-42
    coaxial cable, 265-266
    DOS, 635-637
    DOS Requester, 527
    fiber-optic cable, 271
    file servers
        assigning internal IPX numbers, 570
        copying public/system files, 573-574
        creating partitions, 571-572
        creating volumes, 572-573
        formatting hard drives with DOS,
            568-569
        loading disk drivers, 571
        loading LAN drivers, 574-577
        local support codes, 570
        mounting volumes, 573
        naming servers, 569-570
        NetWare 3.11 versus 3.12, 579-580
        partitioning hard drives for DOS, 568
        required steps, 568
        selecting file name formats, 570-571
        STARTUP.NCF and AUTOEXEC.NCF
            files, 577-579
    high-power/single-frequency radio, 276
    low-power/single-frequency radio, 275
    mesh topologies, 316
    NetWare
        finding drivers/NLMs, 563-564
        hardware requirements, 564-565
        software requirements, 564

NSEPro, 444
point-to-point infrared transmissions, 282
ring topology, 315
satellite microwave transmissions, 280
spread spectrum radio, 277
star topology, 316
STP (shielded twisted-pair) cable, 267-268
terrestrial microwave transmissions, 279-280
UTP (unshielded twisted-pair) cable, 269
workstation software, 600-604
INT numbers, 42
Integrated Drive Electronics (IDE) drives, 494, 663
Integrated Services Digital Network (ISDN) standards, 423-424
Intel microprocessors, 643-646
intelligent hubs, 298-299
interleave ratio, setting, 503-504
internal commands, 624
internal IPX numbers, assigning (file server installation), 570
International Telecommunications Union, *see* ITU
International Telegraph and Telephone Consultative Committee (CCITT), *see* ITU
Internet, 288
Internet Control Message Protocol (ICMP), 384
internet layer (DoD model), 383
Internet Protocol (IP), 384
Internet (TCP/IP) protocol stack, 122, 382-388
Internetwork Packet Exchange (IPX) protocol, 120, 380
    DOS workstations, 524-525
internetworks, 302-306
Interrupt Request Channels (IRQ) conflicts, troubleshooting, 528-529
interrupts, 648
intruder account detection, 26
IO.SYS file, 622
IP (Internet Protocol) protocol, 384
IPX (Internetwork Packet Exchange) protocol, 120, 380
    DOS workstations, 524-525

IPX.COM file, 224-225
IPXNCP VLM, 527
IPXODI.COM file, 10, 42
IPXS NLM, 122
IRMs (Inherited Rights Masks), 28
    changing, 34
IRQ (Interrupt Request Channels) conflicts, troubleshooting, 528-529
ISA (Industry Standard Architecture) bus, 649-651
ISDN (Integrated Services Digital Network) standards, 423-424
ISO 8073 (Connection-Oriented Transport Protocol Specification) protocol, 398
ISO 8327 (Session Protocol Specification) protocol, 399
ISO 8571 (FTAM) (File Transfer, Access, and Management) protocol, 399-400
ISO 8824 (ASN.1 with BER) (Abstract Syntax Notation with Basic Encoding Rules) protocol, 399
isochronous transmission frames (data link OSI layer), 340
ITEM menu command, 90
ITU (International Telecommunications Union)
    ATM (Asynchronous Transfer Mode) protocol, 425-427
    frame relay standard, 422-423
    ISDN (Integrated Services Digital Network) standard, 423-424
    Recommendation X.25, 421-422
    SDH (Synchronous Digital Hierarchy) standard, 424-425

J–K

jukeboxes, 241
jumpers (hard drives), 500

keyboard controllers, 642
keys, 624

L

LABEL command, 627-628
labels, volume, 627
LAN driver NLMs, 61
LAN drivers, 10-11, 42, 114-115
    loading at file server installation, 574-577
LAN file extension, 563
LANalyzer for Windows software, 555
LANs (local area networks), 235
    monitoring, 551
Large Internet Packet (LIP) protocol, 142, 615
lasers, 270
LASTDRIVE parameter (CONFIG.SYS file),
    41, 637
leased dedicated telephone services, 286-288
LEDs (light-emitting diodes), 270
line noise, 437
Link Support Layer (LSL) protocol, 10,
    150, 380
link-state routing, 352
linked-object documents, 246-247
LIP (Large Internet Packet) protocol, 142, 615
LISTDIR command, 46, 209
LLAP (LocalTalk Link Access Protocol)
    protocol, 389-390
LOAD command, 55, 91, 116-117, 562
loading
    applications software, 84-85
    disk drivers, at file server installation, 571
    INSTALL NLM, 571
    LAN drivers, at file server installation,
        574-577
    NetWare DOS Requester, 157
local area networks (LANs), 235
    monitoring, 551
local printers, 73
LocalTalk Link Access Protocol (LLAP),
    389-390
lock SET parameters, 546
logical network addresses, 346
logical topologies, 330-331
logical units (LUs), 403-405

LOGIN directory, 14-15
login scripts
    building, 85-88
    NetWare 2.2, 216-217
    types, 85
login security, 24-26
LOGIN.EXE file, 15
LOGIN_NAME login script command, 87
logs (NetWare 2.2), 222-223
long-term memory, 609
low-level formatting, 503
low-power/single-frequency radio, 275-278
    comparing with other wireless media,
        283-284
LSL (Link Support Layer) protocol, 10,
    150, 380
LSL.COM file, 10, 42
LUs (logical units), 403, 405

M

MAC.NAM NLM, 119
MACHINE login script command, 87
Macintosh
    client support, 594
    expansion buses, 654
magneto-optical (M-O) drives, 518
MAIL command, 94
MAIL directory, 15
MAILbus family of products, 400
main menus, 90
maintenance console commands, 55-56
MAKEUSER utility, 32
management and enhancement utility NLMs,
    58-60
MANs (metropolitan area networks), 235
MAP command, 43-44, 87
Mass Storage Services (MSS), 242
Maximum Rights Masks, 210
MC68000 microprocessors (Motorola), 646
MC68020 microprocessors (Motorola), 646
MC68030 microprocessors (Motorola),
    646-647

MC68040 microprocessors (Motorola), 647

MCA (Micro Channel Architecture) bus, 652

MD command, 628

media access control
    contention-based, 332-333
        versus token passing, 335
    polling, 335-336
    token passing, 333-334

MEM addresses, 42

memory, 111, 642, 654-657
    allocation, optimizing NetWare
      performance, 608-611
    DOS workstations, 530-531
    file servers
        calculating allocation amounts, 134-138
        components, 132-134
        information about, viewing, 138
        monitoring statistics, 184-185
        pools, 130-132
        registering additional, 138-139
        SET parameters, 140-142
    maintaining network performance, 178

memory addresses, 643, 648

MEMORY console command, 138

memory pools, 608-609

memory SET parameters, 543

MENU menu command, 90

MENUCNVT utility, 93

MENUMAKE utility, 92

menus
    converting previous versions to
      NetWare 3.12, 93
    creating, 89-91
      NetWare 2.2, 225-227
    preparing for use, 91-92

mesh topologies, 316-317
    NLSP (Network Link Services Protocol)
      protocol, 381

message identifiers (transport OSI layer), 356

message services, 245-247

message switching, 348

metropolitan area networks (MANs), 235

MFM (Modified Frequency Modulation)
    encoding scheme, 494

MHTL (Micro House Technical Library),
    449-454

Micro Channel Architecture (MCA) bus, 652

microprocessors, 110-111, 642-648

microwave transmissions, 263, 278-281
    comparing with other wireless media,
      283-284

MIGRATE.EXE utility, 587-588

migrating from NetWare 3.11 to 3.12
    across-the-wire migration, 586-587
    comparing migration utilities, 584-586
    housekeeping, 584
    post-migration procedures, 590
    same-server migration, 587-589
    upgrading, 589-590

mirroring hard drives, 511-516

MLID (Multiple Link Interface Driver)
    protocol, 150, 379-380, 525

modems, 301-302

Modified Frequency Modulation (MFM)
    encoding scheme, 494

Modify rights, 28

modules
    linking, 562
    updating with patches, 553-554

MONITOR console command, 137-138,
    180-186, 214

MONITOR NLM, 58-59, 549-553

monitors, 665-666

monochrome video monitors, 666

motherboards, 642
    display devices, 665-666
    expansion buses, 648-654
    memory, 654-657
    microprocessors, 642-648
    ports, 663-665
    storage devices, 658-663

Motorola microprocessors, 646-647

MOUNT console command, 55

mounting forms, 170-171

mounting volumes at file server
installation, 573
MSD utility, 440-441
MSDOS.SYS file, 622
MSS (Mass Storage Services), 242
multi-wire cable connections, 292-293
Multiple Link Interface Driver (MLID)
protocol, 150, 379-380, 525
multiplexing, 324-325
multiplexors, 301
multipoint connections, 312
topologies based on, 312-314
multiscanning monitors, 666

N

NAK (negative acknowledgment), 341
name space support, 118-119, 123
removing from volumes, 188
name/address resolution, 386
transport OSI layer, 356-357
names
files
DOS, 622-623
selecting formats, 570-571
with non-DOS naming conventions,
storing, 118-122
volumes, 12
naming file servers at installation, 569-570
Naming Service (DNA), 400
NAUN (nearest active upstream neighbor), 480
NAUs (network addressable units), 403-405
NBACKUP utility, 227-228
NCF file extension, 191
NCOPY utility, 46-47
NCP (NetWare Core Protocols) protocol,
122, 382
NCP (Network Control Program) protocol,
406-407
NCP Packet Signature, 179-180
NDAY_OF_WEEK login script command, 87
NDIR command, 46, 209
near-line storage, 241

nearest active upstream neighbor (NAUN), 480
negative acknowledgment (NAK), 341
NET.CFG file, 41-42, 598-600
configuring NetWare DOS Requester,
158-159
configuring NetWare ODI environment,
157-158
NetWare
3.11 to 3.12 migrations
across-the-wire migration, 586-587
comparing migration utilities, 584-586
housekeeping, 584
post-migration procedures, 590
same-server migration, 587-589
upgrading, 589-590
features, 8-9
file system, 11
installing
finding drivers/NLMs, 563-564
hardware requirements, 564-565
software requirements, 564
utilities, 16-17
NetWare 2.2
accessing network, 209
application software, 216
backing up and restoring, 227-228
commands/utilities, 211-214
defining networks, 224
distributed processing, 225
expanding networks, 225
file systems/directory structures, 208-209
hardware components, 224
login scripts, 216-217
logs, 222-223
menus, creating, 225-227
printing services, 214-216
resources, 223
security, 210-211
shells, 224-225
software components, 224
system manager responsibilities, 222
NetWare bindery, 24
NetWare Buyer's Guide (NetWare 2.2), 223

NetWare Core Protocols (NCP), 122, 382

NetWare DOS Requester, 11, 154-159

NetWare IPX/SPX protocol stack, 379-382

NetWare Link Services Protocol, *see* Network Link Services Protocol

NetWare Protocol Suite, 120-122

NetWare servers, accessing, 43-44

NETWARE.DRV file, 151

NETWARE.HLP file, 151

NETWARE.INI file, 151

NetWare's Online Help System (NetWare 2.2), 223

NetWire BBS, 449

   NetWare 2.2, 223

network (regular) drives, 43

network access layer (DoD model), 383

network addressable units (NAUs), 403-405

network administrators

   accounting management, 432

   configuration management, 430

   fault management, 430-431

   performance management, 431

   responsibilities (NetWare 2.2), 222

   security management, 432

network board drivers, 379-380

network boards, 112, 296-297

   ARCnet specifications, 460

   Ethernet specifications, 464-465

   optimizing performance, 615-616

   Token Ring specifications, 474-475

Network Control Program (NCP) protocol, 406-407

network directories, installing client software from, 602

Network File System (NFS) protocols, 388

network interface cards (NICs), 8, 297

   see also network boards

network layer (OSI model), 149

   addresses, 346

   connection services, 352-353

   purpose, 345-346

   route discovery, 350-352

   switching, 347-350

Network Link Services Protocol (NLSP), 381

network operating systems (NOSs), 239

   selecting, 251

network security

   attributes, 29

   file server, 29-31

     implementing, 34-35

   implementing, 32-34

   login, 24-26

   rights, 26

   user/group accounts, setting up, 31-32

network services, 236-237

   accessing, 382

   application services, 247-248

   centralized versus distributed, 249-251

   database services, 248-249

   file services, 240-243

   message services, 245-247

   print services, 243-245

   public, 284-288

Network Services Protocol (NSP), 398

Network Support Encyclopedia (NSEPro), 444-449

Network Users (NetWare 2.2), 211

Network Virtual Terminal Service (NVTS) protocol, 400

networking, 234

   centralized computing, 234

   collaborative computing, 235

   distributed computing, 234-235

networks, 305

   communications requirements, 9-11

   components, 235-237

   connecting workstations, 296-297

   defining in NetWare 2.2, 224

   dial-up access, 420-421

   features, 8-9

   file system, 11

   LANs (local area networks), 235

   MANs (metropolitan area networks), 235

   NetWare 2.2, expanding, 225

performance
  maintenance factors, 178-180
  maintenance troubleshooting, 186-189
  monitoring, 180-186
  WANs (wide area networks), 235
NETX VLM, 527
NET*x*.COM file, 224-225
NFS (Network File System) protocols, 388
NICs (network interface cards), 8, 297
  see also network boards
NLM file extension, 112
NLMs (NetWare Loadable Modules), 56-57, 562-563
  calculating memory-allocation amounts, 134-135
  disk driver, 57, 112-114
  EDIT, 118
  finding for NetWare installation, 563-564
  INSTALL, 117-118
    disk duplexing/mirroring, 512-516
    loading, 571
  LAN driver, 61
  management and enhancement utility, 58-60
  MONITOR, 549-553
  name-space, 118-119, 123
  REMOTE, 61
  RS232, 62
  RSPX, 62
  TCP/IP protocol, 122
  TSA_DOS, 104
  TSA_OS2, 104
  VREPAIR, 187-188, 556
NLSP (Network Link Services Protocol) protocol, 381
NMENU command, 92
noise (line), 437
Norton Utilities' System Information, 440
NOSs (network operating systems), 239, 251
notify list (printers), adding users, 171
Novell
  DR (Digital Research) DOS, 532
  ElectroText electronic documentation, 17-18

NPRINT utility, 74
NSEPro (Network Support Encyclopedia), 444-449
NSP (Network Services Protocol) protocol, 398
NuBus, 654
numbers (internal IPX), assigning, 570
NVTS (Network Virtual Terminal Service) protocol, 400
NWADMIN.INI file, 151
NWP VLM, 527
NWPOPUP.EXE file, 151
NWSETUP command, 213
NWUSER.EXE file, 151
NWUTILS.GRP file, 151

O

objects
  communicating, 246
  linked, 246-247
odd parity, 338
ODI (Open Data-Link Interface) environment, 148-150
  configuring, 157-158
  DOS workstations, 525-526
ODI (Open Data-Link Interface) protocol, 11
OFF console command, 214
offline storage, 241
omnidirectional radio signals, 273
online help (NetWare 2.2), 223
online storage, 241
Open Data-Link Interface environment, *see* ODI environment
Open Data-Link Interface (ODI) protocol, 11
Open Shortest Path First (OSPF) protocol, 385
Open Systems Interconnection Reference Model, *see* OSI
operating systems (OSs), 239
operators, > (redirection), 634
optimizing performance, 608
  communications channel, 612-616
  file system, 611-612
  memory allocation, 608-611

system processor, 616
with bridges/routers/hubs/repeaters,
    554-555
with packet burst mode, 556-557
with SET parameters, 542-548
Organizational commands (menus), 90
original cache buffers, 137
OS call interruption, 370-371
OS login script command, 87
OS/2 client support, 594
OS_VERSION login script command, 87
OS2.NAM NLM, 118
OSI (Open Systems Interconnection) Reference
  Model, 148-150, 256-257
OSI model
    application layer, 369
        advertising services to clients, 370
        service access methods, 370-371
    data link layer
        connection services, 340-342
        logical topologies, 330-331
        media access control, 332-336
        physical device addresses, 337
        purpose, 329-330
        transmission synchronization, 337-340
    network layer
        addresses, 346-347
        connection services, 352-353
        purpose, 345-346
        route discovery, 350-352
        switching, 347-350
    peer layers, communicating, 258-259
    physical layer
        allocating transmission media capacity, 323
        connection types, 312
        multiplexing, 324-325
        purpose, 311-312
        signaling, 317-321
        topologies, 312-317
        transmission synchronization, 321-323
    presentation layer, 363-364
        data translation, 364-365
        encryption, 365-367

session layer, 359-362
SNA (Systems Network Architecture)
    protocol stack influence, 401-402
transport layer, 355-358
OSPF (Open Shortest Path First) protocol, 385
OSs (operating systems), 239
output devices, 642
output ports, 642
oversampling, 323
OVL file extension, 623

P

package switching, 349-350
Packet Burst protocol, 122, 143, 614
packet receive buffers, 133, 137
packet sequence control (network OSI
    layer), 353
Packet Signature, 30-31
packets, 119
    LIP (Large Internet Packet) protocol, 142
    NCP Packet Signature, 179-180
    passing to protocol stacks, 380
    reliable delivery, SPX (Sequenced Packet
        Exchange) protocol, 381
    RIP (Routing Information Protocol),
        190-191
    SAP (Service Advertising Protocol), 190-191
    sizes, optimizing communication
        channel, 613
PAP (Printer Access Protocol) protocol, 392
parallel ports, 663-665
parent software, 189
parity bits, 338, 655
partitions
    creating, 635-636, 662
    for DOS, 568
        for file server installation, 571-572
    formatting, 636
    setting, 504-505
passive hubs, 298
passive service advertisement, 370

passwords
  console, 30
  users, 24-25
patches, updating modules, 553-554
PATCHMAN utility, 553-554
PATH command, 629
path control (SNA model), 402
paths, 13-14
  directory, 628
    relative, 629
  mapping, 43-44
  search, 629-630
PAUSE command, 635
  login scripts, 87
PCI (Peripheral Component Interconnect) bus,
  653-654
PCONSOLE operators, 26
PCONSOLE utility, 70-73, 75, 170-172
  NetWare 2.2, 215
PCs (personal computers), expansion buses,
  649-654
PDS (Processor Direct Slot) bus, 654
peer layers (OSI model), communicating,
  258-259
peer-to-peer communications, 407
peers, 236-237
Pentium microcomputers (Intel), 645-646
performance
  maintenance
    influencing factors, 178-180
    troubleshooting, 186-189
  management, 431
  monitoring, 180-186, 549-553
  optimizing, 608
    bridges/routers/hubs/repeaters, 554-555
    communications channel, 612-616
    file system, 611-612
    memory allocation, 608-611
    packet burst mode, 556-557
    SET parameters, 542-548
    system processor, 616
    with packet burst mode, 556-557

Peripheral Component Interconnect (PCI) bus,
  653-654
permanent memory pool, 131
phase, 320
phase shift keying, 321
physical control (SNA model), 402
physical device addresses, 337
physical layer (OSI model), 149
  allocating transmission media capacity, 323
  connection types, 312
  multiplexing, 324-325
  purpose, 311-312
  signaling, 317-321
  topologies, 312-317
  transmission synchronization, 321-323
physical problems, preventing, 436
  printers, 536-537
physical topologies
  bus, 312-314
  cellular, 317
  mesh, 316-317
  ring, 315
  star, 316
physical units (PUs), 403, 404-405
pixels, 665
point-to-point connections, 312
  topologies based on, 314-317
point-to-point infrared transmissions, 281-282
  comparing with other wireless media,
    283-284
Point-to-Point Protocol (PPP), 420-421
polling media access control, 335-336
pools of memory, 130-132
PORT numbers, 42
ports, 663-665
  output, 642
PostScript printers, troubleshooting, 538
PPP (Point-to-Point Protocol) protocol,
  420-421
presentation layer (OSI model), 149, 363-364
  data translation, 364-365
  encryption, 365-367
presentation services (SNA model), 402

prevention
    electrical problems, 436-437
    physical problems, 436
    printer problems, 536-537
    security problems, 437
    viruses, 438
primaries, 335
PRINT command, 633
print jobs
    default settings, 166-169
    managing, 75-78
    redirecting to network printers, 74
    stopping and restarting, 170
Print Queue Operator users
    (NetWare 2.2), 211
print queues, 69, 243-244
    assigning to other printers, 171-172
    creating, 70
    NetWare 2.2, 215
    setup and management design, 165-166
    troubleshooting, 537
Print Server Operator users (NetWare 2.2), 211
print servers, 68
    configuring, 71
    listing, 72-81
    multiple file servers, setup and management
      design, 165
    NetWare 2.2, 214
    troubleshooting, 537
print services, 243-245
    components associated with, 68-69
    setting up, 69-73
PRINT VLM, 527
PRINTCON utility, 75
    default print job settings, 166-167
PRINTDEF utility, 78
Printer Access Protocol (PAP), 392
PRINTER command, 215
printer utilities, troubleshooting, 538
printers, 68
    accessing, 392
    assigning print queues to, 171-172
    checking status, 170

    definitions, 78
    local, 73
    locations, 244
    multiple workstations, 243
    notify list, adding users, 171
    preventing problems, 536
    troubleshooting, 536-538
    types, 244
printing DOS files, 633
printing services
    maintaining, 170-172
    NetWare 2.2, 214-216
    setup and management design, 164-166
private keys, 367
process/application layer (DoD model), 383
Processor Direct Slot (PDS) bus, 654
product documentation (NetWare 2.2), 223
PROGMAN.INI Windows configuration
    file, 152
PROMPT command, 633
Protected mode, 530
protocol analyzers, 555
protocol stacks, 150, 257, 377
    AppleTalk, 389-394
    DNA (Digital Network Architecture),
      394-400
    NetWare IPX/SPX, 379-382
    SNA (Systems Network Architecture),
      401-409
    TCP/IP, 382-388
protocols, 237, 378
    AARP (AppleTalk Address Resolution), 390
    ADSP (AppleTalk Data Stream
      Protocol), 393
    AFP (AppleTalk Filing Protocol), 393
    APPC (Advanced Program-to-Program
      Communication), 408
    APPN (Advanced Peer-to-Peer
      Networking), 407
    ARP (Address Resolution Protocol), 386
    ASP (AppleShare), 393-394
    ASP (AppleTalk Session Protocol), 392

ATM (Asynchronous Transfer Mode), 425-427

ATP (AppleTalk Transaction Protocol), 391-392

CICS (Customer Information Control System), 408

CLNS (Connectionless-Mode Network Service), 396-397

CONS (Connection-Mode Network Service), 397

CSMA/CA (Carrier Sense Multiple Access with Collision Avoidance), 332

CSMA/CD (Carrier Sense Multiple Access with Collision Detection), 332

DAP (Data Access Protocol), 400

DDCMP (Digital Data Communications Message Protocol), 395-396

DDM (Distributed Data Management), 409

DDP (Datagram Delivery Protocol), 390-391

DIA (Document Interchange Architecture), 409

DNS (Domain Name System), 386

ELAP (EtherTalk Link Access Protocol), 389-390

Ethernet Version 2, 395

FTP (File Transfer Protocol), 387

HDLC (High-Level Data Link Control), 396

ICMP (Internet Control Message Protocol), 384

IMS (Information Management System), 408

IP (Internet Protocol), 384

IPX (Internetwork Packet Exchange Protocol), 380

ISO 8073 (Connection-Oriented Transport Protocol Specification), 398

ISO 8327 (Session Protocol Specification), 399

ISO 8571 (FTAM) (File Transfer, Access, and Management), 399-400

ISO 8824 (ASN.1 with BER) (Abstract Syntax Notation with Basic Encoding Rules), 399

LIP (Large Internet Packet), 142, 615

LLAP (LocalTalk Link Access Protocol), 389-390

LSL (Link Support Layer), 380

MLID (Multiple Link Interface Driver), 379-380

NBP (Name Binding Protocol), 391

NCP (NetWare Core Protocols), 382

NCP (Network Control Program), 406-407

NetWare Protocol Suite, 120-122

NFS (Network File System), 388

NLSP (Network Link Services Protocol), 381

NSP (Network Services Protocol), 398

NVTS (Network Virtual Terminal Service), 400

OSPF (Open Shortest Path First), 385

Packet Burst, 143, 614

PAP (Printer Access Protocol), 392

PPP (Point-to-Point Protocol), 420-421

RIP (Routing Information Protocol), 380-381, 384-385

RPC (Remote Procedure Calls), 388

RTMP (Routing Table Maintenance Protocol), 391

SAP (Service Advertising Protocol), 382, 614-615

SDLC (Synchronous Data Link Control), 406

Session Control, 398-399

SLIP (Serial Line Internet Protocol), 420-421

SMTP (Simple Mail Transfer Protocol), 387

SNADS (SNA Distributed Services), 409

SPX (Sequenced Packet Exchange), 381

TCP (Transmission Control Protocol), 385

TELNET (Remote Terminal Emulation), 387-388

TLAP (TokenTalk Link Access Protocol), 389-390

Token Ring, 406
UDP (User Datagram Protocol), 385-386
VTAM (Virtual Telecommunications Access
    Method), 407
XDR (External Data Representation), 388
ZIP (Zone Information Protocol), 391
see also standards
PSC utility, 170-172
PSTN (Public Switched Telephone Network),
    284-286
Public directory, 15, 580
public files, copying for file server installation,
    573-574
public keys, 367
public network services, 284-288
Public Switched Telephone Network (PSTN),
    284-286
Purge attribute, 29
PURGE console command, 214
purging deleted files, 50
PUs (physical units), 403-405

Q

queries with NSEPro, 445-446
question mark (?) wild card, 631
QUEUE command, 215
queues, 69, 243-244
    creating, 70
    NetWare 2.2, 215
    setup and management design, 165-166

R

Radio Frequency Interference (RFI), 437
radio transmissions, 263, 273-278
    comparing with other wireless media,
        283-284
RAID (Redundant Array of Inexpensive
    Drives), 508-510
RAM (random-access memory), 654
    DRAM (Dynamic RAM), 655
    SRAM (Static RAM), 655
    Video RAM, 656

Raw ETHERNET (802.3) frame type, 471-472
RCONSOLE utility, 34-35, 62-63
RD command, 628
Read Audit attribute, 29
Read Only attribute, 29
Read rights, 28
Read Write attribute, 29
read-after-write verification, 101
read-only devices, 159-160
read-only memory (ROM), 654-655
reading e-mail, 94
Real mode, 530
Real-Time Data Migration (RTDM), 242
Recommendation X.25 (ITU) standard,
    421-422
reconfiguring
    bus topology, 314
    cellular topology, 317
    mesh topologies, 316
    ring topology, 315
    star topology, 316
recovering deleted files, 48
Red, Green, Blue (RGB) monitors, 665
REDIR VLM, 527
redirecting print jobs to network printers, 74
redirection (>) operator, 634
Reduced Instruction Set Computer (RISC)
    microprocessors, 647-648
Redundant Array of Inexpensive Drives
    (RAID), 508-510
REGISTER MEMORY console command,
    138-139
relative directory paths, 629
relative expense, 350
reliable delivery of packets, SPX (Sequenced
    Packet Exchange) protocol, 381
REM command, 634
REMARK login script command, 88
remote booting, DOS workstations, 527-528
remote file access, DDM (Distributed Data
    Management) protocol, 409
REMOTE NLM, 61
remote operation, 371

remote printers, troubleshooting, 537
Remote Procedure Calls (RPC) protocol, 388
Remote Terminal Emulation (TELNET)
    protocol, 387-388
REMOVE DOS console command, 56
REMOVE utility, 34
REN command, 46
Rename Inhibit attribute, 29
RENDIR command, 209
repeaters, 299-300
    optimizing performance, 554-555
replication databases, 248-249
RESET ROUTER console command, 214
resolution, 665
resources
    controlling, centralized versus distributed
        network services, 250-251
    monitoring, 553
    NetWare 2.2, 223
restarting print jobs, 170
restoring, 189, 198-201
    in NetWare 2.2, 227-228
    third-party products for, reliability, 556
restrictions, user accounts, 25-26
REVOKE utility, 34
RFI (Radio Frequency Interference), 437
RGB (Red, Green, Blue) monitors, 665
rights security, 26
RIGHTS utility, 33
Ring Management (RMT), 482
ring topology, 315
RIP (Routing Information Protocol) packets,
    190-191
RIP (Routing Information Protocol) protocol,
    121-122, 380-381, 384-385
RISC (Reduced Instruction Set Computer)
    microprocessors, 647-648
RJ-11 connectors, 293
RJ-45 connectors, 293
RLL (Run Length Limited) encoding
    scheme, 494
RMT (Ring Management), 482
ROM (read-only memory), 654-655

ROM BIOS, 656
root directory, 628
routers, 303-305
    brouters, 305
    optimizing performance, 554-555
    tracking, 528
routing, 306
    circuit switching, 347
    information about, viewing, 190-191
    message switching, 348
    OSPF (Open Shortest Path First), 385
    package switching, 349-350
    route discovery, 350-352
Routing Information Protocol (RIP) packets,
    190-191
Routing Information Protocol (RIP), 121-122,
    380-381, 384-385
Routing Table Maintenance Protocol
    (RTMP), 391
RPC (Remote Procedure Calls) protocol, 388
RPLFIX utility, 528
RS232 NLM, 62
RSA VLM, 527
RSPX NLM, 62
RTDM (Real-Time Data Migration), 242
RTMP (Routing Table Maintenance Protocol)
    protocol, 391
Run Length Limited (RLL) encoding
    scheme, 494

S

SALVAGE utility, 48-50
same-server migration, 587-589
SAP (Service Advertising Protocol) packets,
    190-191
SAP (Service Advertising Protocol) protocol,
    121-122, 382, 614-615
SAS (Single Attached Stations), 482
satellite microwave transmissions, 280-281
    comparing with other wireless media,
        283-284
SBACKUP utility, 103-104, 189, 198-201

screen display console commands, 56
SCSI (Small Computer Systems Interface) drives, 495-498, 663
SCSI Address jumper, 500
SDH (Synchronous Digital Hierarchy) standard, 424-425
SDLC (Synchronous Data Link Control) protocol, 406
search drives, 43-44
search paths, 629-630
searching with NSEPro, 445-446
secondaries, 335
sectors, 658
security
    data integrity
        SFT (System Fault Tolerance), 100-101
        SMS (Storage Management Services), 102-103
    encryption (presentation OSI layer), 365-367
    implementing, 32-35
    management, 432
    NCP Packet Signature, 179-180
    NetWare 2.2, 210-211
    network levels
        attributes, 29
        file server, 29-31, 34-35
        login, 24-26
        rights, 26
    problem prevention, 437
    setting up user/group accounts, 31-32
    virus protection, 196-198
seek time, 492
segment sequencing, 357
segments, transport OSI layer management, 357
self-clocking signals, 323
semipermanent memory pool, 131
semistatic patches, 554
SEND console command, 56
sending e-mail, 94
separate clock signals, 323
sequence control, 340

Sequenced Packet Exchange (SPX) protocol, 121, 381
Serial Line Internet Protocol (SLIP), 420-421
serial ports, 665
SERVER.EXE file, 112
servers, 236-237
    advertising services, 382
    fax, 245
    file, *see* file servers
    print, 68
        configuring, 71
        listing, 72-81
        multiple file servers, setup and management design, 165
        NetWare 2.2, 214
    specialization, 251
service access methods (application OSI layer), 370-371
service addresses, 346
Service Advertising Protocol (SAP) packets, 190-191
Service Advertising Protocol (SAP), 121-122, 382, 614-615
service protocol VLMs, 155
service providers/requesters, 236-237
service-provider-initiated address/name resolution, 357
service-requester-initiated address/name resolution, 356
Session Control protocol, 398-399
session layer (OSI model), 149, 359-362
Session Protocol Specification (ISO 8327) protocol, 399
sessions, 361-362
    ASP (AppleTalk Session Protocol), 392
SET command, 116-117
    login scripts, 88
    parameters, 140-142
        optimizing, 542-548
SET TIME command, 189-190
SET TIMEZONE command, 189-190
SETPASS utility, 210
SFT (System Fault Tolerance), 100-101

Sharable attribute, 29
shells
    NetWare 2.2, 224-225
    versus DOS Requester, 595-598
shielded twisted-pair (STP) cable, 267-268
    comparing with other cable types, 272-273
    connections, 293-294
Shift-JIS (Japanese characters), 364
short-term memory, 609
SHOW menu command, 91
signal timing, 321-323
signaling, 317-318
    analog, 319-321
    digital, 318-319
SIMMs (Single In-Line Memory Modules), 657
Simple Mail Transfer Protocol (SMTP), 387
simplex dialogs, 360
Single Attached Stations (SAS), 482
sizes
    data buses, 643, 649
    packets, optimizing communication
        channel, 613
SLIP (Serial Line Internet Protocol) protocol,
    420-421
SLIST utility, 14-15, 45-46, 210
Small Computer Systems Interface (SCSI)
    drives, 495-498, 663
SMDS (Switched Multimegabit Digital
    Service), 427
SMS (Storage Management Services), 102-103
SMT (Station Management), 483
SMTP (Simple Mail Transfer Protocol)
    protocol, 387
SNA (Systems Network Architecture) protocol
    stack, 401-409
SNADS (SNA Distributed Services)
    protocol, 409
SNAP frame type, 120
sneaker-net, 240
SNMP NLM, 122
software
    application software, 84-85
    NetWare 2.2, 216

child, 189
communications, requirements, 10-11
file server components, 112-115
LANalyzer for Windows, 555
NetWare 2.2 components, 224
NetWare installation requirements, 564
parent, 189
third-party backup/restore products,
    reliability, 556
workstation, installing, 600-604
SONET (Synchronous Optical Network)
    standard, 424-425
spanning tree algorithm, 303
specialization of servers, 251
SPOOL console command, 214
spooling NetWare 2.2, 215
spread spectrum radio, 276-278
    comparing with other wireless media,
        283-284
SPX (Sequenced Packet Exchange) protocol,
    121, 381
SRAM (Static RAM), 655
ST506/412 interface, 662-663
standards
    FDDI (Fiber Distributed Data Interface),
        418-420
    frame relay, 422-423
    IEEE (Institute of Electrical and Electronic
        Engineers) 802 family, 414-418
    ISDN (Integrated Services Digital Network),
        423-424
    SDH (Synchronous Digital Hierarchy),
        424-425
    SONET (Synchronous Optical Network),
        424-425
    X.25 (ITU), 421-422
    see also protocols
star topology, 316
start bits, 338
starting file servers, 123
STARTUP.NCF file, 116-117
    installing file servers, 577-579
state transition encoding, 318-319

static, 436-437
static linking of modules, 562
static patches, 554
Static RAM (SRAM), 655
STATION login script command, 88
Station Management (SMT), 483
stop bits, 338
stopping print jobs, 170
storage devices, 642, 658-663
Storage Management Services (SMS), 102-103
store-and-forward networks, 348
storing files, 241-242, 626-627
STP (shielded twisted-pair) cable, 267-268
    comparing with other cable types, 272-273
    connections, 293-294
STREAMS NLM, 122
subdirectories, 628
submenus, 90
Supervisor equivalent users, 26
    NetWare 2.2, 211
Supervisor users, 26
    NetWare 2.2, 211
        commands/utilities, 212-213
Supervisory rights, 28
swap blocks, 597
Switched Multimegabit Digital Service
    (SMDS), 427
switched telephone services, 284-286
switching
    circuits, 347
    messages, 348
    packages, 349-350
synchronizing file updates, 242-243
Synchronous Data Link Control (SDLC)
    protocol, 406
Synchronous Digital Hierarchy (SDH)
    standard, 424-425
Synchronous Optical Network (SONET)
    standard, 424-425
synchronous transmissions
    bits (physical OSI layer), 322-323
    frames (data link OSI layer), 339-340

SYS command, 627
SYS file extension, 623
SYS volume, 14
    creating for file server installation, 572-573
    mounting at file server installation, 573
SYSCON utility, 88
    creating user and group accounts, 32
    creating user trustees, 27
    editing AUTOEXEC.NCF file, 118
    intruder account detection, viewing
        status, 26
    NetWare 2.2, 211
    network/file system security, 32-33
System attribute, 29
system clock time/date, setting, 189-190
system configurations, 529
System directory, 15, 580
System Fault Tolerance (SFT), 100-101
system files
    copying for file server installation, 573-574
    DOS, 622
System Information (Norton Utilities), 440
system login scripts, 85
    building, 85-88
system manager (NetWare 2.2)
    resources, 223
    responsibilities, 222
system modules, monitoring, 552
system processor, optimizing performance, 616
system units, 642
SYSTEM.INI Windows configuration file, 152
Systems Network Architecture (SNA) protocol
    stack, 401-409

T

tables, 133-134
targets, 103
TCP (Transmission Control Protocol)
    protocol, 385
TCP/IP protocol stack, 122, 382-388
TDM (time-division multiplexing), 325

technical support
    MHTL (Micro House Technical Library),
        449-454
    NetWire BBS, 449
telephone networks, 284-288
TELNET (Remote Terminal Emulation)
    protocol, 387-388
temperature, effects on computers, 436-438
terminals
    dumb terminal emulation, 387-388
    virtual, 400
terrestrial microwave transmissions, 278-280
    comparing with other wireless media,
        283-284
thick net (10BASE5) cabling (Ethernet),
    467-469
thin net (10BASE2) cabling (Ethernet),
    465-467
tic count, 350
time
    access time, 657
    DOS clock, setting/displaying, 633
    restrictions, 26
    system clock, setting, 189-190
TIME command, 633
time zones, setting, 189-190
time-division multiplexing (TDM), 325
timing signals, 321-323
TLAP (TokenTalk Link Access Protocol)
    protocol, 389-390
TLI NLM, 122
TLIST utility, 34
token passing media access control, 333-334
    versus contention-based media access
        control, 335
Token Ring specifications, 474-480
Token Ring protocol, 406
token ring topology, 330-331
Token-Ring frame types, 120
TokenTalk Link Access Protocol (TLAP),
    389-390
topologies
    bus, 312-314

cellular, 317
comparing, 485-486
logical, 330-331
mesh, 316-317
    NLSP (Network Link Services
        Protocol), 381
ring, 315
star, 316
total cache buffers, 137
TRACK console command, 190-191, 214, 528
tracks, 658
TRAN VLM, 527
transaction services (SNA model), 402
transaction tracking SET parameters, 546-547
Transactional attribute, 29
transactions
    ATP (AppleTalk Transaction Protocol)
        protocol, 391-392
    identifiers (transport OSI layer), 356
    processing, 408
transceivers, 295, 297
transferring
    data during sessions, 362
    e-mail, 387
    files, 240-241, 387
transients, 437
Transistor-Transistor Logic (TTL)
    monitors, 666
translating data (presentation OSI layer),
    364-365
transmission control (SNA model), 402
Transmission Control Protocol (TCP), 385
transmission media, 237
    allocating capacity, 323
    cable types, 264-273
    characteristics, 263-264
    signals, 262-263
    wireless media, 273-284
transmission media adapters, 297
transmission synchronization
    data link layer (OSI model), 337-340
    physical layer (OSI model), 321-323

transport layer (OSI model), 149, 355-358
transport protocol VLMs, 155
troubleshooting, 438-439
  ARCnet, 462-463
  bus topology, 314
  cellular topology, 317
  documentation for, 439-440
    MHTL (Micro House Technical Library),
      449-454
    NetWire BBS, 449
    NSEPro (Network Support Encyclopedia),
      444-449
  DOS workstations
    connecting to servers, 524-525
    system configurations, 529
  Ethernet, 473-474
  fault management, 430-431
  FDDI, 484-485
  IRQ (Interrupt Request Channels) conflicts,
    528-529
  mesh topologies, 317
  ODI, 525-526
  printers, 536-538
  ring topology, 315
  star topology, 316
  Token Ring, 478-480
  tools
    diagnostic software, 440-441
    protocol analyzers, 555
    tracking routers, 528
trustees, 27-28
  granting/revoking rights, 34
  listing, 34
  removing users/groups from lists, 34
TSA_DOS NLM, 104
TSA_OS2 NLM, 104
TSA_SMS.COM file, 104
TTL (Transistor-Transistor Logic)
  monitors, 666
TTS, 101
twisted-pair cable, 266-269
  comparing with other cable types, 272-273
  connections, 293-294

TXT file extension, 623
TYPE command, 629-630

U

UDP (User Datagram Protocol) protocol,
  385-386
unacknowledged connectionless services, 340
UNBIND console command, 56
United States Department of Defense (DoD)
  model, 382-383
Unix client support, 594
UNLOAD command, 56, 562
unshielded twisted-pair cable, *see* UTP cable
updating
  files
    client workstation, 153-154
    file-update synchronization, 242-243
  modules with patches, 553-554
  previous menu versions to NetWare 3.12, 93
  with MHTL (Micro House Technical
    Library), 449-454
  with NSEPro (Network Support
    Encyclopedia), 444-449
upgrading NetWare 3.11 to 3.12, *see* migrations
upper memory, 531, 656
UPS (uninterruptible power supply)
  controlling, 101
  information about, listing, 60
UPS NLM utility, 58, 60
User account manager users
  (NetWare 2.2), 211
user accounts
  restrictions, 25-26
  setting up, 31-32
User Datagram Protocol (UDP), 385-386
user IDs, 24-25
user login scripts, 85
  building, 85-88
user memory, 656
User Tools for Windows application, 74
USERDEF utility, 32
USERLIST utility, 210

usernames, 24-25
users, 26
   assessing printing needs (setup and
      management design), 164
   e-mail distribution lists, 93
   effective rights, 28-29
      viewing, 33
   passwords, 24-25
   removing from trustee lists, 34
   types, 26
      NetWare 2.2, 211
utilities
   ACONSOLE, 34-35, 62-63
   ADMIN, 93
   ALLOW, 34
   ATTACH, 210
   BINDFIX, 186-187
   BINDREST, 186-187
   CAPTURE, 74, 166-169
   CHKVOL, 45
   command-line, 17
   DOS text, 16
   DOSGEN, 527
   FDISK, 635-636
   FILER, 32, 47-48
   First Mail, 94
   GRANT, 34
   graphical, 17
   MAKEUSER, 32
   MENUCNVT, 93
   MENUMAKE, 92
   MIGRATE.EXE, 587-588
   migration, comparing, 584-586
   MONITOR console, 137-138, 180-186
   MSD, 440-441
   NBACKUP, 227-228
   NCOPY, 46-47
   NetWare 2.2, 211-214
   NPRINT, 74
   PATCHMAN, 553-554
   PCONSOLE, 70-73, 75, 170-172, 215
   PRINTCON, 75, 166-167
   PRINTDEF, 78

   printer, troubleshooting, 538
   PSC, 170-172
   RCONSOLE, 34-35, 62-63
   REMOVE, 34
   REVOKE, 34
   RIGHTS, 33
   RPLFIX, 528
   SALVAGE, 48
   SBACKUP, 103-104, 187, 189, 198-201
   SETPASS, 210
   SLIST, 14-15, 45-46, 210
   SYSCON, 26-27, 32-33, 88, 118, 211
   TLIST, 34
   USERDEF, 32
   USERLIST, 210
   WHOAMI, 210
   see also commands; VLMs
utility NLMs (management and enhancement),
   58-60
UTP (unshielded twisted-pair) cable, 268-269
   comparing with other cable types, 272-273
   connections, 293-294
   Ethernet (10BASE-T), 469-471

V

VAP console command, 214
VER command, 633
VESA (Video Electronic Standard
   Association), 653
VESA Local Bus (VL-Bus), 652-653
VGA (Video Graphics Array), 666
VGA monochrome monitors, 666
Video RAM, 656
VIPX.386 file, 151
virtual circuit packet switching, 350
Virtual Loadable Modules, *see* VLMs
Virtual Telecommunications Access Method
   (VTAM) protocol, 407
virtual terminals, 400
virus protection/prevention, 196-198, 438
VL-Bus (VESA Local Bus), 652-653
VLM file extension, 155

VLM.EXE file (VLM Manager), 10-11, 42
VLMs (Virtual Loadable Modules), 11
    DOS Requester, 527
    types, 155-157
VNETWARE.386 file, 151
voice mail, integrating with e-mail, 245-246
VOLINFO command, 45, 209
volume disk restrictions, 26
volume labels, 627
volumes, 11-13
    creating for file server installation, 572-573
    information about, listing, 45
    managing, 47-48
    mounting at file server installation, 573
    SYS:, 14
    troubleshooting, 187-188
VREPAIR NLM, 187-188, 556
VTAM (Virtual Telecommunications Access
  Method) protocol, 407

W

WANs (wide area networks), 235
    Internet, 288
    telephone networks, 284-288
warm boots, 624
WATCHDOG console command, 214
Watchdog process, 525
well-known addresses, 346
WHOAMI utility, 210
wild cards, 631
WIN.INI Windows configuration file, 152-153
window flow control (data link OSI layer), 341
Windows
    client support, 594-595
    configuration files, 152-153
wireless media
    comparing types, 283-284
    infrared, 281-283
    microwave, 278-281
    radio, 273-278
wiring concentrators, 298-299
workflow management applications, 246

workgroup applications, 246-247
Workgroup manager users (NetWare 2.2), 211
workstation restrictions, 25
workstation software installation, 600-604
workstations
    accessing file servers, 61-63
    backing up/restoring, 189, 198-201
    connecting to networks, 42, 296-297
    DOS
        DOS Requester, 526-527
        DR (Digital Research) DOS (Novell), 532
        IPX (Internetwork Packet Exchange)
          architecture, 524-525
        IRQ (Interrupt Request Channels) conflicts,
          528-529
        memory, 530-531
        ODI, 525-526
        remote booting, 527-528
        system configurations, 529
        tracking routers, 528
    see also clients
Write Audit attribute, 29
WRITE login script command, 88
Write rights, 28
WSUPDATE command, 153-154

X–Z

X.25 standard (ITU), 421-422
X.400 Message Handling System, 400
X.500 Directory standard, 400
XCOPY command, 632
XDR (External Data Representation)
  protocol, 388
XMS (Extended Memory), 531, 657

ZIP (Zone Information Protocol) protocol, 391

WANT MORE INFORMATION?

CHECK OUT THESE RELATED TOPICS OR SEE YOUR LOCAL BOOKSTORE

CAD and 3D Studio

As the number one CAD publisher in the world, and as a Registered Publisher of Autodesk, New Riders Publishing provides unequaled content on this complex topic. Industry-leading products include AutoCAD and 3D Studio.

Networking

As the leading Novell NetWare publisher, New Riders Publishing delivers cutting-edge products for network professionals. We publish books for all levels of users, from those wanting to gain NetWare Certification, to those administering or installing a network. Leading books in this category include *Inside NetWare 3.12*, *CNE Training Guide: Managing NetWare Systems*, *Inside TCP/IP*, and *NetWare: The Professional Reference*.

Graphics

New Riders provides readers with the most comprehensive product tutorials and references available for the graphics market. Best-sellers include *Inside CorelDRAW! 5*, *Inside Photoshop 3*, and *Adobe Photoshop NOW!*

Internet and Communications

As one of the fastest growing publishers in the communications market, New Riders provides unparalleled information and detail on this ever-changing topic area. We publish international best-sellers such as *New Riders' Official Internet Yellow Pages, 2nd Edition*, a directory of over 10,000 listings of Internet sites and resources from around the world, and *Riding the Internet Highway, Deluxe Edition*.

Operating Systems

Expanding off our expertise in technical markets, and driven by the needs of the computing and business professional, New Riders offers comprehensive references for experienced and advanced users of today's most popular operating systems, including *Understanding Windows 95*, *Inside Unix*, *Inside Windows 3.11 Platinum Edition*, *Inside OS/2 Warp Version 3*, and *Inside MS-DOS 6.22*.

Other Markets

Professionals looking to increase productivity and maxmize the potential of their software and hardware should spend time discovering our line of products for Word, Excel, and Lotus 1-2-3. These titles include *Inside Word 6 for Windows*, *Inside Excel 5 for Windows*, *Inside 1-2-3 Release 5*, and *Inside WordPerfect for Windows*.

Orders/Customer Service **1-800-653-6156** Source Code **NRP95**

New Riders Publishing 201 West 103rd Street ◆ Indianapolis, Indiana 46290 USA

REGISTRATION CARD

CNE Short Course

Name _____ Title _____

Company _____ Type of business _____

Address _____

City/State/ZIP _____

Have you used these types of books before? ☐ yes ☐ no

If yes, which ones? _____

_____

How many computer books do you purchase each year? ☐ 1–5 ☐ 6 or more

How did you learn about this book? _____

Where did you purchase this book? _____

Which applications do you currently use? _____

_____

Which computer magazines do you subscribe to? _____

_____

What trade shows do you attend? _____

_____

Comments: _____

_____

_____

Would you like to be placed on our preferred mailing list? ☐ yes ☐ no

☐ **I would like to see my name in print!** You may use my name and quote me in future New Riders products and promotions. My daytime phone number is: _____

New Riders Publishing 201 West 103rd Street ◆ Indianapolis, Indiana 46290 USA

Fax to **317-581-4670** Orders/Customer Service **1-800-653-6156** Source Code **NRP95**

Fold Here

- -

‖‖‖‖

BUSINESS REPLY MAIL

FIRST-CLASS MAIL PERMIT NO. 9918 INDIANAPOLIS IN

POSTAGE WILL BE PAID BY THE ADDRESSEE

**NEW RIDERS PUBLISHING
201 W 103RD ST
INDIANAPOLIS IN 46290-9058**

Using the New Riders Electronic TestPrep

The New Riders Electronic TestPrep testing program is designed to help you become a Certified NetWare Engineer (CNE) or a Certified NetWare Administrator (CNA) by simulating the types of questions you're likely to face on the CNE or CNA exams. If you're already a CNE or a CNA, Electronic TestPrep will help you keep your skills sharpened by presenting you with up-to-date topics and information presented in an easy-to-use graphical format.

Installing the New Riders Electronic TestPrep Disc

The Electronic TestPrep is a Windows-based application that has the following system requirements:

Any IBM PC-compatible computer running Microsoft Windows version 3.0 or above (standard or enhanced mode); DOS version 3.1 or above, 2 MB or more of RAM; a Microsoft Windows-compatible mouse; an EGA, VGA, or compatible monitor (color is recommended); a hard disk drive with at least 3 MB of free space; a CD-ROM drive; a Microsoft Windows-compatible printer is recommended.

Steps To Follow

1. Place the CD-ROM in your CD-ROM drive.

2. From the Windows Program Manager, choose **F**ile, then **R**un.

2. In the **C**ommand Line box, type **D:\TESTPREP\SETUP.EXE** and press Enter. (If your CD-ROM drive is installed to a drive other than the default letter D, type the letter of that particular drive).

4. Follow the instructions on the screen. When the license agreement screen displays, read it and click on the "agree" button if you agree. Also, be sure to enter your name correctly in the Enter Your Name field.

5. Specify the startup directory where you want the TestPrep to be stored. The default is NRP4. Click on Continue.

TestPrep will now install on your hard disk. After TestPrep installs, a program group named New Riders is created in your Program Manager. From here, you can start the TestPrep program by double-clicking on its icon. Or, if you want to review additional books published by New Riders Publishing, double-click on the NRP Books icon.

Pentium—two 486-type chips for dual processing. Independent access to internal data caches (8 KB each), over 120 MHz, 64-bit internal bus and 3 million transistors.
RISC and CISC. Floating-point unit (FPU) uses mathematical firmware for 300% increase in computational speed.

Motorola processors—Graphic orientation rather than math. First ones in 1979— MC68000 and used in Apple—16-bit, 32-bit internal arch and 16-bit data bus. 16 MB RAM and 16 MHz. Brains in: Mac 128KB; Mac 512KB; Mac 512KBe; Mac Plus; Mac SE; Mac Classic; Mac Portable (really uses the MC68HC000 - low powered version of chip).

MC68020—32-bit with 32-bit communications inside and on data bus. 4 GB memory, 16 MHz and math coprocessor: Mac LC; Mac II.

MC68030—Basis of NeXT. Had revolutionary two buses. Two-32 bit buses to serve processor twice as fast! Internal memory caching, math coprocessor, 40 MHz: Mac SE/30; Mac IIx; Mac IIcx; Mac IIci; Mac IIsi; Mac IIfx.

MC68040—64-bit communications and is brain of Mac Quadra.

MEMORY
RAM—100 times faster than from disk
DRAM—Dynamic—most popular. Tiny capicitors storing 0s and 1s. Must be continually refreshed.
SRAM—Static—no capacitors. Mechanical in nature and uses switches. Much faster/no refresh
Most common memory access times = 60-70 nanoseconds
Typical motherboard = 8 SIMM slots—2 banks of 4 providing for 256 MB DRAM
ROM—semipermanent. Stays if power lost, but maintained by a battery that could die.

Five video standards:
Monochrome
RGB—Original IBM color. Added red, green, and blue.
CGA—16 real colors; 320×200 pixels
EGA—64 colors; 640×350—Enhanced Graphics Adapter
VGA—Can switch between high resolution/low color and low resolution/high color. 640×480 with 16 colors or 320×200 with 256 colors

Networking Technologies Test

Error Checking is done at 3 levels of the OSI model:
Data-link; Transport; Session

UTP supports a transfer rate of 1 to 100 megabits per second with the most common being 10 Mb/s. It is restricted to 100 meters or 328 feet. STP is essentially UTP with an aluminum/polyester shield and an electric ground. It is capable of 155 Mb/s, but the most common is 16 Mb/s. It is also confined in length to 100 meters.

Coax has a capacity of 500 Mb/s, but most implementations still run at 10 Mb/s. The effective range is 2 kilometers or 2,000 yards. Variations of it are:
Thick Ethernet—50 ohm RG-8/11
Thin Ethernet—50 ohm RG-58
ARCnet—93 ohm RG-62

Fiber optic cable has a capacity of 2 gigabytes per second and restricted length of 60 kilometers, or 40 miles.
There are two parts to the cable: inner glass cylindrical core and outer concentric glass cladding.

Within the OSI model, Repeaters operate at the Physical level, Bridges at the Datalink level, Routers at the Network level, and Gateways at the upper levels.

Frame format:

1. SOF—Start of Frame
2. Source address
3. Destination address
4. Administration
5. Data
6. Error checking (CRC)
7. EOF—End of Frame

IEEE 802.2 = LLC
IEEE 802.3 = Contention Bus
IEEE 802.4 = Token Passing Bus
IEEE 802.5 = Token Passing Ring

Physical Address = Data link Layer
Network Address = Network Layer
Service Address = upper layers

Service and Support Test

Four types of electrical problems:
1. Crosstalk
2. Static
3. Transients
4. Line noise

Four types of security threats:
1. Destruction
2. Corruption
3. Disclosure
4. Interruption

Three steps to installing software on a client machine:
1. Run INSTALL.EXE. This creates the NWCLIENT directories and copies in the VLMs.
2. Give the Windows path when prompted, if you are using Windows.
3. Give the configuration information when prompted—this will be used to build the NET.CFG file.

Four steps to troubleshooting model:
1. Gather information
2. Develop attack plan
3. Isolate the problem and execute the plan
4. Document what was done

The Twelve files you should see are:

File	Description
AUTO.VLM	Automatic reconnect
BIND.VLM	Protocol bindery service
CONN.VLM	Connection table manager
FIO.VLM	File input/output
GENERAL.VLM	Miscellaneous NETX functions
IPXNCP.VLM	Transport protocol using IPX
NETX.VLM	Shell compatibility
NWP.VLM	Protocol multiplexer
PRINT.VLM	Print redirector
REDIR.VLM	DOS redirector
RSA.VLM	Encryption
TRAN.VLM	Transport protocol multiplexer